# Britain's ( On Turkey

## An Irish Perspective

1914-1924

by

## Dr. Pat Walsh

*To Hasan Saat*
*Best wishes*
*from*
*Pat Walsh*

To Una, David and Aoife

ATHOL BOOKS
www.atholbooks.org

*Also by Pat Walsh:*

**Irish Republicanism And Socialism**, *The Politics Of The Republican Movement 1905 To 1994*

**From Civil Rights To National War**, *Northern Ireland Catholic Politics 1964-74*

***Lionel Curtis* Ireland**. Introduction by *Pat Walsh*

*Major C.J.C. Street*: **The Administration Of Ireland, 1920**; with a substantial extract from his Ireland In 1921 and a review of his other writings on Britain's world role, and inter-war Europe. Introduction by *Dr. Pat Walsh*

**The Rise And Fall Of Imperial Ireland**. Redmondism In The Context Of Britain's War Of Conquest Of South Africa And Its Great War On Germany, 1899-1916

**Britain's Great War On Turkey**
by
*Pat Walsh*

ISBN 978 085034 121 8
2009

*ATHOL BOOKS*
PO Box 339
Belfast
BT12 4GQ

Orders: athol-st@atholbooks.org

## List of Illustrations

# Table of Contents

# Introduction—'Our War' on Turkey

Ireland's Great War on Turkey is probably the most significant thing that Ireland has ever done in the world. And yet there are no histories of it.

In the last months of 2008 (to celebrate the ninetieth anniversary of the armistice on the Western Front) there was an orgy of Remembrance in Ireland, ranging from the efforts of the Lord Mayor of Cork and President of Ireland to rehabilitate British Imperial militarism in the country to an RTE project to re-popularise the War. There was also an RTE book, *Our War*, published in conjunction with the Royal Irish Academy, and presided over by Trinity College Professor John Horne, which now claims ownership of the Great War for Ireland.

The Remembrance project has had the effect of challenging the forgetting reflex of nationalist Ireland toward these events—a reflex that originated in the belief that what Ireland did in the Great War was shameful and was best left unsaid and forgotten (and those who participated in it best left alone to forget).

Nationalist Ireland, when it had a mind of its own, and knew what it had helped to do in the world, knew that this was the best way to deal with these events. And so it left well alone.

However, it is no longer possible to leave well alone.

Remembrance commemoration is presented as a harmless activity and even Sinn Feiners have taken part. And, of course, those who wish to have nothing to do with it are presented as remnants of the bad old days and the bad old ways, that was independent Ireland—a thing that has now fallen into disrepute.

Remembrance has a political dimension and it has started to substitute a political agenda for history, with the effect that real history—cause and effect history—is left unwritten and unknown. That is all very convenient for the objectives of those who wish to substitute another view of history for the independent Irish one.

The Remembrance project has come up against a historical blank in relation to the War on the Ottoman Empire because *there is no history of Ireland's Great War on Turkey*. There are, of course, militarist accounts of Irish participation and the battles fought. But there is no Irish account of why Ireland went to war with the Turks, why the Ottoman Empire was destroyed and dismantled in that war, and the catastrophic effects this had on the world.

And that fact has made this account, of necessity, a long and detailed one.

Most of the aspects of the Great War on Turkey have been forgotten in Ireland because they have never been written about. And yet they haven't gone away. They have come back to remind us, since September 2001, with a vengeance, and to pull the West back into the region, with lessons unlearnt, as if nothing had ever happened. Thus the President of Ireland, at Bailieborough, Co. Cavan on 27th September 2008, referred to the funerals (with full British military trappings) of Irishmen who continue to participate in England's wars in those regions, as 'beautiful' and things demanding 'respect.'

Surely that is the best illustration of the great problem with Remembrance and its accompanying forgetting of history?

Remembrance has required us to remember. So remember again we will.

## Francis Ledwidge Carries Ireland's Cross

It might be worth starting with the obvious question: Why did Ireland go to war on Turkey in November 1914?

Perhaps the poem *The Irish in Gallipoli* explains why. It is, after all, featured [February 2009] on the website of the Taoiseach of the Irish Republic in a section headed *Irish Soldiers in the Great War*. It is by Francis Ledwidge, one of the Irish attackers of Turkey at the Dardanelles in 1915. And the Office of the Taoiseach, in its wisdom, chose it, particularly, to illustrate why Irish soldiers participated in the Great War. So here it is:

> Where Aegean cliffs with bristling menace front
> The threatening splendour of that isley sea
> Lighted by Troy's last shadow, where the first
> Hero kept watch and the last Mystery
> Shook with dark thunder, hark the battle brunt!
> A nation speaks, old Silences are burst.
>
> Neither for lust of glory nor new throne
> This thunder and this lightning of our wrath
> Waken these frantic echoes, not for these
> Our cross with England's mingle, to be blown
> On Mammon's threshold; we but war when war
> Serves Liberty and Justice, Love and Peace.
>
> Who said that such an emprise could be vain?
> Were they not one with Christ Who strove and died?
> Let Ireland weep but not for sorrow. Weep
> That by her sons a land is sanctified
> For Christ Arisen, and angels once again
> Come back like exile birds to guard their sleep.

Francis Ledwidge was a soldier in the 10th Division of the British Army. He was an enthusiastic Home Ruler and had been a founder member of the Irish Volunteers in Slane, County Meath. When the Volunteers split over John Redmond's commitment to the British War on Germany at Woodenbridge, Ledwidge went against the Irish Party leader. But a week later, after Tom Kettle and other nationalists began to engage in fierce anti-German propaganda, he enlisted in the British Army, in the 10th Division, to fight the Germans. He wrote the poem not in 1915, but in February 1917, after the Easter Rising. It therefore represents a justification of Irish participation in the War, particularly against the Turks, after another Ireland had registered its protest.

6

Presumably the Ledwidge poem is on the Taoiseach's website because there was Irish participation in the Imperial assault on the Dardanelles and, as Ledwidge describes, an Irish blood sacrifice in that crusade. These days it is regarded as imperative that equal recognition be given to those who participated in the Great War of 1914-? along with those who helped found the Irish State — and thus this entry in the Taoiseach's website. (I have put a question mark instead of an end date for the conclusion of the Great War as its consequences are still with us.)

There seems to be no understanding of the perversity of this — that an attack on an ally of the 1916 rebels, conducted by the Empire which Ireland had to go to war with to gain independence, should be given pride of place by the senior Office of the independent Irish State.

Have the compilers of the Taoiseach's website read *The Irish in Gallipoli* or thought about the meaning of the poem?

Because there is certainly no explanation of why this Crusader hymn (a quite unrepresentative and most nasty example of Ledwidge's poetry) which talks of the mingling of the crosses of Ireland and England in war, and the sanctifying of (Muslim) land for the Christian Christ, appears under the *imprimatur* of the Taoiseach.

## *Tell England/Ireland*

Within Ireland and England the War on Turkey seemed to bring out something deep, to do with the unity of Christians, not seen since the time of the Crusades. And it is perhaps the case that, when Ledwidge lost his stomach for killing Germans, after the Easter Rising, he kept a belief in what he had been doing for England against the Moslem Turks.

*Tell England* was an enormously popular novel written by Ernest Raymond in 1922. It was published by Cassell and went through forty editions between then and 1969. There is something of what Ledwidge was trying to get across in his poem in the story of three young English Public School boys going off on a great adventure to Gallipoli with the 29th Brigade and 10th (Irish) Division. Here is an extract describing the initial invasion of Turkey, to provide a flavour of the times:

> "The march of History in these wonderful months brought with it an event that stirred the world. This was the first great landing of the British Forces on the toe of the Gallipoli Peninsula, in their attempt to win a way for the Allied Navy through the Straits of the Dardanelles. On April 25th, 1915, as all the world knows, the men of the 29th Division came up like a sea-breeze out of the sea, and, driving the Turks and Germans from their coastal defences, swept clear for themselves a small tract of breathing room across that extremity of Turkey. Leaping out of their boats, and crashing through a murderous fire, they won a footing on Cape Helles, and planted their feet firmly on the invaded territory...

The First Line—we were proud of the fact—had been the first territorial division to leave England. In September, 1914, it had sailed away, in an imposing convoy of transports escorted by cruisers and destroyers, under orders to garrison Egypt. There it had acted as the Army of Occupation till that April day when the 29th Division laughed at the prophecies of the German experts and stormed from the Ægean Sea the beaches of Cape Helles. Scarcely had the news electrified Egypt before the First Line received its orders to embark for Overseas. And every man of them knew what that meant.

So all we of the 2nd Tenth seemed marked down like branded sheep for the Gallipoli front. The Colonel was full of it. With his elect mind that saw right into the heart of things, he quickly unveiled the poetry and romance of Britain's great enterprise at Gallipoli. He crowded all his young officers into his private room for a lecture on the campaign that was calling them. Having placed them on chairs, on the carpet, on the hearth-rug, and on the fender, he seated himself at his writing-table, like a hen in the midst of its chickens, and began:

'For epic and dramatic interest this Dardanelles business is easily top.'

To the Colonel everything that he was enthusiastic about was epic and dramatic and 'on top.' Just as he told us that our day was the day and our generation the generation, so now he set out to assure us that Gallipoli was the front.

'If you'll only get at the IDEAS behind what's going on at the Helles beaches,' he declared, with a rap on the table, 'you'll be thrilled, boys.'

Then he reminded us that the Dardanelles Straits were the Hellespont of the Ancient world, and the neighbouring Ægean Sea the most mystic of the 'wine-dark seas of Greece': he retold stories of Jason and the Argonauts; of 'Burning Sappho' in Lesbos; of Achilles in Scyros; of Poseidon sitting upon Samothrace to watch the fight at Troy; and of St. John the Divine at Patmos gazing up into the Heavenly Jerusalem.

As he spoke, we were schoolboys again and listened with wide-open, wistful eyes.

From the fender and the hearth-rug, we saw Leander swimming to Hero across the Dardanelles; we saw Darius, the Persian, throwing his bridge over the same narrow passage, only to be defeated at Marathon; and Xerxes, too, bridging the famous straits to carry victory into Greece, till at last his navy went under at Salamis. We saw the pathetic figure of Byron swimming where Leander swam; and, in all, such an array of visions that the lure of the Eternal Waterway gripped us, and we were a-fidget to be there.

'Have eyes to see this idea also,' said the Colonel, who was a Tory of Tories. 'England dominates Gibraltar and Suez, the doors of the Mediterranean; let her complete her constellation by winning from the Turk the lost star of the Dardanelles, the only other entrance to the Great Sea.'

This roused the jingo devil in us, and we burst into applause.

Knowing thereby that he had won his audience, the Colonel beamed with inspiration. He rose, as though so enthralling a subject could only be dealt with standing, and cried:

'See this greater idea. For 500 years the Turk, by occupying Constantinople, has blocked the old Royal Road to India and the East. He is astride the very centre of the highways that should link up the continents. He oppresses and destroys the Arab world, which should be the natural junction of the great trunk railways that, to-morrow, shall join Asia, Africa, and Europe in one splendid spider's web. You are going to move the block from the line, and to join the hands of the continents. Understand, and be enthusiastic. I tell you, this joining of the continents is an unborn babe of history that leapt in the womb the moment the British battleships appeared off Cape Helles.'...

'So much for secular interest,'continued the Colonel, dropping his voice. 'Now, boys, follow me through this. You're not over-religious, I expect, but you're Christians before you're Moslems, and your hands should fly to your swords when I say the Gallipoli campaign is a New Crusade. You're going out to force a passage through the Dardanelles to Constantinople. And Constantinople is a sacred city. It's the only ancient city purely Christian in its origin, having been built by the first Christian Emperor in honour of the Blessed Virgin. Which brings us to the noblest idea of all. In their fight to wrest this city from the Turk, the three great divisions of the Church are united once more. The great Roman branch is represented by the soldiers and ships of France: the great Eastern Orthodox branch by the Russians, who are behind the fight: the great Anglican branch by the British, who can be proud to have started the movement, and to be leading it. Thus Christendom United fights for Constantinople, under the leadership of the British, whose flag is made up of the crosses of the saints. The army opposing the Christians fights under the crescent of Islam.

It's the Cross against the Crescent again, my lads. By Jove, it's splendid, perfectly splendid! And an English cross, too!

'Thank you, gentlemen; that's all; thank you.'" (*Tell England*, pp.214-7.)

It seems that the mingling of crosses was all the rage in 1914, on both sides of the Irish Sea.

The title for *Tell England* comes from another passage in the novel, where the three comrades in the 10th Division go to find the grave of their friend, Lieutenant White:

"And not a grave did we pass without examining it to see if it bore the name of White... Whenever we saw an isolated cross some distance away, we left our tracks to approach it, anxious not to pass, lest this were he. And then, quite unexpectedly, we came upon twenty graves side by side under one over-arching tree, which bore the legend: 'Pink Farm Cemetery.'And Doe said:

'There it is, Rupert.'

He said it with deliberate carelessness, as if to show that he was one not easily excited by sudden surprises.

'Where—where?'I asked.

'There—'Lieutenant R. White, Royal Dublin Fusiliers.'

'Good Lord!'I muttered: for it was true. We had walked right on to the grave of our friend. His name stood on a cross with those of six other officers, and beneath was written in pencil the famous epitaph:

'Tell England, ye who pass this monument,

We died for her, and here we rest content.'

The perfect words went straight to Doe's heart.

'Roop,'he said, 'if I'm killed you can put those lines over me.'

I fear I could not think of anything very helpful to reply..." (*Tell England*, p.327.)

It seems that even in death the Irish 10th Division died for England. How little things change.

*Tell England* was made into a 1931 film of the same name. According to American *Time Magazine* of 28th March 1932, the film was received well in the 'liberated' cities of Jerusalem and Baghdad:

"The sight of Turkish soldiers killing British soldiers raised a mighty Arab cheer in Jerusalem last week, causing the British censor to ban showings of a film called *Tell England*. British-made, this film has told England about her unsuccessful onslaught against Turkey at Gallipoli in 1915.

A fortnight ago in Bagdad the Turkish soldiers were cheered and the British soldiers hissed so loudly by subjects of King Feisal of Irak that His Majesty hastily barred *Tell England* from his realm. This year Irak hopes to make her world debut, hoping that Mother Britain will keep her promise to end British tutelage in 1932 and secure for the little kingdom full membership in the League of Nations."

It seems that the 'liberators'of Palestine and Iraq had outstayed their welcome (and their former oppressors were now seen as not so oppressive after all!) despite the efforts of the Irish 10th Division. It seems that Our War was not universally appreciated, even by those it was supposedly waged for.

### The Taoiseach's Account

This is how the Taoiseach's website describes the events at the start of the Great War and the formation of the 10th Division, which invaded Turkey in 1915:

"The Home Rule Bill was given the Royal Assent on the 18th September 1914 but its operation was suspended for one year or for the duration of the war when it would be reviewed with a view to securing the general consent of Ireland and the United Kingdom. On the 20th September, the leader of the Nationalist Party, John Redmond, who was widely expected to be the first Prime Minister of the new Irish Parliament, called on the Irish Volunteers to enlist. Irish soldiers in the British Expeditionary Force had already been in action in Flanders. The German advance through Belgium, the rumours of atrocities and refugees and the near capture of Paris had created an emotional atmosphere. The organisation split with those who followed Redmond being called the National Volunteers. About 12,000 of the 180,000 retained the Irish

Volunteers title and set themselves the objective of gaining full independence for Ireland, by force if necessary. The peaceful achievement of Home Rule was again in doubt due to the failure of the Government to deal with the build-up of arms in Northern Ireland and the public refusal of a cavalry brigade in the Curragh to enforce Home Rule Act if so requested.

About 80,000 enlisted in Ireland in the first 12 months of the war, some half of whom came from Ulster. The First New Army of 100,000 soldiers, K1, contained the 10th (Irish) Division which was formed in late August, 1914. It had three brigades. One had regiments with bases in all four provinces. The second was based in Ulster and the third was based in the other three provinces. The 16th (Irish ) Division of the Second New Army was formed in September, 1914. One brigade was from the province of Ulster. The 36th (Ulster) Division was authorised on the 28th October 1914. It was based on the formation and membership of the Ulster Volunteer Force to which a London based artillery unit was added. It contained men from all nine counties of Ulster. Redmond had sought to have all Irish regiments organised into a single fighting unit."

The 10th Division of Kitchener's New Army was composed of about 12,000 men divided into three infantry brigades, the 29th, 30th and 31st, each containing four battalions. New battalions of existing Irish Regiments of the British Army, such as the Inniskilling Fusiliers, the Connaught Rangers, the Royal Irish, Dublin and Munster Fusiliers were incorporated into the Division. These were 'Service' Battalions—i.e. they were only meant to exist for the duration of the war. So, despite the dreams of the Redmondites, they were not meant to form an Irish army after the end of the war which might have been used to fight for Home Rule.

The 10th Division was made up of a large number of Irishmen from Redmond's Irish Volunteers, along with Englishmen and Punjabis, but it was not an Irish Division. This was because the Unionists who dominated the War Office did not want an Irish Army. They wanted to disable Ireland's military expression, as England always had done, or continue to incorporate it within the confines of the Imperialist State, rather than enhance it. The War Office had given its blessing to an Ulster Division (the 36th), according a national recognition to a part of Ireland that had never sought national recognition. But to the Irish, who craved national recognition, the War Office would not concede any national recognition, despite their enthusiastic support for the Empire, the special circumstances, and the pleadings of Mr. Redmond to Mr. Asquith.

No matter. Home Rule Ireland persisted and it recruited for the Empire War on Germany, despite the snub from Lord Kitchener, the Kerryman who detested Ireland—apart from the bit of it which he could 'take his hat off to' for providing him with cannon fodder for the front.

The 10th Division of the British Army (largely to be composed of Irishmen, but not 'Irish') took up training at the Curragh Camp in Kildare in the early part of 1915. The previous year British officers at the Curragh had staged a

Mutiny against the Liberal Government's Home Rule Bill. But now enthusiastic Home Rulers recruited Irishmen to serve in the same Army, under the same officers, thus thinking to ensure that Home Rule would become a reality. And John Dillon imagined this army could be used against the Ulster Unionists in the circumstance of a quick victory over Germany, sometime in 1915, if they still resisted Home Rule after the War.

In May 1915 the troops were moved to England where General Kitchener, now heading the War Office, inspected them before sending them off against a new enemy that England had procured—the Turk—and Gallipoli.

### Ireland's 'Military Tradition'?

The Taoiseach's website suggests that there was nothing unusual in the Irish participation in the Great War, and presumably, in the assault on Turkey, given Ireland's 'strong military tradition':

> "Ireland has a strong military tradition. Even before the departure of the 'Wild Geese' after the Treaty of Limerick, Irish soldiers had practised their profession abroad. The recent exhibition of prints by Albrecht Durer contained a watercolour of Irish soldiers from 1521. Throughout the 19th century, the British Army in Ireland provided a convenient outlet for young men interested in soldiering. The country was divided into catchment areas for local regiments which offered regular income, attractive uniforms and the opportunity to travel abroad. Others joined the British navy. Irish emigrants to the United States had won distinction on both sides in the Civil War."

Well that's one way of putting it—that the Irish liked a fight and the British Army was a convenient outlet for their natural pent-up aggression!

But, if Ireland had ever had a 'strong military tradition', it was certainly broken in 1690-1, for centuries. England connived in the departure of 'Wild Geese' and subsequent Irish departures to the continent, as a means of draining away any potential resistance to its pacification of the country. There was the added bonus to its balance of power strategy that the extra armed men helped to fuel the fighting in Continental Europe, leaving more of the world to be conquered by the British Empire.

Subsequently, after a century of the Penal Laws, the British Army began to recruit a large part of its cannon-fodder in Ireland. And I'm sure, from hearing the popular songs about Recruiting Sergeants, that the attractions were the King's Shilling, along with 'regular income, attractive uniforms and the opportunity to travel abroad.'

Any military tradition that Ireland had was diverted into safe external channels by Britain, into Empire building, and expanding the British State. Ireland itself remained a most unmilitary society; any expression of Irish militarism was greatly discouraged, by various means. I remember one of John Dillon's speeches, from around the time of the Home Rule agitation, that pointed out to the crowd that if it had assembled any time in the previous centuries in anything like the numbers they mustered that day, they would have been ridden over by cavalry and mown down by grape-shot.

By the end of the nineteenth century Ireland had become thoroughly demilitarised and pacified and there was only a 'cabbage-patch rebellion' (1848) left in living memory. The Fenians had become the object of sentimental ballads and could be safely nodded to by the Irish Party politicians as icons of times past.

Not only that—the political representatives of the Irish and their press were most hostile to militarism, as any reading of the papers around the time of the Boer War clearly demonstrates. Up until the Unionists reintroduced the gun into Irish politics in 1912-14, Ireland had put its fate in the hands of peaceful parliamentary methods. And that is one of the reasons it was disabled in its conflict with the Unionists over Imperial Home Rule, and the reason why some Home Rulers supported the popular militarisation of nationalist Ireland in August 1914.

### A Great War to Unite Us All?

The Taoiseach's website offers the following further explanation for Irish enlistment in 1914:

> "The reasons for enlisting were as varied as the individuals. Some joined out of economic necessity. Others had the hope that the experience of serving side by side against a common enemy would forge friendships that would transcend the historic differences. Thomas Kettle, the former Nationalist MP for East Tyrone who served and was killed as a Lieutenant in the 9th Royal Dublin Fusiliers, believed that:
>
> 'Used with the wisdom which is sown in tears and blood, this tragedy of Europe may be and must be the prologue to the two reconciliations of which all statesmen have dreamed, the reconciliation of Protestant Ulster with Ireland, and the reconciliation of Ireland with Great Britain.'"

Of course, Irishmen, like Englishmen and Scots, always joined the British Army to seek adventure or ward off starvation. But 1914 was different. The Irish were recruited as an expression of national existence, to a make-believe Irish army, by the future Irish Prime Minister, representing a Home Rule Government-in-waiting. And it wasn't just the 'sweepings' or the 'corner boys' that joined up, but, as in England, the poets, the professors, and the solid middle classes.

A book of essays was published in 2002, with the title *Ireland And The Great War: A War To Unite Us All?*, edited by Adrian Gregory and Senia Paseta, two Oxford Fellows. Apparently Roy Foster suggested the title. In the Introduction the contemporary significance of the Great War is discussed:

> "As the Northern Ireland peace process gathered momentum the commemoration of the Great War, which had frequently been symbolic of the massive gulf between and within each of the 'two Irelands',became a forum for

dialogue and reconciliation. In 1987 the IRA had perpetrated one of the most striking human and symbolic atrocities by bombing the war memorial at Enniskillen on Remembrance Day. Eleven years later the Queen and the President of the Republic joined together in unveiling a memorial to the joint martyrdom of the 16th and 36th Divisions at Messines in 1917. Catholic, nationalist and southern Ireland could apparently link hands with northern Protestant unionists over the grave of William Redmond. The spirit of 1914 could be reborn, the clock turned back." (p.6.)

The most despicable of all reasons for Irish participation in the catastrophic *killing-fest* that was the Great War was surely the desire for Irish unity to be attained under Home Rule by killing Germans and Turks in massive numbers. At least the Unionists have never stooped so low as to suggest such a thing and have retained a dignified silence on such a monstrous fantasy — the only unionist contributor to the essay collection, Philip Orr, markedly dissents from the view. The proposal that 50,000 Irishmen should die — and with a proportionate killing rate 50,000 Germans, Austrians, Turks etc., not to mention catastrophic after-effects on Europe and the wider world — to persuade Unionists of Nationalist good intentions under Home Rule, really should be confined to the desperate ranting of the lunatic.

If Nationalist Ireland has the belief that it can connect up with Ulster Unionism by adopting Remembrance and issuing a *mea culpa* about the Great War it will be sorely disappointed. Ulster Unionists will simply pocket the apologies that the Republic is currently making for forgetting *Our War*, and those who served in it, and utilise them as part of the communal grind against the Northern Catholic community. This is because Ulster Unionists have always believed that they were right about the Great War and have always felt comfortable about participating in Imperial wars for the British Empire.

There is, however, something very tragic in the fact that Ulster Unionists and Irish Nationalists went off to kill Germans for the same reasons they formed the Ulster Volunteer Force and the Irish Volunteers. And this continuum of purpose, to kill a third-party in pursuit of their objectives in the Home Rule conflict, was extended by the Redmondites to a fourth party — the Ottoman Turks.

But that is the basis on which some nationalist politicians and academics have recently tried to use the catastrophe of the Great War for political purposes: 'The spirit of 1914 could be reborn, the clock turned back.' Oh what a lovely War!

### Recruiting For Which War?

The Redmondite recruitment propaganda of Irishmen to the British Army was largely directed toward warring on Germany — in defence of 'little Catholic Belgium', for 'the rights of small nations', against 'Prussianism', 'Nietzscheism' etc. I have read the Redmondite papers for late 1914 and for 1915, and the war on Turkey is barely mentioned by the Irish Party politicians and the Home Rule priests on the recruiting platforms. And yet maybe up to half the men who signed up, with the rhetoric against the Hun in their ears, were sent into War against Turkey and against Bulgaria.

There was, of course, the suggestion that the Dardanelles operation was ultimately part of the War on Germany, even if it was directed at Turkey. But that does not explain subsequent operations in the Middle East in which Irish soldiers of the Imperial armies participated, unless one is to believe that these were a kind of improvisation after the event.

The Irish were recruited largely to two divisions of the British Army, the 10th and the 16th (I am not including the 36th Ulster Division as an 'Irish' Division). It is difficult to obtain the numbers of Irish in each Division, but presumably they were fairly similar. So one 'Irish' Division went to France to fight the Germans and one went to the Dardanelles to take on the Turks. This means that Ireland's war effort was actually disproportionately directed against the Turk rather than the Hun. Since the vast majority were recruited to fight the Hun, were they not surprised to find themselves sailing into Gallipoli with the intention of bringing down the Ottoman Empire?

I wonder why has this aspect been ignored—that a substantial part of Ireland's contribution to the Great War on Germany was in fact to wage war on Turkey? Is it, by any chance, because it is difficult to explain?

The 10th (Irish) Division was heavily involved in the British remaking of the Middle East—one could say, making it what it is today. In early August 1915 it participated in landings at Suvla Bay on the Gallipoli Peninsula (with the 5th Battalion Connaught Rangers, which was attached to the 10th Division from this time). The Suvla Bay landings were designed to establish an expanded bridgehead north of Cape Helles and Anzac Cove, which had seen landings from Imperial forces (including Irish soldiers) at the end of April, but which had been contained on the beaches by the Turks. The overall objective was to secure the Gallipoli Peninsula for the minesweeping operation in the narrows of the Dardanelles, that was necessary before the fleet could sail up to Constantinople.

When, in December 1915, it was clear that the operation had been a failure *The Irish News* of Belfast wrote an editorial entitled *The Gallipoli Tragedy*:

"On the 22nd of June, Mr. Winston Churchill, then Chancellor of the Duchy of Lancaster, referred to the operations at Gallipoli in the course of a speech to his Dundee constituents, and said: 'We are within a few miles of the greatest victory that history has ever known.' Divested of Cabinet rank, Major Churchill is now fighting in the trenches in France; and, six months almost to the day after his intimation that the conquest of Constantinople was at hand, the War Office announced that: 'All the troops in Suvla Bay and Anzac, together with their guns and stores, have been successfully transferred, with insignificant casualties, to another sphere of operations.' In plain terms, the Western strip of

Gallipoli coast which had been won with unparalleled gallantry and held at enormous sacrifice has been abandoned... It was at Sedd-ul-Bahr that the Dublin and Munster Fusiliers and battalions of a Hampshire regiment faced storms of shot and shell such had never previously been poured into bands of soldiers... The lives of thousands were sacrificed needlessly... More than 106,000 British casualties were reported on the 9th of November; the total lives lost, and wounded men on the British side in Gallipoli cannot fall short of 120,000. Major Churchill's prophesy reads grimly in the light of events... Undoubtedly, political and strategic advantages accrued from the invasion at Gallipoli—though these may have been overbalanced by the failure of the scheme... The situation in the Near East has materially altered—not for the better... Now the centre of interest is Salonika and its neighbourhood."

And so the 10th Division, having been beaten by the Turks, were evacuated in late September 1915 and moved to Salonika, in Macedonia, during early October 1915. Salonika was part of Greece at this time and there the 10th Division sat, aiming to put pressure on the neutral Greek Government to enter the War.

The situation was complicated by the Bulgarian entry into the War on the Austro-German side and a strong Austrian offensive to the North through Serbia at just this moment. The 10th Division was moved up to Lake Dorian, fifty miles north of Salonika, in Serbia, behind the Serbian army. This left it vulnerable to an attack from the north-east and it was forced by a Bulgarian advance into retreat, back into Greece (whose neutrality the Bulgarians, unlike the British, respected).

In mid-December 1915 the 10th Division retired to Salonika. It spent the next year establishing large fortifications around this part of neutral Greece, for which work it became known as the 'Salonika gardeners.'

The 10th Division in Salonika was ultimately used to help bring about the fall of the Greek Government and prompt Greece's participation in the War. It thus set off a series of events that were to prove catastrophic to the Christians (and to large numbers of Moslems) of the Balkans and Asia Minor.

In September 1917 the 10th was shipped to British-occupied Egypt and on to Palestine, where it assaulted Gaza and assisted in the capture of Jerusalem in the service of the Balfour Declaration.

In September 1918 the Division took part in the battle of Nablus during the final destruction of the Ottoman Empire. The 1st Battalion Connaught Rangers (which was part of the Indian Army) helped secure Mesopotamia (Iraq) for the Empire.

So what Ireland helped achieve in the Great War was the destruction of the Ottoman Empire, the destabilisation of Greek democracy, the capture of Palestine for the British Zionist enterprise and the Imperial conquest and establishment of Iraq, amongst other things. That surely is an achievement that merits some comment.

### General Sir Bryan Mahon and The 10th Division

The 10th Division was led by General Sir Bryan Mahon, a career soldier in the British Empire (who was later rewarded by the Free State with a place in its Senate). The *Freeman's Journal*, the newspaper of the Irish Party, had an editorial on the 30th October 1915 which sought to provide inspiration to the Irish volunteers for the Front, by citing the achievements of an Irish hero in the military service of the Empire:

> "The appointment of General Sir Brian Mahon to the command of the British forces in Serbia will give much satisfaction to his many friends in his native land. The new Commander is a Galway man, and his father and mother are both natives of the county... The new Commander was born 53 years ago at Belleville, Co. Galway. His military career was varied and in many climes, and has won him no little fame as a military commander. He has been the General in command of the 10th Irish Division since 1914. His military career began in the 8th Hussars, with which he served in India from the date of his joining, from 1883 to 1893. He took part in the Egyptian campaign in 1896, and he was mentioned in dispatches for bravery as Adjutant of the regiment. He gained the D.S.O. in the Dongola expedition, and was made Lieutenant-Colonel for his action in the Khartoum expedition. In the Kordofan expedition he took a prominent part in the capture of Kalifa. This won him the generalship of the cavalry brigade. In the South African war he commanded the cavalry brigade, and he was the first to reach Mafeking at the head of the relieving column. He filled the office of Military Governor of Kordofan after the South African War, and left that office in 1909 on being created General of Division, when he assumed command of the Lucknow Division in India. He left India last year to take command of the 10th Irish Division, which has been in the Dardanelles since the spring."

The *Freeman's* biographical sketch was compiled from *The Tenth (Irish) Division in Gallipoli* by Major Bryan Cooper who served in the 10th Division and wrote its history in a rest period from the Front. Major Cooper, Unionist MP for South Dublin until 1910, later became Military Censor for the British Government in Ireland during 1918 before joining Cumann na nGaedheal after the Treaty was signed. (He made a contribution to the debate on the Treaty of Lausanne, included later.)

In his book, Major Cooper describes how the Division that attacked Gallipoli was fortunate to have had such experienced campaigners as General Mahon:

> "The General Commanding the 10th Division had seen the last warriors of Mahdism lying dead on their sheepskins around the corpse of their Khalifa. One of the Brigadiers had witnessed the downfall of Cetewayo's power in Ulundi; another had marched with the Guards Brigade, across the desert to Tel-el-Kebir; while the third had played his part in the desperate fighting outside Suakim in 1884. Nearly all the Colonels and many of the Company

Commanders had served in the South African War and so had a number of the senior N.C.O.s." (pp.59-60.)

General Mahon was the sort of person *The Freeman's Journal* had detested a decade and a half previously when its editorials celebrated the casualties suffered by the Dublin Fusiliers in assaulting the Boer Republics. But in August 1914 all had changed in the pursuit of Home Rule.

The British Imperial campaigns, which General Mahon had commanded forces for, were military aggressions against 'lesser breeds' which the Irish Party and its newspaper, *The Freeman's Journal*, had ferociously denounced in its recent past. Mahon had participated in the celebrated Relief of Mafeking in the Boer War, an event that *The Freeman* frequently jeered at during its previous life—as boisterous, jingoistic 'Mafficking.'

The 'Dongola expedition', in which General Mahon won the DSO, was the first operation in the British conquest of Sudan. In 1897, the Salisbury Government sent General Kitchener to conquer and 'civilize' the Sudan—and teach it a lesson for what had happened to General 'Chinese' Gordon at Khartoum in 1884. In September 1898, Kitchener overwhelmed the Dervishes at the Battle of Omdurman. But Omdurman was more a massacre than a battle— it was the nineteenth century's 'turkey shoot' on the Basra Road from Kuwait. Tens of thousands of Sudanese were slaughtered by Britain's long-range rifle fire, machine guns, artillery and gun-boats. Kitchener ordered no prisoners be taken, and the wounded were killed or left to die in the desert—something that appalled the young Winston Churchill, who was a war correspondent embedded with Kitchener's Army. When Kitchener's Army reached Khartoum the following day, Major Maxwell (the General Maxwell who ordered the executions after the Easter Rising) summarily executed people by the score. The local Islamic leader was cut in two and Kitchener's Army was marched between the two parts of his body. The Mahdi's body was exhumed and Kitchener had its head cut off so that he could have the skull mounted as a cup for his desk. In the end, he had the Mahdi's bones thrown into the Nile. Some Liberal and Irish Nationalist MPs tried to have Kitchener's pay withheld for the barbarous conduct of English revenge in Sudan, that General Mahon won his medals for. They failed.

Michael Davitt MP had strongly condemned the behaviour of the British forces at Omdurman and in the Sudan and had resigned his Parliamentary seat over the South African War and its concentration camps in which at least 40,000 perished (including 25,000 children as well as an uncounted number of blacks). But by 1915 'Home Rule was on the Statute Book' and not a word was said by the Irish Party in condemnation of these Imperial adventures, and General Mahon, a leading participant in them, was held up to the Irish nation as a great hero, to be emulated by other Irishmen.

## Bad History or Revised History?

Here is the Taoiseach's account of Ireland's Great War on Turkey:

"The stalemate on the Western Front prompted an alternative approach to defeating Germany. The capture of Constantinople, now Istanbul, would give a direct link to the Russian ally and a successful eastern front campaign could be undertaken. A British Navy attempt to sail up the Dardanelles on March 18 failed with the loss of several ships. Despite the advanced warning that this gave the Turks, the British and French attempted a land invasion on the 25th April. They went ashore at six locations but the Turkish defence held them close to the beaches. A second attempt was made on the 6th August at Suvla Bay but this also ground to a halt. The campaign was abandoned and last of the troops were withdrawn in January 1916. Churchill, who had proposed the campaign, had to resign from the Cabinet. He subsequently lost his seat in the House of Commons and had to wait until the outbreak of the Second World War to return to a position of power.

The 1st Battalions of the Royal Dublin, Munster and Inniskilling Fusiliers took part in the landing on April 25th at Cape Helles which was a perfect defensive location with gun emplacements housed on steep slopes. The naval bombardment failed to neutralize the Turkish defences. The Royal Dublin Fusiliers and the Royal Munster Fusiliers were the first to disembark from the S.S. River Clyde and of the first 200 men to leave the ship, 149 were killed and 30 wounded immediately. The Dublins had 25 officers and 987 other ranks but only, one officer and 374 other ranks made it ashore. There were 637 casualties in the first 36 hours.

The Allies decided to launch a fresh attack against the Turks and chose Suvla Bay, 25 miles north of Cape Helles. The first Irish volunteer unit to go into battle was the 10th (Irish) Division which contained the new service battalions of the Irish regiments. As a result of administrative incompetence, the Division's artillery had been sent to France and the men arrived without either maps or orders. The Division did not fight as a unit. There was a chronic water shortage and the soldiers ran out of ammunition and had to resort to throwing stones at the enemy. At least 3,411 serving with Irish battalions were killed or missing, 569 from the 1st Battalion Royal Dublin Fusiliers alone...

On September 29, 1915, the 2,454 strong 10th (Irish) Division set sail from Gallipoli for Salonika to fight on the Bulgarian front. On the 3rd October, the Royal Dublin and Munster Fusiliers were at the front line and were ordered to take the village of Jenikoj which is now in Macedonia. In the attack, they lost 385 men killed, wounded or missing. There is a granite Celtic cross to commemorate the 10th (Irish) Division near the village of Robrovo in the Former Yugoslav Republic of Macedonia. This complements the ones at Wijtschate in Flanders and Guillemont in France."

I wonder in which election it was that the proposer of the campaign, Winston Churchill, 'subsequently lost his seat in the House of Commons and had to wait until the outbreak of the Second World War to return to a position of power'? There was, indeed, an election due in 1915, just after the Gallipoli assault. But it was called-off, with a minimum of fuss, and the British Government simply extended its term, rejuvenating itself by a Unionist coup.

There was, in fact, no election until the end of 1918. Winston Churchill was a prominent Government Minister in the Coalition formed thereafter, having a large say in the Irish Treaty negotiations and enforcement, as Secretary of State for the Colonies. And, in the subsequent Conservative Government, he was Chancellor of the Exchequer, one of the most important 'positions of power', I would have imagined. In fact, even in his 'wilderness years' in the 1930s, Churchill was consulted about important affairs of State, such as the Peel Commission on Palestine.

Churchill, in fact, only lost his job at the Admiralty in May 1915 when the Unionist coup forced Liberal Ministers out to make way for them—with Churchill a handy candidate for demotion because of the botching at Gallipoli. He actually remained in the Government as Chancellor of the Duchy of Lancaster until November 1915, when he resigned to do something more substantial at the Front. And he remained an MP all the time! He returned to the Government in 1917, becoming Minister for Munitions for the remainder of the War and then from January 1919 Secretary of State for War.

It was not till over seven years after Gallipoli that Churchill lost his seat as an MP. Churchill lost in Dundee at the General Election of 1922—after the break up of the Coalition in the wake of the Chanak Crisis. This had nothing whatever to do with the Gallipoli operation of 1915, though Britain did come close to resuming the war with Turkey, and thundering into another Gallipoli! And he quickly returned to Parliament in 1924 as a Tory in the General Election of that year.

In his *Seven Pillars Of Wisdom*, Colonel Lawrence—of 'Arabia' fame, recounts Churchill's important input to the making of the Middle East in 1921-22:

> "Mr. Winston Churchill was entrusted by our harassed Cabinet with the settlement of the Middle East; and in a few weeks, at his conference in Cairo, he made straight all the tangle, finding solutions fulfilling (I think) our promises in letter and spirit (where humanly possible) without sacrificing any interest of our Empire or any other interest of the people concerned."

But if the Department of the Taoiseach does not know about Churchill's role in the making of Ireland through the Treaty, one cannot expect it to be informed about his influence on the Middle East.

How is it possible, though, for someone to put the statement: Winston Churchill 'subsequently lost his seat in the House of Commons and had to wait until the outbreak of the Second World War to return to a position of power' on the Taoiseach's website and for it to remain there for two years without anyone noticing it? What does this say about the knowledge of history today in Ireland's ruling circles? Has it too become a victim of Remembrance?

The other noticeable thing about the account is how it virtually ends with Gallipoli and says very little about the 10th Division's exploits in Greece, Egypt, Palestine and Mesopotamia afterwards. There is no discussion about the subsequent political repercussions of Ireland's contribution to the War on Turkey. One wonders, is that bad history or just diplomatic history? Lest we remember...

### Why did Ireland go to war on Turkey?

So the question remains: Why did Ireland go to war on Turkey in November 1914?

The present writer seeks to address this and raise some other questions which Irish historians have not cared to ask. For instance: What were these young Irishmen doing attacking a country that had done Ireland no wrong (that had even provided assistance during the Famine of 1847-8), on behalf of an Empire that had done it plenty of wrong? Why was Ireland at War with the Turks in the first place? And why was the British Empire itself attacking Turkey when, for a century previously, the Ottomans had been allies in arms with Britain?

The answers to these questions have unearthed some forgotten aspects of Ireland's Great War on Turkey between 1914 and 1924.

These include the fact that Ireland actually remained at war with Turkey until 1924. In one respect that is no surprise. Reading the newspapers from 1919-22 the present writer was left with the inescapable conclusion that the Great War did not end in November 1918. What ceased at the time of the Armistice was only military operations on the Western front. A naval blockade of Germany was carried on into May 1919, fighting continued in Poland and many parts of Eastern Europe and the Balkans, and the Near East were aflame for years. This was all part of the working out of the Great War but has been consigned to the footnotes—or 'details'—of British history books for reasons of State (and Remembrance commemorations, of course).

A second forgotten aspect is that the hero of Turkish resistance to Imperialism and the father of the modern Turkish nation, Mustapha Kemal (Ataturk), was greatly admired by the *Catholic Bulletin* (a supposedly Catholic-sectarian publication according to modern Irish historians); and that there were some extraordinary parallels between the British treatment of the emerging Irish and Turkish States.

There was, of course, one major difference. The Irish failed and the Turks succeeded.

Consequently the Irish Free State, having dis-established the Irish Republic, was forced to join the rest of the British Empire in ending their war on Turkey in the Treaty of Lausanne in 1924—even though its members had, as part of Sinn Fein, disassociated themselves from Redmond's war of 1914. By this Treaty, Turkey was recognised as an independent sovereign state—having seen off the Imperialists by a combination of arms and skilful negotiation.

In many ways this story is a tale of three treaties. The Anglo-Irish Treaty of 1921, the 1923 Treaty of Lausanne and the forgotten Treaty of Sèvres, which was imposed on a defeated nation, Turkey, at the point of a gun in 1920. But the diktat was resisted by that nation, so much so that the Empire imposing it went into decline itself as a result of the collapse of its will to enforce the terms of the Treaty.

This story is told by outlining the main events of the period, with extracts from the Irish, British and American press, to give a flavour of the times. It proceeds on the same basis as my previous book, *The Rise And Fall Of Imperial Ireland* (Athol Books, 2003), which used fullish extracts from the time to counteract the misinformation that has been inserted into the popular understanding of past events. I feel this gives the reader a more complete understanding of the thought processes and the reasoning behind the actions of the decision makers of the time.

It also contains a number of selections from Hanns Froembgen's 1938 book on Ataturk, some coverage from the *Catholic Bulletin* (1922-4) of Near Eastern affairs, and transcripts from the debates in the Free State Parliament on the ratification of the Treaty of Lausanne (1924).

The Chapter containing extracts from the *Catholic Bulletin* for 1922 is intended to provide further appreciation of the fact that the War cannot be said to have finished in November 1918, by any stretch of the imagination. It demonstrates the mess made of Europe and the Middle East by Britain's (and Ireland's) Great War. The *Bulletin* summed it up like this at the time:

"For nations and peoples, at home and abroad, the year 1922 has been one of prolonged agony. Horrible as was the World War in its toll of life and in its unnatural methods of destroying humanity, it is incomparable in tragedy and pathos to the fratricidal strifes, the tyrannies, the assassinations, executions and enforced famines that have characterised the existence of Western and Eastern nations during the year that is now drawing to a close."

The *Catholic Bulletin* approach indicates the understanding that had started to develop in Anti-Treatyite Ireland and was to enable Fianna Fail to emerge and follow Ataturk's example and establish Independent Ireland in the following couple of decades. So, perhaps as well as fathering the Turkish State, Ataturk might be also given some credit in forming the view of independent Ireland, having repelled the invaders of Home Rule Ireland from the shores of Gallipoli.

Pat Walsh.
*January 2009*

Note on spelling: I have maintained the diversity of spelling of places and people from the accounts of the time. They are, after all, all part of the rich tapestry of life that was the Ottoman Empire, before Ireland helped Britain to destroy it.

The Rt. Hon. Winston Churchill
First Lord, October 1911-May 1915

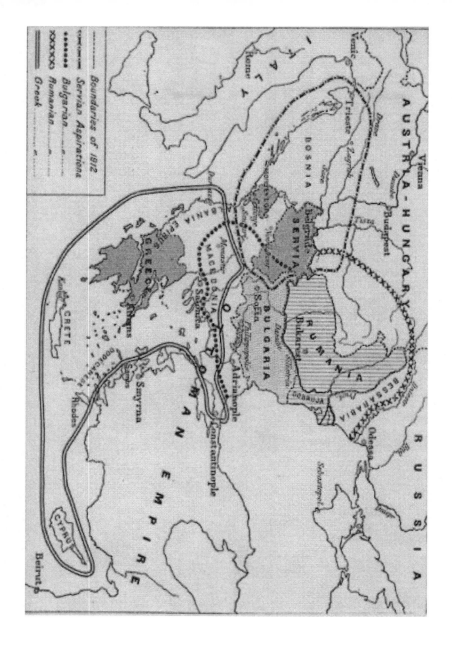

Balkan 1912 Borders
and Nationalist aspirations

# 1. Preliminaries—Britain And The Ottoman Empire

The following description of Turkey in Europe was published in 1919, a few years after the Turks had been expelled from South-Eastern Europe. It is in a book by the Member of Parliament for West Belfast, William E. D. Allen, who had something of an interest in the Near East:

> "For five hundred years an army of occupation has held South-Eastern Europe. When a hostile army occupies a country, all the ordinary life comes to a standstill: there is little trade, no social intercourse, probably misery and privation... When the 'Turkish Night' overshadowed the Balkan lands, all trade, all art, all literature, all education, all social progress ceased. The Bulgaria of Tsar Simeon was as progressive as the England of Edward the Confessor; the Serbia of Stephen Dushan was as advanced as the France of St. Louis. But to-day the Serbs, the Bulgars, the Greeks, and the Albanians are without a national culture, without political institutions, without coherent traditions, without a history. They are the men of the fifteenth century: they understand only the argument of force and the diplomacy of treachery; they have the mentality of medieval brigands...
>
> The Turks' arrogant tolerance of subject religions, if not so oppressive, was more debasing than the brutal proselytising of the Spaniards.
>
> The 'Turkish Night' is the negation of history.
>
> How was it possible for an obscure tribe of nomad shepherds from the steppes of Central Asia to impose its domination upon a dozen nations of Europe?" (*The Turks In Europe—A Sketch Study*, pp.1-2.)

That could be said to be the standard British view of the Turks which increasingly gained credence in Redmondite Ireland. The 'Turkish Night' is a common theme of British propaganda against the Ottoman Empire in this period.

But it is important to understand that this view, though it was a feature of Gladstonian Liberalism in the latter part of the nineteenth century, was adopted by the British State late in the day, as an adjunct to its destroying of the Ottoman State.

W.E.D. Allen (1901-73) is a curious character. He was educated at Eton, wrote *The Turks In Europe* in 1919 and became a military correspondent during Britain's proxy war between the Greeks and the Turks a year later. He was elected at the 1929 election for West Belfast but left the Unionist Party in 1931 to join Sir Oswald Mosley's New Party. He was a close friend of Mosley and helped him to pursue his ambitions by supporting him financially and also by contributing articles to *The Blackshirt*. Allen wrote a book entitled *BUF, Oswald Mosley And British Fascism* in 1934 under the pen name of James Drennan and apparently acted as a conduit between Mussolini and Mosley for financial provision to the British Fascists. It was reported around this time that he was an MI5 agent handled by Sir Basil Thomson, the Head of Special Branch (of whom we will hear more later).

Between Britain's two World Wars Allen travelled widely and conducted extensive research on the history of the peoples of Anatolia and the Caucasus. He was a Foreign Service Officer from 1943 until 1948, heading the British Embassy's Information Office in Ankara, Turkey (despite his tirades against the Turks). He stepped down and returned to Belfast in 1949, running *David Allen's*, the famous Belfast bill-posting company, with his two younger brothers. And he was awarded the OBE in 1948—having seamlessly travelled from Ulster Unionist to Fascist to honoured servant of the Empire.

An explanation for his life's journey may lie in the incisive comment he made in his Fascist book of 1934:

"Far from being alien to the character of the English people, Fascism is rather a new expression of a very strong... historical tendency in English thought." (*Oswald Mosley And British Fascism*, p.217.)

But his views on the Ottoman Empire are very much of the mainstream propagandist type. Despite the fact that Allen was an Ulster Unionist, and Fascist, his views about the Turks were increasingly shared by the Irish Home Rulers. Along with the joint venture of killing Germans that was the second thing that Ulster Unionists and Irish Nationalists had in common.

### The Ottoman Empire—Propaganda And Otherwise

Our understanding of the Ottoman Empire is deeply coloured by the British Great War propaganda of Wellington House (which we shall look at in more detail in a later chapter). This propaganda was designed to counter the view that '*the Turk is a gentleman*'—a view promoted when the British State wished to justify its support for the Ottoman Empire in the face of the hostility of Gladstonian Christian morality (the force that scuppered Parnell).

The Ottoman Empire was characterized in this propaganda as a decrepit and ramshackle affair—the 'sick man of Europe'. The origin of this phrase is older than Wellington House, dating back to the time of the Crimean War. In January 1853, Czar Nicholas I, complaining of a high fever and in agony from gout, had risen from his sickbed to meet Sir Hamilton Seymour, the British Ambassador in St Petersburg. Their conversations turned to the Czar's main preoccupation—Constantinople. Nicholas attempted to convince Sir Hamilton Seymour that the Ottoman Empire was on the point of collapse. He told the British Ambassador:

"we have a sick man on our hands, a man who is seriously ill; it will . . . be a great misfortune if he escapes us one of these days, especially before all the arrangements are made." (cited in Alan Palmer, *The Banner Of Battle; The Story Of The Crimean War*, p.56.)

The 'arrangements' the Czar had in mind were for the sharing out of the Ottoman Empire by the European Powers. But at this time (despite the notable exception of Richard Cobden, the Manchester Capitalist) England was most unwilling to see the Russians in Constantinople and, instead of sharing Ottoman spoils, they went to war with Russia the following year to resuscitate the 'sick man of Europe'.

But a half century later there was a dramatic turnabout and the Ottomans became the 'sick man of Europe' for the British too — an empire of Armenian massacres, peopled by a lazy race of bloodthirsty Turks, incapable of governing themselves, let alone others, who destroyed everything they touched and retarded progress everywhere they had conquered. The Turks were 'a merciless oppressor', 'a remorseless bully', 'pure barbarians', 'degenerate', and had 'strewn the earth with ruins'. These are some phrases used about Turks in *The Clean-Fighting Turk, A Spurious Claim* by Mark Sykes. But they could have come from a hundred similar publications from the period.

The message was that the demise of the Ottoman Empire was inevitable and far too long in coming.

And yet the Ottoman Empire was an amazingly successful and durable construction.

In the 14th Century the Turks had taken in hand the Moslem world and constructed it into a distinct entity that remained in existence for 500 years. The Osman Turks or Ottomans had overthrown the Eastern Roman Empire, capturing Constantinople in 1453, and established the city as their capital. Constantinople, originally known as Byzantium, had been the capital of the Eastern Roman Empire for about a thousand years before becoming the centre of the Ottoman Empire. The Ottoman Government at Constantinople was known as the *Sublime Porte*, or *Porte*, from the name of the gate to the Grand Vizier's office (the Grand Vizier was the Sultan's chief minister).

The city was built mainly on the Western side of the channel separating Europe from Asia. And it was a very cosmopolitan city. Around half its population was Moslem but it had large numbers of Jews, Greeks and Armenians, who dominated the commercial and financial life of the city. The different races lived in different quarters of the city, as they did in most towns in the Balkans and Western Anatolia. The European quarter of the city lay to the North of the Golden Horn, the great bay that dominated Constantinople, whilst the old quarter was to the South, housing the bulk of the Turks.

During the following two centuries the Empire expanded through the Balkans to the gates of Vienna, where it was halted in 1683 by the last military hurrah of the disintegrating Polish State.

By the early nineteenth century the Ottoman Empire was a vast area of land straddling three continents bordered by seven seas. It stretched from Tunis in the West to Mesopotamia and Kuwait in the East, and from Rumania in the North down to Aden and Yemen in the South. It had a small population in relation to its size — only thirty-six million in 1830 — but contained a wide diversity of races: Turks, Arabs, Egyptians, Kurds, Armenians, Greeks, Serbs,

Bulgarians, Macedonians, Albanians and Rumanians as well as a sizeable number of Jews. It also contained the holy places of three great world religions.

A constant theme of Western views of the Turks was that the Ottoman Empire was a more brutal place to live in than Christian Europe. However, in 1925 an American writer and veteran of the Great War, Alexander Powell, who was generally very anti-Turk in his writings, made this contrast between the Ottoman Empire and Christian Europe between the Middle Ages and the early modern period:

> "As a matter of fact, the history of the Ottoman Empire is less marred by religious intolerance and by massacres due to religious hatreds than the history of European states from the thirteenth to the sixteenth centuries. It is well to remember that when the Crusaders were butchering their Moslem prisoners in Palestine, when the horrors of the Spanish Inquisition were in full swing, when Cromwell's troopers were massacring the Catholics of Ireland, when Protestants in France were being exterminated by order of the French king, when Jews were being subjected to countless persecutions and barbarities in every European country, Moslems, Christians and Jews were dwelling side by side, in perfect amity, in Asia Minor." (E. Alexander Powell, *The Struggle For Power in Moslem Asia*, p. 120.)

The fluid and open Ottoman social system and society had the effect of encouraging refugees from other systems to seek their fortunes in the Ottoman Empire rather than in the rigid and closed societies which existed elsewhere in Europe. The Ottoman Turks absorbed peoples into their expanding Empire without eradicating the cultures of the societies they conquered, and allowed them to continue to live their own lives, practise their own religions, and live within their own cultures without interference—whilst at the same time forming part of a very rich and diverse multi-ethnic and religious society.

The Ottoman system seemed peculiar to the West in that it made no distinctions between races or 'nationalities' within it. It viewed nationalities as spurious constructions, cobbled together with a hotchpotch of adopted characteristics, that were largely accidental. And there was a lot to be said for this approach. The intermingling of race, language, religion and culture was so complex within the Ottoman Empire that it was difficult to separate distinct nationalities at all. So, with this in mind, the Ottomans sought to establish a loose framework of administration that would facilitate the different races and religions, that often overlapped socially and geographically, to live together in the way they preferred, and in relative harmony.

The English writer, A. N. Wilson, in his 2002 book, *The Victorians,* notes:

> "Throughout four centuries, it had been the task of the Ottoman sultans to preside over… unedifying squabbles, and to impose, for the sake of civil order, a culture of mutual tolerance on the inhabitants of their empire. In cities as various as Constantinople itself, Alexandria and Sarajevo, Christians, Jews

and Moslems had been taught by their Turkish rulers that where religious difference was in question, there really was one political option: live and let live. Moslems and Jews were nearly always able to accept this, in relation to one another and to the Christians. The followers of Christ, however, while finding it possible to live at peace with their fellow monotheists of the Islamic or Judaic persuasion, could not always resist outbursts of violence against their co-religionists, and the inter-denominational hatred grew hotter, the closer they came to their most sacred shrines." (pp. 172-3.)

The Ottoman Empire was a very different entity to the British Empire. There was no great civilising mission in it, no concerted religious proselytizing, no desire to extirpate conquered inhabitants and their traditional ways of life. It operated a relaxed and easy-going approach to its subjects of 'live and let live', only requiring taxes and some military service of them, in times of necessity.

A Jewish resident of Salonika, Leon Sciaky, who experienced the last years of Ottoman rule in Macedonia, described in his memoir the attitude the Islamic Turks took to other religious groups:

"When the Turks conquered the Balkans they brought with them a theocratic organisation. Islam, 'The Path,' was a code which ruled life in all its details. The Koran settled the conduct of the individual from the caliph down to the beggar. Mohammed II, who by his conquest of Constantinople in 1453 put an end to the decadent and corrupt Byzantine Empire, was confronted with a non-Muslim population to whom the Holy Law did not apply.

It was with a spirit of sympathy and tolerance far ahead of his time that he approached the problem of governing his new subjects. It was the spirit of the Muslim, for whom hospitality is a religious duty, and in whose house or tent even the infidel must be protected, which suggested the solution.

Since he had no conception of civil code or administration, since the individual had for him no entity outside his religious affiliation, each religious group was given virtual autonomy, and its head made responsible for the government and good conduct of his people.

Each millet organised itself around its head, recognised by the sultan as its representative and received at the court as its ambassador. Each was a self-governing state within the empire, independent from the others insofar as its own affairs was concerned. The Turks never made an effort to assimilate the non-Muslims, neither did they attempt to impose upon them their own Koranic laws.

Each people had its own courts in which disputes between coreligionists were settled according to their own laws, and each levied taxes to defray the cost of its schools, charitable institutions, hospitals and government. This organisation, ideal at its inception, in the course of years led to abuses and encouraged the ultimate segregation of the various millets into immiscible groups with ingrown concerns and aspirations often hostile to each other." (*Farewell To Salonica, City At The Crossroads*, pp.122-3.)

The Ottoman system of *millet*, or religious community, formally recognised the rights and obligations of non-Moslems. Ottoman subjects were organized into four religiously-based *millets*, the Muslims, the Jews, the Armenian Orthodox, and the Greek Orthodox, each run by its own religious hierarchy. These *millets* were charged with caring for everything not cared for by the Ottoman Ruling Class. They attended not only to the affairs pertaining to religion, but also to civil society, organizing the sections of the cities in which members of their *millet* lived, and with education, social security, justice, all in accordance with their own religious and cultural traditions.

The Orthodox and Jewish *millets* were allowed full freedom of worship and exemption from military conscription. The only disadvantages in being a non-Moslem within the Ottoman State was in the slightly heavier taxes (to gain exclusion from the army by contributing financially to its upkeep) and the requirement to convert to Islam to hold some of the highest offices of the State.

If Britain had governed Ireland as the Turks administered the Balkans, there would have been no need for Home Rule. But the British Empire was an entirely different organism than the Turkish Empire—being a species which increasingly saw itself as lord of the jungle of humanity within the Darwinian mode of life.

The Ottomans built their Empire through the contributions of all the people they could attract to its service. Alone out of all the states in Europe and Asia at the time, the Ottomans accepted the entry and settlement of refugees fleeing from persecution, regarding them as assets in work of building the Empire. The Ottoman Empire was immensely successful in incorporating the talents of its peoples in the common interest—for, while the Empire was formally Turkish, it seems to have been operated, and been utilised, by its constituent elements, in their own interest. Jason Goodwin describes its achievement well:

"This was an Islamic Empire, though many of its subjects were not Muslim, and it made no effort to convert them. It controlled the thoroughfares between East and West, but it was not very interested in trade. It was, by common consent, a Turkish empire, but most of its dignitaries and officers, and its shock troops, too, were Balkan Slavs. Its ceremonial was Byzantine, its dignity Persian, its wealth Egyptian, its letters Arabic. The Ottomans were not accounted builders by contemporaries—even though one grim old Grand Vizier was remembered as the man who built more churches than Justinian. They came with no schemes of agricultural improvement, although production soared in the lands they conquered in Europe. They were not religious fanatics as a rule; Sunni Muslims, they followed the moderate Hanefi school of Koranic interpretation...

Its most brilliant sailors were all Greek. Its canniest merchants were Armenian. Its soldiers were ineptly led while everywhere admired for their courage... The Ottomans seemed to stand, in their final years, for negotiation over decision, for tradition over innovation, and for a dry understanding of the world's ways over all that was thrusting and progressive about the western world." (Lords of the Horizon, pp. xiv-xv)

But the very thing that produced contentment of life for Ottoman subjects — its lack of thrusting progress—seems to have marked it out for destruction by the West.

The Ottoman Empire was the most successful example of collaboration between different peoples in history. Collaboration was accomplished in Constantinople-Istanbul through bribery, corruption, dealing, trade-offs and, occasionally, violence; that encouraged the settlement of disputes between the various peoples before they became full scale wars. From the fourteenth to the nineteenth centuries peoples of diverse races and religions intermingled for the most part contentedly and successfully under Ottoman administrations and even the Balkans were a relatively peaceful area for the best part of five hundred years.

C.F. Dixon-Johnson was a British hero of the Boer War. He wrote *The Armenians* in 1916 when his nation was at war with the Turks, and when the Armenians were being used by the *Entente* as an instrument to destabilize the Ottoman State. He was certainly not a propagandist for the Turks. Yet Dixon-Johnson described an immensely tolerant and easy-going people, quite contrary to British propaganda of the time:

"In peace the Turks are a good-natured, easy-going race, hospitable, generous to the poor, and particularly fond of animals and children—a sure sign of a kindly and humane disposition, long-suffering, but when provoked, like all the near Eastern races both Moslem and Christian, exhibiting a fury out of all proportion to the insult according to our Western ideas. In war time the Turks are neither fanatical nor intolerant. They are indeed less so than any of the Western nations with all their supposed superiority.

When Greece was fighting Turkey, the Greeks of Constantinople, although Ottoman subjects, actually dared to fly the Greek flag over their houses, and after the death of their archbishop, which occurred at that same time, paraded his dead body, seated upon the Episcopal throne, through the streets of Pera, escorted by their prelates and clergy, without being subjected to any molestation. Annually, too, the Host is borne in procession through the streets of the City of the Khalif. Contrast this extraordinary tolerance with present conditions in London, where German subjects are forbidden to pray in their own churches in the German tongue and where, only a few years ago, the British Government on the occasion of the Eucharistic Congress refused to allow the Host to be borne through the streets of Westminster.

During the Balkan war, when even the mosques were crowded with sick and starving refugees and only the most heroic efforts of the Turkish army, decimated with cholera, were able to keep the victorious Bulgars outside the gates of the city whose very foundations were shaking under the vibration of the enemy's guns, Greeks, Bulgars and foreign adventurers of ever description, feasting and making merry in the cafés of Pera, openly rejoiced at the misfortune of the Turkish Empire. The principal of Robert College, a Christian school on the shores of the Bosphorus, allowed full play to his sectarian bias, boasting that many of the enemy's successful generals had been educated at the College, which was founded under the protection and goodwill of the Sultan. Yet during those bitter days, in spite of all this provocation, not a single alien enemy was interfered with by those 'fanatical Moslems', whose hierarchical chief, the Sheik-ul-Islam, set an example by continuing to employ the Greek gardener who had been in his service for many years. The Turks were either too tolerant or too contemptuous to even notice the unseemly and licentious behaviour of the enemies within their gates. Such is the character of a people who would rather go without their dinner than see a poor man hungry, and who, even at a period when Jews were being burnt alive in Christian Spain, Huguenots hunted out of France and priests guilty of saying Mass executed in England, allowed perfect freedom to every race and sect within her dominions." (*The Armenians*, pp. 44-5.)

A peculiar feature of Ottoman society (peculiar to Westerners) was its absolute social equality. The Turks had no aristocracy and the most important official would converse with the lowliest peasant and there were no barriers to intercourse in everyday life.

There were, of course, social classes. But the Empire facilitated social mobility through a meritocracy and a person of any social position, race or religion could rise to the top of the society as long as they fulfilled a number of requirements.

There were two main political and social groups in the Ottoman Empire. There was on the one hand the Ruling Ottoman Class, which was called the *Osmanli,* who were in charge of providing and maintaining Sultans and of making the rest of Ottoman society function. They did this by running a military force to defend the Empire, keeping order and security within it and by collecting taxes.

And there was on the other hand the vast Subject Class, the *rayas*, who were the 'protected flock' of the Sultan.

To be a member of the Ruling Class an Ottoman citizen had to fulfil certain requirements—all of which were possible for the lowliest of subjects. First, he had to be a loyal 'dependant' of the Sultan. No matter how wealthy or powerful a person was, he had to accept this status. Secondly, he had to be a Muslim, either by birth or voluntary conversion. But unlike in Europe, where someone could not rise in society if he were born a Jew or a Muslim, in the Ottoman Empire a subject could convert to Islam if he wished to rise to the top. Thirdly, he had to know and practise a complicated system of language and behaviour known as the Ottoman Way, including the Ottoman language, which was itself a very difficult-to-acquire mixture of Arabic, Persian and

Turkish. A child of a member of the Ruling Class who failed to learn and practise these duties would fall into the Subject Class, but a Muslim, Jew, Armenian or Greek member of the Subject Class could rise into the Ruling Class by accepting , learning, and practising the required duties of the Ruling Class.

The fluid social structure of Ottoman society compared very favourably with the Europe of its day and resembled modern Western society, in the fact that most people who achieved prominence, wealth and importance did so because they worked at it rather than because they were born into it.

### Ottoman Race Suicide—An English View

There is a view of the Ottoman Empire from the distinct perspective of the British Empire written just before the Great War. It is in *Nationalism And War In The Near East* by George Young, edited by Lord Courtney of Penwith, and published anonymously by Oxford University Press in 1915. (Lord Leonard Courtney was a Liberal Cabinet Minister under Gladstone who left the Party with Joseph Chamberlain and then became a Liberal Unionist. He returned to the Liberal Party of Campbell-Bannerman after the Boer War, which he opposed.)

*Nationalism And War In The Near East* was published in 1915 but it was written in 1914; there is no mention of the Great War in it and at times the author speculates (hopes?) about the possibility of a Balkan war developing into a European war.

It is interesting because it is written just before all writing about the Ottoman Empire derived from the purpose of producing hostile propaganda about the Turks. So there is an element of insightful thought about it, in trying to explain why the Ottomans were being driven out of Europe, and why their Empire was decadent, according to the Anglo-Saxon perspective.

The argument about the defeat of the Ottoman Empire in Europe is based on a racialist conception of government, a common feature of English political writing at the time, as noted by William Allen (a conception maintained until Hitler became inspired by it and put it into operation.)

It argues that the Ottomans were committing race suicide when they adopted the cultural and political features of Byzantium, refused to operate a racial policy with regard to governing, and trusted the administration of their Empire to the hands of the lesser subject races. (The term 'Eurasians,' applied by '*A Diplomatist,*' was used to define British-Indian race-mixing—a practice that was very much frowned upon because of the presumed link between racial interbreeding and degeneracy, and since it could result in the production of an inferior stock of 'half-castes.')

Young asks why, when he is supposedly the closest thing to an English gentleman that can be found in the East, the Turk is a failure at Empire whereas Britain's Imperial mission is thriving. Young makes clear that the distinguishing feature of British Imperialism and its government is that miscegenation was strongly discouraged to keep up a healthy racial stock, whereas the easy-going Turks and their Empire, who seemed to play fast and loose with this kind of thing, lost their Empire as a result:

"The first cause of the Balkan Wars is the failure of the Turks to keep their empire alive. This failure is generally attributed to the physical and intellectual decay of the Turkish ruling class and to the spiritual and intellectual decay entailed in the Islamic religion. It is true that the ruling class of the Turkish race have shown themselves utterly incapable of keeping the empire together and of even keeping themselves going. The result of their five hundred years of power has been that the government was entirely divorced from all vital forces in the governed, so that the measure of development was the measure of decentralization. On the other hand the Turkish peasantry, still on the land, retained their racial health and strength of character, but remained peasants. Their sound stock never became available to revitalize the dying ruling class. So the power fell altogether out of Turkish hands into those of ever lower racial types, as the follies and failures of the ruling Turks brought the government into less worthy hands. The Greek and Roumanian nobles who administered the empire for the Turks, as Hospodars in the provinces or as Dragomans in the capital, threw the Turks over or were overthrown by them. The Armenian or Turkish officials of the middle class that took their place became in turn suspect and were replaced in turn under the Hamidian regime by Levantines, landless men, renegades, rapscallions, and all the outlaws that haunt the borderlands of East and West...

Why, then, did the Turk fail so utterly that we Anglo-Saxons, who have so much in common with him in character and political circumstances as to have a real sympathy for his difficulties, find ourselves to-day with no choice but to welcome as a boon to humanity the end of his empire in Europe?

What is the cause of the failure of the Asiatic in Europe?... his failure does not lie in any moral or mental inferiority of Asiatics to Europeans... But it does lie in the impossibility of Asiatics governing Europeans or of the British governing the Babu unless each retains his alien character and constantly renews his strength from his own homeland. Let us imagine the seat of government transferred from the United Kingdom to Delhi, or from the United States to Manila. Let us suppose the government be left in the hands of Eurasians, inheritors of the Mogul or of Malay culture, with such assistance as they could get from the native races; and that a half-caste government at Delhi or Manila could, by acquired authority of religious and racial tradition and by arbitrary power of money and militarism, impose their imperial yoke on native nationalism. The result would be the same as that which the establishment of the Turkish government in Constantinople has had upon the Ottoman Empire and its races. The ruling urban class would be unable to renew its strength from the rural stock, which would exist only to supply the country with men and money; the ruling class would sink morally and physically lower while

34

the rural mass would be in no way educated but merely exploited. After a few centuries the Eurasian Empire would fall before vigorous young native kingdoms, and the moral would be drawn that Europeans are incapable of governing Asiatics.

In a word the failure of the Turks is due to Byzantinism. Their corruption and impotence were inherited with their national capital—When they reached their promised land they would have done better to have followed the Hebrew policy of smiting the Amalekites hip and thigh until not one of them was saved. But they spared what was most pleasing in their own eyes and ran after strange gods. Byzantine civilization was overflowed, not flooded out, by the Turkish invasion; and all the worst features of the decadent Byzantine social system emerged, and flourished in the soil refertilized by new blood... The decadence of the Turk dates from the day when Constantinople was taken and not destroyed..." (pp.35-40.)

One is tempted to think that 'A Diplomatist' would have thoroughly approved of Ataturk, who moved the Turkish capital out of Constantinople into the heartland of the hardy Anatolian Turk and put his trust in the Turkish peasant, rather than in the Greek or Armenian.

But what comes out of this is the fact that the British and Ottoman Empires had entirely different notions of race and governing. The British Empire was founded on the principle of racial and religious hierarchy whereas the Ottomans played fast and loose with these categories to the extent that, in the English biological view, they contravened the laws of nature, leading to their own extinction.

The Social Darwinism that infused British Imperialism from the 1880s helped bolster the view that the Ottoman Empire was doomed and that the English were destined, as the most vigourous race, to absorb the Ottoman territories. This was the age of Herbert Spencer and Francis Galton, in which the great English racial and eugenic theories became the justifications for the expansion of the Imperial State amongst the 'lesser breeds'. There was general agreement in England that, as in nature, there was an inevitable evolutionary process of the stronger breeds and the higher civilisations prevailing over the weaker and lower ones. England, of course, was one of the strong states—the strongest in fact—and it looked forward to taking the territories of the dying nations and the territories of the empires of the less virile races. (The dying empires of the 'Latin' Catholic races were cited as cases in point).

The expansionist Imperialism, with its Social Darwinist imperative, was subject to no moral law or conscience but that of natural selection and nothing limited its pursuit of progress. Darwin himself identified the Turks and their Empire as one that was ripe for elimination by the higher races, including England. In one letter he wrote:

"Remember what risk the nations of Europe ran, not so many centuries ago, of being overwhelmed by the Turks, and how ridiculous such an idea now is!

The more civilized so-called Caucasian races have beaten the Turkish hollow in the struggle for existence. Looking to the world at no very distant date, what an endless number of the lower races will have been eliminated by the higher civilized races throughout the world." (Francis Darwin, *The Life and Letters of Charles Darwin*, Vol. I, 1888, p.285-286.)

Elimination of lesser races was no problem for the British Empire and it was done under the flag of civilization and democracy. The problem was that others might interfere with this process and there were other 'higher civilized races' that could profit from the elimination of the Turk. The most feared by the English Social Darwinists was the other Teuton race, the German, whom, it was believed, most resembled the English in vigour. And, unfortunately, by the turn of the new century the German had begun to acquire a box seat in Constantinople!

But for all the English racial theories applied to the affairs of men it was British power that led to the demise of the Ottoman Empire, as the Lion sought to extend his law over an extension to his jungle.

### *The Great Game And The Turkish Prey*

The destruction of the Ottoman Empire came about largely as a result of the English calling off their Great Game with Russia, in favour of a Greater Game that emerged in the Imperial consciousness at the end of the nineteenth century.

The Great Game was the British term for the Anglo-Russian rivalry in Central Asia in the nineteenth century. It stemmed from the British fear that the Russian colonising mission in Central Asia would extend into Afghanistan and ultimately India. Slowly but surely Russia had extended its frontiers in Asia and had pushed towards the East and South, and England saw that she had to make immediate preparations, as her own efforts to expand from the direction of India would come up against Russian opposition. The dangerous situation was that Britain, which was mainly a sea power, might easily come off second best in a conflict in the interior of Asia with the vast amount of manpower that could be marshalled there by Russia.

The Imperial ruling class in London viewed the Russian colonising, particularly of the Moslem regions of Asia, as having great dangers for the Indian Empire and they determined that it should be prevented from entering Afghanistan.

Since the time of Peter the Great, Russia had sought to obtain freedom for its shipping from the Black Sea to the Aegean and Mediterranean. The reason for this urge, first of all, was geographical. Russia's northern coast is icebound (except for Archangel, which is free of ice for part of the year). Its Baltic Coast was difficult to emerge from, due to length of passage and interference of other Powers. And its Siberian seacoast was too far from the important, western, part of Russia, to make it valuable as a trade route.

Much of the driving force behind the Great Game emanated from Britain's insistence on blocking Russia's access to port facilities, that would ensure its economic development.

Russia aspired to be a world power for a century before 1914 at least. But the vast Czarist Empire with a population of around 150 million was severely impeded in its industrial and commercial development at a time when the world market was developing and the process of economic growth was essential to global power. In an environment that had been globalized by the Royal Navy, to be a world power Russia had to become a sea power. And it was impossible to be a sea power with only one port and with the rest of the country's vast territory hemmed in by ice and hostile foreign navies.

This geographical difficulty led on to political designs in areas that Russia saw as having potential to free it from its landlocked problem. Its first objective was Constantinople, the ancient Byzantine capital of the Orthodox Church. The Russians had a religious connection with the Slavs in the Balkans and Asia Minor, peoples who mostly inhabited the Ottoman Empire. Under Czar Nicholas, between 1850 and 1854, the Russian State began asserting a claim as the protector of these Orthodox Christians. This claim came up against a similar French claim to look after the interests of Roman Catholic Christians in regard to jurisdiction over the Holy Sepulchre in Jerusalem. And Russia declared herself the champion of the Bulgarian, Bosnian, Serbian and Magyarian Slavs within European Turkey.

The dispute over the Holy Sepulchre led Britain to fear a Russian move on the Ottoman Empire. Throughout the nineteenth century Britain viewed the Ottoman Empire as the main bulwark against Czarist Russia—which it regarded as the major threat to British interests in the East. The great Islamic area around the Ottoman Empire constituted one giant buffer zone between Russia and the trade route between Egypt and India. So the most anti-Catholic state in the world went to war in the Crimea with France and Sardinia to protect Catholic pilgrims in Jerusalem against Orthodox designs! (This was a bit like fighting the Great War for 'poor little Belgium'.)

England's objective in fighting the Crimean War (1854-56) was to preserve the Ottoman Empire, in order to prevent Russia from gaining Constantinople thus becoming a naval power in the Mediterranean. The Dardanelles was strategically important because it controlled the East-West passage between Europe and Asia and the North-South passage between the Black Sea and the Mediterranean. The war in the Crimea ended, as Britain desired, in a treaty that banned passage through the Bosphorus and Dardanelles to all naval units— which for all practical purposes meant Russian naval units. That effectively bottled up the Russian Southern fleet in the Black Sea. And having the Straits in friendly hands meant that the Royal Navy could enter the Black Sea when it chose—despite transient treaty obligations—and bombard the Russian ports, if necessary.

The Peace of Paris (1856) guaranteed the political integrity of Turkey and forced Russia to remove her claim to be sole protector of the Slavs in the Balkans, conferring it, instead, on the French, British and Sardinians and extending it into the Ottoman territories in Asia. This settlement had a hugely destabilizing effect in the Balkans and in the Christian parts of Asia Minor, as the Christian minorities of the Ottoman Empire began to assert themselves in the knowledge that they could use the power politics of the situation against the Ottoman State when they so chose. This tended to take them increasingly into conflict with local Moslem populations and the instances of massacre and counter-massacre increased.

The Peace of Paris succeeded in checking Russia's ambitions for southern waters and in diverting her energies eastward. The Russian State advanced into Turkistan and the Caucasus, and occupied some Persian ports. In 1878, as part of The Great Game, a British army invaded Afghanistan to counter Russian influence in Kabul and this had the effect of checking Russian movement toward the Persian Gulf and Arabian Sea.

Russia then looked further east to find outlets to the sea. The completion of the Trans-Caspian Railway to Vladivostok made it possible for a port on the Siberian coast to be developed. However, here again the Russians found themselves checked by England, which made an alliance with Japan, which was fearful of Russian expansion into Korea and Manchuria.

The victory of Japan in the Russo-Japanese war in 1905 and the sinking of the Czar's fleet closed off the Manchurian possibility. With Russia failing to possess a Pacific port, in Manchuria, it was left with no alternative but to set its eyes back on Constantinople again.

In a 1921 book Joseph Anthony Starke, an American, reveals the significance of Britain's successful blocking manoeuvres on Russia and its connection to the Great War:

"Russia now urged with increasing insistence her 'Slavic race protectorate argument,' her racial and dynastic relationship with Serbia in particular, and by both these agencies worked through the Balkan states for the achievement of her own political purposes: The elimination of Turkey from Europe; possession of or dictation over Constantinople; acquisition of Aegean and Adriatic sea ports; complete freedom of navigation through the Bosporus and Dardanelles for her commercial ships and navy. For the realisation of this programme in Europe, Russia would probably have been willing to renounce definitely any further designs to reach the Persian Gulf and Arabian Sea. This aspect of the matter is important as it carried within itself the possibility of that later rapprochement with England that actually took place and was such an important factor for the war of 1914. The connection is plain: England could afford to look with much less concern upon Russia obtaining her southern-sea outlet policy in European rather than in Asiatic waters because of the lesser danger therefrom to India. For, holding the Suez Canal and Gibraltar, she had it in her power, with her superior fleet, to block any sea aggression from the Mediterranean from any or all the countries bounding thereon." (*Light And Truth After The World Tragedy,* p.40.)

I will return to this aspect later, after an examination of Britain's influence at Constantinople.

### Britain's Protection Racket at Constantinople

Britain protected the Ottoman Empire from Russia in order to make English power indispensable to the Sultan—so that a gradual Ottoman decline would lead to British gains in the region. This was accomplished through a combination of military and financial means.

The Ottoman financial problems began with the Crimean War when the *Porte* had to foot a large bill to pay for the expenses of the British and French armies stationed in Constantinople and the Black Sea coast. Britain and France lent the Turks the money to pay the debt—which came back to themselves with interest. They crippled the Ottoman Exchequer with the interest rates imposed on the loan and through an insistence that the Ottomans restrict their tariffs on British and French imports to below 5%. This forced the Turks to buy all manufactured goods abroad and discouraged the growth of any indigenous industry within the Empire. As a result, in 1874, over half of the Porte's expenditure went on paying off the foreign debt and the Empire began to decay as it was bled dry by the Franco-British protection racket.

The Ottomans were also forced to cede to Western business interests special privileges, called Capitulations, that included freedom from taxes and the Ottoman courts (which amounted to Embassy rights outside the Embassy). The loans and Capitulations were found to be an effective way of both buttressing the Ottoman Empire against Russia and of controlling the *Porte* by holding its purse strings.

The lack of finance had a dramatic effect in 1873-4 when a famine killed tens of thousands in Istanbul and Anatolia. The *Porte* had to go to private bankers to overcome financial problems and in 1875 it defaulted on a large debt. The bankers forced the Ottomans to hand over the administration of its finances to the foreign banks, including duties—which meant that the Ottomans were no longer masters of their own Treasury or Customs.

In effect the countries that were later to form the Triple *Entente* against Germany developed a cartel in Turkey that would persist unless some Power disturbed the balance:

"Astride across Europe and Asia, the Ottoman Empire represented, for all the nations of the old continent, the cosmopolitan centre where each had erected, by dint of patience and ingenuity, a fortress of interests, influences, and special rights. Each fortress watched jealously to maintain its particular advantages in face of the rival enemy. If one of them obtained a concession, or a new favour, immediately the commanders of the others were seen issuing from their walls to claim from the Grand Turk concessions or favours which should maintain the existing balance of power or prestige. . . . France acted as protector of the Christians; England, the vigilant guardian of the routes to India, maintained a privileged political and economic position; Austria-Hungary mounted guard over the route to Salonica; Russia, protecting the Armenians and Slavs of the South of Europe, watched over the fate of the Orthodox. There was a general understanding among them all, tacit or express, that none should better its situation at the expense of the others." (Pierre Albin, *From Agadir to Sarajevo*, p. 81.)

Another Frenchman, Gaston Gaillard, summed up the effects of the privileges gained by the European Powers within the Ottoman Empire in his 1921 book *The Turks In Europe*:

"Such privileges... soon brought on unrestricted and unjustifiable interference by Foreign Powers in Turkish affairs... The Capitulations damaged the Turkish treasury by binding the Ottoman State and preventing it from establishing differential duties at a time when a war of tariffs was being carried on by all States.

During the reign of Abdul Hamid, owing to the facilities given by this state of things, the interference of the Powers in Turkish affairs reached such a climax that they succeeded not only in bringing Turkey into a condition of subjection, but in disposing of her territories, after dividing them into regions where their respective interests were paramount. The greediness of the Powers was only restrained by the conflicts their rivalry threatened to raise...

Of course, Turkey, being thus brought into subjection, did not develop so rapidly as the nations, which, not being under any foreign tutelage, enjoyed independence; and it is unfair to reproach her with keeping behind them." (pp.22-3.)

The 'sick man of Europe' was, in effect, diseased by Europe and put on his death bed by the very people who sought to inherit his earthly goods. And they jockeyed for a favourable position about his bed calculating the most favourable moment of the patient's demise.

Britain nearly went to war again with Russia in 1877 when it looked like the Czar was going to take Constantinople. The Russians took the opportunity, when Britain was preoccupied with India, to drive through the Balkans and into Rumania. The war fever in the London Music Halls against the Russians produced the term 'Jingo.' Disraeli ordered the fleet to the Dardanelles to block the Russian advance. And Britain refused to accept the Treaty of San Stefano, which the Russians concluded with the Turks, and which gave independence to the Christian states of the Balkans.

Instead, on Bismarck's invitation, Russia and Britain agreed to conclude arrangements for the Balkans at Berlin. There Disraeli exerted British influence in the Treaty of Berlin to preserve as much of the Ottoman possessions in Europe as possible, and an independent block of states, to act as a barrier against the expanding influence of the Russians. Lord Beaconsfield famously described this as '*peace with honour.*' And Bismarck remarked: '*There is once again a Turkey in Europe.*'

England then made a deal with the Sultan. Justin McCarthy describes the arrangement made between Britain and the Turks in his *History of Our Own Times, Vol. IV*:

> "The English Government undertook to guarantee to Turkey her Asiatic possessions against all invasion on condition that Turkey handed over to England the island of Cyprus for her occupation... Lord Beaconsfield now declared it to be the cardinal principle of his policy that England specially, England above all, was concerned to maintain the integrity and independence of the Turkish Empire; that in fact the security of Turkey was as much a part of the duty of English statesmanship as the security of the Channel Islands or Malta." (p.486-7.)

T.P. O'Connor of the Irish Parliamentary Party had a racialist explanation for Disraeli's sympathies:

> "His general view... upon the question of the Turk is that as a Jew he is a kinsman of the Turk, and that as a Jew he feels bound to make common cause with the Turk." (Cited in Bernard Lewis, *Cultures in Conflict; Christians, Muslims And Jews In The Age Of Discovery*, p.34.)

But the new vigorous Imperialism that emerged in England saved the Ottoman Empire from Russian designs — merely so that it could feast on it itself, in its own time. Britain began to nibble at the edges of the Ottoman carcass and then bite off chunks of it, before digesting them whole. The occupation of Egypt was a case in point — violating the terms Britain had signed up to in the Treaty of Berlin of 1878. And hand in hand went the continual process of the removal of free Moslem States in the East by Britain to provide commercial fields for its merchants.

England was not alone in coveting the Ottoman possessions; France acquired influence in Syria and Italy then looked for its share around Tripoli. But what occurred around 1901-03 was a qualitative departure in British foreign policy that put the very existence of the Ottoman Empire and the future of the region into question.

### The Reorientation of British Policy

The genesis of the British project to dismantle the Ottoman Empire — that Ireland became accessory to in 1914 — lay in the re-orientation of British foreign policy which began just after the Boer War. It represented a fundamental adjustment in Britain's Balance of Power Policy (with a change of enemies), the consequences of which can only be described as monumental.

The reverses suffered in the Boer War set off great worries in England that the Empire, which had expanded massively over the previous two decades, had reached a turning point. For years Imperial writers had made parallels between the British Empire and Rome. Comparisons began to be made between the fall of Rome and the potential demise of the British Empire. Greater Britain perceived itself as the new Rome and Germany began to be seen as its Carthage. And it was well known what Rome had done to Carthage. And so a Grand Alliance, in the manner of 1688 against France, began to be assembled against Germany.

The first sign of a British reorientation came when Leo Maxse, the influential Imperial propagandist, wrote a series of articles in his *National Review* during 1901-02, which proposed a radical departure in British policy. It was argued that Britain should make concessions in order to make friends with her traditional enemy in the East, Czarist Russia, as the first part of an alliance that was to later include Britain's traditional enemy in the West, France—aimed at destroying what was seen as the new emerging threat, Germany.

England needed alliances with France and Russia because it could not destroy Germany on its own. Britain was primarily a sea power, with most of its resources concentrated on controlling the world's commerce and communication. Its armies were designed for extending the Empire in areas of the world where it did not come up against equally well-armed opponents. And it had a Liberal ideology against military conscription that was possible because of its island situation.

So, in waging Balance of Power wars on continental Europe, continental allies were indispensable.

Maxse's articles, signposting Britain's new policy, were no ordinary anti-German propaganda such as characterised the period 1900-14. The articles were high level collaborations with Edward Grey, soon to be Liberal Foreign Minister; Lord Rosebery, the leader of the Liberal Imperialist faction in the Liberal Party; George Saunders, the *Times* Berlin correspondent; Sir Roland Blennerhasset, President of Queen's College, Cork; Charles Hardinge, Secretary of the St. Petersburg Embassy and Permanent Under-Secretary at the Foreign Office 1905-10; and William Tyrrell, Grey's future Private Secretary at the Foreign Office. Hardinge made sure the articles found their way into important hands in Russia and later actually put the policy into operation in conjunction with his immediate superior, Grey.

The Redmondites presented the Great War as the 'great English democracy' going to war to stop the aggressions of the 'Prussian Oligarchy'. But the 'great English democracy' did not plan, organise or arrange the Great War on Germany and the Ottoman Empire. It was the work of a political and military Oligarchy within the British Foreign Office and Committee of Imperial Defence, led by a small Liberal Imperialist coterie—all done behind the back of the British democracy, which the Irish Party was enthralled by.

In 1914 England was a minority democracy in that its Parliament was still elected by only a third of its adult population. But it was democratic, in semblance at least, by being the most democratic of aristocracies. Although the semblance of a democratic parliament existed for sure, the guidance of foreign policy had never been entrusted to democracy in the democratic age. It was the fear that it *would* be entrusted to it that led to the establishment of the Committee of Imperial Defence after the Boer War and the ensuring that Edward Grey, the aristocratic Imperialist, became Foreign Minister, rather than a more representative Liberal, so that continuity of foreign policy was maintained. It was the thing that Leopold Maxse's *ABC etc.* articles in the *National Review* made a great point to address to the Russians and French, so they could rest assured of England's continued commitment to a war on Germany, when the British State came under new Liberal management in 1906.

The Oligarchic British State established in 1690 became gradually more democratic in 1832, in 1867 and in 1918, but one aspect of it remained true to its origins – the part concerned with Foreign Policy. The British Foreign Office maintained the privilege of acting in secret and it retained the right to report treaties, either not at all, or only in such parts, as it deemed advisable and necessary to the democracy. Parliament was only given the right to question such arrangements if it found out about them first, and then could only question the Minister in formal interrogatories. Only general questions could be put to him, as to whether a Treaty had been made or not, and he was not obliged to reveal its terms, if he chose not to. The security and safety of the British State, the most important function of government, was thus only entrusted to its Oligarchy, officered by the gentry and aristocracy, who confided their policy solely to the memory and honour of English gentlemen.

In August 1914 Ireland, through John Redmond, who saw himself as Ireland's future Prime Minister, entrusted its destiny to these gentlemen and their secret plans for the remaking of the world.

## *Trouble For Turkey*

The alliances that were constructed by England in anticipation of War on Germany fundamentally altered the British strategy toward the Ottoman Empire. Prior to the alliances with Russia and France, England was intent on preserving the Ottoman State as a buffer against the Czarist State whilst manoeuvring itself into a position to move on the territories it coveted if the Empire showed signs of collapse (or if the Sultan could be persuaded to part with them).

But the alliance with Russia, in particular, made this strategy untenable and drew England into planning for the destruction of the Ottoman State and the taking of its best bits—the Straits, Palestine and Mesopotamia.

The first hint of trouble for Turkey, out of this new policy, is contained in the first of Maxse's articles. It includes the essence of the strategic reorientation that was being mooted in Imperial circles in relation to Germany, Russia and, by implication, the Ottoman Empire. And, for that reason, it is worth quoting at length. Maxse and his high-level collaborators set down the future direction of Foreign Policy of the British State in the following record:

"Closely connected with the subject of inter-Imperial relations is the policy which the British Empire should pursue as regards other nations and empires. We shall have to reconsider our position with regard to them one by one; for it must be owned that some of our Ministers seem to be living under the spell of a diplomacy which the wisest of them has declared to be 'antiquated.' ... Perhaps the main fact which has impressed itself upon Englishmen in considering the actual international outlook is not merely the extraordinary growth of Germany—who has achieved greatness by trampling upon her neighbours— but the fact that this formidable community is becoming increasingly dependent on a foreign food supply, as well as on foreign supplies of raw and partially manufactured articles. This necessarily involves the development of Germany as a Sea Power, and it is a matter for every European state to ponder over. She is already stronger at sea than either France or Russia...

At the present time it is estimated that a substantial proportion of the food of the entire population of Germany is sea-borne. She is becoming transformed from an agricultural into an industrial community, and if this process continues for another quarter of a century, while remaining secured against actual starvation by her land frontiers, she will become no less dependent on the ocean highways for her prosperity than we are. Great Britain is therefore confronted with the development of a new Sea Power founded on the same economic basis as herself, and impelled by a desire to be supreme. But *l'océan ne comporte qu'un seul maitre*. We have secured in the past the sovereignty of the seas, and our sceptre cannot be wrested from us without a desperate and bloody struggle...

If once the sea power of England were overthrown, Germany would be free to execute her hostile policy towards Russia, who is not less in her way than we are. There is an idea growing steadily amongst Germans that Germany should expand into an Empire branching from the Bosphorus to the Persian Gulf; thus would territories be secured ensuring an excellent climate, to which the surplus stream of German population, which now flows to the United States and to the British Empire, might be diverted, without being lost to the German flag. This is by no means a new idea; it is the revival of an old idea, and it means of course the supremacy of Germany in the Near East and the supersession of the Slav by the Teuton. Such is the objective of those ambitious dreamers known as the Pan-Germanic League...

Whatever the effect of recent developments may have been upon Russia, the attitude of the German nation and the suspicious policy of the German Government has led a continually increasing number of Englishmen to inquire whether it would not be worthwhile for England and Russia to discuss their differences with the objective of arriving at a workable understanding, and, if possible, a comprehensive settlement? Very distinguished Russians have frequently expressed an earnest desire that their country should seek an *entente* with England...

The chief political obstacle to an Anglo-Russian understanding is, no doubt, due to the desire of Russia to come down to the Persian Gulf. If we are able to recognise and tolerate her ambition in that quarter our antagonism would come to an end, at least for a generation... It is clearly our interest, as it is our intention, to preserve intact the status quo in the Gulf unless we can come to an arrangement with Russia by which we get a *quid pro quo*. That status has been lately threatened by the Sultan of Turkey at Koweit, the port at the head of the Gulf which the Germans are believed to have marked as their future naval base, and which is to be the southern terminus of the great trunk line which will cross Asia Minor from Constantinople...

It cannot be too often repeated that the condition precedent of such an agreement is the active goodwill of the powers that be in St. Petersburg. It is for them to reflect as to whether the co-operation of England might not be of enormous use in promoting Russian trade in the Far East...

In another part of the world it is for the Russians to consider whether the goodwill of England might not be worth cultivating. The question of Manchuria naturally rankles in the mind of the Japanese, who can clearly see that a Japanese *Pied à terre* constituted a menace to the integrity of the Chinese empire, which was the pretext on which she was ordered out of Port Arthur, then the establishment of Russia in Manchuria may become a very formidable menace to Japan... The keystone to British policy in the Far East is a friendly understanding and cooperation with Japan; that being recognised, there is nothing to prevent this country from supporting a settlement of the Manchurian and Corean questions on lines which would be regarded as fairly satisfactory both in St. Petersburg and in Tokio...

Russian Statesmen have to make up their minds whether, in the present condition of Russian industries, Russian agriculture, and Russian finance, a friendly understanding with England, which would relieve her anxieties in the Far East, and which might result in her being able to continue her Trans-Caucasian and Siberian Railways to the shores of the Persian Gulf, and which, last but not least, might enable her to carry out her historic mission in the Balkans, is not worth the high price... But in the interval we venture to sketch in outline some suggestions for a comprehensive settlement between Russia and Britain with the objective of demonstrating to sceptics that at any rate the raw material for an Anglo-Russian agreement abounds...

PROPOSED ANGLO-RUSSIAN UNDERSTANDING.

The understanding would naturally fall under three different heads:

1. THE NEAR EAST.

With regard to the Near East the basis would be that while Russia abstained from any attempt to interfere with the *status quo* in Egypt, we should frankly recognise that the fulfilment of what Russia regards as her historic mission in the Balkan peninsula conflicts with no vital British interests, and that in Asiatic Turkey we should abstain from favouring the development of German schemes of expansion.

## II. PERSIA AND CENTRAL ASIA.

With regard to Persia and Central Asia, we might offer Russia our cooperation in the development of railway communications between the Caspian and the Persian Gulf, and in securing for her a commercial outlet on the Gulf in return for an undertaking on the part of Russia to respect the political *status quo* along the shores of the Gulf.

## III. THE FAR EAST.

With regard to the Far East the question is necessarily more complicated, as Japan would have to be taken into the counsels of the two empires and the basis of agreement arrived at which would satisfy her as well as Russia and Great Britain. As far as Japan is concerned, such a basis might be found in the recognition by Russia and England of the Japanese claim to an exclusive sphere of influence in Corea...

To those foreign statesmen who say, or are supposed to say, that 'it is impossible to do business with England, seeing that one government is up to reverse the foreign policy of its predecessor,' we would reply that of late years there have been various influences at work to steady public opinion in this country on questions of foreign politics, and that the break on a change of government is practically imperceptible. The credit of this continuity is principally due to Lord Rosebery and his adherents in Parliament and the Press. No one familiar with the personnel of our politics can seriously suggest that if Lord Salisbury and Lord Lansdowne were to pursue the policy set forth in this paper their successors would fail to keep the engagements they might inherit...

We seek no quarrel with any power; but if Germany thinks it her interest to force one upon us, we shall not shrink from the ordeal, even should she appear in the lists with France and Russia as her allies. Germany would, however, do well to realise that if England is driven to it, England will strike home. Close to the foundations of the German Empire, which is hardly emerged from its artificial stage, there exists a powder magazine such as is to be found in no other country, viz. Social Democracy. In the case of a conflict with Great Britain, misery would be caused to large classes of the German population, reduced by the total collapse of subsidised industries; far-reaching commercial depression, financial collapse, and a defective food supply might easily make that magazine explode." (*The National Review*, November 1901.)

The three articles in Maxse's *National Review* became the basis for the secret Foreign Policy pursued by the Liberal Imperialist coterie of Asquith, Grey and Haldane (the other two deal with the other part of the alliance jigsaw, France). It began with the *Entente* with France in 1904 and was completed in 1907 with the Anglo-Russian Agreement. Secret arrangements were then instituted by the military cadres of each state to be activated in the event of war with Germany. And it all culminated in August 1914 with the Great War.

Walter Bagehot wrote in *The Economist* around the time that

"the old idea that Russia is already so great a power that Europe needs to be afraid of her... belongs to the pre-Germanic age." (David Fromkin, *A Peace To End All Peace*, p.31.)

Britain, with the aid of Japan, had stopped Russian expansion in the East and this signalled to Britain that the Czarist threat was in decline and Russia could be enlisted against the new, emerging and more vigorous menace in Central Europe.

In January 1902 Maxse published an article entitled *A Plea For The Isolation Of Germany* under the name, *C.P.* In it he urged Britain to utilise the expansionist and irredentist designs of Russia and France in an encircling policy toward Germany:

"Combat, therefore German Anglophobia, I would say, by working all round at the isolation of Germany. Bring home to her the perils of her detestable geographical position between France, watching for a *revanche*, and Russia at the head of irreconcilable Slavism." (*National Review*, January, 1902.)

The Czarist State was expansionist by impulse and had pursued a policy of continuous expansion for the previous three hundred years. Its ambitions had focussed on driving the Turks from Europe and, in particular, on the capture of the former capital of the Orthodox world, Constantinople. Britain now intended to turn these impulses into a positive force in the British interest, directed at the elimination of Germany and the Ottoman Empire was going to be an inevitable casualty of this process.

### Settling Accounts With Russia

Britain agreed in 1907 to the 'Macedonian Reform' giving Russia the go ahead for a major sphere of influence in the Balkans which Britain had always blocked in the past. Once Grey gave the nod for a Russian expansion in the Balkans, a war to crush Germany was possible (and the Balkan Wars of 1912-13 were made inevitable). As one disillusioned English Liberal writer subsequently put it—after the consequences had begun to work themselves out:

"This cold blooded pretext of the Imperialist Cabinet to again leave to the wisdom and justice of the despotic government of the Czar, the promulgation of reforms... as well as settle the racial rivalries of the different religious nationalities in Macedonia, and at the same time ignore Turkey and isolate the German Empire in the Balkan councils, inevitably created conditions which made peace in the Balkans an impossibility. It was, however, what allied 'civilisation' and British 'peacemakers' dictated for the protection of little States! It was, in truth and in fact, a political device to cover nothing short of the establishment of the hegemony of Russia in Europe, although it must never be forgotten, that when in 1853 the proposal was made that Russia should take over the protection of the Balkan Christians, it was regarded with scorn by both England and France, and rather than yield a single inch of that claim, the Crimean War with all its horrors was the result. The price of the Anglo-Russian alliance was apparently Britain's reversal of the policy that kept Russia out of Europe in 1853. The deliberate continuation and renewal of the old policy of making these struggling little nationalities the cockpit to future struggles for World Empire marks, at this epoch, the *causa causans* of the dreadful calamity that came to Europe six years after King Edward's state visit to Russia, for every European diplomat knew, that neither Germany, nor Austria, would be likely to submit to Russian domination in the Balkans. It was, therefore, no surprise to Europe then to find revolution immediately breaking out at Monastir and Constantinople, that in October, 1908, Prince Ferdinand of Coburg proclaimed the independence of Bulgaria and assumed the title of Czar, and that, on 4 October, Austria-Hungary annexed Bosnia-Herzegovina." (E.G. Jellicoe, *Playing The Game*, pp.76-7.)

Britain thus began playing the nationalities game again, as in the days of Wordsworth and Lord Palmerston, in the empires of its rivals—only this time with far more devastating and long-lasting consequences.

In Grey's 1907 Agreement with Russia, England also made a settlement of frontier disputes in Asia very favourable to the Czar. Britain agreed not to make Afghanistan a British protectorate and drew up with Russia a scheme of spheres of influence in the Persian Gulf. The Liberal Government's agreement with Russia earmarked the Southern part of Persia for Britain, assuring domination of the Persian Gulf, as an extension to British India. And a neutral zone of mainly desert, under cover of Persian independence, was left as a buffer state between Russian and British interests. E.G. Jellicoe commented:

"Persia at this time by her geographical situation was at the confluence of British influences from India and Russian interests in the North. In 1906... some violent influences had provoked a revolution in Tehran, and this immediately strengthened the hands of Russian and British diplomats, and afforded them a pretext for agreeing the terms of still another 'understanding,' which followed in the spirit of the Anglo-French precedent. This was intended, either verbally or by implication, to secure, in Lord Haldane's words, 'the assistance of Russian pressure' on the 'eastern' frontier of Germany, and which, while affirming the integrity and independence of Persia, expressly divided that country into three zones.... Except as part of the policy of a great military enterprise, there never could have been any necessity to negotiate with Russia to secure British interests in the Persian Gulf or for bribing Russia in order to secure the peace of Asia... Germany alone stood in the way of our foreign policy in diplomacy. The Bagdad Railway was the stumbling block to the development of Persia on the lines of both Lord Curzon's book and Disraeli's 'Tancred'." (*Playing The Game*, pp.65-6.)

Here we see the first mention of a significant factor in the waging of the Great War on Turkey—the Bagdad Railway.

The Persian Government refused at first to recognise the Anglo-Russian agreement, but with the Lion and the Bear now in the same camp, what could it do? Russia sent in troops to the richest part of the country and the Persian Government was then replaced by one more favourably disposed towards Russia and England.

One of the main reasons for the Turkish alliance with Germany during the Great War was the fear of the Turks that their country would end up like Persia—divided up and parcelled out to the Christian Powers.

## Settling Accounts With France

At the same time as the understandings with Russia, it was calculated that France could be employed in an alliance against Germany by utilising her irredentist desires for Alsace-Lorraine. These largely German-speaking provinces had been absorbed by France in the seventeenth and eighteenth centuries. They had been lost as a result of the war in 1870-1 when France had invaded German territory with a view to preventing the process of German unification led by Prussia. But the manipulation of France's irredentist claim on them for the purposes of war on Germany now formed the basis of the *Entente Cordiale*.

A year before the Great War Georg Brandes, the left-wing Jewish writer from Copenhagen, and a frequent commentator on events in France, noted a transformation of attitude in the country:

> "Since 1870, and until very recently, France wanted nothing but peace. The defeat of that year convinced the people of Germany's military superiority, and even thirty years afterwards their belief in it was so great that, at the time of the Dreyfus affair, French generals and men of high standing declared that war with Germany would be fatal to France.
>
> In 1912 a change had crept into the French attitude, however. Confidence in the army had been restored. People spoke with assurance of the army's equipment and France's preparedness for war; in many circles the French army was even considered capable of challenging Germany's...
>
> In 1913... another change had taken place. Belief in the maintenance of peace seemed to have vanished. War was inevitable—why not look facts in the face?" (*The World At War*, pp.36-7.)

France had been transformed by the *Entente Cordiale* with England. After decades of moving away from the irredentist hankering over the lost provinces the revanche had been reinstilled by Britain's military backing, which made successful war with Germany a possibility again.

Russia and France were already in open alliance before the arrangements with each were concluded by Britain. It was understood, under the Franco-Russian alliance, that it would be activated only in a situation which enabled both countries to attain their objectives. The alliance which Britain joined was, therefore, a combined venture to gain for France Alsace-Lorraine, from the Germans, and for Russia Constantinople, from the Turks (although this latter objective had a problematic aspect to it for Britain).

Both Russia and France had an interest in provoking a European war in pursuit of expansionist or irredentist aims which neither could pursue unaided. And Britain used this knowledge as a lever to build up an encircling alliance against Germany by offering its services in the event of war—and thus encouraging such an eventuality.

So between 1904 and 1914 British Foreign Policy was turned upside down. Once the Liberal Imperialists had the Foreign Office, the wheels of State began to turn toward the German and Ottoman demise—and Grey described himself, according to Roger Casement, as merely 'a fly upon those wheels'.

In July 1906, the Committee of Imperial Defence—which had already reorientated itself away from planning wars with France and Russia and toward planning for war against Germany a couple of years earlier—first discussed the question of war with Turkey. The Admiralty and General Staff were instructed by Campbell-Bannerman, the new Liberal Prime Minister, to examine options and plan for an operation against the Dardanelles in a war against the Ottoman State.

That fact became public knowledge only in the meetings of the Dardanelles Commission, held in 1916, to enquire into the failure at Gallipoli. A General Staff memorandum, advising the politicians against an attack was presented to the Commission and was made public:

> "When the question of dispatching a military expeditionary force to the Gallipoli Peninsula comes to be passed in review, the first point to be considered is the general one of whether a landing is possible at all, in the face of active opposition under modern conditions. In regard to this history affords no guide. The whole conditions of war have been revolutionised since such an operation was last attempted."

The memorandum then goes on to discuss the pros and cons of the operation before concluding:

> "However brilliant as a combination of war, and however fruitful in its consequences such an operation would be, were it crowned with success, the General Staff, in view of the risks involved, are not prepared to recommend its being attempted." (*The World War I Collection—Gallipoli and the Early Battles 1914-16*, p.114.)

But, despite the opposition of the military, the plans were dusted off and put into effect nine years later.

### Germany and the Ottoman State

England had by now a new rival for the heart of the Ottomans and whilst Britain increasingly ill-treated its heart's desire, in the manner that a pimp manages his whore, its younger rival engaged in some serious courting.

Thirty years before Germany emerged as a state, Count Von Moltke (who later became a famous Field Marshall) considered the future prospects of the Ottoman Empire, and came to a very different conclusion to that which Britain, France and Russia had arrived at. He believed that the 'sick man of Europe' could be helped to make a recovery and to bloom again:

"If it is possible to regenerate the Turkish Empire as such, it can proceed only from a generation which must be educated to it, and that, too, from Mussulman roots. All proselytism and attempts at Europeanization, all hostile attacks, as well as friendly interpositions, lead only to complete dissolution... A few voices have dared to declare that there is no life inherent in the body of the Turkish state; that Islam permits neither progress nor change; that reform has broken Mussulman strength, and it cannot be replaced by foreign institutions; that a great, helpless and defenceless country having entered into the circle of European powers is a continual source of jealousy, of terror, of contention; that whatever cannot exist naturally must perish; that Turkey must be divided.

Such a step is contrary to moral right, with which policy by no means accords, though it strives to do so." (*Germany and Palestine,* from *Essays, Speeches and Memoirs, Vol.1.* p.272.)

Despite this view—a view that went totally against the idea of progress that the Imperialist Powers had in mind for the Ottoman Empire—England seemed to look back at the era of Bismarck with some fondness:

"The estrangement between Great Britain and Turkey that followed Mr. Gladstone's return to power in 1870 gave Germany an opportunity, of which Bismarck promptly availed himself, to step into England's shoes as the friend of Turkey, and to secure an influence over the Porte to which she had never hitherto aspired. Bismarck was not, however, prompted to this new departure by any desire to embark on aggressive adventures. The acute resurgence of the Eastern Question, which brought England and Russia to the brink of war, had threatened to defeat the policy of peaceful, if armed, conservation to which all his energies had been directed since the Franco-German War of 1870. He knew the limitations of Germany's power, and all that he contemplated at Constantinople was another of the many adroit manoeuvres on the international chessboard, by which he hoped to maintain, without any fresh resort to arms, the hegemony he had achieved for Germany on the European continent at the cost of three marvellously successful wars." (*The Turkish Empire From 1288 To 1922*, p.24.)

This passage is from a 1923 book by Lord Eversley and Valentine Chirol, the celebrated Foreign Affairs editor of *The Times*. It builds up Bismarck to knock down the Kaiser, by suggesting that, whilst Bismarck practised a kind of wise Statesmanship that preserved the peace of Europe, the Kaiser did not know what he was doing when he adopted a policy of Imperialist expansionism with regard to Turkey.

Of course, there is one sense in which the argument is correct, in its positive assessment of Bismarck as against the Kaiser. Bismarck was a fierce Anglophobe who knew how to handle Britain, whereas the Kaiser was a naïve Anglophile who thought that England would tolerate German behaviour in the world if it only aspired to 'a place in the sun' of the sort Britain had achieved.

But that is not the argument that is in the minds of Lord Eversley and Valentine Chirol. Their argument is that something occurred between the time of Bismarck and the time of the Kaiser that made Germany intolerable to Britain; and that something was the Kaiser's quest for 'world domination'.

The great fly in the ointment of British designs on the Ottoman Empire was Germany. But despite the view amongst the English Social Darwinists that the German was very dangerous because he was of the same Anglo-Saxon racial stock as the vigourous Empire-building English, Germany was, in fact, very different. It had only recently became a State (as a defensive reaction to French aggression in 1871) and was new to the world stage. In contrast to the Imperialist Powers, it had a very conservative foreign policy which tended to look favourably on the older states of the world. It saw in them something of itself and had the instinct of wanting to preserve them as a consequence of this.

The Kaiser declared in a celebrated visit to Palestine in 1898 that a strong Moslem state was essential to the stability of the world. He stated that he desired no territorial annexations for Germany, in what he saw as an established civilisation that ought to be preserved. This declaration came as a bit of a shock to Britain, which was used to thinking in terms of an inevitable Ottoman demise — particularly because none of its Imperialist rivals had ever suggested such a thing, even to gain an advantage over the other Powers. England, Russia, France and Italy had all just concentrated their eyes on the rich pickings to be had and had merely concerned themselves with making sure they would get their share. So although it was generally scoffed at, as the grossest of opportunism, the Kaiser's declaration came as something of a bombshell to them.

Germany's involvement with the Ottoman Empire followed on from this view. It recognised Islam as one of the great cultures of the world, and sought to actually consolidate the Islamic system, and not undermine it. It had as its intention to preserve the traditional Islamic frameworks of life rather than the desire to atomise the Moslems in order to make them amenable to progress. It was an involvement not of the normal Imperialistic type — it was not a predatory relationship. In the years ahead Germany attempted to produce economic development and a modernisation of the infrastructure of the Ottoman Empire along with protection of the Islamic Turks against the other Imperialist powers in return for the facilitating of its own commercial interests. And this startled and outraged Britain, which was just not used to business being done in such a way.

In some of the English press reports of the Kaiser's visit to Jerusalem, he is depicted as a Crusader, receiving land in the city for German Catholic pilgrims as a gesture of good-will from the Sultan! These were attempts to work up Islamic passion against the Teutonic ambassador, and they were used, as we shall see later, to try to incite any Fundamentalists that could be mustered into rebellion against the foreign infidel.

### The Holy War of 1911

The German support for the consolidation of the Ottoman State in the Middle East was one of the major reasons Britain made war on Germany in August 1914. In the nineteenth century the Islamic State had served the purposes of British Imperialism as a buttress against Russia and its existence was facilitated by Britain. But when the strategic reorientation in Imperial affairs occurred around 1903, all that changed and it was decided that the Ottoman State was to be reduced to a hollow shell. So, despite the fact that the new government of the Ottoman State, the Young Turks, were Western in orientation, they were damned because they threatened, with the Kaiser's help, to reinvigorate the Islamic State.

The last thing Britain wanted was a consolidation of a state that would be a beacon to other Moslems, particularly those ruled by Britain. That would give the Mussulmen dangerous ideas of an alternative existence that might be fatal to Britain's control over its Indian Empire. Britain's lordship over the Indian Moslems presented Germany with a great advantage with Turkey, since it had no part in the oppression of Islamic people. It could stretch out the hands of friendship to Islam, taking it as it found it, and leaving it as it was. On the other hand, England, to maintain its dominion over the Moslem world, had to operate in a devious and manipulative manner towards the Islamic world to ensure the subjection of large numbers of people, of different races and varieties of Islam, to the Imperial will.

In the course of reading up the background to British-Ottoman relations in the period before the Great War I came across something I was completely unprepared for. I had understood that Britain had planned for the destruction of the Ottoman Empire in the decade before the Great War. But I had never realised that England had indicated its intentions so openly to the world. And the fact that it did throws a completely different light on the War declared on Turkey in 1914—proving the case further that Turkey was the victim of an Imperial predator, despite all the muddying of the waters produced by Imperial propagandists.

The intentions of Britain toward the Ottoman Empire were openly advertised on 5th March 1911 in a prominent article in *The New York Times*. This was entitled, 'England Bent On Ousting Turkey From Mecca.' The article's subheading declared that it was Britain's aim to:

> "Seek To Restore Complete Independence Of Arabia And To Help The Tribes Set Up One Of Their Princes As The True Caliph—Great Advantages That Would Follow.'

The obviously well-informed article was penned, 'By A Veteran Diplomat' who seemingly was one who was kept in the know about England's policy. The 'Veteran Diplomat' wrote:

> 'George V. may be described as the greatest Moslem ruler of the universe. In this sense: that of the near 200,000,000 members of the human race who accord their spiritual allegiance to the Prophet, some 140,000,000 are subject to his sway, and are content with his rule... In India alone, there are nearly 900,000 Mohammedans... and their loyalty to Kaisr-i-Hind constitutes the strongest bulwark of his throne against internal revolution and foreign invasion.

> These are considerations which dominate all others in the policy of England with regard to Turkey, and indeed toward the entire so-called eastern question in which Austria, Italy, France, Russia, but above all, Germany, are also concerned. It is necessary to bear them in mind, in order to understand the role which the British Government has been playing for a number of years past in Arabia, where it is credited with a determination to emancipate from the despotism of the Turks the cradle of Islam, namely, Arabia, and the Holy cities of Medina and Mecca, which mean even more to the Moslem than Jerusalem to Christian or Jew.

> The English have never dreamt of attempting to subject Arabia to their own control. Their aim is to restore the complete independence of Arabia, and to help the tribes to set up as their sovereign one of their princes, who by reason of his authentic membership of the family of the founder of Islam, would as the true Caliph, command the homage of all the various tribes of Arabia, and the spiritual allegiance of Mohammedans in every further part of the world.

> A Prince who thus owed his temporal throne, and his religious supremacy, to England's assistance, might fairly be expected to entertain sentiments of gratitude, which would be shared by his people in connection with the recovery of their national independence, and emancipation from Turkish misrule.

> It would be of inestimable advantage to Great Britain to have Arabia, and above all, the Holy cities of Mecca and of Medina, in the possession of friends rather than of foes, and to have as Caliph, that is to say, as chief representative of the Prophet, here on earth, one who is imbued with sentiments of good will toward the English, rather than an enemy, such as the present Sultan of Turkey and his three immediate predecessors.

> The Turkish Sultans, in the same way that they secured possession of Arabia, and of the holy places of Islam, by conquest, obtained the title of Caliph by fraud, which while they fail to deceive the more highly educated

Mohammedans, impress the masses of the believers.

Until about forty years ago or so the English, for some reason or another, believed in the pretensions of the Sultans to the Caliphate. It was, indeed, this impression, even more than the dread of seeing Constantinople fall into the hands of Russia, that led Great Britain to champion the cause of the Ottoman Empire and to expend vast quantities of British blood and treasure in its defence at the time of the Crimea War, and to subsequently, in 1877, threaten to open fire on the Russian army if it ventured to enter Constantinople...

The English thought that they owed it, as a great Mohammedan power, to their Moslem fellow-citizens in India to protect the chief of the latter's church. But the now deposed Sultan Abdul Hamid, by his readiness to lend himself to every anti-British intrigue at Constantinople, and by his reluctance to accept English advice, ere long convinced the statesmen at Calcutta and at Downing Street that as the spiritual head of Islam he constituted not only a perpetual source of trouble but likewise a very serious danger to the Moslem possessions of the British crown.

Realizing the hopelessness of the situation at Stamboul, where the Sultan, with his policy of playing one European power against another, was always certain to find some foreign government ready to outbid England, for the sake of temporary advantages at the latter's expense, the British authorities in Downing Street and at Calcutta proceeded to investigate the claims of the Turkish Sultans to the Caliphate, and after a most careful inquiry, in which the most learned members of the Mohammedan Church took part, came to the conclusion that the pretensions of the Turkish ruler were unfounded, and were based wholly on usurpation and on false assertions.

The Koran... strictly and explicitly provides that the Caliph of Islam—its supreme Pontiff—must be a linear descendant of the Prophet who founded the faith... The Sultan cannot be considered as being even in the remotest degree descended from Mohammed...

On making this discovery, England ceased to protect and champion the cause of the Sultan, and turned from him, in the first place to the late Grand Sherif of Mecca, who was an authentic descendant of the Prophet, and since his death, some years ago, to the Sheikh Hamid Eddin, ruler of Hadramaut... whose rights to the Caliphate have the strong endorsement of the great Mohammedan university El Ashar at Cairo... the headquarters of the orthodoxy of Islam.

Sheikh Hamid Eddin who enjoys the enthusiastic support of the population of the southern half of Arabia and most of the important Sheikhs and tribes of Northern and central Arabia has now the entire peninsula up in arms against the Turks, with an army of over 100,000 warriors under his command... who, bye the bye, are splendidly armed and possessed of abundant... arms and resources... according to Turkish and German assertions, supplied by the English, and certain it is that while England is very strict in her punishment of gun-running in the Persian Gulf when the weapons, the ammunition, and the machine-guns are destined for Persia, or for the Indian frontier tribes, she offers no opposition whatsoever to the landing of war material of this kind at points on the coast of Arabia...

Slowly but surely is England extending her influence among the various Arab tribes... In fact, Great Britain, which already controls the Persian Gulf and the Red Sea, and which has secured footholds on the southwestern and southeastern corners of the peninsula is in a fair way of becoming the principal friend, the recognised protector, and predominant power in Arabia, the cradle of Islam.

No English statesman contributed more to the cultivation of English friendship with Arabia than Lord Curzon... Viceroy of India...

I do not know for certain whether it was Lord Curzon who first instituted this policy. But, at any rate, his name has been identified therewith throughout the Orient, and it was largely owing to his action that in Persia, Afghanistan and Morocco... the pretensions of Sultan Abdul Hamid to the Caliphate were not only denied but also derided to such an extent that any Moslem who ventured to offer the Friday prayer for him in a mosque as Commander of the Faithful would have been summarily executed as a traitor...

Every follower of the Prophet, no matter what his station in life, is expected to make at least once before he dies a pilgrimage to Mecca and Medina. Some of the pilgrims are men of great wealth... exposed to... the certainty of being shamefully robbed, owing to the appalling conditions of Turkish misrule at Mecca and Medina.

The opening of the railroad from Damascus to Medina, a little over a year ago, has not to any extent improved matters. For owing to the chaos which now prevails in all parts of the Ottoman Empire the railroad in question from which so much was expected no longer furnishes any safety of conveyance...

The cause of the present rebellion in Arabia... is the indignation on the part of the Arabs against the Young Turk Party now in control in Constantinople in giving the infidel within the gates equal political rights with the faithful, at the expense of the latter.

At Constantinople German influence has long since superseded that of Great Britain and has become dominant with the Sultan and his ministers who affect to look upon the Kaiser as the protector of Islam. Indeed the Germans have every thing their own way at Stamboul. When last summer the Sublime Porte was in desperate straits for money, it found the English and French money markets closed to it, but was able to get the funds from Germany...

It is to offset this that England is bent on ousting Turkey, Germany's friend and ally, from Arabia, and from possession of the Holy Places of Islam. If the Turks lose Mecca and Medina, the last vestige of the Sultan's claim to obedience on the part of the faithful, as Caliph, will disappear. Indeed, it would mean the break up of the Turkish Empire, as now constituted, and the transfer of whatever influence the Padishah at Stamboul has enjoyed in the past, over Mohammedans, to the new guardians of the cradle of their faith, the friends of Great Britain."

I had to check the year of publication of this New York Times article—

that it was really 1911 and not 1915, when the policy became fully activated through the Arab Revolt. The thing that surprised me was the annunciation of a prepared Arab revolt by Britain in 1911. I had never read of any substantial uprising against the Ottoman administration in this period and then searched for information about it without success. So what had happened to England's scheming in 1911?

It seems that England was scratching around in the region trying to incite rebellion against the Ottomans by taking it upon itself as 'a Great Mussulman Empire' to confer Islamic legitimacy on any rebels she could find. There was indeed a small conflict between Sheikh Eddin of Hadramaut, an area on the South-Western tip of the Arabian peninsula, and the Ottomans in 1911. But it does not seem to have come to very much. And it certainly had nothing to do with Arab nationalism.

Hadramaut and Aden, at the Southern tip of the Arabian Peninsula, had, in fact, been taken into the British sphere of influence after the purchase of the Suez Canal and the Sultan had been 'persuaded' to recognise them as a 'protectorate' of England back in 1873. They were treated to a carrot and stick approach by Britain ever since (the carrot being some commercial opportunities, the stick being the Royal Navy).

The 1911 event occurred during the emergency of the Italian invasion of Libya when Ottoman forces were stretched in defending the Moslems of North Africa from European Imperialism. Turkey's difficulty was England's opportunity, it seems. The Sultan requested that the Shereef of Mecca help in relieving a besieged Turkish garrison in Obha in the Asir territory, which he duly did with an army of Bedouins, slaves and mercenaries. And the Turks dismissed the whole affair as "a quickly suppressed uprising of roving robber-bands in the pay of England." (C.S. Hurgronje, *The Revolt In Arabia*, p.27.)

When Sheikh Eddin disappointed, England returned to the Husseins five years later (having courted Ibn Saud and the Wahhabis in between) and the Arab Revolt of 1911 became a dry-run for the main event which was to take place in 1916.

George Antonius's *The Arab Awakening* (1938) is a search for Arab nationalism. What emerges from this search is the clear fact that Arab nationalism hardly existed. Prior to the Great War, it was confined to a small group of largely European-educated intellectuals. Most of these had been part of the Arab elite that had been patronised by the former Sultan and had been neglected by the Young Turks to the extent that they took umbrage. Some of it was also the result of American Protestant missionary activity in the region and could be mostly located in its hinterland of activity.

Arabs had their representatives in the Parliament in Constantinople, in both the lower and upper chambers. They were found in the Sultan's Cabinet, in high administrative posts, as *Valis* or provincial governors, and in 1909 an Arab had been appointed Prime Minister. There was considerable local autonomy and Arabs were frequently in charge of the regions in which they lived when things were stable.

The position of the Arab in the Ottoman Empire was, in fact, far superior to that of the Irish in the British Empire—even if Home Rule had been conceded to John Redmond.

Arab leaders may have desired greater influence in Constantinople and more local autonomy—fearing the encroachment of Young Turk centralisation and secularizing—but they did not desire to be ruled by the Husseins, for instance, as a cover for the control of non-Moslems. The mass of Arabs seem to have lived lives of reasonable contentment within the loose Islamic state of the Ottomans and did not want 'liberation' by the self-styled 'great Moslem Power of England.'

Antonius's book reveals that nothing came of England's intrigues in Arabia in 1911. When Sheikh Eddin disappointed, the Shereef of Mecca did not respond either, despite all the arms flooding in to assist him in a Holy War. There just seems not to have been the will for *jihad* against the Ottoman 'oppressor' on the behalf of the Imperial 'protector' of Islam. And many Arabs, I would guess, would curse the day that there ever was.

In 1911 Britain's efforts proved to no avail. It required the catastrophe of a Great War to lure the Arabs into nationalism and the disruption of the structures in which they existed.

### *Persia, England And The Kaiser*

I wondered though what had set off such a significant manoeuvre in 1911 that it was revealed to the world by the New York Times. I think the answer lies in what Britain was doing in Persia the previous year—and the reaction it produced in the Moslem world.

One of the chief bones of contention between Russia and England had been spheres of influence in Persia. The British agreements with the Russians to settle differences over Persia were designed so that war could be made on Germany. Persia, it was decided, was to be divided in two by the two Powers with a buffer zone in between (which England later grabbed). The zones were supposed to be 'spheres of influence' but Southern Persia was gradually absorbed by Britain into the Empire.

And this British absorption of Southern Persia also facilitated the opening of the gateway to Arabia. This event, in which the main Christian Powers divided up Moslem lands between them, seems to have outraged the Islamic world. The *New York Times* of 5th November 1910 reported the reaction in its headline: *Islam's Call To Kaiser, Emperor Hesitates to Answer Appeal to Save Persia from Aggression.* The article explained:

"Political interest was concentrated on the remarkable Mohammedan meeting held at Constantinople last week, in which thousands of frenzied Turks and Persians acclaimed the German Kaiser as the 'true protector of Islam,' and appealed to him to save Persia from Anglo-Russian aggression, as he had saved Morocco and Macedonia.

The meeting has made a profound impression in German political quarters, although there is little prospect that the Kaiser will accept the role his Mohammedan devotees would assign to him... Meanwhile the German press, especially the rabid Anglophobe section, urges the government not to miss the opportunities now awaiting Teutonic diplomacy in Constantinople... German newspapers recall the Kaiser's solemn words when he stood at the grave of Saladin in 1889 and assured 'three hundred million Mohammedans that the German Emperor would always be regarded as their friend.' It is pointed out that this utterance was delivered in the presence of Count Von Bulow, then German Foreign Secretary, and therefore became a formal act of State for which the German Government could not then and must not now evade the responsibility."

But despite the Moslem appeals for help, the Kaiser thought better of it and desisted from interfering on their behalf. And furthermore he did nothing to restrain his ally, Italy, when she invaded Libya in 1911, another Moslem province of the Ottoman Empire.

The whole history of this pre-War period belies the British propaganda about Germany and Turkey being aggressive expansionists. In fact, the reality is that both the Kaiser and the Ottoman Administrations seemed to do everything they could to avoid confrontation with Britain and her allies and try to keep on their right side, as a matter of survival.

In the end, of course, they failed.

Britain, whilst it was whittling away the Ottoman Empire, urged reform on the Sultan. Reform came with the Young Turks in 1908. But British policy toward the Ottoman Empire was not governed by the character of its government but by England's — and, after the alliance of 1907, Russia's — long-term ambitions concerning its territories.

### The War On The Bagdad Railway

The disparaging mention in the *New York Times* article of the Hijaz branch line of the Berlin to Bagdad Railway, that was to run through Palestine to Mecca, reveals a sore point for Britain. This great feat of German engineering was going to be hugely beneficial in bringing pilgrims to Mecca and Medina through difficult conditions — and this was not an aspect of German-Turkish cooperation which Britain wanted to succeed or wanted to acknowledge. Instead it began to try to convince the Shereef that the lucrative trade in camel transportation, that the Husseins ran, for the purposes of the Pilgrimages, would be ruined by the coming of the German railway.

Within the five volume *The Great Events Of The Great War*, by C.F. Horne, W.F. Austin and L.P. Ayres (1923), there is a section in the first volume, *Causes*, about the Berlin-Bagdad Railway. Maurice Jastrow, Professor at the

University of Pennsylvania, is quoted:

"In the last analysis the Bagdad Railway will be found to be the largest single contributing factor in bringing about the war, because through it more than through any other cause the mutual distrust among European Powers has been nurtured until the entire atmosphere of international diplomacy became vitiated. The explanation of this remarkable phenomenon, transforming what appeared on the surface to be a magnificent commercial enterprise, with untold possibilities for usefulness, into a veritable curse, an excrescence on the body politic of Europe, is to be sought in the history of the highway through which the railway passes. The control of this highway is the key to the East—the Near and the Farthest East as well—Such has been its role in the past—such is its significance today." (p.194-5.)

Jastrow further explained:

"It was felt in England that if, as Napoleon is said to have remarked, Antwerp in the hands of a great Continental power was a pistol levelled at the English coast, Bagdad and the Persian Gulf in the hands of Germany (or any other strong power) would be a 42-centimetre gun pointed at India." (p.197.)

Professor Jastrow's book, *The War And The Bagdad Railway: The Story Of Asia Minor And Its Relation To The Present Conflict*, published in 1917, is the most substantial argument in print for the building of the German Railway being the single biggest cause of the War. In one part he states:

"British policy was determined that the railway should not reach the Persian Gulf under German control. This was clearly enunciated by Lord Cranbourne, Under-Secretary for Foreign Affairs, in January 1902, who stated that the 'maintenance of the *status quo* was incompatible with the occupation by any Great Power of a port on these waters.' The Bagdad Railway, if extended, even to Basra, would destroy the trade that English merchants and English capital had built up in the most important centre between India and the Suez Canal." (p.99.)

George Brandes argued that it was the German proposal of a share in the venture to the French that finally motivated Britain to make its approach to France for an alliance. England looked with concern on the developing *détente* between the French and the Germans and decided to counter it with an *Entente*—driving a wedge between Franco-German reconciliation and turning France's eyes back to Alsace-Lorraine.

Firstly, however, Brandes outlined why the Berlin-Bagdad Railway was viewed as such a threat in Britain:

"During the nineteenth century England controlled the industry of Europe by means of her coal and iron as well as her... unrivalled sea power. France alone was a feeble competitor and after the Fashoda incident she dropped out of the race. But then a new rival suddenly appeared; which until 1870 had been an agricultural nation. She began to abound in foundries, mills, chemical works, and shipyards. She acquired new railroads, new canals and even a budding navy.

At first Germany's industrial attempts caused no uneasiness in England. But as the years passed and the Germans progressed England discovered that many an article supposed to be of home manufacture was German in reality. And as German consuls and German salesmen were active in every part of the world, England and Germany soon began to conflict in Brazil as well as Asia Minor.

The first move in this international game of chess was Joseph Chamberlain's attempt to strengthen the bond between England and the colonies by abandoning free trade and introducing a protective tariff for the mother country and the colonies... Then Edward VII planned to encircle Germany by a network of allied powers. He came to France in the second year of his reign as soon as the Boer situation was cleared.

About this time — 1902 — the German Government, having obtained the concession of the Bagdad Railway from the Sultan, tried to bring about a financial understanding with France.

The Bagdad Railway was to unite the suburbs of Constantinople with a German port on the Persian Gulf and as first planned it was to have followed the old Roman road, creeping around the Taurus Mountains and linking together the flowering cities in the plain of Nineveh. This line would have been the shortest and the cheapest. But Russia protested and... the German company therefore had to follow a southern route, that taken by Xenophon's ten thousand, which afterwards branched into the plains of Mesopotamia.

The German-Anatolian Railway Company also secured concessions to the side roads already in operation. The two most important belonged to French companies. These were bought. One of these controls the direct line to Smyrna; the other leads to Adana and the port of Alexandretta. Finally the German company obtained the rights to the long important line which was to connect Aleppo, Damascus and Mecca, and which would be used by all pilgrims going to the Prophets' city...

The road would have brought Bagdad five hours from Constantinople instead of fifty-five days, and made it possible to transport Turkish troops easily from the centre to the most distant parts of the country. There would be rich harvests of corn and cotton on the banks of the Tigris and Euphrates; a new way would be opened up to India, and the value of the Suez Canal would be incalculably decreased. Turkey would become an economic vassal of Germany and England's domination in India would be severely menaced.

As Germany did not have the requisite capital, she turned to France and a Franco-German company was formed. The president was Arthur von Gwinner, President of the Deutsche Bank, and the vice-president was a M. Vernes, an associate of the Rothschilds in the Compagnie du Nord et du Midi. On the Board of trustees he also represented various banks and interests...

As soon as this financial understanding had been reached between France and Germany a diplomatic rapprochement was inevitable. It must be remembered that in France, as in all other countries, the financial and industrial interests are centred in the hands of a very few men who practically control the nation... And when these men had determined to co-operate with the German bankers, the two nations had to become friends again. The first steps were taken. Jules Lemaitre, who at that time had not become a nationalist, proposed that by-gones be by-gones and advocated friendship with Germany.

At this England began to show signs of nervousness... If Germany was to secure the backing of France, she would become a very serious rival.

The consequences of the Franco-German understanding was King Edward's visit to Paris in 1903... As an onlooker in the crowd I witnessed his reception and was struck by the rather uncertain attitudes of the masses. The tension between France and England was still strong after the Fashoda incident. During the Boer War, which had just ended, sentiment in Paris had been entirely for Kruger.

But now King Edward appeared as the old friend and admirer of France... as a diplomat he knew what he wanted and was bent on making use of every opportunity to ensure England's supremacy in her competition with Germany. He realised it would not be very difficult to stir up the old French grudge against Germany, the hatred from 1870-1.

During his stay in France King Edward met Delcassé, who for about eight years had directed the foreign policy of his country and who was delighted at the thought of co-operating to encircle Germany. In 1901 he had been to Russia to strengthen the Russian alliance and he was *persona grata* at St. Petersburg; he tried to dissolve Italy's connection with the Triple Alliance and he was active in Constantinople: he was at hand wherever he thought he could further the interests of France by means of an isolated Germany.

King Edward's stay in Paris was well spent. The day after he left for London it was announced that M. Vernes and his associates withdrew from the Bagdad company and that the Franco-German company was dissolved." (*The World At War*, pp.140-5.)

Having seen off the French, the Liberal Imperialists then had to see off the Tories, who were slower to readjust to the new strategic orientation.

In 1903 it looked as though a deal had been struck between the Germans and the British Unionist Prime Minister, Balfour, which would have led to the Railway becoming a joint venture between the Germans and Britain, as well as the French. But after pressure from the Liberal Imperialists, Balfour withdrew from the conciliatory German offer. This proved a watershed in Anglo-Ottoman relations.

Professor Zaki Salah, a Westernised Iraqi academic, commented on the significance of this in his *Mesopotamia 1600-1914, A Study in British Foreign Affairs*, published in Baghdad in 1957:

"It has generally been conceded that the year 1903 witnessed a turning point in the British attitude toward the German enterprise... Prior to that date, it may be noted, Great Britain viewed the issue quite favourably as a manifestation of the 'white man's burden,' and as, primarily, a sort of business expansion in which she hoped to participate. It was in 1902, for instance, that Earl Percy stated in Parliament what was common to many another Britisher with similar concern. He said: 'Germany is doing for Turkey what we have been doing for Persia. She is making for the social improvement and the material well-being of the native races; and for my part I believe that if the struggle of the future is to be between the Slavonic policy of compelling stagnation or the Teutonic policy of spreading the blessings of enlightenment and civilisation the victory will lie with those nations which are striving selfishly or unselfishly, consciously or unconsciously, to fulfil the high aims which Providence has entrusted to the Imperial races of Christendom.' ...

From 1903 onwards, however, the issue was to the British dominated by strategic considerations... The menace was now specifically that of Germany, rather than that of Russia; and the occasion was Germany's astounding Bagdad Railway convention of the same year... What came to be regarded at stake by the British was, thenceforward, their control over the Persian Gulf, their preponderance in Mesopotamia, and, consequently their interests in India... It strove consistently, from 1903 onward, to bar the German line from reaching the Persian Gulf, and German influence in Mesopotamia from matching her own... and that was finally settled by war." (*Mesopotamia 1600-1914, A Study in British Foreign Affairs*, pp.266-7.)

Britain had been the pioneer in the idea of a Bagdad Railway. In 1837 she spent vast sums on a survey of the Euphrates valley and in 1851 England obtained a concession from the Sultan for the construction of a line between the port of Alexandretta and the Persian Gulf. The objective was to shorten the journey to India. But when the Suez Canal was purchased in 1876 Britain abandoned the project, only to see it taken up by the Germans a couple of decades later. In the intervening years the first track of the railway, the Ismid line, was still a British concern, but there was no enthusiasm to develop it after the Suez purchase had seemingly created a shorter route to India, and the Deutsche Bank subsequently acquired it.

The British attitude to the Railway went through a metamorphosis with the strategic orientation toward Russia and France, and against Germany. But this was not always made clear to the Turks. Some ambiguity remained—convincing Constantinople that, if they satisfied British concerns with regard to it, all would be fine. As with Belgium in 1914 (and Saddam Hussein's Iraq in 1990-1) signals were deliberately confusing. Mixed messages acted as an invitation to come on, to ensure a reason for conflict.

*The Commercial War*

When General Townsend's army came to disaster in attempting to capture Baghdad in a hasty gamble during 1915 *The New York Times* asked what on earth was on Britain's mind in launching such a risky military adventure?:

"Why all this strain about Bagdad, a caravan town outside of this world? The answer, so far as it is unromantic, is this: Bagdad lies on the overland railroad route from Europe to India... Moreover, the time from Europe to India via this imagined overland route would be half as long as now is required to go from London to India via the Suez Canal. Besides Bagdad is supposed to command the best trade route to Persia, and therefore, ought not to be in Turko-German hands." (*New York Times*, 30th April 1916.)

The Bagdad Railway was feared in England because of its potential to link up mercantile interests on the European heartland with Asia and thereby develop the commercial potential of Germany (and in consequence, Europe and Asia) free from the seas.

The Railway proposal came about because the increasing industrial production of Germany made the question of raw materials, new markets and security from outside interference an acute one. The outside interference that threatened the economic development of Germany was the State that controlled the commerce of the world market through its control of the seas—Britain.

Percy Evans Lewin of the Royal Colonial Institute wrote *The German Road To The East* in 1916 and it describes how German economic expansion was forced toward the East by Britain's dominating position on the sea to the West. Lewin argued that the whole of Germany's sea commerce came out of a small triangle of which Heligoland formed the centre. From there it passed through the narrow waters between Denmark and Norway which could be easily blocked by the British fleet. Ninety-five per cent of it went through the English Channel, and the only alternative route around the Orkneys also took it through an area controlled by the Royal Navy. And even if it successfully managed to negotiate these routes it would run into British sea power again at Gibraltar.

The Railway promised not only to meet the economic needs of Germany but would have also opened a much shorter and safer route for its trade than that through the Baltic and North Sea, through the English Channel, the Straits of Gibraltar and the Suez Canal—all controlled by the guns of the Royal Navy.

Eastern Europe, the Near East, the East coast of Africa and the Far East all offered Germany raw materials and potential new markets free from blockade. If a railroad could be arranged through Austria, Bulgaria, Turkey, Mesopotamia to Baghdad and the Persian Gulf, along with the necessary conventions with the countries concerned, the economic potential of the Eurasian heartland would be unleashed.

In 1898 an Agreement was reached between the Kaiser and the Sultan for German construction of the Railway. It was begun in 1900 and this great engineering project's tracks climbed huge mountains and crossed vast deserts, following one of the oldest and richest trade routes in the world, where caravans had previously travelled from India to Europe. It was due for completion in 1915 and would have linked up the Ottoman Empire with central Europe and provided an alternative route to India. The Railway was also planned to extend to Basra and through Palestine to Mecca to facilitate the Moslem pilgrimages.

The transportation of merchandise by such a route would also be far cheaper than by Britain's roundabout shipping road through the Suez Canal. The Railway would also provide great economic advantages, putting the new European heavy industries in touch with the metal resources of Anatolia; the textile industry in contact with the cotton, wool and hemp of the Balkans and Middle East; it would also provide a route for oil from Persia.

In short, the Berlin-Bagdad Railway had revolutionary consequences for the commerce of the world and threatened a fundamental realignment in the economic axis of the world market in favour of continental Europe and away from maritime England. And it was estimated that it would increase Germany's commercial opportunities ten-fold through the shipping lines that would emanate from its terminus in the Persian Gulf to African, Asian and Australasian ports.    What England was concerned about was the fact that this economic development would take place outside the reach of the Royal Navy. Britain controlled the world market and commerce by its control of the seas, and the creation of a powerful land-based market, free from British interference, would threaten the British military dominance of commerce (and undermine the effective use of the Balance of Power Policy being applied to continental Europe in future).

Midway through the nineteenth century Britain was the 'workshop of the world' producing half of all the industrial products made. By 1910 this share had dropped to only an eighth, as America and Germany ate into its cut, with Germany being particularly adept in the new chemical and machine-tools industries. The Bagdad Railway had the potential to overwhelm British competition by eroding Britain's greatest competitive edge—its power on the seas.

### Frederic Howe—An American On The Railway

Frederic Howe, an American who was very sympathetic to England's cause during the War, put himself in the position of Britain in imagining the threat of the Berlin-Bagdad Railway. The following extensive passage is from a chapter entitled 'Menace To The British Empire' from his 1919 book, *The Only Possible Peace*:

"British investments in Egypt, Eastern Africa, Australia, India, and the Far East amount to at least $6,000,000,000. This represents government loans, investments in rail-roads, docks, mines, oil, plantations, and development work of all kinds. England is the great creditor nation of the world. Her overseas investments in 1913 amounted to $20,000,000,000, or more than the foreign investments of the rest of the world combined. And the investing classes of England come from the old aristocracy, which owns the land, the mines, the railroads, shipping, and the other financial interests of the kingdom. This investing class is powerful politically. It controls the House of Lords. It controls the Conservative party. It moulds the policies of the Foreign Office and the diplomatic service.

Great Britain controls a great part of the carrying trade of the world... Fifty years ago England feared French control of the Suez Canal. That was one reason for its purchase...

British shipping interests and the profits of the carrying trade were also menaced by the trade route overland to the East. The Bagdad Railway was to be an integral part of the marvellously organized German railway system from the centre of Europe to the Persian Gulf. It would connect with Hamburg, Berlin, Essen, and the lower Rhine region; it would pass through Austria-Hungary, the Balkan states, Turkey, Asia Minor, and Mesopotamia. It would place western Asia and Persia in direct railway connection with German industry. It would enable German merchants to place their wares in Africa and the Far East in much less time than England could transport them by water. The Bagdad Railway would do to shipping what the trans-Pacific railways did to water transportation around Cape Horn. It would shorten it by many days. It would substitute carriage by rail for carriage by water. Thus the Bagdad Railway threatened billions of British investments in shipping.

England's shipping amounted to 21,000,000 gross tons in 1913 or about 40 per cent of the ocean tonnage of the world. A great part of this is employed in Oriental trade. Two-thirds of the tonnage passing through the Suez Canal is of British registry. Thus the Bagdad Railway was a maritime as well as a financial drive at the British Empire. And when we consider the extent to which German shipping had increased in recent years, and the inroads already made on what Great Britain considered her rightful monopoly of the seas, we can understand that the ship-owners of England, always alert to their interests, were alarmed at the prospect.

No nation has made use of its railways for the development of commerce as has Germany. It has been the greatest single agency of German industry. Special rates are made to encourage foreign trade. Through tariffs are provided. Materials and supplies are carried below cost to develop industries or communities. The railways are closely linked with the German merchant marine. They are operated as a unit. Transportation in Germany is an engine of industrial development just as it is of military power...

London is the financial centre of the world. England acquired financial supremacy from the Netherland states during the Napoleonic wars. Her financial power was increased by her shipping and overseas trade. And she has guarded this supremacy most zealously. Free trade increased her economic power, for free trade made England the natural clearing-house for the shipping of every country, and the marketplace to which the wealth of every clime could be brought for exchange. In her harbors goods are warehoused or trans-shipped to other countries without the payment of tariffs. The financial supremacy of Great Britain is closely related to and dependent upon the control of commerce and shipping. British exports and imports passing through the Mediterranean in 1916 amounted to $1,650,000,000. This was carried almost exclusively in British ships. It was cleared through British banks. It was handled almost wholly by British merchants. It was produced almost wholly by British labor.

Here again the Bagdad Railway touched the nerve-centre of England. And no other activity is as responsive to economic change as is banking and finance. British banks have connections all over the world. These connections reflect every change, no matter how obscure it may be. The banks form a reporting agency like a world-wide seismograph which records the slightest vibrations of the world. Such is Lombard Street. It is the nerve-centre of the commercial world.

This, too, was threatened by a land route from Hamburg to the Orient. The dislocation of shipping from water to rail, the bringing of the trade of the Orient to Germany, the possibility of developing Constantinople as a great port, meant that Berlin might become a great financial clearing-house; and Hamburg and Constantinople, working in that close scientific relationship that characterizes German economic operations, might supplant London as a financial centre. If carried far enough, England's financial power might pass to Germany, just as in earlier centuries it passed from northern Italy to south Germany, thence to the Hanseatic cities and the Netherlands.

The opening up of a new transportation route by land, the substitution of rail for water transportation, the development of German ports in the Mediterranean threatened the economic and financial power which has come to England as a result of her long, almost unchallenged monopoly of the industry and the carrying trade of the world. And the bankers and the financiers of Great Britain form part of the ruling classes. As stated before, they are as sensitive to every economic change as is the nervous system of the human body.

British industry was also threatened by the Bagdad Railway. A land route to the East was an industrial peril. During the years which preceded the war, German foreign trade was advancing by leaps and bounds. In 1914 it had almost reached the total of British trade. In that year the foreign commerce of Great Britain was $5,021,655,000; while that of Germany was $4,966,660,000. And the press of both countries as well as the jingo writers had been urging these facts on the attention of the people. 'Made in Germany' had become a British nightmare. It had alarmed the manufacturers just as the increase in German tonnage had disturbed the shipping interests.

The Bagdad Railway and its advantages to German industry was a further menace to the industrial structure of Great Britain. For three generations Great Britain had enjoyed something like a monopoly in iron and steel, in wool and cotton, in machines and cutlery. The fact that four-fifths of her people live in towns and cities indicates how exclusively industrial she is. The Bagdad Railway would bring the products of Germany to the 110,000,000 people about the Mediterranean, as well as the hundreds of other millions of the Far East, in far less time than the output of the mills of Manchester, Leeds, and Sheffield could reach them. It was an express service. It would enable German business men with the most skilful agents in the world at their command to place their products in the Far East — in India, China, East Africa, and the Pacific islands much more quickly than they could be brought by sea.

In addition the British colonial service, which offers opportunities for the younger sons of the aristocracy in Egypt, India, Africa, and elsewhere, was in jeopardy, as were the tens of thousands of young men who annually leave the mother country to enter the foreign service. The economic life of the British Empire is involved in the protection of the supremacy which has been built up in shipping, in industry, in overseas trade, in finance, and in the handling of the wealth of the outside world. And... the same interests in Great Britain were menaced or thought they were menaced by the German drive to the East. That is why the Bagdad Railway was so portentous. That is why the control of the Mediterranean forms the keystone of one empire and the imperialistic dream of another." (pp.146-153.)

If the reader is still sceptical about the view that a war was required to bring about British commercial supremacy over Germany, when economic competition was going against the Empire, this record of a 1910 conversation between Arthur Balfour and Henry White, the United States Ambassador in London, should be considered. It is taken from a book of White's experiences, written in 1930. White, a strong Anglophile, treats the conversation as a humorous aside. But, as they say, many a true word was spoken in jest:

"Balfour (somewhat lightly): We are probably fools not to find a reason for declaring war on Germany before she builds too many ships and takes away our trade.

White: You are a very high-minded man in private life. How can you possibly contemplate anything so politically immoral as provoking a war against a harmless nation which has as good a right to a navy as you have? If you wish to compete with German trade, work harder.

Balfour: That would mean lowering our standard of living. Perhaps it would be simpler for us to have a war.

White: I am shocked that you of all men should enunciate such principles.

Balfour (again lightly): Is it a question of right or wrong? Maybe it is just a question of keeping our supremacy." (Henry White and Allan Nevins, *Thirty Years Of American Diplomacy*, p.257-8.)

The Berlin-Bagdad Railway was the economic link that, for Britain, marked off the destruction of the Ottoman Empire together with that of Germany.

And so England could not permit a neutral Turkey. With regard to British hostility to the Bagdad Railway, its War on Turkey, and the Mesopotamian campaign, that began a day after the Declaration of War, Professor Salah noted:

"Of all the Ottoman regions Mesopotamia held out the main reason for

British dislike of continued Turkish neutrality: A neutral Turkey was bound by international agreements to allow Germany to continue the construction of the Bagdad Railway down to Basra. The project was going ahead with remarkable success. The British were at a great disadvantage there, and they had to act before it was too late. By Autumn (1914) they were prepared to attack Southern Mesopotamia at short notice. The Turks made no preparations for such an eventuality, as they probably suspected no immediate war with Great Britain... On November 6th the British subjugated the lone Mesopotamian port of Fao, almost without a fight. Sixteen days later the all-important maritime city of Basra was occupied." (*Mesopotamia 1600-1914, A Study in British Foreign Affairs*, p.276.)

## Charles Woods—An Englishman In New York

H. Charles Woods, a British Balkan and Middle-East expert, was on a speaking tour of America as British forces advanced again through Mesopotamia in 1917 to cut off the Bagdad Railway. Woods, a Fellow of The Royal Geographical Society, was one of those Geographers of the time, like Halford Mackinder, who lent his academic abilities to the Imperial Service in the form of Geopolitics. His particular speciality seems to have been the danger of the Berlin-Bagdad Railway to the interests of the British Empire. And he wrote and lectured on this subject, and others, extensively at the time. He was the author of a number of books, including *Washed By Four Seas* and *The Danger Zone of Europe*, and a contributor to Geographical and Political publications such as *The Fortnightly Review,* on the subject of the Railway. When the Great War was extended to the Middle East his time had come as a propagandist, and as part of this work he went off to the United States, like many other English writers and academics during 1917, to convince the Americans of Britain's good intentions in the world.

Woods visited the New York Geographical Society in January 1918 and this is from a report by *The New York Times*:

"Mr. Woods described the British campaign in Mesopotamia and Palestine as essential to the defense of the British Empire, for the reason that, if these expeditions had not been undertaken, the Turks, with German aid would have been able to complete both railroads, and with these lines of communication could have launched attacks against British power in Egypt and the East.' (January 9th 1918.)

Woods' explanation is illustrative of the fact that the British were possessed of the unshakeable belief that the defence of their Empire impelled the attacking of neighbouring adjacent territories. And this, of course, was a recipe for, and a justification of, almost continuous expansion in the world for defensive purposes.

This is the *New York Times* report of Charles Wood's address to the *Lowell*

*Institute* in Boston on the first leg of his American tour, in November 1917, in which he explicitly connects the British advance into Palestine with the perceived problem of the Bagdad Railway:

'To understand the movement undertaken against Jerusalem and to appreciate its importance one must go back into recent history. This done and one will see that any blow against this Holy City is also an Allied blow against Germany. Ever since the Kaiser came to his throne he has been infatuated with the desire of a German drive to the East, an attempt to dominate from Hamburg to Bagdad. For instance in 1889, and in 1895, he made visits to Turkey and really played the role of a royal carpet-bagger. On the second of these occasions he even went so far as to declare himself the friend of the Sultan and of all Moslems, who have in consequence venerated him always. He appointed to that country his best Ambassador, Von Beiderstein, who well carried out the war-lord's intrigues before he was brought, shortly before his death, to London. The Kaiser lent German Officers to train the Turkish Army and German engineers to build her railroads.

It is for these reasons that the interests of Turkey and Germany are so closely bound up that a defeat of the Ottoman Army is an actual defeat of the German Army." (25th November 1917.)

Joseph Anthony Starke makes a comment in his 1921 book, *Light And Truth After The World Tragedy,* about the morality of Britain's behaviour in the matter of the Bagdad Railway that is worth noting, although it was no defence against British intention:

"Looking at this matter dispassionately we may well ask this question: Wherein was the moral or political wrong in Germany's plans in as much as her enterprise was merely commercial and economic and did not emanate from any design of conquest or annexation? Have not other nations carried out similar schemes of commercial extension or improved transit facilities: Suez Canal, Panama Canal, Cape-to-Cairo railroad plan, and others, all of which carried with them political measures and rearrangements? Why is that which is approved, accepted and done by England, France or America wrong when done by Germany? Why should a nation so fit not aspire to its fullest development, to an equal position and facilities with the others?...' (pp.52-3.)

'It is peculiarly illustrative of England's intense jealousy of her commercial and shipping supremacy in the world that she should have thrown all this opposition in Germany's path... while England herself was in possession of numerous similar trade routes and special privileges in every part of the world, the most of them acquired by forceful conquest or arbitrary political measures and not by peaceful diplomacy and equitable agreements as in the case of Germany in her Asia Minor project. In view of all the facts, a serious doubt arises as to whether England's final apparent acquiescence in the German Berlin-Bagdad scheme was sincere and actuated by genuine desire to secure world peace by removal of the acute friction over that question... Even while England was officiously pretending to give Germany the right of way in her enterprise Earl Grey was busy with... the military convention pledges between England and France, and soon thereafter entered, together with France, into definite marine-policy arrangements with Russia for the case of a European war." (p.73.)

Starke was dealing with a very important point here—the argument that, if Britain waged its Great War over the Bagdad Railway, why did it seemingly make an agreement with Germany permitting it just before the War broke out? To make sense of this, it should be realised, firstly, that this agreement neutered the more dangerous aspects of the Railway, secondly, that British control was conceded on various aspects of its development and thirdly, and most importantly, that the Great War was seen as imminent and therefore the Railway could be dealt with, finally, through other means. The final agreement was the diplomatic dressing to a weak link in the propaganda, aimed at diverting attention from the Railway as a cause of the War.

Frederic Howe pointed out, in his aforementioned book, (a book otherwise in all ways hostile to Germany), that the very attitude that England and France took to Turkey made it become a willing partner in the German scheme:

"Turkey was desirous of developing her Asiatic possessions. She wanted to protect her territory from Russia and Great Britain, one ambitious for the Dardanelles and Armenia, the other for the Mesopotamia region. As Great Britain and France controlled the Mediterranean, this was only possible by railroad connections. Unfortunately for the Allied Powers, as it afterward developed, they had discouraged the development of Turkey. They had kept her in economic subjection. There was danger that she might become too powerful. A strong Turkey might interfere with Russian plans for Constantinople. It might interfere with the British Protectorate over the Sublime Porte. For Great Britain had assumed the guardianship of Turkey as a means of protection against Russian advance to the East." (*The Only Possible Peace*, p.72.)

The war propaganda, issued by Britain in service of its conquest of Palestine and Mesopotamia, sought to justify their absorption into the British Empire on the basis of the relative economic underdevelopment that persisted in the Ottoman Empire. And yet it was England and France who had been responsible for that economic stagnation and the same two countries which had engineered a European War when economic development and prosperity was becoming a threatening possibility, under German auspices.

The English writer, G. Lowes Dickinson, made no secret of this in his 1917 book, *The European Anarchy*:

"Here had been launched on a grandiose scale a great enterprise of civilization. The Mesopotamian plain, the cradle of civilization, and for centuries the granary of the world, was to be redeemed by irrigation from the encroachment of the desert, order and security were to be restored, labour to be set at work, and science and power to be devoted on a great scale to their only proper purpose, the increase of life. Here was an idea fit to inspire the most generous imagination.

Here, for all the idealism of youth and the ambition of maturity, for diplomatists, engineers, administrators, agriculturists, educationists, was an opportunity for the work of a lifetime, a task to appeal at once to the imagination, the intellect, and the organizing capacity of practical men, a scheme in which all nations might be proud to participate, and by which Europe might show to the backward populations that the power she had won over Nature was to be used for the benefit of man, and that the science and the arms of the West were destined to recreate the life of the East. What happened, in fact? No sooner did the Germans approach the other nations for financial and political support to their scheme than there was an outcry of jealousy, suspicion, and rage. All the vested interests of the other States were up in arms. The proposed railway, it was said, would compete with the Trans-Siberian, with the French railways, with the ocean route to India, with the steamboats on the Tigris. Corn in Mesopotamia would bring down the price of corn in Russia. German trade would oust British and French and Russian trade. Nor was that all. Under cover of an economic enterprise, Germany was nursing political ambitions. She was aiming at Egypt and the Suez Canal, at the control of the Persian Gulf, at the domination of Persia, at the route to India." (*The European Anarchy*, p.101-3.)

### *The Railway and The Origins of Kuwait*

Before the Great War England was determined that Russia would not reach the Persian Gulf with her railways and obtain a sea-port there. The division of Persia between England and Russia had secured an agreement from the Czar that this objective would be given up. So, having seen off Russia Britain turned her attention to Germany.

In order to prevent Germany extending the Railway to the Persian Gulf, Britain moved to block it beyond Baghdad, even though the territory it was planned to cross, to the Gulf, was part of the Ottoman Empire, and had been for centuries.

Kuwait was an administrative unit of the Basra *vilayet* in Mesopotamia. Its ruler was subordinate to the Governor of Basra and it was regarded as part of Mesopotamia. In 1871 the Sheikh of Kuwait had accepted the title of *Qaim-Maqam*, or official ruler of the Ottoman district.

In 1899 England got the local ruler (and Ottoman Governor), the Sheikh of Kuwait, to sign a secret treaty in which, in return for £1000, he agreed not to sell or lease any of his territory to anyone without the prior consent of Britain (the treaty was cancelled in 1961). And in 1904 Britain established a Political Agent there to keep an eye on things. But Kuwait had no defined boundaries as a territory. So Britain encouraged Sheikh Mubarak bin Sabah to object to the possible extension of the line to the Warba and Bubiyan Islands, by claiming these islands (which British surveyors had identified as the probable termini for the Railway) on the basis of fishing rights.

In helping to detach Kuwait from the Ottoman Empire, Britain wished to command all the possible Railway outlets on the Western shore of the Persian Gulf. And the Government of India decided to buy up the best land for the site of a terminus in 1907.

Professor Salah cites Lord Curzon's statement to the House of Lords regarding Britain's position in the Gulf being based on the belief that the Gulf constituted the defensive frontier of India:

"Our position in the Gulf... rests upon the unassailable ground of our trade in the Gulf; upon our services there for the last hundred years; upon the capital sunk; upon the naval position we kept up; upon the political predominance which we maintain; and most of all upon the fact that the Gulf is part of the maritime frontier of India, and that in the politics of the Gulf are involved the security, integrity, and peace of India itself. This is no new fact but an admitted truism accepted by all parties on both sides in both Houses of Parliament." (*Mesopotamia 1600-1914, A Study in British Foreign Affairs*, p.274.)

Professor Salah then describes the British diplomatic attempts to separate Kuwait from Mesopotamia to prevent port facilities being available at the terminus of the Railway:

"Situated at the head of the Persian Gulf, about 80 miles due south of Basra, Kuwait proved to be the focal point of British tactics against German and Ottoman in the field of lower Mesopotamia and the Gulf. The Sheikdom of Kuwait, with inhabitants at the time of 15000 souls lay on the south side of a bay... forming a fine natural harbour with good anchorage. Administratively it belonged to Mesopotamia; its ruler (the Sheik) was subordinate to the Governor of Basra province. The British paid special attention to the Ottoman outpost since the inception of the Bagdad Railway project, lest a terminus for the Railway be procured there. And it was in the year 1899 that they reached a secret agreement with Sheik Mubarak of Kuwait who pledged, accordingly, to alienate no territory without British consent.

By the turn of the century Kuwait was fast becoming a British Protectorate, notwithstanding British denial of their anomalous protection over the same Ottoman territory." (*Mesopotamia 1600-1914, A Study in British Foreign Affairs*, p.275.)

In 1913 Britain, ignoring the Sheikh of Kuwait, demanded that the Ottoman Government cede Kuwait (and Qatar) to them so that they could become an official British Protectorate. The Turks agreed not to extend the Railway south of Basra and conceded the right to Britain to control any extension to the line if they consented to it reaching the Gulf. But the matter of Kuwait's formal status remained unresolved when England declared War on Turkey a year later.

The chipping away of Kuwait from Mesopotamia and the Ottoman Empire was obviously not an attempt to 'free a small nation' and no pretence was ever made that it was. Kuwait was not a nation in any sense but a product of the military power of the Royal Navy and a strategic weapon to be used against the Germans (or any other Power that might emerge in the region that might require cutting down to size).

In March 1914 the Turks announced plans to establish an oil company for Mesopotamia. This was followed by a subsequent statement from the British Foreign Office warning Constantinople that the boundary between Mesopotamia and Kuwait be strictly observed, even though the latter was still part of the Ottoman Empire.

The Sheikh of Kuwait agreed to help the British capture Basra in return for recognition of his territory as a Protectorate. But when he died in 1916 his son, the new Sheikh, went over to the Ottomans and Britain blockaded Kuwait from the Gulf until the Armistice with Turkey.

When Britain established Iraq in 1920 it decided not to include within it the territory of Kuwait. By this point Iraq had become restless and had to be given a measure of self-rule. So it was considered useful to keep Kuwait apart from it.

### The Balkans Detonator

Whilst England's desire to destroy the Bagdad Railway was a significant cause of the Great War on Germany and Turkey it could not be the detonator for that War. That had to be found in the Balkans, for a number of reasons that I will now explain.

In the course of the nineteenth century the Ottomans were gradually forced back through the Balkans after the spread of nationalism in Europe. At the turn of the twentieth century much of South-Eastern Europe, including Thrace, Bulgaria, Bosnia, Albania, Macedonia and Rumania was still nominally under Ottoman control but Greece and Serbia had become independent, Bulgaria was practically independent and Bosnia was administered by the Austro-Hungarian Empire.

Nicolae Batzaria was a Rumanian-speaking Christian from Monastir in Macedonia who became a Young Turk. His Memoirs, *Din Lumea Islamului*, contain a useful analogy concerning the Ottoman attitude to the races contained in their Empire. He notes that from the time the Turks conquered the Balkans, in the fourteenth century:

> "Turks did not, either at that time or later, think about denationalizing other peoples or about imposing upon them a different culture... The Turk rule from this viewpoint had a good effect upon nationalities. This rule could be compared to the snow that covers the crops and protects them from winter freeze. The Young Turks desired to depart from this policy and sought to introduce a policy of denationalization. It was too late and the policy was doomed to fail. It was too late because, due to the regime of tolerance adopted by Turks with regard

to ethnic groups in national and cultural matters, the existing national groups had developed and strengthened themselves to the point where they could cope with any action likely to threaten their existence and ethnic structure." (Nicolae Batzaria, *Din Lumea Islamului*, p.123.)

The Balkans cockpit became the detonator for the Great War on Germany. It was an unstable region that for centuries the Turks had managed to govern effectively and keep remarkably stable. But after the Peace of Paris of 1856, the sponsorship of the minorities by the Europeans, and the intrigues of the Great Powers in the region, the Ottomans began to fight a losing battle in stabilizing the region.

The American, Joseph Starke, argued in 1921 that England had utilized the inherent instability of the region to further its interests in preparing the ground for the Great War on Germany:

"Within a comparatively small territory there are thrown together in that area some seven or eight nationalities, and semi-nationalities: Greece, Roumania, Bulgaria, Servia, Bosnia, Herzegovina, Montenegro and Albania, to which we must add Hungary, Croatia, Slavonia, Turkey and Italy to make this political crazy-quilt complete. The Balkan and adjoining Slavic nationalities are largely intermixed along their real and imaginary boundary lines, and the whole area is permeated by Greeks, Turks, Italians and numerous Jews, also some Austrians and Germans. Each country claims parts of the others on ethnological and historical grounds; each has proud traditions of former independence; they all claim the glories of ancient Greece and Rome as their heritage. In reality they are a collection of 'wreckage peoples,' evolved from the transition periods of ancient civilizations, mixed with nomadic settlers from the east, and hence, of most indefinite lineage. In character they are turbulent... and of the worst political reputation...

England is directly responsible for this exasperating and baffling state of affairs. By nourishing in these peoples, under the impulse of Gladstone's humanitarian eloquence, an inordinate sense of importance quite beyond their deserts and the nationalistic possibilities of the situation as it stood at that time, she directly encouraged their restlessness and violence, increased the racial jealousies between them and interfered with the natural evolution of these related countries to a strong and united Slavic state under Austrian guidance—the fertile scheme of the murdered prince Francis Ferdinand." (*Light And Truth After The World Tragedy*, p.39.)

The achievement of the Ottomans in managing these 'wreckage peoples' was put into perspective during the twentieth century when the Balkans and Middle East passed out of the Ottoman sphere and into the realm of Christian European control and influence. When the Ottoman administration began to retreat from the region the Balkans and Middle East became killing grounds for the best part of a century. Millions died and millions more were uprooted by the 'march of progress', when nationalist passions were unleashed and nation states on the Western model were constructed out of the peoples of these regions.

But, as Starke contended, the Balkan region might still have remained stable if the other great Empire in the region had been allowed to stabilize it.

The Austro-Hungarian Hapsburg Empire, like the Ottoman Empire, was not an Empire in the same sense of the word as the European Empires, with far-flung colonies ruling over 'lesser breeds'. It was a single land block of territories combining together a number of different nationalities of mostly German, Hungarian and Slavic origin, which were being added to the governing of what originally had been a Viennese Empire of the Hapsburg dynasty. Since 1867 it had been governed as a Dual Monarchy, with a single King governing two Austrian-German and Hungarian State systems. And it was greatly admired by Arthur Griffith's Sinn Fein as an improvement on the Union between Britain and Ireland. In 1914 it was in the process of becoming a triple monarchy by incorporating the Slavs into the system. The principal advocate for introducing a distinct Slav component to the dual monarchy was the Archduke Franz Ferdinand, the heir to the Hapsburg throne.

In 1908 Austro-Hungary annexed Bosnia-Herzegovina, and this event formed the basis of conflict with Serbia—which was being encouraged by Russia in its expansionist ambitions to incorporate all Serbs into a Greater Serbia. Serbia, with Russia at her back, became increasingly confident in challenging Austria after 1912 because the Ottoman Army had been removed from the equation by the First Balkan War.

Serbia and Bosnia-Herzegovina had both been part of the Ottoman Empire but by 1878 they had become independent. Bosnia-Herzegovina had a mixed religious population of Orthodox and Catholic Christians and Moslems. The territory was claimed by the Serb nationalists and to prevent a Serb takeover of the area the Hapsburgs took it over as part of the agreement at the Congress of Berlin in 1878, with the agreement of Britain and Russia. The reasoning behind this was that the mixed population of Croats, Serbs and Moslems would be best administered by a powerful state that had experience of reconciling these elements together effectively. Austria initially incorporated it as a protectorate, while it was legally still part of the Ottoman Empire, but then exercised her right of annexing it, in 1908, which she had been given by Russia and Britain in various treaties.

The annexation of Bosnia-Herzegovina would have been a matter of routine if it had not been for two factors. First, the fact that Russia had turned her eyes back to the Balkans as a result of being blocked from an outlet to the ocean in the Middle and Far East—by Britain in Persia and her Japanese rival in the war of 1905. And second, the Anglo-Russian understanding that removed the main barrier toward Czarist expansion in the Balkans.

The effect of this latter factor was seen almost immediately. Russia had had a secret agreement with Austro-Hungary from May 1897 to preserve stability in the Balkans. But this was undermined by the 1907 Agreement between the Czar and London. In January 1908 the Austrians obtained a concession from the Sultan to conduct survey work on a railway line across a strip of territory between Serbia and Montenegro. Over the previous decade this would have presented no difficulties for the Russians, but the circumstances of the 1907 Agreement meant that the Austrian railway began to be seen as a German attempt to link up with the Turks and the Bagdad Railway.

Austria-Hungary and Russia had reached an understanding that, if Russia was supported by the Hapsburg State in her desire to have free passage through the Straits for her navy, the Russians would not object to the annexation of Bosnia-Herzegovina. But when the Russian Minister informed the British and French of the agreement, they found the *Entente* objecting to it as an infringement of the terms of the Triple Alliance. Having found themselves rebuffed, the Russians began to attack the Austrian annexation of Bosnia-Herzegovina and work up the Serbs about it.

What was happening here was that Britain and France were blocking the means by which Russia could achieve her objectives in the Balkans diplomatically and in agreement with the Austro-Hungarians, so that she was maintained in a position to welcome a general European war conducted against Germany when a favourable opportunity came.

A German compromise on the Bosnia-Herzegovina annexation was accepted — largely because Russia herself was not ready for war at this point — only three years after her defeat by Japan.

### The Irishman 'Who Broke Up The Turkish Empire'

The Young Turks (Committee of Union and Progress) were a product of the nationalism that spread across Europe during the nineteenth century after the French Revolution. But this nationalism was largely encouraged by England through the globalizing tendencies of its Free Trade policies and in order to disrupt the multi-national Empires of other States. The C.U.P. attempted to rejuvenate the multi-national Ottoman State by making concessions to the way the world was turning, with a nationalism based on French Revolutionary principles. But there were many contradictions in such a project that were open to exploitation by those who wanted to see the break up of the Empire, from both within and without.

The Young Turks, influenced by European notions of progress, took the traditional *millet* system, which permitted each nationality to have its own law, to be incompatible with the modern national state and began to abolish it. But in abolishing it, in the pursuit of progress, they presented those who aimed at the break-up of the Empire with their opportunity.

Perhaps it was the case that only a resurrection of the Ottoman Empire under German assistance would have saved it. But the Young Turks' *Entente* orientation and efforts to bend-over backwards to buy off the European predators did nothing to save it. And the last throw of the dice was a failure.

Sir Edward Grey and the British Foreign Office maintained a front of goodwill toward the Young Turks — how could they not since reform had been urged on the Ottomans in the belief that it was unlikely to occur (Britain had insisted that the terms of the Cyprus Convention, which guaranteed Ottoman rule in Asia Minor, were dependent on reform under British Consuls).

But behind the *façade* there were worries that a rejuvenated Empire (buttressed by Germany) might result and Turkey might cheat its fate and rise from its death-bed, with unforeseen consequences. Grey warned his Ambassador in Constantinople on 7th August 1908:

> "If Turkey really establishes a Constitution and keeps it on its feet, and keeps strong herself, the consequences will reach further than any of us can foresee. The effect in Egypt will be tremendous and will make itself felt in India... If Turkey now establishes a Parliament and improves her government, the demand for a constitution in Egypt will gain great force, and our power of resisting the demand will be very much diminished. If, when there is a Turkish Constitution in good working order and things are going well in Turkey, we are engaged in suppressing by force and shooting a rising in Egypt by people who demand a constitution too, the position will be very awkward." (Cited in Feroz Ahmed, *Great Britain's Relationship With The Young Turks 1908-14*, Middle Eastern Studies, July 1966, p. 303.)

A healthy democratic Ottoman State was feared by Britain for its potential to provide inspiration to the Islamic world against Western control. Whilst Turkey was presented as a sick man on his deathbed the Ottoman State posed little problem for England. But if it recovered all bets were off.

In April 1909 there was an attempted coup in Constantinople which aimed to get rid of the Young Turks and restore the Sultan, Abdul Hamid. Britain was behind this, according to Gaston Gaillard:

> "On April 13 1909 a reactionary movement set in which failed only because of Adbul Hamid's irresolute, tottering mind... The reaction of April 13 seems to have been partly due to foreign intrigue, especially on the part of England, who, anxious at seeing Turkey attempt to gain a new life tried to raise internal difficulties by working up the fanaticism of the hodjas, most of whom were paid and lodged in seminaries, and so were interested in maintaining Abdul Hamid's autocratic government. These manoeuvres may have even been the original cause of the reactionary movement.
>
> Mr. Fitzmaurice, dragoman of the English Embassy, was one of the instigators of the movement, and the chief distributor of the money raised for that purpose. He seems to have succeeded in fomenting the first internal difficulties of the new Turkish Government. After the failure of the reactionary movement the Committee of Union and Progress demanded the dismissal of Mr. Fitzmaurice, who later settled at Sofia, where he continued his intrigues." (*The Turks In Europe*, (1920), pp.16-7.)

A dragoman is an interpreter, fluent in local languages; dragomen were used as a kind of official go-between between the European Embassies in

Constantinople and the *Porte*. Gerald Fitzmaurice, the Irish spoilt-priest, who was a British dragoman, was intensely opposed to the Young Turks, whom he believed to be a bunch of up-start foreigners, freemasons and crypto-Jews in the pay of Berlin. The dragomen had great influence in the Foreign Office due to their language skills which, it was supposed, gave them a greater appreciation and understanding of the situation in Constantinople; thus they were seen as a vital source of intelligence.

But the intrigues of Fitzmaurice failed in 1909. The Young Turks, having survived the reaction, were then to be disabled by the encouragement of nationalism in south-eastern Europe that set off the Balkan Wars and threw the Ottoman State into turmoil (and, of course, set off the chain-detonation that blew up in August 1914.).

I had not expected to come across open evidence supporting Roger Casement's view that England was behind the Balkan wars, since these things are usually accomplished through quiet diplomacy and are never owned up to, for good reason. But there is actually a book devoted to another 'Irishman' — a man after Gerald Fitzmaurice's heart — who acted as England's agent in this, and, apparently, accomplished wonders in that area.

*The Inner History Of The Balkan War* by Lt.-Col. Reginald Rankin, Special War Correspondent of *The Times,* was published in early 1914, and is dedicated to James David Bourchier. Lt.-Col. Reginald Rankin called Bourchier 'the unattached diplomatist who has broken up the Turkish Empire in Europe' on the opening page of his book. Quoting *Who's Who* of 1913 the author has this description of Bourchier's background, which reveals him to be Anglo-Irish:

> "fourth son of the late John Bourchier, J.P. of Bagotstown, Co. Limerick and Maidenhall, Co. Cork. Educated Cambridge... previously scholar and Gold Medallist of Trinity College, Dublin. Was for some years Assistant Master at Eton; in 1888 acted as Special Correspondent of The Times in Roumania and Bulgaria and has subsequently represented that journal in South-Eastern Europe..." (p.1.)

The bulk of Lt.-Col. Reginald Rankin's book is made up of articles written by Bourchier and published by *The Times*, *Daily Telegraph*, *Daily News, Fortnightly Review* and other periodicals. But Chapter I of this book, entitled *James David Bourchier*, describes the rise to power of the Young Turks, Bourchier's hostility toward them, and his role in organizing the Balkan Alliance, which expelled the Ottoman Empire from Europe. The reader familiar with the history of Ireland will note that Liberal England seemed appalled at the Turks doing the same things on a minor scale that England had itself done on a much greater scale, and over a much longer period of time, in Ireland, and across the globe. Here is Rankin's account of the Irishman 'who has broken up the Turkish Empire in Europe':

> "The behaviour of the Young Turks in Macedonia in 1910 convinced Bourchier that only a resort to arms could free the subject Christians from an

intolerable persecution. In that year ten thousand peasants were beaten on the feet so mercilessly that many of them were crippled for life... and yet not a government issued a Blue Book stating the facts; there was a conspiracy of silence.

This silence was due largely to the influence of the financiers and Jews who control the European Press and whose interests are wrapped up in the preservation of Turkey. The Young Turk movement started in Salonika, a Jewish town, and from the first Jews were at the back of it. That movement may be said to have been a combination of two or three factors. A group of exiles in Paris, driven out by Abdul Hamid, had imbibed French revolutionary ideas. Long away from their own country, they had ceased to understand it; and they believed, or professed to believe, that Turkey might be regenerated... They preached Liberte, Egalite, Fraternite, and imagined that the principles of the French Revolution could be applied in Turkey...

Another factor was the military element in Macedonia. The young Chauvinist officers were indignant at the presence of an international gendarmerie in their own provinces, and at the prospect of the institution of foreign control for Turkish rule. The meeting at Reval between Edward VII and the Tsar, and the discussions between England and Russia in 1908... frightened them. The movement was thus in the nature of a revolt against foreign interference...

Salonika and Monastir became the rallying-points of the movement — Salonika, as has been said, being the home of many rich and influential European Jews, and also of many Mohammedan or Crypto-Jews, who formed a link between the Jewish community and the soi-disant reformers. The movement spread with great rapidity in the army, chiefly amongst the junior officers. The Sultan became alarmed and... issued orders for the arrest of thirty or forty of the chief officers in the conspiracy, amongst whom was Enver Bey.

This precipitated a revolt... The thing spread rapidly. The Young Turks captured Monastir and Salonika and the Constitution was proclaimed. The Sultan finding that he could no longer depend on the army... agreed to proclaim the Constitution...

Parliament met in the winter, and a few months after a reactionary movement took place at Constantinople... The Young Turks... entered the Palace and made the Sultan sign his abdication. He was hurried into a train and taken to Salonika... There he remained till November 1912, when the victories of the Allies forced the Turks to take him back to Constantinople. The new Sultan... was a mere puppet of the Young Turks...

Having got the army behind them the Young Turks were now secure and began to show the real character of their government. They began to put into practise their principles of Ottomanism, the doctrine that all Turkish subjects, regardless of race or religion, were to be made simply 'good Ottomans'; to abandon their native habits and inherited traditions and give up all their privileges that had been accorded to subject races by former sultans. Thus, under the outward form of a liberal constitution, they aimed at the obliteration of the various nationalities and the extinction of their national ambitions...

The curtailment of the old privileges of the Christian races was based on the pretext that, as all were equal under the Constitution, these special privileges no longer need be maintained...

At the same time the Young Turks tried to Ottomanise the half-Ottomanised Albanians... Then a series of revolts followed, and after the suppression, with ferocious cruelty, of one in the north of the country in the spring of 1910, the Turks decided on a general scheme of disarmament. At first it was applied to Albania only but it was then extended to the whole of Macedonia...

For the sake of appearances, the disarmament was carried out in the Turkish villages, but no one there was beaten or molested. At the same time the Young Turks encouraged the immigration into Macedonia of a large number of Bosnian refugees; these they planted in the Christian districts, often ousting the Christian proprietors, and gave them arms with which to terrorise their Christian neighbours.

All these outrages went on without any effective protests from the Great Powers; the Press of the world was gagged, the conspiracy of silence, under Jewish auspices, meant the silence of extermination for the subject races of Turkey in Europe. For money had been laid on the Young Turks, and what do financiers of the Hebrew or any other brand care about torture and outrage, and suffering and death, so long as they get their proscribed rate of interest? From Shylock to Putumayo the fearful story is ever the same.

Bourchier, with a knowledge of the conditions prevailing in Turkey and in the Balkans, on the one hand, and at the councils of the Great Powers, on the other... realised that the only remedy was a combination of the free nations, kinsmen of the oppressed peoples, either to bring pressure on the Young Turks... or to put them out by force.

He came to this conclusion at the end, I believe, of 1910. He did not want an immediate war; the first thing to be done was to apply pressure...

But there was little possibility that this would succeed... So Bourchier turned his attention to the other possible solution to the problem. What forces could the four states of the Balkans—Bulgaria, Servia, Greece and Montenegro—command for the purpose of bringing pressure, of one kind or another, on the oppressors of their co-religionists and kinsmen?... Here was the germ of the Balkan League, the first cause of the war which drove the Turks out of Europe after nearly five hundred years of misrule—a calculation simmering in the brain of an unofficial Irishman, who, for love of them, had given half his life in service to the Balkan people.

So it came about that during the winter of 1910-11 Bourchier had long talks with M. Venizelos, the Greek Prime Minister, and the two men discussed the scheme of a defensive, and then offensive, alliance between the Balkan States against the Turk.

Events marched rapidly in favour of the project. The difficulty in achieving secret unity and cooperation between nations whose sole common ground was their hatred of the oppressor, gave way before the blundering rancour of the Jew-inspired Young Turks.

However... the trade of the Near East is in the hands of Jews and Greeks, and rival traders never love each other very much. Possibly that is why the Jews have found it impossible to accept the New Testament...

It has been pointed out that the Young Turk movement was backed by Jewish funds and influence... Turks never make money themselves; they watch others make it, and then take it. In an access of generosity they informed the Jews that, as an *ad hoc* and temporary measure only, they would relax their salutary rule that no plundering was to be done by anybody but themselves. The Jews were delighted. A boycott of Greek goods was organised...

The disastrous boycott of Greek products and the treatment of their kinsmen in Crete roused the Greeks to fury, and their Prime Minister and King to embark on the great enterprise counselled by the unofficial Irishman.

The pressure put on Bulgars and Greeks alike caused a rapprochement between the peasants of the two races. Warfare between them, almost chronic in the past, ceased between them... This... naturally strengthened the hands of Venizelos and Bourchier. At this time the latter was striving to bring about a Greco-Bulgarian alliance, which the other states might subsequently join, and to this end he directed all his influence to the sedulous fostering of the nascent friendliness between the two races.

M. Venizelos is a very old friend of Bourchier, and their talks, those talks that were to change the face of Europe for all time, were not held in the official atmosphere of council chambers; they met in various places and made a pilgrimage to the tomb of Byron at Mesolonghi...

At last one day in 1911, the decisive step was taken... Venizelos told Bourchier that he had finally approved the draft treaty of an alliance with Bulgaria against Turkey.

Thus did Bourchier achieve his purpose that will make his name ever famous... Some months later Bourchier went to Sofia and... persuaded the Bulgarian Government to fall in line with Greece... Bourchier had not left Servia out of the hunt. At the end of December 1911 he went to Belgrade and broached his plan to M. Milovanovitch, the Foreign Minister. He urged on him the idea of a combination between the Balkan States... In due course, the Serbo-Bulgar Treaty was signed a week or two before the Bulgar-Greek Treaty.

Bourchier went back to England in July 1912 and at that time the Balkan League was practically formed... He had done his part in the great task, and none too soon, for the futures of the peoples his statesmanship was to liberate... At last on September 30 the four States mobilised simultaneously...

The four States, temporarily united by the force of his genius, by common respect for his abilities, and by common knowledge of his devotion to their cause, sank their ancient differences; allied themselves; simultaneously made war; conquered the Turk and drove him out of Europe... Vast tracts of territory have changed hands; millions of people have changed their rulers; a power and a creed that at one time threatened to dominate Europe have been practically evicted. Christianity has triumphed over Islam, civilisation over barbarity; the European has proved himself a better man than the Asiatic; the apple of discord has been lifted out of the reach of the Great Powers;... Fifty years hence, or much less, the Crescent will not float over Constantinople...

The names of Byron, of Gladstone, of Bourchier, will be remembered and treasured in the hearts of millions... The statues that will rise in the Macedonian towns will be time-bound witnesses to the love and admiration which the unofficial Irishman... excited in the hearts of the people he liberated." (*The Inner History Of The Balkan War*, pp.7-21.)

### Casement On The Balkan Wars

Roger Casement wrote *The Problem Of The Near West* in March 1913 as the Second Balkan War was taking place. *The Problem Of The Near West* is part of his only book, *The Crime Against Europe*, which is a collection of articles written between 1911 and 1914 about British Foreign Policy and how it was leading to a Great War.

The First and Second Balkan Wars were two wars in South-Eastern Europe in 1912–1913 in the course of which the Balkan League of Bulgaria, Greece, Serbia and Montenegro, encouraged by Russia, attacked and conquered the Ottoman territories of Albania, Montenegro and most of Thrace—and then fell out over the division of the spoils—leading to Turkey recovering Eastern Thrace up to Adrianople.

Casement placed the Balkan Wars in the context of Britain's attempts to stop German commercial expansion into the Ottoman Empire, by utilising the nationalist impulses of the Christian Balkan countries against the Turks. He saw the result of these wars, the expulsion of the Ottomans from most of South-Eastern Europe, as having placed a barrier, once and for all, in the way of German activity in the Near/Middle East—or '*The Near West,*' as he called it. He believed that this should have satisfied British fears of a German 'colonisation' of the region, but reasoned that, knowing Britain, it would not satisfy her. She would only be satisfied with the total destruction of Germany.

At the same time, the consequences of these wars meant an encirclement of German commercial activity that she could only break by turning increasingly to the seas and building a bigger fleet; this move placed her on a collision course with England.

It had been a long-standing view of British strategists that Germany was vulnerable on the seas because her commerce and her food and vital materials came into her ports via the oceanic waterways, controlled by the Royal Navy. It was reckoned that by 1900 Germany had become incapable of feeding her rising population. And plans had been drawn up to utilise this weakness—for a blockade of Germany to cut her down to size. Therefore, in preventing another source of overland commerce for Germany, the Balkan Wars were a very helpful thing for Britain—forcing Germany toward the seas again.

To protect its expanding merchant navy and vital supplies Germany needed a bigger navy. But the seas were owned by Britain, who could not permit such a thing. So Germany was being boxed into an inevitable conflict with the controller of the seas. And that would lead not only to the destruction of Germany but also to the break-up of the Ottoman Empire—unless, of course, Germany could win.

Casement was writing as the outcome of the Second Balkan War was still unclear:

"That war is still undecided as I write (March 1913), but whatever its precise outcome may be, it is clear that the doom of Turkey as a great power is sealed, and that the complications of the Near East will, in future, assume an entirely fresh aspect. Hitherto, there was always the possibility that Germany might find at least a commercial and financial outlet in the Asiatic dominions of the Sultan... It is true that the greatest possible development, and under the most favoured conditions of German interests in that region, could not have met the needs or satisfied the ever increasing necessities of Teutonic growth; but at least it would have offered a safety valve, and could have involved preoccupations likely to deflect the German vision, for a time, from the true path to greatness, the Western highways of the sea.

An occupation or colonisation of the Near East by the Germanic peoples... of the lands of Turk and Tartar, of Syrian and Jew, of Armenian and Mesopotamian, was never a practical suggestion or one to be seriously contemplated. 'East is East and West is West,' sings the poet of Empire, and Englishmen cannot complain if the greatest of Western peoples, adopting the singer, should apply the dogma to themselves. Germany, indeed, might have looked for a considerable measure of commercial dominance in the Near East, possibly for a commercial protectorate such as France applies to Tunis and Algeria and hopes to apply to Morocco, or such as England imposes on Egypt, and this commercial predominance could have conferred considerable profits on Rhenish industries and benefited Saxon industrialism, but it could never have done more than this. A colonisation of the realms of Bajazet and Saladin by the fair-skinned peoples of the North, or the planting of Teutonic institutions in the valley of Damascus, even with the benevolent neutrality of England, is a far wider dream (and one surely no German statesman ever entertained) than a German challenge to the sea supremacy of England.

The trend of civilized man in all great movements since modern civilization began, has been from East to West, not from West to East. The tide of the peoples moved by some mysterious impulse from the dawn of European expansion has been towards the setting sun. The few movements that have taken place in the contrary direction have but emphasized the universality of this rule, from the days of the overthrow of Rome, if we seek no earlier date. The Crusades furnished, doubtless, the classic example...

But whatever value to German development the possible chances of expansion in the Near East may have offered before the present Balkan war, those chances to-day, as the result of that war, scarcely exist. It is probably the perception of this outcome of the victory of the Slav States that has influenced and accelerated the characteristic change of English public opinion that has accompanied with shouts of derision the dying agonies of the Turk. 'In matters of mind,' as a recent English writer says in the Saturday Review, 'the national sporting instinct does not exist. The English public invariably backs the winner.' And just as the English public invariably backs the winner, British policy invariably backs the anti-German, or supposedly anti-German side in all world issues. 'What 1912 seems to have effected is a vast aggrandizement of the Slavonic races in their secular struggle against the Teutonic races. Even a local and temporary triumph of Austria over Servia cannot conceal the fact that henceforth the way south-east to the Black Sea and the Aegean Sea is barred to the Germans.' (Mr. Frederick Harrison in the English Review, Jan., 1913.)

That is the outstanding fact that British public opinion perceives with growing pleasure from the break up of Turkey.

No matter where the dispute or what the purpose of conflict may be, the supreme issue for England is 'Where is Germany?'

Against that side the whole weight of Great Britain will, openly or covertly, be thrown. German expansion in the Near East has gone by the board, and in its place the development of Greek naval strength in the Mediterranean, to take its stand by the Triple Entente, comes to be jauntily considered, while the solid wedge of a Slav Empire or Federation, commanding in the near future 2,000,000 of armed men is agreeably seen to be driven across South-eastern Europe between Austro-German efforts and the fallow lands of Asia Minor. These latter can safely be left in Turkish hands yet a while longer, until the day comes for their partition into 'spheres of influence,' just as Persia and parts of China are to-day being apportioned between Russia and England. This happy consummation, moreover, has fallen from heaven, and Turkey is being cut up for the further extension of British interests clearly by the act of God.

The victory of the Balkan States becomes another triumph for the British Bible; it is the victory of righteousness over wrong-doing.

The true virtue of the Balkan 'Christians' lies in the possibility of their being moulded into an anti-German factor of great weight in the European conflict, clearly impending, and in their offering a fresh obstacle, it is hoped, to German world policy...

Not the moral argument, but the anti-German argument, furnishes the real ground for the changed British attitude in the present war...

The present apparent injury to German interests by the closing of South-eastern Europe, and the road to Asia Minor, will inevitably force Germany to still more resolutely face the problem of opening the Western seaways. To think otherwise is to believe that Germany will accept a quite impossible position tamely and without a struggle.

Hemmed in by Russia on the East and the new Southern Slav States on the South-east, with a vengeful France being incited on her Western frontier to fresh dreams of conquest, Germany sees England preparing still mightier armaments to hold and close the seaways of the world...

Thus while the Eastern question is being settled while I write, by the expulsion of the Turk from Europe, England, who leads the cry in the name of Europe, is preparing the exclusion of Europe from all world affairs that can be dominated by sea power...

That war of the seas is inevitable. It may be fought on a continent; it may be waged in the air—it must be settled on the seas and it must mean either the freeing of those seas or the permanent exclusion of Europeans from the affairs of the world. It means for Europe the future, the very existence of European civilization as opposed to the Anglo-Saxon world domination. In that war, Germany will stand not alone as the champion of Europe, she will fight for the freedom of the world.

As an Irishman I have no fear of the result to Ireland of a German triumph. I pray for it; for with the coming of that day the 'Irish question' so dear to British politicians, becomes a European, a world question.

With the humbling of Great Britain and the destruction of her sea ownership, European civilization assumes a new stature, and Ireland, oldest and yet youngest of the European peoples, shall enter into free partnership with the civilization, culture, and prosperity that that act of liberation shall bring to mankind." (*The Crime Against Europe,* pp.100-5, Athol Books Reprint.)

Casement saw German commercial expansion in the Near and Middle East as a useful outlet for German energies, that would distract them from competing with England on the seas—a project Casement knew would not be let go by in Britain without a war. But the whole purpose of British policy became to bottle up German energy and encircle it, creating a kind of pressure-cooker effect that would produce revolution within or be destroyed from without. And Germany, because it needed to participate in the world market without fear of strangulation, was therefore forced back to the seas.

It is interesting that Casement marks the Balkan Wars as the point where the fate of the Ottoman Empire was sealed, because when Turkey was forced into the War in November 1914 it was pretended that she had made the fateful choice herself—a kind of suicide. But Casement's insight is revealing in that it locates the Balkan Wars as all part of a process on England's part designed to achieve the demise of both Germany and the Ottomans.

The Balkan Wars certainly came about as a result of the Anglo-Russian Agreement of 1907. Without the restraining forces of England and France, Russia saw itself as having a free hand in the Balkans and initiated the first steps of its movement down to Constantinople. The Balkan League was largely a creation of Izvolski, the Russian Foreign Minister, who hoped to use it as an instrument to finally drive the Austrians from the Balkans and the Turks from Europe. And all restraints were removed from the various Balkan nationalisms.

When the Young Turks assumed power in Constantinople in 1908, Britain was presented with the opportunity to stabilize relations with the Ottoman

Empire and preserve peace in the region generally. The Young Turks were enthusiastically pro-British and it was believed they were eager to ditch the German connection. But the 1907 Agreement with Russia, entered into by England in order to destroy Germany, made the normalisation of relations with Turkey impossible. Russia was indispensable in the destruction of Germany so, at the very moment Britain could have secured many of its interests in the region, it chose to subordinate this to its 'supreme issue', as Casement called it. And this is what made War with the Ottoman State nearly inevitable — no matter what the Turks did to accommodate England.

## *The Balkan Wars—A False Start*

The Balkan Wars of 1912-13 did not lead *directly* to a Great War because the other parties to the *Triple Entente*, England and France, had no interest in seeing Russia grab the Straits without bringing Germany into the conflict. As the French historian Alfred Fabre-Luce concluded in his 1926 book, *The Limitations Of Victory*:

> "England's representatives had been instructed, ever since 1909, at all costs to prevent the eastern crises from becoming general; and in 1914 she still maintained this point of view, as she refused to intervene until France and Belgium were drawn into the conflict. 'Our idea,' Grey said to Cambon on the 29th July, 'has always been to avoid being drawn into a war for a Balkan question." (pp.97-8.)

In order to destroy Germany, England needed her to be involved in a war. So a Balkan war was useless to England unless Germany could be implicated in it. Germany could only become involved through the intervention of Austria, and the Hapsburg's attitude in the Balkans after 1909 was purely concerned with the preservation of order among the diverse nationalities inhabiting the Empire, to ensure its survival. A much greater provocation would be necessary to bring about Austria's entry into any conflict in the Balkans. Fabre-Luce, considering the understanding England had with France to go into a war with Germany and the preparations her military men had made for this War, put it like this:

> "There was only one doubt in the midst of all this optimism: under certain circumstances, public opinion, which is the final arbiter of English policy, might refuse to sanction intervention. It was consequently necessary for France to avoid any open provocation to Germany, and to endeavour to make out a favourable case, which would enable the Prime Minister, Mr. Asquith, to solve this domestic question, the only unknown quantity of the problem. Now, if the many repercussions of the alliances are carefully considered, they lead to the paradoxical conclusion that nothing but a Balkan conflict, in which, however, neither France nor England would be directly interested, could have brought about a combined Triple *Entente* offensive... It was consequently necessary for Germany to be indirectly involved in the quarrel. This was also essential in

order to be sure of Russia's co-operation...

On the other hand, it would not have done for the claim to Constantinople to have appeared responsible for the conflict, for this would have been risking an Anglo-Russian conflict, even before Austria's hostility had been raised or Germany intervened... Their (Russia's. P.W.) only chance of inducing England to recognize their right to Constantinople was to formulate it after the outbreak of a war waged in common for another cause, at a moment when anxiety for victory was the chief concern and made the most painful concessions easy between allies (This is, in fact, what happened in 1915.).

Here, then, we have the whole Triple Entente interested in Balkan crises. This was something new, and it brought about an analogous change in the policy of the enemy group, whose alliance was correspondingly firmly cemented, its centre of gravity being similarly shifted to the east." (*The Limitations Of Victory*, pp.158-9.)

And that is another reason why Turkey became drawn into the world conflict—because the *Entente's* special interest in the Balkans as the site of detonation that would bring about the chain reaction required for the Grand Alliance to go to War on Germany shifted the centre of gravity of the conflict eastward.

If Russia had taken Constantinople in 1913 as a result of a Turkish collapse, the Czar would have had little motivation for joining in a war against Germany. And since a war with Germany was necessary for the French recovery of Alsace-Lorraine and the general destruction of the German State, desired by Britain, then Britain and France used diplomacy (in conjunction with Germany) to end the Balkan conflict, for another day, and prevent it leading to a Russian takeover of Constantinople.

Edward Grey's conducting of affairs in relation to the Balkans in 1913 is sometimes cited as an example of Britain's peaceful intentions in Europe. But it was simply the case of the 1913 situation not proving a suitable detonator for the European conflict desired to achieve the overall objectives of the *Entente*. In 1908-9, only a year after the Anglo-Russian Agreement, Grey had blocked a Russian deal that would have coupled their occupation of the Straits with the Austrian occupation of Bosnia-Herzegovina.

After the First Balkan War, the French were fearful that the Russians might secure the Straits without a European war, so Paul Cambon wrote to Grey to pin him down on what the exact circumstances would be in which he would commit England to a war on Germany, with France and Russia. Grey replied in a rather shifty manner that implied commitment to the objective but stopped short of formal alliance. And that was why, when Grey informed Parliament of the secret understandings he had made with France in his famous speech of August 3rd, the War was presented as a matter of honour rather than as a formal commitment. (And, of course, the informality of it all worked wonders in luring Germany, who was unsure of Britain's position or intentions, into

Belgium.)

The Balkans remained important, however, as the one area over which a European war might be provoked and over which a Russian attack on Germany might take place, so that the general conflagration necessary to ensure the German and Ottoman destruction could be brought about.

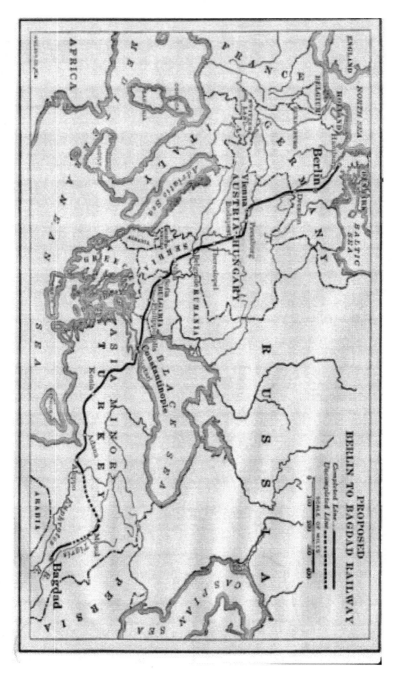

The Bagdad Railway

# II. The Great War On Turkey

The opportunity for the Triple *Entente* to generate a full European conflict emerged in the summer of 1914 when a suitable provocation was found to engage the Austro-Hungarians in a war in the Balkans.

In June the Austrian Archduke, Franz Ferdinand, heir to the throne, was assassinated by a Bosnian terrorist group of mainly Orthodox Serbs who supported unification with Serbia. The Hapsburgs demanded satisfaction from Serbia and when none was forthcoming the Austro-Hungarians had no choice, if they were to retain any credibility, but to make war on Serbia.

In the 1990s Serbia was proclaimed a pariah state and bombed for having similar intentions to the Serbian expansionists of eighty years previously. And Afghanistan was attacked for sheltering terrorists who had perpetrated a terrorist act against a major state. But in 1914 the Great Powers acted in precisely the opposite manner, supporting Serb expansionism and denying the right of Austria to obtain justice for the assassination of its future head of state, in order to turn a local war in the Balkans into a full-scale European war, and then, with the participation of Britain, into a world war.

The logic of the *Entente*, in engaging in war, can only have been that this was an opportunity that might not come along again, and could not be missed. It was in this way that the Third Balkan War (of July 1914.) was turned into a European war, and then, by Britain's participation, into the Great War.

## The Turks Rebuffed

The Great War on the Ottoman Empire is usually treated as an incident in the War against Germany, with the Ottoman administration taken as a military ally of the Kaiser. But the activity and behaviour of the Turkish Government in the years preceding the Great War suggest that the Ottoman Government did everything possible to establish good relations with the *Entente* formed to make war on Germany, and the alliance with Germany was a defensive act of the last resort, when the Ottoman Government were left with no other option.

Between November 1908 and June 1914 the Young Turk Government made at least six attempts to establish defensive alliances with Britain, Russia and France—but all were rebuffed. Abdul Hamid, the Sultan who had undertaken the establishment of relations with Germany, was overthrown in 1908 by the Young Turk revolution. Lord Kinross outlined the Young Turk attempts to pacify the *Triple Entente* in his book, *The Ottoman Centuries—The Rise And Fall of The Turkish Empire* (1977):

> "The new regime became distinctly pro-British, revering Britain in constitutional terms as 'the mother of parliaments,'and responding to British advice.
>
> British policy, however, still remained that of a benevolent but aloof neutrality. In November, 1908, the Young Turks sent two high-level emissaries

to London to propose an Anglo-Turkish alliance, which they hoped would be joined by France. Grey replied with expressions of goodwill to the new government and offers of British advisers, who were in fact to materialize in several ministries. But he insisted that it was Britain's policy to keep her hands free in terms of alliances.

A similar approach was made in July, 1909, after the counter-revolution, through a Turkish parliamentary delegation concerned to counterbalance German influence. This met with a similar reception. With Turkey's defeat in the First Balkan War, the Sick Man of Europe was evidently dead and beyond saving... At the same time, weakened and insolvent as they were, isolated and at the mercy of acquisitive neighbours, they saw that their survival depended, as never before, on the protection and support of a great power.

In June, 1913, Tewfik Pasha, as Grand Vizier, reopened with Grey the question of an Anglo-Turkish alliance. Once more it was rejected... Turkey as he saw it, was now the 'Sick Man of Asia', and it was in his Asiatic dominions that the European powers should now combine, as formerly in Europe for the sake of their mutual interests. Through 1913 Britain, Germany, Austria, France and Italy, without Russia, held talks with the Turks and with one another which amounted in effect to the establishment in Asiatic Turkey of zones of economic influence — and could indeed, if events so materialized, amount to a blueprint for the ultimate political partition of Asiatic, as already of European, Turkey. Most significant of all, as August approached, these resulted in the signature of a satisfactory Anglo-German agreement with regard to the Baghdad Railway. Germany retained the right to exploit it, with all its accompanying commercial implications, in the Anatolian and Cilician sectors. But it was agreed that it should not proceed beyond the planned terminus of Basra. This safeguarded Britain's imperial interests in the river valleys of Mesopotamia and in the Persian Gulf." (pp.600-1.)

The Young Turks were admirers of Britain and France and leant toward the *Entente* in their general political outlook. They consequently wished to disentangle Ottoman Turkey from the German connection and to establish closer ties with Russia, Britain and France.

The 1911 proposal made by Djavid, the C.U.P Minister of Finance, for a permanent alliance with England was vetoed by Grey and the British Foreign Office. The 1913 Young Turks plenipotentiary was sent to London with instructions to 'leave no stone unturned to settle outstanding differences' with England. Some humiliating economic concessions were granted to Britain along with recognition of the British position in the Persian Gulf and Kuwait. England was granted a monopoly on navigation of the Euphrates and Tigris rivers. And it was agreed that the Berlin-Baghdad Railway should not alone terminate at Basra but also have two British directors on its board. And as part of this conciliating process, and as a token of goodwill, the Young Turks entered into a naval agreement with Britain in which British dockyards took orders for Turkish battleships, under the supervision of Winston Churchill and the Admiralty. In fact, by 1914, the size of the British naval mission to Constantinople was as large as the German military mission, and they were looked on as counter-balance to each other by the Turks. And so, if it could be said that Turkey had a military alliance with Germany in 1914, it could be equally said that she had a naval alliance with England.

Lord Kinross also reveals that Britain and France were responsible for the blocking of a Turkish alliance with Russia in 1914, to ensure that the Czar would still report for duty when duty called:

"... if British action was inclined to be negative, Russian action was vigorously positive. In the spring of 1914 the Russian Ambassador to Istanbul, firmly supported by Sazanov (the Foreign Minister, P.W.) in St. Petersburg, discussed with the Turkish ministers proposals for such an agreement between Russia and Turkey as should solve the problem of the Straits in the interests of both. Russia would provide Turkey with the protection she needed. In the event of war, Turkey, as the ally of Russia, would close the Straits to all enemy powers...

The Russian proposals were eagerly welcomed by Talaat, who went to St. Petersburg in May, 1914, to propose a formal Turco-Russian alliance. In the following month Jemal went to Paris, where he proposed, as more effective, an alliance with all three powers of the Triple Entente. He received the cautious reply — which amounted to a veiled refusal — that this must depend upon agreement among them, and that France on her own could not take the initiative. In fact no agreement materialized. The French rejected outright territorial guarantees required by the Turks at the expense of the Balkan states. The British agreed with them, insisting still on a policy of Turkish neutrality and remaining sanguine in their hope that it would be adopted as being in Turkish self-interest.

For the sixth and last time Turkey's plea for an alliance with the Western powers had failed. Talaat and Jemal returned to Istanbul empty-handed and disconsolate at its failure. Soon they were turning with reluctance to the last resort of the triumvirate's militant War Minister, Enver Pasha. This was the hazardous gamble of an alliance with Germany. It was a situation that boded ill for the ultimate fate of both the Russian and Ottoman empires." (pp.601-2.)

One of the leading members of the Young Turk Government, the Naval Minister, Djemal Pasha, wrote his recollections of these events after the War. *Memories Of A Turkish Statesman* describes the frantic attempts of the Turks to achieve understandings with France and England in order to stave off war and preserve the Empire. Djemal describes the outlook of the Government, firstly in 1913, in the wake of the Turkish defeats in the Balkan War:

"As a result of the Balkan War the Committee of Unity and Progress adopted the principle that the old passive policy must be abandoned in favour of an active foreign and domestic policy. Their reason was that it had become clear that this was the only way of saving Turkey from the complications which threatened on every side, building up her strength and giving her her true place among the nations... if we were to be safe against Russia we had no other resource but to win the sympathy of France and England, and particularly of public opinion in those two countries...

In these circumstances we were determined to cultivate the best relations, primarily with the French, but also with the English, and to convince them beyond any possible doubt that our only desire was to introduce serious reforms at home and assure ourselves of their protection against a Russian attack.

We were extremely anxious that the negotiations of the Foreign Ministry and Hakki Pasha should lead to a final solution of the various questions at issue between the English and ourselves. We had delimited the Turkish and English zones of influence in the Gulf of Basra and in the Southern part of the Arabian peninsula, and we had also solved the problem of Aden in a way which satisfied the English.

We had not opposed the English demands in the question of the extension of the Bagdad Railway to Basra, nor in the matter of shipping routes on the Euphrates and Tigris. We gave English companies the concessions for petroleum in Mesopotamia, for the extension of the Aidin Railway, the construction of several new sections and the development of the harbours of Trebizond and Samsun... we had called in an English Inspector-General and several English inspectors to reform the Ministry of the Interior and the organisation of the Civil Service... The reorganisation of our customs system was entrusted to Sir Richard Crawford, and we had decided to appoint a number of English inspectors for our customs offices.

We had considerably enlarged the powers of the English naval mission which we had called in for the reorganisation of our navy, and we now began to enjoy the fruits of its labours...

We had handed over the reorganisation of our arsenals to English companies, the administrative committee of which was under the chairmanship of gentlemen like Sir Adam Block, long known as an advocate of Anglo-Turkish friendship... Unfortunately, owing to Russian opposition, England declined our proposal that we should call in English officials to administer the vilayets inhabited by Armenians." (pp.97-100.)

The Turks had offered England extraordinary positions of influence in the Ottoman State—positions that no other country with concern for its sovereignty would offer. They had entrusted to Britain the most vital components of the defence of their capital—the reorganisation of their navy under Rear-Admiral Douglas Gamble and Admiral Arthur Limpus and a English Naval Mission of 72 officers, and the modernisation of the arsenal at the Golden Horn by Armstrong and Vickers. Admiral Limpus offered advice to the Turkish Admiralty on such matters as the location of mine fields in the Straits and mine laying techniques as well as torpedo lines. The work on the arsenal was handed to a committee consisting of representatives of the British arms company and an English Director-General was put in charge of it.

It is not surprising that the British took on this constructive work, even though their long term ambitions with regard to the Ottomans were entirely destructive. It counter-balanced German influence at Constantinople, gave the English a unique, inside knowledge of the defences of the Turkish capital and the Turkish Navy — and made sure that the Russians, French and Germans did not possess such influence or information themselves.

But what this reveals is that the last thing on the minds of the Turks was to wage war on Britain. For to have had this intention and to entrust England with such expert knowledge of the defences of the Turkish State would have been tantamount to suicide.

In Volume II of Arthur Marder's three Volume *Fear God And Dread Nought: The Correspondence of Admiral of the Fleet Lord Fisher of Kilverstone*, one of Fisher's letters of 20th August 1911 has the Admiral writing, 'The Turks love us, but all we do is kick their arses.' Marder comments in another book on Fisher's career:

> "The Admiral had a shrewd, realistic political sense. He was one of the architects of the Triple Entente; but he went further. Regarding war with Germany as inevitable, he always maintained that Britain needed above all a quadruple alliance, with France, Russia and Turkey as the other partners. For a naval war he held that Britain needed especially the alliance of Russia and Turkey — Russia for the naval diversion she could create in the Baltic, and Turkey so that communications with Russia via the Black Sea would remain open, and because of the influence of Turkey on Islam... His Turkish policy goes back at least to the time of his Mediterranean command. The stupidity of the official policy of alienating Turkey was a favourite theme." (*From The Dreadnought To Scapa Flow: The Royal Navy In The Fisher Era, 1904-1919, Volume I, The Road To War, 1904-1914*, p. 26.)

Admiral Fisher was, of course, under the impression that the upcoming War on Germany would be waged with all things taken into account to defeat the Germans. He had, from 1904, begun the process of concentrating the then scattered Imperial fleet in the North Sea, whilst leaving the Mediterranean to the French allies, in preparation for War on Germany. He did not seemingly know that the Liberal Imperialists had other ambitions in the Middle East that they wished to achieve under the cover of this War.

Djemal continues with his description of how the Young Turks went to very great lengths to conciliate the English and French:

> "We strengthened all our private ties and endeavoured to remove English prejudices with regard to the Turks in the hope of finding some means of bringing England back to her former views, England which had always shown herself disposed to support and strengthen Turkey, but had revolutionized her traditional policy as a result of her understanding with Russia... The Government in general and its individual members worked tirelessly, both officially and in private, to strengthen the bonds of friendship with the English,

and also let no opportunity slip of bringing about a rapprochement with France.

The reorganisation of our gendarmerie had long been committed to the French General Baumann. His powers were continually being extended, and with a view to pleasing the French he was also asked to reorganise the gendarmerie of the Lebanon, which had hitherto held a special position.

As the construction of the roads of the Ottoman Empire had been entrusted to a French company, the Minister of Public Works engaged a number of French engineers. Their pay was to be increased.

For the purpose of putting our financial house in order... we appointed a Frenchman, Monsieur Joly, Inspector-General of Finance, and gave him a number of French officials to assist him." (*Memories Of A Turkish Statesman,* p.101.)

The only aspect of Ottoman reorganisation entrusted by the Young Turks to the Germans was the army. The Turks initially saw this as a kind of insurance against being taken complete advantage of by the English and French and also as a kind of balancing act between the Powers to ensure that everyone was kept onside. But the Turkish Government was so concerned at placating the *Entente*, knowing their hostile intent, that they even contemplated the possibility of transferring this aspect to the French, if it would buy them off"

"At that time the desire to win the friendship of England and France was so strong that we should not have hesitated even to entrust the organisation of our army to a French mission if that had been in any way possible. But it was, in fact, impossible. In the first place a large number of our officers had completed their training in Germany, and the rest of them had been trained and educated according to German military methods. It is a fact recognised by all experts that when the organisation and training of an army have proceeded on certain principles it is impossible to revolutionise that organisation offhand, and particularly to force new methods on it, without great confusion...

Besides, it would have been very foolish to offend a State which had no evil designs upon us in order to please other governments which, very probably, contemplated doing us a bad turn. For these reasons we had no intention of reversing our decision so far as the army was concerned, and we paid no attention whatever to the noisy agitation which followed on the arrival of Liman von Sanders'military mission." (*Memories Of A Turkish Statesman,* p.102.)

Later, as a further act of goodwill, the Turks and Germans agreed to the *Entente* demand that the head of the German military mission, Liman Von Sanders, be moved from his position of Commander of the Constantinople Army Corps to a non-command role. No reciprocal demands were made by the Germans of the British naval mission at Constantinople.

Djemal Pasha was invited by the French Government to observe their naval manoeuvres in late June 1914, in recognition of his work in his efforts at friendship. Later, at the Foreign Ministry in Paris, Djemal offered the French an alliance to complete the encirclement of Germany — in return for their help in recovering the Dodecanese islands from Italy and some other islands off Smyrna from the Greeks:

"The Ottoman Government says to itself: 'The object of the policy of France and England is to forge an iron ring around the Central Powers.'That ring is closed except in the south west. If Turkey associated herself with the plans of the Entente, Bulgaria, which would then be left entirely isolated in the Balkans, would necessarily be compelled to come in too.

'If you want to close your iron ring once and for all, you must try to find some solution of this question of the islands between us and the Greeks. You must take us into your Entente and at the same time protect us against the terrible perils threatening us from Russia. If you support us in our upward strivings, you will soon have a faithful ally in the East!'...

The proposal was straight and unambiguous; in the question of the islands a solution must be found acceptable to Greeks and Turks alike, then an alliance with Turkey, and Germany is completely cut off from the road to the east." (*Memories Of A Turkish Statesman*, pp.105-6.)

Djemal Pasha was told that his offer would be communicated to France's Allies. But nothing was ever heard of it after.

It would certainly have made sense for the Powers of the *Triple Entente* to bind the Turks to an alliance, that they would have been amenable to and grateful for, in early 1914. But the decision was taken to do without Turkey in the War on Germany.

The inescapable conclusion is that the *Triple Entente*, and in particular, Britain and France, decided that it was in their interest that Turkey should not be given guarantees of territorial integrity at this point, for reasons of future intentions toward the Ottoman territories.

### A Reluctant Alliance of Last Resort

After having their offers of alliance rebuffed by Britain, France and Russia, the Turks approached the Germans in July 1914, on the eve of the War. Their intention was to secure one of the Great Powers as security from hostile attacks from the others in the event of war. As Djemal Pasha recalled:

"A few days after my return to Constantinople Talaat Bey said to me: 'What would you say, Pasha, if Germany proposed an alliance with us on such and such terms? Would you accept it? You can see for yourself that we have nothing to hope from France. As France has declined, would you decline Germany's suggestion too?'

I immediately answered: 'I should not hesitate to accept any alliance which rescued Turkey from her present position of isolation." (*Memories Of A Turkish Statesman*, p. 107.)

Djemal then recounts how he found out that talks had been held between other members of the Young Turk Government (who had despaired of an accommodation with England or France) and the Germans, talks from which he had been excluded. He recalled how he began to mull over the significance of this move in his mind on being informed by the Grand Vizier that there was now an alliance with Germany. And he realised that Turkey's options had been narrowed down by the rebuffs she had received from those intent on her destruction:

"After the Treaty of Berlin... Czarism had fully realised that it would be impossible for Russia to get Constantinople, her ambitions had been turned toward India. As the artful policy of England had then blocked her path in that quarter, she turned her eyes to the Far East. But the hand which she stretched out to Port Arthur received a hard knock from the Japanese, and she had to withdraw the bleeding member. Thus her only course was to return to the object of her century-old ambition, and was making her preparations to begin her last mighty onslaught on poor Turkey, the booty for which she had been yearning for hundreds of years. Her allies, so far from opposing her design, were now entirely in agreement with that design. The circumstances prevailing at the time of the Crimean War and the Treaty of Berlin had now wholly changed. England, mistress of Egypt, looked with far more jealous eyes at Germany's economic plans in the Gulf of Basra than at Russia's ambitions with regard to Constantinople and the whole of Anatolia. Russia was to have Constantinople as compensation for Mesopotamia. As for France, she was not of those who would oppose the partition of Turkey so long as she was given a free hand in Syria...

In view of all these considerations, I had turned to France in order to secure her support and that of England in case we found ourselves exposed to attack by Russia. While I was in the grip of these phantoms my colleagues had found themselves presented with extremely plain and important proposals—an association with the Powers of the Triple Alliance, or, to speak more accurately, an alliance with Germany.

A mighty Empire like Germany was offering us an alliance based on equality of status, we who five or six months before had tried to escape from our isolation and associate ourselves with a group of Powers by making an attempt—a vain attempt—to form an alliance with Bulgaria, from which we promised ourselves great profit...

Among the Entente Powers, England had got Egypt completely in her power, and would undoubtedly try to possess Mesopotamia, possibly Palestine also, and secure her exclusive influence over the whole of the Arabian Peninsula...

Germany, whatever else might be said, was the only power which desired to see Turkey strong. Germany's interests could be secured by the strengthening of Turkey, and that alone. Germany could not lay hands on Turkey as if she were a colony, for neither the geographical position nor her resources made that possible. The result was that Germany regarded Turkey as a link in the commercial and trading chain, and thus became her stoutest champion against the Entente Governments which wanted to dismember her, particularly since the elimination of Turkey would mean the final 'encirclement'of Germany. Her south-western front remained open thanks to Turkey alone. The only way in which she could escape the pressure of the iron ring was to prevent the dismemberment of Turkey.

Thus we had two groups of Powers before us, the ideal of one of which was to get us in its power, while the aim of the other was to make friendly approaches to us in view of certain prospective advantages, and to conclude an alliance with us based on equal rights and obligations...

Although this alliance made us the enemy of the Entente Powers in case of a European war, as long as the conflict was postponed for between five and ten years we should have brought up the fortifications of the Straits and our different coasts to such a standard, made our army so strong, and developed our country to such a degree that we need not hesitate to take our part in such a war." (*Memories Of A Turkish Statesman*, pp.111-14.)

Below is the account of Talaat Bey, the third of what England called the 'Young Turk Triumvirate' (along with Enver and Djemal Pasha). It is from the *Posthumous Memoirs of Talaat*, published in the October volume of *The New York Times Current History*, No. XV., 1921 (Talaat was assassinated by an Armenian in Berlin in March 1921). In this account Talaat describes the course of events from the start of the War until Turkey's entry in November:

"After the disasters of Turkey in 1913, she was left without a friend among the European nations. Russia then began a series of exactions, and Britain abandoned us to Russia. In this strait Germany alone assisted us, and by her protection enabled us to escape or at least postpone the Russian demands.

This amiable attitude on the part of Germany encouraged us to suggest to the German Ambassador at the Porte that we might enter a permanent alliance with Germany. But while the ambassador seemed most favourable to this, the Berlin government was not. It answered in effect that Turkey was too weak, and that an alliance at the moment would be detrimental to both governments.

This, in fact, explains our failure to find an ally anywhere. The European powers wished only for powerful allies, who could help rather than be a burden.

In June, 1914, however, we were surprised by an approach from the German government, which suggested that the project for an alliance be again considered. As we were in the same unhappy isolation as before, there seemed no reason for refusing this proposal. The alliance was discussed in a series of meetings with the German ambassador, and agreement proved easy. A preliminary document was then prepared and signed, outlining the main points of the alliance, which was to be both military and political.

Just afterward there followed the series of events which culminated in the World War. We realized that Germany's change of attitude toward us must be due to her having foreseen some such warfare; but we still thought the alliance would benefit us. No European power would have welcomed us without expecting something valuable in return.

During the opening months of the War our position was very difficult. Practically we were already allied with Germany, and every day the German and Austrian ambassadors came to me urging our immediate entrance into the War. It would have been easy to have evaded them by pointing out that Italy, though a member of their alliance, had not joined them, or by showing that in invading Belgium, Germany had ignored her own signature to an alliance.

But we were unwilling to break away completely from the partnership we had so anxiously sought and so much valued. So we told the Teutons we would gladly join them as soon as possible, but that to do so while Bulgaria remained undecided would be as dangerous for them as for us.

Constantinople was wholly unprotected against a Bulgarian army. Since the Bulgars hated the Serbs, Germany should be able to persuade Bulgaria to join our alliance. Then, but not till then, Turkey could make good her agreement to fight in aid of Germany.

This logical answer enabled us to delay entering the War. So we waited and watched the course of events. Germany next urged us to conduct our own negotiations with Bulgaria; and as we could not well refuse this, Halil Bey and I went in person to Sofia.

There, after many conferences with the Bulgarian leaders, we realized that they dared not act for fear of Rumania. If Rumania joined Russia, the combined armies could at once overwhelm Bulgaria; hence the latter could promise us nothing unless we could guarantee her against a Rumanian attack. For this reason we left Sofia and proceeded to Bucharest.

There we became convinced after many conferences that Rumania was really determined on a strict neutrality. Radoslavoff, the Bulgarian premier, asked us to get a written promise of this neutrality; but Bratianu, the Rumanian premier, refused this. He said that such a written contract would be un-neutral, but that he could assure me by word of mouth that even if Bulgaria attacked Serbia, Rumania would continue neutral. This promise seemed to Radoslavoff valuable but insufficient. So we returned unsuccessful to Constantinople...

We played only for delay, which became constantly more difficult..."

It was the Turks, rather than the Germans, who initiated the proposal of an alliance for defensive purposes. In July 1914 the only, and fundamental, intention of the Ottoman State was to survive the War. It knew that Britain had its eyes on grabbing the Arab parts of the Ottoman Empire and that its ally Tsarist Russia coveted Constantinople as a warm water base for its battleships.

However, the German Government refused Turkey's approach.

At that point the Germans wanted to do everything possible to avoid war with Britain, so they steered clear of a full alliance with the Turks — an alliance they knew would provoke the *Triple Entente*. But when the mobilisations against Germany began, and the encirclement was complete, the Kaiser had no choice but to send his Ambassador back to the Turks. The agreement that emerged on August 2nd committed Germany to defend the Ottoman Empire from attack but did not oblige the Turks to enter the war on the side of Germany.

Talaat and Djemal convinced the Germans that it was in the best interest of both that Turkey remain neutral.

It would have been logical for the Ottomans to look for support from the Kaiser, and with this in mind the Turks had kept up the connection with Germany. But, to protect its own survival, Turkey remained neutral in the War and played for time by putting Germany off with preconditions for the activation of a fully-fledged alliance (One was that Bulgaria had to join the war on Germany's side first—a development the Turks judged to be very unlikely).

The agreement with Germany did not mean that Turkey was committed to entering the War on Germany's side. As Basil Liddell Hart noted in his *History Of The First World War*:

> "... the news of Britain's entry into the war was a shock that nearly burst the new treaty like a paper balloon. Indeed, so much hot air was generated during the next few days that it even sufficed to blow out another ballon d'essai—the astonishing offer to Russia of a Turkish Alliance. But this offer did not suit Russia's ambition, even though it promised her the one chance of having a channel through which she could receive munitions from her Western allies. She preferred isolation to the sacrifice of her dream of annexation, and did not even report the offer to her Allies." (p.158.)

It was perhaps convenient that Russia did not report the offer to her Allies because, on the experience of the previous years, it would surely have been rejected. And it would have simply added to the weight of evidence that, whilst the Ottomans were desperately trying to manoeuvre themselves free of war, the Allies were determined to hook them at the convenient moment.

### The Goeben And Breslau

A week before the British Declaration of War on Turkey, *The Times* produced a long editorial explaining that England did not want war with the Ottoman Empire, despite all the 'provocations'of the *Porte*. And it rounded it off with the following final paragraph:

> "The present mighty struggle will mean for Europe not only the end of Prussian militarism, but also the end of the Turks in Europe. These have been the chief menaces to the peace of the Old World for more than fifty years. Syria, Arabia and Mesopotamia will also be freed from the blighting influence of the Turk, who will be relegated to the obscure valleys of Asia Minor." (*The Times*, 31 October 1914.)

Of course, there was a problem—Turkey was not a combatant in the War that had been engineered against Germany. It took a couple of months for Britain to find a *casus belli* against the Turks. But it did so in early November 1914 over a couple of German ships, an obscure incident in the Black Sea—and then the conquest of the Ottoman territories was on.

The incident in the Black Sea came about as a result of a chain of events beginning with the confiscation of Ottoman vessels that the Royal Navy was building for the Turkish navy. On August 3rd, Churchill, the First Lord of the Admiralty, seized two Turkish Dreadnoughts which had just been fitted in English dockyards.

The Turks had paid for these ships by popular subscription and had declared a naval week to celebrate their arrival. The Turkish fleet had put to sea to receive them and to honour the Royal Navy for building them. But they never turned up. (One of them, the *Sultan Mehmet Rachid V,* was rechristened *The Erin* in honour of Ireland's loyalty to the Empire's cause.)

Quite apart from the breaking of the naval alliance with Turkey, Churchill's actions were without precedent, and he was warned by the British Attorney-General that what he was doing could not be supported by law. Of course, it could be argued that what he was doing was in the national interest, in time of war. But the problem was that war had not yet been declared—even with Germany, let alone Turkey. So Churchill detained the ships in expectation, or knowledge, of war and the law just turned a blind eye.

And War turned up a day later!

All this has been obscured by propagandist writing on behalf of the British version of history. But the chronology and causation of events are clear.

In the days before the British declaration of War on Germany, the Germans decided to move two of their battleships, the *Goeben* and the *Breslau,* from the Mediterranean toward Constantinople to cement the relationship with Turkey, and by way of compensation for the loss of the Dreadnoughts. The Royal Navy permitted the two ships to sail across the Mediterranean and to the Dardanelles, blocking their retreat at Messina in Sicily, where they went for coaling. Whilst coaling, the German Admiral, Souchon, received a message from Berlin to turn back because the *Porte* were concerned at how the British might interpret the German action. England had just declared war on Germany. But he was surprised to find his way home blocked and the way to the Aegean clear. The British Admiral Milne could have trapped the German ships in the Messina Straits by placing his ships at both ends but instead chose to block the Western end of the Straits alone, permitting their 'escape'to the Dardanelles.

In the subsequent Inquiry over the 'escape' of the *Goeben* and *Breslau,* Admiral Milne, who directed the German ships toward Constantinople, was congratulated for 'understanding the spirit of his instructions' and Admiral Troubridge, who failed to attack them outside the Straits, was found, as 'a danger to the State', to be 'not trustworthy to receive any other command'.

The Turks did not welcome the appearance of the German ships at Constantinople but were presented with a dilemma: if they refused them permission to enter the Straits they would be destroyed by the chasing pack, much to Germany's displeasure. But, under the rules of neutrality if the ships entered the Turkish port they had to be disarmed and interned.

So Constantinople permitted the ships entry and invented the fiction that they had purchased them off the Germans, as compensation for those illegally appropriated by Churchill, to protect Turkey's neutral status in the War.

One often sees references, in publications of the time, to Britain's great reluctance to make War on Turkey. But it was all just a question of timing. The Allies could have rejected the Ottoman explanation about the ships and used it as the occasion for War on Turkey. But at this point, with the French and British Armies in full retreat toward Paris, taking on another enemy would have been ridiculous. Sir Louis Mallet advised: 'No one but a madman could have contemplated war in the Near East at that moment'. And it was not until the Germans had been halted at the Battle of the Marne, in September, that this course became possible.

Edward Grey set down British intentions toward Turkey in early October in an internal memo at the Foreign Office:

"To delay the outbreak of war as long as we could, to gain as much time as we could, and to make it clear, when war came, that we had done everything to avoid war and that Turkey had forced it." (A.L. Macfie, *The Straits Question In The First World War*, *Middle Eastern Studies*, July 1983, p.49.)

Churchill laid a blockade on the Dardanelles to prevent the ships coming out. He then organised a series of meetings at the Admiralty on September 1st-3rd to discuss a pre-emptive strike on Constantinople — to 'Copenhagen' it, as Nelson had done in destroying the fleet and port of neutral Denmark in 1801. Kitchener vetoed this plan, however, because he was moving an Indian force into Egypt at that moment and feared the effect of an unprovoked British attack on Constantinople on Moslem opinion (*The Straits Question In The First World War*, p.48.)

At this point the British began to put pressure on the Turks by making demands of their neutrality that the Ottoman Government could not concede without leaving themselves open to a Russian occupation. Basically, the British demanded that Turkey send the German military mission packing at once and reopen the Straits to all shipping. The Turks realised that, if they did this, they would not only let the Royal Navy into the Dardanelles but also have the Russian fleet bearing down on Constantinople. They would be faced with an offer they could not refuse: letting the *Entente* take care of the Straits until the War was over, and having the problem of a temporary occupation turning into a permanent one. In such circumstances, after victory, the Russians, or the British, would be impossible to shift, without a war. And what hope would Turkey have in such an event?

At the same time Ambassador Mallet informed the Sultan that the Royal Navy would not allow Turkey's ships to leave the Straits — a violation of Turkish neutrality that Constantinople accepted without retaliation. When the Turks tried to send a ship through, it was stopped and sent back by the Royal Navy blockade. In response the Turks closed the Straits at the end of September, laying a minefield across them to prevent the entry of hostile vessels.

Along with the rejection of repeated attempts at alliance, and the seizure of the Turkish battleships, this was the event that more than any other pushed Turkey into Germany's camp.

### The Black Sea Affair

The Turks decided to test the intentions of the *Entente* by a final attempt at alliance. The British Ambassador was presented with an offer: Turkey would join the *Entente* if the *Entente* consented to the abolition of the Capitulations, the restoration to the Ottoman State of the islands taken by Greece, a solution to the Egyptian question and a guarantee against Russian interference in domestic matters.

Britain made vague proposals in return, amounting to a settlement of these issues by some conference or other after the War, rather like Irish Home Rule. But the Turks decided not to buy the pig in a poke and were confirmed in their opinion that England and its allies did not desire Turkey on their side, because they had other plans for the Ottoman Empire.

Djemal Pasha later explained the choice open to the Ottoman Government, in a situation where neutrality was no longer an option:

"In short, we had only two safe courses open to us. We could either ally ourselves with the English and French, declare war on the Central Powers, and in that way secure ourselves against further attack by Russia, or we could join the Central Powers and assist in the destruction of Russia. After declining our alliance, France and England had required us to remain neutral and keep the Straits open for the benefit of our worst enemy. The Central Powers on the other hand allowed us to come in with them, though they felt themselves strong enough to destroy Russia, but they bound us to put every possible obstruction in her way... There was, of course, a possibility that the Central Powers might be beaten, and in that case a catastrophe for us was a certainty. But it is also an undeniable fact that if we had remained neutral and left the Straits open the inevitable victory of our enemy would have sealed our fate with equal certainty."
(*Memories Of A Turkish Statesman*, p.125.)

Admiral Souchon took the *Breslau* and the *Goeben* into the Black Sea. The Russians had stated that if they entered the Black Sea they would be regarded as hostile vessels, despite Turkish neutrality. The battleships were attacked by the Russian fleet and, in response, the German Admiral began bombarding some Russian ports. The Turkish Government, in a last attempt to avoid war, proposed a joint enquiry to ascertain which fleet had attacked first, so that the commander of that fleet could be held responsible, but the Russian Government rejected the proposal. And in any case, Britain had her excuse for war and she was not about to let it go.

On the last day of October, Churchill gave the order to 'commence hostilities with Turkey' without informing the Cabinet or formally declaring war, or even consulting the War Council. The Royal Navy began bombarding the Dardanelles on 3rd November. (This pre-emptive strike was cited by Sir Thomas Mackenzie to the Dardanelles Commission, as having the disastrous effect of warning the Turks as to Allied future intentions, with the result that defences were improved.) And, according to Margot Tennant's (Asquith's wife) *Recollections,* Churchill had been advocating a Copenhagen-style pre-emptive strike on Constantinople two months before War had even been declared on Turkey.

Turkey did not take this provocation as an act of war, or indeed Asquith's Declaration the next day that 'we are now frankly at war with Turkey'. But on 5th November a formal Declaration of War on Turkey was made by Britain.

The Turks themselves waited another week to declare war on Britain, when they found a British army coming up from Kuwait and heading for Baghdad (Kuwait had been one of the bits of the Ottoman Empire that England had been chipping off prior to the War. It was supposedly an independent state in 1914, but it had a sizeable British Indian army camped inside it, ready to expand the Empire into Mesopotamia).

In the course of writing this book I have come across numerous publications that state, or infer, that Turkey came into the War on Germany's side of her own volition. The inference is made that Turkey was in alliance with Germany and it was only a matter of time before she joined the War. Some books pin the blame on the Germans whilst others argue that the Turks simply made an error of fatal proportions.

In the light of this, it might be of value to consider also the account of Sir Edward Pears. Pears was a British lawyer who had practised law in Constantinople for forty years; he had contributed articles to the Liberal *Daily News* on the 'Bulgarian atrocities'that began Gladstone's campaign against the Turks. He wrote his impressions of what was happening in October 1914 in *Forty Years in Constantinople*:

> "We all saw by the middle of October that Turkey was drifting into war. We all regretted the situation and asked ourselves whether it might not have been avoided by England. Briefly resumed the position was the following: The Turkish Ministry had repeatedly declared its intention of remaining neutral. The Grand Vizier, Prince Said Halim, had given almost daily assurances, first to Mr. Beaumont and then to Sir Louis Mallet (the British Ambassador, P.W.) on his return to Constantinople, to this effect. Talaat Bey, the Minister of the Interior, who impressed those whom he met in England five years ago with a certain openness and frankness of character, was mainly anxious to have the integrity and independence of the empire guaranteed by England and France, and this guarantee had been given. No one would have pronounced him weak. Jemal, the Minister of the Marine, I have already described as having friendly

feelings toward the Entente. Hallil Bey was also regarded as friendly. The two Christian members of the Government, Biscani and Oscan, were avowedly in favour of the Entente if the attitude of neutrality could not be maintained. The Sheik-ul-Islam was understood to be in favour of the policy proclaimed by Said Halim and spoke of attacks on Russia as madness. The only Minister who was openly unfavourable to the Entente was Enver, and it had already become clear that he had thrown in his lot heart and soul with the Germans." (*Forty Years in Constantinople*, pp.347-8.)

Sir Edward also noted that even after the appearance of the *Goeben* and the *Breslau* in Constantinople the Turks still desired to remain neutral:

"In spite of all the inducements held out to them they were unwilling to join in the war. They would have been unanimously and heartily on the side of England and France had it not been known that we were in alliance with Russia. It was perhaps too much to expect that a people should suddenly forget the tradition of many generations during which Russia has always been the enemy...

Nevertheless the Ministry believed that neutrality could be maintained as long as Turkey was inactive. In spite of the urgent demands of the Germans, the Turkish Government would not declare war. A family council was held at the palace in the early days of October at the demand of Izzedin, the Crown Prince, when a resolution was adopted that no declaration of war would be made without the consent of such body. The meaning of the resolution was that Enver Pasha, to whom the majority of those present were opposed, was already doing his utmost to rush Turkey into an act of war. The Grand Vizier himself had declared that under no circumstances would he consent to make war on France or England. Such was the position at the end of October." (*Forty Years in Constantinople*, pp.352-3.)

The American Ambassador to Constantinople, Henry Morgenthau, who was extremely anti-Turk, wrote the following about the *casus belli*:

"I have often speculated on what would have happened if the English battle cruisers, which pursued the Breslau and Goeben up to the mouth of the Dardanelles, had not been too gentlemanly to violate international law. Suppose they had entered the Strait, attacked the German cruisers in the Marmora, and sunk them. They could have done this, and, knowing all that we know now, such an action would have been justified. Not improbably the destruction would have kept Turkey out of the war. I am convinced that, when the judicious historian reviews this war and its consequences, he will say that the passage of the Strait by these two German ships made it inevitable that Turkey should join Germany at the moment that Germany desired her assistance, and that it likewise sealed the doom of the Turkish Empire. There were men in the Turkish cabinet who perceived this, even then." (cited in *Great Events of the Great War, Volume II*, pp.102-3.)

Morgenthau conveniently forgets the 'ungentlemanly' behaviour of the Royal Navy regarding contraband that his own Government protested about to the British a few months later. And he doesn't seem to regard the Royal Navy's starvation blockade, which illegally treated food as contraband, that starved to death a million German civilians six months into 1919 as 'ungentlemanly'. But Anglophile Americans often have blind spots for that kind of thing (England started out in 1914 by making 'a scrap of paper' of the Declaration of London governing rules regarding contraband in wartime. President Wilson proceeded to allow the Royal Navy to make use of armed merchant ships as if they were peaceful commercial vessels. And on the whole England was allowed to violate U.S. neutral rights far more extensively between 1914 and 1917 than she did before the War of 1812.)

Wilson came to believe, however, that Great Britain was fighting for civilization and that so trivial a thing as international law must not be allowed to stand in her way.

The Great War has been written up as a natural occurrence with seamless extensions of Allied operations and enemies. But the waging of war is, in its fundamentals, a matter of choice, a matter of decision, based on interests. Those interests were revealed during the course, and at the end, of the conflict.

Morgenthau's speculation of what might have been is one of the best explanations—quite contrary to the author's purpose—of why Britain *chose* to make war on Turkey and of how Turkey became a reluctant participant in the catastrophe that engulfed the Near and Middle East.

The Ottoman Empire joined a European war for which it was not at all prepared. The Ottomans had a far smaller population and economic base than any of the other participants on both sides in the War. Its army had just been largely destroyed in the Balkan Wars and its home front had been devastated. It had no system planned to provide for mass mobilisation or aggressive warfare—the Empire had been shrinking for centuries. And it could not afford to finance a war of any duration out of its empty Treasury, whose purse strings were held by the enemy.

When the Ottoman authorities tried to mobilise its population for the crisis, they called up the entire male population in one day, telling them to bring enough food with them to maintain themselves. After three days the vast majority of recruits had to be sent home as food ran out, and men were needed to work the land. This shambolic response by Constantinople to the events in Europe show that it was completely unprepared and unorganised for the events that lay ahead of it; that represents the final proof of its lack of aggressive intent in 1914.

A last word about this matter should go to Sir Basil Thomson, Director of British Intelligence during the Great War. Thomson described the disposition of the Turks in October 1914 as it appeared to the Intelligence services:

"A majority of the Turkish Cabinet was strongly in favour of neutrality. The Sultan was for peace; Youssuff Izzadin, the Heir Apparent, was openly pro-Ally; the Grand Vizier favoured England rather than Germany, but the Turks were incensed at the commandeering by the British Admiralty of two war vessels ordered by them from a private yard in England, and, intended by them to be used against the Greeks, and Baron Wangenheim, the German Ambassador, had offered them the Goeben and the Breslau as 'compensation'. The fiction that Turkey had purchased the ships deceived no one." (*The Allied Secret Service in Greece*, p. 40.)

Britain did not have to go to war with Turkey and there were even good strategic reasons why it should not do so. But the desire to conquer in the region over-rode those reasons and the issue of the German battleships provided the excuse for hostilities. Turkey, on the other hand, had nothing to gain by going to war and everything to lose.

Neutrality ultimately proved impossible for the Turks in relation to Britain, rather than in relation to Germany—which might have desired the Ottoman participation but could not bring it about themselves. Germany gained an ally because of England's intentions toward the Ottoman Empire.

Britain was not prepared to accept that neutrality was an option in the 'war for civilisation' and cordial relations were not a long-term British objective— since Britain viewed the Ottoman Empire in the manner the predator views the prey.

### Why did Ireland Make War on Turkey?

So much for the Empire. But what of Ireland?

It could be stated that Ireland went to War with the Turks because Ireland was part of the United Kingdom and Empire in 1914, and Britain was at war with Germany.

That statement is of course a fact—and the logic of it seems unquestionable; at any rate it has remained unquestioned for nearly a century.

It is accepted as a fact that, because Britain went to War with Germany in August 1914 and Redmond had promised Irish help for the Imperial War on Germany and Austro-Hungary, Ireland should naturally have fallen in line when the Empire extended its War to Turkey and the Middle East.

John Dillon put it like this to the Irish in Glasgow, who he feared might come under the influence of the doubters:

"Some of them advocate the doctrine of neutrality—neutrality in a struggle like this—as if anybody under the flag of England could remain neutral. To be neutral is to be hostile and to be a coward. (hear, hear)" (*Freeman's Journal*, 19 April 1915.)

That was indeed the position: Liberal Britain had made the Great War a war for civilisation, a fight to the finish between good and evil—reserving the right to determine who was good and who was evil. How was it possible to be neutral in such a conflict? And if the Irish were lacking in the required moral fibre they would have to ask themselves: How would Ireland have got Home Rule in such circumstances?

But it was never asked what Turkey had ever done to Ireland to have brought Irishmen to invade its country and kill its inhabitants under the flag of Empire, in the name of civilisation, for a measly measure of devolution. It was just taken as a natural extension of the War. Or as John Redmond told a recruiting meeting in West Belfast in October 1914, and Irish Volunteers destined for Gallipoli: 'Ours not to reason why, ours but to do and die...'

The Irish press went along with it. *The Irish Independent* was the most popular nationalist daily newspaper in 1914. It was owned by the capitalist Home Ruler, William Martin Murphy, who was critical of the Irish Party on some of the financial details of Home Rule. But this is how the *Independent* commented on the British declaration of war on Turkey—which was effectively also an Irish declaration:

> "The air is cleared with regard to Turkey. England has formally declared war, and has annexed the island of Cyprus... The men who have control of the (Turkish P.W.) government are nothing more than German agents, and they have put a period to the existence of the Ottoman Empire. They can make no appeal to Islam to help the Caliph in a fight against 'the unbelievers'..." (*Irish Independent,* November 6th)

The following day, on November 7th, The *Irish Independent's* editorial turned its attention to the financial implications of the war:

> "For many years, Turkey has been financed mainly by France and Great Britain... During the wars with Italy over the Balkan Allies Turkey paid the interest on her foreign debt, the total of which is £134,000,000. Financially she is in a very weak condition, and she has probably to fall back on Germany for monetary resources to conduct the war. In these circumstances interest payments on the debt money may be suspended. This default cannot cause more than a temporary inconvenience, because when the Allies have disposed of this anomalous Empire all financial difficulties can be settled."

In other words, it was unfortunate that, because of Germany, Turkey could not be held in hock to the Allies, but accounts would be settled at the close of business. It is quite clear from this analysis that what was happening was fully understood in Ireland—that this was not a 'war for small nations' that was being taken on, but a war of expansion for an Imperialist division of spoils.

The Devlinite *Irish News* of Belfast made no comment about the Declaration of War and simply reported it along with the British statement justifying it. But the *Irish News* had been preparing Northern Catholics for war on the Turks in the days preceding the official Declaration. On the 2nd of November, in an editorial entitled, *Allies And The Turks*, it warned its readers:

"The last hope of bringing Turkey to reason seems to have vanished with the determination of the Allies'Ambassadors to abandon Constantinople to its fate. Until yesterday there was still presumptive evidence that the action of the Porte in breaking its own fresh neutrality rules was due, not to any viciousness of its own, but rather to the timidity of a Government under the guns of powerful German warships. Only diplomacy could have regarded the excuse as entertainable; commonsense remembered that it was due, in the first instance, to Turkish duplicity that the Goeben and Breslau were admitted to the shelter of Turkish waters... The treachery of the Turk is a byword in history; and no one but a confirmed believer in the mere science of diplomacy could have failed to remember the traditions of Abdul Hamid... The terrorism of the Kaiser and the bribes of his Treasury have tempted the Ottoman Government to the ruin of Turkey in Europe... and when the cowardice and perfidy of the cabal in Constantinople have been sufficiently punished, an operation which cannot take too long, both the Kaiser and the Sultan's advisers will be inclined to regret the most stupid and incomprehensible blunder yet committed since the war began."

It might be worth explaining the difference between the Redmondites and Devlinites at this point. Joe Devlin was, of course, one of the major figures in the Home Rule Party, of which Redmond was Chairman. Whilst the Imperialist development originated in London with Redmond and his Parliamentary colleagues, Devlin and his followers were the real life and substance of the Irish Party in Ireland. Devlin and the Hibernians were the actual activist core of the Home Rule movement, radiating out from West Belfast into Ulster and the rest of the country. A number of commentators took Devlin to be the real power in the Parliamentary Party and this was demonstrated at the Baton Convention when William O'Brien and his followers were driven from the Party by Joe Devlin's men. While Redmondism lasted for about a decade in the South of Ireland and was largely swept away by the result of the 1918 election, the legacy of Joe Devlin persisted in its Northern heartland.

When Ireland was in the process of joining the Great War on Germany, *The Irish News* was not as enthusiastic in signing up for Imperial duty as the Southern Redmondite papers. Of course, the paper did not persist with this attitude—which was in some ways similar to the actions of the Liberal press in Britain in the days leading up to the British Declaration of War. When Redmond declared his intention of supporting England in the conflict, the Belfast paper started to fall in line with the Redmondite press in the South and adjust its attitude.

By the 4th of November the paper had substantially readjusted and, in an editorial entitled, *The World War*, signalled the extension of the conflict to the Near East. But *The Irish News* at least reminded its readers of the British change in policy, that had brought about the new situation with regard to the Turks:

"The world has altered since the distant days when Lord Beaconsfield and Salisbury ruled England, and when the 'refrain' that moved millions to enthusiasm was—

We don't want to fight: but, by Jingo, if we do,

We've got the ships, we've got the men,

We've got the money too —

And the Russians shall not have Constantinople!

That was in 1879. In all human probability, the Russians will have Constantinople before the end of 1915. Germany has lured the Turks to their doom as a European 'power'. Gladstone's 'bag and baggage'policy will at last be put into practical operation—nearly forty years after its promulgation by the great old Liberal."

This was a reorientation it thoroughly approved, of course. The view from Catholic Belfast was that England was about to put into action the Gladstonian dream of expelling the Turk from Christian Europe—including Constantinople, at long last.

*The Irish News* readjusted and became a virulent supporter of British War aims by placing them in a Gladstonian Liberal context. Thereafter it could be argued that it was Britain which was, in fact, changing, not Ireland (as Liberal England had over Home Rule). There was a kind of ethical Imperial policy that Radicals could call their own—and Irish Nationalists too.

But *The Irish News* never asked the obvious question—whether Ireland should reorientate itself to Britain's changes in foreign policy, as if it did not have a mind of its own. And it did not pose the question whether this alteration in attitude towards Turkey was a requirement of Imperial Home Rule; it did not ask if Ireland should abandon its own view of the world—the view that had prompted the Irish Party to oppose vigorously the Empire's conquest of South Africa only a decade or so before, and the paper itself to put the blame for the European War initially on the Allies.

Along with the editorial commentary, the *Irish News* published the British Foreign Office Statement that signalled the beginning of hostilities against Turkey. Three days later, on the day War on Turkey officially began (November 5th), the Belfast daily headlined:

"Dardanelles—Turkey Tastes First Fruits of Perfidy' 'Porte's Treachery, Dardanelles Shelled' 'Successful Russian Invasion of Turkey' 'Anglo-French Bombardment Continuing Effectively"

No one asked how it came about that the Allied forces found themselves so quickly in a position to pounce on their prey.

John Redmond did not issue any declaration of war against Turkey, as he had against Germany, and he sought no electoral mandate to go off in pursuit of the new British war aims in the Middle East. And it was never questioned what these war aims were—whether they were part of the 'war for small nations', or maybe for 'democracy',or were they for the old style Imperial expansion that England had given up, according to the Redmondites?

"The intervention of Turkey in the war has had no effect in changing the purpose or direction of the allies in this great struggle", declared the Irish Party's own daily newspaper, *The Freeman's Journal,* on the 10th of November, and the great extension of the war was fitted in with the previous struggle Redmond had pledged Ireland to:

> "The war of liberation would not be complete unless the power of the Turk went with the power of the German. The Hun and the Turk come from the opposite ends to scourge Europe."

In this way the war on the 'unspeakable Turk' was integrated into the war on the 'shameless Hun'.

And so Ireland fell into line with Imperial requirements, taking the addition of a new enemy and expansion of the war objectives in its stride—without asking any awkward questions about it all.

But a reading of the main nationalist newspapers in the weeks after the extension of Ireland's war to the Turks suggests that the Home Rule leaders did not have the same enthusiasm for it as they did in taking on the Hun. Redmond, Devlin and Dillon fulminated on the platforms against Germany and its misdeeds—but there was a noticeable absence of comment on the new War against the Ottomans. But they recruited for it all the same, up and down the country, and gave it their unconditional and unqualified support. And the Nationalist Press did most of the running for them.

However, there was a marked difference in the editorial coverage of the War on Turkey between the Redmondite papers in the South and the Northern Devlinite *Irish News.* Whilst *The Freeman's Journal* and *The Independent* covered events connected to the War on Turkey extensively throughout 1915, *The Irish News* mentioned them only in passing. And curiously *The Irish News* commented on the departure of a large number of Irish recruits from Belfast on 12th February 1915 with the following hope:

> "These Irish soldiers... are trained in three or four months; and when they are trained, they want to fight the Germans, who know how to fight; and they do not seek service against the poor Turks in the sunny land of Egypt."

### Limited Or Unlimited War?

One of the most important questions that arises from a consideration of England's Great War on Germany and Turkey is whether it was meant as a limited or unlimited war. Now that is a question I have not seen discussed by historians since the end of the Great War, although one finds it implicitly in many accounts of the period.

It is not discussed because of the prevalence of the British view of the Great War, which has become uncontested, particularly after the crushing of Germany in the Second World War.

When one tries to think outside the parameters of thought which have been set by the prevalence of the British view, one is struck by the question of what England intended in 1914 with regard to Germany and the Ottoman Empire and how much the actual waging of the Great War changed the original intentions and created trouble for the future. For it is clear that Britain found itself in 1918-19 with a situation very much removed from what it had imagined it would face in its War plans, and particularly in relation to the Ottoman Empire.

One thing that really struck me in relation to this was the presence in accounts written in Britain during the Great War of a presumption of danger of a revival of German influence in the Near East after the end of the conflict. That does not square at all with the propaganda that was being produced at the time about destroying Germany and its evil for good etc. It seems to suggest that a limited war was the original objective in England and that somewhere along the line this aim became corrupted. There were, of course, numerous accounts prior to the Great War depicting Germany as Carthage to England's Rome and a 'Carthaginian Peace'was the intention—up to a point. But there was always the consideration of the Balance Of Power to take into account.

There is an interesting book called *The German Empire's Hour Of Destiny*, which is a translation of a German publication by Colonel H. Frobenius. It was published in London with a Preface by Sir Valentine Chirol, former editor of *The Times*, Foreign Office diplomat and associate of Leopold Maxse. It is one of those books written by Germans that were translated and republished under different titles to prove that Germany was intent on world-domination. But reading it (which perhaps the publishers did not intend the average citizen actually to do) suggests otherwise; it is, in fact, quite a well-considered account of what Germany should do in the light of the *Entente's* intention of attacking her.

In the section of this book dealing with Britain, the author reveals that Germany, whilst believing France and Russia to have every intention of waging a war of destruction against her, understands England as only wishing to conduct a limited traditional Balance of Power war which would destroy Germany's navy and ability to be a commercial competitor, but would leave her army largely intact, to balance England's continental allies at the close of play. In the light of what subsequently happened, this seems like wishful thinking on the part of the German but when one thinks of what happened at the end of the War there is strong reason to suggest that Colonel Frobenius was not so wide of the mark in his understanding of Britain. It was simply that British intentions were messed up by a factor that intervened in the waging of the War, that Colonel Frobenius and many others did not take sufficient account of.

The Liberal Imperialist War plan was based on the understanding that the Allies would make short work of Germany—and some even imagined that the

War would be all over by Christmas. The Liberal Imperialist coterie (Asquith, Grey, Haldane, Churchill) who planned the War had a view of it as a limited commitment based on the usual naval operations — with a small expeditionary force to keep the French happy. The War Minister, Haldane, had, over the preceding decade, built up an Expeditionary Force of 100,000 to fight on the French left wing. But it was imagined that this minimum force, coupled with the main contribution of the Royal Navy on the seas, would be enough to see off Germany, by keeping the Allies engaged, and with the 'Russian steamroller' coming at Berlin from the East.

While this was happening, another British Expeditionary Force from India would surprise the Turks and grab as much of Mesopotamia as possible.

England had not fought a continental war since the time it organized a grand alliance against Napoleon, and much of the understanding of the Liberal Imperialists was based on that experience. The Napoleonic wars conformed to the principles of England's aristocratic wars. Britain fought in continental wars to preserve the Balance of Power in Europe and obtain overseas territory when the continental Powers were busy fighting. It did so by letting its Allies do most of the fighting on land whilst the Royal Navy controlled the seas around Europe. English military interventions were conducted around the edges of conflict by small armies which never got bogged down in a long war. In the Napoleonic Wars, the Royal Navy quickly saw off the French Navy and Britain used its war chest to pay other armies to do the fighting on land. The war chest had been increased by the naval blockade of France which stopped the French Republic's trade and increased Britain's revenue. French forces were engaged by small scale amphibious operations at the fringes, most notably in the Iberian Peninsula. And Napoleon was drawn into a war with Russia which sapped the French strength through the weight of numbers and vast territorial battlegrounds that confronted his armies.

One Liberal writer, Laurie Magnus, described the War of 1914 as another round with absolutism in Europe in a book entitled *The Third Great War*. (The First Great War was that of the Grand Alliance against Louis XIV. The Second was against Napoleon, a century later. And the Third was a century after that.) And Winston Churchill, the descendant of Marlborough, announced the naval blockade on Germany in Napoleonic terms on February 15th, 1915: 'We shall bring the full force of naval pressure to bear on the enemy. It may be enough without war on land to secure victory over the foe'. (*Daily News*, 16th February 1915.) The Liberals still had the notion that the old limited warfare of their Whig ancestors would be enough to see off the Hun as it had the little Corporal.

England's War strategy had always been based on the principle that, if things went wrong, she could cut her losses quickly without any great effects on her fighting power or martial spirit. And it was imagined that the European war of 1914 would follow a similar pattern to that of wars between 1793 and 1815.

114

In 1793 Edmund Burke called for something like an unlimited war to be waged on the French Revolution but William Pitt, whilst utilizing Burke's polemics against the Republic, was careful to limit the war to a Balance of Power contest. But in 1914 the Liberals turned the Balance of Power war into an unlimited commitment by waging it as a war of good over evil that could never be called off until the evil had been vanquished.

Haldane's institution of a British Expeditionary Force was undoubtedly an innovation in military strategy that had unforeseen consequences. It committed England to a large scale continental engagement, something that it had carefully avoided for a century. But in itself this innovation might not have had the catastrophic effect it subsequently did. The Expeditionary Force might have been used up, stalemate might have ensued and the War might have been called off in some way — either by a general peace settlement or through letting the French and Russians find their own solution.

But the War propaganda produced in conjunction with the waging of it, which was seen as essential in bringing the Liberal backbenchers and the Irish along, turned what might have been a limited commitment into an unlimited struggle to the death. And this encouraged Britain to go much further in Eastern Europe and the territories of the Ottoman Empire than it originally intended.

A 1917 book, *England And The War (1914-1915)*, by a sympathetic Frenchman, André Chevrillon, gives an excellent description of the War propaganda, as having all the character of the missionary work of Puritan England; indeed the Liberal Government of 1905-15 contained the greatest number of Nonconformists since Cromwell:

"... the continuous, urgent exhortation to every young man's conscience, an indefatigable propaganda of meetings, sermons, processions, open-air speeches, and all the activity of recruiting sergeants. The root idea was that a man should enlist just as he might join the Salvation Army, by virtue of a certain working of his mind, a new conviction, a perception of good and evil, justice and injustice, awakened in him by this active and well-organized campaign. The moral, protestant, and puritanic character of this campaign was apparent from a first glance at the picture posters which covered the walls. They mark in one's memory forever the profound crisis in the English national conscience. Through all their gaudiness one word incessantly recurs: Duty. The feeling of imperative duty is the suggestion aimed at by all these pictures, that form a matchless document on the inner nature of the English soul." (p.96.)

And the propaganda paid dividends, staving off for over a year of War the necessity of compulsion — something that was natural to the Frenchman, surrounded by continental neighbours, but which was anathema to the Liberal Englishman, who could choose when and where to fight.

At first all went well. Within a fortnight of the outbreak of war, the Russians had driven into East Prussia, forcing the Germans to withdraw two army corps from the West, just prior to the battle of the Marne. The Germans were halted at the Marne by the British Expeditionary Force and, by November 1914, the 'Russian steamroller' was expected to drive through the Austrian forces and Silesia, into the heart of Germany. And this gave an over-optimistic impression in England of the general position.

The reasoning was that, in a war of attrition, the Allies held all the trump cards. *The Irish News* publicised this view in an editorial called *A Matter of Staying Power?*:

"Asked to give reasons for his confidence in the ultimate and complete victory of the Allies an experienced Student of War writes:—'There are two: firstly, the Germanic Powers have challenged Powers which altogether possess four times the resources in men which they do, and at least twice the resources in wealth; and secondly, because the Prussians have never in all their history fought a long war to a successful issue. The first advantage is only one that could be frittered away by sheer imbecility—a defect that even the enemy dare not attribute to the four Great Powers at war with them... The policy of England in war has always been diametrically opposed to that of Prussia. England has been in all the long wars of history, and out of nearly all the short ones. She was at war with France for more than one hundred years, from 1338 to 1449; the War of the Spanish Succession lasted twelve years; there were nine years of war between 1739 and 1748; five years from 1756 to 1761, seven years from 1775 to 1782, and twenty-two from 1793 to 1815. Prussia, on the other hand, has always preferred a policy of short wars and quick results; and the periods of her wars have always been brief. During the Thirty Years War her main anxiety was to keep out of it... During the Napoleonic period Prussia, for the most part, held aloof. She stood aside while Austerlitz was fought, and crumpled up in a few weeks when Napoleon smote her at Jena. The War of Liberation lasted only fifteen months, and that was longer than any war in which Prussia had previously been engaged. But wars fought prior to 1815 were not to be compared in any respect with the struggle of to-day." (20th November 1915.)

The Irish Party had made the calculation at the time of the Declarations of War that with the range of forces arrayed against Germany and the Ottoman Turks, the War would be concluded within a year—so that it was in the interests of Home Rule that the Irish should be there at the conclusion, with the forces for good.

However, the facts in this editorial conflict greatly with the War propaganda which flooded Britain and Ireland in 1914 about Prussian militarism, and to which the Redmondites greatly contributed, to send Liberal England on its mission of destruction in the world. It quite correctly points out that the Allies possessed a massive advantage in men and material over the Central Powers and, in consequence, would have been more inclined to war than their opponents. Also, it is recognised that England and her Allies had a much greater record of warring, a more likely tendency to engage in war and a much greater propensity to wage war for longer than the enemy.

But the knowledge of these facts tended to give the *Entente* an over-confidence in relation to Germany and Turkey which was not borne out after the opening phases of the Great War.

### Enter Kitchener

It was in early 1915 that the decision to make War on Turkey began to have implications for the War on Germany.

Just after the British Declaration of War on Turkey there was a change in the general military situation that focussed British attention on the Eastern front. The Russian ally possessed massive resources of manpower, but their artillery was using as many shells per day as their factories could produce in a month. The Czar had not calculated that such a supply of munitions would be necessary, because the vast superiority in numbers were expected to tell before Christmas against Germany. So, in early 1915, The Czarist armies became incapable of further offensives until they could be rearmed by their factories — or by the *Entente*. The 'Russian steam-roller' ground to a halt, just like its Allies in the West, and stalemate set in.

Because the Allies had made War on the Turks, the Dardanelles had been closed; however, the Straits were the main means by which the Russians could be supplied by their Allies in the West. So the Allied Declaration of War on Turkey handicapped the Allies (although this could never, in fact, be said).

In August 1914, as a result of the Curragh Mutiny, the Prime Minister, Herbert Asquith, found himself acting as his own Secretary of War. The Prime Minister had taken the War Office in hand after he had sacrificed his War Minister, Colonel Seeley, to placate his Home Ruler backbenchers over the Mutiny. (Seeley had gone beyond his remit in making a deal with the Mutineers, who were, of course, essential for the coming War on Germany.)

It was important that the backbenchers did not find out about the arrangements made with the French for the War with Germany until the *fait accompli*. So, to prevent anyone else, beyond the inner circle, being made aware of the details, the Prime Minister became War Secretary himself.

But now there was a War, and all was out in the open (although not spoken about, in the interests of waging the War) and there needed to be a War Secretary.

Lord Kitchener, the great Colonial war hero, just happened to be home on leave from Egypt in August 1914. So Asquith recruited the General to give his Government a more national character, in the absence of a coalition with the Unionists, for the purpose of waging the War.

This appointment had a big effect since Kitchener, off in Egypt, was not clued in to the Liberal Imperialist War plans. The Liberals had envisaged a limited War on a voluntary basis but had attached to this a moral dimension to encompass the doubters in their ranks. But Kitchener had a different war in mind—a long war of attrition on the Western front. This would involve a much greater commitment on the continent, over a much longer time-frame, with conscription essential, to wear the Germans down. When Kitchener saw the resources planned for the job in hand, by the Liberal Imperialists, and contrasted them with the job he saw ahead, he realised that new armies were needed.

Owing to the conflict over Home Rule, England was deeply divided in August 1914. The War against Germany came at a most opportune time, preventing this division from becoming a civil war. But although the War had the desired effect of bringing the country together again in the face of an external enemy, it was almost as if England was divided about the War it intended to fight—particularly because the Liberal Imperialist War had been such a secret and had involved such subterfuge that Unionist England was not at all clear about what it was going to be like.

That is why British War objectives appear incoherent to the observer. England did know what it wanted out of the War, but different interests within the British State had differing priorities in relation to the War objectives. And they had come to the War from different sides in the conflict over Irish Home Rule that had only been (very luckily, as Asquith and Churchill put it) averted by the European conflict.

What gave the Great War its unique character was the investing of a limited Balance of Power War with a strong moral imperative that made a total war, using conscription, the only logical way of fighting it. This produced the worst of all wars—an endless process of wearing down the enemy that, because of the moral dimension, could never be called off until the job was finished, no matter what the consequences for Europe and beyond. And in that way the British Empire overstepped and overreached, losing control of itself in proportion and judgement.

### Westerners And Easterners

The first military assault on the Ottoman Empire by land, during the opening days of the War, took the form of an invasion of Mesopotamia by Britain's Indian Expeditionary Force. This was to do with directly seizing Ottoman territory for the Empire. But the assaults on the Dardanelles and Gallipoli, which began a few months later, were much more products of the War on Germany. In fact they were so much products of the War on Germany that the planning for them was begun over two months before Turkey entered the War. And yet it was still claimed in England that Turkey was the aggressor!

H.C. O'Neill, the Liberal Imperialist writer, described the objectives behind the Dardanelles assault in the valuable *A History Of The War* (1920), which in its quest for causation tends to blur out interesting facts long forgotten:

> "The Straits very early attracted the attention of Mr. Churchill's vivid imagination. On the last day of August he arranged with Lord Kitchener for

two staff officers to work out with two naval officers plans for the seizure of the Gallipoli Peninsula by a Greek army. This was one of the few known cases of true prevision in the war, for it was a month before Turkey joined Germany. Mr. Churchill not only foresaw the set of events, but also correctly gauged their chief implication. Turkey's entrance into the war would seal the Straits, but if they could be forced, how many desirable results would follow. Even economically, Russia would benefit to a very great extent by unfettered intercourse with her allies... and her armies might take the field as victoriously as their numbers, fine leading, and fine spirit deserved. Moreover, the Balkan nations — Rumania, Bulgaria, and Greece — living spiritually and sympathetically so remote from Great Britain, would receive a lesson which might quite reasonably dispose them to cast in their lot with the Entente Powers. And finally, if the Dardanelles should be forced and Constantinople taken, this would mean the end of Turkey as a fighting power to be reckoned with." (p.271.)

Kitchener and Churchill collaborated on the initial planning for the Dardanelles operation but there lay a fundamental conflict of understanding between them.

The different interests within the British State with their differing priorities in relation to the War were expressed in the dispute between 'Westerners' and 'Easterners' over the War on Germany. On the whole Unionists tended to be 'Westerners' because they saw no option but in grinding Germany down, where it mattered, in the West. Liberals tended to be 'Easterners' because they fancied the quick-fix that would head-off compulsion.

The static War that had developed in Europe, and that had not been taken account of in the Liberal Imperialist War plans, led to the main conflict between these 'Westerners'and 'Easterners'in early 1915.

Churchill, the Liberal Imperialist at the Admiralty, saw the problem of a war without flanks in Europe. He argued that, despite the fact that the War Office pinned its hopes on a spring offensive where the new armies could be brought into play against the Germans, the Western front was settling down to a kind of stalemate in which high casualties could be expected.

In his *World Crisis*, published in 1923, Churchill argued that he was proposing a controlled and decisive escalation of the War in order to prevent the uncontrollable escalation that subsequently took place from the start of 1915:

"Governments and individuals conformed to the rhythm of the tragedy, and swayed and staggered forward in helpless violence, slaughtering and squandering on ever-increasing scales, till injuries were wrought to the structure of human society which a century will not efface, and which may conceivably prove fatal to the present civilization. But in January 1915 the terrific affair was still manageable.' (p.461.)

Churchill was against the war of attrition that Kitchener and the Unionists at the War Office with their mass armies were proposing to fight. He wrote:

> 'No war is so sanguinary as the war of exhaustion. No plan could be more unpromising than the plan of frontal attack. Yet on these two brutal expedients the military authorities of France and Britain consumed, during three successive years, the flower of their national manhood... It is a tale of the torture, mutilation or extinction of millions of men.' (p.463.)

Churchill reasoned that it would be better, therefore, to open up other fronts. He saw two possibilities:

> 'There were, at this juncture, two great plans of using sea power to relieve the murderous deadlock in the west. Both aimed at breaking into and dominating the land-locked waters which guarded the Teutonic fronts... Both would affect in a decisive manner a group of neutral states... Should we look to Holland, Denmark, Norway and Sweden, or to Greece, Bulgaria, and Roumania? Should we strike through the Belts at the Baltic, or through the Dardanelles at Constantinople and the Black Sea?" (pp.32-3.)

The second alternative was decided upon over the first. An attack on the northern flank of Germany was very much in keeping with the traditional Balance of Power wars in which English armies had acted in conjunction with, but independently from, their continental allies to secure specific British objectives. In this, an attack and occupation of the North German coast would be aimed at the destruction of the German fleet—a primary objective of the War.

However, the Unionist presence in the War Office complicated things; they argued that an attack on the North German coast would involve a high stakes decisive battle which they were loathe to take on. And the southern option had the advantage of falling in with British strategic objectives in the Near East.

Churchill reasoned that a naval attack on the Dardanelles Straits would destabilise the Balkan region sufficiently to convince the War Office of the value of diverting sufficient numbers of soldiers away from France, for a larger assault on the Ottoman Empire than originally envisaged.

Kitchener did not survive the War to put his side of things before the public. But after the War, Lieutenant-Colonel Charles a Court Repington, who helped organise the initial military arrangements with the French and worked at the War Office to implement the strategy, wrote a reply to Churchill's arguments in *The World Crisis,* in a book called *Policy And Arms* (1924.). The charming Lieutenant-Colonel Repington wrote:

> "Those of us who were resolutely opposed to the Easterners during the war, and attributed our great defeat in France in March, 1918, mainly to the political folk who had scattered our armed forces far and wide over the face of the earth, have kept silent since the Armistice in the belief that these gentlemen had recognised their folly. We now see by Mr. Churchill's second book on the

war—namely, The World Crisis, 1915—that this is not the case...

The Eastern school affected with its poison very few soldiers, but it appealed to some of Mr. Churchill's political friends who had not made strategy a life study, and this deadly heresy led our armies to the Dardanelles, to Salonika, to Bagdad, and to Jerusalem, and to many other distant and unprofitable objectives...

This policy—for it was policy, and not strategy—was based on the illusion that there was a complete deadlock in France towards the end of 1914, and that we could afford to run about and try to win the war elsewhere without persisting in our endeavours to break the heart of our principal enemy. It was an illusion because the German Higher Command never believed that the war could be won anywhere else but in France, and returned to their original conception whenever the defeats of the Russians permitted it...

We wanted to defeat the main forces of our principal enemy, persuaded that when this was accomplished his satellites would fall from him and the war would be won, whereas, in the contrary course of defeating the satellites, Germany would not surrender. We sought for, and readily found, the centre of gravity of these main forces of our principal enemy, and desired to concentrate against it every man and gun that we could place in the field until he cried for mercy, as he eventually did before the Armistice...

Who first invented the seductive phrase about the 'politico-strategic flank attack'? Who was the genius that discovered the Central Powers were, in Mr. Churchill's words, 'vulnerable in an extreme degree on either flank'? Possibly it was Mr. Churchill himself. Possibly Sir Maurice Hankey, in his paper of December 28, 1914, on the Dardanelles... So we get his picture of the 'swaying and the staggering, the 'helpless violence,'the 'slaughtering and the squandering,'the 'sanguinary war of exhaustion,'the 'dull carnage'and much other unmitigated balderdash... I have not yet discovered how Mr. Churchill expected to work through the 13 or 14 million Germans who took part in the war except by killing them...

I do not know why Mr. Churchill should give such hard names to the wearing-out battles in France and to the war of attrition which all our armed forces conducted. A war of exhaustion is not a novelty." (pp.197-205.)

Churchill could have been talking about Colonel Repington when he was describing General Munro, who had been sent out to the Dardanelles to replace Sir Ian Hamilton as the Gallipoli expedition was being abandoned by the War Office:

"He belonged to that school whose supreme conception of Great War strategy was 'killing Germans'. Anything that killed Germans was right. Anything that did not kill Germans was useless, even if it made other people kill them, and kill more of them, or terminated their power to kill us. To such minds the capture of Constantinople was an idle trophy, and the destruction of Turkey as a military factor, or the rallying of the Balkan states to the Allies, mere politics, which every military man should hold in proper scorn." (*The World Crisis*, p.592.)

And Churchill's verdict on Munro at the Dardanelles was memorable: 'General Munro was an officer of swift decision. He came, he saw, he capitulated'. (p. 593.)

Britain had only two choices for winning the War against Germany. A war of attrition on the Western front (and on the seas) that was based on the calculation that even if the killing rate was only 1:1 the Germans would be exhausted by their inferior population in the long run. Or spreading the War across Eastern Europe and Asia, drawing in other countries, letting them do the killing and dying, and setting the world ablaze, so that out of the inferno, Germany would collapse. Repington and the Unionists favoured the former and Churchill and others argued for the latter.

Churchill believed that the static, grinding, war of attrition was a long and expensive wastage of British Army personnel on the Western front. Repington believed that the flank attack was a fantasy short cut that pointlessly involved far flung regions in war and nearly led to defeat in the principal theatre of war. And they were both right and both wrong, in their own ways! (They were both wrong because the German defeat was ultimately brought about by a combination of the mobile warfare brought by the American forces and the Wilsonian propaganda offensive of 1918 which combined to win the war in the mind of the German command.)

The War Office were loathe to divert resources away from what they saw as the main conflict in the West against Germany. Many Unionists believed that there was little military necessity for a British war on Turkey in the context of the War on Germany and that, in many respects, it was a diversion from the main conflict. France had commercial interests in the Near East, Russia was suspicious of England's intentions there and senior British military figures were against an attack on the Straits. The Turks, by any stretch of the imagination, represented no threat to British interests in the region (although it was pretended that they threatened the British occupation of Egypt and India!) and they could only be anticipated to mount a largely defensive campaign when drawn into the war.

The Dardanelles operation came about through a compromise between 'Westerners'and 'Easterners'. The Easterners got their operation at the Dardanelles but did not get the resources to carry it through effectively.

Churchill, making the best of a bad job and against his better judgement, persuaded Admiral Fisher to go along with a purely naval attack on the Straits. This was partly to do with the War Office opposition to transferring the military forces from the Western front necessary for a combined operation at the Dardanelles. But the British were also obviously in a hurry, with their eyes on the Czar.

So the old Committee of Imperial Defence plan of attack on the Dardanelles, from 1906, was put into operation when England launched its naval forces at the Straits in February 1915. The Royal Navy was sent by Churchill to overawe the Turks and make them acquiesce in the British plan for the Middle East.

## Britain And The Dardanelles

A good summary of England's objectives in storming the Dardanelles is contained in the 1915 book *The Dardanelles: Their Story And Their Significance In The Great War, By The Author of 'The Real Kaiser'* (which contains a review or recommendation from *The Times* and *Times Literary Supplement* on its title page). In *Chapter I, The Significance of the Dardanelles*, the unattributed author explains the importance of the Dardanelles operation for the British Empire — not only to win the War against Germany and Turkey but also to keep the Moslem and lesser races in general in their place, below the white man:

"The first result will be the restoration of communications between Russia and her Western allies. The declaration of war by Turkey almost coincided with the freezing over of the Russian port at Archangel, and so deprived our Eastern ally of any means of communication by sea with the friendly world outside...

In the early spring of 1915 the Russian army sustained severe reverses in Galicia and the passes of the Carpathians. The official explanation of these reverses was a simple one; the Russians were overmatched in heavy guns, the deciding factor in the war of Europe. But big guns and huge stores of ammunition, indeed, military equipment of all kinds, were ready for them in the West, only waiting until a means could be devised of carrying it to Russia...
The autumn of 1914 saw a heavy wheat harvest garnered on the shores of the Black Sea. It was a food supply of infinite value to the allied forces, at a time when the price of wheat was mounting by leaps and bounds over all the world. But so long as the Dardanelles are closed to our merchant ships, the Russian wheat must lie useless in the granaries. And so, if only to restore trading communication between East and West, the attempt upon the Dardanelles had to be made.

It is almost equally important to destroy the present means of communication between Germany and Turkey. These means are maintained through some of the neutral Balkan States, and more particularly through Rumania and Bulgaria. These communications can only be stopped by some event which will force the Balkan States to declare themselves... the Balkan States, one and all, are supremely concerned in the ultimate mastery of Constantinople.

The reasons which caused its founder to select the city as the new capital of the Roman Empire apply with equal force to-day. Apart from its naval importance, as the key to the Straits, Constantinople occupies a position of the highest strategical significance, from the military point of view alone. Its possession would mean to any of the existing nations of South-east Europe a nucleus spot for the creation of an Empire that might well vie in might and influence with the great Empires that have already had their seat there.

When Constantinople passes into the hands of the Allies the momentous choice can no longer be deferred by the Balkan States. It will indeed be strange if, when the magnitude of their interests has been considered by them, they cannot set aside the differences that have paralyzed them through the first months of the war. In the great settlement that is before Europe the question of paramount importance to them is the disposal of Constantinople. Only one way exists for any of them to claim a voice in the settlement of that question. Which of them will refuse to take that way when Constantinople shall have fallen into the hands of the Allied Powers?

It would seem, therefore, that the forcing of the Dardanelles will drive between Germany and what is left of Turkey a wedge of far greater extent than is represented by the mere strip of territory that will fall into the possession of the Allies. The Turks will be cut off from their supplies of weapons, ammunition, and skilled advisers. There will be a rapid end of them as a fighting possibility, and a deadly menace to the whole of our Eastern Empire will be removed. For the plot to rouse the fanaticism of the 300,000,000 Mohammedans of the world into a religious war against Great Britain has still to be considered... the idea itself is an insidious poison, that has been diligently scattered by German emissaries in all the dark and uncivilized places of the earth. It has been sedulously fostered by such lies as Germany alone knows how to disseminate. It would be impossible to exaggerate the danger it still holds for civilization. Savage and half savage tribes in Africa and the East are watching the issue with true homicidal interest. All their latent savagery is stirred by the return of an era of unchecked violence and bloodshed. The Kaiser, who has already figured in their eyes as the protector of Mohammedanism, and has even been represented to them as a renegade Christian, has led his armies into the lands of the Christian...

The prestige of Great Britain, in which they have an inherited belief, the more implicit because it has never before been challenged, is now at stake. It suffices still to hold them in check, though every baser instinct in them is stirred by the daily record of carnage and savagery. All heathendom waits expectant for the next turn of fortune.

The great Sultan has declared a holy war. It is sedulously reported that the English are determined to crush the Mohammedan faith; that, as far as they can, they will prevent pilgrimages to Mecca; that the Ameer of Afghanistan has taken up arms for the faith. All Islam looks on, rapt and intent. In these circumstances an attack is launched at the very heart of Turkey. The Holy War becomes for the Sultan a war of self-preservation. The seat of the Turkish Empire is threatened; it seems about to pass away from his possession into the hands of the all-conquering English. The heathen must still wait for the event, sullen and watchful. And this mighty issue, the prestige of the British flag in all the dark places of the world, is being decided in the Straits of the Dardanelles.

While Constantinople stands, the few white men who are holding hundreds of thousands of coloured men in check, not in one place but in many, live in a deadly peril. Had Constantinople never been attacked, they might well have been carried away ere now in a flood of barbaric licence. When Constantinople falls, the floodgates will be securely fastened again, and the British prestige will stand higher than ever, both in Africa and in the dangerous Far East.

In view of these considerations, it is easily possible to regard the attempt on the Dardanelles as the main point of the Allies'offensive... The Allies, on their part, display that coherence of plan which has marked their conduct of the war since its very beginning... In confident unison they are enduring all, until the determining factor in the struggle has been revealed. May not that factor be declared when the Christian God is once more worshipped under the dome of St. Sophia?... So we find that the line which separates the continent of Europe from that of Asia is in no way artificial ; it is a line established from the beginning of things by Nature herself...

It is the object of this book to show that the policy which dictated an attack on the Dardanelles, with the ultimate object of capturing Constantinople and driving a wedge between Turkey in Europe and Turkey in Asia, is a policy dictated by the necessity of bringing an early end to the war, which is exhausting the resources of Europe at such breakneck speed." (pp.9-19.)

The Irish Parliamentary Party, which had entered into the spirit of the War on the basis of propaganda about 'the rights of small nations', was also beginning to see things in Imperialist terms as they became pulled into the War effort. The *Freeman's Journal* began having the same understandings and making the same calculations as those who had played the game for many seasons past. *The Freeman* greeted the first Allied naval attack on the Straits in February 1915 with the following strategic analysis, in an editorial called *The Dardanelles*:

"The bombardment of the Dardanelles opens up a new phase in modern war. The last successful bombardment by a fleet was that of Alexandria in 1882... Admiral Mahan put the position tersely when he wrote—'A ship can no more stand up against a fort costing the same amount of money than the fort could run a race with the ship.'The attack on the forts of the Dardanelles, therefore, is of the highest military and naval interest. It is also of the greatest political importance... The attack was a wonderful spectacle... The forts were unable to aim at the moving targets which the battleships offered; and the attack on both days was a one-sided affair, in which the forts were subjected to a heavy and destructive fire, whilst the attacking fleet escaped without being hit once...

There is much speculation as to the object of the bombardment. The Germans and Turks anticipate that it is the first step in the forcing of the Dardanelles... The forcing of the Dardanelles would be a formidable task. But it would be a great achievement. It would raise the blockade on Russia, which has been closed in from the sea since the outbreak of war. It would determine the attitude of the Balkan States and other neutral States in the war. It would end the power of Turkey and bring the threatened invasion of Egypt and the attacks on the Suez Canal to an end. There would be little difficulty in landing troops on the Gallipoli peninsula from the Gulf of Saros or on the eastern side of the Straits, as Turkey has no fleet that could come out to oppose them. But a large army would be required, as the Turks would send large forces there, and the garrison of Constantinople alone numbers 100,000 men. The difficulties are great, but the enormous gains would make the attempt attractive." (*Freeman's Journal*, 23 February 1915.)

*The Freeman* described Turkish military operations around Suez as a 'threatened invasion of Egypt'. That is a strange use of the word 'invasion', since Egypt was actually officially a part of the Ottoman Empire. Britain had simply occupied it, unofficially, in 1882, without the consent of the Ottoman Sultan or the local Moslem inhabitants. Within a few weeks of the Declaration of War on Turkey a large British, Australian and Indian army was landed at Alexandria, the Khedive in Cairo deposed and the country turned into a full Protectorate of the Empire. Yet *The Freeman* saw Turkish forces not as liberators of fellow Moslems but, in Imperial terms, as an 'invasion'!

The Churchillian version of history is becoming accepted fact in Ireland today. Churchill himself understood the importance of the control of history writing. 'History will be kind to me. I know that because I intend to write it myself', he is once reported to have said. And write it he did, finding time to do so as he conducted the important affairs of State and all the wars those affairs of State involved planning and waging.

### Shock and Awe, 1915

The attack on the Dardanelles, which began in late February and continued until mid-March 1915, was conducted by the greatest fleet of ships ever assembled in world history. It was led by *The Queen Elizabeth*, the largest battleship on the seas.

It enjoyed initial success as the Royal Navy destroyed the outer forts of the Dardanelles in the first few days of operation, enabling the fleet to penetrate the Straits (it must be borne in mind that these are over a hundred miles long). But upon entering the Straits the fleet hesitated when it came across more sustained Turkish resistance, much to the chagrin of Churchill. So, on March 18th, the whole fleet was ordered to attack with full vigour the intermediate and inner forts.

Included below is the story of the British naval attack on the Dardanelles from the point of view of the Turks from this moment. It is the version of events told by the recipients of the 'shock and awe' provided by the greatest military force of the day.

It comes from a book that is very hard to come by these days. Written by a German, Hanns Froembgen, in 1935, it was translated into English by Kenneth Kirkness for the Jarrolds Publishing House in 1937 under the title *Kemal Ataturk*. Its original German title was *Kemal Ataturk: Soldat und Fuhrer*, but the last part of the German title was not retained for its British edition.

The book is interesting and well-written with the old style narrative that has lately fallen into disrepute, at least in Ireland. Most importantly, it describes the chain of events that led to the most important defeat of the British Empire —

suffered at the height of its powers—that was to have immense repercussions for the world, told from the point of view of the victors. A victory that has all but been written out of the history books because it does not fit into the Churchillian version of history. But here is its account of the assault on the Straits in March 1915:

"CONSTANTINOPLE on 17 March, 1915.

In Pera, where the hoarse cries of haggling Armenians, Levantines, Greeks and Jews echoed day and night, a rumour passed from mouth to mouth: 'They are coming —The Inglis! The English!'No one dared to say it aloud, but grinning lips whispered it into ears which eagerly received the message...

Assembled outside the Straits, near the Aegean Islands, were the united British and French Fleets, consisting of dreadnoughts, armoured cruisers, destroyers, torpedo-boats and submarines. In Pera people spoke of a fantastic force numbering a thousand ships and a hundred thousand men.

For some time past spies had been secretly spreading information that the obsolete, tumbledown Dardanelles forts were without munitions. The Germans were said to be taking shells from the fortress of Bosporus to Chanak, the principal fort in the Dardanelles, while the Bosporus was being left completely defenceless. If the Russians attacked from the Black Sea, and if both sides attacked at the same time—the British from the west, from the Mediterranean, the Russians from the east...

Pera trembled with impatience, joy and hatred, and the street scene was, if such a thing were possible, livelier than usual. Spies and traitors were active everywhere, and invisible threads connected Pera with the Gallipoli positions and, beyond them, the enemy fleets lying in the shelter of the Aegean Islands.

This under-current of excitement was not confined to Pera. It had spread over the whole of Constantinople. The old Imperial City at the Golden Horn seemed to realize that the eyes of the whole world were upon her, and that a decision of the Great War was to be forced at her gates.

How impertinent the Levantines had become! Now they were quite openly stating that special trains had been got in readiness to take his Majesty Sultan Mohammed V and his Court to Asia Minor, that the outer forts had been completely demolished by shell-fire and that Constantinople was to be evacuated.

Turks had disappeared from the streets. In the cafés and bazaars there remained a few old men, solemnly and anxiously sipping their coffee. All the others, on orders from the military authorities, had made themselves scarce. Constantinople had been transformed overnight into an armed camp. The foreign element, spying and foretelling evil, alone remained visible.

At the Ministry of War there was a big conference. His Excellency the Vice-Commander-in-Chief, Enver Pasha, was receiving the Head of the German Military Mission, General Liman von Sanders; behind closed doors negotiations were being pursued and plans discussed.

Dependable news had been received. During the last few days the Queen

Elizabeth, England's mightiest ship, had been lying off the Dardanelles. The whole world impatiently waited to be told of the effect of her 16-inch guns, which were mounted in her at the Southampton Docks.

The decisive action was expected hourly. The forts had just enough munitions to last them for a single day's fighting. They were short of everything. Moreover, there was no communication with Germany, from whom war supplies could have been obtained. A hundred and eighty ancient guns, vintage 1879, faced the Anglo-French Fleet, equipped with the most up-to-date artillery, which was approaching in overwhelming force.

The fall of Constantinople, the capital of the Ottoman Empire, Germany's ally, would at a single blow have altered the entire war situation to the disadvantage of the Central Powers, and it was evident that the British, with their well-known tenacity, would leave no stone unturned to reach this goal.

The faces of those in the Turkish Ministry of War bore anxious expressions. Sleep was not easy in Constantinople that night. Some distance away, along the Narrows, beyond the Sea of Marmora, all was silent. Long and slender, the Gallipoli Peninsula gradually lost itself in the black expanse or the Aegean Sea. Away on the other side Asia approached to within a few kilometers. The silhouettes of the forts, like giant tombs, rose from the dark strip between sky and water which represented the other shore...

Over on the Asiatic side, behind Fort Kum Kale, lay the ruins of Troy, the oldest memorial of the struggle for the Straits which separate Asia from Europe. On the walls of Nagara stood two officers, field-glasses held to their eyes, scrutinizing the glittering sea. They were Colonel Wèhrle, who had charge of the fortifications, and Colonel Jevad, the Dardanelles Commandant...

Suddenly the German whistled softly. The Turk quickly picked up his glasses and turned them towards the horizon, and whispered:'Allah!'

A minute cloud of smoke could be distinguished in the distance above the dancing waves. Quickly it developed into a dense wall of black-grey cloud. Heavy, dark shadows fell across the sea. The sun disappeared behind an impenetrable smoke-screen. The arrows of the Persian Army, which crossed from here to Greece, are said once to have similarly obscured the light. England's Fleet was steaming from Tenedos and Imbros. The frightened sea divided to allow the armoured giants of battleships to pass. Leading the way was the speedy pack of torpedo-boats, destroyers, mine-sweepers and pinnaces. Behind them followed the big fellows. Ten battleships, a French squadron and two British squadrons. Hydroplanes circled above the Kum Kale Fort, which had been demolished in February, and light cruisers reconnoitred the coasts. With uncanny rapidity the advance developed. In this battle 318 of the latest guns were to be used against 180 aged pieces, ripe for the museum.

The Fleet now arrived at the entrance to the Narrows. Level with Troy, within sight of the ruined Fort Kum Kale, a 'round-about' was formed affording to all ships the maximum fire scope. Flags of smoke fluttered wildly, spreading themselves like giant cloths, screening the sky.

Suddenly there came sounds of music! The ships' bands had paraded on deck, and their marches echoed across the water. As in an opera, the Fleet advanced into battle with martial music, triumphantly.

But listen! Sounds of music came from the land, too, but a different kind of music. The muffled sounds of drums. Turkish kettledrums sounding the alarm. And from Chanak, on the other side, the subdued notes of the bugles could be heard. Then thunder shook the world. It burst forth from the mouths of the guns. The iron roundabout began to open fire. The reports of the guns eclipsed all other sounds; and the bursts were frightful. Under blows from the Queen Elizabeth's 16-inch guns the earth writhed.

The forts swallowed the rain of iron in silence, for the Fleet was still beyond range of the Turkish guns, and the strictest account had to be taken of every shell fired. Great ribbons of flame illuminated the opposite shore — burning villages.

At noon signs of life were no longer visible in the outer works. But fountains of earth continued to ascend skywards, and walls continued to crumble. Victory was assured. France was eager to be first at the finishing post. Rather surprisingly, the French passed the British lines and steamed full speed into the inner Dardanelles, in the direction of Fort Chanak.

Gaulois led the way, casting up a great wash as she progressed, ploughing her way towards the Sea of Marmora, en route for Constantinople.

They were now within range of the Turkish guns, which at once opened fire. The armoured giants trembled under the first hits. Shell-fire from the battered forts continued without interruption. In all cases the Turkish gunners had managed to hold out under the murderous bombardment. The works were destroyed, but the soldiers were still living beneath the ruins to serve the guns which were still capable of firing, for, luckily, the Briton had exhausted most of his energy upon skilfully mounted dummy batteries.

The French continued to advance deeper into the inner Narrows, and failed to observe the vivid flames which suddenly shot forth from the battleship Inflexible, which only a short while before, near the Falkland Islands, had run down the valiant Spee. The giant ship took a serious list. A howitzer shell had found its way through the deck and reached the magazine. With difficulty the Inflexible limped from the scene.

Two o'clock in the afternoon. The French had advanced ten kilometres into the Dardanelles, and commenced to pound the main defences at Chanak. In the meanwhile, the British hurled salvo after salvo at the Peninsula of Gallipoli. A new line of battleships now arrived and took the position formerly occupied by the French.

The break-through had succeeded. There remained one more obstacle — Fort Hamidie — and then Chanak!

A hurricane of iron swept the fort away, transforming it into a huge burial ground. The earth opened up and swallowed the ruins. The Gaulois continued on her course. The way was free. Pennants fluttered, cannons roared. The ruins that were Fort Hamidie had just been passed. Four French battleships had broken through to the Dardanelles. En avant!

129

Then, suddenly, to the horror and dismay of the French, their misfortune became apparent. From the heap of ruins, Fort Hamidie, there came deadly fire. Shot after shot. With superhuman strength, the occupants of Fort Hamidie, most of them severely wounded, dug their way out of the wreckage and fought a way back to the light. With blood coursing over them, the gunners ran to the few guns that were still serviceable and — with more than one foot in the grave — did their duty, to save Constantinople, to save the Sultan.

The Gaulois was hit, put out of action, and listed. Helpless, she drifted with the current and ran aground at Tenedos in the Aegean Sea.

The British steamed ahead at full speed. But they were too late to avert a catastrophe. The Bouvet foundered and in a few minutes she sank, 600 of her crew of 660 perishing with her. Fort Hamidie continued to fire shot after shot. The dying gunners were delivering deadly blows. The Suffren, the French flagship, sprang a leak, and appealed for help, maintaining herself above the surface with the utmost difficulty.

The French squadron was destroyed.

The British were now on the scene and poured concentrated fire on Fort Hamidie, finally bringing the ruins to silence. Four o'clock in the afternoon. The British Commander-in-Chief wirelessed a message of victory to the Admiralty. A little later, the Queen Elizabeth, the pride of the British Fleet, went about and, severely hit, fled from the scene of battle.

Fort Hamidie was now firing spasmodically — every round was precious — but she was still scoring telling hits. The other forts were in no way inclined to lag behind her. The battle reached its peak. A Turkish shell struck the armoured turret of the Irresistible and carried it away. Hardly had the British curses died away when a fearful detonation rent the air. The Irresistible had struck a mine.

The Ocean rushed forward to her assistance, but in a short time collapsed under Turkish howitzer fire and, together with the Irresistible, began to drift, relentlessly pursued by the Turkish artillery. Level with Troy, at the entrance of the Dardanelles, the Ocean met her fate and foundered. The Irresistible, sorely stricken, was taken in tow.

The Commander-in-Chief, Admiral de Roebuck, witnessed these misfortunes. He had no need to wait for them to be reported to him. The thunder and noise of battle in the Straits increased to a frenzied pitch. At any moment one expected the heavens to break asunder. He glanced at his staff-officers. Their features, grey and grim, betrayed emotions of excitement, tension, intense anxiety, fear.

Who would have imagined such a resistance possible? The enemy's fire continued to increase.

'Break off the battle!'

'Hold out!'

'Return to the harbour of Mudros!'

'Fight on, sir, for God and England's sake!'

The Admiral hesitated; cast a glance at the sky, then at his watch.

'Withdraw! To Mudros!'

Dry and hard were his words. The great roar of the coastal batteries continued unabated. The huge ships turned and sought refuge in the Aegean Sea, from whose waters night would presently rise, to cover the scene of battle a dark mantle of silence. From the ruins, dust and smoke along the shores a hoarse, guttural cheer was raised.

Constantinople and the Straits were for the present saved. Torchlight processions marched through the streets of the capital. In the mosques foreheads touched the ground in a prayer of thanksgiving.

The muezzin's cry from the minaret echoed louder:

'Allah is great! There is no god but Allah! This day He has shown us His blessing. Come to Allah!'

A more serious view of the events was taken by the men at the Ministry of War. While endless torchlight processions were filling the streets with lights and noise, the pashas were conferring. They knew that only the beginning had been seen..." (*Kemal Ataturk,* pp.9-16.)

In all, three attempts at storming the Straits failed. The Turkish will to resist was maintained whilst the nerve of the Royal Navy crumbled, even though they were within sight of victory. And so the Allied naval forces had to wait for a military force to gather to press home a larger amphibious assault, two months later at Gallipoli.

### The Freedom Of The Straits?

Most of the Irish publications relating to the Great War on Turkey are about the Allied assaults on Gallipoli and the Dardanelles. But they do not concern themselves with why these assaults took place. And they do not wonder, at all, about the reasoning put forward to justify them. If they bothered to read the newspapers of the time they would have found that the Dardanelles operation was seen very much by the Redmondite press in terms of the principle of the 'freedom of the Straits'.

In September 1922 Britain conducted a 'reappraisal' of the idea of the 'freedom of the Straits' after it had been forced to reappraise by what happened at Chanak. What this 'reappraisal' involved was a reconsideration of the principle of the 'freedom of the Straits' in relation to the question of whether it was worth the resumption of full-scale war. The Official Memoranda, produced by Harold Nicolson at the Foreign Office, on the instructions of Lord Curzon, are enlightening in the way they mull over the historical and strategic nature of the 'freedom of the Straits'.

The first thing of importance Nicolson pointed out, in a Memorandum of 25th September, was that Britain had only recently adopted the principle of 'the freedom of the Straits'. It had maintained the exact opposite position for most of its history, insisting on the closure of the Straits by the Turks:

"The purpose and logic of this theory was dependent, as we now see, upon the assumption that Turkey would always be on our side as against Russia.

131

This assumption has altered in a very radical manner, and with it the old expression the 'closing of the Straits'has been transferred into the new formula 'freedom of the Straits.'

The difference between those two catch-words, is not only obvious but essential. For whereas up to 1914 our object was to prevent the Russian Black Sea Fleet entering the Mediterranean, our object is now to ensure the British Mediterranean Fleet can, in the last resort, enter the Black Sea." (A.L. Macfie, *The Straits Question, Middle Eastern Studies*, May 1979, p. 211.)

In a follow-up Memorandum, sent on October 3rd, Nicolson developed his analysis further:

"The apparent divergence between these two policies—between the Nineteenth Century policy of the 'Closing of the Straits' and the Twentieth Century policy of the 'Freedom of the Straits'- is not as fundamental as might be supposed: both policies are ultimately defensive policies against Russia: they represent, in fact, an identic and hereditary policy, adopting different forms, or more accurately, different formulae. The 'Closing of the Straits', as Lord Salisbury indicated in 1878, was inspired by the assumption that in the last resort Turkey, as in the Crimean war, would let us in. The 'Freedom of the Straits' is based on the conviction that, as in 1915, she most assuredly will not."

Nicolson was clear about, and did not disguise, the pivot for change—the 1907 Agreement with Russia—and its consequences:

"Turkey abandoned the hope of our naval protection, for the security of Germany's military support. The essential readjustment of the Straits Question was not realised in England until, on 12 August 1914, the Goeben and the Breslau escaped to the Golden Horn. From that moment the doctrine of the 'Closing of the Straits'was destroyed, and the Gallipoli campaign only emphasized its destruction. It became obvious that Turkey could no longer guard the Straits in the interests of Europe and that some other method should be devised. The 'Freedom of the Straits' was the natural corollary." (*The Straits Question, Middle Eastern Studies*, May 1979, p. 212.)

But there is something missing here in the search for continuity. Perhaps it could be summed up in the phrase: 'Don't mention the war!'

Nicolson was correct in identifying the Straits Question as being primarily about Britain's fear of Russia. Before the War, or more accurately before 1907, England insisted on the 'Closing of the Straits' to keep the Russian fleet out of the Mediterranean and, after the War, Britain insisted on the 'Freedom of the Straits' so that the Royal Navy could get at Bolshevik Russia. In between there was the War on Germany and Turkey, with Russia as a vital component, which needed supplying, and whose supply route was blocked by the closing of the Straits. So the period from 1908 to 1917 was something of an aberration— in that it was a temporary break in which, instead of the Straits being used by

Britain against the Russian State, the objective was to open them to support the Czar.

Lloyd George later told the House of Commons that the collapse of Russia was almost entirely due to the closure of the Straits. If that was the case, it should be concluded that the Russian Revolution, the rise of Hitler, the Second World War, and the Russian conquest of Eastern Europe followed on from Britain's decision to make War on the Ottoman Empire, and the ensuing closure of the Dardanelles.

If that is the case then the issue of the Straits, and the British decision to make War on Turkey, assumes an importance that it has not been credited with by historians. But that would make it all very much worse, would it not?

Before the War, the 'freedom of the Straits' was only denied to one nation by another. The Russian Navy was restricted from passing through the Straits largely on the insistence of England. The Treaty of Paris of 1856, imposed on the Russians after the Crimean War, severely limited the size of Russian vessels on the Black Sea and forbade her to have arsenals on her coasts. The Conference of 1871 relaxed these restrictions on the Russians, mainly on Bismarck's insistence. But Russian warships still could only proceed through the Straits with the permission of the Sultan — and of course, the Sultan, at this time, was England's man. (The Ottomans, by themselves, could not prevent the Russians from having access to the Straits, if the other Great Powers insisted upon it.) So during the Russian-Japanese War of 1905 the Black Sea fleet had to remain passive as their sister ships were destroyed by Britain's ally in the Far East.

In 1908, a year after the Agreement with England, the Russians asked for the concession that warships belonging to the Black Sea States be allowed passage through the Straits when Turkey was not at war. They proposed the provision that not more than three ships belonging to one State be allowed to sail between the Black Sea and Aegean at any one time and that the Straits be closed to warships belonging to other nations. The Austrians supported this solution to the Straits question but England blocked it. Grey insisted that Russia was acting outside the terms of the *Triple Entente* by negotiating with Austro-Hungary alone. He put up the counter-proposal that the Straits should be completely open to warships of all nations at all times. This was a proposal that Russia (and the Turks) were most against as it would mean that the Royal Navy could enter the Straits at will from the Mediterranean and bombard the Black Sea ports, as it did in the Crimean War. Because it was so unacceptable to all parties (except England) it effectively closed the question of the Straits again.

Three years later, in 1911, Russia sought to take advantage of Turkey's difficulties after the Italian attack on Tripoli by proposing that in return for free passage of her ships Russia would act as guarantor of the Straits. In return the Russians would recognise the Ottoman right to Constantinople and its European hinterland. But Grey again refused to give his sanction to the deal.

In contrast, both the Austro-Hungarians and the Germans approved the Russian proposals. And Germany acted in accordance with Bismarck's principle that the problem of the Straits should be settled by treaty between Russia and the Porte.

The question of the 'freedom of the Straits' therefore was kept alive primarily by England. Settlement of the issue, which would have reduced antagonisms in the region between Russia, Austro-Hungary, Turkey and Germany, was impermissible from the position Britain had adopted with regard to the destruction of Germany. Russia could not be allowed to attain its objectives at the Straits by diplomacy. She must be only allowed to gain them by taking Constantinople by force and in the context of a European war.

The problem over the 'freedom of the Straits' would also have been settled if Britain had not pushed Turkey into the War. The attack on the Dardanelles was supposed to be about the 'freedom of the Straits'. But there had been no lack of freedom to merchant shipping of any nation before the War. There were no restrictions or instances of Constantinople hampering the commerce of the world prior to the appearance of hostile Allied war ships threatening the city. The closing of the Dardanelles and Bosphorus was a purely defensive measure on the part of the Turks to the Allied threat.

The idea of a neutralised Straits, which began to be advocated as a war aim, was as ridiculous as that idea applied to any of the other waterways in the world. It was a 'principle' made available to the British war effort, like the idea of the 'freedom of the seas'.

In both these phrases the word 'freedom' could be used interchangeably with the words 'British controlled'. England, through the power of its navy, 'owned' practically all the main commercial waterways of the world, save for the Panama Canal—which she knew better than to interfere with, because of the Monroe Doctrine.

For about three centuries Britain had set herself the task of controlling all the important routes of the seas. By means of the acquisition of Gibraltar the entrance to the Mediterranean could be closed, through Malta the connection between its western and eastern sections, sentineled. Through the holding of Cyprus, England assured the entrance to the Suez Canal, which, with Egypt, she appropriated. By that means the Royal Navy controlled the shortest water-way to India, the Indian Ocean and the Pacific. But she also put herself in a position to exercise her influence over the longer route round Africa by means of occupying St. Helena and the Ascension Islands as well as through her African colonies. The gate from the Red Sea to the Straits of Bab-el-Mandeb was capable of being closed by possession of the Island of Perim. The road to the Pacific which went through the Straits of Malacca was also controlled through a British naval base built at Singapore.

Britain also threatened with war or blockade countries who considered offering ports to its rivals for the process of coaling. These coaling stations were essential, in the era of ironclads, for the movement of navies and all the dreadnoughts in the world could not be of any use if they could not be moved (The Agadir affair of 1911 was an example).

And, as I have noted, great care was taken to prevent the continental Powers from breaking this grip, by stopping them from building railways to points that might undermine Britain's control of the world's maritime commerce and communication.

The other great waterways of the world, such as the Suez Canal or Gibraltar, or the mouth of the Danube, were no more free in peacetime than the Straits. When war came, the Powers with the available naval forces (usually the Royal Navy) rushed to close them to the enemy. (A case in point was the Suez Canal. An 1888 Suez Treaty signed by Britain committed her to leave the Canal open to shipping in times of war but, in 1914, the Suez Canal was closed to all shipping that the Royal Navy deemed unfriendly. All pretence of a neutral internationalised waterway was dropped and the surrounding land incorporated into the Empire.)

The issue of the 'freedom of the Straits' for Britain became intimately connected to the Turkish relationship with Germany that Britain encouraged through its 1907 Agreement with Russia. England never raised the issue of the 'freedom of the Straits' when it believed Turkey to be in decrepitude, ripe for the picking, and powerless to resist British threats to the maritime traffic passing Constantinople. However, when an Ottoman rejuvenation was threatened by the German assistance, England took fright at the thought that Turkey might, in the future, be able to defend its sovereignty against the Royal Navy.

The least valid reason cited by the *Freeman* for the forcing of the Dardanelles was to

"raise the blockade on Russia, which has been closed in from the sea since the outbreak of war."

Russia's Northern ports had, as always, been isolated due to winter freezing. But the Straits had only been closed by the War on Turkey itself. Russia was only the subject of 'blockade' because of the appearance of the Royal Navy there in November 1915. And after the Bolsheviks took power in 1917, and made peace with Germany, the British Navy placed its own, proper, 'blockade' on Russia.

H.C. O'Neill has this informative passage in his discussion of the Dardanelles operation:

"The isolation of Russia in winter, only recently understood sympathetically in Western Europe, was the reason for her consistent desire for... an entry into the Mediterranean as the possession of Constantinople and the Gallipoli Peninsula would have given her. Constantinople was the door; the Dardanelles was the vestibule. Both had, for hundreds of years, been in the possession of Turkey, and the fact became of cardinal importance when that country entered upon the war with its traditional friends, Great Britain and France." (*A History Of The War* (1920), p.271.)

What a marvellous expunging of history this is—as if England had never had anything to do with closing the Straits on the Russians, as if the Crimean War had never taken place, as if Disraeli had never had a foreign policy...

Public sympathy is a thing that is very consistent in England with State policy. It was 'By Jingo' to the Russians prior to 1908, sympathy from 1914 to about 1917, and then sympathy ebbed away again as Russia became an enemy again, just as H.C. O'Neill was putting pen to paper.

The 'freedom of the Straits' was another of those principles, like the 'war for civilization', the 'war for small nations' etc. invented to support British Imperial interests during the Great War and in the Peace Settlements after, and selectively applied by England according to the circumstances.

In September 1922 Britain had to take into account a new situation, with Ataturk's Turkey no longer amenable as guardian of the Straits for Britain, against Russia. And the other consideration was France, the new object of Britain's Balance of Power policy, after the defeat of Germany.

If the Redmondites believed they were fighting for another great principle of humanity in the assault on Gallipoli, they were seriously naïve in their understanding of how England operates.

### The Russians *Shall* Have Constantinople

Five days into the War on Turkey a note of concern was raised by *The Freeman's Journal* over Russian successes in the East. On 10th November *The Freeman's* London Correspondent wrote:

"Yesterday's news contains much ground for satisfaction, but also much for anxiety. The military position on both the eastern and western battle fronts is undoubtedly good. In the east the Russians have cleared the Germans out of every part of Poland, and are now pursuing them into their own territory. At this moment they are within less than 200 miles of Berlin itself, and if they chose to follow up their success with full vigour they should be able in a comparatively short time to put an entirely new face upon the whole situation...

It is upon this point that the ground for anxiety exists. Will Russia, having cleared the enemy out of her own territory, follow up her own brilliant success in this direction, or will she merely leave a sufficient force in East Prussia to hold the Germans while she devotes her chief energies to crushing Turkey and seizing Constantinople? The 'Morning Post' of yesterday printed a message from its Petrograd correspondence which is full of significance on the subject... He explains the fact that Russia, having already done so much to break the power of the Germans, now looks to France and England to do something equally big, and that meanwhile she intends to complete the pulverising of Austria-Hungary, drive out the Turks, set up a new state of Armenia, and hold Constantinople for herself. The possibility of such a complication arising has of course been contemplated from the moment it became evident that Germany was trying to drag Turkey into the war, and it goes to explain the great tolerance shown to the Porte Government even in the face of its repeated and flagrant violations of neutrality." (*Freeman's Journal*, 10 November 1914.)

This raises the issue that Ireland (and the 'great English democracy', for that matter) did not quite realise what they had signed up to in the War. The understanding of *The Freeman's* London Correspondent is that Britain was prepared to tolerate Turkish provocations because it wanted to avoid Russia coming down to Constantinople.

War is a catastrophic activity. When a country signs up for war it can never be quite sure what it is buying into. And that is why the decision of the Redmondites to give England a blank cheque in August 1914 was so problematic. The Redmondites had a completely different understanding of the War that was being entered into than the War that was about to be fought. They were not privy to the Liberal Imperialist ambitions and War plans, which had been kept a very tight secret. And they did not seem to realise that the War they entered, in support of their Home Rule allies, would not remain just a Liberal War. It was a War conducted by and in the interests of the British State as a whole. But, having entered into the bargain with the Government of the British State there was no going back on it without endangering Home Rule. And so the Irish Party became hostage to fortune in a game for higher and higher stakes.

Edward Grey viewed 'the Russian Steamroller' as the vital force in the War on Germany: 'Everything in the war', Grey informed his Ambassador in St. Petersburg, 'depends upon the Russian offensive upon Germany and... nothing should be allowed to divert Russian forces from this object.' (*The Straits Question In The First World War*, p.50.) And so, from the time of the Declaration of War on Turkey, Grey moved to conclude an agreement with the Russians that would give them Constantinople.

The British attack on the Dardanelles brought the conclusion of a formal agreement closer because it raised Russian fears that the British and French Allies would proceed from Gallipoli on to Constantinople and hold it for themselves. So the secret Treaty, the *Constantinople Agreement*, that promised the Czar the Byzantine capital, would encourage him to keep the bulk of his forces engaged against the Germans, instead of diverting them to take Constantinople.

The *Constantinople Agreement* between Tsarist Russia, Britain and France was completed between March 4th and April 10th, 1915. It was agreed by Britain and France to let Russia take Constantinople and the Straits. Included within the territories earmarked for Russia was the Gallipoli Peninsula, where British and Imperial troops were at that moment being killed in thousands. Britain did not guarantee carrying on the War until Constantinople was captured, but merely consented to its annexation by Russia, in advance of its capture. For Britain, in return, the Persian section of the Anglo-Russian Agreement of 1907 was revised so as to include 'the neutral zone of Persia in the English sphere of influence'.

Sir Edward Grey handed over Constantinople to the Czar to prevent him making a separate peace with the Kaiser. This amazing capitulation by Grey, brought about by the failure to break German resistance, despite all the advantages of men and materials, went against all the fundamentals of British foreign policy down the ages—'the Russians shall not have Constantinople'.

There was the suspicion in some quarters that what the Dardanelles operation was partly about was the British securing of the Straits as a kind of hostage—so that the Czar could never afford to make a separate peace with Germany and Turkey before they were destroyed. (In early 1915 the Turks and Germans offered the Czar right of passage through the Straits if he declared an end to hostilities. But the prize of Constantinople proved too attractive to him to conclude a separate peace.)

It occurred to some people in Britain during the summer of 1915, when Turkish resistance had proved stiffer than had been anticipated, that the War against Turkey had not been a good idea—that England had become over ambitious and had taken on one enemy too many. Sir Maurice Hankey, Secretary to the Committee of Imperial Defence, proposed that a separate peace be concluded with Turkey, in order to concentrate all resources on Germany, and reopen the Straits for Russia, and his idea received support from the British General Staff.

But Grey would have none of it. He had concluded a deal with the Czar and Russia was indispensable to winning the War. So Constantinople and the Straits were to be given over to Russia.

### Gallipoli And Ataturk

Anyone who doubts the role of the individual in history should reconsider in the light of Ataturk. The Turkish nation's recovery and its achievement of establishing a functional state in the teeth of Imperialist aggression was due in large measure to producing a leader of exceptional military and political ability at the vital hour.

Mustapha Kemal was born in Salonika, the son of an Ottoman Customs Officer. The city was regarded as a hot-bed of revolution by the British Embassy at Constantinople, as well as by the Sultan. It was supposedly a centre of Freemasonry, apparently since the arrival in the area from Italy of the followers of Mazzini. There was a large Jewish population, many of whom were involved in socialist organisations. And also there were Turks, opposed to the Sultan's rule and organised in secret societies—chief of these being the Young Turks.

The character of the city must have rubbed off on Kemal. As a young man, he attended the nearby military academy in Monastir, (where he taught himself French to read Voltaire and Montesquieu) and won a place at infantry college in Constantinople.

The military academies were centres of Young Turk revolutionary sentiment and Kemal formed the opinion that the Ottoman administration under the Sultans was increasingly inept. He joined a number of secret societies which aimed at a reform of the Constitution, which had been suspended by Abdul Hamid, along with the Ottoman Parliament.

Kemal was transferred to Jaffa by his superiors but he secretly made his way back to Salonika a year later. In 1908 the officer corps of the army in Salonika, which was a centre of influence for the Young Turks (including Talaat, Enver and Djemal), was involved in the Young Turk (Committee of Unity and Progress) *coup d'état* against Abdul Hamid. Kemal led a division to Constantinople to help depose the Sultan, replace him with his brother, and restore the Constitution and Parliament.

Mustapha Kemal, however, soon found himself in serious disagreement with the Committee. He grew disillusioned with the Young Turks after their incompetent handling of the Empire's affairs and their defeats at the hands of the Balkan Alliance. The Greeks captured Salonika and threatened Constantinople before another coup brought a different faction of Young Turks, led by Enver and Talaat Pasha, to power. The new Government rallied the army against the now squabbling enemy and Kemal was appointed to the General Staff. He led a force that managed to drive the Greeks back through Thrace and out of Adrianople.

Ataturk seems to have concluded, pretty early on, that the Young Turk movement was doomed to failure. He reasoned that there were only two possible futures for the Turks: either a declining multi-national Empire being eaten away by the West or a thoroughgoing national development based on a Turkish State.

In July 1913, during the Second Balkan War, Kemal was appointed Chief of the Staff to the army corps based in Gallipoli, where he made a detailed first-hand study of the problem of defending the Dardanelles. After the war, however, Kemal was posted to Sofia, as military attaché, to keep him out of the way. He only returned to the Dardanelles after the Great War broke out and Liman Von Sanders took over, after the shock of the Allied naval assault. At this time he was of the opinion that Turkey should have avoided siding with Germany, whom he saw as doomed to ultimate defeat, given the strength of forces ranged against her.

And that was how Mustapha Kemal found himself in a pivotal position when the British Imperial forces landed at Gallipoli.

Hanns Froembgen's account continues with a narrative of the events at Gallipoli, written from the Turkish perspective, and the first appearance on the world stage of Ataturk:

> "An endless procession of troop-transports ploughed deep furrows in the disturbed waters of the Aegean. The ships came from Gibraltar, from England, from Northern France, from Marseilles, from the South, from Egypt, from

India, from Australia. In the mighty depots at Malta there was feverish activity. Mountains of supplies and equipment were unstacked and loaded into the ships — in addition to munitions and war materials of the latest kind, of which the Anatolian soldier had not even heard.

Forward against Constantinople! Forward to the Straits!

The British were no longer willing to tremble for India's sake and no longer prepared to leave their armies as helpless victims of the German cannons in Northern France; they wanted more than anything to establish communication with the Russian ally, supply him with munitions and instruments of war, and transform him into a really dangerous opponent of the Central Powers. In London there was a man who visualized the bold way by which England could achieve a quick victory: Winston Churchill, the First Lord of the Admiralty. If God were with him, he would discover the right men to bring his daring plan to fruition.

Under General Sir Ian Hamilton's command were one hundred thousand men — Scots, New Zealanders, Australians, Gurkhas — the finest troops at England's disposal. In their ranks was an enthusiasm that had not been known since the days of Nelson. Gallipoli! It was the greatest war adventure that had come England's way for many decades. Who would miss such a chance? The flower of Britain's youth rushed to join the Dardanelles Army, the great Expeditionary Corps that was assembling off the Greek islands.

Time passed, precious time. English military bureaucracy, a superabundance of men and materials. Already four weeks had passed since the naval battle. In the Turkish War Ministry nerves were getting frayed. How much longer did the enemy need for his preparations and plans?

It was a lucky thing that he needed so long! Each day was of inestimable value to the defender. In all haste, the Vth Army was formed. No less a soldier than Marshal Liman von Sanders, the Head of the German Military Mission, was appointed its commanding officer. Here, too, we have the same picture. The best men had one ambition: to be transferred to the Vth Army.

Their strength was rather less than half that of the enemy. It was impossible, therefore, to guard the whole coastline, and the only thing to do was to mass troops at points where a landing attempt might be expected. The long strips of coast between these points were watched only by small formations of the military and by gendarmes. The Briton had a clear picture of what was happening, had maps showing the minutest details, and an intelligence service which functioned perfectly.

On 25 April people were surprised by the sound of gunfire. The Briton was manoeuvring up and down the coast with the object of causing confusion on the other side. Torpedo-boats, as though possessed, darted here and there, firing whenever the slightest target presented itself. This continued all through the day. Lucky was the man who possessed strong nerves!

For the present Liman von Sanders had to content himself with relying on the training which he had given to his army and divisional commanders. At the decisive moment everything depended on the right man giving the right orders quickly.

Night came. At the southern end of Gallipoli, near Sedd-el-Bahr, the Briton had disembarked and set foot on land. There a battle had been raging for several hours. What was happening on other sectors of the front was still not clear.

In the vicinity of Cape Ariburnu, under cover of the darkness, a giant flotilla of boats neared the unguarded coast. A landing was difficult, especially as the strong current began to carry the boats slightly to the north. Soon it would be dawn. On shore nothing stirred, though several pairs of eyes kept a constant watch on the black surface of the sea.

As quietly as possible the boats worked their way towards the shore, and before it was yet light a party of Australians set foot on Gallipoli. The Turkish sentinels were noiselessly liquidated, only a few gendarmes succeeded in escaping. They took to their heels and disappeared into the darkness.

A little way inland rose the heights of Ariburnu. It was known that they were not defended, and it was essential that they should seized without loss of time. Their possession meant victory half gained, for from there the whole Peninsula could be commanded. From there the Turks could be shot to pieces in their trenches without being able to do very much in their own defence. The heights of Ariburnu were of first-class importance.

They drew nearer and nearer to their goal and the first men of the Anzac Corps were commencing to climb the slopes, when they suddenly and noiselessly collapsed under Turkish bayonets. Immediately there was confusion. In the uncertain light of dawn Turkish fezes could be seen rising over the crest. With fixed bayonets, and bending low, the Anatolian infantry advanced at the double, and in the next few moments the full force of their attack struck the British. There was a brief and vicious hand-to-hand skirmish, in the course of which the English were defeated and forced to retreat to the beaches. There fresh troops were still being landed. Fearful confusion broke out. Fugitives and landing parties collided and got in each other's way. Then the Turkish artillery opened fire, and wrought fearful havoc among the masses of men assembled on the unsheltered beaches. What had happened? What was the solution of the mystery? The secret of this gruesome surprise?

Liman von Sanders gave instructions for the time of calm before the storm to be employed by the troops in practice manoeuvres to prepare them for their task of repulsing the enemy invasion, and none showed greater zeal in carrying out this order than the young commander of the 19th Turkish Division, to whose sector of the front the Ariburnu area belonged.

He was a sharp-spoken, rather unapproachable gentleman, with a completely un-Turkish conception of military service: he was as severe and as demanding as any German officer of the Military Mission. He was a harsh disciplinarian, and had all the officers and men under his command on tip-toe. It went hard with the man who was found guilty of the slightest breach of discipline or neglect of duty. But no one—not even in the Arab regiments—in the 19th Division was ever convicted of those offences. The young lieutenant-colonel had only recently taken over the command. He had come from Sofia, where he held the post of Military Attaché, had set to work with fierce energy and in a few weeks transformed his men into soldiers who would not hesitate to face the Sheitan himself, if the Kumandan were at their head.

Also on this night, instead of sleep and rest, there was a field exercise—on the heights of Ariburnu. A battery of artillery accompanied the infantry on this manoeuvre. When he was asked whether ball ammunition was to be issued to the men, he replied briefly: Yes. Some extra sense must have warned him of the coming danger.

Practising modern war tactics, the soldiers slowly advanced towards the heights. Presently they were close to them. In the chilly atmosphere which immediately precedes daybreak, the men shivered. It was at this time that they noticed the Turkish gendarmes breath-lessly running towards them.

'Inglis! Inglis!'

Immediately the Kumandan's voice echoed over their heads: 'Forward against the enemy!'

What was formerly an exercise was now the real thing. The troops ascended the slope at the double. Every minute was costly. The Australians were scaling the other side of the mountain. Soon the sounds of fighting, quiet at first, gradually swelled into a furious crescendo. The Kumandan himself remained with the battery of artillery, shouting orders and encouraging the gunners ...

The thunder of the guns echoed over the Peninsula and the sea, sounds gradually losing themselves in the bays, coves, valleys and vines. The battle speedily developed, and the invaders, taken by surprise, were driven back to the sea.

The Anatolians rushed after them, eager to make a thorough job of their work. But, at the moment they occupied the beach, the first salvo from the British naval batteries burst forth, and an iron screen of death parted the two adversaries.

Against the ships'heavy artillery the Turks, with their small calibre guns were unable to make any headway. The Kumandan cursed to himself. He had to leave the British in occupation of the beaches, for to send his men through that screen of death was more than he could dream of attempting.

But that did not minimize the victory. The enemy's attempt to make a successful landing at the most vulnerable spot on Gallipoli had been frustrated, brilliantly frustrated, thanks to the masterly generalship of the Officer Commanding the 19th Turkish Division, Lieutenant-Colonel Mustafa Kemal.

At once his name became known in the streets, cafés, the bazaars and drawing-rooms of Constantinople. With Eastern extravagance the Turks named him the Saviour of Constantinople; and the Commander-in-Chief, Liman von Sanders, realized better than any that they had in him a soldier in a million.

We must not forget the Anatolian soldiers, whose leader he was. In the loneliness of his uneventful peasant existence, the Anatolian in remote Asia Minor was by nature a philosopher and deep thinker. The world, as he knew it, consisted of a plot of land and a strip of sky bordered by a high wall of jagged mountains. At night the stars shone powerfully in this strip of sky. Time then seemed to stand still; the pulse-beat of world history appeared to cease. The

Anatolian sat lost in thought, losing count of the march of the hours.

He was seldom known to translate his thoughts into words, and, indeed, was hardly able to do so, for no one had taught him this. The thoughts of his peasant nature were profound; he was closely bound up with those things which, he was aware, were round him: his soil and his limited strip of star-strewn sky.

Far from the world, he built for himself his own world, a world of belief, of the miraculous and of the supernatural. His life turned him into a philosopher, and he claimed to be conscious of the presence of higher, mysterious powers, which the reason of the inhabitants of big cities refused to recognize. He recognized them, fanatically, devoutly, and with every atom of his being.

His wretched mud hut often concealed thousands of good Turkish gold-pounds, enough to enable him to build a fine country house, enough to permit him to travel—but he had no wish for such things. The money continued to rest where it had already long rested. Once a month he visited the nearest market, sold his cattle, and, if the Beiram Festival was at hand, sold them in herds, bringing home with him more gold-pounds, which he placed in the chest with the others. And there they stayed. He continued to sleep on the bare floor; his life consisted of caring for his soil and of silent thought; occasionally in the evening he smoked his old water-pipe; maize was his principal food.

He was a man of great stature and formidable strength. A long battle with the hard soil had made him so. He was accustomed always to carry arms, for he had to defend himself against wolves. About five centuries ago he came from the dark lap of Turkestan, when the great drought descended upon Asia, driving the nomad Turks westwards.

When the Sultan declared war, he suddenly found himself a soldier, and he displayed in his new profession the same tranquillity that had characterized him as a peasant and philosopher. He was amenable to discipline, loyal and fearless; he demanded little for himself, placed not the slightest value on his own life, and looked up in quiet confidence to the officer whom Allah had destined to be his master and leader.

His uniform was ragged, and the boots given to him by his Supreme War Lord were worn out—but he made no complaints. In the other world Allah was preparing every luxury for those who in this world humbly and loyally served His representatives.

Of such stuff were the soldiers with whom the Divisional Commander, Lieutenant-Colonel Mustafa Kemal, defended his front near Ariburnu against the Anglo-Australian 'Anzac' Corps.

It is only to-day that we are able to see these men and their leader in their true light. He was a man who inspired confidence in his subordinates. The Anatolians regarded him with a mixture of awe and admiration, and placed absolute trust in him. There was something about him—they could not explain to themselves what it was— something of magic. . ." (*Kemal Ataturk,* pp.16-20.)

Mustapha Kemal's successful defence at Gallipoli had repercussions for countries other than Turkey. Blocked at the Straits, England began to turn its attention toward the neutral countries of the Balkans to fight its war for civilisation.

# III. Britain and Greek Neutrality

When it found itself unable to defeat Germany quickly, Britain interfered in Greek affairs from 1915 (to 1922) to further the War and and protect its interests in the Balkans and the Near East. In the war for small nations that England was supposedly waging, the small nation of Greece suffered from espionage, threats, blockade and invasion—all at the hands of the Allies, attempting to use the Greeks as cannon-fodder in the War. And the 'Irish' 10th Division was part of this assault on Greek neutrality that culminated in a mad adventure in Asia Minor and tragedy for Greeks across the Balkans and Asia Minor.

These events, I presume, are almost unknown to modern Ireland, and perhaps they are forgotten in Britain these days too.

## *The Balkans At The Crossroads*

The chain of events that led to the Allied violations of Greek neutrality originated in the British determination that Turkey should be drawn into the conflict.

At the end of August 1914, the Rumanians, who had kept out of the Balkan Wars of 1912-13, attempted to form a neutral Balkan bloc of States that would keep the whole region out of the War. The Rumanians invited the Bulgarians, Greeks and Turks to a conference at Bucharest. The objective was to sort out the differences between them so that the Balkan States would not be lured into the general conflagration and start fighting over disputed territories in the Balkans. However, the belief that the Turks were going to find it impossible to remain neutral seems to have scuppered the negotiations, and left King Constantine of Greece having to tread a delicate course between those at war and the other Balkan States who might be open to offers to take the plunge.

The *Entente* saw the situation regarding Greece and Rumania in much the same way as they did that of Italy. While neither of these two countries was a member of the Triple Alliance, unlike Italy, there was some reason to believe that some treaties of 'material and moral obligation' had been signed with Germany to cover certain situations. There were also personal ties which were expected to prove helpful to further the relationship with Germany: the Queen of Greece was a sister of the Kaiser, and the King of Rumania was originally a Hohenzollern Prince.

Greece and Rumania, like Italy, also had irredentist movements for the acquisition of adjoining territories populated in part by their respective peoples or by peoples of related ethnic stock. Moreover, in Greece there was an ongoing strong agitation for ending the monarchy and establishing a republic.

The position and purpose of the Entente towards both Greece and Rumania was, therefore, similar to that of Italy: to tempt them to break any arrangements they had previously made with Germany, by pledging to them the realisation of their irredentist ambitions in exchange for their support in the War against the Central Powers.

Here again the Bagdad Railway loomed large. If Rumania and Greece had been allowed to persist with their arrangements with Germany, in order to provide a stable territory for the route of the Railway, there would, in all probability, have developed a political accommodation of necessity between the two countries and Bulgaria in the Balkans. The extension of the Berlin-Bagdad Railway would also have made an accommodation between the Christian Balkan nations and Turkey necessary and this would have been accomplished under German influence. And if the Railway had begun to provide the economic development that it potentially could along its route, there is everything to suggest that the Balkan region might have settled down to become a stable region with a pragmatic interest in working with a rejuvenated Ottoman Empire.

The alternative was ethnic and religious conflict across the region with every nation looking to satisfy its own *Irredenta*. And that was the situation Britain sought to encourage and attempted to manipulate in the War effort.

### *England's Holy War*

One of the most interesting books written about the Great War is *England's Holy War* by Irene Cooper Willis, who usually wrote commentaries about subjects in English literature. *England's Holy War* was published in New York in 1928, with the subtitle *A Study Of English Liberal Idealism During The Great War*. It is a devastating criticism of the moral collapse of English Liberalism in August 1914, its resort to an idealistic crusade against evil to justify its collapse, the effect this had on the waging of England's Great War, and on the 'Peace to end all peace' afterwards.

Willis located the Holy War that England decided to fight in the Liberal necessity to wage an idealistic crusade to salve their conscience:

> "That idealism arose largely from the necessity of finding reasons for intervention other than those balance of power arguments which had evoked such opposition from the Liberal Press in the days before our actual entrance. The change of attitude on the part of the Liberals, from opposition to the war to support of it, required a transformation of the issues involved. Idealism accomplished that transformation.' (*England's Holy War*, pp.175-6.)

And this had fundamental repercussions on the character of the War:

> 'It was the Liberal aversion to war, the extreme Liberals'dissatisfaction with the vital interest argument, combined with their final submission to the fact of war, which made this war different from previous ones and consecrated it from the outset as a war on behalf of civilisation." (p.87.)

The Liberal War propaganda, produced by its Press, from *The Daily News* to *The Manchester Guardian*, involved promoting the idea that the Great War was fundamentally different to all of England's previous wars. It was the 'war to end wars', in which 'the sword was drawn for peace'. And Redmondite Ireland, quite apart from its absorption of English Liberal ideas, had its own reasons to pretend this was a different British War that it was signing up to.

It is for that reason that Liberal England and Redmondite Ireland bear a greater responsibility for the catastrophic effects of the Great War than the traditional warmongering element in Britain.

Irene Willis's *England's Holy War* has a chapter on *The Mobilisation Of Neutrals* which is very perceptive on why Liberal England showed such interest in drafting in neutral countries to fight in its Holy War on Germany:

> "As the talk about conscription grew louder, the Liberals became increasingly interested in the mobilisation of other belligerents. The Conservatives were more concerned to conscript at home than abroad. But the Liberals' dislike of compulsion did not extend to unwillingness to see it operated in other countries. Neither did their aforetime interest in neutrality and in the attempt to localise the conflict incline them to discourage interventionist movements in Italy, Rumania and Greece. On the contrary the Liberal Press was most active in advertising war fervour in these countries and in pointing out the moral and material advantages which would accrue upon their entrance into the war." (p.211.)

Liberal England was opposed to intervention in the Great War right up until it was faced with a *fait accompli* by the Liberal Imperialist leaders'plans for War on Germany and the activation of those plans in August 1914. To justify their moral collapse in the face of the situation Edward Grey presented to them, they created and cultivated the Holy War for civilisation against Prussianism and evil. But they were handicapped in waging this War by their opposition to compulsion. The Tories were strong advocates of Conscription and pointed out that, if this was a War for civilisation, as Liberal England claimed, and a great struggle to the death against evil, surely it was the duty of the Government to wage it to the fullest by instituting compulsion.

But Liberal England hesitated to compel in their own country and went looking for manpower elsewhere to wage their Holy War. And, in looking for that manpower, they went to the neutral countries of Europe, carrying the message to their people that this was a War of good versus evil, that it would be morally inexcusable to abstain from. So compulsion to kill became a moral imperative in Liberal England's dealings with the small neutral nations of Europe.

### Sir Basil Thomson And Greece

Sir Basil Thomson, Director of British Intelligence in the Great War, and the head of Special Branch after it, is best known in connection with Ireland for being instrumental in the apprehending of Roger Casement and for the subsequent campaign to secure his execution through the use of the Black Diaries. It was said, at the time of Casement's arrest, that Scotland Yard had in its possession a diary in Casement's handwriting of indecent experiences. And these indecent experiences would so disgust any right minded Irishman that, if they read them, they could not see what Casement did in 1916 in terms of patriotism. Thomson gave a number of accounts of how he acquired the diaries, that made out Casement to be a homosexual pervert, and which led to the desertion of the high profile figures who were attempting to get Casement's death sentence commuted to imprisonment.

The propaganda emanating from Scotland Yard served its purpose and silenced any campaign for a reprieve. But, ironically, Sir Basil Thomson— head of Special Branch and son of the Archbishop of York— was himself caught by a humble bobby in a lewd act with a young prostitute in Hyde Park in 1925, after he had fallen out with his superiors and voiced some criticism of the Police in a book. His claim that he was merely doing research failed to save him and the phrase: 'He who lives by the sword...' comes to mind.

All the same, Basil Thomson knew a thing or two about what had happened in Greece during the Great War.

Thomson, in fact, wrote a very good book about Britain's behaviour in Greece, a book which seems to have been motivated by his distaste for the activities of Allied Intelligence Officers there. Thomson believed that the Intelligence Services were responsible for painting a picture, in the Allied capitals, of a situation that did not really exist in Greece. And in acting on such information the Allied Statesmen justified a blockade and an invasion of the neutral country, that led to the deposition of its head of State.

Basil Thomson's reasoning, that Allied Intelligence in Greece was primarily responsible for what happened to that country, is not one I would entirely subscribe to. Spies are flies on the wheels of state, at any rate, more so than Foreign Ministers. The British State had the power to take or leave the reports of its network of spies and more often than not it left them. But I would say that, in Greece, the true nature of the Allies' Great War emerged, even though the British State, through its Intelligence Services and communications/ propaganda infrastructures, did everything to minimise information about this to the outside world.

Thomson's book is called *The Allied Secret Service In Greece* (1931) and in the early pages he describes the political situation in Greece at the start of the European War:

"Greece was in a state of internal peace which has been rare in her history. In 1913 she had emerged victorious from two consecutive Balkan wars in which her King had led her so successfully in the field that her territory had been greatly enlarged. But her people were war-weary, and since the quarrel between Austria and Serbia seemed in no way to concern them, their feeling was for a neutrality benevolent toward England and France. Their sympathies were with the Allies, and if the vital interests of Greece required the sacrifice, the great majority of people were resolved that their country should range herself on the side of the Allies... Not a voice was raised in favour of the Central Powers. No individual Greek could have been described as pro-German, for all the Greek material interests were linked with one or other of the Allied countries." (*The Allied Secret Service in Greece*, p. 37.)

It was at this time that differences between the King and his Premier began to emerge. Prime Minister Venizelos argued for an unqualified and unconditional Greek entry into the War on the side of the *Entente*, arguing that there was no time to lose — since the War would last less than a month. Venizelos wanted to use the War to advance Greek interests against the Turks and he seemed to be aware of the British plans to extend the conflict to the Ottoman Empire, even though it was neutral at this time. (Churchill was forming a plan to involve the Greek Army in a naval attack on the Dardanelles at this moment and this seems to have been communicated to Venizelos.)

King Constantine was himself predisposed to the Allies but he believed that it was in the interests of Greece that she remained neutral in the European War. He felt that the newly enlarged Greek State required a period of consolidation, and not war, if it were to incorporate and develop the new territories and peoples it had acquired in the course of the Balkan Wars.

He believed that Turkey and Bulgaria, the two countries which had issues with Greece regarding territory that the Greeks had prised off them in the Balkan wars, would ultimately join the Central Powers. And he determined to keep Greece out of conflict with them, if at all possible. Also, the King was well aware of the situation of the million or more Greeks inhabiting Constantinople and other parts of the Ottoman Empire, whose position would be made very difficult in the event of a full-scale conflict between Greece and Turkey.

But Venizelos did not hold this view and as soon as the War broke out he began to agitate for Greek participation in it for the purposes of further expansion of the Greek State. Thomson relates:

"It was not long before the restless spirit of Venizelos began to chafe at the inaction of neutrality... Actually, before the middle of August, without the knowledge of the King or any of his colleagues, he had asked each of the Allied Ministers in Athens whether, if Greece were to go to the aid of Serbia and attack Bulgaria, she would be regarded by the Allied countries as one of themselves... M. Venizelos called upon Sir Francis Elliot and M. Deville and offered them the services of the Greek army without conditions. On this occasion the reply was prompt; the Allies thanked the Greek Government, but declined the offer because they thought it undesirable that the war should spread into the Balkans." (*The Allied Secret Service in Greece*, p. 42.)

At this point in the War, England did not require the military services of Greece. Britain foresaw a short war — over by Christmas, or certainly by Spring,

1915—in which her new Expeditionary Force on the left flank of the French would complete the encirclement of Germany in conjunction with the 'Russian steamroller'. The Royal Navy would do the rest. Her other expeditionary forces in Africa and Asia would grab the parts of the world adjacent to the Empire's current territory. In the context of the Great War, the Balkans served merely as a detonator and England did not want the complication of Balkan allies demanding parts of the Ottoman Empire which she herself coveted. So Venizelos was rebuffed.

And, for another thing, King Constantine's benevolent neutrality was aiding the Serbs in a number of ways, including the provision of artillery shells and financial services, aid that was enabling them, unexpectedly, to hold off the Austrians.

### The Allies And Venizelos

G. F. Abbott wrote a number of well informed books at this time on the Balkan region, including *Greece And The Allies 1914-1922*. (The *Preface* to this book is by Admiral Kerr, the Commander-in-Chief of the British Naval Mission to Greece.) In this 1922 book G. F. Abbott gives the following estimation of the differences between Constantine and Venizelos:

> "King Constantine, a practical soldier, estimated that the European War would be of long duration and doubtful issue: in this battle of giants he saw no profit for pygmies, but only perils. At the same time he did not forget that Greece had in Bulgaria and Turkey two embittered enemies who would most probably try to fish in troubled waters. If they did so he was prepared to fight; but to fight with a definite objective and on a definite military plan which took into account the elements of time, place, and resources.
>
> The King's standpoint was shared by most Greek statesmen and soldiers of note: they all, in varying degrees, stood for neutrality, with possible intervention on the side of the Entente at some favourable moment. But it did not commend itself to his Premier. Caution was foreign to M. Venizelos's ambitious and adventurous temperament. Military considerations had little meaning for his civilian mind. Taking the speedy victory of the Entente as a foregone conclusion, and imbued with a sort of mystical faith in his own prophetic insight and star, he looked upon the European War as an occasion for Imperialist aggrandizement which he felt Greece ought to grasp without an instant's delay." (*Greece And The Allies 1914-1922*, pp.11-12.)

Venizelos had begun his career as an obscure lawyer from Crete, before becoming a liberal politician; he took part in the rebellion there in 1897, which began a war with Turkey in which the Greeks were defeated. But he made a name for himself by helping to construct, with British assistance, the alliance between Greece, Bulgaria and Serbia-Montenegro in 1912, the alliance that engineered (with David Bourchier) the First Balkan War, resulting in Turkey's expulsion from practically all of Europe.

150

Through this war, Greece finally took control of Crete, Southern Macedonia, part of Thrace, the Aegean Islands and the Aegean Sea. Particularly significant was the Greek occupation of Chios and Mitylene, two islands that guarded the approaches to the chief Anatolian port of Smyrna. Thanks to this war, Venizelos doubled the Greek territory and population in just a year. King Constantine, who was to become Venizelos's great adversary, was also prominent in this war, leading the triumphant Greek Army into Salonika.

The difference between Constantine and Venizelos was that, whereas the King believed in consolidating the expanded Greek State, the Prime Minister had bigger ideas and unlimited ambitions, on the lines of a new Byzantium.

The very qualities that made Venizelos very dangerous to the Greek national interest endeared him to England. Apparently Venizelos told Colonel Metaxas, of the Greek General Staff:

> "I know that my proposal is rash, but I insist upon it because I have every confidence in my star.' (*Greece And The Allies 1914-1922*, p. 48.)

Here is a view of Venizelos's positive irredentist virtues from Ronald Montague Burrows, Professor of Greek and Principal of King's College London, (a prominent figure in England's designs on Greece):

> 'The party leaders of pre-Venizelish Greece, who have come to life again to back the King's policy, have not only proved themselves incompetent to carry through the ideal of a Greater Greece, but do not possess the ideal at all. Just as they felt no thrill when Venizelos aimed at gathering the Greeks of Asia Minor under the flag, so in their heart of hearts they care not at all for securing the maritime power of Greece by alliance with England and France... It is because the future of Greece lies with Venizelos, that we are justified in asking Greece to take the risk." (*The New Europe*, 9th November 1916.)

The Greek War of Independence (1821-1829) had the effect of separating large sections of Greeks from the new Greek State. That, like the original Italian case, presented the possibility of future Greek irredentist claims on parts of Turkey, and this had the effect of creating a natural antagonism with the Ottoman Turks. The Greeks were spread right across the Ottoman Empire; from Greece itself, across the islands in the Aegean, to Constantinople, Asia Minor, and the Middle East. The Greek contribution to the Ottoman Empire was substantial and the Greek communities prospered in many areas of commerce, shipping, language and culture; they also enjoyed privileged positions with the *Porte*. But the division between the free Greeks and the large communities of Greeks still inhabiting parts of the Ottoman Empire had great implications for what happened to Greece between 1915 and 1922, since it inspired the dream of a 'Greater Greece' taking in territories in Asia Minor at that point belonging to the Turks.

Owing to Greece's geographical position, her existence—and potential expansion—depended on the Powers who controlled the Mediterranean, as her merchant marine could be destroyed, her islands captured and Athens easily shelled by anyone controlling the Sea. King Constantine, in refusing the overtures of his brother-in-law, the Kaiser, told him:

> "It is impossible for me to see how I could serve the Emperor by mobilizing my army... The Mediterranean lies at the mercy of the combined British and French fleets. Without being of any use to the Kaiser we should be wiped off the map." (*The Allied Secret Service in Greece*, p. 39.)

But Venizelos decided that the way to build a new Byzantium was to throw in the lot of his country with England, the chief of the great Powers.

An early sign of Venizelos's decision to subordinate Greek interests to those of England was his opposition to King Constantine's desire for a Serbian alliance after the First Balkan War. Constantine calculated that there would be an inevitable falling out between the victors of this war and he wanted to make sure Greece was in the strongest possible position to retain Macedonia against Bulgarian attack in a future conflict. But Venizelos, who was aware that Britain wanted a permanent Balkan Alliance as a buffer against German commerce, opposed the Serbian Alliance, against the Greek national interest. Constantine's foresight enabled the Greeks to win the Second Balkan War.

However, Venizelos argued that Greece would never again be presented with an opportunity like the European War to achieve its irredentist programme—the chance of fighting with so many powerful allies to gain a 'Greater Greece' in Asia Minor. Constantine, being a trained military man, realised such a venture would be extremely unwise and, unlike his Prime Minister, he listened to military advice on deciding on military matters. The Chief of the General Staff, General Metaxas, who had been involved in compiling a report on taking and holding Western Asia Minor during the Balkan Wars, believed that such an enterprise would be beyond the Greek Army. (The General concluded that, since the basis of a Greek colonial venture would be the mild and refined commercial classes of Greeks and Armenians in the vicinity of the town of Smyrna, who were surrounded by seven million hardy Turkish peasants, the long term prospects of survival of such a colony were not good.) So Constantine informed the *Entente* that, in line with his policy of 'benevolent neutrality', he would not fight Turkey unless she attacked Greece.

When the Allies asked again in November, 1914, upon Turkey's entry into the War, whether Greece would aid the Serbians, Venizelos decided to decline. The Premier had altered his attitude, because he realised by then that the War was not going to be an affair of three weeks, and it was better to wait and see how circumstances developed.

Despite this rejection, England violated Greek neutrality on the first day of the War on Turkey by occupying the harbours of three Greek islands in the vicinity of the Straits. In justifying this action, Britain came up with a very ingenious argument. It said that, since these islands had been taken by Greece from Turkey in the Balkan Wars, they were formally still part of the Ottoman Empire. So there was no violation of neutrality, there was simply a conquest of enemy territory.

### The Greeks And The Dardanelles

On 24th April, 1915 the *Freeman's Journal* presented a strategic view of the Allied landings at Gallipoli:

"The reports from the Dardanelles are somewhat conflicting. One feature is common to all of them — that the British and French land expedition has arrived and appears to have landed from the Aegean Sea... When the first attack on the Dardanelles was made the allies apparently believed that they would have the assistance of Greece to conduct their land campaign. It seemed appropriate that the Balkan States should be the power to drive the Turks out of Europe. The forcing of the Dardanelles was feasible with the combined land and naval operations. The intervention of the King of Greece and the change of Ministry put an end for the time being to the hope of the Balkan States undertaking the clearing out of the Turks. It was impossible to abandon the attack on the Dardanelles, for it would be an admission of defeat that would have had a serious effect all around the Aegean Sea and in the Mediterranean. It has therefore been decided to go on with the work, though the advance to the Black Sea has itself all the magnitude of a big war...

It has been said that the operations in the Dardanelles are subsidiary to the Great War. That is true in the technical sense. The main operations and the main purpose of the war are those directed against Germany from France and Belgium. But the opening of the Dardanelles and the Bosphorus is a vital issue in the war. It will be the defeat of Turkey. Turkey has been powerful as a defender of Germany's eastern frontier. We have frequently called attention to the powers of resistance unexpectedly displayed by Austria... Austria has saved the German southern flank during the past seven months against the Russian advance. The Russians had been unable to bring their full forces into play because of the shortages of ammunition. The opening of the Dardanelles will enable Russia to bring out vast resources and men to bear against Germany in Silesia. This will be as decisive a blow against Germany as any that could be struck against the western frontier. With Russia equipped in munitions and the material necessary for the vigourous prosecution of her campaign, the military problem in the west will be in great measure solved. Russia's vast resources in food and raw material will at the same time be set free for the use of the allied armies in France as well as the people at home in these islands. The impression on the Balkans that a defeat of Turkey must cause will be all for the good. The attacks on the Dardanelles are therefore a vital issue in the war, necessary for the success of the operations in France and in Poland and in Silesia."

The statement in *The Freeman* that 'the allies apparently believed that they would have the assistance of Greece to conduct their land campaign' points to the offer made by England to Venizelos in January 1915.

Assuming the Greek Premier could deliver Greek participation in the War, Edward Grey offered him the vague promise of 'important territorial concessions in Asia Minor' in return for military assistance. Britain thus attempted to draw Greece into the Great War on irredentist grounds, as it was to do with Italy four months later.

Crawfurd Price in a 1915 book, *Light On The Balkan Darkness*, attempted to restore a degree of sense into the view of Greek affairs that was developing in England, where War propaganda was making neutrality an impossibility. He pointed out the salient fact that it was the decision to make war on Turkey that had transformed the situation in the Balkans and made Venizelos into a man of destiny for Britain—and at the same time massively raised the stakes for Greece:

> "The extension of the arena of war to the Middle East was of vital moment to Greece. A great struggle was to be fought on a territory largely peopled by Greeks, the Turks were to be driven from the capital whence the national Church had been governed for centuries, and probably also from lands historically, ethnographically, and ethnologically Hellene. The issue had developed from a simple question of the expediency of assisting friendly Powers into a direct challenge to Greece to enter the conflict or lose, possibly for ever, all claim to her great heritage in Asia Minor. In the opinion of this remarkable man the hour of destiny had struck. He felt that the time had arrived for Greece to take such action as would plant her in Asia Minor and bring into the fold some 4,000,000 Hellenes of Ottoman nationality. He subordinated the dangers which he had hitherto realized might arise from hostile neighbours to the vastness of his political outlook. He deemed that the mere right of representation at the Peace Conference justified the risks attendant upon intervention. Therefore, presuming the division of Turkey-in-Asia among the Entente Powers, he seized on the suggestions of territorial compensation which had been put forward by Sir Edward Grey in January and went to King Constantine with a proposal that an expeditionary corps of 40,000 Greek soldiers should be dispatched to the Dardanelles. He subsequently reduced the number to 15,000." (*Light On The Balkan Darkness*, p.90-1.)

Grey's offer excited Venizelos's imagination; the Greek Premier attempted to flesh out the detail for the King (without Grey's assent), arguing that Greece should cede Cavalla (in Eastern Macedonia) to the Bulgarians, provided the Bulgars immediately joined the Allies. Venizelos was aware that the King and General Staff were concerned that Greece could be attacked by the Bulgarians whilst her army was off fighting elsewhere. However, the King was totally against the ceding of Cavalla to the Bulgarians. It was the richest agricultural province within the Greek State and it had been hard won, from the Turks, in the Balkan Wars. Venizelos suggested to the King in Memoranda that trading Cavalla to the Bulgarians for a hundred times that amount of territory in Asia Minor would be good business. And he argued that the Greek inhabitants of Cavalla could be used as colonists in Anatolia and could be employed, with the local Greeks, to maintain order in the future Asia Minor colony.

Commenting on Venizelos's *Memoranda to the King* urging Greek participation in the War, the American war correspondent, Paxton Hibben, wrote:

"As political documents Venizelos's two memoranda to King Constantine are without precedent in history. He transplants the populations of whole provinces; he outlines Bulgaria's probable future course as if he himself were directing it; Serbia is moved about like a pawn on a chessboard; he disposes of the armies of the Entente as if he were their commander-in-chief; and brushes aside as a mere detail the administrative difficulties of Ottoman territory double the size of present Greece. Throughout he writes with the exaltation of one carried away by a great enthusiasm; 'an opportunity furnished by Divine Providence to realize our most audacious national ideals'is his phrase. Moral considerations in favor of the action he supports appear only parenthetically in his first memorandum; they disappear altogether in the second. His whole argument is that Greece will again be doubled in size,—quadruple what she had in 1912,—and the tone of the memoranda is that of a man who has been taken up into a high mountain and shown the world, and has chosen the world." (*Constantine I And The Greek People,* 1920, p.19.)

Venizelos calculated that, under his scheme, Greece would double her territory and add another million to her population. But the General Staff still refused to have anything to do with it, seeing it as the utmost madness.

The *Freeman's Journal,* apparently in the know, reported this on April 5th 1915:

"M. Venizelos expresses the conviction that the sacrifice of Kavalla would be the means of doubling the extent of the present Greek kingdom, and proceeds to sketch the extent of territory which would be ceded to Greece in Asia Minor... These territories exceed in area 125,000 square kilometres...

As regards population, while Greece would be ceding 30,000 inhabitants she would be claiming more than 800,000 in Asia Minor.

M. Venizelos consequently urges the abandonment of all hesitation, inasmuch as an occasion like the present may never recur, and adds—'If we do not participate in the war we shall, whatever be the result of the same, undoubtedly definitely lose Asia Minor. If the *Triple Entente* is victorious these powers will divide between them or even with Italy not only Asia Minor but the remainder of the whole of Turkey... The general evolution of events coupled with the proposals made to Greece is proof that certain powers repose confidence in us, and consider Greece an important factor in the reorganisation of the East, and that at the moment of the collapse of the Ottoman Empire these powers would furnish us with financial and diplomatic means in order to enable us to face the difficulties which a sudden increase of territory would entail.'"

All this talk of conquest involving transfer of land and uprooting of people on a gigantic scale passed without comment from *The Freeman's Journal.*

The Allied naval assault on the Dardanelles occurred on 19th February 1915. When it was repulsed, the *Entente* Powers realised that, if they wanted the Straits, they would have to come back a second time with a military force. On 1st March Venizelos, without the knowledge or authorization of the King or Cabinet, offered three Greek Divisions to the Allies for the Dardanelles expedition. Even though the King was totally opposed to such an operation, the Premier led the British to believe that he had given his assent to it.

When the Greek General Staff learnt that the Premier had been offering their forces without thought of the military implications, they were furious, and General Metaxas, the Chief of Staff, resigned in protest. They had made a systematic study of the forcing of the Dardanelles and had concluded that such an operation was doomed to failure because of the strengthened Straits defences, the increased efficiency of the Turkish Army under German direction, and the advance warnings already given by the Royal Navy through its earlier attacks.

When the plan to take part in the assault of the Dardanelles was submitted to the Greek Cabinet, Venizelos reduced the proposed Greek commitment to one Division. The Premier was a very persuasive advocate, arguing that the *Entente* would be in Constantinople in a week and it was best not to miss the opportunity. There was some enthusiasm in the Cabinet for adopting his proposal, but the King offered to abdicate if the Cabinet agreed to participate in the venture, saying he would rather step down than sanction a disastrous course that would ruin Greece. The General Staff were very reluctant, believing that the one initial Division would be the first of many, and that, if the Allies got bogged down, the Greeks would be supplying them with cannon-fodder for months, in a hopeless pursuit.

Constantine and the General Staff were proved correct by the events in the Dardanelles over the succeeding months, as the dangerous implications of the Premier's plans became evident. Venizelos, finding his proposal rejected, resigned as Premier on 6th March.

On the day of his resignation, Allied representatives were signing a secret Treaty in London assigning Constantinople to Russia. So the Czar was becoming the arbiter on all questions affecting Constantinople and he placed a veto on the Greek offer of participation, seeing the Greeks as a potential rival for the possession of the Byzantine capital. And, because of the secret nature of this Treaty, the Allied Powers could not communicate its terms to the Greeks. So they had to create a smokescreen around their rejection of Greece's offers of help which involved black propaganda against the King.

Although the British press made a great fuss over Venizelos's fall from power, after the King blocked his proposal to bring Greece into the War, *The Irish News* treated it as an event of no democratic consequence:

"Venizelos announced his permanent retirement from public life; and really nothing in the news from Greece indicates that the people are profoundly concerned."

And it made the following point about the Balkan countries that England was attempting to lure into the War:

"All these Kingdoms are waiting for the issue of the attack on the Dardanelles, which has just been resumed. They know more about the position of affairs in the Straits, the Sea of Marmora, and Constantinople than we have learned in Ireland or Great Britain... and it would be the merest hypocrisy to pretend that Italy, Rumania, Greece, or Bulgaria will fire a single shot because they deem any cause just. They will 'chime in' to guard their own interests, and to lay the foundations to claims to grab something for themselves." (4th April 1915.)

At this point, in mid-1915, there seemed to be a contrast between the Redmondite and Devlinite press in war reporting. The Redmondite *Freeman* was indulging in all manner of Imperial strategic deliberations, making calculations and examining scenarios, imagining itself as a player in the Imperial intrigues that were shaking up the world. But there was a noticeable absence of this kind of thing in *The Irish News*, which still had something of a healthy scepticism toward the Imperialist intrigue in the Balkans. It was clear that the Redmondite press in the South was much more comfortable with the Imperialist reordering of the world than the Home Rulers in the North. And it was as if the Redmondites were rushing headlong into the Imperialist mission whilst the Devlinites retained more of the old world thinking, which made them follow events in a more restrained fashion.

### Britain And Neutral Greece

After the resignation of Venizelos there was a gap of two months before a General Election could be held, owing to the finalising of the electoral rolls in the newly conquered Balkan territories. An interim administration was formed under Gounaris which adhered to the same policy as the previous administration. However, the new Government submitted to the Allies certain proposals, as a basis for discussion concerning the conditions under which Greece might enter the War. The new Government, in conversations with the *Entente*, ascertained that Venizelos had exaggerated the vague territorial offer made by Grey, who, in fact, had only offered Smyrna and its hinterland, rather than large tracts of Anatolia. So the new Greek administration sought clarification of the deal that might be on offer, if Greece decided to enter the War, on a calculation of its own interests.

The Greeks wanted the Allies to guarantee the territorial integrity of Greece after the War; they wanted the dissolution of the Ottoman Empire (to secure any Greek gains in Asia Minor); they wanted to know the exact details of the war materials and finance that would be made available to them, as well as the details of the territorial gains on offer. If these asssurances were provided, the Greeks, Gounaris offered, would fully commit to the War on the Allied side.

But the *Entente* preferred the Venizelos offer—unlimited Greek commitment for undefined objectives, and did not take any notice of the new, more limited, Greek offer.

Constantine and the Cabinet felt they could not allow any ambiguity or uncertainty in their dealing with the Imperialist Powers. George Abbott summarised the position:

> "The Greek position was plain: Greece made proposals which constituted a break with the policy pursued deliberately since the beginning of the war—proposals for an active partnership... There were certain things she could do and, therefore, wished to do. There were certain things she could not do, and must be assured she would not be made to do them. The Entente Powers, on the other hand, would bind themselves to nothing... If you come with us in a courageous forward campaign for the liberation of the world and righteousness, how could we fail to be with you in every question affecting compensations or the integrity of your territories? That's all very fine, said the Greeks. But -"
> (*Greece And The Allies 1914-1922,* pp.89-90.)

It seems to me that the kind of blank cheque England was expecting from the Greeks, and which Constantine refused to give them, was what Redmond gave England in August 1914 in relation to Ireland and Home Rule. And if the Greeks could have looked into the future, they would have seen what a disastrous bargain they had rejected, and Ireland had accepted.

There is another parallel to Constantine's decision and that is to Poland in 1939. If Greece had unconditionally joined the Allies in early 1915, she would have had Turkey, Bulgaria and the Central Powers marching on Athens with only Allied assurances to protect her. At that time the Allies, owing to their war of attrition in the west, could not field enough men to capture the Dardanelles, or even aid Serbia, so it was most unlikely that they could have assisted Greece. And Greece would probably have gone the way of Poland in September 1939, who, fortified by the British guarantee, felt confident enough to take on the Germans, and then found her Allies were not forthcoming and their guarantees worthless.

Just after Constantine's offer was made, there was good reason to show why great care was required in dealing with the Imperialist Powers. Serbia, the ally, and Greece, neutral, found out that the *Entente* had already made formal offers of parts of their territories to Bulgaria to encourage her into the War. In the case of 'gallant Serbia' this was an outrageous stab in the back, because it was, supposedly, for her integrity that the *Entente* had gone into the European War. And in the case of Greece, the *Entente* was offering pieces of the territory of a neutral state, and a friendly one at that, to which naturally they had no claim, to another State that had always inclined toward the enemy

(England always had a much higher opinion of the Bulgars as fighters than of the Greeks).

That knowledge brought the relations of the *Entente* Powers with the Gounaris Government to an end.

The effect of the Venizelist offers was to create a situation whereby Venizelos began to regard himself alone as representing the national will of Greece and the *Entente* to regard Venizelos alone as synonymous with the national will of Greece. According to George Abbott:

> "It was impossible for M. Venizelos to admit that others besides himself might be actuated by patriotic as well as by personal motives... His egoism was of that heroic stature which shrinks from nothing. His nature impelled him to this labour; his privileged position as the particular friend of the Entente supplied him with the means.
>
> M. Venizelos had taken a long stride towards that end when he insinuated that King Constantine's disagreement with him was due to German influence. Henceforth this calumny became the cardinal article of his creed, and the 'Court Clique'a society for the promotion of the Kaiser's interests abroad and the adoption of the Kaiser's methods of government at home... M. Gounaris, though in name a Prime Minister, was in reality a mere instrument of the sovereign's personal policy—so were the members of the General Staff—so was, in fact, everyone who held opinions at variance with his own; they all were creatures of the Crown who tried to hide their pro-Germanism under the mask of anti-Venizelism. Their objections to his short-sighted and wrong-headed Asiatic aspirations—objections the soundness of which has been amply demonstrated by experience—were dictated by regard for Germany, the patron of Turkey. Their offers to fight for the dissolution of Germany's protégé were not genuine: the conditions which accompanied them were only designed to make them unacceptable. The Entente should beware of their bad faith and learn that M. Venizelos was the only Greek statesman who could be trusted...
>
> England was much annoyed by the Greek Government's hesitations, which she attributed to King Constantine's opposition, and asked herself whether she could even then or in the future treat with a country governed autocratically... they ceased to have any eyes, ears, or minds of their own; they saw and heard just what M. Venizelos willed them to see and hear, and thought just how M. Venizelos willed them to think...
>
> Hence, every proposal made to the Entente by M. Venizelos's successors was rejected. Greece was kept out of the Allies camp, and Servia was sacrificed. For it should be clearly understood that the fate of Servia was decided in the months of June and July 1915, not only by the development of the Germano-Bulgarian plan, but also by the failure of all co-operative counter measures on the part of the Serbs, Greeks and Entente Powers while time was still available."
> (*Greece And The Allies 1914-1922*, pp.47-8.)

And all this was to have disastrous effects for Greece seven years later when Venizelos was gone and her armies were stretched across Anatolia.

## The Allies' Bulgarian Bribes

On August 3rd 1915, the Allies passed a note to the Greek Government calling on them to cede Eastern Macedonia to Bulgaria, on a promise of compensation in Asia Minor. This was an eleventh hour bribe to keep the Bulgarians out of the ranks of the Central Powers, by offering them part of a country the Allies had no jurisdiction over—friendly Greece. After the First Balkan War, the Balkan Alliance fell out over the spoils; Bulgaria, which had done most of the fighting against the Turks, had been defeated in the Second Balkan War and its newly acquired territory divided up by its former Serb, Rumanian and Greek allies. The Serbs and Greeks grabbed Macedonia between them at the close of that war, excluding the Bulgarians, who had a majority around Salonika and Cavalla. So it was well known by the *Entente* that the main thing that would get Bulgaria into the War was a promise of a recovery of parts of Macedonia and some other territories at the expense of the Greeks and Serbs.

The Allies tried to enlist Bulgaria into the War first, but a problem arose. In May 1915 the Serbian leadership discovered the details of the secret *Treaty of London,* whereby Italy was promised large areas on the Adriatic Coast (that the Serbs had their eye on for a Greater Serbia) in return for their entry into the War. This prevented Britain from offering any other Serbian territory to Bulgaria in order to bribe her into the War.

In September 1915 Bulgaria mobilised her army, signalling her intent to join the Central Powers.

The Allied Ministers let it be known that, if Greece refused to hand over Cavalla to the Bulgarians, pressure would be brought to bear; to demonstrate this was no idle threat the Royal Navy began to detain Greek shipping in a harassing manner, to show what was in store for the country if it resisted.

Constantine held his ground. However, the Greek King's refusal to surrender territory for a Bulgarian bribe increased the Allied pressure on Greece.

Venizelos was returned to power in August 1915 after the resignation of Gounaris. The Greek public were unaware of the manoeuvring that the ex-Premier had been doing behind the scenes with the Allies and saw him as the representative of a neutral Government, in unity with the King. But Venizelos viewed the result as a mandate for whatever policy he wished to pursue and bided his time.

The dispute over Greek neutrality between Venizelos and the King was seemingly patched up when Venizelos returned as Prime Minister, having accepted to serve in the Government under a policy of neutrality. The publication of the Allied demand for Eastern Macedonia had produced a wave of indignation in Greece and Venizelos would have found it very difficult to openly advocate joining the War at this point and remain in power. Despite advocating the very policy the Allies were now demanding of Greece, he dared not endorse it publicly and it seemed as if he had bowed to the King's wisdom in affairs of State.

### Venizelos's Invitation And Allied Intervention

*The Irish News* reported the situation on 23rd September 1915, but began to suggest that there was an inevitable pull of irredentist character on Greece entering the War on the side of the Allies:

> "M. Venizelos was triumphantly returned to power some months ago in the face of the King's avowed opposition to his policy, and a sort of compromise was arranged on the 'neutral'principle. There are reasons for believing that the first naval attack on the Dardanelles was undertaken on the assumption — if not definite understanding — that the Greek Army would march toward Constantinople while the warships operated in the Straits... All Greece's ambitions are centred in the demolition of the Turkish Empire. Territories historically connected with Hellas since the days of her ancient glory are still under the Ottoman flag."

The event that encouraged *The Irish News* into thinking like this was the Greek mobilisation in response to the mobilisation of the Bulgarian Army. After the Bulgarians had begun to mobilise, Venizelos urged the King to enter the War on the side of the *Entente*, using his election as a sign of the popular will. The King agreed to mobilise the Greek Army in response to the Bulgarian mobilisation but refused to go any further than a position of armed neutrality.

At the start of the European War the question of Greece's stance in relation to Serbia had emerged. Greece had a mutual defence Treaty with Serbia, thanks to King Constantine's efforts between the First and Second Balkan Wars. There were those in the *Entente* who hoped this Treaty would bring Greek assistance to the Serbs but in fact the Treaty provided for Greek assistance to Serbia, and vice-versa, only in relation to a Bulgarian attack. When Austro-Hungary declared war on Serbia, Greece saw herself as having no obligations to the Serbians, unless Bulgaria entered the war against Serbia as well. So King Constantine declared benevolent neutrality in the conflict.

However, in late August 1914, Constantine made an offer to the Allies of aiding the Serbians with 180,000 men, on strict condition that this army was not used anywhere other than in the immediate theatre of war, so that, in the event of a Bulgarian attack, it could be pulled back to defend Greece.

Bulgaria was neutral at this point, but one of Constantine's concerns was that a Greek mobilisation would provoke a parallel Bulgarian mobilisation and an alliance of Sofia with the Central Powers. Britain had the same concern, but was secretly making plans for an offer of territory, at the expense of Greece and Serbia, to gain the Bulgarians as part of the Allies. So the King's offer was turned down by Edward Grey.

According to the 1913 Treaty Convention between Greece and Serbia, the

Serbs were required to supply 150,000 troops in the event of a conflict with Bulgaria. Under an annex to the Treaty the two armies were to form a line facing north-east, with the Serbs taking the north flank and the Greeks the south. If one of the parties failed to take up their position, the overall stipulations of the Treaty were deemed to fall. But overall, the Treaty was meant to defend Macedonia from Bulgarian attack and never envisaged to deal with a conflict with the Austro-Hungarians, or indeed a World War.

Throughout late 1914 and the early part of 1915 when the *Entente* were trying to induce the Greeks to march to the aid of Serbia, and offering them Ottoman territory as an inducement to do so, the Greeks pointed out that they could not send their army to the north, leaving Salonika open to attack from Bulgaria, whereas, if they stayed put, Bulgaria was unlikely to move. The Greeks urged the Serbs to abandon their line on the Danube, which was getting dangerously exposed, and to join them on a line against Bulgaria, which would activate the Treaty of 1913. But the Serbs, under pressure from the Allies, declined.

With the Serbians fighting on the Danube line the Greeks were in no position to supply their contingent. So Venizelos sought to use the Convention in another way to end Greek neutrality. The Premier, without the knowledge of the King or Cabinet, contacted the *Entente* in private, inquiring if they were willing to make up the Serbian contribution with French or British troops. The Allies, seeing an opportunity to break the Greek neutral status, replied immediately that they would send 150,000 soldiers. When King Constantine got wind of what was happening, he warned Venizelos of the consequences of the violation of Greek neutrality, particularly since the activation of the Convention was only supposed to come into effect in the event of war with Bulgaria—and Bulgaria was still neutral. He argued that the landing of *Entente* troops in Greece was most likely to be the provocation that would bring the Bulgarians into the war. The Premier communicated the King's views to the *Entente* governments and that seemed to be that.

But the *Entente* still despatched an army to Salonika—in spite of the Greek Government's wishes. Even Professor Burrows disapproved of this opportunism, describing the claim made by Government Ministers in the British House of Commons, that their forces were in Greece by invitation, as a fiction:

"What Venizelos did, on September 23, 1915, was to ask the English and French Ministers whether, in case Bulgaria declared war on Greece, and Greece, standing by her treaty, asked Serbia to provide the 150,000 men stipulated for in that treaty, France and England would undertake Serbia's obligation for her. Forty-eight hours later, an answer came from France and England that they would be ready to undertake this obligation. Venizelos at once reminded Sir Francis Elliot, the British Minister, that he had only asked a question, and that the conditions under which it would become a request were not yet fulfilled. In the meantime, however, the

English and French Governments proceeded with plans for the landing of troops without further ado, and, on October 2nd announced the fact to Venizelos." (*The New Europe,* 9th November 1916.)

Burrows was supported by Compton Mackenzie, a British Intelligence Officer in Greece, who described the affair as an example of Edward Grey's Whig 'capacity for self-deception':

> "I call it self-deception but of course it is really an example of Whig mentality. Sir Francis Elliot... was contemplating putting an end to his diplomatic career by asking to be recalled rather than be the mouthpiece of such Whiggish self-righteousness." (*Greek Memories*, p.152.)

The reason why these anti-Constantine figures were appalled at Grey's 'capacity for self-deception' was because they understood the negative effect such claims would have with the Greek people, regarding the position of Venizelos.

Professor Burrows believed that England should simply have invaded Greece under Article VIII of the Protocol of 1830:

> "No troops belonging to one of the contracting Powers shall be allowed to enter the new Greek State without the Consent of the two other Courts who signed the Treaty."

Since England, France and Russia had been the contracting Powers of Greek independence, they had the right to overrule that independence indefinitely, according to the Professor. Here was casuistry called in to mask the exigencies of policy. The dethronement of the monarch was advocated not because it was lawful but because it was required as a war necessity by England and France.

Venizelos himself protested in a telegram to London that his question had been improperly turned into an invitation — but he did so with a winking eye. And he then proceeded to announce in the Greek Parliament, with the knowledge that *Entente* forces were on their way, his belief that Greece should fight Turkey, Germany and Austria as well as Bulgaria, under the terms of the 1913 Treaty.

### Britain And The Greek Constitution

Venizelos's virtual declaration of war in Parliament was entirely contrary to the Greek Constitution, which laid it down that declarations of war and conclusions of peace were solely Crown prerogatives.

In Britain it was pretended that it was King Constantine, the 'agent of the Kaiser', who had acted unconstitutionally in dismissing the Venizelos Government. Venizelos went along with that fiction, even though he knew better, and it is in numerous British accounts of the affair. But Article Thirty-One of the Greek Constitution, that was given to Greece by Britain and France, stated: 'The King appoints and dismisses his Ministers.' Article Ninety-Nine stated that 'No foreign army may be admitted to the Greek service without a special law, nor may it sojourn in or pass through the state.' It was also part of the Greek system that the King's consent was required before the Constitution could be amended.

George Abbott, in the following passage, explains why, under the Greek system of government, the King acted both constitutionally and rightly, and the great democrat, Venizelos, acted the autocrat in over-stepping the limitations placed on a Minister of the Crown by the Constitution:

"This action, it was alleged, violated the spirit, though not the letter, of Constitutional Law, because the dissolved Chamber represented the will of the people. But, the other side retorted, it was precisely because there was ground for believing that the Parliamentary majority had ceased to represent the will of the people that the King proceeded to a dissolution; and in so doing he had excellent precedent. His father had dissolved several Chambers (specifically in 1902 and 1910) on the same ground, not only without incurring any censure, but earning much applause from the Venizelist Party. In fact, the last of those dissolutions had been carried out by M. Venizelos himself...

... the whole case of M. Venizelos against his Sovereign rested, avowedly, on the theory, improvised for the nonce, that the Greek Constitution is a replica of the British — a monarchical democracy in which the monarch is nothing more than a passive instrument in the hands of a Government with a Parliamentary majority. It is not so, and it was never meant to be so. The Greek Constitution does invest the monarch with rights which our Constitution, or rather the manner in which we have for a long time chosen to interpret it, does not. Among these is the right to make or to refrain from making war. That was why M. Venizelos in March, 1915, could not offer the co-operation of Greece in the Dardanelles enterprise officially without the King's approval, and why the British Government declined to consider his semi-official communication until after the King's decision. Similarly M. Venizelos's proposals for the dispatch of Entente troops to Salonica in September, so far as that transaction was carried on above-board, were made subject to the King's consent. Of course, if the King exercised this right without advice, he would be playing the part of an autocrat; but King Constantine always acted by the advice of the competent authority — namely, the Chief of the General Staff. In truth, if anyone tried to play the part of an autocrat, it was not the King, but M. Venizelos. His argument seemed to be that the King should acquiesce in the view which a lay Minister took of matters military and in decisions which he arrived at without or in defiance of technical advice.

In this again, M. Venizelos appears to have been inspired by British example. We saw during the War the responsibility for its conduct scattered over twenty-three civil and semi-civil individuals who consulted the naval and military staffs more or less as and when they chose, and the result of it in the Gallipoli tragedy. We saw, too, as a by-product of this system, experts holding back advice of immense importance because they knew it would not be well received. The Reports of the Dardanelles Commission condemned this method. But it is to a precisely similar method that the Greek General Staff objected with such determination. 'Venizelos,' they said, 'does not know anything about war. He approaches the King with proposals containing in them the seeds of national disaster without consulting us, or in defiance of our advice. Greece cannot afford to run the risk of military annihilation; her resources are small, and, once exhausted, cannot be replaced.'The King, relying on the right unquestionably given to him under the terms of the Constitution, demanded from his chief military adviser such information as would enable him to judge wisely from the military point of view any proposal involving hostilities made by his Premier. It was this attitude that saved Greece from the Gallipoli grave in March, and it was the same attitude that saved her a second time at the present juncture. But, in fact, at the present juncture the King acted not so much on his prerogative of deciding about war as on the extreme democratic principle that such decision belongs to the people, and, finding that the Party which pushed the country towards war had only a weak majority, he preferred to place the question before the electorate, to test beyond the possibility of doubt the attitude of public opinion towards this new departure. From whatever point of view we may examine Constantine's behaviour, we find that nothing could be more unfair than the charge of unconstitutionalism brought against it." (*Greece And The Allies 1914-1922,* pp.71-3.)

Under the Greek Constitution the King had the final say on external affairs, and the King demanded the Premier's resignation. A new Government, formed after the resignation of Venizelos, pledged to continue to uphold Greek neutrality—despite the presence of Allied troops on its territory.

Bulgaria then entered the War. The Bulgarians had been determined to hold out to the highest bidder, and the Allies were left with no more cards to play in terms of territorial concessions, so King Ferdinand decided to throw in his lot with Germany to avenge the Second Balkan War. The Bulgarians joined the War in October but then proceeded to concentrate their army against the Serbs and Serbian-occupied Macedonia, respecting Greek neutrality, and insuring that the Greco-Serbian pact did not become operative.

This seemed to disappoint *The Irish News.* The Devlinites had previously acknowledged Greek approval of the King's policy of neutrality, and had viewed Venizelos's scheming as immaterial. But they had built up their hopes that a united Greece would enter the War through the intervention of the Bulgarians on Germany's side. And when the Bulgarians failed to attack Greece and Constantine disappointed them by not using the opportunity to reactivate the Balkan alliance of the Second Balkan War to go to war with Bulgaria and thus enter the conflict against Germany, *The Irish News* rounded on the two Balkan 'small nations':

"These two small nations, Bulgaria and Greece, are helping, actively and passively, the furtherance of German designs in the Balkan Peninsula. Greece owes its liberty and its existence as a sovereign State to Britain, France and

Russia. Each of the three Powers fought for Grecian freedom against the Turks... And now Greece is 'neutral', at best, when Britain, France and Russia are fighting for their lives. The Russians freed Bulgaria. Muscovite blood flowed in torrents that Bulgaria might be emancipated from Turkish rule." (October 30th 1915.)

*The Irish News* was obviously informed by the Irish example. England had—supposedly—given Ireland Home Rule and so there was a debt of honour involved to fight for the liberator for ever—even if the liberator had been the oppressor until very recently.

But Greece and Bulgaria did not feel under the same obligation as Ireland to support their liberators, even though their respective liberators had not been their former oppressors.

### The Salonika Expedition

Britain's use of Irish soldiers to intimidate Greece into the Great War has been all but erased from the Irish memory and the history books. But it remains in a corner of the Irish mind through that musical medium that retained the Irish identity in the years when its eradication was nearly accomplished by those whom the Irish were now fighting for. I suppose if Salonika is known about at all in Ireland it is because of the anti-recruiting ballad of the same name mocking the Irish in British uniform in Macedonia. I think it is of Cork origin and here are a few verses:

Oh me husband's in Salonika, I wonder if he's dead,
I wonder if he knows he has a kid with a foxy head,
So right away, so right away,
So right away Salonika, right away me soldier boy.

When the war is over what will the slackers do,
They'll be all around the soldiers for the loan of a bob or two,
So right away, so right away,
So right away Salonika, right away me soldier boy.

And when the war is over what will the soldiers do,
They'll be walking around with a leg and a half,
And the slackers they'll have two,
So right away, so right away,
So right away Salonika, right away me soldier boy.

They taxed the pound of butter and they taxed the ha'penny bun,
And still with all their tax they can't bate that bloody Hun,
So right away, so right away,
So right away Salonika, right away me soldier boy. Etc, etc.

hat sort of humour obviously would be in very bad taste these days when more respect is demanded for those who served (and serve) in foreign adventures.

166

By the end of 1915 a British (with its Irish contingent) and French army composed of thirteen divisions and 350,000 men had landed at Salonika, in spite of Greek neutrality—even though a similar German violation of Belgian neutrality had supposedly brought Britain to declare war on Germany in the first place. Initially it was claimed that the Allied armies in Salonika were there to fight for the Serbs. But by November 1915 the Serbian front was collapsing. So it made little sense to move forces to the area, where they would be effectively bottled up. So, in Salonika the Allies stayed.

Churchill talks openly about the real purpose of the Salonika expedition in his *World Crisis*, where he states:

"As a military measure to aid Serbia directly, the landing at this juncture of allied forces at Salonika was absurd. The hostile armies concentrating on the eastern and northern frontiers of Serbia were certain to overwhelm and overrun that country before any effective aid, other than Greek aid, could possibly arrive. As a political move to encourage  and determine the action of Greece, the despatch of allied troops to Salonika was justified." (p. 585.)

The Salonika operation which was bolstered by the evacuation of the 10th Division from Gallipoli was mostly about putting pressure on neutral Greece and Rumania. And Asquith, with this threat of force in mind, warned the Greeks and Rumanians of the consequences of their continued neutrality:

"A united Rumania, a united Greece, is possible if these nations can rise to the height of their opportunity. If Greece or Rumania consider Greek Irredenta, or Transylvania, not worth fighting for they will never receive them in the end, for a government and nation which will not risk its life for its enslaved brethren is a government and nation unfit by such cowardice to be given the privilege of ruling over them, even if liberated by other hands." (*Freeman's Journal*, 15th November 1915.)

If that principle, 'if you fight for it,you deserve to have and keep it', was applied generally, it would mean in Ireland that the only group deserving to reincorporate the Six Counties into an Irish State would be the Provisional I.R.A. And Hitler should have been rewarded with Danzig in 1939 and Saddam Hussein would still be in Kuwait. Expediency, however, is the mother of principle for British Statesmen.

To encourage this new principle of international relations, Cyprus, which had been annexed by Britain on the opening day of the War, was offered to the Greeks as a down payment for their help in deposing the German agent (the King) and joining the conflict. But Greece continued to resist temptation and protested at the violation of their neutrality by the Allied armies.

Irredentism is seen universally as a bad thing these days. But it was a positive virtue for Britain in 1915 in waging its War. To fail to be an aggressive nationalist eager for the conquest of all the territory a nation claimed, was tantamount to cowardice—except within Britain's Empire, of course, where it was prone to be treated as mutiny and treason.

*The Freeman's Journal* and the Redmondites in general made no comment on the type of war Ireland had become involved in—a War that was to involve vast Imperialist expansion, irredentist conquest, and presumably, partition, plantation and ethnic cleansing on a massive scale, in this reordering of the East. It just went along with it as part of its Imperial duty, with the recruiting of Irish cannon-fodder to facilitate the grand design of Britain and the Allies— and to get Home Rule, of course. But the Redmondites never considered what would happen to the large Christian populations of Asia Minor if a Greek colonial adventure were to come to grief, not to mention the destabilizing effects of another war in the Balkans. It seems to have been taken for granted in the Redmondite Press that it was inevitable that the Empire, like Rome, could do no wrong.

With an Allied army occupying Salonika, in neutral Greece, *The Irish News* urged Britain to quit pussy-footing around with King Constantine, and his pathetic insistence on Greece neutrality, and show him and his nation who was the master in the world:

> "The Greece which counts—the Greece of the King, the oligarchy, the army, the capitalists and the interested traders—is as hostile to the Allies and their cause as Turkey and Bulgaria are... The King is hypocritical by nature; in the war against Turkey during the 'nineties he was regarded as a coward by the volunteers who left these countries and fought for Greece...
>
> M. Venizelos has 'thrown in the sponge'; he has practically followed the example set in 1797 by Grattan and the other leaders of the Irish Patriot Party in Parliament who took no part in the elections of that year and withdrew from the political scene, leaving the country and the overwhelming majority of its people at the disposal of Pitt, Camden and Castlereagh. We have had bitter experience in this country of an unorganised, leaderless, distracted, and unarmed majority, no matter how 'overwhelming,'against the merest minority who control the power and resources of the State and act unitedly under authoritative guidance in pursuit of a definite object... Perhaps the basis of an understanding with Greece may be discovered even yet, but no one... can believe that any treaty or arrangement made with Constantine and the clique which have, under German direction, smashed the Greek Constitution, defrauded the masses of the people, and established the Kaiser's rule as firmly at Athens as it is in Berlin, will be respected for a moment after the treacherous gang and their Teutonic masters think it can be outraged and broken with safety to themselves. Clearly the hour for resolute action in the Balkan regions—beginning with Greece—has arrived if the Near East is not to be wholly delivered up to the Teutonic Powers for many a month to come." (9th December 1915.)

What is particularly offensive about this editorial is its depiction of Constantine as a 'coward'. It is unlikely that *The Irish News* would have applied the same reasoning to DeValera in 1940 as he exercised Ireland's right to neutrality. But that just goes to show how the Imperialist influence of Home Rule was such a perverting phenomenon.

Clearly, there was little sympathy left in Ireland for neutrals as the 'war for civilisation' hotted up. But *The Irish News* was very badly informed if it believed that the popular will in Greece was for war and a small Royalist clique was holding back the march of a nation. But perhaps that is not surprising given the experiences of Paxton Hibben.

### Paxton Hibben—An American Radical in Athens

Despite the threats from *The Irish News* and their army—the British one—to Greek neutrality, the King stood firm. In January 1916 Constantine reemphasized his policy of 'benevolent neutrality' toward Britain and he requested the Allies to leave Greek territory—since, with Serbia knocked out of the war, they had no purpose in being there. He restrained his Army from defending Greek territory from the Allied occupation forces—perhaps sensibly—and simply requested the invaders to leave.

Churchill explained later why Constantine failed to be intimidated by the landing of allied forces in Salonika (which he refers to as 'allied help'):

"King Constantine had been trained all his life as a soldier. He had studied very closely the strategic situation of his country and conceived himself to be an authority on the subject. The road to his heart was through some sound military plan and this he was never offered by the allies. When he learned that the allied help was to take the form of withdrawing two divisions from the Dardanelles, he naturally concluded that that enterprise was about to be abandoned. He saw himself, if he entered the war, confronted after a short interval not only with the Bulgarians but with the main body of the Turkish Army now chained to the Gallipoli Peninsula. He read in the British and French action a plain confession of impending failure in the main operation whose progress during the whole year had dominated the war situation in the east... He thought it was the beginning of the abandonment of the expedition and would release the whole Turkish Army to reinforce the Bulgarians." (*The World Crisis,* pp. 585-6.)

About this time, the King set forth his views to Paxton Hibben of the Associated Press, including, as he saw it, the infringements of Greek neutrality that the Allies were engaged in. And he appealed to the American public for help in encouraging the Allies to leave.

Hibben's telegraph of the interview, however, was stopped by the British censors and it was only released when the journalist made representations to the U.S. Government. Basil Thomson, the Director of British Intelligence, who obviously knew a lot about these matters from his doings, has this surprisingly honest piece in his book about it:

"Mr. Paxton Hibben's experiences during his mission in Athens are illuminating on the processes by which public opinion was formed in the

169

western countries. He sent frequent circumstantial reports to his newspaper in America, but the version that reached the editor was so meagre and so colourless that the Associated Press found the luxury of keeping a special correspondent in Greece too costly if he could make no better use of his opportunities, and Hibben was recalled... Having to stop in Malta to await a boat he made enquiries and found that many of his dispatches were still piled up in the censor's office untouched; that others had been so thoroughly expurgated of the truth by the British and French censors in turn that what was left was not worth reading. He was indignant and then and there declared his intention of writing a book setting forth the facts about Greece as he knew them. The book was ready in 1917 but watchful eyes were on him. The United States were now moving into the war; the Intelligence Services began to pull the strings and Hibben was prevailed upon to postpone the publication of his book. He volunteered for the American Army and fought in France until the end of the war. His book— Constantine I and the Greek People—appeared in 1920. It was the first independent exposition of what had been going on behind the smokescreen of an over-zealous war propaganda. The author is now dead and the book out of print. It was becoming rare in 1921 when a friend of the writer, who was interested in Greek affairs, obtained a copy in a bookshop in Piccadilly and was told that there were still fifteen copies unsold. A few days later he returned for another copy and was told that the book was sold out—that M. Venizelos, who was then in London, had come in on the previous day and bought up the lot!..." (*The Allied Secret Service in Greece*, pp. 114-5.)

Thomson's account was challenged by another spy in Greece, Compton Mackenzie, during the 1930s. Mackenzie wrote a series of books about his espionage activities in Greece, including *Athenian Memories* and *Greek Memories*. In these publications Mackenzie was critical of Thomson's book and others that were hostile to Venizelos. But Thomson's account is consistent with both of the other major accounts—those of George Abbot and Paxton Hibben—despite their differing political perspectives. And much of Mackenzie's criticisms are in the nature of nit-picking and personal abuse. Wider political understanding certainly was not his strength—instead of pursuing a career in an area of power he became an accomplished and celebrated novelist (of *Whisky Galore* fame).

Compton McKenzie, in his *Greek Memories*, contested Thomson's account of Hibben's treatment at the hands of the Censor. This is the spy's vindication of his version of events with regard to Hibben:

"I showed the drunken little correspondent this censored dispatch myself and warned him time after time that if he persisted in telegraphing such lies the Censorship would mutilate his messages. Yet Sir Basil Thomson states that Hibben did not know his dispatches had been stopped until he found them in the Censor's Office at Malta." (p.257.)

Paxton Hibben was an American war correspondent who arrived in Athens sometime in 1915, and who became a political radical out of his experiences there. When America joined the War he volunteered for the front. And after leaving the U.S. Army in 1919 he went to Ukraine and organised a great humanitarian effort to rescue starving children in the famine of 1921-23, which cost him his life. For his services, the Russians honoured him with a hero's burial in Moscow.

Hibben had intended his interview with Constantine to be ammunition for the Allies in undermining the King's authority. But, despite being a Francophile and Republican, and by inclination opposed to the Royalists in Greece, Hibben became drawn toward the honest patriotism of King Constantine, and was, at the same time, repelled by the behaviour of the 'democrat' Venizelos. His later reports from Greece caused consternation amongst Anglophile Americans and in one Foreign Relations Committee meeting he was accused of being on the pay-roll of King Constantine and of speaking with 'a slight German accent'.

Before the *Foreword* to Paxton Hibben's book on Greece there is a dedication to Constantine which is a useful antidote to *The Irish News's* poison:

> "SIRE! I do not believe in Kings nor in the business of Kings.
>
> But I believe in you, Sir, as a man.
>
> It is therefore not to the King of the Hellenes that I dedicate this book, but to the sincere democrat, the leader and comrade of his people, the brave and able soldier, the loyal friend, the devoted patriot and the generous, open hearted man that I have found you.
>
> Athens, January 25, 1917."

Paxton Hibben has the following analysis of the Salonika expedition, in which the 'Irish' 10th Division played its part:

> "If the expedition was political (and only the chancelleries of London and Paris know what they had in mind in ordering the expedition), calculated to induce the Greeks to enter the war, it was both childish and dishonest; dishonest because it assumed that the Greeks would be led by sentiment to throw themselves into the war at the first appearance of Allied troops on Greek soil, and that, once precipitated thus into the hostilities, they would be compelled to fight it through even to the destruction of Greece, without further help from the *Entente* Powers... The enterprise, if undertaken with the hope of persuading the Greeks to go to war, was childish because it assumed that the Greek Staff would not know an expeditionary force of serious proportions from a handful of armed men—the Greeks who, in the present generation and before the outbreak of the European War, had seen more real war than France and Britain combined.
>
> It is almost impossible to conceive of the adventure as having been seriously undertaken as a military emprise. If so, however, it is perhaps the greatest single folly of the war, not excluding the Dardanelles affair. For the Saloniki adventure involved the possibility of a far worse disaster to the Allied arms

than that of Gallipoli. General Sarrail's troops were saved from destruction when they retired upon Saloniki only by the purely fortuitous circumstance of the presence of friendly Greek troops on both his flanks... had the Greek Staff and the Greek King actually favoured the Germans, as both Mr. Venizelos and the *Entente* press insist with such vehemence is the case, a combined Greco-Bulgarian attack upon Sarrail's retreating army would have meant its capture or its complete annihilation. It was these mad risks that the expedition ran.

There were greater military and moral issues involved in the adventure than the fate of an Allied army of less than 60,000 men. The whole prestige of the *Entente* in the Balkans was at stake. Serbia had been promised help. She did not get it. Serbia and Montenegro were crushed, because the promised help was not brought in time, or indeed, ever. It is of no avail to blame the Greeks. This is not the war of the Greeks; it is the war of the Entente, and the Entente Powers had no business to stake the very life of two of their allies on a mere gamble...

The haphazard manner of planning and pursuing the Dardanelles adventure merely strengthened the Greek Staff in its conviction that the Entente were both badly informed in respect to conditions in the Near East and inclined to take the military problems of the Balkans far too lightly." (*Constantine I And The Greek People*, pp.55-8.)

On January 21st, 1916, the Liberal *Daily News,* which fulminated about the German violation of Belgian neutrality to encourage its pacifist readership to become warmongers, had this to say about the Allied violations of Greek neutrality:

"It is evident that the business-like measures the Allies are taking for their protection on land and sea have inspired the King with lively resentment. That is not altogether astonishing. The conditions under which the Allies are encamped, and will soon be fighting, on neutral soil are an anomaly without parallel in modern warfare, and they involve inevitably an attitude equally anomalous towards the neutrality of Greece. Apart from the occupation of the Salonika zone, her railways have been cut, her bridges blown up, certain of her islands borrowed, and Consuls accredited to her put under arrest. Such facts cannot and need not be disguised. They call for no defence from the Allies, for Greece has no one to thank for them but herself."

That was further evidence of the moral collapse of English Liberalism as its principles were whittled away in the Great War effort.

### Greece—Made in England

On 21st June, 1916, the Allies issued an ultimatum to King Constantine. The Allied Governments stated that they were not demanding an end to Greek neutrality but they put forward demands that, it was thought, would ensure the establishment of conditions under which the Greeks could only do the Allies' bidding.

Under the terms of the ultimatum, the Greek Government had to demobilize their Army immediately and totally, replace the present Cabinet by a new Coalition Ministry to the satisfaction of the Allies, dissolve the legislative Chamber and hold fresh elections, and replace the senior police in Athens with those acceptable to Britain and France. And it was made clear that, if the Greeks did not oblige, Athens would be flattened by the Royal Navy and the King and his family dealt with like Louis XVI.

This ultimatum was backed up by a demonstration of force in Allied occupied Greece. The French General Sarrail, in command of the forces at Salonika, had recommended that the Allies 'strike at the head, attack frankly and squarely the one enemy—the King'. Britain concurred, and on St. Constantine's Day, when Salonika was honouring the King with a *Te Deum*, martial law was proclaimed. Allied detachments with machine guns occupied strategic points, the Macedonian gendarmerie and police were expelled, and the local press was placed under an Allied censor.

On 6th June a blockade of the Greek coasts was established in pursuance of orders from Paris and London and on the 16th, to back up the ultimatum, a squadron was ordered to be ready to bombard Athens, while a brigade was embarked at Salonica for the same destination. Before the guns opened fire, it was planned that hydroplanes would drop bombs on the royal palace; then troops would land, occupy the town, and proceed to arrest, among others, the royal family that the English and French had formerly put on the Greek throne.

Paxton Hibben made the following comment on the ultimatum, comparing it to the Austrian ultimatum to Serbia that had 'produced' the European War:

"Nothing would be gained by seeking to deny that the four demands constituted a very grave interference in the internal affairs of Greece in behalf of Venizelos and his party. The Greek Constitution was to be applicable only where convenient: the cabinet, which constitutionally must be responsible to the people and whose term had expired, was to be dismissed; elections were to be held within the constitutional period, only if the demobilization had 'restored the electoral body to normal conditions'— *in fine*, only if it were evident that Venizelos could carry the country; otherwise, the Constitution was to be suspended and elections were not to be held. The success of the Venizelists in the elections might depend upon having a Venizelist chief of police in office, therefore this also was required.

The latter point recalls Sir Edward Grey's protest to Count Mensdorff against the Austrian demands upon the Serbian Government on July 23, 1914, which were the moving cause of the European War... Quite as effectively as Austria with regard to Serbia, the *Entente* proposed to require the appointment of a chief of police, Colonel Zymbrakakis, devoted to the interests of Venizelos... All that Great Britain complained of in Austria's attitude toward Serbia two years previously, Great Britain was now imposing upon Greece, with a fleet off the Piraeus to back her—all, and more besides." (*Constantine I And The Greek People*, pp. 237-8.)

How was it that a military and naval occupation of over half of Greece, with the imposition of martial law, could be taken as constituting the normal conditions of the electoral body in Greece? and how could demands on the part that was unoccupied to regulate itself to the occupation's satisfaction conform to a notion of democracy?

It was because the *Entente* claimed they had the right to interfere in the internal affairs of Greece due to the Treaty of London (1863-4) between England, France and Russia on the one hand and Greece on the other. This recognised the independence of Greece—but now it was claimed that it also entitled the guarantors of that independence effectively to end it.

England had a long history of interference in the affairs of the Greeks and by 1914 regarded this interference as a matter of routine. Arguing for further interference during 1916, Ronald Montague Burrows, Professor of Greek and Principal of King's College London, noted:

> "As we created Greece at Navarino, so we recreated it in 1863, and the letter of the original guarantee must be construed in the spirit of the Treaty of 1863, and of the interference in the internal affairs of Greece which that Treaty crystallized." (*The New Europe*, 19th October, 1916.)

*The New Europe* was a weekly periodical which sought to develop ideas from various contributors amongst the Allied nations about the type of Europe they would construct after the defeat of the Central Powers. It was founded by R.W. Seton-Watson, a British academic, whose purpose was 'to provide a rallying ground' for those favouring 'European reconstruction on the basis of nationality, the rights of minorities and the hard facts of geography and economics' as opposed to 'the Pan-German project and Berlin-Bagdad'. Those who wrote for it included Masaryk, Benes, Harold Nicolson and Sir Samuel Hoare. So it could be said it was in large part responsible for the Europe between the Wars, which was designed to prevent the growth of a European community based on German commercial power. It succeeded and instead it produced economic collapse, Anti-Semitism, the breeding ground for Hitler, and another World War.

Professor Burrows became adviser on Greek affairs to the British Cabinet and simultaneously to Venizelos during 1915. *The Encyclopaedia Britannica* has this entry for him:

> "He taught at the University of Manchester (1908–13) and was principal of King's College, London, from 1913 to 1920, the period when he devoted much time to modern Greek affairs. His plan for bringing Greece into World War I was adopted by the British Cabinet in 1915. A confidant and adviser to the Greek statesman Eleuthérios Venizelos, he was chosen to be the Greek provisional government's semiofficial representative in London (1916)."

Greece had been part of the Ottoman Empire until the Greek War of Independence in the 1820s. Britain (with Lord Byron) had intervened in this war on the Greeks' behalf in the decisive naval engagement, destroying the Turkish fleet at Navarino, and making a Greek victory possible.

In 1832 the Greeks had wanted a Liberal Republican State but they had been straight-jacketed by a monarchy complete with foreign King by the guarantors who, at that time, not long after the French Revolution, did not want to promote liberal democracies in Europe. So the Greek King, to a great extent, was the representative of the three great Powers of Europe, because his position was derived from their power over Greece, and they were always inclined to believe he should be their man (or not be king at all).

Burrows referred to the fact that the Greek King Otho had been forced to accept a Constitution by Britain and, when he had refused to abide by it, he had been deposed in 1862. In 1863 England put Prince William of Denmark (father of King Constantine) on the throne of Greece and defined the political status of the Greek State as 'a monarchical, independent and constitutional state' in a Treaty with Denmark.

Interestingly, in 1855, at the time of the Crimean War, Greece, under King Otho, was in favour of going to war against Turkey, on the side of Russia. But France and England, who were in alliance with Turkey against Russia, would not allow it. King Otho was told that strict neutrality was the only policy consonant with the interests of Greece. And the Allies landed troops at Athens to compel obedience to their will. The Greek sovereign was put on notice for daring to adopt an independent Greek policy.

Half a century later King Constantine was portrayed in British propaganda as a pro-German for declaring his country neutral. And much was made of the fact that he was the Kaiser's brother-in-law (despite having the same relationship to the British King). But the truth of the matter was that the King had rejected generous German overtures and had, in fact, offered to come into the War on the side of the *Entente* on several occasions—but on certain conditions.

The difference between 1855 and 1915 was that, in the former time, the English and French compelled the Greeks to neutrality whilst in the latter they were attempting to compel the country to make war. In both cases Greece was taken to have no independent existence, or an independent existence only when it suited.

So Professor Burrows, who regarded the Greek State as a creation of England, urged the Government to keep up the tradition of interference, which, he argued, had been given formal status by international Treaty. The Liberal *Daily News* concurred with this view, declaring in its leader of June 23rd 1916 that because England had freed the Greeks at Navarino, drafted their Constitution, and become the country's guarantor, it was 'warranted in taking any measures for the protection of their ward'.

Neither Burrows nor Compton Mackenzie were advocates of the ultimatum. They were more in favour of the British Government putting its money where its mouth was, recalling the Ambassador, and declaring open support for

Venizelos. This course, if Grey had been prepared to take it, would have logically resulted in a Venizelist *coup d'état* and probably Greek civil war. But Grey did not feel predisposed to risking it.

## Lord Carson And Salonika

Professor Burrows, Compton Mackenzie and Sir Edward Carson came together in London during October 1915 to try to organise a renewed effort to get Greece into the War. Mackenzie has an account of it in his book *Greek Memories*:

> "Burrows... suggested that I should have an interview with Sir Edward Carson who had resigned from the Cabinet over the Salonica muddle in October 1915. Burrows told me that he was now inclined to interest himself in the Greek question... I no longer had any hesitation in putting the state of affairs in Greece before Sir Edward Carson. Burrows took me along to the Law Courts where we found Sir Edward Carson in a dark little room, his wig lying on a table beside him. His large swarthy face looked larger and swarthier for the dimness and dinginess of the surroundings. A sombre and impressive figure, he sat there nursing a knee and listening to my appreciation of Greek affairs.
>
> 'Well,' he said in the end, 'I might overthrow the Government over this if matters grow worse in Greece.'
>
> He mentioned the number of members who were ready to vote with him when the time came. I am under the impression it was one hundred and fifty-three, the number of the miraculous draught of fishes.
>
> 'But, Sir Edward,'I went on, 'the situation might develop rapidly at any moment... What is required is a positive assurance that the British Government will support Venizelos...'
>
> 'Well,' said Sir Edward Carson, if you find the situation becoming graver you can communicate with me through Professor Burrows, and I shall probably decide to act.'...
>
> Perhaps if the disastrous events of the First of December in Athens had happened a fortnight earlier Sir Edward Carson would have succeeded in overthrowing the Government without those tortuous negotiations which Lord Beaverbrook relates so vividly in the second volume in *Politicians and the War.*" (*Greek Memories*, pp. 315-7.)

Mackenzie's sentence about 'the disastrous events of the First of December' was a reference to the Battle of Athens of December 1916 when a large force of French and British troops were landed in Athens after the King had protested against the positioning of ten battalions of Allied Artillery on neutral Greek territory. When Greek soldiers drove them off, with over a hundred fatalities to the French and British, a state of official war was only just avoided.

Whilst the Redmondites insisted there was supposed to be a truce over Home Rule during the War, Edward Carson applied his political efforts to undermining the Liberals, who had instigated the Home Rule Bill. His reasoning would have been that, if there were no Home Rulers left in the Government at the close of the War, there would be no Home Rule. At the start of the War, Carson set about agitating for coalition and, when he was made a Minister in the Coalition Government of May 1915, he immediately set about to ensure the end of Asquith, the Prime Minister who had originated the Home Rule Bill, and of the other Liberals who wished to hand over Ireland to Redmond. Churchill was seen off after the Gallipoli fiasco (as were Haldane and Grey) and in October 1915, only four months after joining the Government, Carson resigned from the Coalition using the Dardanelles-Salonika debacle as his opportunity. At the time of Carson's resignation there was extensive speculation about the Unionist leader's reasoning in leaving the Coalition, when this did not appear to be the done thing in war-time. But it became even harder to state the obvious, that Carson was continuing the political struggle over Home Rule when the War on Germany was supposed to be the overriding priority.

The Irish Home Rulers put their faith in British democracy but what went on at Westminster during the War was anything but democratic. The Government's electoral mandate had run out in 1915 and it began preserving itself through a series of internal coups in which power became increasingly concentrated within a small cabal within the Executive. And its political character was totally transformed by these executive coups as the Government began the War as a Liberal one and went into its third year as a Unionist one with a Liberal figurehead.

This Government which preserved itself against the democracy in Britain by avoiding elections, while championing democracy around the world, was the same Government who plotted in Greece against the Greek democracy. And the same administration that the Easter Rising — that great 'undemocratic' event — in Dublin was conducted against.

### The Hunger Blockade of Greece

To save the capital from the guns of the Royal Navy, Constantine complied with the Allied four demands, and a new Ministry, under the leadership of M. Zaimis and with *Ententists* included, was appointed to carry on the administration of the country until the election of a new Chamber. The chief of police was replaced to the Allied satisfaction and the Army began to be demobilised.

The demobilisation of the Greek Army had an immediate effect, as irregular bands of Bulgarians invaded Cavalla. Instead of the Allies resisting this action, the King was condemned for being unwilling to defend his country with his demobilized army, with the suggestion that the Allied Army could do this for him.

In response to the Greek acquiescence to their demands, the Allies lifted the blockade but restricted the importing of foodstuffs into Athens — thereby keeping the people on short rations, with the understanding that they were existing in freedom under Allied sufferance.

The General Election, which the *Entente* demanded through the guns of their battleships, was due to be held in September 1916 and this time the issue was clear. It would have given the Greek people an open choice between neutrality and war (discounting the threat levelled at them from the Royal Navy).

Perhaps it would have been like the Treaty election of 1922 in Ireland, with the Greeks bowing to the threat of force. But we will never know.

Rather than contest the election, Venizelos stole out of Athens with the help of the French Secret Service, went on to Crete, and headed of a rival Greek Provisional government established by the Allies in Salonika. In so doing, he determined that he could only return to Athens with an Allied Army.

On November 19th 1916 the British announced a full blockade of Greece and demanded the withdrawal of Greek troops from Salonika, the handing over of road and rail networks in the area and supply bases in Greek territorial waters.

The Royal Navy blockade of Greece was designed to force Greece into the War, or else to bring about a regime change in Greece that saw Venizelos in charge at Athens, so that he would bring the Greeks into the War.

Charles J. O'Donnell in his book, *The Irish Future With The Lordship Of The World,* made the following comment about the morality of blockading:

> "Infinitely the most inhuman act of war is the blockade, which avowedly is not aimed at soldiers or sailors, but at the aged and the child, the babe and the woman. In the Middle Ages the Catholic Church inflicted the major excommunication on any general who blockaded a town before he had given full opportunity for the withdrawal of women and children. In those uncivilized days there was such a thing as 'the truce of God'." (p.220.)

Blockading was, of course, the main weapon in the armoury of the Royal Navy, Britain's senior armed service. But in international law, including the Declaration of Paris (1856), to which Britain had enthusiastically signed up, contraband was supposed to be confined to enemy materials of war specifically used by its armed forces, and blockading was certainly not to be permitted against civilians. (Contraband of war means the commodities not to be supplied by neutrals to belligerent powers.)

Irene Willis argues that the Liberals, because of their aversion to compulsion, became even greater enthusiasts, and were even more responsible for blockading, than the Tories, who all along advocated *Delenda est Germania.* Here is her reasoning about why this was so and how it came about:

> "'The Triumph Of The Navy'was the trump card of the Liberals throughout the war, displayed by them with immense flourish whenever the military situation was inconclusive... It was this jealous pride in the naval weapon which carried the Liberals so wholeheartedly into the policy of the blockade.

Their anxiety to parade and to make political capital out of the supremacy of the Fleet made them insensible to the legal and moral arguments with which America disputed the British policy of contraband... and consequently, put imports of foodstuffs, even when destined for civilians, into the contraband list." (*England's Holy War*, pp.195-7.)

The blockading of the enemy was one thing, but England, during 1915, began also to stop neutral shipping, and to seize their cargoes as contraband. It defended this by claiming it had the right to seize goods that might find their way to the enemy. Asquith announced the policy to the Commons on March 1st:

"The policy indicated by Mr. Asquith did not... commend itself to neutral opinion, which ranged from mild remonstrance to angry criticism concerning his determination to ignore those 'judicial niceties'which were the accepted principles of international law. The judicial network was an international agreement—the Declaration of Paris—to which England had set her hand and seal, but which she now proposed to violate... That Declaration was subscribed to by Great Britain, France, Austria, Russia, and several other nations. The United States did not sign because the Declaration did not come up to the terms of the historic American contention that all private property at sea should be exempt from capture. But the Declaration laid down specifically that 'the neutral flag covers enemy goods with the exception of contraband of war.'It was in view of this and other agreements that Admiral Mahan wrote, in his *'Influence of Sea Power'*: 'The principle that the flag covers the cargo is for ever secure.' That principle was now openly flouted by the British Government. 'The right of the belligerent ends where the right of the neutral begins' declared America and neutral opinion generally. The war, as conducted by British Liberals, brought other counsel." (*England' Holy War,* pp.206-7.)

This was the thin end of the wedge. Once the Royal Navy began stopping and seizing the goods of neutral shipping bound for German and Austrian civilians, it began extending this strategy to stopping the shipping of neutral countries it desired to influence into joining the War. And then, in the case of Greece, it went the whole way and treated her simply as an enemy to be subjected to the terror of a hunger blockade.

Below is George Abbot's powerful description of the Allied Blockade of Greece and the effects it had on its people. And it describes why blockade is such an insidious weapon of war:

"Among the acts sanctioned by International Law, none is more worthy of a philosopher's or a philanthropist's attention than the 'pacific blockade.'... It denotes 'a blockade exercised by a great Power for the purpose of bringing pressure to bear on a weaker State, without actual war. That it is an act of violence, and therefore in the nature of war, is undeniable;'but, besides its name, it possesses certain features which distinguish it advantageously from ordinary war.

First, instead of the barbarous effusion of blood and swift destruction which open hostilities entail, the pacific blockade achieves its ends by more refined and leisurely means: one is not shocked by the unseemly sights of a battlefield, and the wielder of the weapon has time to watch its effects as they develop: he can see the victim going through the successive stages of misery—debility, languor, exhaustion—until the final point is reached; and as his scientific curiosity is gratified by the gradual manifestation of the various symptoms, so his moral sense is fortified by the struggle between a proud spirit and an empty stomach—than which life can offer no more ennobling spectacle. Then, unlike crude war, the pacific blockade automatically strikes the nation at which it is aimed on its weakest side first: instead of having to begin with its manhood, one begins with its old men, its women, and its infants. The merits of this form of attack are evident: many a man who would boldly face starvation himself, may be reasonably expected to flinch at the prospect of a starving mother, wife, or child. Lastly, whilst in war the assailant must inevitably suffer as well as inflict losses, the pacific blockade renders him absolutely exempt from all risk. For 'it can only be employed as a measure of coercion by maritime Powers able to bring into action such vastly superior forces to those the resisting State can dispose of, that resistance is out of the question.'

In brief, the pacific blockade is not war, but a kind of sport, as safe as coursing, and to the educated mind much more interesting. The interest largely depends on the duration of the blockade, and its operation on the victims' physical and moral resources. When the blockade was proclaimed on the 8th of December, Allied journalists predicted that its persuasive force would be felt very soon. The country, they reasoned, owing to the manifold restrictions imposed upon its overseas trade by the Anglo-French Fleet, had been on short commons for some time past. The total stoppage of maritime traffic would bring it to the verge of famine within a week. And, in fact, before the end of the month Greece was feeling the pinch. As might have been expected, the first to feel it were the poor. Both the authorities and private societies did their utmost to protect them by keeping prices down, and to relieve them by the free distribution of food and other necessaries. But, although the achievement was great, it could not prove equal to the dimensions of the need. The stoppage of all maritime traffic caused a cessation of industry and threw out of employment thousands of working-people. As the factories grew empty of labourers, the streets grew full of beggars. The necessary adulteration of the flour produced epidemics of dysentery and poisoning, especially among children and old people, while numerous deaths among infants were attributed by the doctors to want of milk in their mothers' breasts. Presently bread, the staple food of the Greeks, disappeared, and all classes took to carob-beans and herbs... Next to bread, the most prominent article of Greek diet is fish...

The ultimate object of the blockade was to propagate rebellion. Other things spoke even more eloquently. The few cargoes of flour that arrived in Greece now and then were sequestered by the Allies and sent to the Salonica Government, which used them as a bait, inviting the King's subjects through its agents to sell their allegiance for a loaf of bread. Generally the reply was: 'We prefer to die.'Of this stubborn endurance, the women of modern Greece gave instances that recall the days of ancient Sparta...

Never, indeed, in the hour of his triumphs had King Constantine been so near the hearts of his people as he was in this period of their common affliction. Although the operation-wounds in his ribs were still open, he met the emergency with dauntless fortitude, and never for a moment forgot his part, either as a prince or as a man...

The people who had formerly admired their sovereign as a hero, now revered him as a martyr; and the man upon whom they visited their anger was he whom they regarded as the true cause of their misery. After his flight to Salonica M. Venizelos was never mentioned except by the name of The Traitor; after the events of 1 December he was formally impeached as one; and after the blockade had been in force for some weeks, he was solemnly anathematized: on 26 December, the Archbishop of Athens, from a cairn of stones in the midst of a great multitude, pronounced the curse of the Church upon 'the traitor, Venizelos.'...

Appeals from the Holy Synod of the Greek Church to the Pope and the heads of other Christian Churches availed as little as the appeals of the Greek Government to Allied and neutral Governments. Month after month the blockade went on, and each month produced its own tale of suffering: deaths due directly to starvation; diseases due to the indirect effects of inanition; a whole nation wasting for want of food; horses starved to provide it; mothers praying to God for their daily bread with babes drooping at their desiccated bosoms. Yet of yielding there was no sign: 'Give in?'said a woman outside a soup-kitchen at the Piraeus, in March. 'We will eat our children first!'

In such a manner this ancient race, which has lived so long, done so much, and suffered so much, bore its martyrdom. By such an exercise of self-discipline it defied the Powers of Civilisation to do their worst. In spite of the licence given to brute force, in spite of the removal of the machinery of civil control, in spite of the internment of the army and its arms, in spite of the ostentatiously paraded support to the Rebel, in spite of actual famine and the threat of imminent ruin, the people held to the institutions of their country, rallied to their King; and expressed their scorn for the usurper of his authority by inscribing over the graves of their babies: 'Here lies my child, starved to death by Venizelos.'"
(*Greece And The Allies 1914-1922,* pp. 172-6.)

Basil Thomson had this to say about the effects of the blockade:

"If the blockade played havoc with the defenceless civilian population, its moral effect was even more severe. The country was now entirely cut off from the outside world. All postal communications to and from Greece were intercepted. Private correspondence, especially correspondence from other neutral countries, when not detained or destroyed, was returned to the senders... Thanks to the blockade Greece was cut off from the world as if it were in an air-tight compartment." (The Allied Secret Service in Greece, pp. 205-6.)

But the blockade failed in its ultimate objective to get the people to abandon their King and force the Greeks into regime change.

So, in May 1917 the British and French decided on a three stage programme to ensure Greek entry into the War. It was agreed that the semblance of freedom of action should be left to the Greeks so that the Allies would not be seen to be involved in a direct military coup against Constantine. The Allies decided to seize the wheat crop of Thessaly, upon which the entire Greek population depended for bread; to seize the Corinth Isthmus, cutting off the Greek Army from the capital; and to deliver an ultimatum to Constantine demanding the immediate entry of Greece into the War. And it was decided that direct force would then be applied to the situation in Athens if Constantine refused to comply.

### The Man From The Daily Mail

George Ward Price, *The Daily Mail* correspondent, who was with the Allied Army in Macedonia, wrote a book from the spot: *The Story of the Salonica Army;* (it had a Foreword by Viscount Northcliffe, the press baron). The book is really a defence of the Salonika operation against the criticism it received concerning the inactivity of the Allied Army, at a time when a life or death struggle was taking place on the Western front during the German offensive of 1918.

In his Introduction, *Has Salonica Been Worth While?*, Ward Price outlined the practical achievements of the Salonika expedition and then turned to higher strategic objectives:

"... there are considerations of a larger nature to be borne in mind. England, especially, cannot afford to disinterest herself from the Balkans, because the Balkans are one of the principal stepping-stones on the way to India. Whatever else might be the conditions on which the war were brought to an end, a peace which left Germany with undisputed rule or even undisputed influence over the Balkans would be a German victory, and the vast sacrifices which she and her allies have made would be held by Germany to be justified, if, as a result of them, she could consolidate this first great stage of her thrust towards India and that dominion in Middle Asia which has always been the traditional goal of world-conquerors and the possession of which is the historical symbol of world-supremacy.

It is therefore of the first importance to the British Empire that there should be in the Balkans a barrier-state across the path of this German *Drang nach Osten* [Drive to the East. P.W.]. Egypt and the Suez Canal have lost much of their importance as the gatehouse of the East now that the trans-Balkan railway runs straight through from Berlin to Bagdad. To quote a distinguished officer who has much studied the strategic problems of the Mediterranean : 'The frontier of India should be at Belgrade; we are actually defending it at Bagdad, and if the war leaves Germany with a strengthened position in the Near East, the day may come when we have to defend it at Bombay.'

All that seems, indeed, to presume a perpetuation of the state of semi-hostility that we all hope the war will somehow abolish as the normal peace-time condition of international affairs, but until there are more signs than are at present manifest that the German leopard is going to change his spots and that German schemes for substituting Germania for Britannia throughout the world have ceased to be cherished the defence of our Indian Empire will have to be taken into the consideration of our statesmen.

Our interest in Serbia, then, is not merely the sentimental one of a big ally for a small; it is based on something more tangible than sympathy for 'gallant little Serbia.'In the Serbians, with their strongly marked national character, their passion for independence, their traditional Slav hostility towards the Teuton, we find the natural buffer-state which should bar Germany's way towards India and the East and cut her off from that outlet to the Mediterranean at Salonica, which, if she gained it, would change the world's naval balance of power, and force us for the defence of Egypt constantly to maintain a large fleet in the Levant.

Our going to Salonica has had, then, this advantageous consequence: it has been a practical guarantee that the great and vital interests which the Allies, especially ourselves, possess in the Balkans, should not be lost sight of; that public attention should be kept alive and well-informed upon a part of the world where our diplomatic blunders in the past have wrought us only too much harm, and that the Serbs, that virile little people whom destiny and the situation of their country have called to play so important a part in the modern history of Europe, should have received a practical gage of the Allies' support." (*The Story of the Salonica Army,* pp. 6-9.)

Some readers may know Ward Price for his books of the 1930s, such as *I Know These Dictators* and *Year of Reckoning,* in which the author, who was on personal terms with the Nazi and Italian Fascist leaders, tried to explain Hitler and Mussolini to the English (meaning he tried to convince them of the Fuhrer's admiration and good intentions toward Britain).

This is interesting in view of Ward Price's fear of the Kaiser's Germany in 1918. Price was another of those who believed that the Bagdad Railway was such a threat to the British Empire that India needed to be defended at Belgrade. And yet in 1937 he had no such fears of the Anglophile Adolf Hitler—whom he had become convinced had learnt the lessons that the Kaiser had been taught by England. Hitler presented no threat to the British Empire, he had made it clear that he was interested only in an eastward extension through the Ukraine, and therefore should be appeased. But the Kaiser's Germany and its Railway—that was a far more serious matter!

### Ward Price On The Invasion Of Thessaly

In the following passage in *The Story of the Salonica Army* Ward Price, explains how, when the naval blockade was proving unsuccessful in bringing

Constantine to order, a military push into Thessaly was launched to put a stranglehold on the Greeks and their bread supply:

"Though King Constantine never actually attacked us, he was always posing as being on the point of doing so, and by that means distracted the attention and drew off some of the strength of the Allied Army in the Balkans from its main objective—the Bulgarian and German forces in front of it. The Allied fleets were blockading the coasts of Greece all through the spring of 1917, but though this caused a certain shortage of bread, which forms a much larger part of the food of the Balkan peoples than of our own, it did not reduce the King to obedience by bringing him into danger of starvation, one reason being that a country which produces vegetables, fruits and sheep in such abundance as Greece can hardly lack seriously for food, and the other that the granaries of the country were well stocked with reserves of wheat. As these reserves dwindled, however, it became evident that the King's passive attitude was chiefly due to the fact that he was anxious to be allowed to reap the Thessalian corn crop undisturbed. Once this was garnered he would again be independent of foreign supplies for seven or eight months and could begin once more with impunity to flout the Allies. By that time, indeed, with the turn that things were taking in Russia since the Revolution, he might hope that the Germans would be able to withdraw 100,000 men from that front and send them to attack us in the Balkans, which would give him an opportunity for co-operation. The French Higher Command at Salonica and M. Venizelos both urged upon the Allied Governments the need for occupying Thessaly and seizing the corn-crop—on payment, of course, to its owners. Not only was this a measure of self-defence, for we needed the food. The islands which had adhered to Venizelos were indeed very short of corn. At the beginning of May the occupation of Thessaly was decided in principle by the Allied Powers." (*The Story of the Salonica Army,* pp. 150-1.)

So the Allied blockade which failed to starve the Greek people into submission actually threatened to starve the occupation forces on Greek territory. And therefore it was necessary to commandeer the only food the Greeks had left to feed the forces occupying their country!

Thessaly, which had been annexed to Greece in 1885 through the Treaty of Berlin, organised by Disraeli, was occupied again by Turkey after the war with Greece in 1897. Turkey had aimed to reintegrate it into the Ottoman Empire but Britain and France disagreed and forced the Turks to return the area to the Greeks. Now in 1917 they were taking it back from the Greeks due to the Greek refusal to join another War on the Turk.

The military occupation of Thessaly and Corinth coupled with a threat to bombard Athens finally had the desired effect for the Allies and forced Constantine's abdication. The King decided to save his people by sacrificing his throne on 11th June 1917. There were scenes of turmoil in Athens as large crowds tried to prevent the King's departure but Constantine was left with no alternative and he urged his people to remain calm and resolute in the face of the invasion forces. Prince Alexander, the 23 year old second son of Constantine, took the throne and Venizelos entered Athens with the French Army. Greece then formally joined the War on the Allied side.

## The Conversion Of Greece

In *Salonica And After: The Sideshow That Ended The War* Harry Collinson Owen, the editor of a British propagandist organ in the Balkans, described the events in Greece from the failed Allied coup of December 1916 until the overthrow of King Constantine. The passage is from a chapter entitled, *The Conversion Of Greece*:

"Constantine was King in the South, and Venizelos, under the sheltering wing of the Allies, the power in the North. The Allies pressed their demands, and with his eye on the battle line in Rumania Constantine gave way just as much as was necessary, and no more, to keep the Allies dangling...

The Allied ultimatum, which insisted on disarmament of Greece as a guarantee of her neutrality, was drawing to a close. It expired on December 1st. On that day came one of the Allies' greatest muddles and Constantine 's supreme treachery. The Allied marines landed by Admiral d'Artige du Fournet, were caught in ambush and shot down by machine-gun and rifle fire, and for the best part of twenty-four hours the French Admiral was a prisoner, and his meals brought to him. The Allies' long duel with Constantine seemed to have fizzled lamentably. For the moment 'My dear Tino'was on top....

Who could have thought then, that within less than six months King Constantine would have become ex-King Constantine, and... on June 24th, 1917, M. Venizelos would re-enter Athens... with full powers, backed by the Allies, to guide his country along the road which he had long foreseen truth and courage had traced for her ? The mills of the Allies ground very slowly, but in the end they ground to some purpose.

The bloody events of December 1st, 1916, and the days immediately afterwards, were followed by another ultimatum on December 14th, in which Royalist Greece was ordered to transfer her troops and munitions to the southern province of the Peloponnese, where, joined to the mainland only by the narrow Isthmus of Corinth, they would no longer be a source of danger to the Salonica Allies; and to cease immediately all movements of troops and material towards the north. For nearly six months longer Constantine played his astute game, but always losing a little; never living up to his promises to the demands made on him, but never having quite the courage to defy them entirely. Gradually, but ceaselessly, the pressure of the Allies went on... and still German help did not come to Athens. And at last we had drawn sufficient of his teeth to make it possible to apply the final pressure without any danger of an armed Greece rising in our rear at the bidding of its pro-German King.

A strong French force, joined by a small detachment of British (500 men of the East Yorkshire Regiment) advanced down into Greece with the double object of securing the corn crop of the Thessaly plains, and threatening Athens from the north. The Isthmus of Corinth was occupied, so that all the Greek troops and material south of it in the Peloponnese were cut off. And a strong Allied Fleet had Athens at the mercy of its guns. On June 11th the King departed for Switzerland, the first of the enemy '*rois en exil*'. His fall was partly one of the many quiet triumphs of sea power. Without the sea open to her, Greece sooner or later must capitulate. The blockade was an argument against which the wireless messages from Berlin had no answer." (pp.177-8.)

*The Irish News,* which had earlier recommended the overthrow of Constantine, commented on the King's leaving in its editorial of 14th of September 1917. It was called *King 'Tino' Departs* and it made a comparison between the people's revolution in Russia and the foreign-induced *coup d'état* in Greece:

"When the late Czar of Russia realised that his deposition had been accomplished he solemnly 'nominated'his brother as his successor. But the Soldiers and Workers Council had no further use for Czars of the Romanoff or any other breed. Poor Nicholas is in captivity now; he does not 'enjoy'even the privileges of a prisoner of war; and the Soldiers and Workers of Russia are ruling themselves — somehow. Constantine of Greece is first cousin to the ex-Czar of Russia and to King George V.; and 'Tino'is now among the 'exes'also. But the act of 'deposition'was not performed by the people of Greece; there never has been any valid evidence to prove that the people wished to get rid of him. He was invited to depart by the representatives of England, France, and Russia — the guarantors of Greek independence: and he thought it wiser to accept the invitation. The three Powers also barred Constantine's eldest son — evidently regarding him as too much 'a chip of the old block'; and the removed monarch bestowed the throne of Greece, with his blessing more or less, on his second son, whose name is Alexander... M. Venizelos probably thought he would be President of a Greek Republic; if he is lucky he may regain his position as Prime Minister to a King of Greece... ex-King Constantine has decided to leave Greece — not for England, the home of many ex-monarchs, we may feel certain..."

Britain skilfully used the precedent set in Russia to get rid of King Constantine in the general atmosphere of democratic revolution but, as *The Irish News* stated, Venizelos returned to power 'with foreign bayonets'.

The new Greek democracy was hardly a revelation, though. Venizelos returned to Athens as Prime Minister, dismissed calls for an election and had the opposition leaders immediately deported to imprisonment on Corsica. There were large scale executions of army officers loyal to the King, hundreds were interned and a number of Ministers died in custody in the Venizelist reign of terror. The Liberal dictatorship of Venizelos was to last for three years before it was overturned when an election was finally pressed upon the Prime Minister. But by that stage Greece was over half-way to disaster.

At the end of his book, Ward Price sums up what he witnessed in Salonika and dwells on some considerations of high politics for the future relations between Britain and Greece:

"Such is the most plain and straightforward story of our relations with the Greeks and the occupation of Thessaly by the Allies. What secret reasons of state or what varied motives may have controlled the development of the Allies' action in all these matters, hastening or retarding it, I have not discussed here... There is much, indeed, that is mysterious in this complicated Balkan situation which has resulted in a vastly expensive Allied force being held up for two years in a barren region at the other end of Europe without accomplishing anything proportionate towards the aims of the war. The cryptic influence of the Jew; the restraint upon strategy imposed by the Parliamentary politics of some Allied countries; the alleged existence of financial aims to be gratified in Greece, — these are some of the explanations, probable and improbable, that you will hear from people who profess to be acquainted with the facts of the situation... The leading factor of the future of our Balkan army still remains a moot question. Just as the failure of the Greeks to keep their treaty pledges and their plighted word handicapped and limited the Salonica Expedition at its beginning, so the tardy atonement of the Greek nation for that defection may yet advance the successful end of the enterprise.

The value to the Allied cause of the Greeks as soldiers is increased by two facts: First, they are soldiers on the spot; you have not to go through the slow, costly and risky process of shipping them out there first. Secondly, as regards supplies, they can to a great extent be fed from the resources of their own country, since they are already living on those resources as civilians.

As fighting material they are not at all bad... Of course, they have much to learn, like all raw troops in this war. Their own idea that the Balkan campaigns had proved them warriors by instinct as well as experience brought them one or two rude shocks at the beginning.

As regards personnel, the Greeks naturally lacked good generals, capable of commanding such a campaign as this...

When I was in Thessaly with the French troops the peasants were saying, 'Rather than go to war I would take refuge in the mountains.'But it is in the character of the Greek to accept authority without much trouble if it is firmly enforced, and M. Venizelos will probably be able gradually to put his army into the field on condition that the Allies make up the defects in its existing equipment." (*The Story of the Salonica Army,* pp. 188-9.)

Having entered the war, Greece helped knock Bulgaria out of the conflict and ultimately joined the triumphal procession into Constantinople.

One of the most significant remarks in Ward Price's book is that: 'Venizelos is a European and not merely a Balkan statesman. He can take big views.' Similar things were said about John Redmond by his admirers in England. But, as Redmond's star was falling, the great Hellenic mission was only just beginning, because Britain had further uses for Venizelos and his Greek Army.

Paxton Hibben, the American correspondent in Athens who had followed events closely since 1915, made this judgement on the importance of the whole affair regarding Britain and the undermining of Greek neutrality in 1920:

> "What is of great consequence... is that during the war and after our entry into it as an ally of France and Great Britain, without our knowledge and consent the constitution of a little, but a brave and fine, people was nullified by the joint action of two of our allies; the neutrality of a small country was violated, the will of its people set at naught, its laws broken, its citizens persecuted, its press muzzled. By force a government was imposed upon this free people, and by force that government has and is today maintained by absolute power. In the words of General Sarrail, 'Venizelist Greece has become a British Dominion.'" (*Constantine I And The Greek People*, pp. xv-xvi.)

And that was the first great achievement of Ireland's Great War on Turkey.

King Constantine of Greece

# IV. Britain, America and the Turks

The U.S. declared war on Germany and Austro-Hungary in 1917, but it never actually declared war on Turkey. This was despite a strong Protestant lobby in the country (which was fed information by the American missions in the Ottoman Empire) that wanted to take Constantinople back for Christianity. Questions were asked in Congress about the obvious omission of not taking on the Turks as an enemy but no satisfactory answer was ever given. So one has to conclude that America viewed the war on Turkey to have been outside the one it had joined—i.e. an Imperialist war which the U.S. wanted to avoid getting its hands dirty with. And this is confirmed by the American refusal to have anything to do with the Mandates Britain attempted to foist on it in the region after the War when the U.S. passed on being implicated in the land grabbing under cover of Mandate.

The United States had remained neutral in the Great War between 1914 and 1916. So, when it joined the conflict, it had to insist that it was fighting a different War from the one it had abstained from previously. So it made out that the character of the War Germany was fighting, rather than the War itself, had brought America into the conflict, and that, as a result of the U.S. entry, the character of the Allies' War had also changed.

America was not taken in as easily as were Ireland's political leaders by British War propaganda. By late 1917 Americans had become engaged, through their utopian-minded President, in the 'war for civilisation'. But many would still have had a very cynical view of the Imperial adventures of the British Empire in the Middle East. What were ordinary Americans to make of the Imperialist predators that America was fighting in alliance with, campaigning in the Middle-East to carve up territorial gains for themselves with secret treaties? Was this not the kind of thing the U.S. entered the War to destroy?

In late 1917 England was crying out for American cannon-fodder for the Western front while, at the same time, many of its own resources of men and materials were being employed in gaining territory for the British Empire in Mesopotamia and Palestine. So it was in the brief of Charles Woods and others to convince the Americans that the two campaigns were really part of the same War that the U.S. had signed up to, to dispel any worries on the part of Americans that they were supporting naked Imperialism.

### When The Turk Was A Gentleman

I have described the strategic reorientation that Britain accomplished in the years before the Great War. This policy change, however, came up against the sentiment that existed among the masses, instilled by the music hall and other forms of popular culture, as a corollary to the anti-Russian jingoism, that saw the Turk as 'a gentleman'.

Prior to the Great War, the British public had what could be described as an ambivalent attitude towards Turks. Before England made war on Turkey, the Turk was well regarded in England, having been an ally against Russia for the best part of a century. During the time of the 1876 Bulgarian uprising, Gladstone blamed the Turks for the 'Bulgarian atrocities'. But, soon after, the positive British attitude toward the Turk was reasserted, when Disraeli worked up the masses into calling for war with Russia to defend the Ottoman Empire — along with the British interest. And, in the last couple of decades of the century, a number of English travellers, diplomats, and others wrote very sympathetic accounts of the Turks, which contrasted to the writings of Protestant missionaries whose interests lay in doing down the Moslem Turk in order to re-establish Christianity in the region.

Overall, the impression developed in the public mind was that the Turks, whilst being unchristian and not constituting a 'first-class race', as such, had many good and noble qualities. They were honest, could be relied upon and the word of a Turk was his bond. In short, despite not being British, 'the Turk was a gentleman'.

But the Declaration of War on Turkey necessitated a different approach to the Turk—especially because, once the Turks started fighting the British, favourable reports of Turkish soldiering came back to England, and these appeared in some newspapers. These reports, in contrast to the atrocity propaganda about the Germans, happened to describe the Turks as 'clean fighters' and generally as being men of honour.

This was not the kind of thing that the British Government wanted people to believe about the enemy. In the 'war for civilisation' it was not ideal that one of the enemy was exempt from damnation—as if this was some kind of old aristocratic war. It might then have been asked why England was sending its men to fight the decent Turk when its armies were engaged in a life or death struggle with the barbarians in the West. So something had to be done to change this perception. And Liberal England soon obliged.

On the 20th of February 1917 a letter appeared in *The Times* with the heading, *The Clean Fighting Turk, A Spurious Claim.* Its author, 'a distinguished authority on Oriental Affairs, has had exceptional experience of the Turk,' it was claimed. The anonymous writer was Mark Sykes, the man charged with dividing up the Ottoman Empire with the French in anticipation of victory.

This is how it begins:

"During the present war we have heard a good deal of the good nature of the Turks, yet they have pursued the most devilish policy that ever this war has seen."

Sykes then goes on to accuse the Turks of the deaths of 700,000 Armenians, as well as of the creation of an artificial famine in the Lebanon, the ill-treatment of British POWs, and the conscription of Jewish colonists into the Ottoman

Army (without noticing any parallel with the British State's attempts to do the same with the Irish).

Here are some further extracts from it:

"Nevertheless, the sportsmanship and chivalry of the Turks is a favourite theme of some writers. How is the paradox to be explained?

The plain fact is, that the Turk as a ruler is a merciless oppressor, as a negotiator a cunning Byzantine, as a soldier a tough fighter, as a victor a remorseless bully—but when he feels he has met his match he is chivalrous, when he is defeated he is a pathetic and distressed gentleman...

The Turk has strewn the earth with ruins and has made the prettiest nursery rhymes; he has shattered civilizations, both Moslem and Christian; he has coined the most witty and delightful proverbs. He is a thoughtful and solicitous host, an easy-going master, and a mild landlord, but he is a merciless misgovernor, a feckless squanderer, and as revengeful as a camel.

Take again the Young Turk with a German uniform, a German parade voice, and German technical education. He has been reared in a Stamboul harem... His German Professors taught him all there was to know about mass-suggestion, weltpolitik, and high explosives... The Young Turk who snubbed his mother, pulled his sister's hair, kicked the Armenian porter, cringed before his father, gobbled up the dogmas of the German Professor, mastered the formulae of the Prussian military instructor and resuscitated the dormant lusts of his savage ancestors in his heart, is the man who counts...

In England the Young Turk still hopes to maintain a certain sentimental hold on public opinion, which interested politicians and romantic travellers have secured for him in the past. His spurious reputation as a clean fighter he is glad enough to keep as a war asset.

His success we must acknowledge; he has massacred, pillaged, outraged; for two years and a half he has broken every convention, maltreated our prisoners, killed our wounded, held our women hostages, but he remains the 'clean fighting Turk.'"

Harems were very much part of the mysticism of the Orient beloved of the Orientalists. But it is very unlikely that many Turks were 'reared in a Stamboul harem'. As far as I am aware, the only harem that existed then in the Ottoman Empire was the Sultan's. It is perhaps the case that some powerful men enjoyed the pleasures of the harem too, but ordinary Turks certainly did not have harems. Harems were, in fact, a Byzantine tradition, appropriated by the Sultans of Constantinople. And other cultures had harems which really put the harem of the Sultan to shame. India's Moghal emperor, Akbar, for instance, was supposed to have had 5,000 women in his harem and it is reputed that a Persian King might have had as many as 10,000.

A hundred thousand copies of Sykes's letter were produced as an off-print and distributed, with thirty thousand being sent across to America. It became the model for anti-Turkish propaganda and its ideas about the Turks have become firmly established in the Anglo-Saxon mind (within which we might include Ireland).

Sykes had made two predictions in 1914. One, made when opposing war on Turkey, was that

"the disappearance of the Ottoman Empire must be the first step towards the disappearance of our own."

Secondly, after War had been declared, that it had

"rung the death-knell of Ottoman dominion, not only in Europe, but in Asia." (Cited in David Fromkin, *A Peace To End All Peace*, p. 75.)

They say that the only true prophet is the one who carves out the future he himself predicts. Sykes was to be proved right on both counts.

### Wellington House and the Turk

The organisation which arranged the print run of Sykes's letter to *The Times* was Wellington House.

The bulk of the work aimed to change the opinion of the Turk in the Anglo-Saxon world was carried out by this secret organisation of the British State. It got its name in the Autumn of 1914 when the War Propaganda Bureau was a part of the Foreign Office and was stationed in Wellington House—later destroyed in a mysterious fire—near Buckingham Palace. It was part of the Foreign Office because the target of its work was overseas opinion, particularly in America. (A detailed examination of it can be found in *Wellington House And British Propaganda During The First World War* by M. L. Sanders, from *The Historical Journal*, XVIII, 1975.)

The Director of the War Propaganda Bureau was Charles F. Masterman, a Liberal MP, former Cabinet Minister in Asquith's Government, and literary editor of *The Daily News*, who before the War had run a campaign in favour of Lloyd George's National Insurance legislation. When Asquith called Masterman to direct the propaganda of the British State in August 1914 he invited twenty-five leading British writers to Wellington House. The agenda of the meeting was to discuss ways of best promoting Britain's interests during the War. It was attended by J.M. Barrie, Gilbert Murray, H.G. Wells, John Galsworthy, Arthur Conan Doyle, Thomas Hardy, John Masefield, Arnold Bennett, G.K. Chesterton, and G.M. Trevelyan among others.

The meeting was the largest gathering of creative and academic writers for an official purpose in English history. And a second meeting attracted all the great newspaper editors like Geoffrey Dawson, Edward Cook, J.L. Garvin and J.A. Spender. All of the authors at the conference agreed to the utmost secrecy regarding their future work and very few people, even in Parliament, knew of the existence of Wellington House until well after the War.

A Department of Information Document listing its sections shows two Irish contributors, both under the control of a T.L. Gilmour: Denis Gwynn, the Professor of History and future biographer of Redmond and Casement, and

Hugh Law, Redmondite MP and later Cumann nGaedheal T.D. for Donegal.

Propaganda was a game played by English gentlemen but it was not considered to be a gentleman's game. Arnold Toynbee, a gentleman from Winchester College and Balliol, and a respected classical historian, apparently remarked that he would like to get out of it for that reason, and as soon as it was practically possible. Nevertheless it was something that had to be done and British gentlemen did it as their duty. And to relieve their consciences all the records of their activities at the Propaganda Office were destroyed immediately after the War.

The Wellington House brief was very simple — to make the enemy look as evil and conniving as possible and make Britain and her allies look as decent and upright as could be. The main focus was Germany, but much of its effort was later to be expended against the Turks, who had been getting too much of a good press.

One of the reasons writers were assembled together at the start of the War was due to the following:

> "Amateur propagandists were in abundance. The activities of voluntary organisations were both useful and a problem to Wellington House. Masterman testified that there was an unconscionable growth of work directing, coordinating, and often restraining the propagandist intentions of private individuals." (*Wellington House And British Propaganda During The First World War*, *The Historical Journal*, XVIII, 1975, p. 120.)

The nature of the War, which was infused with a great moral dimension at its opening in England, led to a natural desire in private individuals to do their bit in propagandising. But Britain realised that propaganda is an art. It considered German attempts at it as amateurish and gross, and consequently of limited effectiveness. So Wellington House spent a great deal of its time discouraging casual amateur enthusiasm that might be damaging to its subtle and professional work.

Wellington House issued two types of publications in book form: books specifically written for it, and books written by independent authors, which it bought and distributed because they furthered the objectives of propaganda. But its publication operation was kept a secret. All the writers present at the conference agreed to work in the utmost secrecy, and it was not until 1935 that the activities of the War Propaganda Bureau became known to the general public.

Randal Marlin cites an insider's view of this from an official (marked 'secret') document lodged in the Imperial War Museum:

> "The existence of a publishing establishment at Wellington House, and, *a fortiori*, the connection of the Government with this establishment were carefully concealed. Except for official publications, none of the literature bore overt marks of its origin. Further, literature was placed on sale, when

possible, and when sent free was always sent informally, that is to say, through and apparently from some person between whom and the recipient there was a definite link, and with a covering note from the person to whose private patriotism the sending of the literature seemed due." (*Propaganda And The Ethics of Persuasion*, p.64.)

Because it was necessary that publications should never bear any mark of a Government Department, commercial publishers like Hodder and Stoughton, Methuen, Macmillan, Oxford University Press and John Murray were used for distribution. And even the method of delivery was organised with care. When important people were targeted, they received a copy of the publication with a card from an influential person of high renown to give it the personal touch—so that it did not appear to be mass propaganda. This was particularly important in the U.S. where people with new money were often impressed by the card of an English gentleman with a royal title.

Wellington House had many of England's finest minds working for it, amongst them the best historians England could muster. It included in its offices people such as G.P. Gooch (of Gooch and Temperley) and Arnold Toynbee. Toynbee was employed by Wellington House as a propagandist, not as a historian. In nothing Toynbee, the respected historian, wrote was there ever an indication of who he was working for. For all the world he remained the individual academic historian he had been prior to the War, with all the gravitas that went with his name, whilst in reality he was writing propaganda for Wellington House with a large organisation of like-minded people.

The Wellington House publications directed against the Turks included the following: British Palestine Committee (Mark Sykes), *The 'Clean-Fighting Turk', a Spurious Claim*, E.F. Benson's *Crescent and Iron Cross* and *Deutschland über Allah*, Israel Cohen's *The Turkish Persecution of the Jews*, Edward Cook's *Britain and Turkey*, E.W.G. Masterman's *The Deliverance of Jerusalem*, Basil Mathews, *The Freedom of Jerusalem*, Esther Mugerditchian's *From Turkish Toils*, Martin Niepage's *The Horrors of Aleppo*, Canon Parfit's *Mesopotamia: the Key to the Future*, R.W. Seton-Watson's *Serbia, Yesterday, Today and Tomorrow*, Josiah Wedgwood, MP, *With Machine-Guns in Gallipoli*, Chaim Weizmann, R. Gottheil, *What is Zionism?*, Anon., *Subject Nationalities of the German Alliance*, Anon., *Syria During March 1916: Her Miseries and Disasters*, S. Tolkowsky's *Jewish Colonisation in Palestine*, Arnold J. Toynbee's *Armenian Atrocities: The Murder of a Nation, Turkey— A Past and a Future*, and *The Murderous Tyranny of Turks*.

Here is an example, the *Preface* to E.F. Benson's *Crescent and Iron Cross*, which shows the method used in these publications, which were propaganda masquerading as fact. (Benson, the son of the Archbishop of Canterbury, was a hugely popular novelist, famous for his ghost stories.):

"In compiling the following pages I have had access to certain sources of official information, the nature of which I am not at liberty to specify further. I have used these freely in such chapters of this book as deal with recent and contemporary events in Turkey or in Germany in connection with Turkey: the chapter, for instance, entitled 'Deutschland über Allah,' is based very largely on such documents. I have tried to be discriminating in their use, and have not, as far as I am aware, stated anything derived from them as a fact, for which I had not found corroborative evidence. With regard to the Armenian massacres I have drawn largely on the testimony collected by Lord Bryce, on that brought forward by Mr. Arnold J. Toynbee in his pamphlet *The Murder of a Nation*, and *The Murderous Tyranny of the Turks*, and on the pamphlet by Dr. Martin Niepage, called *The Horrors of Aleppo*. In the first chapter I have based the short historical survey on the contribution of Mr. D.G. Hogarth to *The Balkans* (Clarendon Press, 1915.). The chapter called 'Thy Kingdom is Divided' is in no respect at all an official utterance, and merely represents the individual opinions and surmises of the author. It has, however, the official basis that the Allies have pledged themselves to remove the power of the Turk from Constantinople, and to remove out of the power of the Turk the alien peoples who have too long already been subject to his murderous rule. I have, in fact, but attempted to conjecture in what kind of manner that promise will be fulfilled."

Below are the first couple of pages of Chapter One of *Crescent and Iron Cross*, which is entitled *The Theory Of The Old Turks*. It takes as a starting point the phrase 'the sick man of Europe', referring to Turkey, and it is a pretty typical example of the output of Wellington House:

"For at whatever period we regard Turkey, and try to define that monstrous phenomenon, we can make a far truer phrase than Lord Aberdeen's. For Turkey is not a sick man: Turkey is a sickness. He is not sick, nor ever has been, for he is the cancer itself, the devouring tumour that for centuries has fed on living tissue, absorbing it and killing it. It has never had life in itself, except in so far that the power of preying on and destroying life constitutes life, and such a power, after all, we are accustomed to call not life, but death. Turkey, like death, continues to exist and to dominate, through its function of killing. Life cannot kill, it is disease and death that kill, and from the moment that Turkey passed from being a nomadic tribe moving westwards from the confines of Persia, it has existed only and thrived on a process of absorption and of murder. When first the Turks came out of their Eastern fastnesses they absorbed; when they grew more or less settled, and by degrees the power of mere absorption, as by some failure of digestion, left them, they killed. They became a huge tumour, that nourished itself by killing the living tissues that came in contact with it. Now, by the amazing irony of fate, who weaves stranger dramas than could ever be set on censored stages, for they both take hundreds of years to unravel themselves, and are of the most unedifying character, Turkey, the rodent cancer, has been infected by another with greater organisation for devouring; the disease of Ottomanism is threatened by a more deadly hunger, and

Prussianism has inserted its crab-pincers into the cancer that came out of Asia. Those claws are already deeply set, and the problem for civilised nations is first to disentangle the nippers that are cancer in a cancer, and next to deprive of all power over alien peoples the domination that has already been allowed to exist too long.

The object of this book is the statement of the case on which all defenders of liberty base their prosecution against Turkey itself, and against the Power that to-day has Turkey in its grip.

Historical surveys are apt to be tedious, but in order to understand at all adequately the case against Turkey as a ruler and controller of subject peoples, it is necessary to go, though briefly, into her blood-stained genealogy. There is no need to enter into ethnological discussions as to earlier history, or define the difference between the Osmanli Turks and those who were spread over Asia Minor before the advent of the Osmanlis from the East. But it was the Osmanlis who were the cancerous and devouring nation, and it is they who to-day rule over a vast territory (subject to Germany) of peoples alien to them by religion and blood and all the instincts common to civilised folk. Until Germany, 'deep patient Germany,' suddenly hoisted her colours as a champion of murder and rapine and barbarism, she the mother of art and literature and science, there was nothing in Europe that could compare with the anachronism of Turkey being there at all. Then, in August 1914, there was hoisted the German flag, superimposed with skulls and cross-bones, and all the insignia of piracy and highway robbery on land and on sea, and Germany showed herself an anachronism worthy to impale her arms on the shield of the most execrable domination that has ever oppressed the world since the time when the Huns under Attila raged like a forest fire across the cultivated fields of European civilisation. To-day, in the name of Kultur, a similar invasion has broken on shores that seemed secure, and it is no wonder that it has found its most valuable victim and ally in the Power that adopted the same methods of absorption and extermination centuries before the Hohenzollerns ever started on their career of highway robbery. But like seeks like, and perhaps it was not wholly the fault of our astonishing diplomacy in Constantinople that Turkey, wooed like some desirable maiden, cast in her lot with the Power that by instinct and tradition most resembled her. Spiritual blood, no less than physical blood, is thicker than water, and Gott and Allah, hand-in-hand, pledged each other in the cups they had filled with the blood that poured from the wine-presses of Belgium and of Armenia." (*Crescent and Iron Cross*, pp.1-2.)

Wellington House produced and distributed similar, and in some cases almost identical, propaganda against the Turks as they did against the Germans. The same techniques and formulas were systematically applied by the academic lie producers.

Atrocity propaganda was realised to be the most potent weapon with the masses. Lord Bryce (President of the British Academy and a former Liberal Cabinet Minister) and Toynbee wrote a very similar but shorter book about

German atrocities in Belgium as the *Armenian Blue Book* they compiled directed against the Turks. The German book used unknown and fraudulent sources designated by letters, X,Y,Z, etc.. After the war, the concerned Belgians investigated and found that the book, and its eye-witness accounts of babies on German bayonets etc., were almost all pure fiction. And Austen Chamberlain described it in the House of Lords on 24th October 1925, when a different attitude was required in the public mind about Germany, as factually baseless. (The Trinity College History Professor who has overseen the RTE *Our War* book, John Horne, has recently attempted to resurrect this War propaganda in a publication called *German Atrocities 1914: A History Of Denial*, presumably to justify the Great War on Germany to a new generation. This book is a tirade against 'pacifism' and the belief that Germans were not an especially wicked and frightful race.)

Lord Bryce had been for neutrality at the outbreak of War and had only become an enthusiast for British participation when he read accounts of the 'violation of Belgium' written by Tom Kettle, amongst others. He became the British Ambassador to Washington and had many connections in the American political elite. But he was merely a figurehead for the real workers. The writing of his book, *The Treatment of Armenians in the Ottoman Empire* (more widely known as *The Blue Book*), was actually done by Arnold Toynbee and it was issued as a companion volume to the Report on German atrocities in Belgium. Toynbee himself was the named author of three books on the Armenian issue: *Armenian Atrocities—The Murder Of A Nation*, *The Murderous Tyranny Of The Turks* and *Turkey: A Past And A Future*. The Bryce Report and Toynbee's books became the basis for Wellington House propaganda which constructed the lasting negative image of the Turk in the Western mind.

The propaganda against the Turks utilised the American missions in Armenia, who concentrated their activities on converting the Armenians to Protestantism, and whose work was threatened by the Russian-Turkish conflict. Nearly half the sources used by Bryce and identified as 'foreign residents' were, in fact, unnamed American missionaries. But they were not identified as such, leading readers to believe they were simply independent and trustworthy foreigners with no interest in the matter. The American missions then helped the process in two ways: they provided the information for the propaganda and helped distribute it in America.

The other sources, presented as those of objective individuals, were largely collected from Armenian nationalist organisations, with axes to grind against the Ottomans.

England latched on to the fact that anti-Turkish feeling already existed among some sections of the American public due to the pre-War accounts of their missionaries in Armenia. These people had characterised the Turks as persecutors of Christians (when the Ottomans had, in fact, rather liberally, tolerated the presence of these proselytising and disruptive Christian missions in their Empire). The Christian missionaries had often been presented, in the American media, as long-suffering martyrs, and Britain saw a chance to utilise the sympathy they engendered in the public as a lever to help bring America into the War.

There never was a formal retraction by the British Government of the contents of *The Blue Book*, even though Toynbee later described it as 'propaganda' in his *Western Question in Greece And Turkey* (p.50)—in 1922, at a time when the issue was dead, the Greeks had been cast adrift, and the British were keen to make peace with Ataturk.

A British historian, Trevor Wilson, recently put it like this:

> "Bryce did not have the choice of telling the truth or telling falsehood. If he proved so scrupulous in his investigations that he might have to deem the tales of sadistic crimes unproven—then, inadvertently but inescapably—he would be helping to propagate a much larger untruth: that the whole notion of deliberate and calculated atrocity by Germany on Belgium was unfounded." (*Lord Bryce's Investigation Into Alleged German Atrocities in Belgium, Journal of Contemporary History,* July 1979, p.381.)

Liberal propagandists for the War felt it was their duty to publish unfounded tales in the service of the War effort because not to do so would nullify the reasons for the War itself—and their own support of it. By telling lies about the Germans and Turks in the service of the State, they were salving their own Liberal consciences about having become warmongers.

But the British Government did attempt to try 144 Ottoman officials interned in Malta during 1920-1 on the basis of its evidence. After a two year investigation the Prosecutor released the prisoners due to the lack of concrete evidence, even though the information on the sources used in *The Blue Book* was readily available to the prosecution (this technique will be familiar to readers in Northern Ireland).

It is therefore tempting to conclude that *The Blue Book* was placed on the shelf handy for dusting off on some future date when leverage was required by Britain on the Turks.

The Wellington House publication output was really immense. By June 1915 about two and half million books, pamphlets and leaflets had been distributed. In 1916 there were over 200 individual publications and in 1917 over 400 individual works produced in 17 languages. Pamphlets were placed in libraries, barber shops and doctors' surgeries across America. During the course of the War over 7 million newspapers, books and pamphlets were sent to opinion formers around the world.

The particular target was, however, always America. Gilbert Parker, who directed this work in the United States had over 13,000 names of influential Americans in his notebook. And the important American individuals and organisations who were targeted believed that they were receiving material from Britain's intellectual elite rather than from a State propaganda department.

But it was not just the production of information that was important to Wellington House. Pamphlets and books were expensive and largely read by the upper social classes only. Newspapers were the real medium to influence the masses. And Wellington House printed its own newspapers, in many languages, on the presses of *The Illustrated London News.*

However, the independence of the American Press meant that propaganda production was not so effective within this medium. So England took care to control as well as produce the information provided to American journalists by cutting the German communication cables to America on the opening day of the War, and from then on being the chief supplier of information to the American Press, financing visits to the fronts for U.S. journalists and cultivating them as 'friends' of Britain.

The British Government was able to control all the information going to America because it had already established control over the British Press through the Press Bureau, established in August 1914 to 'supervise' information, and through the Defence of the Realm Act to suppress it, if need be. H.C. Peterson, whose 1939 book, *Propaganda For War*, makes extensive use of the Wellington House American Press releases, commented:

> "With the cables to Germany cut, American newspapers had to secure their war news where it was available—and that was in England. The only way in which they could get complete and dependable (?) news was to buy the advance sheets of London newspapers. Otherwise they were limited to official communiqués from the British or French governments. News obtained from other European countries had to be filtered by the British censor also. Hence it can be seen that it was truly British news that became American news." (H.C. Peterson, *British Influence On The American Press 1914-17, American Political Science Review*, February 1937, p.81.)

It was important that England convince the American public that Ottoman rule was the most murderous and despicable in existence, because the U.S. was not enamoured of the idea of British or French Imperialists extending their rule into the Near East. America had to be persuaded that the extension of Imperial armies into the area was a moral imperative and that the establishment of Colonial administrations was immensely preferable, and indeed an altruistic act on the part of Britain.

### The Armenians And The Jews

Another reason why it became necessary to construct propaganda against the Turks was to counteract the information spreading to America that Britain's Allies, the Russians, were responsible for the massacre of large numbers of Jews in Eastern Europe. These reports had a very negative effect in the U.S. which had a sizeable Jewish community. Britain feared that the negative publicity that this brought on the Allies, combined with the supposed 'power of the Jews' could keep America out of the War. It was therefore essential to hide these reports in a fog of propaganda about Armenia etc. so that the American public would be distracted from the anti-Semitic activities of England's Ally.

I make no claim to know the truth of the Armenian issue—one way or another. All I can do is point out the context of it. During the Great War, the infrastructure of life in the Ottoman Empire, which had been seriously weakened as a result of the conflicts in the Balkans, was almost completely destroyed. In the process of this destruction, up to one third of the population of the Ottoman Empire perished. In the main war zones, in Macedonia and Thrace, western Anatolia, the north-east and south-east, that percentage was as high as two thirds—a much higher number of fatalities suffered than in any other country that was involved in the War.

In the decade between 1912 and 1922, as a result of Allied pressure on the Empire and resulting ethnic cleansing and massacre in the areas seceding from it, the Ottoman Empire was deluged by millions of refugees. The effect of this was compounded by the Great War. Thousands of people moving around as refugees from invading armies and blockade, in chaotic conditions, with the transportation system collapsing, with bandits preying on them under the collapse of order, with the general shortage of food and with primitive sanitation conditions leading to famine, hunger and disease, inevitably resulted in a general breakdown of society in much of the outlying areas of the Empire.

The invading French and Russian armies brought with them Armenian groups armed with Allied weapons whose main purpose was to kill Moslem Turks and Kurds—which they proceeded to do. British and Russian spies circulated amongst the Armenians and Kurds and provided them with weapons and money to enable them to create general disorder. And when the Ottoman authorities moved various groups of people out of the war zones, these groups fell prey to other groups with scores to settle, such as in the case of the Kurds on the Armenians.

The British blockade of the Empire was carried out in order to kill enough Ottoman citizens to force them into surrender and in order to encourage a general collapse of Ottoman society into anarchy. The successful destruction of civil society, caused by the blockade and by the invading Allied armies, was the major factor in turning the position of Armenians and other Christian groups from one of mainstays of the commercial infrastructure, into one of malevolent elements within the Ottoman Empire. And since the objective of the Allies was the destruction of the commercial life of the Ottoman State through invasion and blockade, what future had the Armenians within it, since they were the main traders?

It is not clear whether more Turks and Kurds died at the hands of Armenians and their Russian backers than Armenians died at the hands of Ottoman

Moslems. The only comparable situation I can see would be in the Nazi invasion of Eastern Europe during 1941-2 when society was reduced to its elements, when people did not know under what authority they might live the next day, and different groups did what they had to for the purposes of sheer survival.

But understanding the historical context of events is not conducive to the production of propaganda, of course. So it has to be removed from consideration by separating the event from the context. And then propagandist atmospheres, once produced, have a tendency to persist for longer than is necessary for its producers' purposes, as the recipients have a general disinclination to let go, having been worked up to the cause by the propaganda.

### John Buchan—Jews, Gypsies, Turks and Thieves

John Buchan is famous for his novels, and in particular for *The Thirty-Nine Steps*. But he was not merely a novelist. He had been with Alfred Milner's Kindergarten in South Africa, a group of Britons who served in the South Africa Civil Service, and were responsible for the foundation of the *Round Table* group. He acted as the Proconsul's Private Secretary and remained close to the *Round Table* group for the rest of his life. He was made Director of Intelligence for the Government in the Great War.

In December 1916, when the Propaganda Bureau became the Department of Information, it was placed under the direction of Buchan, on Lord Milner's recommendation to Lloyd George, with Masterman becoming his Deputy. In February 1917 Buchan was put in charge of coordinating all the State's propaganda activities, under the direction of Lord Carson. Later, in 1918, upon Carson's resignation from the Cabinet, a Ministry of Information was created under Lord Beaverbrook, the press baron. However, throughout all these organisational changes, people involved in the propaganda formation business continued to refer to it all as 'Wellington House'.

Colonel Buchan worked as war correspondent for the *Times* and the *Daily News*, sending back reports from the Front that were designed to raise the masses' confidence that they were winning the War. His work involved placing selective information in the public domain, writing books on battles, and compiling the lengthy *History of the War* over 24 volumes, published by Nelson's in monthly instalments.

In his pamphlet, *The Battle of the Somme*, Buchan described the offensive as an Allied victory and stated that it would enable Britain to utilise its superior cavalry. He informed his readers that it was so successful that it marked 'the end of trench fighting and the beginning of the campaign in the open.' He did not tell his readers that the British Army had lost 400,000 men to advance six miles. Propaganda production involved not only using deliberate falsehoods but also being economical with the facts.

Buchan was also responsible for the notorious 'corpse factory' story which alleged that the Germans were boiling the corpses of their soldiers to produce oil from body fats in order to overcome the shortages produced by the Royal Navy blockade.

Buchan saw his novel-writing as very much part of the War effort. *The Thirty Nine Steps*, published by Hodder and Stoughton in 1915 but set before the War, capitalised on the German spy fever, prevalent in England, to sell 25,000 copies in three months (Erskine Childers' *Riddle Of The Sands* was an earlier example of this).

Here is a passage from *The Thirty Nine Steps* which is quoted to show some of the underlying assumptions of Buchan's world view. The main character, Richard Hannay, relates his conversation with another character who acts as a cipher for Buchan's own views.

"I am giving you what he told me as well as I could make it out. Away behind all the Governments and the armies there was a big subterranean movement going on, engineered by very dangerous people. He had come on it by accident; it fascinated him; he went further, and then he got caught. I gathered that most of the people in it were the sort of educated anarchists that make revolutions, but that beside them there were financiers who were playing for money. A clever man can make big profits on a falling market, and it suited the book of both classes to set Europe by the ears. He told me some queer things that explained a lot that had puzzled me—things that happened in the Balkan War, how one state suddenly came out on top, why alliances were made and broken, why certain men disappeared, and where the sinews of war came from. The aim of the whole conspiracy was to get Russia and Germany at loggerheads. When I asked why, he said that the anarchist lot thought it would give them their chance. Everything would be in the melting-pot, and they looked to see a new world emerge. The capitalists would rake in the shekels, and make fortunes by buying up wreckage. Capital, he said, had no conscience and no fatherland. Besides, the Jew was behind it, and the Jew hated Russia worse than hell. 'Do you wonder?' he cried. 'For three hundred years they have been persecuted, and this is the return match for the pogroms. The Jew is everywhere, but you have to go far down the backstairs to find him. Take any big Teutonic business concern. If you have dealings with it the first man you meet is Prince von und Zu Something, an elegant young man who talks Eton-and-Harrow English. But he cuts no ice. If your business is big, you get behind him and find a prognathous Westphalian with a retreating brow and the manners of a hog. He is the German business man that gives your English papers the shakes. But if you're on the biggest kind of job and are bound to get to the real boss, ten to one you are brought up against a little white-faced Jew in a bath-chair with an eye like a rattlesnake. Yes, Sir, he is the man who is ruling the world just now, and he has his knife in the Empire of the Tzar, because his aunt was outraged and his father flogged in some one-horse location on the Volga.'" (*The Thirty Nine Steps*, pp.11-12.)

Belief in 'the power of the Jews' was a common preconception in Britain during the first half of the twentieth century. And, as we have seen, it made connections between Germany and Turkey in the worrying English mind.

The other great fear lay in the power of Islam, and its supposed potential to unite all Moslems in the British Empire, in a *jihad*, to throw out Westerners. And Germany and Turkey, along with the Jews and Islam, come together in the Buchan imagination in his 1916 War novel, *Greenmantle*.

*Greenmantle* was the sequel to *The Thirty Nine Steps*. It featured the same main character, Richard Hannay, and was also published by Hodder and Stoughton.

In *Greenmantle* the hero, Hannay, is called in to investigate rumours of an imminent uprising in the Muslim world, and he undertakes a journey through enemy territory in Germany and Austro-Hungary to meet up with his friend Sandy in Constantinople. Once there, Hannay and his colleagues attempt to thwart the German plot to use Islam in a *jihad* to help them win the War.

The book opens in November 1915, with Hannay and his friend Sandy convalescing from wounds received at the battle of Loos. Hannay is summoned to the Foreign Office by Sir Walter Bullivant, a senior intelligence operator, whom Hannay had previously assisted in *The Thirty-Nine Steps*. Bullivant gives Hannay an outline of the political situation in the Middle East, and tells him that the Germans and their Turkish allies are plotting to cause a great uprising throughout the Muslim world, that will throw the whole of the Middle East, India and North Africa into a Holy War against the British infidel and his Empire:

> "Sir Walter lay back in his arm-chair and spoke to the ceiling. It was the best story, the clearest and the fullest, I had ever got of any bit of the war. He told me just how and why and when Turkey had left the rails. I heard about her grievances over our seizure of her ironclads, of the mischief the coming of the Goeben had wrought, of Enver and his precious committee and the way they had got a cinch on the old Turk. When he had spoken for a bit, he began to question me.
>
> 'You are an intelligent fellow, and you will ask how a Polish adventurer, meaning Enver, and a collection of Jews and gipsies should have got control of a proud race. The ordinary man will tell you that it was German organisation backed up with German money and German arms. You will inquire again how, since Turkey is primarily a religious power, Islam has played so small a part in it all. The Sheikh-ul-Islam is neglected, and though the Kaiser proclaims a Holy War and calls himself Hadji Mohammed Guilliamo, and says the Hohenzollerns are descended from the Prophet, that seems to have fallen pretty flat. The ordinary man again will answer that Islam in Turkey is becoming a back number, and that Krupp guns are the new gods. Yet—I don't know. I do not quite believe in Islam becoming a back number.' 'Look at it in another way,' he went on. 'If it were Enver and Germany alone dragging Turkey into a European war for purposes that no Turk cared a rush about, we might expect to find the regular army obedient, and Constantinople. But in the provinces, where Islam is strong, there would be trouble. Many of us counted on that. But

we have been disappointed. The Syrian army is as fanatical as the hordes of the Mahdi. The Senussi have taken a hand in the game. The Persian Moslems are threatening trouble. There is a dry wind blowing through the East, and the parched grasses wait the spark. And that wind is blowing towards the Indian border. Whence comes that wind, think you?' ...

'Have you an explanation, Hannay?' he asked again. 'It looks as if Islam had a bigger hand in the thing than we thought,' I said. 'I fancy religion is the only thing to knit up such a scattered empire.' 'You are right,' he said. 'You must be right. We have laughed at the Holy War, the jehad that old Von der Goltz prophesied. But I believe that stupid old man with the big spectacles was right. There is a jehad preparing. The question is, How?' 'I'm hanged if I know,' I said; 'but I'll bet it won't be done by a pack of stout German officers in pickelhaubes. I fancy you can't manufacture Holy Wars out of Krupp guns alone and a few staff officers and a battle cruiser with her boilers burst.' 'Agreed. They are not fools, however much we try to persuade ourselves of the contrary. But supposing they had got some tremendous sacred sanction—some holy thing, some book or gospel or some new prophet from the desert, something which would cast over the whole ugly mechanism of German war the glamour of the old torrential raids which crumpled the Byzantine Empire and shook the walls of Vienna? Islam is a fighting creed, and the mullah still stands in the pulpit with the Koran in one hand and a drawn sword in the other. Supposing there is some Ark of the Covenant which will madden the remotest Moslem peasant with dreams of Paradise? What then, my friend?' 'Then there will be hell let loose in those parts pretty soon.' 'Hell which may spread. Beyond Persia, remember, lies India.' ..." (pp.15-17.)

On his journey through enemy territory Hannay meets one of Buchan's stereotypical German characters, Colonel Von Stumm, which gives the author an opportunity to give rein to his anti-German prejudices:

"The middle of Germany was a cheerier place than Berlin or the western parts. I liked the look of the old peasants, and the women in their neat Sunday best, but I noticed, too, how pinched they were... Stumm made an attempt to talk to me on the journey. I could see his aim. Before this he had cross-examined me, but now he wanted to draw me into ordinary conversation. He had no notion how to do it. He was either peremptory and provocative, like a drill-sergeant, or so obviously diplomatic that any fool would have been put on his guard. That is the weakness of the German. He has no gift for laying himself alongside different types of men. He is such a hard-shell being that he cannot put out feelers to his kind. He may have plenty of brains, as Stumm had, but he has the poorest notion of psychology of any of God's creatures. In Germany only the Jew can get outside himself, and that is why, if you look into the matter, you will find that the Jew is at the back of most German enterprises." (p.99.)

In Constantinople Hannay meets Blenkiron, a German-American agent, who explains how dangerous German designs are on the Middle-East:

"Blenkiron stopped to light a fresh cigar. He was leaner than when he left London and there were pouches below his eyes. I fancy his journey had not been as fur-lined as he made out. 'I've found out one thing, and that is, that the last dream Germany will part with is the control of the Near East. That is what your statesmen don't figure enough on. She'll give up Belgium and Alsace-Lorraine and Poland, but by God! she'll never give up the road to Mesopotamia till you have her by the throat and make her drop it. Sir Walter is a pretty bright-eyed citizen, and he sees it right enough. If the worst happens, Kaiser will fling overboard a lot of ballast in Europe, and it will look like a big victory for the Allies, but he won't be beaten if he has the road to the East safe. Germany's like a scorpion: her sting's in her tail, and that tail stretches way down into Asia. 'I got that clear, and I also made out that it wasn't going to be dead easy for her to keep that tail healthy. Turkey's a bit of an anxiety, as you'll soon discover. But Germany thinks she can manage it, and I won't say she can't. It depends on the hand she holds, and she reckons it a good one. I tried to find out, but they gave me nothing but eyewash. I had to pretend to be satisfied, for the position of John S. wasn't so strong as to allow him to take liberties. If I asked one of the highbrows he looked wise and spoke of the might of German arms and German organization and German staff-work. I used to nod my head and get enthusiastic about these stunts, but it was all soft soap. She has a trick in hand—that much I know, but I'm darned if I can put a name to it. I pray to God you boys have been cleverer.'..." (pp.196-7.)

In the following passage the similarities between the German character and Islam are outlined to explain why they made the perfect partners in crime. Greenmantle is the name of the Prophet who will lead the Islamic uprising:

"The Turk and the Arab came out of big spaces, and they have the desire of them in their bones. They settle down and stagnate, and by the by they degenerate into that appalling subtlety which is their ruling passion gone crooked. And then comes a new revelation and a great simplifying. They want to live face to face with God without a screen of ritual and images and priestcraft. They want to prune life of its foolish fringes and get back to the noble bareness of the desert. Remember, it is always the empty desert and the empty sky that cast their spell over them—these, and the hot, strong, antiseptic sunlight which burns up all rot and decay. It isn't inhuman. It's the humanity of one part of the human race. It isn't ours, it isn't as good as ours, but it's jolly good all the same. There are times when it grips me so hard that I'm inclined to forswear the gods of my fathers! Well, Greenmantle is the prophet of this great simplicity. He speaks straight to the heart of Islam, and it's an honourable message. But for our sins it's been twisted into part of that damned German propaganda. His unworldliness has been used for a cunning political move, and his creed of space and simplicity for the furtherance of the last word in human degeneracy. My God, Dick, it's like seeing St Francis run by Messalina.'...

'Germany's simplicity is that of the neurotic, not the primitive. It is megalomania and egotism and the pride of the man in the Bible that waxed fat and kicked. But the results are the same. She wants to destroy and simplify; but it isn't the simplicity of the ascetic, which is of the spirit, but the simplicity of the madman that grinds down all the contrivances of civilization to a featureless monotony. The prophet wants to save the souls of his people; Germany wants to rule the inanimate corpse of the world. But you can get the same language to cover both. And so you have the partnership of St Francis and Messalina. Dick, did you ever hear of a thing called the Superman?' 'There was a time when the papers were full of nothing else,' I answered. 'I gather it was invented by a sportsman called Nietzsche.' 'Maybe,' said Sandy. 'Old Nietzsche has been blamed for a great deal of rubbish he would have died rather than acknowledge. But it's a craze of the new, fatted Germany. It's a fancy type which could never really exist, any more than the Economic Man of the politicians. Mankind has a sense of humour which stops short of the final absurdity. There never has been, and there never could be a real Superman ... But there might be a Superwoman.' 'You'll get into trouble, my lad, if you talk like that,' I said." (pp.250-2.)

What we see in John Buchan and Wellington House propaganda is the application of fiction writing to the production of a general consciousness that becomes 'fact'. And it was no accident that so many novelists were employed in the production of propaganda, alongside the academics and historians who turned their hands to fiction; fiction which passed as fact, in the case of historians, thanks to their previous reputations.

### How To Produce Propaganda On The Turks

In 1917, with conscription on the statute books and America entering the War, Lloyd George instructed Buchan to concentrate his efforts on the Turks.

Justin McCarthy, Professor of History at Louisville University, Kentucky, has done a lot of work in the area of British propaganda about the Turks and has delivered a number of speeches on the activities of Wellington House. In a 2001 article entitled *The Bryce Report: British Propaganda and the Turks,* McCarthy cites a document in the Foreign Office files written by Buchan describing what producing anti-Turk propaganda should entail and the formula it should follow to be most effective:

> "We must organize an elaborate campaign in Britain, in Allied countries, and to a limited extent in neutral countries on the text, 'The Turk must go'. If Turkey in its present form disappears the German *Drang nach Osten* [Drive to the East. P.W.] fails, and with it the major purpose with which Germany entered the war. We may have difficulty with the Allies and neutrals on some of our peace terms, but the impossible position of Turkey is a point on which we should be able to secure general unanimity. We have got to make it a platitude among Allies and neutrals.

The points we must emphasize are:

(a) The ancient riches and the great prosperity of Asia Minor and Mesopotamia.

(b) The blighting influence of the Turk on social and Commercial progress.

(c) The incapacity of the Turk for absorbing conquered peoples or for administering equitably subject races. For this we want a historical argument and an account of the recent treatment of Jews, Armenians, Syrians and Balkan races, et cetera.

(d) The impossibility of reforming the Turkish state. The Turk is a military power and nothing else. He has never shown any capacity for civil government.

(e) The danger of allowing a reactionary and incompetent state to control the avenue between Europe and Asia. Such a state must always be a satellite of a reactionary military bureaucracy like Germany.

(f) The religious element might also be pressed. Turkey at present governs a sort of museum of opposing religions, and toleration in the modern sense is alien to her theory of government.

There is no necessity to present detailed themes for the future of Turkey. All we have to do is to convince people that the present situation is impossible and must be drastically dealt with." (Cited in Justin McCarthy, *The Bryce Report: British Propaganda and the Turks,* p.4.)

The general themes of propaganda against the Turks were made deliberately consistent and they were repeated over and over in the whole range of Wellington House publications. The Turks' rule was depicted as arbitrary and illegitimate, they were stated to have retarded the progress of the lands they ruled, they were characterized as fanatical Moslems, haters and slaughterers of Christians and perpetrators of unspeakable attacks on Christian women.

All this propaganda had a number of objectives, including bringing America into the War, as explained. But the final purpose was to prepare the world for the transfer of the Ottoman territories over to the Western Powers, who would bring progress where there was stultification and reaction, civilization where there had been barbarism, paradise where there had existed hell, and light where there was darkness.

Propaganda is an important feature of warfare in the democratic era. And it is pretended that Hitler and Dr. Goebbels were the masters of it. But Hitler explained who the masters of it were in *Mein Kampf*—and it was not the Germans.

I think that the great effort England put into the production of propaganda in 1914 was something altogether different than anything that ever went before—and its main effect was to change Britain for ever. To conduct affairs in the world effectively, States need to produce propaganda in the service of their interests, but they also need to be able to ignore it in practical politics. The United States is still capable of acting like this. But from 1914 Britain began to take its own propaganda in earnest and it has never been the same since.

Today, it seems that Britain and its agencies of State do little more than produce propaganda in the service of the British State and then work to universalise this propaganda. But in the century since 1914 this propaganda production has had nothing but a disabling effect on England's ability to conduct its affairs in the world wisely. And all those who are taken into its orbit seem to be affected likewise. But then again that might just be the point of it!

## The Armistice and Imperial Objectives

Britain managed to bring the United States into the War and in time this produced the victory that would have been impossible without such an intervention. But the American participation in the War complicated things for England in the Middle East and the first issue on which this was evident was over Turkey and Constantinople.

On January 5th, 1918, Lloyd George made a speech, in which he promised that Britain was not fighting for Constantinople or for Asia Minor and Thrace, 'the homelands of the Turkish race'. But at the end of the war, the Prime Minister claimed that this statement had not been intended as an offer to the Turks. It had presumably been aimed at disorganising Turkish resistance to the advancing Imperialist armies, in the same way as President Wilson's Fourteen Points had been used against the Germans.

On New Year's Day, 1919, *The Irish News* published a report by Mr. Collinson Owen, the 'Special Representative of the British Press with the British Naval Forces at the Dardanelles', indicating Imperial objectives with regard to Constantinople and Turkey. It is a good summary of what the British thought about doing to the Turks, before they were forced to hesitate by the turn of events and plans began to go awry:

"The Allies have now been in Constantinople since November 13th, on which day their great fleet anchored off the Golden Horn, and on the surface it would seem that little has been done towards the solution of the greatest problem of the Near East, viz: the proper government of Turkey and its capital. (As a matter of fact this is not one of the tasks of the Allies under the Armistice, however persistent the idea of it may be in everybody's mind.) And yet in spite of appearances one great step forward has been made. It is that everybody concerned is convinced once and for all that the Turks are not competent to govern themselves, much less subject peoples; that they have recklessly thrown away all the many generous chances Western Europe has given them in the past and that there is not the slightest chance that they would do any better with any further opportunities for reform that might unwisely be given them in the future... Now this conviction is common to all the Allies who hold the fate of Turkey and her peoples in their hand and with the bonds that now exist between them, born of common sacrifices, it should be possible to consider the problem in a spirit free from the jealousies and the diplomatic manoeuvres which in the past were Turkey's chief strength...

Tewfik Pasha's Government is a weak government (and Tewfik Pasha himself cannot be called a strong man), but it is at any rate the Government which was formed to treat with the Allies after the armistice. But the Chamber, which ought to realise this, and give some support, does nothing but criticise and hinder... They become angry at the mere suggestion that Turkey has been vanquished in the war... but believe that honours on the field of battle were even and the Turkish Palestine Army was preparing to fight again...

What is to be done with a people which loves domination over other races, but possesses no power for good government?.. An international control drawn from the various Allied Powers is often suggested, but this would have its own inherent weaknesses... and when the binding effects of the Great War had worn off the Turk would take advantage of this situation just as he juggled with the various European Powers in the past. Here and there the situation is made that the United States should take charge of Turkey's affairs... But Turkey is a long way from the United States and it would seem difficult for a country which has lived by the Munroe Doctrine to form a sort of protectorate on the far edge of Europe...

The suggestion one oftenest hears here, from Turkish sources amongst others, is THAT BRITAIN SHOULD TAKE CONSTANTINOPLE AND TURKEY IN HAND [capitals in original] and do much with them as she has done with Egypt. It is impossible, when considering the question of Turkey, not to think continually of the question of Egypt. No doubt we could do the same here as we have done elsewhere, regarding Turkey simply as an extension of 'the white man's burden', and shouldering this responsibility as we have done so many others. It is certain that nobody wants it for its own sake, and that if we undertook the task it would be from disinterested motives—as the best solution to an age-old problem. It is equally certain that we could do it better than any other people, having both the genius and experience for that sort of thing. But the chief difficulty would be to persuade other peoples to believe in our complete lack of material interest in undertaking the regeneration of Turkey... They might thoroughly believe in our competence, but very much hesitate that we would attempt this purely for the sake of civilisation. The British are still only a vaguely understood people, and finally we might shrink from it ourselves foreseeing the difficulties and, no doubt, the thankless nature of the task, and realising that we have already a little too much on our hands."

Before the Great War, Britain had used the policy of establishing Protectorates to expand the frontiers of Empire over regions that they did not officially control. When the Empire had established a Protectorate, British authority was projected across these areas, as in Egypt, and other Powers (like France) were warned off. Then British Power was gradually assembled in these Protectorates until they became Imperial possessions in all but name.

There is something of the pre-War spirit and the temptation to continue the traditional expansionist policy in Collinson Owen's report—Britain 'having both the genius and experience for that sort of thing' and 'regarding Turkey simply as an extension of 'the white man's burden'.' But it is tempered by the effects of the alliance built up to destroy Germany and the pretensions adopted in the 'war for civilisation'. And there is the understanding that the Empire, in fighting the 'war for civilisation' and acquiring its vast expanses of territory in the course of it may have over-extended itself and had 'already a little too much on [its] hands'. So England knew what it wanted to do with the Turks, but it no longer believed it could accomplish it in the straightforward manner that was possible in the past.

### The American Complication

The Paris Peace Conference, which opened in January 1919, did not immediately start dispensing judgement on the Turks, due to the conflicting interests of the Allied Powers and the numerous secret arrangements that had previously been entered into by Britain regarding the dividing up of Ottoman territory (these numbered ninety-nine in all!). This made some people think that the Turks had been forgotten about altogether.

In the Constantinople Agreement of May 18th 1915, Britain had agreed that the Czarist Empire should obtain Constantinople and the Straits. However, in 1918 this Treaty was considered no longer valid — since Russia had relinquished her Imperialist claims against Turkey in 1917 shortly before the Bolshevik revolution. So what was to be done with Constantinople and the areas earmarked for the Czar in the Constantinople Agreement?

A writer under the pen name 'Seleucus' outlined the British dilemma over the control of the Middle East in *The New Europe* of 17th January 1917. At the bottom of the problem lay the abrupt change of policy that the British State undertook in the first decade of the new century, according to 'Seleucus':

"During the 19th century we had tried to insulate our Oriental Empire from continental Europe by maintaining a barrier of neutral independent states, and since these states were chiefly Moslem, our policy was in effect an *entente* with Islam."

But then came the understanding with Russia of 1907,

"which in Germany is known as 'the policy of encirclement' ... a profound modification of the policy we had pursued for a century before."

So, Britain dropped the Moslem states in favour of its new Russian partner

"and the partition with her of the 'insulating region' or in other words, the Middle East, which the Anglo-Russian *Entente* ultimately involved, cost us inevitably the friendship of the Moslem world."

But then Britain's new Russian partner imploded in waging the War on Germany and its cut of the Moslem world was repudiated by the new regime in Moscow. This opened up the problem of the 'insulating region' again:

"We cannot carry on the policy of 1907 alone. We cannot step into Russia's shoes and take over her former sphere in the Middle East as well as our own. It would involve extending the range of British responsibility."

And there was already the understanding that in expending such a huge effort in the War on Germany 'this would be altogether beyond our strength.'

However, 'Nor can we confine ourselves to what, under the agreements, seems to have been regarded as the British sphere, and stand on the defensive in Palestine, Mesopotamia and Southern Persia' because of the presence of other Powers.

'Seleucus' then pondered on the idea of resurrecting the 'Moslem *entente*' and 'indirect annexation to the British Empire' of Persian, Arab, Jewish, Armenian, Georgian and Tatar areas and their construction into states, until they could achieve 'self-determination.' 'Seleucus' finally concluded:

> "There is no solution unless we can find some third party disinterested enough to take this area in trust and hold its peoples in wardship until they are capable of standing by themselves. No power can do this except some authority constituted by a League of Nations, and it is difficult to see how the particular problem of the Middle East can be solved at the Peace Conference unless the League of Nations is called into existence at the same time."

And this is where the United States starts to come in handy for Britain at the Peace Conference.

On May 19th 1919 *The Irish News* editorial, *Dividing Up*, reported on the tricky process England was engaged in at Paris:

> "Official sanction has not yet been proclaimed in connection with the Allies' dismemberment of the 'Turkish Empire.' There was a time—and that within the memory of men who yet deem themselves far from aged—when the preservation of the Turkish Empire in Europe and Asia was a cardinal point of British 'Imperial' policy... England fought the Crimean War to secure Turkish integrity... and now the Turkish Empire is to pass from existence, as greater 'combinations' have faded out of sight. Assyria, Greece, Rome, Carthage, where are they now?...
>
> America, according to the report, will take charge of Constantinople, which, with an adjacent area, is to be fashioned into an 'International State.' No one will envy America her task—and we are convinced that many Americans will not relish it. Palestine and Mesopotamia are to pass to Great Britain as her share of the great 'divide.' France is to have Syria—and she is not satisfied. Adalia (Anatolia), a historic port in Asia Minor, and control over Konia go to Italy. Parts of 'Turkey in Europe' will be handed over to Greece. Thus the Turkish Empire will be ended—when these arrangements have been put into practical effect: and the Caliphate of the Moslem world will be a-begging.
>
> There is a certainty of 'trouble' amongst Mohammedans in Asia and Africa; we await a formal intimation before accepting the statement that America will put her hand into this dangerous mass of 'inflammable materials.' But we do not question England's desire to get Palestine and Mesopotamia. The Suez

Canal will then be as completely under English control as the passage through Panama is under American, and the Red Sea will become an 'English lake.' Some years ago Russia (of the Czar) and England 'partitioned' the ancient Kingdom of Persia into 'spheres of influence.' Russia has vanished from the 'Imperialist picture'; we shall soon learn that Persia's genuine interests demand the supervision and 'protection' of the European Power whose new territories adjoin the Dominions of the Shah."

With regard to Constantinople, Britain, hesitating at the prospect of establishing an Egypt style Protectorate over Turkey, believed it could use the United States in the region against the interests of France and Italy. There was some opposition from the British Admiralty to the proposal that the U.S. Navy take Constantinople in hand, but this was regarded as a useful ploy to deter the French interest in the city and also save money, in the event of an American agreement.

### The Round Table And The Holy Grail

The scheme for United States involvement in the Middle East is argued out in *Windows of Freedom*, an article published by Lionel Curtis in *The Round Table* of December 1918, and disseminated to Anglophile Americans in the hope of converting them to the Imperial civilising mission. It began with the contention that: 'The future position of America in the world, not that of Germany, Austria, or Turkey, is the great issue that now hangs on the Peace Conference.' Here is an extended extract:

"If five years ago a responsible American had foretold the present position, his friends would have summoned a mental specialist. Not Theodore Roosevelt himself would have thought that today, with two million men in Europe, an American President would be taking the lead in dethroning Emperors, in erecting Republics, and re-drawing the map of the world. The incredible has happened, and now it seems so obvious, that people are apt to assume that it could not have happened otherwise. America no longer stands, contrary to her old habit, clean outside the world-old struggle of freedom with despotism. The British and American Commonwealths are now together in that struggle and will stand together by the law of their being, once for all... Provision must be made for peace, order and good government in all the derelict territories severed from Turkey, and in the colonies taken from Germany; and some Power must be made responsible for each of them... Provision must be made for the control of the Dardanelles and the Bosphorus...

The crux of the problem lies in the fact that none of the territories outside Europe detached by this war from the German and Turkish Empires can in the near future provide peace, order and good government for themselves. How to provide good government for these territories is the most difficult of the questions which the Conference has to face... Egypt is an example of the countries of the Near East for which there is at present no hope except in the guardianship of some civilized State. As powerful financial interests of Europe gained a footing in Egypt, her native despotism developed typical symptoms. Corruption, indebtedness, over-taxation, rapacity, torture and anarchy followed each other in turn. Less than forty years ago Egypt was one of the most miserable countries on earth. To-day she is one of the most prosperous, and is gradually contracting the habits of order from which progress toward self-government can begin...

Let America apply the same reasoning to the problem of Mexico, which is at their doors... Is it too much to ask that in this crisis of human destiny America shall forget to think of herself, and rather think of the wider interests, to vindicate which she has sent two million Americans to Europe...

If only America can discard her traditional aloofness and... make herself answerable to a League of Nations for peace, order, and good government in some or all of the regions of the Middle East. Her very detachment renders her an ideal custodian of the Dardanelles. For exactly similar reasons her task in preserving the autonomy of Armenia, Arabia and Persia will be easier than if it were to rest in our hands. Her vast Jewish population pre-eminently fits her to protect Palestine. Her position between India and Europe removes all our objections to the railway development which these regions require... Above all she has the capital for these works, while we, with less than half her population will be hard put to it to find enough for the vast territories we already control."

In *The Anglo-American Establishment*, Professor Carroll Quigley wrote that the Mandate system 'was first suggested by George Louis Beer in a report submitted to the United States Government on January 1, 1918, and by Lionel Curtis in an article called *'Windows of Freedom'* in *The Round Table* for December 1918.' (p.168.).

*Windows of Freedom* was the first expression in print of the Mandates idea and this proposal originated with Milner's Kindergarten/*Round Table* Group (which later became the Royal Institute of International Affairs/Chatham House). Along with the Mandates proposal drawn up by Lord Milner was *The League of Nations: A Practical Suggestion,* a policy which was introduced into the Peace Conference by the *Round Table* group.

George Louis Beer became Wilson's expert on colonial questions at the Peace Conference in Paris. While the *Round Table* group served at the Conference as advisers to Lloyd George, they managed to install Beer as head of the Mandate Department of the League of Nations. Beer was one of the originators of the Royal Institute of International Affairs in London and its American branch, The Council on Foreign Relations, which still has an influential role in American Foreign Policy.

*The Round Table* published replies to Curtis's article from two sympathetic Americans in its next edition, under the heading, *America And World Responsibility: First And Second Thoughts.* (It is not unreasonable to suggest that one of these replies might even have been penned by Beer, considering the way the Milnerites worked.) The gist of these replies was that it would be very difficult to get America to see the world in the same way Britain saw it and utilise the United States entry into the War as a lever to make her into an Imperial Power, as Curtis desired, and ultimately as the foundation of Anglo-American world government. Here is an extract from one of the American replies to *Windows of Freedom*:

"I may lack the vision or the imagination to follow you, but to my mind there is at present little chance that our country will embark on such altruistic ventures... It rests upon too idealistic a conception of the reasons which prompted us to enter the world war, and upon the altruistic considerations which it claims... America did not enter the war to vindicate the wider interests in question, nor has she the welfare of the world at large at heart, if in opposition to her own interests... Our participation in the world war, or rather the cause of the participation, has been obscured by the use of slogans like 'Make the World safe for Democracy.' We would never have gone to war for that. We saw the German monster in its ugliest and most inhuman form, and we commenced to fear that it might some day 'get us' if we did not help to kill it...

Now, as to 'the welfare of the world at large, as the polestar of its policy,' I think that no country can be expected to steer by that polestar unless its citizens are accustomed to think and feel in world terms. The Britons are; the world has been an open book to them since centuries. Not so with Americans, who, until the beginning of the recent catastrophe, had been taught to fight shy of any political combination outside their own territory. The war has widened our horizon immensely, but it will take more than that to prepare us for so serious and novel a task as to shoulder the white man's burden.

There are in this country certain large financial interests that have world connections and investments, and they might well be disposed to adopt and further a policy along the lines advocated in the article under review. But their advocacy of it would destine it to failure. The general public, on the other hand, is, in my opinion, not prepared to undertake the trusteeship over territory and alien peoples in Europe, Asia or Africa, and would, I believe, strongly resist any attempt to fasten such a responsibility upon our Government." (*The Round Table,* March 1919.)

The article was correct in suggesting that America did not go to war in 1917 for altruistic reasons. Putting it another way, she did not enter the conflict on the basis of an Anglo-Saxon racial affinity that the Mother Country claimed in order to obtain the American entry. If she had, there would have been widespread opposition from the large German-American and Irish-American populations as well as the Eastern Europeans, including the Jews (who had tasted Czarist oppression).

I have read many accounts which suggest that ordinary America, outside of the Anglophile elite, was largely more sympathetic to Germany than to the Imperialist Allies and I have no reason to doubt that there was little enthusiasm amongst ordinary Americans to enlist in the War on the Central Powers.

America entered the war at a time of her own choosing, at the moment that suited her own interests. At the point of her entry into the War, the prospective outcome was so advantageous to the United States that interests must have been the determining factor in the calculation.

America's initial view of the War had been that there was nothing morally at issue between the belligerents, it could only be bad to get involved in it, and a settlement should be made between the combatants without the destruction of any of the nations fighting it. President Woodrow Wilson, however, had converted to the idea of intervention long before January 1917. A year earlier, he had sent Colonel House to Europe with a plan to put America in the war on the side of the Allies, if Germany would not accept peace terms obviously unfavourable to her. But even though his peace terms for Germany were almost unacceptable for her, they were in fact rejected by Britain, who was determined to crush Germany before the President or Pope Benedict could bring about a settlement. The British rebuff did not lead Wilson to lose heart in his efforts to bring the U.S. into the War but he was convinced that there was no hope of getting the country into war until after the election. The American sentiment was for peace, so Wilson played on this general sentiment in his election campaign of 1916. (The influence exerted by American finance upon U.S. entry into the Great War is revealed in Ray Stannard Baker's *Life and Letters of Woodrow Wilson* and in Professor C. C. Tansill's *America Goes to War*.)

Whilst the U.S. remained neutral, at the same time it set about making Britain financially dependent upon it—largely through J. P. Morgan's banking empire—by giving Britain the necessary credit to keep waging war. At the beginning of the War, America declared against loans to any belligerent, on the ground that credit is the basis of all forms of contraband. But this declaration was made at a time when the situation did not operate seriously against the Allies, for the balance of trade and investment was against the United States, and the Allied countries could simply pay for their purchases by cancelling the debts owed abroad by Americans. This situation took care of matters for the first few months of the War. But Allied war purchases became so great that, by the end of 1914, there was a credit crisis.

The Banks appealed to Wilson and he gave them the nod to issue loans to the Allied governments. Loans were in violation of American neutrality but Morgan's got around this by issuing $2 billion in credit to the *Entente*.

On September 8th 1915, Wilson assented to pressure and the first public loan, the $500,000,000 Anglo-French loan, was floated. American industry, in propping up the British Exchequer, became an adjunct of the British war effort. Of the five million pounds the British spent on weaponry and supplies each day during 1915-16, two million pounds was being spent in the United States. By 1916, 40% of Britain's war material was being supplied by the U.S.

Whilst this factor helped America in the medium term to undermine the

British Empire's power and eventually replace it on the world stage, it also tended to place the U.S. in the position of having to make a necessary defence of its investments if there was danger of its client going under with its debts unpaid.

Formal loans to the Allies, amounting to over $2,500,000,000, financed their purchases for a little over a year, but their purchasing was so heavy that even the great U.S. banking houses could not supply their needs. By January 1917, the Allies had overdrawn their credit by nearly $500,000,000 and only the U.S. Government could save their great banking houses and the Allies.

By the end of 1916, France and Russia were broke and London was paying for its war on American credit. In March 1917, only 114 million pounds of gold were left in the Bank of England's vaults to cover further loans. If this had been exhausted, British finance would have collapsed and brought down a large section of American industry with it, with a catastrophic effect on the U.S. economy.

Wilson was influenced by a message from the American ambassador to England, Thomas Nelson Page, a strong Anglophile, that Britain would be bankrupt within two weeks if the U.S. did not enter the war and provide her with funds. Also in the picture were cables from the U.S. embassy in Paris, warning that French morale was cracking. These were communicated to Congress.

But American participation in the War brought about a problem for England—there were strings attached, namely Wilson's Principles.

When *The Round Table* heard the Wilsonian principles, they believed they could be worked on in the Imperial interest but they underestimated the substantial reasons for the American participation, which were far from altruistic.

But the Round Tablers persisted in searching for the Holy Grail of Anglo-American co-operation in world empire establishment.

### The Americans and Mandates

Before the War, and until the moment America joined it, the Imperialist Powers would have intended the conquered territories of the vanquished to be directly absorbed by their respective Empires. The Sykes-Picot agreement was an example of this. But the necessity of taking on America as an ally, to bail out the *Entente*, changed the character of the War and complicated things for the Imperialist Powers at the Paris Peace Conference.

The Mandates idea was an attempt to square traditional Imperialist objectives with America's appearance on the world stage and the War for small nations propaganda. It is probable that, if the Allies had been able to win the War without America, there would have been a simple Imperialist division of spoils—or a war over those spoils between the Allies. But the entry into the War of anti-imperialist America, with her strong disdain for the European

Imperialist mission, and her presence at the conference table complicated matters somewhat for the Imperialist Powers and they were forced to proceed in a tricky fashion, through the Mandates.

From the very start the intention was to draw the United States to her 'world responsibilities'—which meant convincing the Americans that they should take up the Imperialist project of bringing the 'lesser breeds' up to civilisation whilst 'supervising' their countries in the meantime.

Of course, this suggestion had never been made prior to the Great War, when an American intrusion into the feeding grounds of the Imperialist Powers would have produced the utmost dismay in Europe. However, in late 1918, England needed the United States because it had come to possess a vast amount of new territory as a result of the Great War. And it had bitten off more than it could chew: after its efforts in the War, it had neither the blood nor the treasure to expend in purposefully governing these acquisitions. England was now the 'dog in the manger' who did not want anyone else taking on its role—particularly not France, or indeed Italy or Russia. Even up to mid-1918 a collapse of the enemy was not a certainty, so a resurgent Germany or Turkey was also a possibility that needed to be blocked off. It was also determined in London that these new territories should not be permitted to go their own way, lest they develop minds of their own or fall into the clutches of others with a mind to rival Britain.

That is where America came in. The Anglo-Saxon cousin was the perfect Imperialist—since she was anti-Imperialist in nature and inclination. She could not be a rival to England in the Imperialist sense but could keep the other Imperialists out and could do the work Britain would have done herself if she had emerged from the Great War as victor in 1915, still plentiful in money and men. (I am aware that in some circles a war between England and America was predicted after the conclusion of the War on Germany. But this view faded in Britain as it realised the extent of its exhaustion after seeing the War on Germany through to the bitter end.)

George Washington had insisted, as a fundamental of Foreign Policy, that the United States should never become involved in European entanglements. His policy was adhered to throughout the nineteenth century. But it was abandoned by President Wilson in 1917. Now Britain, which had achieved American involvement in Europe, hoped that the United States would do the difficult and expensive work in the troublesome and less profitable areas of Britain's Imperial acquisitions, on Britain's behalf. And, by being given the most difficult jobs in the world, perhaps America could even be worn down, and cut down to size as an emerging Power.

### An American in Paris

Frederic C. Howe was sent by President Wilson to the Paris Peace

Conference in 1919. Howe was the author of the book *Socialized Germany*, which James Connolly published extensive extracts from in *The Worker's Republic* during 1915-16. Howe was not a socialist himself and this probably helped him to produce such an extremely interesting book on the character of the pre-War German State, which he characterized as socialist. He was Governor of New York Immigration Authority when he published this book on the German system of State Socialism. (Connolly agreed with Howe that Germany was virtually a Socialist state, prior to its destruction in the War.)

Although Howe was an admirer of the pre-War German accomplishment, he was, like his President, still an Anglophile at heart, as his reminiscences of 1925, *The Confessions Of A Reformer*, reveal:

"Early in the war I wrote to the President about the Near East. I was intensely interested in that part of the world which began with Constantinople and ended with Persia, including Egypt, Syria, Mesopotamia, and the control of the Mediterranean. I felt that here was the origin of the war, here was danger to the British Empire, to France, to the Allied cause... My Anglo-Saxon instincts were strong enough to revolt at this. I did not want Germany to take the place of England and America in their dominance of the world. I did not believe the war propaganda, did not accept the singleness of German guilt. Still something within me was aroused at the thought of German ascendancy in the world. The thought of America seemed to be fixed on the western front; our minds were being filled with hatred and desire for revenge. Vistas of permanent security and peace that the President's eloquence painted were unrealizable, to my mind, unless the problems of the Near East were taken into account. Here was the tinder-box of Europe, the source of repeated modern wars. Over its control Russia, England, and France had warred and negotiated from the time of Napoleon." (p.284.)

Howe's 1919 book, *The Only Possible Peace,* is a fierce denunciation of Germany, which the author believed to be intent on world conquest through its Bagdad-Berlin Railway. And it is clear that until Howe encountered Britain in reality, in the peace-making process at Paris, he held the idealist Anglophile notion of English civilization and benevolence. But that was all to change from the time of his experiences in Paris.

Howe developed a special interest in the Near East and believed that if the Wilsonian philosophy of the Fourteen Points were applied to its administration by the victorious Allies then the Near East would prosper, as of old. Obviously he was taken in by the English view of the Ottoman Middle East as derelict. The following extract explains his idealist conception of the prospects for a peace settlement in the area:

"In correspondence with the President I urged on him my conviction of the economic causes of the war; that it was not the Kaiser, nor the Czar, but imperialistic adventurers who had driven their countries into conflict. Secret diplomacy, the conflict of bankers, the activity of munition-makers, exploiters, and concessionaires in the Mediterranean, in Morocco, in south and central Africa, had brought on the cataclysm; glacial-like aggregations of capital and credit were responsible for the war. His vision of peace was only possible with imperialism ended and the world freed from the struggle over the control of backward countries, embroiling now one country, now another. Permanent peace meant that Gibraltar, the Suez Canal, and the Dardanelles should be internationalized; the Bagdad Railway completed by an international consortium, so that Asiatic Turkey might again become as in ancient days a great granary and storehouse of wheat and cotton. I pictured the territory of the old Roman Empire freed from imperialism and developed by international arrangement, with Constantinople a free port and great cosmopolis, serving as the distributing centre of three continents.

I pictured a renaissance of this part of the world, a renaissance in industry, in culture, and in art that would make it again the centre of a civilization of its own.

When the armistice was signed I felt that the international millennium was at hand. The President's idealism had carried the world; his Fourteen Points had been accepted; armies were to be disbanded, armaments scrapped, imperialism ended. Self-determination was to be extended to all peoples, hates were to be assuaged, and peace to reign.

I was ready to embrace a league of nations, even a league to enforce peace. Any international arrangement that would prevent war was worth while. I believed that the negotiators at Paris wanted peace and were willing to make any sacrifices for it; that war was going to be forever ended on the earth. Such facts as did not fit in with my enthusiastic vision, I suppressed... The men in Europe would be of one mind with [the President]; war had all but destroyed civilization, war should not happen again. I was captivated by the President's eloquence and thoroughly believed in his programme. And I wanted to have a part in it; a share in the settlement of the Near Eastern problems. I wanted to be around when the hand of the Western world should be lifted from the peoples of the Near East, the glories of whose ancient civilization I dreamed of seeing restored." (pp.287-288.)

However, when Howe began to get to grips with the future of the region, he found all sorts of obstacles and complications in the way of Wilson's Fourteen Points, due to the secret deals concluded by the Allied Powers during the War:

"Shortly after my arrival, Colonel House sent for me and said that the President planned to send a mission to Syria to ascertain the wishes of the Syrians themselves in regard to a mandatory. He desired me to familiarize myself with all the treaties and engagements of the allied powers relating to the Near East, and to hold myself in readiness to leave for Syria at a moment's notice. Doctor Barton of the Armenian Relief Fund, was to be my associate on the mission.

The assignment called for much preliminary work. I reread the pre-war investigations of the Germans on the Near East. The secret treaties were placed at my disposal by Colonel House and the English authorities, who seemingly approved of the mission. There was no help to be had from the French, who did not want the inquiry made. These secret treaties, like others, had been kept from President Wilson; it was claimed he knew nothing about them until his arrival. They furnished astounding revelations. Our allies, like Germany, scrapped treaties—not with traditional enemies, but solemn agreements with friends and with each other. The documents showed that England and France had pleaded with the King of the Hedjas to throw the Arab forces in with the allied cause, and drive the Turks from Arabia. The Arabs were promised their freedom in exchange; England would get out of Mesopotamia, France would get out of Syria; the whole of Arabia was to be divided into three parts, to be ruled by the three sons of the King of the Hedjas – one of whom, Emir Feisal, was in Paris. Dignified, meditative, richly turbaned, he was there to see that the compact was lived up to. But France and England were unwilling to give up this rich territory. Scarcely was the ink dry on their compact with the Arabs when they negotiated with each other the secret Sykes-Picot Treaty, under whose terms England was to retain Mesopotamia, France was to keep Syria, and Russia take Armenia. Then the Jews asked for Palestine, and Balfour, the gentleman-statesman, agreed on behalf of England that they should have it, although Palestine had already been promised to the Arabs and given to the French. And England, I soon found, was reluctant to hand over Syria to France...

My vision of a free world was clouding. Self-determination for peoples began to ring like an empty phrase. Still I believed that President Wilson had guaranties that would permit him to turn a trick at the proper time and restore the situation. I would not believe that we were going back to the old order; would not credit what I saw about me." (pp.291-295.)

### Lord Milner's Men and America

Howe then met 'Lord Milner's men,' to exchange ideas about the Near East. *The Round Table* group seemed to be allies in the Wilsonian project, given the idealist conceptions abundantly present in their writings. But Howe found Milner's group to hold objectives and intentions for America that were far from idealist. The following extract from Howe's reminiscences is an excellent summary of the differences between England and America, which left *The Round Table* group profoundly disappointed in their attempts to get the United States to take up the Imperial burden. What is particularly noticeable is how the American saw Imperialism fundamentally in terms of economic exploitation—a thing which the *Round Table* group with their background and their perspective just could not bring themselves to countenance. The following extract, I believe, is one of the most enlightening explanations of the nature of the British Empire and its transition after the Great War:

"One evening a number of young Englishmen visited me at the Hotel

Chatham. They were Oxford and Cambridge men, brilliant, friendly, amiable. A few days later I was invited to breakfast with them. Arriving, I found that I was at the house of Lloyd George; that Philip Kerr, my host, was Lloyd George's secretary. He and his associates, Lionel Curtis, Arnold Toynbee, and others, were known as 'Lord Milner's men.' They were editors of the periodical known as *The Round Table*, and had organized an imperial conference in each of the British colonies. We talked about the Near East. They too were interested in the subject. I took it for granted that they were interested in self-determination for peoples; that they understood, as a matter of course, the crimes committed by imperialistic adventures in Egypt, Persia and Africa. I talked about my discoveries of conflicting treaties, about the activities of British oil interests in Mesopotamia and Persia. I warmed to the theme of financial imperialism and the necessity of being rid of imperialistic exploiters in order to have permanent peace. I felt that they would help in solving the Near Eastern problem.

It astounded me to find that they scarcely knew the meaning of the words 'economic imperialism.' Imperialism was not economic, it was a white man's burden. A sacred trust, undertaken for the well-being of peoples unfitted for self-government. The war was in no way related to the conflict of financial interests. Unfortunately things were done sometimes by business bounders— true—but they did not influence the Foreign Office. The flag followed the investor, perhaps, but only because the investor was a British citizen who was sacred wherever he ventured. This imperialism, which was not imperialism, must be carried to the end. It must be carried by Anglo-Saxons, and England was no longer able to carry it alone. She had lost much of her best blood in the trenches; Oxford and Cambridge, which recruited the Foreign Office, had been depleted of a generation of talent. The only country which could be trusted to share the white man's burden was America; America must help. She must carry it in Armenia... 'But,' I parried, 'Armenia is a danger-spot. It is a buffer between Europe and Asia. The power that holds Armenia may have to defend the British Empire in Mesopotamia, Persia and India—defend it against Turkey, central Europe, certainly against revolutionary Russia. If we should take Armenia we would need a huge military and naval force; we might be embroiled with every power in Europe; certainly we would be embroiled with the Turks and Arabs.' 'It looks to me,' I ended, 'as if America is to be asked to carry the bag; to police Europe and remove from England and France the burden of protecting imperialistic ventures. You are asking us to assume the biggest, most dangerous, and costliest job of all.' The young men admitted the danger. They felt, as all Englishmen whom I met seemed to feel, that America owed a debt to England, much as did Canada, Australia and other colonies. We ought to be proud to pay our debt to the empire. That America was a colonial dependence, not yet a sovereign nation, seemed to be their fixed idea.

I had seen British university men of this type at Ellis Island, had met them in Washington and at the clubs in New York. But I understood them better in Paris. The civil service of which they are a part is one of the marvellous things about England. Made up of Oxford and Cambridge men who enter the Foreign

Office after the hardest kind of competitive examinations, it forms them into servants devoted, like Jesuits, to the empire. Before the war these men, especially the Lord Milner group, had gone to Canada, Australia, and South Africa. They gave up home, companionship, and everything to which they had been accustomed; they often lived isolated lives in distant places of the world. They mobilized opinion for imperialistic ends. Conservatives or Liberals, the empire was their passion. It was to be served, strengthened, carried on. Where the empire was in question they were impervious to facts, blind to obvious evils, untouched by argument... This extraordinary efficient organisation knew everything except the suppressed wants of subject peoples; granted everything to subject peoples except political liberty. It was not willing to dignify by discussion the questionings of others as to the sanctity of England's imperial trust.

As I talked with these young men I reflected on the nature of English gentlemen and Oxford scholars — their unwillingness, perfected by long practice into inability, to recognise issues that touched their economic interests. India, Egypt, Africa, Mesopotamia provided careers for the younger sons of the aristocracy; England was crowded, trade undesirable, the service of the state was their opportunity. To end Imperialism was to end jobs, opportunities for preferment. It was like suggesting abolishing the church to the clergy, the army to the military caste, the navy to marines. Men receive unwillingly ideas that destroy a livelihood; and vocal England is a unit in the protection of its privileged sons — they would be left to starve if the colonial service were ended, they would have to compromise their dignity in trade or emigrate as workers.

Another interest touched them in a way they refused to see. England exploited her dependencies; billions of pounds were invested in backward countries, in bonds, in oil, in diamond and gold mines, in rubber plantations. The landed aristocracy was the investing class. It kept aloof from things economic at home; business was vulgar, outside of recognised interests. The bombardment of Alexandria or the Boer War was not in any admissible way related to gold and diamond mine owners. Yet when the British purse was touched, the investing class felt the hurt. Then the press spoke, the Foreign Office responded, Britain bristled, gunboats were despatched; the cry was that the rights of British citizens were in danger. In reality British pounds sterling were affected. Economic reasons for imperialism were consistently ignored. Even the Labor Party had a confused veneration for the empire, a veneration springing from tradition. Oxford young men wanted our dough-boys to do their policing, to help protect economic interests that they dignified as sacred. That was the objective of the Armenian drive; America's duty was always being held before my eyes." (pp. 295-9.)

Howe found the French and their Imperialism, in comparison, far more honest and straightforward to deal with:

"Representatives of French interests talked no bunk. They were always realistic. They were opposed to our mission to Syria. Syria was French in influence; France claimed it from the time of the Crusades. She had contracts with the British for exclusive control that were exhausting to Syria... The French point of view was straightforward. It embodied complete historical realism. France could only protect herself by force. President Wilson was a dreamer, his ideals were foolish or worse. France would prepare in every possible way for war that was inevitable; imperialist possessions where black troops were recruited was one important way. About the Turks, whom the Allies had promised to drive into Asia, the French were equally succinct: 'They owe us money,' was their summary of the Turkish question—'huge debts contracted before the war. If we drive out the Turks and take Constantinople, there will be no Turks left to pay our debts. The Turks must keep Constantinople.'

England's attitude was that Constantinople must remain British to save it from Russia. Turks were better than Russians in that debated city, better than the French. The Greeks should be invited in to help strengthen British power.

Allied opinion about the Bagdad Railway, which I had visualised as a great international highway to open up a rich storehouse of lands, was that it should be left to rust. It had done enough damage already; completed it would disturb the balance of power. What would happen to British shipping interests if the freight of Europe travelled by rail? What would happen to the Suez canal, the majority of whose shares were held by Britain?...

France took Syria, England Mesopotamia. Palestine went to the Jews. The Arabs had driven back the Turks and had perhaps saved the British Empire. Their sacrifices were ignored; agreements were thrown to the winds and betraying friends took possession of their ancient towns and countryside. The Arabs rebelled; their rebellion was crushed by the same friends with aeroplanes and machine-guns. Emir Feisal, son of the desert, was exiled to Switzerland. A free Mediterranean was the idlest of dreams." (pp.298-302.)

## A Disillusioned American

The behaviour of the Allies at Paris left Howe thoroughly disillusioned with the Peace Conference and the League of Nations, particularly as it became evident that the good intentions of the President, and America, were being used by the Powers in the service of the same old Imperialism:

"Truth meant little at Paris. Paris did not expect men to tell the truth. The President worked in a net of duplicity; he was surprised when apparently satisfactory agreements turned into betrayals of his position... Officially Paris was not interested in things economic. It was fixing boundaries, agreeing on reparations. The President was not interested. Nor were Balfour, Lloyd George, or Clemenceau—ostensibly. But economic forces moved the conference, like players about a chess-board. Boundary-lines were shifted to include harbors, copper, oil, mineral resources. Races were split, natural demarcations ignored. The imperialist interests that had kept the world on edge for thirty years before the war were making a killing; they would end the old controversies; would sanction their loot by treaty agreements; perhaps rivet them by the League of Nations. The British Admiralty wanted oil; it had talked oil for years. British maritime prescience saw that oil was the fuel of to-morrow. The French steel trust wanted a grip on coal and iron ore, to gain command of the Continent and strip Germany of her war-making power. Munition-makers were busy. They were getting ready for the next war...

One evening at dinner a friend of President Wilson's, a man thoroughly conversant with the conference, said despondently: 'It is impossible to tell yet whether the peace is being drafted by the international bankers or the munition-makers. It is not being drafted by America.'

America had no business at Paris. That was the outstanding thing about which we almost all agreed. President Wilson should have stayed at home. We were amateurs, amateurs seeking to right the world by moralistic appeals; we had fought as religious crusaders, and, like Joshua, had expected the old world to fall at a trumpet-blast. Our emotions were honest, the sacrifice genuine, whole-hearted, but Europe only smiled at our naiveté. The righteousness of Wilson was one of the Allies' greatest assets. Confronted with the realism of old Europe, it was almost childish. It was the morality of the church seeking to function against alarmist war lords, ministries tenacious of power, lords of finance—all moved by elemental motives of individual, class, and nationalistic aggrandizement. The evangelism of Wilson had turned America from her traditions; it made no impression on the realism of the old world.

My Still-born vision of the Near East was the child of kindly American ignorance. It partook of our righteousness; possibly it was the idlest dream of all. Only a Europe dedicated to renunciation would have considered it. And old Europe was thinking of spoils and the next war." (pp.303-306.)

This is Howe's summing up of the wider Peace arrangements at Paris and Wilson's outmanoeuvring by the Allied leaders, that led to America's withdrawal from the arrangements for governing the world:

"When Woodrow Wilson landed in France he was hailed as a Messiah. His presence would bring in the millennium. ...Men even expected a new economic order. They dimly hoped for deliverance from war, a deliverance that was to come through the great American emancipator, Woodrow Wilson. For a time Lloyd George, Clemenceau, and Orlando were apprehensive of this veneration; it was whispered that Wilson might appeal to the people, and the people might repudiate their rulers. He might continue to talk to the world as he had talked from Washington; might refuse to confer, to barter, to sit in secret sessions.

At Paris, President Wilson stood on a pinnacle. He had lifted the world to his own idealism, and the world seemed ready for a messianic dispensation...

He had only the scantiest knowledge of Europe, of the men whom he had to meet. He professed to be ignorant of the secret treaties that confounded his pledges. The Peace Conference was to be a personal affair; he hoped that it would be largely personal to him and Mr. Arthur Balfour. It was to be guided by his Magna Carta, the lineal issue of other great Anglo-Saxon charters, beginning with the barons at Runnymede and ending with Thomas Jefferson. Men had conquered with the pen as well as with the sword. He would bring liberty to a distracted world by the pen. He would bring it alone.

England fed this isolated grandeur. And England knew Woodrow Wilson better than did we. She knew him as she knows so many things that no other country thinks it worth while to know. She had studied his written words; had penetrated into his hidden psychology. She knew his strength and his weakness. England had sent Mr. Arthur Balfour to Washington to win him to the war. Mr. Balfour was the statesman-philosopher, the model of President Wilson's university aristocrat. He best represented the England that Mr. Wilson knew from Walter Bagehot. The England he had written about, the mother of America. The Balfour family had always been a family of rulers. They had no interest in trade. They knew nothing of the vulgarity of practical politics. Other British emissaries had been picked with the same insight. And England bowed to the Messianic Wilson; she accepted him on his own measure of himself. The King received him with sovereign honors at Buckingham Palace. Peers, commoners, people claimed him as their own. The press sanctioned his idealism as the idealism of English peoples. They seemed to accept his leadership of the world.

While England swelled this Messianic vision, France pricked it. The Paris press was cynical; under government direction it sneered. Daily editorials questioned the President's vision of himself. Clemenceau said: 'God gave us Ten Commandments—we have not followed them; but Wilson has given us Fourteen.' ... Balfour, the man on whom Wilson relied, was first of all a Briton. He spoke as a philosopher but acted as a politician...

To these men Woodrow Wilson was impractical, naïve. His peace without victory had aided in breaking down German morale. His idealism had deceived the world and helped win the war. But why did he think his words were so different from other war propaganda? It was ridiculous that he should think them so important; his Fourteen Points so sacred. They had never been agreed to anyhow.

The secret treaties were now brought forward; plans for the distribution of the spoils, for the dismemberment of Germany, the destruction of middle Europe. Mr. Wilson professed to have no knowledge of the secret treaties, which confounded all his pledges, although they had been printed in America. He was indifferent, if not irritated, over imperialism, and was wholly unprepared for criticism and attack from sources from which he had least expected it. Neither France nor England felt gratitude; rather they felt resentment that we had not come in earlier. We had made money from their necessities. That, too, could not be forgotten. Among his confreres he was the inexperienced colonial, to be confused, outwitted, played on; now a savior of the world, now an obstructionist to speedy peace, now an ingrate to the sufferings of England and France. That it was primarily their war, not ours; that we had come in because of appeals for help; that we had abandoned our traditions and made our own sacrifices, was a point of view to which they were impervious. That we had made these sacrifices because we sincerely believed that they too wanted an end of war, received no credence.

The President's Fourteen Points had no supporters. England would not even consider his freedom of the seas; command of the seas was protection to her empire. She would not renounce conquest. Conquest was a word she did not know. Her empire was a trust, a sacred burden, which could not be discussed. She had seized her winnings by war in Africa, in Mesopotamia, in the islands of the sea. She had gained control of the raw materials of the earth. She would hold them as her spoils. They were not open to disposition by the Peace Conference.

France would draw a cordon about Germany—Poland, Czechoslovakia, the Baltic States, and the Balkans. Austro-Hungary would be dismembered and new countries created. France needed allies, more enemies of Germany. Italy would have the Adriatic; Greece demanded Smyrna, part of Turkey. Japan would have Shantung; she had taken it herself from Germany.

The President was unable to cope with the men about him, who used every device to confuse, to cheat him. He did not trust his advisers. He could not possibly know the significance of what was being proposed, of decisions made, of the things he concurred in. He wanted approval, but was met with a sneer; he reached out for support, but found deceit.

And when he had delivered his sermon he had exhausted his armor. When he abandoned one principle he abandoned all... For the first time in his political life Woodrow Wilson was compelled to do battle with equals, who knew every detail of what was being discussed, but of which he had only the superficial information provided on a sheet of paper. He had expected an afternoon tea; he found a duel. He expected to dictate; he descended to barter... As the politician he failed. But his words carrying promise of a new dispensation fell on soil that had been made ready by the pledges of the war and the common sufferings of peoples. And the winged words of the President ripened these aspirations into revolution in Ireland, in Egypt, in Mesopotamia, in Africa, in India. As an evangelist he achieved what he possibly least wanted to achieve. He helped to free Ireland. He heartened the Egyptians, the Arabs, and the Indians. He set aflame fires that are slowly driving the white men from other people's countries...

The peace the President had promised to the world would not come through the treaty... There was no price that he could have paid that would have satisfied the men who for four years had planned the partition of the world under treaties that double-crossed each other and that violated every assurance that had been given to America. And the League of Nations, which issued like the Treaty of Versailles, was a league of conquest rather than a covenant of freedom. It was an international sanction of servitude to make permanent the conquests of the war. Like the Treaty of Versailles, it provided a moral approval of economic and imperialistic exploitation. It was this that was offered President Wilson in exchange for his ideals; it was this that was urged upon America, for with America sanctioning the league there was no great power left to sympathize with or assist the aspirations of subject peoples." (pp.307-314.)

England believed America to be easy to manoeuvre since its idealist President was proving a soft touch and Lloyd George was running rings round him. Earlier on in his book Howe actually touches on why the Anglophile academic Wilson was such a push-over for Britain:

"Woodrow Wilson fell under the spell of Walter Bagehot, one of the greatest of British essayists. He urged his students to read and reread Bagehot as he himself had done. His Congressional Government was said to have been inspired by Bagehot's British Constitution, as were many of his essays on public men. Bagehot gave the student Wilson that which his mind wanted; a picture of what a great constitutional statesman should be. Through Bagehot's eyes he saw British statesmen as he saw himself. They were drawn from the best families, trained from youth for the service of the state. They grew up in the atmosphere of Oxford and Cambridge, and were exalted by traditions of disinterested public service. They had no private ends to serve; because of their independent wealth they were influenced only by the welfare of the empire. They were the natural rulers of the constitutional state. England was a gentleman's country. And Mr. Wilson believed in gentlemen, in selected men, in the platonic sense of the term. To Woodrow Wilson the scholar it was easy to idealize a country that put its scholars in politics and kept them there as it kept Arthur Balfour, James Bryce, and other men of his own type...

Woodrow Wilson loved England as the mother of civil liberty and of parliamentary government. She had given us the Magna Carta, the Bill of Rights, and Petition of Rights. She had exiled the Stuarts for their betrayal of English liberties and had called in Cromwell and William of Orange to re-establish them. In his mind England was the literal mother of America. From her we had taken our political institutions. Also our system of jurisprudence. His chief criticism of the American Constitution related to those features which failed to follow the British parliamentary model. It was this love for British forms that led him to read his messages to Congress in person and to treat himself as a Premier rather than as a President. As a matter of fact he was better fitted by temperament to serve as a parliamentary leader than as a President, and he would have felt much more at home at Westminster than in Washington...

Woodrow Wilson the President is to be found in these early influences. He never outgrew them. He lived in a world of dreams rather than with men." (pp. 36-40.).

Britain humoured Wilson's Principles, treating them as war propaganda to disorganise the enemy—and disorganise the enemy they did. The League of Nations was supposedly set up to institutionalise these Principles but Britain quickly saw it instead as a vehicle to utilise America in a new balance of power operation against its Allies, saving money and trouble in the world for Britain. Lloyd George achieved this through repeatedly threatening Wilson with British withdrawal if he did not give way. And the British Prime Minister always had it in mind that England and France would go back to settling

Imperialist business between themselves when Wilson had been seen off.

If Britain's general objectives in 1919 could be defined, they would be something like this: to continue Imperial activity to the best of its ability, to maintain naval supremacy, and to combine this with an Atlantic partnership to bail out the Empire with men and materials, so that it could continue its activities in the world and play the Balance of Power again.

Britain used America in Paris, with regard to the Balance of Power in containing French Rhineland ambitions through the Anglo-American guarantee. Collaboration between England and America also prevented the French desire for security through resistance to France's proposal for a League of armed allies. Instead only a Covenant was provided by Britain and America.

There was a crucial vote in the United States Senate on 19th November 1919 which put up conditions before the League of Nations could be ratified. These conditions chiefly guarded against America being pulled into military conflicts not of its choosing. Lloyd George was urged to accept these conditions, by, among others, Sir Edward Grey. Grey had been persuaded out of retirement to go to the U.S. to try to secure limitations of American naval expenditure. But Grey, who was used to dominating the Great Powers in the pre-War days, found it a very dispiriting experience. When the Americans stonewalled, he asked London if he could be recalled, saying he had 'not come out of retirement to accept this indignity and nonsense.' (George Egerton, *Britain And The Great Betrayal*, *Historical Journal*, December 1978, p.899.)

Grey urged the Prime Minister to accept the Senate's reservations, in order to pull the United States into 'world responsibilities' and wrote a letter to *The Times* to make his position public. But Lloyd George did just the opposite. In Parliament, in December 1919, he stated that the League must be a League of 'equal members', with no member (such as the U.S.) having a right to have fewer responsibilities than the others. He said that, whilst Britain would support the League, she would now tend to her own specific interests in the world, without regard to the League. The Prime Minister also stated that, in his opinion, the hope of cooperation with America in the post-War world was ending and the British and the French needed to finish outstanding business to do with the Peace Conference—particularly regarding the Turks. And in a follow-up speech in his native country Lloyd George accused the Americans of playing party politics with peace.

America, unlike England, was more than its Executive head. It was a very democratic system with a deliberating legislature which considered national interest in a way the British Parliament was not capable of. And Congress, through the Senate, decided not to be railroaded by propagandist morality into foreign adventures, or buttered up by *Round Table* platitudes. So it steered clear of the 'entangling alliances', consequent from the Peace Conference and the League. And it determined to be nobody's pawn in the world. America finally rejected Versailles and the Mandates in March 1920—after it began to see the behaviour of Britain and France in relation to them.

It is probably as well that America took on no mandatory responsibilities if this report of a statement made by Woodrow Wilson at a White House Party on 28th February 1919 is anything to go by. Apparently the President said:

> "I am not without hope that the people of the U.S.A. may agree to be the trustee of the interests of the Armenian people and see to it that the unspeakable Turk and the almost equally difficult Kurd have their necks sat on long enough to teach them manners." (Joseph Tumulty, *Woodrow Wilson As I Know Him*, (1921) p.377.)

### Britain And The League

The failure of Britain to secure American assistance in the reordering and governing of the world after 1919 had profound consequences. Lloyd George took it as giving England the freedom to go back to Imperialist work in conjunction, or competition, with the French. And this led him back to the Greeks, and the Anatolian adventure that ended in tragedy for them (and finished his career). George Egerton comments in his *Britain And The Great Betrayal*:

> "With the failure to sustain an Anglo-American *entente*, the Imperial dimensions of British strategy would be given greater priority under Curzon's Foreign Secretaryship. Chanak, however, would soon demonstrate the limitations of this strategy as orchestrated by Lloyd George." (*Historical Journal*, December 1978, p.899.)

Lloyd George had a practical understanding of what America could do for Britain, and when the U.S. would do no more he was only too willing to let it go its own way. But *The Round Tablers* had a much more idealist conception of America and what it could do for the Empire and it was they who would inherit the future.

Before the Peace Conference the *Round Table* group had considered the idea of abandoning the traditional British Balance of Power policy in Europe. Lionel Curtis, their chief thinker, wrote in the *Round Table* of December 1918 that England, despite being 'an island fortress', and predisposed to 'remaining aloof', could not refrain from making war in Europe:

> "the narrowness of the moat that divided her from Europe compelled her to support the weaker side in diplomacy, and again and again to preserve the balance by engaging the stronger side in war.' And he saw the cause and solution as follows: 'the balance of power policy has outlived its time by a century and that the world has remained a prey to war, was due to the continued alienation of the British and American communities."

The objective was to encourage the Americans into a relationship that would provide Britain with the men and materials she lacked to continue her world dominance — and mastery over Europe. Such a relationship would establish an Anglo-American hegemony in the world to replace the Balance of Power policy which, it was conceded, after the event, had led to the Great War. And how could Wilsonian America turn down the chance of putting an end to the alliances and policies that created war?

*The Round Table* was enthusiastic about the League when they thought they could involve the United States in it and make the new Europe and the New World Order an Anglo-Saxon one. But they were devastated by the American refusal to take part in their scheme and the Senate's decision to reject the Treaty of Versailles and any obligations under it toward the League. *The Round Table* complained in March, 1920:

> "The League has failed to secure the adhesion of one of its most important members, the United States, and is very unlikely to secure it... This situation presents a very serious problem for the British Empire. We have not only undertaken great obligations under the League which we must now both in honesty and in self-regard revise, but we have looked to the League to provide us with the machinery for united British action in foreign affairs."

The phrase 'united British action'—meaning Anglo-American action—was surely revealing. But from this time onwards the Milnerites started to take an increasingly hostile view of a League of Nations free from Anglo-American hegemony. And the *Round Table* began to blame the problems of post-War Europe and the chain of events that would lead to the Second World War on American 'isolationism'.

One of the concrete manifestations of Britain's changing attitude to the League was the refusal by Lord Hankey of the position of first General Secretary of the League. Hankey was one of the most important figures in British politics, having been a secretary to the Committee of Imperial Defence from 1908-12 (when it was planning the War on Germany and Turkey), private secretary to Lord Milner, and a secretary to the War Cabinet and Peace Conference. He was also a member of the *Round Table* group. His declining the post of General Secretary of the League signalled England's distancing itself from the League.

Professor Carroll Quigley concluded that from 1920 to 1939 the Milner group, which dominated British policy in this period,

> "sought to weaken the League of Nations and destroy all possibility of collective security in order to strengthen Germany in respect of both France and the Soviet Union, and above all to free Britain from Europe in order to build up an Atlantic bloc of Great Britain, the British Dominions, and the United States. They prepared the way for this Union through the Rhodes Scholarship organisation (of which Lord Milner was the head in 1905-25 and Lord Lothian was secretary in 1925-40), through the *Round Table* groups, through the Chatham House organisation, which set up the Royal Institute of International Affairs in all the Dominions and a Council on Foreign Relations in New York... and the Institutes of Pacific Relations. This influential group

sought to change the League of Nations from an instrument of collective security to an international conference center for 'non-political matters' like drug control or international postal services, to rebuild Germany as a buffer against the Soviet Union and a counterpoise to France."' (*Tragedy and Hope* (1966) p.582.)

Between the two Wars on Germany, the Milnerites attained their greatest influence on British policy and Britain began to view the League of Nations as an instrument of national policy, useful for propaganda purposes, but otherwise ignored. *The Round Table* group, which had a great influence on the policy of the British State from 1920 to 1939, aimed to maintain the Balance of Power in Europe, by building up Germany against France and Russia, while at the same time maintaining British freedom of action. The aim was also to encourage Germany to look Eastward as she grew back to something of her former power; clearly, Germany—as a self respecting nation—could not be confined within the Versailles straight jacket, and war was practically an inevitability. That war, it was hoped, could be directed against the Bolsheviks.

But in 1939 it all unravelled with the guarantee to Poland and round two with Germany was on.

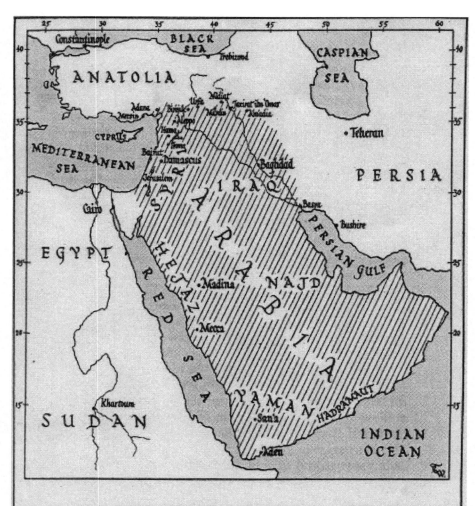

# THE EASTERN ARAB WORLD

❖

The shaded portion represents the area of Arab independence as defined in the Sharif Husain's note of July 14, 1915

# V. Remaking The Middle East

The conflict between Arab and Jew in the Middle East is a direct product of the Great War on Turkey. And it should be added to Ireland's tally of achievement in what a recent history has called *Our War*.

Having failed to dispatch the Turks in the time expected, England lured the Arabs into the War against the Moslem Ottoman State, on the promise of a great Moslem Arab state after the War. To achieve this, the seeds of nationalism were sown amongst this people, which had, up until then, proved impervious to it. And Palestine, they were led to believe, would be part of the nationalist inheritance at the harvesting of victory.

At the same time, in secret agreements with their Allies, Britain divided up the Arab lands, including Palestine, despite knowing that this would confront the new Arab nationalism which they were cultivating.

In 1917, in a moment of great difficulty during its Great War, Britain launched the project of a Jewish Colony in Palestine. The object was to win over what it believed to be the considerable force of international Jewry to the Allied cause. To do this it announced the Balfour Declaration and set about the process of large-scale Jewish colonization of Palestine under the auspices of the Mandate system of Versailles. The plan was not to establish an independent Jewish State but a Jewish colonial state of the British Empire.

So, having created an Arab nationalism in the region, England made sure it was to be frustrated and then given a rival nationalism to conflict with.

The Arab world was not the victim of a British double-cross, it fell foul to a triple-cross. And, in the ninety years from 1918, there has been a working out of what emerged from the activities of the British State between 1916 and 1918 in winning its War on the Turks and Germans.

## Britain And Arab Nationalism

In 1911 Britain had sought to raise a revolt against the Ottomans using everyone and anyone in Arabia. However, just after the British declaration of War on Turkey, Britain rejected an offer of alliance from a real Arab nationalist group in Basra, organised by Said Talib, who was offering his services to the Empire.

Said Talib, a very influential figure in the Basra area, was well connected to the town's merchant class as well as to the local Sheikhs from the areas outside. Before the War he was the virtual ruler of Basra. He was a great admirer of Britain, and although his nationalism was confined to a rather narrow social base, his popularity and connections made it possible that he could have carried off an alliance. In February 1911, he had written a letter to Hussein in Mecca urging him to overthrow the Ottomans from the Arab lands and pledging his support for such a venture. Talib called on the British Ambassador in Constantinople in early October 1914, a month before War was declared on

Turkey, to offer his services. Talib asked the Ambassador, Sir Louis Mallet, to remind Lord Kitchener of a conversation he had had with him in 1911 and to tell him that 'the time had come'.

But Britain turned a deaf ear to Said Talib's overtures and when its army took Basra, without his assistance, the Foreign Office declared that he had forfeited all claims to consideration. Sir Percy Cox then deported Talib, as a troublemaker, to Bombay, where he sat out the War.

At this point the British viewed alliances with nationalist groups as unnecessary and a complicating factor in any conquests that were going to be made in the region. Just prior to the launching of the expedition to conquer Mesopotamia, for instance, it was decided that 'policy was to be pursued by restraining, rather than inciting, an Arab rebellion.' (*British Policy In Mesopotamia 1903-14*, Stuart Cohen, 1976. p.305.) And the Indian Expeditionary Force was given explicit instructions to preserve order rather than instigate revolt:

> "keeping uncivilised bodies of fighting men out of reach of Basra as far as possible... the aim of the force—to control an Arab uprising—... demonstrated the continuity of British policy." (p.308.)

The Indian Expeditionary Force to Mesopotamia was given these instructions because England had the intention of setting up an Indian-type administration in the conquered area and did not want any nationalists to disturb the process. But by the end of 1915, when the Dardanelles assault had been repulsed and the Mesopotamian expedition defeated (see next section), Britain began to reactivate the plans of 1911, as it became clear that the Ottoman Empire was going to prove more difficult to destroy than expected.

### Origins Of The Arab Revolt

England ignored the nationalists who existed in Mesopotamia and sought out nationalism where it hardly existed and was most inappropriate—in Arabia.

Arabia was certainly not the stuff of nations in 1914. It was composed of at least ten areas ruled by local chieftains. These included: Kuwait, ruled by Ibn Saba; Bahrain, ruled by Ibn Kalifa; Oman, ruled by Ibn Said; Hadramaut, ruled by Ibn Auda; Yemen, ruled by Ibn Mohammed Hamid; Nedj, ruled by Ibn Saud, the leader of the Wahhabis, and the Hejaz, including the Holy cities of Mecca and Medina, ruled by Shereef Hussein. These tribal fiefdoms were not territorially fixed and each area tended to expand or contract according to the strength and influence of the local Sheikh and his followers at the time. There were also significant differences between the settled Arabs of the towns and the desert tribes around them.

But, of all the Arabian Sheikhs, Shereef Hussein of Mecca was of the most interest to Britain, for two reasons. Firstly, he had the strategic advantage of ruling the area that dominated the centre of the Peninsula, next to Egypt. And secondly, the prestige he derived from being the descendant of the Prophet, and Custodian of the Holy Places, made him a very useful asset to England.

Lord Kitchener and other English Statesmen and soldiers who had spent much of their lives ruling over and fighting in the Moslem world had developed a great fear of Holy War and the prospect of all Moslems uniting against the Westerners who occupied their lands. This had become something of an obsession, based on the belief that the Moslems, as long as they could be divided, could be easily bought or controlled by the superior resources and technology of the West. Only a Holy War, waged by vast numbers of Moslems prepared to fight to the death, could make the Moslem world—which included British India— ungovernable for England.

This was not a problem whilst the Sultan-Caliph of Constantinople, who had the supreme authority to call for a *jihad*, was an ally of Britain. But with England's reorientation against the Turks and Germany's growing friendship with the Turks, the prospect of a Holy War aimed against England began to worry those concerned with the Orient. One Imperial administrator put it like this:

> "As the great foster-mother of Islam we have always retained the diplomatic friendship of Turkey, whose ruler is the Khaliph... The importance of such an alliance to our hold on our Moslem subjects of India, cannot be over-estimated... To the orthodox believer, the Khaliph represents the whole of Islam in his own person. The shock, therefore, to the sensibilities of Moslems in India when he declared war against us must have been shattering. The immediate necessity was to discover some means to counteract or at least mitigate the effect... A return to the *status quo ante* was quite impossible during the war, but the situation could at least be considerably improved by setting up Mecca in opposition to Constantinople. There was, however, an obvious risk in this policy of offending Islam, because the Sultan was not only the spiritual but also the temporal Chief of the Shariff." (Thomas Lyell, *The Ins And Outs Of Mesopotamia*, p.160.)

The Custodian of Mecca began to assume a new significance in this situation. If the Lord of Mecca and Medina dissented from the call for *jihad,* the call, coming from Constantinople, would not have the desired authority with Moslems. So it became essential that Shereef Hussein become Britain's man, to counter the influence of the Caliph in a situation of war between the English and the Ottomans.

Shereef Hussein's second son, Abdullah, was particularly ambitious and the Ottomans, before the War, had offered him a seat in the Cabinet and then the post of Governor-General of the Yemen. But, like his father, Abdullah was trying to win further autonomy for the Hejaz and to achieve dominance over the other Arabian chiefs—so he declined the offers and went to see Kitchener instead.

This was in February 1914, when Kitchener was British Agent in Egypt (the title was later changed to High Commissioner when Sir Henry McMahon replaced him). Abdullah sounded Kitchener out as to England's position in the event of a conflict between Constantinople and Mecca. Kitchener was circumspect, replying that Britain had traditionally been an ally of the Turk, but he sent Sir Robert Storrs, the Oriental Secretary at the Agency in Egypt, to a private meeting with Abdullah to investigate further. Nothing came of this meeting, or of a later one, but Kitchener banked the idea of an alliance with the Hashemites in the event of a new situation developing.

When that new situation developed, Kitchener made a firm offer to Hussein. If Hussein and his followers were to side with England in the War (that was to be declared in the week) the British Government would guarantee his position against all outside force.

Hussein decided not to accept Kitchener's offer. By this time the Caliph had issued a *fatwa* against Britain, and Constantinople was expecting support from the faithful, and in particular, from the Shereef of Mecca. Hussein's third son, Feisal, who at that time favoured standing by the Ottomans against the West, advised caution. Hussein replied to the Sultan that he gave his 'silent blessing' to the *jihad* but could not openly endorse it due to the presence of the Royal Navy in the Red Sea, which could easily bombard his ports and blockade the Hejaz. (The British put a blockade on the Hejaz on 15th November 1915, which induced a famine, in order to encourage the Arabs to act). He felt sure the Sultan would, in his wisdom, understand his predicament and, as gestures of support, he sent the green banner of the Prophet and a force of *mujahidin* to accompany an expeditionary force destined to attempt the liberation of Egypt.

By this manoeuvre, Hussein managed to placate, if not satisfy, the Sultan whilst he provided the greatest service to England, by not endorsing the *jihad*, when his endorsement would have had the greatest effect on the Moslems of the British Empire and elsewhere.

From October 1914 to July 1915 there were no significant moves on Britain's part to cement an alliance with the Arabs. Hussein's offer was put aside for a rainy day. England hoped that the Gallipoli expedition would drive on to Constantinople, Mesopotamia would be taken by the Indian Army, and that would be that. Allies would merely be an unnecessary complication. But by July 1915 the Gallipoli force had been confined to the beachhead and the rainy day had come.

Sir Henry McMahon, Britain's High Commissioner in Egypt, later stated in a memorandum that the Arab Revolt was originally intended to draw Arab support away from the Ottoman Empire in order to create a new destructive nationalism in the region:

> "It was the most unfortunate day in my life when I was left in charge of this Arab movement... It began at the urgent request of Sir Ian Hamilton at Gallipoli. I was begged by the Foreign Office to take immediate action and draw the Arabs out of the war. At that moment a large portion of the Turkish force at Gallipoli and nearly the whole of the force in Mesopotamia were Arabs, and

the Germans were then spending a large amount of money in detaching the rest of the Arabs... Could we give them some guarantee of assistance in the future to justify their splitting with the Turks? I was told to do that at once and in that way I started the Arab movement." (Cited in Elie Kedourie, *The Chatham House Version*, p. 16.)

So far from utilizing a nationalism that existed in any substantial form against a supposed oppressor, Britain in fact worked up the Arab Revolt, to divert the active support that ordinary Arabs were providing the Ottoman State in resisting Imperialist aggression.

In June 1915 British aeroplanes dropped leaflets over Arabia; the text, signed by Sir Henry McMahon, guaranteed the recognition and the security of an independent Arab State on the Arabian peninsula. This was a significant advance on the offer of October 1914, and in July 1915 negotiations were reopened between Hussein and Britain.

Hussein began to get ambitious with his demands. For an Arab Revolt, he stated that his price was an Arab State of

"an area bounded on the north by latitude 37 from Mersina to Persia; on the west by the Red Sea and the Mediterranean; on the south and east by the Indian Ocean, the Persian Gulf and the frontier of Persia." (H.M.S.O., *Military Operations, Egypt And Palestine*, Vol. I, p.215.)

The Arab State, which would be independent and headed by Hussein, would comprise all the Arab-speaking south-west of Asia, except Aden, and would include many non-Arab minorities. McMahon replied enthusiastically but stated that discussion of territorial boundaries was 'premature'.

By October, when it had become clear that the Gallipoli expedition had failed, McMahon contacted the Shereef to give him the astonishing news that his demands for an independent Arab State had been accepted, save for Syria, West of Damascus. This encouraged the Arabs to believe that once the Ottoman Empire had been destroyed, through the joint efforts of England and an Arab revolt, Britain would recognise the Middle East as a great Arab State stretching from Adana in the North-West across to Amadia in the North-East, down along the Persian frontier to Basra, the Indian Ocean and Red Sea in the South and the Mediterranean Sea to the West. So, to all intents and purposes, an alternative independent Islamic State (without the Christian areas West of Damascus, and Aden) would be erected with a simple change of owners—the Arabs for the Ottoman Turks.

In the early part of his memoirs, Ronald Storrs, who made the early contacts with Hussein and was involved in the McMahon correspondence, considered the question of the promises made by England to the Arabs during the War. And he argued that the Shereef of Mecca had asked for too much and England had promised too freely:

"It was at the time and still is my opinion that the Sharif opened his mouth and the British Government their purse a good deal too wide. It seemed to me that having been little more than a sort of Erastian Administrator for the Turks, the Sharif and his people would be well treated and amply rewarded if they were gratuitously enabled to defeat and evict their traditional enemy, and were guaranteed immunity from external aggression in their permanent possession of the two Holy Cities, together with the independent sovereignty of their country of origin, the Hejaz. If to this a sufficient majority of Moslems chose to add the Khilafat, that was their business and not ours; though, as uniting the strongest religious with the weakest material power, it would be greatly to our interest. But Husain... claimed to wield a general mandate as King of the Arabs for a Spiritual Pan-Araby, to which he knew better than we that he could lay no kind of general claim... The Christians of the Lebanon could never acknowledge him, Mesopotamia was mainly Shia, regarding his Islam about as benevolently as Alva did the Protestantism of the Low Countries; to the South the Imam Yahya recognised him as nothing at all; whilst with Ibn Saud on his immediate East (feeling for him as an Ebenezer Chapel might for Rome) he had long been on the same terms... When in addition we reflected that 90 per cent of the Moslem World must call Husain a renegade and traitor to the Vicar of God we could not conceal from ourselves (and with difficulty from him) that his pretensions bordered upon the tragic-comic." (*Orientations*, pp.160-1.)

Storrs obviously had a purpose in this—to demonstrate that Hussein was an unsuitable ruler outside of his own Hejaz, and that, therefore, not to follow through with the promises made to him had been the right thing to do. And Storrs was also speaking with the benefit of hindsight, as future Governor of the Jewish Colony. But his assessment was nonetheless sound.

The people who were involved in British Statecraft were very skilled in justifying the unjustifiable. And Storrs presents his argument as a justification for Britain's subsequent behaviour in relation to the Arabs. However, the question that arises from it, that Storrs does not ask, is why England made such promises to the Arabs if they knew they were untenable in practice and would result in chaos after the War?

### Lawrence Of Arabia

Thomas Lyell describes the role of 'Lawrence of Arabia' in all this, as chief briber of the Arabs, and suggests an answer to the question of why England made promises that it knew would result in chaos after the War:

"Negotiations were conducted by those who knew. There is only one way by which to obtain anything substantial from an Arab—and that is hard cash. The policy that followed has been associated with the name of Colonel Lawrence.

Lawrence was the accredited purse-bearer of the British Treasury to Hussein, Shariff of Mecca. The wealth of our Empire is well known throughout the

238

East, and so soon as his mission was thoroughly understood, he was naturally welcomed with open arms.

Hussein, under the circumstances, was in a position to demand his own terms, and his natural aptitude for the part was in evidence. So vitally necessary was his support, that it was tentatively suggested he should himself become supreme Khaliph of All Islam. Now this suggestion was about as absurd as it would be for some Buddhist Power to propose inviting the Patriarch of Eastern Christendom to reign in the Vatican after dethroning the actual Pope!

Hussein coyly and courteously declined the offer; but it served to show him how far we were prepared to go for his support. And he named his terms. These were what could naturally be expected from any member of the Religious Hierarchy of Islam—hard cash and power...

Since, at all costs, the war had to be won and our Empire maintained intact—it is difficult to see what other policy we could have adopted. It is perhaps not impossible that cheaper 'terms' might have been obtained, but in such matters the Arab is a wily bird. Its immediate effect, at any rate, was noticeably to our advantage, through a definite steadying of Moslem thought... The influence of the Shariff being paramount over the tribes of the Hedjaz, our right flank in the Palestine advance was not only secure, but supported by active help, while Moslem opinion in Egypt became no longer definitely anti-British.

In fact all went well until the time came for the fulfilment of the promises." (*The Ins And Outs Of Mesopotamia*, pp.160-3.)

Lawrence was recruited at Jesus College, Oxford, by Professor David George Hogarth, Keeper of Antiquities at the Ashmolean Museum, and an academic spymaster on the lookout for bright young men. Hogarth was a *Round Table* member, and sat on the Royal Geographical Society (at a time when Geography was intimately connected with Geopolitics and virtually a branch of Imperialism). In 1911 Lawrence was sent on an archaeological dig to Syria, which was really a cover for a spy mission against the Bagdad Railway. Lawrence was aware that the purpose of his map-making was military intelligence and noted: 'we are obviously only meant as a red herring to give an archaeological cover to a political job.' (J. Wilson, *Lawrence of Arabia,* p.136.)

Colonel Lawrence seems to have entered into it all with great self-delusions, which was convenient for the War effort, but very inconvenient for the Arabs:

"The Cabinet raised the Arabs to fight for us by definite promises of self-government afterwards. Arabs believe in persons, not in institutions. They saw in me a free agent of the British Government, and demanded from me an endorsement of its written promises. So I had to join the conspiracy and, for what my word was worth, assured the men of their reward. In our two years' partnership under fire they grew accustomed to believe me and to think my Government, like myself, sincere. In this hope they performed some fine things, but, of course, instead of being proud of what we did together, I was continually and bitterly ashamed.

It was evident from the beginning that if we won the war the promises would be dead paper, and had I been an honest adviser of the Arabs I would have advised them to go home and not risk their lives fighting for such stuff: but I salved myself with the hope that, by leading these Arabs madly in the final victory I would establish them, with arms in their hands, in a position so assured (if not dominant) that expediency would counsel to the Great Powers a fair settlement of their claims. In other words, I presumed (seeing no other leader with the will and power) that I would survive the campaigns, and be able to defeat not merely the Turks on the battlefield, but my own country and its allies in the council-chamber. It was an immodest presumption: it is not yet clear if I succeeded: but it is clear that I had no shadow of leave to engage the Arabs, unknowing, in such hazard. I risked the fraud, on my conviction that Arab help was necessary to our cheap and speedy victory in the East, and that better we win and break our word than lose." (T. E. Lawrence, *Seven Pillars of Wisdom: a Triumph*, p. 24.)

I think the question of why England offered so much to the Arabs, knowing that it would not, or could not, fulfil its promises afterwards, can be only answered through the understanding that Imperial Britain had invested so much more than it initially thought necessary to destroy its Carthage; with the result that it would do anything to achieve the defeat of Germany and its allies, and it would worry about it all later. To hell with the consequences for the world — they were for another day.

Taking on Turkey as an enemy compounded the problem, since it then became necessary to placate the Islamic subjects of the Empire to ensure their continued pacification and to hold together the Indian Empire, in preparation for its expansion.

In putting the bravest face on it, England, perhaps, believed that after it had emerged victorious it could put right any problems that it created in the course of winning the War. It would be the greatest Power on earth, the greatest of all time, after all — so anything would be possible.

But that is not how Britain emerged from the War. It emerged as a shadow of its triumphal projection, with Allies to satisfy, who had made great sacrifices; and it began to struggle with the problems it had created, which then became far beyond its capacities.

The dissatisfaction of Lyell and Storrs is to do with the fact that Britain never intended that such a thing would occur. It was clear to those in the know that England planned to conquer the region (or as much of it that they could before the French got there) and use it as a land bridge between India and Egypt. An Arab State would have been a barrier to this project. But England needed allies and so it couched the Treaty with Hussein in such language that it convinced the Arabs of England's benevolent intentions — the Arab world would be theirs — but left it also open to a reading that would enable it to be got out of at the end of the War.

## England's Holy War

Following the Treaty with England, Hussein issued a Proclamation of a most reactionary character against the Ottoman Government, on 27th June 1916. In it he announced himself, a direct descendant of Mohammed, as the true leader of the Islamic faith and people. As such he was effectively seeking to depose the Sultan as Caliph, whom he represented as a mere tool of the Young Turks.

The Proclamation, issued through the *Ulema* (the body of priests of Mecca), attacked the Young Turks for the progressive reforms they had brought to the Empire and condemned them for allowing freedom of the press in Constantinople, favouring equal rights between men and women, and decreasing the Executive power of the Caliph. The text of it was issued in London as a pamphlet (along with Sir Stanley Maude's speech after the occupation of Baghdad) under the title *The King Of The Hejaz And Arab Independence*.

The Sultan had responded to the British Declaration of War by declaring a *Jihad* and he was ridiculed as a Medievalist in England for doing so. But Britain secured a Holy War against Constantinople, courtesy of the Shereef in Mecca, and an Arab revolt against the Turks, on the promise of replacing the rule of the Young Turks with a Moslem state of a much more reactionary character.

Here is just a sample of the Shereef in Mecca's *Jihad* (The *'Unionists'* are the Young Turk Committee of Union and Progress):

"...In truth we were one with the Government until the Committee of Union and Progress rose up, and strengthened itself, and laid its hands on power. Consider how since then ruin has overtaken the State, and its possessions have been torn from it, and its place in the world has been lost, until now it has been drawn into this last and most fatal war. All this they have done, being led away by shameful appetites, which are not for me to set forth, but which are public and a cause for sorrow to the Moslems of the whole world, who have seen this greatest and most noble Moslem Power broken in pieces and led down to ruin and utter destruction... They made weak the person of the Sultan, and robbed him of his honour, forbidding him to choose for himself the chief of his personal Cabinet. Other like things did they to sap the foundation of the Khalifate... Then the Union and Progress rejected God's Word, 'A man shall have twice a woman's share,' and made them equal... We are absolutely certain that the secret committee of the Young Turk Party has notoriously disobeyed God. No words stayed their hand from crime, and no opposition prevented the evil consequences of their actions... We shall bring forth these facts and lay them before the Mohammedan world when necessity demands. Now we content ourselves with begging those of our brethren who oppose us to send some reliable person or persons to Constantinople, the capital of the Unionists, and there witness personally, as we have ourselves witnessed, Moslem women employed by the Government and exposed in public places unveiled before men of strange nations. What do our true Moslem brethren who oppose us in haste think of this matter, an example of an evil that will greatly injure us if it increases and of which we publicly complain?…We endeavoured to please God and avoid a rebellion so long as it was possible. We rebelled in order to please God, and He gave us victory and stood by us in support of His law and religion, and in accordance with a wisdom known to Him which would lead to the uplifting of this people… We have done what we ought to do. We have cleansed our country from the germs of atheism and evil. The best course for those Moslems who still side with and defend this notorious gang of Unionists, is to submit to the will of God before their tongues, hands, and feet give witness against them.'"

The Proclamation was backed up by military action as the Hashemites, with the help of the Royal Navy, forced the Turkish garrisons of Mecca and Jidda to surrender. Britain landed 60,000 rifles and gave £500,000 for the Hashemite army but they failed to take Medina, which, further inland from the coast, was out of range of the Royal Navy's guns. This reverse, however, did not stop Hussein from declaring himself *Malik el Arab*, King of all Arabs, in late October 1916.

The Arab Revolt was backed up by a blockade of the coasts. In the summer of 1916, reports began to appear in *The Times* about famine in Syria. A 'neutral correspondent' reported on 12th August that: 'The state of the people of Syria is past all belief… It is estimated that from 60,000 to 80,000 have died of starvation in Northern Syria.' Further reports from Americans leaving the country described women and children dying by the roadside and even cases of cannibalism. Famine casualties far exceeded military ones, and death rates for Syria and Lebanon were afterwards put at between 12 and 18 per cent of the population.

The British public would never have guessed that the famine in Syria was a result of the British blockade of the coast. Western reports blamed Ottoman requisitioning of animals and foodstuffs, but the requisitioning was done in response to the blockade itself—which encompassed the Mediterranean Sea, the Persian Gulf and the Red Sea.

### Professor Snouck Hurgronje's Warning

Much of the 'knowledge' Britain had of the Middle East came from its Imperial Administrators in Egypt. Britain had unofficially absorbed the Ottoman province of Egypt in the 1880s and ruled the country through the Khedive and some native ministers who acted on British 'advice'. The British occupation of Egypt was always declared to be a temporary measure, until 'law and order' was restored amongst the unruly locals. Some in Britain had wanted to formally annex Egypt and the Sudan. But General Kitchener, the hero of Omdurman, had always opposed this move. The area, however, appeared in red on British maps of the world by the turn of the new century, and at the outset of the War it was officially incorporated into the British Empire—despite still being officially part of the Moslem Ottoman State.

A large number of the British Administrators in Egypt ended up in the War Office with their boss, Lord Kitchener, in August 1914. These 'experts' from Cairo seem to have developed the view that Islam was like Roman Catholicism, with a centralised authority based around a 'Pontiff of Islam', or Caliph. Britain's historic anti-Catholicism often coloured its understanding of Islam. In the Middle Ages, European Powers had threatened, or even captured, the Pope, and bent his authority to their interests, sometimes against England. Islam and the Caliph were thought to function in a similar manner and it was imperative that the Caliph should be England's man. He who controlled the Caliph, so the reasoning went, controlled the Moslem world.

And ultimately that reasoning went a long way to seal the fate of the Caliphate.

Before the War, Britain's Administration in Egypt had toyed with the idea of promoting the Khedive of Egypt as a new Caliph. But it was realised that in the Moslem world the Egyptian puppet would not have the authority to carry off such a function. So interest shifted to the Shereef of Mecca—since the Shereef was a real descendant of the Prophet.

Britain wanted to displace the Ottoman Sultan as Caliph because it believed he was Germany's man. There was also the worry that he might become Russia's man if Constantinople fell to the Czar in the event of war.

The Shereef of Mecca was an ideal replacement because he had the legitimacy of the Prophet and was the guardian of the Moslem Holy Places. He could also be protected (and isolated) from the other Powers by the presence of the Royal Navy off the coast of Arabia. And so England decided to promote the Hussein family as a new papal dynasty of Islam at Mecca.

Professor Snouck Hurgronje of the University of Leiden in Holland was the most knowledgeable Western authority on Arabia. When the Arab Revolt became a reality in 1916, a collection of his writings was issued, with an Appendix containing Hussein's Proclamation against the Young Turks. It is a very informative explanation of why England's strategy was fundamentally misconceived and would only end in distress for all concerned.

Hurgronje began with some history of the Shereefate of Mecca and of relations with the Caliphate and Constantinople in the light of events in 1916. In this account, it becomes clear that the relationship between Constantinople and Mecca was far from being one between conqueror and conquered, because the Shereefate of Mecca had proved incapable of independent existence and depended for its continuance on the sufferance of the wider Islamic world:

"According to a Reuter despatch, the Great Shereef of Mecca has revolted against Turkish authority... If Reuter be right... then it is well worth while to consider what may be the possible consequences of the Arab movement. In either case, to comprehend the matter rightly, the political significance of the Shereefate of Mecca should be understood and the reading public should have a clearer idea of what the title 'Grand Shereef of Mecca' covers than is possessed by the majority.

Mecca, the birth-place of the Prophet Mohammed, was not the centre from which he extended his sovereignty over a great part of Arabia. The capital of the realm founded by him was Medina, situated a ten-day caravan journey to the north. Moreover, when, about twenty years after his first appearance as Allah's messenger, Mohammed conquered Mecca, he did not think of transferring the seat of government thither. He had his own good reasons for this, which we can pass over here. Still weightier were the reasons that influenced his successors in the administration of the theocracy of Islam from such a step. Mecca was far too remote from the then existing centres of civilisation…

Out of the chaos in West Arabia, resulting from the disintegration of the Islamic Empire, was born the Shereefate of Mecca. The head of the reigning family in Mecca is 'The Shereef of Mecca' … and the people call him Sayyidana, that is 'Our Master' (or Our Lord). How far the realm of these Shereefs was extended beyond Mecca depended, as long as the petty dynasties existed, entirely on the chances of circumstance; the more that confusion reigned in the surrounding Mohammedan realms and the greater the energy manifested by the ruling head of the family, the greater the portion of the Hijaz that came under his authority. The reverse was equally true. The defects of the most respected race of Islam were, to a great extent, the peculiar characteristics of the Mecca branch. They were incapable of carrying out any great undertaking…

Further, there were among the members of the noble race one quarrel after another about their heritage, so that it was almost the normal state of affairs for one head of two rival branches of the family to fill the Shereefate while the other besieged Mecca or rendered the roads thither unsafe. The stable population of Mecca were sacrificed to this struggle for mastery; the blessings of peace were an unknown luxury to them.

The Shereefate of Mecca differed from most of the states and principalities into which the great Islam Empire was divided, because it had not been developed gradually from a governorship to a condition of greater independence, but was born, spontaneously, during a period of confusion. At Bagdad, as well as in other neighbouring capitals, people had accepted the change as a *fait accompli*. The Shereefate was neither expressly recognised nor expressly objected to as unlawful. Its centuries-long existence attained, moreover, a sort of virtual legitimacy through its acceptance by many Moslem tribes, who were represented in the Holy City by the annual deputations of pilgrims. These visitors were constantly exposed to ill treatment on the part of the Shereef.

Yet, in spite of that, they held to a belief that domination over the Holy City belonged rightfully to a branch of the Holy Family. The fact was simply accepted as irrefutable. The chief Islam powers have always attached a certain reservation to their tacit recognition of the Shereefs of Mecca which the latter have found themselves forced to accept.

He was never an independent ruler and, in the long run, had to recognise the suzerainty of the protecting states. If the Shereefate of Mecca continued, it was to these accidents of origin that the Shereefate of Mecca owed its peculiar standing. Its status was not a little enhanced by the unique significance of the city of Mecca for the Mohammedan world at large. From the tenth century, no one of the foremost Islam princes possessed the machinery to keep West Arabia under an administration even approximately orderly...

Egypt long held an uncontested position so that it is correct to speak of a protectorate exercised by her Sultans over the territory of West Arabia from the thirteenth to the sixteenth centuries... It was always an unequal strife between the trained soldiers of a great Moslem power and the Shereef's little force, consisting as it did, of a few hundred slaves, the same number of mercenaries, and the timely aid of a few Bedouin clans. Domestic dissension, moreover, always assured the punitory leader of the cooperation of one party within the disturbed territory...

When Egypt was conquered in 1517 by Sultan Selim, Turkey, automatically, took over the protectorate of the Holy Land. The Turkish Sultans styled themselves, with unassuming pride, 'the servants' of both holy cities... From that epoch on, their names immediately preceded that of the Grand Shereef in the official prayers. Later, the significance of the honour was enhanced by the addition of the title of Caliph assumed by the Turkish Sultans as sign and seal of their unrivalled power in Islam.

The Osmans made as little effort to reform the hopelessly muddled administration of the holy cities as their predecessors in the Protectorate had done. By that date, the Shereefate had obtained for more than three centuries, and no Mohammedan thought of questioning either the legality or the desirability of the institution. The administration methods of the Osmans were as little adapted for permanent centralization as those of the earlier Mohammedan empire had been. The provinces speedily assumed the character of feudal holdings, each possessing a large measure of independence...

In the eighteenth century, the Shereefs were not troubled by the pressure of a heavy hand from without, but they were forced to depend on themselves, and their inadequate equipment was a source of danger to them when an unexpected opponent threatened to destroy their power. The Wahhabis of Central Arabia, roused by a puritanic zeal to protest against what they declared was the dishonour of Islam, launched out on a campaign of reform. This 'holy war,' directed, primarily, against the Turkish domination, succeeded in exciting a religious fervour throughout a great part of Arabia, similar to that awakened by Mohammed twelve centuries earlier, and, at the turn of the eighteenth into the nineteenth centuries, these Wahhabis succeeded in obtaining the mastery of the Holy Cities and in forcing the Shereefs to recognise their authority.

With infinite difficulty the Pasha of Egypt, Mohammed Ali, later the first Khedive, succeeded in fulfilling the mission entrusted to him by the Sultan of

Turkey and in reconquering the Holy Land in his turn... With the expulsion of the Wahhabis from the Hijaz in 1813, begins the latest historical phase of the Shereefate. The Protectorate exercised by the first Khedive of Egypt down to 1840, partly in cooperation with, partly in opposition to, Turkish authority, was completely effective and so, as the Sultan was regularly represented in the Holy Land by a governor sent from Constantinople, the good old tumultuous times did not return for this free dynasty. The understanding between the Shereefs and their protectors at Stamboul were, however, never cordial; the aspirations and interests of the two parties were too far asunder for that. The Sultans of Turkey considered the Shereefate as a necessary evil that prevented them from making the Hijaz into an ordinary wilayet or province.

They stationed there military and civil officials similar to those in other wilayets, but the functions of these subordinates were hampered by the unrestricted power of the Shereef. After the Wahhabi war, this ruler was selected by the suzerain and the rival kinsmen could no longer oust an incumbent of the hereditary office by force of arms. They were obliged to resort to the weapons of intrigue with the Sultan and the Sublime Porte. Still, even with this appearance of stable administration, it was not until 1880 that the Shereef finally relinquished as fruitless all armed resistance to the Sultan's deputies. The theory had been that the Sultan was to be obeyed, but that his servants in the Hijaz were unfaithful and could not be accepted.

At Constantinople, meanwhile, certain members of the Shereef's family were kept in a kind of honourable captivity, partly as hostages for the good faith of the reigning Shereef, partly to relieve him from the burden of having rivals in his vicinity, and also it was a convenience to have those rivals in readiness in case the Shereef proved untrustworthy..." (*The Revolt In Arabia*, pp. 33-40.)

By 1916 England had successfully whittled down what was left of independent Moslem existence to Ottoman Turkey (after dealing with Egypt, India, Afghanistan and Persia) and it was about to destroy this last vestige of Moslem power. Therefore it was up to Britain to sustain the Shereefate (and the Caliphate) for the Moslem world, if it had any real pretensions to be 'a great Mussulman power', as it often called itself. But, as Professor Hurgronje noted, the Hussein Shereefate was a poor basis on which to construct an Arab nation. It was riven with rivalries, had a largely parasitic relationship with the wider Moslem world, and there were serious doubts whether it could sustain itself in the absence of an exterior power to support it.

In the next piece, Professor Hurgronje dealt with England's intentions regarding Mecca and Constantinople and the plan to replace the Turkish Caliph with a Mecca one, and explained why this project was fundamentally flawed:

"Various writers on Islam have commented on the impropriety, according to Mohammedan law itself, of the assumption of the title of 'Caliph' by the Sultan of Turkey. It was, indeed, for more than nine centuries, regarded by the

Moslem world as obligatory for the Caliphs to be able to trace their descent from the Arabic line of Koreish, the line from which Mohammed sprang. The pretensions advanced by the Sultans since the sixteenth century have never been generally approved. That they did not excite any vehement open opposition was partly owing to the imposing puissance of the Turkish Empire at the moment when the Sultans decorated themselves with the name, and partly to the circumstance that the usurped dignity had no practical sequence. The Caliph added no patch of ground to the territory that the Sultan had conquered with the sword, and spiritual authority has never been ascribed to the Caliph by the Moslem congregations...

Such Moslems as were under Turkish authority were not affected by the Caliphate of their Sultan. The relation of subjects to their rulers in Mohammedan realms not subordinated to Turkey were even less affected; and least of all did the matter signify to those followers of Islam ruled by non-Mohammedans. These are numerous and have steadily increased during the last centuries. An effective Caliphate, however explained, presupposes the political unity of all the faithful.

The Caliph is the very personification of such unity and is, primarily, the leader of Islam's armies against the foes of the Faith, or he bears a name bereft of all significance. In international life there is no room for mediaeval structures, and Turkey can live in peace with other states, especially with those possessing Mohammedan subjects, only if Caliphate pretensions be honestly put aside, even though the title be maintained as a formal one. This was well understood by Turkish statesmen of later times, and they either banished the Caliphate idea in all their international discussions, or they permitted their European colleagues, who mistakenly regarded the Caliph as a sort of pope or prince of the Church to continue to entertain this false conception as it was harmless.

Unlettered Mohammedans, who, ignorant of the modern point of view, went on assigning an important place to the Caliphate legend in their framework of the political system, were, however, often presented with panislamic visions in order to retain, fictitiously, at least, what had long vanished from real life...

Taking all these points into consideration, it becomes hardly needful to reply to the question as to how the Shereef of Mecca might, perhaps, try to become a rival of the Sultan Mehmed Reshad as a pretender to the Caliphate.

A Caliphate, no matter who holds the dignity, is wholly incompatible with modern political conditions. And this will be as true after the present war as it was before. Only as an empty title can it be tolerated at all.

For the rest, it can be seen, from what we have already written about the history and the current condition of the Shereefate, that any lofty aspirations would be especially ill adapted for local principalities. The idea of a Caliphate of the Shereefs of Mecca has been ventilated, more than once, by this or that European writer on Islam, but, in the Moslem world, it has never been broached, and no one of the Shereefs from the House of Katada rulers in Mecca and in varying portions of West Arabia ever since the year 1200 A.D. ever thought of such a thing. It is improbable that even foreign influence could prevail on a

Shereef of Mecca to attempt to gamble for the Caliphate. They all know too well how little chance of success there would be in such an attempt, and they feel themselves limited by tradition and by their resources to the Hijaz.

Perhaps it is not superfluous to controvert another error into which many fall, the opinion, namely, that the wresting of the Hijaz from Turkish domination would, automatically, end the Turkish Caliphate, since the Caliph bases his claim to the title partly on his protection of the Holy Cities. This opinion is supported by neither Mohammedan law nor by Mohammedan history. Mecca and Medina have known periods when, for instance, they were in the hands of the unbelieving Karmathians, when again they submitted to the heretical Fatimide-Caliphs, when all relations with the seat of the Caliphate were suspended, when the Wahhabis drove the Turks from the Holy Land; on none of these occasions did it occur to a single Moslem to question the right of the Caliph to his dignity. The Caliphate and the Holy Land have, more than once, existed independently of each other...

In the Great War, the Shereefate of Mecca cannot possibly take part. The forces at its disposal are nothing more than a bodyguard, a few mercenaries, and the contribution made by some Bedouin tribes, difficult to hold together, undisciplined, untrained. The population of the holy cities furnishes no elements for the formation of a military force, and in that population, Shereef Ali, whom the Turks now wish to use, will assuredly find some adherents. Arabia is still, as it was of yore, hopelessly divided by conflicting interests and by century-long feuds. It is not ready for great undertakings. But, for the moment, a revolt in West Arabia against Turkey, under the lead of the Great Shereef and aided by England, can cause serious trouble to the Turkish Government, and all the more, because it is at Mecca, familiar to, and cherished by, the entire Mohammedan world..." (pp. 33-40.)

It had, of course, been a tactic of Britain to work up nationalist passions in the empires of its enemies in Europe during the previous century as part of the Balance of Power policy. But there were no authentic nationalisms in the Ottoman Empire for England to work up. There were only different races and different varieties of Islam. So Britain sought to work up religious passions within Islam by using Mecca to incite fundamentalist impulses to destabilise Ottoman Rule in the Imperial interest.

But interference in the Ottoman Empire for gain was not a simple matter. The Ottoman Empire was composed of a wide variety of races, religions and branches of religions. Most of the subjects were Moslems, but Islam was very fragmented, with only the Sunni Moslems (who were the majority) regarding the Caliph as having any legitimacy as a temporal and spiritual authority of the Prophet. What England was attempting to do in 1916, then, was to detach a part of the Sunnis from their allegiance to the Sultan and to establish in Arabia an alternative Caliph, who would exercise moral authority over the other Sunni Moslems both in the British and Ottoman Empires.

It does not seem to have been understood that other Moslem leaders, many of whom were not Sunni, would not accept the Caliph as spiritual leader. This was not only to do with doctrinal issues. It was also because the Caliph had potentially more than just spiritual authority—he was also a prince, a governor and a military commander. (Moslems did not make the same distinction between the spiritual and the temporal that had developed in the West since the decline of religion there. If the Caliph was accepted as leader of Islam, he was also accepted as overlord, so to speak. And many chiefs did not want him interfering in their affairs.)

So Moslem leaders were disinclined to accept the Husseins of Mecca as Caliphs because of the implications for their own authority. And for that reason they were inclined to prefer the distant and less hereditary legitimate incumbent in Constantinople. (That became apparent after the Great War when Hussein's House of Hejaz and Ibn Saud's Wahhabi followers went into battle for control of Arabia. Britain supported Hussein as their client ruler in Arabia—and his sons as rulers of Mesopotamia and Trans-Jordan—but found that the real power in the region lay with Ibn Saud, whom they tried, unsuccessfully, to buy off.)

### British Desiderata In The Middle East

Having invited the Arabs onto history's stage with the promise of a leading role, England then conspired to reduce them to a bit part.

In March 1915, Britain had consented to Russia's possession of Constantinople after the War and, to secure the agreement of France in this, had agreed to French designs on Syria. Taken with its own designs on parts of Mesopotamia, this amounted to a break-up of the Ottoman Empire. At a meeting of the War Council, later in the same month, Asquith stated:

> "If for one reason or another, because we didn't want more territory, or we didn't feel equal to the responsibility, we were to leave the other nations to scramble for Turkey without taking anything ourselves, we should not be doing our duty." (Cited in Aaron S. Klieman, *Britain's War Aims In The Middle East In 1915, Journal Of Contemporary History*, July 1968, p.242.)

In April 1915 Asquith appointed an Interdepartmental Committee under the Chairmanship of Sir Maurice de Bunsen to consider 'British Desiderata In Turkey-in-Asia'. The Report concluded:

> "Our Empire is wide enough already, and our task is to consolidate the possessions we already have, to make firm and fast the position we already hold, and to pass on to those who come after an inheritance that stands four-square to the world. It is then to strengthen ragged edges that we have to take advantage of the present opportunity, and to assert our claim in settling the destiny of Asiatic Turkey. " (p.244.)

Around the turn of the century, Joseph Chamberlain put forward a proposal for Imperial consolidation. But it was rejected in favour of unlimited free trade expansionism, after a campaign by the Liberal Imperialists. The de Bunsen

Report suggested that: 'to strengthen ragged edges [of the Empire]... we have to take advantage of the present opportunity'. But Imperial consolidation could not take place, given the continual appearance of more 'ragged edges' every time that the Empire undertook its latest expansion.

In the atmosphere of the Great War, ambitions had a tendency to become unlimited, in any case. And so it was concluded that the main area of importance for Britain in the Middle East was the Persian Gulf and that Basra was essential to the control of the Gulf, and Baghdad was important in relation to Basra, and that Mosul had to be taken to protect the area north of Baghdad, and Persia had to be controlled on the Eastern flank, and to the West the acquisition of Palestine was essential to protect Mesopotamia, and Egypt, and the Suez Canal, and on and on...

The Report of this Committee shows that Britain desired a belt of territory between Arabia and the French in Syria and would not permit a Foreign Power to occupy the area next to Egypt and the Suez Canal. But, after considering a number of possible policies toward Turkey after the War, it recommended support for a devolutionary scheme which would preserve the Ottoman Empire in five regions, Anatolia, Armenia, Syria, Palestine and Jazirah-Iraq, with the latter four being capable of being detached if necessary in the future.

Despite the flexibility this policy might have provided, the Report's recommendations were shelved and the Government took up one of its rejected policy options instead—the partition of the Ottoman Empire between the Imperialist Powers. The Committee described this option as having the advantages of providing Britain with freedom of commerce, as well as a granary and oil reserves in Mesopotamia, an area in which an Indian colony could be established; plus the chance of detaching the Southern part of Syria (Palestine) from Turkey (and France) to construct a buffer zone linking up the Indian Empire to Egypt.

The process of implementing this policy began with the Sykes-Picot Agreement of May 1916.

### The Sykes-Picot Agreement

At the same time as the McMahon correspondence and Treaty with Shereef Hussein, England began making secret treaties with the French (The Sykes-Picot Agreement of May 1916) which sought to divide up the Middle East amongst the Western Christian Powers after the War was won.

Under this Agreement, Russia was to have the Dardanelles, Constantinople and a large area around Erzurum and Trebizond. France was to get Cilicia and Lebanon, above Acre, whilst the vilayet of Mosul, north of Mesopotamia, and Syria were to be included in a large 'Arab State A', under French control. England was to have the vilayets of Basra and Baghdad, and a large tract of land stretching from Kirkuk in the north down past Mesopotamia to the Persian Gulf and west to the Jordan, called 'Arab State B'. Palestine was to become a condominium of England, France and Russia.

Hussein knew nothing of this Agreement, which aimed to balkanise the region and prevent the Moslems from operating a State that would amount to anything.

This plan of balkanisation was a most unsuitable way to administer the region, because divisions within the Arab world were not national in any way. They were religious and cultural. But the different religions and cultures were spread right across the region and could not be delineated by national boundaries or through nation states drawn out of the sand.

That was why the Ottoman structures worked — because they enabled different religious groups, clans and families with different cultures, ways of life and allegiances to live next to each other with no lines in the sand to bother them.

When the lines in the sand were imposed on the Arabs, they were made to see themselves as nationalities — but with no historical meaning — and to see others (who had the same history, religion or culture as themselves) as alien and a threat, because they were from without the newly imposed lines in the sand.

When the Bolsheviks took power in Russia in October 1917, they published the secret treaties from the Czar's Ministry of Foreign Affairs. Amongst those was the text of the Sykes-Picot Agreement. Upon obtaining these papers, the Turks forwarded copies to Hussein with an offer of forgive and forget and a separate peace. This was contained in a letter from Djemal Pasha:

> "The letter addressed to Faisal was worded as an appeal from one serious-minded Moslem to another... that Faisal and his father had been misled by the promises of Arab independence into rebelling against the supreme authority in Islam: that those promises had now been shown to have been utterly mendacious since the true intentions of the Allies were to partition the Arab countries and place them under foreign masters; French in Syria, British in Iraq, and International in Palestine; and that the only course left for the Arabs to take was to return to the Ottoman fold and secure their legitimate rights by coming to an understanding with the Turks... It also contained... an outline of the terms on which the Turks were prepared to negotiate. These terms envisaged the grant of the fullest autonomy to all the Arab provinces of the Empire... secured not only by the Sultan's ratification, but also by the collateral guarantee from the German Government." (George Antonius, *The Arab Awakening*, p. 255.)

The Ottomans gave the fullest publicity to the peace offer to Hussein and this raised doubts in the Sheriff's mind as to the wisdom of his alliance with the British. When he contacted his Allies he was told that the treaties were not concluded agreements but simply records of provisional exchanges and conversations from the early part of the War to avoid any disagreements at the conclusion. The English assured Hussein that the Arab Revolt had altered the situation completely and made the Sykes-Picot Agreement null and void.

Antonius explained that this reply proved enough for Hussein:

> "The reply he received was obviously designed to deceive him, for it not only evaded the issue... of whether or not it was true that the Allied Powers had concluded secret agreements affecting the future disposal of Arab countries, but it clothed the evasion in language which implied that no such agreements had been concluded. And Hussein, with his faith in British standards of fair dealing still unshaken, took the disingenuous message at its face value and set his mind at rest." '(*The Arab Awakening*, p. 258.)

And perhaps the presence of the British Army at the ramparts of Jerusalem also convinced him that there was no going back.

But Hussein was in for another shock. One part of the territory he had been expecting in his Arab State, Palestine, had not only been earmarked for the European Powers but, unbeknown to the leader of the Arab Revolt, it was also meant to become a homeland for another people — who would return to displace the Arabs already living there.

### Asquith Puts Turkey-In-Asia Up For Grabs

Only four days after the British Declaration of War on Turkey, the British Prime Minister delivered a momentous speech in the Guildhall in London, in which he announced the end of the Ottoman Empire in Europe — and in Asia. *The Jewish Chronicle*, published in London, was quick to understand the unprecedented and significant content of the speech. In its edition of 13th November 1914 an editorial entitled *What About Palestine?* noted:

> "The Prime Minister in his speech at the Lord Mayor's banquet at the Guildhall on Monday last... predicted that the Ottoman Empire as it had drawn the sword so will perish by the sword. Mr. Asquith added words which must be of the utmost significance to the Jews. 'It is the Ottoman Government', he said, 'and not we who have rung the death-knell of the Ottoman dominion, *not only in Europe but in Asia*'. We have italicized the last words because, so far as we recollect, this is the first time that any responsible Minister has extended the 'bag and baggage' policy as applied to the Turkish Empire, further than to European Turkey. If, as a result of the War, the dominion of Turkey in Asia is to be ended, then what is to be the fate of Palestine?"

Zionism had little influence with the British Government in the decades leading up to the Great War. And what political influence it did have was largely due to anti-Semitic sentiment in England. Some notable individuals in high places had shown sympathy to the Zionist ideal but it was anti-Semitism that had briefly placed it on the political agenda between 1902 and 1905.

The 1905 Aliens Act, which was really an anti-Jewish immigration Act, was a product of a Royal Commission on Alien Immigration that was set up after flamboyant displays of Jewish wealth in Park Lane outraged aristocratic sensibilities in London. England had absorbed many immigrants in its history, most notably the large numbers of Irish after the Great Famine, but the Jews were different. The unceasing work of these Jewish immigrants coupled with their skills in finance threatened the social structure of English society. The class system of Britain was very rigid and generally did not look kindly on the accumulation of wealth by individuals from classes outside the gentry. But Jews began to buck the system and their ostentatious wealth was troubling to London Society, as a sign of things to come.

These displays and the influx of thousands of Jews into London's East End since the 1880s, after Russian pogroms, prompted England's first substantial interest in Jewish colonization. This interest was almost entirely motivated by anti-Semitic attitudes—which Theodor Herzl, the leader of the Zionist movement, recognized and saw as the only possible lever for winning British Imperial support for the Zionist project.

Lord Rothschild, the leader of English Jewry, was so concerned that Zionism might be used as a useful vehicle by British anti-Semites, to rid England of Jews, that he refused to meet Herzl. Rothschild saw Zionism as the negation of Jewish assimilation and very dangerous to it; he only joined the Commission on Alien Immigration to try to silence Herzl and counter his efforts to gain a platform for his Colony by becoming a pawn of English anti-Semites.

The Jewish colonization proposals offered by the Commission did not involve a settling of Palestine, since at this time England still regarded the Sultan as an ally, and the suggestions for settlements in East Africa, Egypt and Uganda ultimately came to nothing .

The Great War on Turkey and Asquith's pronouncement, however, re-stimulated the Zionist movement. Albert Montefiore Hyamson ('*A.M.H.*'), a Jewish civil servant, penned an article for *The New Statesman* on 21st November, entitled *The Future Of Palestine*, which apparently had a great effect on Lloyd George. Here is an extract:

> "More than once in the past Turkey has received notice to quit Europe, but this is the first time that the liquidation of Turkey in Asia has become a definite prospect, and with Mr. Asquith's words at the Guildhall the hopes of the Zionists have suddenly passed from an ideal into a matter of practical politics...
>
> With the advent of Young Turkey... all possibility of such an event disappeared; with it passed away Zionism as a political movement... Zionism... became entirely a movement for the recreation, after the lapse of two thousand years, of a Jewish center in Palestine. Jerusalem was to be, not the capital of a Jewish State, but the center of Jewish culture...
>
> Left alone the future of the Jews in Palestine would have been secure... But the country is now in the melting-pot and the crisis has come too soon for the Jews to be able to cope with it unaided. The crisis, however, is not one for the Jews of Palestine alone, but for the Jews of many other lands...
>
> Today we are told is the day of small nationalities. Their interests are to be

considered when peace is concluded. It should not be overlooked that the Jews of Palestine... are also a small nationality... the weakest of the nationalities and they cannot stand alone. For many years, perhaps for centuries, they will need a protecting Power while they grow into a nation. To give Palestine self-government today would be a blunder and a crime...

Christendom owes a debt to Jewry for the persecutions of the past nineteen hundred years. It would seem that she now has the opportunity of commencing to pay it. Let Britain remember her past and think of her future, and secure to the Jews under her protection the possibility of building up a new Palestine on the ruins of her ancient home."

This could be described as bait. It was certainly crafted with great care and contained all the essential elements of what the Jews could do for the British Empire, when required. But it would be a mistake to believe that the raised hopes of British Zionists produced the British interest in Palestine. It was the British designs on Palestine that made the Zionist project a possibility and then a reality.

Hyamson played on the reality of the situation England was creating in the Middle East:

"Left alone the future of the Jews in Palestine would have been secure... But the country is now in the melting-pot and the crisis has come too soon for the Jews to be able to cope with it unaided."

By throwing the region into the 'melting-pot' England was disrupting the comfortable and profitable position the Jewish communities enjoyed within the Ottoman Empire. And it was removing them from a stable order to place them amongst Arabs who had been stirred up by notions of nationalism. In such circumstances Britain owed a responsibility of protection to the Jews, particularly given the history of 'the persecutions of the past nineteen hundred years'.

Hyamson did not bother himself with the difficulties this seemed to present in balancing up the interests. For one thing he thought that if the decadent and decrepit Ottomans had for centuries been able to maintain the equilibrium, the British Empire certainly could. How wrong he was!

### *The Conquest of Palestine*

It should be understood at this point that Britain coveted Palestine long before it discovered the Zionists. It was not Zionism that drew England to Palestine, or the Zionists who brought the issue of Palestine up within the British corridors of power. England had its eye on the territory long before the Balfour Declaration or the negotiations that brought it about (which were instigated by Britain and not by the Zionists).

For the first two years of the War England showed little interest in Zionism and pursued its objective of getting hold of Palestine without reference to it. Zionism didn't interest the de Bunsen Commission. Britain negotiated the

Sykes-Picot Agreement and the deal with Hussein of Mecca without reference to it and basically took the future of Palestine to be decided without taking into account the views of either ordinary Jews or Zionists. All it was concerned about was whether it could wrest the area from France at the hour of victory.

Palestine had not been explicitly mentioned in any of the agreements concluded between Britain and Hussein. The Arabs naturally took this to mean that it was simply included within the area of an Arab State, because it had not been specifically excluded, as other areas west of Damascus had been. However, England carefully avoided mention of the area because they had other ideas for Palestine after the War, and they had other deals to make with other people.

Under the Sykes-Picot Agreement the status of Palestine had also been left unclear. England, France and Russia all had an interest in administering it, but Britain, despite having the least claim to it, set its heart on acquiring it for the Empire.

The problem, from Britain's standpoint, was how to devise a scenario whereby the Empire could get control of Palestine. And that is where the Jews started to play a role, and Zionism became significant in Imperial affairs.

Here is a straightforward view of Britain's strategic interest in Palestine, published in *The New Europe* on 19th April 1917, by a writer using the pen-name 'Ibri'. (*The New Europe* was a weekly discussion periodical that presented a forum for prominent people to outline their views on what Britain should do with Europe and beyond when they had won the War. By writing under pen-names people in prominent positions could be freer and more direct in their thoughts than was otherwise possible in public life.):

"For us the moral is that Turkey must no longer keep Palestine. Can we suffer Palestine to fall into the hands of any European Power? States have to think not only of the present but also of the future. This is particularly true of the Suez Canal and Palestine, where our apprehensions, and, therefore, our precautions, are not for the present but for the future. Our traditional policy has been to have no great military Power within striking distance of the Suez Canal, and the development of the art of war has widened that idea so as to mean that we cannot allow any great military Power other than ourselves in Palestine. There has been some suggestion on the other side of the Channel that France might have Palestine. Let us be candid so that there may be no ground for misunderstanding... We predominate in the commerce of Palestine. It will be by British blood and British treasure that the Turks will have been driven out of Palestine. Palestine is a vital need of British Imperial strategy. That is why we are conquering it and mean to hold it. We are driven forward by the irresistible logic of that policy which compelled us to buy the controlling interest in the Canal, occupy Egypt, and absorb the Sinai Peninsula."

When reading this passage, it must be borne in mind that it was written when England was only just holding its own in the Great War and no-one knew how much longer it would continue. Russia had begun to collapse and the new ally, America, had only just entered the War and had not been able to put the required men and material in the field, as yet, to compensate for the loss of the Czarist armies in the East. And it looked as if the main beneficiary of this turn of events would be the Turks.

And yet England was already working out how to keep their Allies from the spoils of victory!

### *Keeping France Out*

It was certainly the case that the French had much greater historical ties to Palestine than the English. If any of the Imperial Powers had rights to supervise the region it was the French. Here is the view of Albert Hyamson, a British Zionist, on this matter:

> "Among the Allies the principal claimant to the inheritance of Palestine was France, who, reaching back to the Middle Ages, argued that as the heir of the Crusaders, whose forces and leaders were largely French, she was morally, almost legally, entitled to recover her lost territory. These claims she reinforced by the contention that Palestine had no longer any separate entity and that, as a part of Syria... Palestine should also come under her control... France, also had for centuries, back to the days of Charlemagne and Harun ar Rashid, claimed to be the protector of the Christians in the Turkish dominions." (*Palestine Under The Mandate*, p.26.)

And Hyamson could also have noted that Western Europeans tended to be called 'Franks' as a result of the French cultural influence in the region.

As far back as the 1840s, Lord Palmerston had recognized the potential value of utilizing the Jews to gain influence within the Ottoman Empire. Palmerston noticed that both of England's rivals, France and Russia, had achieved leverage over the Sultan by adopting religious minorities in Jerusalem. But England had no such influence due to the lack of Protestants there. So, to achieve influence in the region, another religious group would have to be adopted and the obvious candidates, consistent with England's Old Testament proclivities, were the Jews. In the 1880s Laurence Oliphant contacted Lord Salisbury with a scheme for Jewish colonization in the Holy Land, advising the Prime Minister:

> "Owing to the financial, political and commercial importance to which the Jews have now attained, there is probably no one Power in Europe that would prove so valuable an ally to a nation likely to be engaged in a European war, as this wealthy, powerful and cosmopolitan race." (*Life of Laurence Oliphant*, p.503.)

These ideas were ahead of their time because of England's very different objectives with regard to the Ottoman Empire before 1907—but they came together, in a different context between 1916 and 1918.

The first argument used by England to oppose the French claim to Palestine was that the existence of the Holy Places in and around Jerusalem called for a special régime. But when this did not convince the French they produced the Jews as a trump card. With regard to Britain's manoeuvrings against France, Lady Hamilton explains the use that England had reserved for the Jews:

> "Imperially minded Britons knew that ever since Napoleon's massive fleet had landed in Alexandria in 1798 the French had wanted to hold the Holy Land. French missionaries were active throughout Syria and Palestine, and their schools had transformed thousands of intelligent but illiterate Arabs into well-informed intellectuals, writers and poets. A Jewish homeland would provide a rational reason to block the French from taking too much territory in the Levant, and create a reliable and strong client population. Their presence would guarantee Britain a hold on this strategic area. If the Allies won the war, France would take the place of Germany and would be the most powerful nation on the continent. France's power would need to be checked. Britain did not want France also to be the dominant power in the Middle East." (*God, Guns and Israel* (2004) p.136.)

Britain calculated that the insertion of a Jewish Homeland into Palestine, buttressed by British power, would tip the balance in moral claims to the territory in England's favour. Since it was England who would give the Jews a solemn undertaking of a National Home in Palestine, it was only fitting that Britain should govern the territory to see that this promise was fulfilled. So England would get Palestine for the Jews and the Zionists would get Palestine for Britain.

Mayir Verete in *The Balfour Declaration And Its Makers* put it like this:

> "The propaganda value of the 'Palestine scheme' could now become a forceful argument in trying to convince the French and Russian Governments. It could thus, in addition, neatly help in eventually securing Palestine for Britain, the aim Sykes, Samuel, Kitchener and Lloyd George... had in mind and sought to achieve. In this sense, from the British point of view, besides being a war measure the idea comprised a long-range interest. The thought that with the help of the Zionists and 'the international power of the Jews'... the Governments of France and Russia were offered a device which on the surface was meant to serve the Allied cause as a whole while in the long run it was designed to be of value for Britain alone. In this respect... there is an interesting similarity between England's diplomacy in the Zionist question and in her alliance with Sharif Hussein: his refusal to join in the Jehad and his revolt against the Sultan were supposed to be serving the Allied cause in general, but from her alliance with him Britain alone was meant to profit." (*Middle Eastern Studies*, January 1970, p.58.)

It could be said that England cheated the Arabs by saying Palestine had been promised to the French and then cheated the French by promising it to the Jews. And all the time the objective was to keep it for the British Empire.

## Liberal Colonialists And Palestine

'Ibri' noted the potentialities of the conquered territories:

"Palestine is a natural fortress... The climate is healthy and bracing, and the land has great industrial, agricultural, and commercial potentialities."

Just the place for British colonists.

But, of course, the colonists ear-marked for this territory were different. 'Ibri' went on to outline that it was Jews who would be the colonists cementing Britain's strategic interests in the region:

"Our strategic needs have sent us to Palestine. They conspire with the British instinct for liberty and nationality to induce us to encourage the development in Palestine of a Jewish dominion under the British flag. The strongest of all bulwarks is a large and progressive population devoted to the soil upon which it dwells and loyal to the British cause, which only the Jewish people can constitute in Palestine. They alone can bring a passionate love for the land of their ancestors and the goal of their longing through 2,000 years; they alone can bring along with this spiritual force, knowledge, technical skill, and material resources for the full expansion of Palestine's natural powers. Experience has taught us that the self-governing Dominions, so far from being an extension of burdens, are towers of strength in the days of trial. A self-governing Dominion in Palestine, in like fashion, could assume in the process of time responsibility for its own defence and proportionately relieve the Mother-country. No doubt that could not be achieved in a moment, but only a self-governing Dominion could achieve it, and only the Jews could build up in Palestine a self-governing Dominion."

And the Liberal writer made a comparison between the new Jewish home and Irish Home Rule:

"The British Empire which will have created that home will be assured of the spontaneous affection and gratitude of all conscious Jews throughout the world. What England can gain in that way we can measure by what she has lost through the failure to satisfy Irish national sentiment."

English Liberals were the driving force behind the Imperial plans for Zionism. Under the influence of Herbert Sidebotham, a prominent Liberal journalist, and C.P.Scott, the influential editor of *The Manchester Guardian*, there developed a Manchester school of Zionism. *The Manchester Guardian* was the driving force in support of Zionism through a number of editorials from the middle of 1915 (such as '*Jews And The War*' on June 25th, which suggested that a Jewish State would be a good idea to draw Jewish soldiers away from allegiance to the Central Powers; and '*The Defence Of Egypt*' on 22nd November, which proposed Palestine as a Jewish buffer-state between Egypt and 'the hostile North'). The leaders of Jewish nationalism in England, Dr. Weizmann and Harry Sacher (also of *The Manchester Guardian*), were situated in Manchester themselves and the city became the hub for an Imperial Zionist project.

The first book in support of the Balfour Declaration published in England by an English political writer was *England And Palestine: Essays Towards The Restoration Of The Jewish State*. The author, Herbert Sidebotham, a famous journalist on the *Manchester Guardian* (writing a regular column as 'Student Of War' in the paper) was a member of the British Palestine Society, whose purpose was to establish a 'community of ideals and interests between Zionism and British policy.' He was also Secretary to Lloyd George. Sidebotham explained that the colonization policy would, of necessity, involve non-British subjects in Palestine:

> "Nothing is more certain than that if Palestine became part of the British Empire it would never be colonized in any real sense by the sort of Englishmen who have made Canada and Australia. The only possible colonists of Palestine are the Jews. Only they can build up in the Mediterranean a new dominion associated with this country from the outset in Imperial work, at once a protection against the alien East and a mediator between it and us, a civilization distinct from ours yet imbued with our political ideas, at the same stage of political development, and beginning its second life as a nation with a debt of gratitude to this country as its second father." (p186.).

Liberals of the Manchester Capitalism variety had traditionally opposed costly expansion of the Empire but Sidebotham advised that the new Imperialism, in bringing Zionism into the Imperial 'family', would present no drawbacks but only benefits for England:

> "Let us beware of making the mistake of the mid-nineteenth century politicians who regarded every fresh extension of territory as an increase in responsibility that ought to be avoided. Quite a different standpoint of judgement has to be applied to increases in the family and increases in the rest of the establishment. The Dominions, as this war has proved, have brought no fresh responsibility but greater increased strength: so it will be in the future British Dominion of Palestine. And the increase in strength will not be direct only, but indirect, by reason of the headship of Jewry that Jerusalem, as a city of the British Empire, would confer upon us." (*Palestine*, March 1st 1917.)

When the Balfour Declaration was issued in November 1917, it was *The Manchester Guardian* which went the furthest of any newspaper of the British Press in interpreting it—far further than the authors of it would have wanted at the time. The organ of Liberalism proclaimed:

> "What it means is that, assuming our military successes to be continued and the whole of Palestine to be brought securely under our control, then on the conclusion of peace our deliberate policy will be to encourage in every way in our power Jewish immigration, to give full security, and no doubt a large measure of local autonomy, to the Jewish immigrants, with a view to the

ultimate establishment of a Jewish State." (November 9th 1917.)
The Declaration merely stated that the British Government

"view with favour the establishment in Palestine of a national home for the Jewish people, and will use their best endeavours to facilitate the achievement of this object, it being clearly understood that nothing shall be done which may prejudice the civil and religious rights of existing non-Jewish communities in Palestine, or the rights and political status enjoyed by Jews in any other country."

It is now apparent that *The Manchester Guardian* knew more about what the Balfour Declaration had in store for Arab and Jew in Palestine than its authors dared disclose in 1917.

### The Fall of Jerusalem

On December 9th 1917, Jerusalem was recaptured by Britain, apparently on behalf of Christendom. The event was treated in England at the time as the major event of the War. Lloyd George imposed a news embargo on reporters until he could announce the news to the House of Commons (in those days Parliament was still important). To celebrate the liberation of the Holy City from the Moslem after 730 years, the bells of Westminster Abbey rang for the first time in three years and they were followed by thousands of others across England.

General Allenby, the liberator of Jerusalem, and a descendant of Cromwell, declared in Jerusalem that the Crusades were over. On hearing him, the Arabs, who had been encouraged into fighting for the British and who had been fooled into seeing them as liberators, wandered away. And they have found themselves wandering ever since, in one way or another.

Allenby revealed that he carried two books with him to Palestine. The first, recommended to him by Lloyd George, was *Historical Geography Of The Holy Land* by Sir George Adam Smith, Professor of Old Testament Studies at Glasgow. The other was the Bible, which he read every day and consulted to draw historical information that would inform his movements.

The great outpouring of Christian triumphalism produced by the capture of Jerusalem was not confined to England. This is how *The Irish News* in Belfast saw the culmination of the last Crusade in its editorial of December 11th 1917:

"'Fallen is thy throne, O Israel!' The power of the Moslem in 'the Land of Promise' has fallen at last: we may assume that with the entrance of General Allenby's troops to Jerusalem an end has practically been made of Turkish rule over Palestine... When the Holy Land has been fully rescued from Turkish domination, who will possess and administer it? Official statements regarding the re-colonisation of the country by the scattered Jewish race have been made. Observers can discover no traces of enthusiasm for the project amongst Hebrews themselves. As an idea, nothing could be more sentimentally attractive; as a practical proposition, we believe each child of Abraham would bestow a benison on his brother who migrated from the lands of the Gentiles to the shores of Lake Galilee and the slopes of Mount Olivet. Thus might the storied little territory become once more 'a land flowing with milk and honey'—greatly to the content of the descendants of Abraham, Isaac and Jacob who remained where they were. But an independent Jewish State cannot be established all at once, even did all the Rothschilds lead all their compatriots back to Jerusalem. The country must be 'protected'—in plain terms, annexed: a useful synonym in dealing with Oriental transactions might be 'Egyptised.' And the conquerors are, of course, the natural 'protectors' of the territory won by force of arms. Such has been the rule and practice from before the era of Moses and Joshua. We know all about it in Ireland. When the objects of the campaign in Palestine and Mesopotamia have been completely achieved, a solid 'block' of Asian territory will lie between the Germans and the Indian Ocean. The Turks gave the Kaiser's people a free passage from Constantinople to the Persian Gulf. The new occupants of Palestine and Mesopotamia will not be quite so accommodating. No one has hinted as yet at the ultimate fate of Constantinople itself: it was to have been the Czar's property, but poor Nicholas would rest satisfied with less nowadays. England, at all events, is carefully building up a wall against German 'aggression' along a line on which German eyes were cast covetously many years ago... There are really some arguments against a precipitate disclosure of the Allies 'war aims' : one excellent reason for silence being that the Allies do not know how much they can aim at with a prospect of getting it."

Those who fought to liberate the Holy City went on to produce a considerable amount of reminiscences. One such is the memoirs of Major Vivian Gilbert, published in 1923, under the title of *The Romance of the Last Crusade—With Allenby to Jerusalem.* The memoirs open with a piece about King Richard the Lionheart and Sir Brian de Gurnay riding away from Jerusalem after their failure to capture the city: 'In the heart of Sir Brian de Gurnay was the thought of another and a Last Crusade that for all time should wrest the Holy Places from the Infidel.'(p.1.) Major Gilbert and a host of other Englishmen saw themselves in this vision.

Chapter XII of Major Gilbert's book is called *When Prophecies Come True* and is about the capture of the Holy City itself. In one part it describes the exhilaration felt by those who won back the city from the Moslem:

"At last Jerusalem was in our hands! In all ten crusades organised and equipped to free the Holy City, only two were really successful,—the first led by Godfrey de Bouillon, and the last under Edmund Allenby... then at last we found ourselves inside the walls themselves—the first British troops to march through the Holy City!... I recalled a quaint hymn I read many years ago. It was written by Saint Augustine, or founded on words of his, and was passed from mouth to mouth in the Middle Ages to encourage recruiting for the

Crusades... As I rode through Jerusalem the words were on my lips... We were proud that Jerusalem after languishing for over four hundred years under the Turkish yoke should be free at last... But above all, we had a great and abiding faith in God, Whose mercy had granted us this victory... to free the Holy Land forever, to bring peace and happiness to a people who had been oppressed too long!" (pp.171-77.)

Here is a passage from another example. It is from *How Jerusalem Was Won—Being The Record Of Allenby's Campaign In Palestine* by W.T. Massey, the 'Official Correspondent of the London Newspapers With The Egyptian Expeditionary Force':

"I have asked many men who were engaged in the fight for Jerusalem what their feelings were on getting their first glimpse of the central spot of Christendom... Every man or officer I spoke to declared that he was seized with emotion... Possibly only a small percentage of the Army believed they were taking part in a great mission, not a great proportion would claim to be really devout men, but they all behaved like Christian gentlemen. One Londoner told me... he felt that sense of emotion which makes one wish to be alone and think alone. He was on the ground where Sacred History was made, perhaps stood on the rock the Saviour's foot had trod. In the deep stirring of his emotions the rougher edges of his nature became rounded by feelings of sympathy and a belief that good would come out of the evil of this strife. That view of Jerusalem, and the knowledge of what the Holy Sites stand for, made him a better man and a better fighting man, and he had no doubt the first distant glimpse of the Holy City had similarly affected the bulk of the Army. That bad language is used by almost all troops in the field is notorious, but in Jerusalem one seldom heard an oath or an indecent word. When Jerusalem was won and small parties of our soldiers were allowed to see the Holy City, their politeness to the inhabitants, patriarch or priest, trader or beggar, man or woman, rebuked the thought that the age of chivalry was past, while the reverent attitude involuntarily adopted by every man when seeing the Sacred Places suggested that no Crusader Army or band of pilgrims ever came to the Holy Land under a more pious influence. Many times have I watched the troops of General Allenby in the streets of Jerusalem... These soldier missionaries of the Empire left behind them a record which will be remembered for generations." (pp.134-5.)

As the British advanced into Jerusalem many of them began to see themselves as taking part in the last Crusade—forgetting all about the 'war for small nations'. All the Old Testament fundamentalism imbued in English gentlemen by their Biblical education in the Public Schools came flooding out in a great surge. They had reconquered the Holy Land for Christendom after 700 years of Moslem occupation.

### Christian Zionism And The New Jerusalem

During the nineteenth century in England a Christian Zionist impulse developed within the Nonconformist wing of Protestantism. This English Christian Zionism actually predated the Zionism of Jewish nationalists and developed from the Bible. As early as the 17th August 1840 an editorial in *The Times* called for a Jewish Homeland in Palestine.

Christian Zionism worked its way into the political classes of the British State as the Nonconformists came to political power and it became part of the political culture of Liberal England even as, toward the end of the century, Darwinism seemed to undermine the religious impulse.

Tory High Church Evangelicals and the English Puritans who dominated the Liberal Party were always strongly inclined toward the Old Testament part of the Bible—much more so than Catholics, who had the Priest to shield them from it. Their Bible reading bred a familiarity with the idea of reviving the Holy Land and creating a new Jerusalem. Another factor exerted a gravitational pull on England from the Holy Land: Since the break with Rome, the English Church had lacked a spiritual home. The Catholic Church had rebuilt the spiritual home of Christianity in Rome, but when Henry VIII made himself pope of the English he had to be content with Canterbury. The more the English Protestants read their Bibles, the more they yearned for their own spiritual home—in the original Holy Places of Judea and Samaria. And what could be more of a riposte to Rome than to expose its spiritual inauthenticity by trumping it with the original article.

And there was even the notion, encouraged by reading the Old Testament, that a Second Coming of Christ depended upon the return of the scattered Jews to the lands of their ancestors. So what happened to the Holy Land came to matter to Christian fundamentalist England, since great Messianic promises and millenarian predictions depended upon it.

There was seemingly nothing ridiculous in the belief (and desire) that Imperial power could be used to bring about an end to history and the Second Coming.

Lloyd George, the Prime Minister who authorised the Balfour Declaration, was raised by an uncle, a lay preacher in a millenarian Baptist Church, and 'brought up in a school where there was taught far more about the history of the Jews than the history of [his] own land.' His biographer John Grigg described how the Prime Minister

> "had been brought up on the Bible, and the story of the ancient Jews was as familiar to him as the history of England... the idea of reuniting the Jewish people with the land of their forefathers appealed to him."

In 1903, as an ordinary Member of Parliament, he had drawn up a *Jewish Colonisation Scheme* for Theodor Herzl, the founder of the Zionist movement. The colony was meant for British East Africa but by 1917 the real thing became possible.

The Prime Minister was not alone. According to Lady Hamilton in her book, *God, Guns and Israel*, of the ten men who had formed the War Cabinet at one time or another, seven had come from Nonconformist families. Three were the sons or grandsons of Evangelical preachers. They all had a close acquaintance with the Old Testament and the People of the Book.

And what would the Holy City and the New Jerusalem be without the Jews?

A British official who came into contact with the chief persuader of the British Government for the Zionist project, Dr Weizmann, summarized his diplomatic method, which utilized English Christian Zionism to cultivate the notion of the sharing of the New Jerusalem:

> "When the War began, his cause was hardly known to the principal statesmen of the victors. It had many enemies, and some of the most formidable were amongst the most highly placed of his own people . . . He once told me that 2,000 interviews had gone into the making of the Balfour Declaration. With unerring skill he adapted his arguments to the special circumstances of each statesman. To the British and Americans he could use biblical language and awake a deep emotional undertone, to other nationalities he more often talked in terms of interest. Mr. Lloyd George was told that Palestine was a little mountainous country not unlike Wales; with Lord Balfour the philosophical background of Zionism could be surveyed; for Lord Cecil the problem was placed in the setting of a new world organization; while to Lord Milner the extension of imperial power could be vividly portrayed. To me, who dealt with these matters as a junior officer of the General Staff, he brought from many sources all the evidences that could be obtained of the importance of a Jewish national home to the strategical position of the British Empire, but he always indicated by a hundred shades and inflections of the voice that he believed that I could also appreciate better than my superiors other more subtle and recondite arguments." (Robert John, *Behind The Balfour Declaration: The Hidden Origins Of Today's Mideast Crisis*, pp. 88-9.)

Interestingly, for most of the duration of the War, Zionists were simply aiming at obtaining a hearing at the Peace Conference for their cause (and could have ended up like the Armenians). It was not until April 1917 that the proposal of a Declaration in favour of a Homeland was sprung on them by the British. Britain presumed that, at the stroke of a pen, it could assume the responsibility for all the Jews of the world and harness them to the War effort and Imperial objectives. And that was an offer the Zionists could not refuse.

### The Balfour Declaration

Imperial ambitions and the English Christian fundamentalist impulse became fused in the remaking of the Holy Land and Middle East. The culmination of all this Old Testament zealotry was the Balfour Declaration, issued just a week before Jerusalem was captured for the Empire.

The strategic reason for the alliance between British Imperialism and the

Zionist Movement was the British desire to enlist the support of International Jewry in the War effort against Germany, and then to manoeuvre itself into control of Palestine, through the use of the moral right of the Jews to settle there.

Writing to *The Times* on the thirty-second anniversary of the Balfour Declaration, the official biographer of Lloyd George, Malcolm Thomson, suggested it was a 'suitable occasion for stating briefly certain facts about its origin which have recently been incorrectly recorded.' What made it a suitable time as well was the events of the previous couple of years, when the true implications of the Balfour Declaration and the Zionist project were made clear to the world. Thomson revealed:

"When writing the official biography of Lloyd George, I was able to study the original documents bearing on this question. From these it was clear that although certain members of the Cabinets of 1916 and 1917 sympathized with Zionist aspirations, the efforts of Zionist leaders to win any promise of support from the British Government had proved quite ineffectual, and the secret Sykes-Picot agreement with the French for partition of spheres of interest in the Middle East seemed to doom Zionist aims. A change of attitude was, however, brought about through the initiative of Mr. James A. Malcolm, who pressed on Sir Mark Sykes, then Under-Secretary to the War Cabinet, the thesis that an allied offer to restore Palestine to the Jews would swing over from the German to the allied side the very powerful influence of American Jews, including Judge Brandeis, the friend and adviser of President Wilson. Sykes was interested, and at his request Malcolm introduced him to Dr. Weizmann and the other Zionist leaders, and negotiations were opened which culminated in the Balfour Declaration.

These facts have at one time or another been mentioned in various books and articles, and are set out by Dr. Adolf Boehm in his monumental history of Zionism, *'Die Zionistische Bewegung,'* Vol. 1, p.656. It therefore surprised me to find in Dr. Weizmann's autobiography, *'Trial and Error',* that he makes no mention of Mr. Malcolm's crucially important intervention, and even attributes his own introduction to Sir Mark Sykes to the late Dr. Caster. As future historians might not unnaturally suppose Dr. Weizmann's account to be authentic, I have communicated with Mr. Malcolm, who not only confirms the account I have given, but holds a letter written to him by Dr. Weizmann on March 5, 1941, saying: 'You will be interested to hear that some time ago I had occasion to write to Mr. Lloyd George about your useful and timely initiative in 1916 to bring about the negotiations between myself and my Zionist colleagues and Sir Mark Sykes and others about Palestine and Zionist support of the allied cause in America and elsewhere.'

No doubt a complexity of motives lay behind the Balfour Declaration, including strategic and diplomatic considerations and, on the part of Balfour, Lloyd George, and Smuts, a genuine sympathy with Zionist aims. But the determining factor was the intervention of Mr. Malcolm with his scheme for engaging by some such concession the support of American Zionists for the allied cause in the first world war." (*The Times*, 2 November 1949.)

Malcolm was an Oxford educated Armenian who acted as an adviser to the British Government on Eastern affairs. He was a personal friend of Mark Sykes and, upon hearing Sykes's concern that Britain was having no success in persuading Jews to support an American entry into the War, advised him that he was approaching the wrong Jews. It was the Zionists who were the key to the problem, he suggested.

Sykes was not happy with this solution because he knew the terms of the secret Agreement he had concluded with the French. Although he told Malcolm that to offer to secure Palestine for the Jews was impossible, Malcolm insisted that there was no other way and he urged Sykes to take the suggestion to the Cabinet. The matter was taken up by Lord Milner who asked for further information. Malcolm pointed out the influence of Judge Brandeis, of the American Supreme Court, on Wilson and the fact that the President himself held strong Zionist sympathies. Sykes and Malcolm were then authorized to engage in a series of meetings at Chaim Weizmann's London house, with the knowledge and approval of the Cabinet Secretary, Sir Maurice Hankey.

*A Programme for a New Administration of Palestine in Accordance with the Aspirations of the Zionist Movement* was issued by the English Political Committee of the Zionist Organization in October 1916, and submitted to the British Foreign Office as a basis for discussion and in order to give an official character to the informal discussions. It contained the main Zionist demands for an International recognition of Jewish rights to Palestine, nationhood for the Jewish community in Palestine and the creation and recognition of a Jewish chartered company in Palestine with rights to acquire land.

But the *Programme* did not reach the Cabinet because Asquith was known to be unsympathetic to the Zionist ideal. With Lloyd George replacing Asquith as Prime Minister (and Balfour replacing Edward Grey as Foreign Secretary) from December 1916, Zionist relations with the British Government gathered momentum. Dr. Chaim Weizmann, in his autobiography, described the developing relationship between Britain and the Zionists, which became something equating to a partnership:

"From now on our preoccupation was not with obtaining recognition for the Zionist ideal, but with the fitting of its application into the web of realities, and with preventing its frustration by unwise combinations and concessions. The chief danger came always from the French. I had a long talk with Balfour on March 27, 1917—he had become Foreign Minister, replacing Sir Edward Grey—and the situation then looked so serious that Balfour made a rather startling suggestion: if no agreement could be reached between England and France, we should try to interest America, and work for an Anglo-American protectorate over Palestine. It was an attractive, if somewhat farfetched idea, but, as I wrote to C. P. Scott, 'it is fraught with the danger that there always is with two masters, and we do not know yet how far the Americans would agree with the British on general principles of administration.'

It was again the attitude of the French which came to the fore in my talk with Herbert H. Asquith, the Prime Minister, on April 3. In spite of what we have seen, from private notes published years later, of Asquith's personal unfriendliness to the Zionist ideal, his official attitude was helpful. Neither he nor Mr. Balfour, however, mentioned the Sykes-Picot treaty. I learned of its existence on April 16, 1917 from Mr. Scott who had obtained the information from Paris. The arrangement was: that France was to obtain, after the war, not only northern Syria, but Palestine down to a line from St. Jean d'Acre (Acco) to Lake Tiberias, including the Hauran; the rest of Palestine was to be internationalized.

This was startling information indeed! It seemed to me that the proposal was devoid of rhyme or reason. It was unjust to England, fatal to us, and not helpful to the Arabs. I could easily understand why Sykes had not been averse to the abrogation of the treaty and why Picot had not been able to defend it with any particular energy. On April 25 I went into the matter thoroughly with Lord Robert Cecil, the Assistant Secretary for Foreign Affairs, one of the great spirits of modern England, and a prime factor in the creation of the League of Nations. Like Balfour, Milner, Smuts and others, Lord Cecil was deeply interested in the Zionist ideal; I think that he alone saw it in its true perspective as an integral part of world stabilization. To him the re-establishment of a Jewish Homeland in Palestine and the organization of the world in a great federation were complementary features of the next step in the management of human affairs.

We did not talk openly of the Sykes-Picot treaty. I alluded only to 'an arrangement which is supposed to exist', and which dated from the early days of the war. According to its terms Palestine would be cut arbitrarily into two halves—a 'Solomon's judgment', I called it—and the Jewish colonizing effort of some thirty years wiped out. To make matters worse, the lower part of Palestine, Judea, would not even pass under a single administration, but would become internationalized: which in effect meant—as I had recently written to Philip Kerr—an Anglo-French condominium. What we wanted, I said to Lord Cecil, was a British protectorate. Jews all over the world trusted England. They knew that law and order would be established by British rule, and that under it Jewish colonizing activities and cultural development would not be interfered with. We could thus look forward to a time when we would be strong enough to claim a measure of self-government. Lord Cecil then asked what were the objections against a purely French control. I answered that of course a purely French control was preferable to dual control, or internationalization, but the French in their colonizing activity had not followed the same lines as the English. They had always interfered with the population and tried to impose on it the *esprit français*...

We had long pointed out to the British, and I repeated it again in my interview with Lord Cecil, that a Jewish Palestine would be a safeguard to England, in particular in respect to the Suez Canal." (Chaim Weizmann, *Trial And Error:*

*The Autobiography of Weizmann*, pp. 190-2.)

(It is interesting that, as part of this developing relationship, the Zionists learnt of Sykes-Picot six months before the Arabs were made aware of it by the Bolsheviks.)

Weizmann was a skilful operator in relation to his British partners. He was presented with a problem when the Czarist State began to collapse during 1917. This threatened to remove some of the rationale behind providing a Home for the Jews (persecuted by the Czarist state) and the antagonism they had for the *Entente* (the Czar's allies), which Zionists promised they could counter if they were given a Declaration. He overcame the fall-out from this event and used it to the advantage of Zionism by planting the idea in Lloyd George's head that Russian Zionists could affect the course of the Russian Revolution and undermine the defeatist policy of the Bolsheviks, saving Russia for the Allies.

The Balfour Declaration appeared for the first time in public view in *The Times* on 9th November 1917 — a month before the capture of Jerusalem. This momentous announcement was produced from behind closed doors and was never debated in Parliament. Its timing was important. To have made it earlier would certainly have had a disorganising effect on the Arabs who were doing the fighting for Britain against the Turks.

## *'The Taming of the Jew'*

There is a memorandum to Lord Peel and the other members of the Royal Commission on Palestine in 1936 marked 'Private & Confidential', written by James Malcolm, which sets out the British reasons behind the Balfour Declaration:

"I have always been convinced that until the Jewish question was more or less satisfactorily settled there could be no real or permanent peace in the world, and that the solution lay in Palestine. This was one of the two main considerations which impelled me, in the autumn of 1916, to initiate the negotiations which led eventually to the Balfour Declaration and the British Mandate for Palestine. The other, of course, was to bring America into the War.

For generations Jews and Gentiles alike have assumed in error that the cause of Anti-Semitism was in the main religious. Indeed, the Jews, in the hope of obtaining relief from intolerance, engaged in the intensive and subversive propagation of materialistic doctrines productive of 'Liberalism', Socialism, and Irreligion, resulting in de-Christianisation. On the other hand, the more materialistic the Gentiles became, the more aware they were subconsciously made of the cause of Anti-Semitism, which at bottom was, and remains to this day, primarily an economic one. A French writer — Vicomte de Poncins — has remarked that in some respects Anti-Semitism is largely a form of self-defence against Jewish economic aggression. In my opinion, however, neither the Jews nor the Gentiles bear the sole responsibility for this.

As I have already said, I had a part in initiating the negotiations in the early autumn of 1916 between the British and French Governments and the Zionist leaders, which led to the Balfour Declaration and the British Mandate for Palestine.

The first object, of course, was to enlist the very considerable and necessary influence of the Jews, and especially of the Zionist or Nationalist Jews, to help us bring America into the War at the most critical period of the hostilities. This was publicly acknowledged by Mr. Lloyd George during a recent debate in the House of Commons.

Our second object was to enable and induce Jews all the world over to envisage constructive work as their proper field, and to take their minds off destructive and subversive schemes which, owing to their general sense of insecurity and homelessness, even in the periods preceding the French Revolution, had provoked so much trouble and unrest in various countries, until their ever-increasing violence culminated in the Third International and the Russian Communist Revolution. But to achieve this end it was necessary to promise them Palestine in consideration of their help, as already explained, and not as a mere humanitarian experiment or enterprise, as represented in certain quarters." (Robert John, *Behind The Balfour Declaration: The Hidden Origins Of Today's Mideast Crisis*, p.84.)

An aspect that has been largely forgotten about in considerations of the Balfour Declaration was its perceived role in the 'taming of the Jew'. It is referred to in a number of places in James Malcolm's 'Private and Confidential' submission to the Peel Commission of 1936 about the reasons for the Declaration. It is proposed as an answer to the Jewish Question: 'to take their minds off destructive and subversive schemes... owing to their general sense of insecurity and homelessness'.

The view that the Jews could function in Europe only as a disruptive influence was not new. Disraeli publicized it over half a century previously in his biography of Lord George Bentinck, (a Tory who, with Disraeli, opposed the repeal of the Corn Laws):

"An insurrection takes place against tradition and aristocracy, against religion and property... the natural equality of man and the abrogation of property, are proclaimed by the secret societies who form provisional governments, and men of Jewish race are found at the head of every one of them. The people of God co-operate with atheists; the most skilful accumulators of property ally themselves with communists; the peculiar and chosen race touch the hand of all the scum and low castes of Europe!... had it not been for the Jews, who of late years unfortunately have been connecting themselves with these unhallowed associations... the uncalled-for outbreak would not have ravaged Europe. But the fiery energy and the teeming resources of the children of Israel maintained for a long time the unnecessary and useless struggle. If the reader throws over the provisional governments of Germany, and Italy, and even of France, formed at that period, he will recognise everywhere the Jewish element." (*Lord George Bentinck: A Political Biography,* p.324.)

James Malcolm's was just one of the voices encouraging the establishment of a Jewish Nation in Palestine as a solution to this English Jewish problem. Halford Mackinder, one of the founding fathers of (Imperial) Geopolitics, founder of the London School of Economics, and an advisor to the British Delegation at Versailles, pointed to a desirable aspect of doing so in his book, *Democratic Ideals and Reality,* written a year after the capture of Jerusalem:

> "The Jewish national seat in Palestine will be one of the most important outcomes of the war. That is a subject on which we can now afford to speak the truth. The Jew, for many centuries shut up in a ghetto, and shut out of most honourable positions in society, developed in an unbalanced manner and became hateful to the average Christian by reason of his excellent, no less than his deficient qualities. German penetration has been conducted in the great commercial centres of the world in no small measure by Jewish agency, just as German domination in southeastern Europe was achieved through Magyar and Turk, with Jewish assistance. Jews are among the chief of the Bolsheviks of Russia. The homeless, brainful Jew lent himself to such internationalist work, and Christendom has no right to be surprised by the fact. But you will have no room for these activities in your League of independent, friendly nations. Therefore a national home, at the physical and historical centre of the world, should make the Jew 'range' himself. Standards of judgement, brought to bear on Jews by Jews, should result, even among those large Jewish communities which will remain as Going Concerns outside Palestine. This, however, will imply the frank acceptance of the position of a nationality, which some Jews seek to forget. There are those who try to distinguish between the Jewish religion and the Hebrew race, but surely the popular view of their broad identity is not far wrong." (pp.173-4.)

The Jews were viewed within the British Foreign Office and other Imperial Departments of State as a unitary collective entity rather than a diverse collection of individual communities across the world. They were seen as powerful and they were seen as pro-German, or, at any rate, disruptive of British interests. And no distinction was made between one Jew and another until a distinction was made between Zionist and other Jews.

Two Irishmen, Gerald Fitzmaurice and Hugh O'Beirne, both products of Beaumont Public School (a Catholic equivalent of Eton, situated near it at Windsor, and run by English Jesuits), and contemporaries of Mark Sykes (a Catholic convert) were particularly obsessed with the power of the Jews over the Young Turks. O'Beirne, a Foreign Office official from Jamestown, Drumsna, County Leitrim, suggested in a memo that:

> "If we could offer the Jews an arrangement as to Palestine which would

strongly appeal to them we might conceivably be able to strike a bargain with them as to withdrawing their support from the Young Turk government which would then automatically collapse." (*Peace To End All Peace*, p.198.)

I have been informed by James Bowen that, in February and March 1916, O'Beirne wrote two memoranda in favour of the idea of a declaration for a Jewish homeland. Although O'Beirne died before the Balfour Declaration was issued, his influence is described in detail in various Zionist books on the evolution of the document. O'Beirne and Lord Crewe—who was married to a Rothschild, a woman who boasted that all in her house were 'Weizmannites'— devised a formula for a Jewish state that was, in fact, much more Zionist than the eventual Declaration. O'Beirne, a good Irish Catholic member of the British Imperialist machine, knew what he was proposing; he wrote:

> "It is evident that Jewish colonization of Palestine must conflict, to some extent, with Arab interests. All we can do, if and when the time comes to discuss details, is to try to devise a settlement which will involve as little hardship as possible to the Arab populations."

O'Beirne died with Kitchener in the North Sea in June 1916 when their ship was struck by a mine while en route to Archangel—presumably O'Beirne was accompanying Kitchener to Russia because he had spent several years as Counsellor in the British embassy in St. Petersburg. There is a famous photograph of Admiral Jellicoe shaking hands with O'Beirne on the deck of the HMS Hampshire, as Jellicoe was bidding the Kitchener party *bon voyage*.

Sir Gerald Lowther, British Ambassador in Constantinople before the War, sent a 5,000 word report to Edward Grey on 10th May 1910 which contains the flavour of English understanding of the Young Turk revolution, as a 'Judeo-Masonic conspiracy' inspired by French Revolutionary ideals. Here are some extracts:

> "Some years ago Emannuele Carasso, a Jewish Mason of Salonica, and now deputy for that town in the Ottoman Chamber, founded there a lodge called '*Macedonia Risorta*' in connection with Italian Freemasonry. He appears to have induced the Young Turks, officers and civilians, to adopt Freemasonry with a view to exerting an impalpable Jewish influence over the new dispensation in Turkey, though ostensibly only with a view of outwitting the Hamidian spies... The inspiration of the movement in Salonica would seem to have been mainly Jewish, while the words '*Liberté, Egalité, Fraternité*', the motto of the Young Turks, are also the device of the Italian Freemasons. Carasso began to play a big role... and it was noticed that Jews of all colours, native and foreign, were enthusiastic supporters of the new dispensation, till... every Hebrew seemed to become a potential spy of the occult Committee, and people began to remark that the movement was rather a Jewish rather than a Turkish revolution...
>
> Talaat Bey, the Minister of the Interior, who is of Gipsy descent... and Djavid Bey, the Minister of Finance, who is a Crypto-Jew, are the official

manifestations of the occult power of the Committee. They are the only members of the Cabinet who really count, and are also the apex of Freemasonry in Turkey... The invisible government of Turkey is thus the Grand Orient with Talaat Bey as Grand Master. Eugene Tavernier... describes the French Republic as the 'Daughter of the Grand Orient.' The same epithet perhaps might be appropriately applied to the Ottoman Committee of Union and Progress... Like French Republicans and Freemasons, the words most frequently on its lips are 'reaction' and 'clerical.' Its first tendency was not to modify and modernise the Mahommedan sacred law, but to undermine and smash it. Most of its leaders, while frankly rationalist, also paradoxically endeavour to use the Islamic fervour of the masses as a political weapon and to divert it into chauvinistic channels on the lines of national, i.e. Asiatic Pan Islamism. It is intolerant of opposition, and one of its principal methods of destroying its adversaries is to drive them into opposition and crush them as 'reactionaries.'

The Turk is mainly a soldier and... the economic organism of the Turk is of the feeblest kind, and unsupported could not stand alone a week. It was hoped in the beginning that the Armenians, Bulgarians, Greeks and the Ottoman Jew would serve as economic props, but the Young Turk seems to have allied himself solely with the Jew... The latter seems to have entangled the pre-economic-minded Turk in his toils, and as Turkey contains the places sacred to Israel, it is but natural that the Jew should strive to maintain a position of exclusive influence and utilize it for the furtherance of his ideals, viz. the ultimate creation of an autonomous Jewish state in Palestine or Babylonia... He would kill two birds with one stone if he could obtain from the Turk unrestricted immigration of Jews into Turkey, an aim that he has been pursuing for years back, and transfer to Mesopotamia millions of his co-religionists in bondage in Russia and Rumania... Mesopotamia and Palestine are only, however, the ultimate goal of the Jews. The immediate end for which they are working is the practically exclusive economic capture of Turkey and new enterprises in that country.

It is obvious that the Jew, who is so vitally interested in maintaining his sole predominance in the councils of the Young Turkey is equally interested in keeping alive the flames of discord between the Turk and his (the Jew's) possible rivals, i.e. Armenians, Greeks etc... This aspect of the Turkish revolution... is not without its direct and indirect side-problems of the Near East. The Jew hates Russia and its Government, and the fact that England is now friendly to Russia has the effect, to a certain extent, of making the Jew anti-British in Turkey and Persia—a consideration to which the Germans, I think, are alive. The Jew can help the Young Turk with brains, business enterprise, his enormous influence in the press of Europe, and money in return for advantages and the eventual realization of the ideals of Israel... The Jew has supplied funds to the Young Turks and has thus acquired a hold on them... Secrecy and elusive methods are essential to both. The Oriental Jew is an adept at manipulating occult forces, and political Freemasonry of the continental type has been chosen as the most effective bond and cloak to conceal the inner

272

workings of the movement...

Young Turkey regards itself as the vanguard of an awakened Asia. It fancies itself bound to protect the nascent liberties of Persia 'now endangered by the selfish and over-bearing policy of Russia and England .' ... It is also coquetting, assisted by the Jews... to create a sympathetic current in Afghanistan and among Indian Moslems.

The Young Turks, partly at the inspiration of Jewish Masonry, and partly owing to the fact that French is the one European language extensively spread in the Levant, have been imitating the French Revolution and its godless and levelling methods. The developments of the French Revolution led to the antagonism between England and France, and should the Turkish Revolution develop on the same lines, it may find itself similarly in antagonism with British ideals and interests." (Sir Gerald Lowther, cited in Elie Kedourie, *Young Turks, Freemasons and Jews*, *Middle Eastern Studies*, January 1971, pp.95-102.)

The British Ambassador's Report goes on, for page after page, about Jewish influence here, there and everywhere in the Ottoman Empire and their nefarious schemes of creating a Jewish state in Palestine and Mesopotamia in return for Jewish financial help to the Young Turks. And in one part it even recommends an alliance with the Arabs — who, it suggests, would have the most to lose from this creeping conspiracy.

These views were widespread across British officials and their departments and persisted through the War. In the opening months of the War *The Times* accused the Jews of attempting to keep America neutral on Germany's behalf (in its *Washington Despatch* of 23rd November and the *Correspondence Column* of 26th November). During the War itself Britain's Ambassadors bombarded London with dispatches about the sinister power of the Jews being exercised on the German behalf. George Buchanan, Ambassador in Petrograd, complained of the 'large number of Jews in German pay acting as spies during the campaign in Poland' against the Russian Ally. In the correspondence of the British Ambassador at Washington, Cecil Spring Rice, between 1914 and 1917, there are continual references to the Jews as German agents ( e.g. 'the pro-German Jewish bankers toiling for our destruction'. See Mark Levene, *The Balfour Declaration: A Case Of Mistaken Identity*, *English Historical Review*, January, 1992.); the character of the views expressed can only be described as anti-Semitic.

A number of influential British writers noted that the Jews had been a significant element in the vigour and success of German commerce prior to the War and that it was a priority that they should be removed from this useful function in German life. Germany and Austria were the closest thing that the Jews had to a homeland in 1914 and many found refuge there after the pogroms and massacres directed against them by Britain's ally, Russia. Their talents in commerce were not held back in Germany or in the Hapsburg State.

Added to this was the growing perception of the Jews as a force in the

Turko-German relationship. The British Embassy in Constantinople, for instance, believed that the Young Turks were a Jewish conspiracy that had got control of the Ottoman Empire and orientated it toward the Germans; a belief largely based on the fact that Salonika, where the revolution had originated, tended to be an area of large numbers of Jews and secret societies.

This aspect had a bearing on the Balfour Declaration because some in Imperial circles began to fear that the Germans, who were believed to be themselves under the influence of Jewry, were about to launch a Zionist project of their own, in conjunction with the Jewish conspiracy in Constantinople. In this way some of the most dyed-in-the-wool anti-Semites in British Imperial affairs became some of the most ardent supporters of the Zionist project. (See Fromkin, *Peace To End All Peace*, pp.41-3 and p.92.)

In 1915 Wellington House published *Crescent And Iron Cross* by E.H. Benson. This was a propagandist work aimed at connecting German and Turk with various acts of brutality within the Ottoman Empire. In Chapter IV of *Crescent And Iron Cross, 'The Question of Syria and Palestine'*, there is the following account of Germany's interest in the Jewish colonies in Palestine. It comes immediately after Benson's assertion that the Germans had saved the Jews from a general massacre for their own political purposes:

"Her policy with regard to them is set forth in a pamphlet by Dr. Davis Treitsch, called *Die Jüden der Türkei*, published in 1915, which is a most illuminating little document. These Jewish colonies, as we have seen, came from Russia, and as Germany realised, long before the war, they might easily form a German nucleus in the Near East, for they largely consisted of German-speaking Jews, akin in language and blood to a most important element in her own population. 'In a certain sense,' says Dr. Treitsch, 'the Jews are a Near Eastern element in Germany and a German element in Turkey.' He goes on with unerring acumen to lament the exodus of German-speaking Jews to the United States and to England. 'Annually some 100,000 of these are lost to Germany, the empire of the English language and the economic system that goes with it is being enlarged, while a German asset is being proportionately depreciated.... It will no longer do simply to close the German frontiers to them, and in view of the difficulties which would result from a wholesale migration of Jews into Germany itself, Germans will only be too glad to find a way out in the emigration of those Jews to Turkey--a solution extraordinarily favourable to the interests of all three parties concerned.'

Here, then, is the matter in a nutshell: Germany, wide-awake as ever, saw long ago the advantage to her of a growing Jewish population from the Pale in Turkey. She was perhaps a little overloaded with them herself, but in this immigration from Russia to Palestine she saw the formation of a colony that was well worth German protection, and the result of the war, provided the Palestinian immigrants were left in peace, would be to augment very largely the number of those settling there. 'Galicia,' says Dr. Treitsch, 'and the western provinces of Russia, which between them contain more than half the Jews in the world, have suffered more from the war than any other region. Jewish homes have been broken up by hundreds of thousands, and there is no doubt whatever that, as a result of the war, there will be an emigration of East European Jews on an unprecedented scale.' This emigration, then, to Palestine was, in Germany's view, a counter-weight to the 100,000 annually lost to her through emigration to America and England. With her foot on Turkey's neck she had control over these German-speaking Jews, and saw in them the elements of a German colony. Her calculations, it is true, were somewhat upset by the development of the Zionist movement, by which those settlers declared themselves to have a nationality of their own, and a language of their own, and Dr. Treitsch concedes that. 'But,' he adds, 'in addition to Hebrew, to which they are more and more inclined, the Jews must have a world-language, and this can only be German.'"

Benson's work provides a further example of the fear that the German-Jewish connection and its relation to the Ottoman Empire produced in English minds. However, the understanding that runs through all British writing about the Germans is that they might, being an Anglo-Saxon race, prove to be more devious and efficient exponents of all the things England had been doing in the world themselves. And much of British propaganda is simply the nightmare produced by gazing at the looking-glass and imagining the policy Britain practised in the world being performed in the future by another, more virile race, of the same character.

The British offer to the Jews of a Homeland in Palestine presented a means of taming and 'turning' the Jews from their German, internationalist-socialist proclivities, to being harnessed to more progressive, nationalist, and British Imperial, purposes. As quoted above, 'a national home, at the physical and historical centre of the world, should make the Jew 'range' himself.' (Of course, it was Halford Mackinder who later inspired Herr Hitler with the geopolitical inspiration required to facilitate what happened to the Jews, through Dr. Karl Haushofer. And it was the Imperial power politics that created the conditions in Europe for the destruction of the Jewish 'Going Concerns' outside of Palestine. But that is an aspect of the Nazis that is seldom thought about, despite their prominent position on television screens and in the school curriculum today.)

The anti-Semitism that shot up in Europe from 1918 did not have its source in Germany or Fascism. The great surge of anti-Semitism that gripped Europe after the War came in the new States set up by Britain and France out of the Hapsburg Empire at Versailles. In the Empire the Jews had blended in as a socially and economically useful part, with many other minorities, in a large cosmopolitan Empire. The weak national development of peoples in the Austro-Hungarian State resulted in Jews occupying a large proportion of business and professional positions. But the Jewish Middle Class of the Hapsburg Empire could never occupy a similar position within the new States, with their emerging national bourgeois classes established by the victors at Versailles. And they began to be subjected to strong anti-Semitic pressures from the developing national elites of these states who wanted to squeeze them out.

In these new creations of the Imperial Powers, the Jews began to be seen as anti-national elements—and they were treated accordingly by the vigorous new nationalist bourgeoisies who governed them during the 1920s and 1930s. (At the same time the indigenous Arab people of Palestine began to be treated by the Jewish nationalists, under the aegis of the Imperial Power, in a similar fashion).

And the German attitude toward the Jews, which had been favourable up until the end of the Great War when Jews were seen as a valuable asset to the country, changed radically in the conditions that manifested themselves in the Germany of the Post-War settlement.

This change of attitude was one outcome of the Imperial scheme to turn the European Jews into a nationality with their own nation-state, along with the concocting of new 'nations' in Europe in which the Jews had no place, in circumstances of politics being reduced to fundamentals, in a state of economic meltdown.

Therefore, the anti-Semitism produced in the Middle East, in Central Europe and in Germany is traceable back to the actions of the British Empire in the latter stages of the Great War.

### *Strange Bedfellows? — Anti-Semitism and Zionism*

There was always a deep anti-Semitic strain in English culture but the flamboyant anti-Semitism exhibited in other European countries was frowned upon in polite Society. When the Balfour Declaration was published and England announced her intention of repatriating the Jews of the world to where they belonged there was a natural tendency for the anti-Semite to become a Zionist.

In 1905 *The Aliens Act* set a precedent in Immigration control in Britain. It was aimed specifically at preventing the entry of Russian and East European Jews, fleeing Czarist oppression, into the country. The Prime Minister and author of this Act was none other than the same man responsible for the Balfour Declaration, Arthur Balfour himself. Anti-Semitism and Zionism were no strangers to each other.

Al Carthill's *The Lost Dominion,* from 1923, reveals some interesting assumptions held about Jews in Imperial circles at this time:

> "Many subversives have been Jews. But there is no evidence that the forces of anarchy were directed by any purely Jewish corporation. *The Protocols of the Elders of Zion*, though possibly published in good faith, were based on older tendentious forgeries or mystifications. *A priori*, it is extremely unlikely

that the Jewish race, which has profited so much in the last century by Western civilisation, should wish to destroy it.

That many subversives should be Jews is not a matter of surprise... It may perhaps be admitted that the Jew, while using our civilisation, has a poor opinion of it. This is not unnatural. He has seen so many civilisations pass. He has used them all. The more degenerate they became, the greater the influence, and thus the greater the profit of the Jew... He was generally able to exercise great influence over the Government, and always found aiders and favourers among the powerful...

The heathen imagines a vain thing, and their devices come to nought, but the Kingdom of Zion is an enduring Kingdom...

The Jew, then, may be perfectly loyal to the ideas of the society in which he lives. Yet his belief in them is not of the degree that is requisite of martyrdom. Just as the most valiant and loyal mercenaries will break and fly after suffering losses which a national and volunteer army would bear without wincing, so the Jew is rarely prepared to stake all on the maintenance of a social state in the absolute value of which he has no belief...

It is but recently that the influence of the Jew in politics, and particularly in foreign and imperial politics, has awakened uneasiness in England... In a country like England, where the small share of power which is not monopolised by wealth was wielded by intelligence, there was thus every probability of the Jew becoming one of the dominant castes. Jews were welcomed as intimates, advisers, and sons-in-law by leaders of both the great parties. Jews provided the empire with statesmen, lawyers, men of the pen, and men of science... For many years they have abstained from an active share in politics...

This latter policy has been abandoned in recent years, to the regret of the old-fashioned pious Jew. And here, I think, the *Fromme Jude* [the pious Jew] was right. No one can be blind to the beginning of a reaction against Jewish control... The alleged monopolisation by the foreign Jew of certain reprehensible traffics has revolted the pious. There is therefore a vague anti-Jewish feeling floating about in solution in England which needs but a shock to crystallise it. The fall of the Coalition is principally to be ascribed to an uneasy and probably erroneous idea that the Jew exercised too much power in the counsels of that remarkable body, and that that influence was being applied to unpatriotic ends. Erroneously, no doubt, it was supposed that the last rags of honour of the British people, the last pieces of gold in an exhausted treasury, the last drops of the blood in the lacerated body of the republic, were about to be jeopardised, in order to decide which of certain Jewish financial houses were to have the profitable business of liquidating the Turkish Empire. The mere absurdity of the supposition is convincing proof of the reality of the general uneasiness.

And as usual the uneasiness of the people, though in itself apparently baseless, was not actually without a rational basis. To return to first principles, it is inexpedient, in a world where rightly or wrongly the idea of nationalism has such power, that the affairs of the nation should be conducted by men who, in so far as they are not citizens of a foreign nation, are cosmopolitans by birth, training and inclination...

For the last three generations organised labour must be counted among the subversive forces. In the propagation of Socialistic doctrine individual Jews have taken a considerable part. But to suppose that the diffusion of Socialism among the labouring classes is due to the efforts of a small subversive secret society is ludicrous. All attempts to make Socialism an international church directed by an extra-nationalist directorate have hitherto failed." (pp.109-116.)

Readers may be unaware of the foundation of Carthill's suspicion of the 'influence of the Jew in politics'. Just before the War, the Marconi and Silver Bullion scandals involving Jewish Ministers of State, Herbert Samuel, Rufus Isaacs and Edwin Montague, occupied the British Press. Allegations were made that the family commercial interests of Jews made them untrustworthy public servants, in that one could never be quite sure for whose interests they were acting (that being a taken for granted trait of the Jew).

Carthill was not in favour of anti-Semitism and he was arguing that it was unfounded in many of its beliefs and manifestations. What is uncomfortable about his description is his failure to give an outright condemnation of it in his attempts to understand it in England. That would not have been politic after 1945 when a taboo was put on thought about anti-Semitism — and condemnation of anti-Semitism became incorporated into the Churchillian myth of history. And then it became a weapon to be wielded against anyone who dared to criticise the expansionist Zionism of the Jewish nationalist state — even against those who had suffered directly at its hands.

### Warnings To Assimilationist Jews

The British propagandists for Zionism realised that they had to counter Jewish assimilation in the various societies Jewish communities lived, demoralise those Jews who might be anti-Zionist, and make them, at least, fear for their future without Zion. This was essential, not only for propagandist purposes centred around the establishment of a Jewish Home, but also because there were not enough Jews available, or willing, in 1917, to make such a project viable.

In 1916, as the Zionist campaign gathered force, Harry Sacher of *The Manchester Guardian* published *Zionism And The Jewish Future*. It was a volume containing a series of essays by Sacher, Hyamson, Weizmann, Moses Gaster and Nahum Sokolow, the leading Zionists in England. This was a full-blooded assault in the name of Zion on assimilationist Jews.

In Sokolow's contribution *'Judaism As A National Religion,'* he argued that it was impossible to be both an Englishman and a real Jew:

"the claim to be Englishmen of the Jewish persuasion—that is, English by nationality and Jewish by faith—is an absolute self-delusion... the Jewish faith is a profession of national and religious unity in the past and in the future."

278

(p.93.)

Weizmann in his essay, *Zionism And The Jewish Problem*, went even further, arguing that authentic Jews were not found in England but in Eastern Europe—the true nucleus of the Jewish nation:

> "the position of the emancipated Jew, though he does not realize it himself, is even more tragic than that of the oppressed brother... East European Jewry has been for some centuries the real center of Jewish life, and its disruption, not accompanied by the establishment of another center, would threaten the very existence of the Jews as a people." (p.8.)

A number of interesting reviews were written on Sacher's collection. There was, of course, a complimentary one by *The Manchester Guardian*. But Lord Cromer, the former Proconsul of Egypt, dismissed the view that there was a 'Jewish Question' at all in England in *The Spectator* of August 12th, partly because of tolerance and also because

> "the relatively small number of Jews in the United Kingdom... has prevented them from exercising so commanding an influence over national life as has been the case in some other countries. There is not, as in Austria, a Jew moneylender in almost every village in the country, who often holds the future welfare of the noble in his castle and of the villager in his cottage in the hollow of his hand."

Cromer was involved with the earlier Commission which investigated the setting up of a Jewish plantation in Egypt and had been obstructive toward the Zionists. He appeared to believe that it was only in Europe that there was really a Jewish Question that required a solution. Britain's small number of Jews did not require the disruption of the Empire that satisfying the Zionists would entail.

But the most controversial reply to Sacher was made by 'An Englishman Of The Jewish Faith' in *The Fortnightly Review* of November 1916, which called Zionism 'a very dangerous movement' for Jews. It said that the existence of 'this strange and retrograde movement' was 'entirely due to anti-Semitism'. And it predicted disaster for European Jews if they forsook assimilation for Zion.

The article in *The Fortnightly Review* produced a welter of replies from Zionists and a sustained press campaign against assimilationist Jews, attacking their desire for equality in Western Europe at the expense of Jewish nationalist separatism.

One example of this message, from *The New Europe* of 27th September 1917, penned by 'Josephus', warned assimilationist Jews that trying to settle down in the new Europe was going to be an unhealthy pursuit:

> "Changes in Russia, Poland and Rumania may lessen to some extent the tendency of the great Jewish reservoirs in Central and Eastern Europe to overflow into other countries, but they cannot serve as a substitute for the

Jewish national ideal nor can they remove the danger of anti-Semitic outbreaks. Dispersion and eventual assimilation can never be the ultimate aims of a healthy people. Reunion and national self-affirmation are worthier objects."

Jews who believed they could assimilate and become 'British' were warned that Gentiles could recognize them and tell them apart by their Jewish 'stamp', no matter how hard they attempted assimilation:

"They feel themselves to be something more than one hundred per cent British, and are comfortably oblivious of the fact that the average Briton regards them as British indeed by choice or education, but as little more British than any Armenian or Syrian Arab might be after a period of naturalization. Voice, gesture, gait, and, in most cases, physical conformation stamp them as Jews quite apart from their religious tenets, and cause them to be recognised even when the oriental swiftness of their intellectual processes passes unnoticed."

But this line of argument left the English propagandists for Zion open to the suggestion that the establishment of a Jewish State would provoke a negative reaction against the existing Jewish communities in Europe: For wouldn't a Jewish homeland encourage the view that Jews should leave the countries of their birth and residence, and encourage anti-Semitic acts to help them on their way home?

A letter from prominent anti-Zionist British Jews appeared in *The Times* of 24th May 1917 and suggested that the establishment of a Jewish homeland in Palestine

"would have the effect throughout the world of stamping the Jews as strangers in their native lands, and of undermining their hard-won position as citizens and nationals of those lands."

With this argument in view 'Josephus' replied:

"Behind the arguments of Jewish assimilationism in its various forms lurks the fear that, should Jewry ever acquire a national territorial status of its own, the non-Jewish world would turn upon the Jews and say: 'Now you have a country of your own; go to it.' ... The existence of a Jewish State would certainly react healthily, upon the position of the Jews who might elect to remain in the Dispersion. They would perforce, become more closely identified with the countries of their adoption, and would have less and less justification for internationalism or for those rapid changes of political allegiance to which they have been addicted in the past."

In 1820 the German-Jewish historian Isaac Jost published what was the first serious historical work on Jews, his *History of the Israelites*. Jost chose to avoid the Biblical period and started his review with the Judean Kingdom, compiling an historical narrative of different Jewish communities around the world. In attempting this, Jost realised that the scattered Jewish communities of nineteenth century Europe did not form an ethnic continuum but were very different from place to place. Jost therefore thought there was nothing in the world that should stop Jews from assimilating in their various societies, particularly with the general spirit of enlightenment he perceived in Romantic Germany.

Perhaps this was an over-optimistic view of the possibility of Jewish assimilation, from Jost's position in Germany. But it must be said it was immensely preferable to what England was engaged in a century later. Britain wanted to treat the Jews as an alien racial entity in Europe, in order to construct them into a nationality and insisted they had better look to their 'homeland' for security.

The Balfour Declaration had the effect of establishing a Zionist hegemony over world Jewry and the effect of the Jewish Colony was to marginalise Jews who were not of a Zionist disposition. It was calculated that this could only be a good thing for Britain and that the Jew, remaining in the West, without Zion, could disappear from the scene; his untrustworthy 'internationalism' and socialism would no longer be an 'addiction' or a menace.

And of course the 'political allegiance' that England wished the Jews most strongly to forsake was the German one, which was the one to which they seemed most naturally attracted.

Al Carthill talked of 'a vague anti-Jewish feeling floating about in solution in England which needs but a shock to crystallise it'. One wonders what would have happened if it had crystallised? Maybe if England had lost the War, been blamed for starting it, had a punitive settlement put on her, and been subject to economic collapse, the crystallization would have happened. As it was, Britain warded it off by instituting a British version of fascism through coalition during the inter-war years and making it a problem for others.

In the post-War Europe that Britain instituted at Versailles, there were many shocks that led to such crystallisations—in countries that had substantial Jewish communities that had hitherto lived in peace with their neighbours. But then there was a reordering of Europe along the lines of small nationalistic States that were inherently unstable, and crystallisation began to take place.

It is said that the founder of modern Zionism, Herzl, once stated that the chief asset of the Zionist Movement's campaign for a Jewish Homeland was anti-Semitism. I think that the truth of that statement is indisputably demonstrated by the behaviour of the British State toward the Jews from 1916 on to the 1930s. It was this anti-Semitism that led to the Balfour Declaration and made Zionism into a going concern. So it is an anti-Semitism that was indispensable to Zionism.

### Doing Business With The Jews

*The Round Table*, the Liberal Imperialist periodical of the movers and shakers in the Empire, explained the background to the Zionist project in its edition of March 1918:

"There was, of course, a Zionist movement that also had the same objective of establishing a national state. But the Jewish nationalists did not have the power to realise it themselves in the region. Though various Governments had on occasion expressed sympathy with the aims of Zionism, and the British Government in particular had made the Zionist Movement an offer (which proved abortive) of a territory in East Africa as the home of a Jewish settlement with some measure of autonomy, Zionism was not, and had no apparent prospect of becoming, a factor to be reckoned with in international politics.

Now, almost suddenly, all that is changed. Thanks to the breadth and sincerity of British statesmanship, to the inherent justice of its own aims, and to the ability with which those aims have been presented, Zionism has received the official approval of the British Government— an approval which, in the circumstances in which it was given, makes the realisation of the objects of Zionism one of the avowed war-aims of the Allied Powers. The way in which the Government's declaration of support has been received shows that substantially it speaks the mind of the whole British nation, and indeed of the whole Commonwealth."

England offers nothing for nothing. British control of Palestine was impossible without the Jews and a Jewish Homeland in the area was inconceivable without the political influence and military power of the British Empire. So this was the deal: Britain would reward the Zionists with a Homeland for the Jews and the Jews would reward Britain with Palestine for its Empire.

The same article outlined the reasons why a substantial Jewish colonisation of Palestine was impossible under the loose Ottoman administration—but became a realisable possibility under British Imperial control:

"The potential value of the Jewish colonisation of Palestine—its value as an indication of what the Jews, and they alone, can make of Palestine—is enhanced by the fact that it has been carried out hitherto in spite of difficulties created not only by the absence of any State organisation behind it, but by the shortcomings of Turkish government. It must indeed be said, in fairness to the Turk, that from the Jewish national point of view his rule has had its good as well as its bad side. Talaat Pasha, in a recent interview, made much of the fact that anti-Semitism was unknown in Turkey, and that the Jewish colonies in Palestine had been allowed freedom in local administration and in the use of the Hebrew language for educational and general purposes. He had a right to take credit for this tolerance, which, if it resulted rather from passivity than from active goodwill on the side of the rulers, was none the less of great value to the ruled. It may well be that if during the last thirty years Palestine had been in the hands of an efficient and centralised government, Jewish colonisation might have progressed more rapidly on the material side, though the settlers might have been much less easily able to learn the rudiments of self-government and to retain and strengthen their specific national consciousness. But there is a heavy account on the debit side. Not only has Jewish colonisation been hampered by burdensome taxes, restrictions on the sale of land, and the neglect of the Government to provide those material facilities without which a country cannot be developed on modern lines; but the absence of security has kept out of the country much Jewish energy and capital which would otherwise have flowed into it, to the benefit both of the Jewish national movement, of Palestine, and of Turkey as the overlord of Palestine. The Turkish revolution of 1908, which Zionists welcomed as the dawn of a new era of freedom and opportunity, turned out in fact to be the precursor of a policy of Turkification which was even more fatal to Jewish national effort on a large scale than the laxity of Abdul Hamid's régime; and since the war broke out much has happened to destroy whatever lingering belief Zionists may have retained in the possibility of achieving their object under Ottoman suzerainty. It is clear, therefore, that Zionism imperatively needs a substantial change — whether or not accompanied by a formal change — in the political position of Palestine if the work of a generation is not to be practically wasted, and if the Jewish people is not to be doomed once more to fall back on hopes and prayers."

Clearly Britain was proposing a great innovation in Jewish settlement in the region. Jews had always been welcome and happy in the Ottoman Empire but they had not shown any great desire for a Homeland in Palestine. That had been the design of Zionists outside of the Ottoman possessions, people from communities in Christian Europe that had felt persecution.

This all begs the question: Why did the Jews, who fled from persecution, choose to seek a better life in the great Islamic Empire of all places, but not in the Holy Land part of it? Especially when Britain began to proclaim this as the great desire of Jews across the world.

The 5th 'Herbert Samuel' lecture is significant because of the (Jewish) audience to whom it was being addressed:

"The Jews might suffer terrible persecutions and pogroms in Russia or Poland; but somehow when they left, with the Holy Land on their lips, their feet carried them resolutely in the other direction, to Germany or England or America. Even when, like the expelled Sephardim of Spain, they went to the hospitable, tolerant Turkish empire, that land of promise as it seemed in the sixteenth century, it is odd how few of them went to Palestine, which was after all an easily accessible and under-populated part of that empire. There was a trickle, but not a stream. To most of them Constantinople, with its opportunities of government finance, or Salonika, with its opportunities of army-provisioning, seemed more tempting than what Gibbon was to call the 'mournful and solitary silence' of Arab Palestine." (20.10.1961; Weidenfeld & Nicholson, pp.14-15.)

Prior to the emergence of Zionism, the Ottoman authorities had never imposed any controls over the freedom of movement or residence of Jews in the Empire. Only for a brief period, around the turn of the century, were there any restrictions. So the Jews had centuries to vote with their feet and return to their homeland in Palestine.

## Salonika—The Jewish Home

The first non-Turks to come and settle in the Ottoman Empire were the Jews of Byzantium, who had been subjected to persecution by the Byzantine Emperors and the Greek Orthodox Church before the arrival of the Ottomans. The Jewish population of Anatolia had been drastically reduced by the time of the Ottoman Conquest as Jews were required to convert to Christianity (See Steven Bowman's *The Jews of Byzantium*).

The remaining Jews of the Byzantine Empire helped in the Ottoman conquests, particularly in the capture of Bursa and Constantinople and were rewarded for this with a privileged position among the non-Muslim *millets*.

Salonika, in Macedonia, was part of the Ottoman Empire in the nineteenth century, before it was captured by the Greeks in the First Balkan War. It was a very ethnically diverse city, made up of Turks, Jews, Greeks, Macedonians and Bulgarians and was regarded as the greatest Jewish city in Europe because the Jews practically owned it and ran its civic and commercial life. It contained a large Jewish proletariat, who were of a strongly socialist disposition, as well as a commercial bourgeoisie.

In the fifteenth century persecuted Jews from various parts of Europe took refuge in the Ottoman Empire, before the Spanish Jews were compelled to follow them after the Inquisition. There were also Jews who fled into the Ottoman Empire from the Ukraine and Poland to escape massacre from the Cossacks and Poles; and some Jews captured by Christian pirates in the Mediterranean were ransomed off by the Jewish communities of the Ottoman Empire, and came to settle among those who had rescued them.

The Ottomans welcomed the Sephardic Jews to Salonika, and other cities in the Empire. And Salonika was the main area of the Dunmehs (from the Turkish, 'to turn'), Jews who had followed their leader, Sabbetai Cevi of Smyrna, and converted to Islam during the seventeenth century.

The Jews who arrived in the Ottoman Empire sent out declarations to the persecuted Jews of Europe, usually written in the names of rabbis and important scholars, praising the security and prosperity that they found under Ottoman rule and these declarations encouraged even more Jews to come.

Leon Sciaky was born in 1893 and grew up in Salonika during the last years of the nineteenth century and the final years of the Ottoman Empire. Salonika was taken by the Greeks in December 1912 and Sciaky left with his family for a new life in America during 1915. This is what Sciaky had to say about Salonika and the experiences of Jews in the Islamic State:

"The Jewish population in Turkey was concentrated in the cities, with Salonica ranking first as a predominantly Jewish capital. Jews had resided in the land since the dawn of its history, tradition having a colony in Thessaly at the time of Alexander the Great.

Contrary to popular belief, Muslims have always been more tolerant toward other nationalities and other faiths than has the Christian world, and with the coming of the Turks in Europe the indigenous Jewish population grew apace, steadily increased by migrations of persecuted Jews from other parts to the more hospitable and liberal treatment in the Muslim empire.

They were invariably well received. In the early Turkish casteless social order they rapidly rose to prominence in positions of confidence at the court of the sultans. History speaks of several Jewish physicians, able ministers and trusted councillors.

The largest influx, however, began toward the end of the 15th century and continued well into the middle of the 16th. The Jews torn from their Spanish homeland by the edict of expulsion signed in 1492 by its Catholic monarchs, Ferdinand and Isabella, flocked to Turkey, and principally to Salonica, where their coreligionists had been living in freedom.

Sultan Bayezit II, in a letter to his governors, ordered that they be received with kindness and that all possible assistance be extended them in their resettlement. Oppression or ill-treatment of the newcomers was to be considered a major offence and severely punished. 'They say that Ferdinand is a wise monarch,' he exclaimed before his courtiers, 'How could he be one, he who impoverishes his country to enrich mine.'

In a short span of years some 25,000 émigrés arrived in Salonica, to find a peaceful and secure haven, free from the persecutions and terrors of the past. Their enthusiastic messages to friends and relatives who had found a temporary and precarious surcease to their miseries in France, Italy or Holland, urging them to join them in the land of freedom, steadily increased their numbers. Not a ship anchored in the gulf that did not bring families of Spanish or Portuguese Jews, come to dwell under benevolent Muslim rule." (*Farewell To Salonica, City At The Crossroads*, pp.124-5.)

Rena Molho, one of the leading experts in the history of Salonica's Jews, described in *The Jewish Community Of Salonika And Its Incorporation Into The Greek State 1912-19* how the poorer Jews of the city, as well as the business class, regretted the end of Ottoman authority and feared the Greek State:

"It should… be noted that a majority of the Jewish working class was active within socialist organizations and it was clear to them that the dissolution of the Ottoman Empire put paid to any hope of a confederate state. Consequently the Jewish proletariat came to reject the newly created establishment and to consider it as 'foreign occupation.' Furthermore the Jews suspected that annexation would be followed by the systematic settlement in the city of Greeks, given special distinctions and privileges as inducements, so that the Greek element would finally prevail, and also become dominant in the economic, social and cultural life of the city… As a result the Jewish community embraced the Austrian plan for an internationalization of the city, seeing it as the only way to preserve the city in its present form and meet the expectations of the working class... By adopting this plan, the Salonika Jews considered that they would be ideally suited since they would secure the support of the powerful Austrian Empire, whose economic interests would be promoted by maintaining the autonomy of the Jews. It should also be noted that the Jews welcomed and were eager to fall under Austrian influence rather than that of any Balkan people." (*Middle Eastern Studies*, October 1988, p.392-3.)

Baghdad was also the home of 80,000 Jews in 1917, a third of the population of the city. When General Maude 'liberated' Baghdad in March 1917, there was some surprise that there was no mention of the Jews in his famous proclamation in the city. This was a few months before the Balfour Declaration and *The Manchester Guardian* went out of its way to address this omission in its editorial of 20th March. It was a first signal to the Arabs that all might not be forthcoming with regard to their great Arab State, and that for the Jews of the Ottoman Empire there would be a different future planned, away from Baghdad:

"The proclamation of General Maude speaks of a union between Arabs, north, south, east and west of Bagdad. This is no time to ask what will be the precise extent of an Arab State with boundaries so vague as these; but we may suppose that these vague words are used to give the widest possible scope for the new state or, it may be, confederation of states... In a portion of this region, that which lies south of Damascus and west of the Hejaz Railway, the Jews have the prior political claim, and it is one which we cannot, by the very reasoning which makes one anxious to revive the political existence of the Arab State, deny to them."

But *The Manchester Guardian* did not seem to have a great inspirational effect on the Jews of Baghdad. Arnold Wilson, Political Officer with the Mesopotamian Expedition, recorded in his memoirs the later effect (or lack of it) of the Balfour Declaration on the Jewish community there:

"The announcement aroused no interest in Mesopotamia; nor did it leave a ripple on the surface of local political thought in Baghdad, where there had been for many centuries a large Jewish population... I discussed the declaration at the time with several members of the Jewish community, with whom we were on friendly terms. They remarked that Palestine was a poor country, and Jerusalem a bad town to live in. Compared with Palestine, Mesopotamia was a Paradise. 'This is the Garden of Eden,' said one; 'it is from this country that Adam was driven forth—give us a good Government and we will make this country flourish—for us Mesopotamia is a home, a national home to which the Jews of Bombay and Persia and Turkey will be glad to come. Here shall be liberty and with it opportunity! In Palestine there may be liberty, but there will be no opportunity'." (*Loyalties, Mesopotamia, 1914-1917*, pp.305-6.)

The Jews who flocked to the Ottoman Empire over the centuries did not bother to settle in their 'homeland'. They preferred the 'flesh-pots' of Europe and Asia (as *The Irish News* called the great Ottoman commercial centres) to their Homeland.

The tolerant, easy-going and cosmopolitan Ottoman Empire was a magnet to the Jews and a great facilitator of their prosperity. Ottoman Salonika became the greatest Jewish city on earth; Baghdad was the Garden of Eden; Ben-Gurion recruited a Jewish militia to defend Palestine from the British in 1914, Moshe Sharett (later Prime Minister of Israel) and many other Jews joined the Ottoman Army. But this is hardly the same Ottoman Empire of British war propaganda?

During the eighteenth and nineteenth century the Ottoman Empire had continued to be a magnet for Jews escaping persecution in Christian Europe, particularly the Jews in Russia suffering the pogroms of 1881. But the forcing of the tolerant Ottoman Empire from Europe by the new Balkan nationalisms sealed the fate of the Jewish communities. Many of the Jews fleeing from the Russian pogroms settled in Rumania, where they were subjected to further persecution, aimed at forcing them to convert to Christianity or to move on to Ottoman territory. The newly-independent state of Serbia expelled what had been extremely prosperous Jewish communities in both Sarajevo and Belgrade. The Greek occupation of Salonika sparked a wave of emigration. The result of all of this was that around 100,000 Jews fled from Southeastern Europe into the Ottoman Empire throughout the late nineteenth century up to the Great War.

During the War the Czech traitor/patriot Thomas Masaryk wrote the following portrait of Enver Pasha, one of the Young Turk Triumvirate, who also hailed from Salonika, for a British propaganda organ, *The New Europe*:

> "Entering the army in the Hamidian era, he became aide-de-camp to Hilmi Pasha when the latter was Governor of Macedonia, and plunged with a will into the labyrinth of conspiracy and treachery which centred on the Masonic lodges of Salonica. He had a greater share than any other Turkish officer in the formation of the Committee of Union and Progress, which these crypto-Jewish intrigues — with their ramifications among the *haute finance* of Vienna, Budapest, Berlin, Paris, and London — did so much to produce." (*The New Europe, 9th November 1916.*)

Reading Masaryk's portrait of Enver gives a clue to why the Allies' destruction of the Hapsburg and Ottoman Empires proved so devastating for their respective Jewish communities. Masaryk went on to lead the newly constructed 'nation' of Czechoslovakia and it was not surprising, given his view of the Jews in the Hapsburg Empire, that their fortunes took a drastic turn for the worse in 'The New Europe', that he helped Britain produce.

In fact there is a strong argument to suggest that what happened to the Jews in Europe in the twentieth century has its origin in the destruction of the Ottoman and Hapsburg Empires by Britain in 1918.

For about two thousand years, Jews were taught to long for a return to Judea. But they refused to return — and not because they couldn't. They did not return because their religion taught them that they were to await the return of the Messiah before they could return. And the Ottoman Empire provided them with plenty of places that they preferred in their secular pursuits.

There is little doubt that the Jews were at the centre of progress in the world in all its facets—capitalism, socialism and internationalism. But what Britain did with the Jews in 1917 was akin to turning the clock back and remaking them in their Old Testament image, as a Biblical people, in modern times.

### *Ronald Storrs, Governor of Palestine*

So much for the theory of the Jewish Colony. What of its practical reality?

Ronald Storrs was an important figure in the Imperial designs for the region, and in particular, Palestine. He was from that great producer of men who took up 'the white man's burden'—a vicarage family. A gifted linguist, he was the official in the Foreign and Colonial Office who made the initial contacts for Kitchener with the Husseins. In 1917 he became Political Officer in the Egyptian Expeditionary Force in Mesopotamia as the Empire expanded North-Westward. And in 1918 he was appointed Military Governor of Jerusalem and oversaw the start of the process of putting the Balfour Declaration into practice. From 1920, after the award of the Mandate, he acted as Governor for Jerusalem and Judea until 1926. He published his memoirs, *Orientations*, in 1939, which detail the mess that began to be created in Palestine as a consequence of the promises made by Britain to the Zionists. As an Imperial servant Storrs never saw the situation as a mess, of course, but simply the burden that had to be borne by the Empire in the name of civilizing and progress.

The part of *Orientations* that is of most interest is a Chapter entitled, *Excursus on Zionism* with the subtitle: *Vere Scire Est Per Causas Scire (To Know Truly is to Know Through Causes)*, where Storrs ponders on the problems of establishing and administering the Jewish Colony, particularly in relation to the effects this project was having on the local Arabs.

One thing becomes clear early on—Britain did not know the material it was using to construct its Colony in Palestine at all well. And the class of people who traditionally handled such things and were sent to establish and govern the new Colony had no experience in dealing with authentic Jews or in handling them. If anything, they tended to see the few Jews they had encountered in their earlier lives as their superiors—in things apart from race, of course. Storrs recounts:

> "What does the average English boy know of Jews? As Jews, nothing. At Fretherne House, between the age of seven and ten, I had met a Ladenburg and a charmingly mannered Rothschild who seemed to know everything, in the sense that you could tell him nothing new, and who impressed me (as have other Jews later in life) with a sense of unattainable mental correctness... Of

Temple Grove I have no Jewish recollections. At Charterhouse were two pleasant brothers Oppé (very much cleverer than myself)... At Cambridge Ralph Straus was one of my best friends. There must have been other Jews in these institutions, but neither I nor my companions knew them as Jews. I never heard my father mention Jews save in connection with the Old Testament, outside of which apart from an occasional Rabbi he had hardly met one...

This then, apart from the Old Testament (Psalms almost by heart) and Renan's *Histoire du Peuple d'Israel*, was the sum of my knowledge of Jewry until the year of 1917, an ignorance that Providence was pleased to mitigate for me in middle life. My wife had never met a Jew until she reached Jerusalem after our marriage in 1923. I had much and still have much to learn." (*Orientations*, pp.351-2.)

When I read this passage, I tried to imagine it written about any other people the English set out to rule. I could not imagine an Englishman governing, for example, the Irish writing that he had much to learn about, and from, them — let alone about or from races they saw on the lower reaches of the racial hierarchy. Even the Boers, who seemed to be most like the Jews, in that they were an alien, but 'first-class', race inhabiting a British colony, would not have attracted such sympathy. For it was generally thought that in the governing of the lesser races Mother England knew best.

What this passage does show is that in the English imagination, because of the Book, the Jews were different — they were Special Ones.

And governing Special Ones is, I'm sure, a very problematic exercise, even for a Master-Race with the whip-hand over them.

England was familiar with the Moslem and Arab world through its centuries of conquest in India and its experiences in Egypt and the Near East. But it had much less knowledge of dealing with or governing the Jews which it now intended to form into one of the props of its Empire. It had less knowledge, certainly, compared with any of its former enemies. Austro-Hungary and the Ottomans all had much greater experience of successfully governing Empires with small but substantial Jewish communities, and so did Germany, which had a sizeable number of Jews within its borders.

But, apart from a small community of émigré Jews in the East End of London, added to by the Russian pogroms, and some Jewish capitalists in its South African colony, the only Jews that England was familiar with were the refined Anglicised variety who did everything possible to negate their Jewishness, in order to be accepted as Englishmen. And the immersion of English Protestants in the Bible tended to give them an idealised picture of the People of the Book, that, to a considerable degree, would have given positive expectations of them as Imperial material.

### An Experiment In Jewish Irredentism

Storrs, the Military Governor of the Occupied Enemy Territory

Administration (O.E.T.A.), characterizes what England was doing in Palestine as a novel and alien pursuit in which it had no experience:

"Europe had learned before, during and particularly after the War, the full significance of Irredentism (invented but unfortunately not copyrighted by Italy): practical Zionism, or irredentism to the nth, was new to most and stood alone. I happened to have learned something of it from the chance of my few weeks in the War Cabinet Secretariat, but with 95 per cent of my friends in Egypt and Palestine (as in England) the Balfour Declaration, though announcing the only Victory gained by a single people on the World Front, passed without notice; whilst the few who marked it imagined that the extent and method of its application would be laid down when the ultimate fate of Palestine (assuming the conquest of its northern half and final Allied victory) had been decided. Those who had heard of the Sykes-Picot negotiations in 1916 cherished vague hopes of Great Britain being awarded Haifa as a British Possession. Mandates were unknown, though President Wilson's Fourteen Points seemed to indicate that Palestinians (then generally considered as Southern Syrians) would be allowed some voice in their political destiny. By the early spring of 1918 O.E.T.A. was already beset with, and its seniors working overtime upon new and strange problems.

When therefore early in March Clayton showed me the telegram informing us of the impending arrival of a Zionist Commission, composed of eminent Jews, to act as liaison between the Jews and the Military Administration, and to control the Jewish population, we could hardly believe our eyes, and even wondered whether it might not be possible for the mission to be postponed until the status of the Administration should be more clearly defined. However, orders were orders; and O.E.T.A prepared to receive the visitors." (*Orientations*, pp.352-3.)

The process of establishing colonies which ultimately expanded territorially so that they displaced native populations and extirpated them was not something that was 'new and strange' to England. What was 'new and strange' was that the War propaganda about the 'rights of small nations' and the fact that the small nations were being taken them on as Allies in the 'War for civilization' meant that England had to give some consideration.to the native populations in this process of colonising.

So administering a process of colonization, with all the ultimate effects of ethnic cleansing that it logically entailed, was much more difficult in the post-War world than it had been in the past.

There was also the nature of the Colony itself. In previous situations colonies had been made up of those serving England's State interests, with the necessary filler who had to do the dirty work of extirpation in order to survive in the hostile conditions in which they had been placed. Colonies were simply established and governed, until a few generations after, when the colony had stabilized and a class of people emerged who felt they could handle a greater share in their own government, and then an adjustment in their administration was necessarily made (In the case of the Thirteen Colonies, which went on to form the United States of America, a miscalculation was made about the timing of this). Colonial Government then was largely a problem of logistics. But in Palestine the Colonists had a special relationship with the Colonial undertakers — they were a Special People on a special mission who believed they had special rights. And it came as something of a shock to the Colonial Administrators, who were used to the routine of doing what they thought best, when a body exterior to them instantly arrived to 'help' with the process of governing.

The Arabs were greatly alarmed when the International Zionist Commission, composed of British, French and Italian Jews, appeared in Palestine in April 1918. The Commission was provided with official status by the Foreign Office to represent the Zionist Organisation in Palestine and to act as an advisory body to the British Authorities in all matters related to the Jews and establishment of the National Home. So, another layer of authority and influence, representing the ten per cent of the population who were Jewish, was being established between the British Administration and ninety per cent of the population.

M.F. Abcarius, who served in the Government of Palestine for twenty years, comments in his book *Palestine — Through The Fog of Propaganda*, that a repressive military administration would have been better for the Arab than being made a third class citizen in his own land by the Zionist Commission 'which formed a veritable *Imperium in Imperio*[an Empire within an Empire]'. (p.62.) Early on in its activities the Zionist Commission secured a Land Commission for the Jewish Colony and put a block on loans to Arab farmers, to pressurize them into selling up.

At one point in his book Storrs puts himself in the Arab's position to understand how, from the Arab's perspective, the Bible was the crucial debilitating factor for his cause, being responsible for his '*ultimate subjection or extinction*':

"With the British 'Liberation' of their country they found their hopes not accomplished but extinguished. Throughout history the conqueror had kept for himself the territory he conquered (save in those rare instances where he returned it to the inhabitants): and that Britain should take and keep Palestine would have been understood and welcomed. Instead she proposed to hand it, without consulting the occupants, to a third party; and what sort of third party! To the lowest and... the least desirable specimens of a people, reputed parasitic by nature, heavily subsidized, and supported by the might of the British Empire. If the Jews were 'not coming but returning' to Palestine... on the strength of a Book written two thousand years ago; if there were no international statute of limitations and the pages of history could be turned back indefinitely, then let the Arabs 'return' to Spain, which they had held quite as long and at least as

effectively as the Jews had held Palestine. That it was the Book that counted...
could hardly be expected to appeal to Moslem or Christian Arabs of Palestine
as a justification for their ultimate subjection or extinction." (*Orientations*,
pp.364-5.)

It is not clear whether Storrs was referring to the English or Arab view
when he called the Jews 'the lowest and... the least desirable specimens of a
people, reputed parasitic by nature...' But there were certainly people in high
places in England who thought of them like this.

The Zionist Commission was composed of the sort of Jewish chaps that
Storrs had looked up to in the course of receiving his education: Major James
de Rothschild, Lieut. Edwin Samuel, Dr. Chaim Weizmann etc. Weizmann,
who had begun to win the War for Lloyd George with his explosives,
pronounced on the noble virtues of the Zionist mission in terms that excited
the English affinity with the Book and the traditional understanding of the
relationship between Colonial Government and Colonist began to evaporate.
Storrs wrote the following after hearing Weizmann:

"It had been from a sense of previousness, of inopportunity, that Clayton
and I had regretted the immediate arrival of the Zionist Commission; certainly
not from anti-Zionism, still less from anti-Semitism. We believed (and I still
believe) that there was in the world no aspiration more nobly idealistic than
the return of the Jews to the land immortalized by the spirit of Israel. Which
nation had not wrought them infinite harm? Which had not profited by their
genius? Which of all was more steeped in the Book of Books or had pondered
more deeply upon the prophecies thereof than England? The Return stood
indeed for something more than a tradition, an ideal or a hope. It was The
Hope — Miqveh Yisrael, the Hope of Israel, which had never deserted the Jews
in their darkest hour... In the triumph of the Peace the wrongs of all the world
would be righted; why not also the ancient of wrongs?" (*Orientations*, p.354.)

Dr. Weizmann had the belief that all Gentiles were anti-Semites in their
genes and the only way they could atone for their anti-Semitism was by
submitting to the Zionist view. What gave Weizmann's view moral force was
the Balfour Declaration itself. Before the announcement of a Homeland for
the Jews, the scattered Jews of the world were merely taken to be members of
a religion. And people who described them in terms of being a separate race
were prone to being called Anti-Semites. But once the Balfour Declaration
was made and the Jews redefined as a separate race and nation, with a right to
their own nation-state, to deny this was considered Anti-Semitic.

Following on from this was the requirement of Gentiles to accept the
irredentist nationalist position that the absentee Jews had as much (or more)
national rights to Palestine than the actual inhabitants of the country. So, if
you were keen to avoid the charge of being anti-Semitic, all you could do was
to adopt the belief that the Zionist was always right and could put you right—

which was very handy for Zionism in its dealings with Gentiles.

Storrs, if his memoirs are anything to go by, seems to have been just the man for Dr. Weizmann.

But the captivating spell of Zionism cast itself upon bigger things than Storrs. Arthur Balfour himself wrote in a private memorandum in 1919:

> "Zionism, be it right or wrong, good or bad, is rooted in age-long tradition, in present needs, in future hopes, of far profounder importance than the desires and prejudices of the 700,000 Arabs who now inhabit that ancient land"' (Noam Chomsky, *Fateful Triangle*, p.90.)

And the word 'now', in the last line, has all the qualities of a temporary and transitory state in its use, when contrasted with 'age-long tradition' and 'future hopes'.

So what chance had the Palestinian Arabs of a level playing field when those who were in control of their land and destiny were in such awe of the Zionists and the People of the Book, from their Old Testament upbringing?

The ethnic cleansing of the natives of Palestine was colonization with a good conscience — given the special status in English hearts of those who were making up the Colony. The logic of Storrs's argument was that it was a wrong visited on the Arabs, that had to be done in order to right all the wrongs that Europe had inflicted on the Jews. The 'ancient wrongs' against the Jews would be compensated for by current wrongs against the Arabs inflicted as a service to the Jews.

And it was more than that. It was an off-shoot of the millenarianism that gripped England from August 1914. Putting the 'ancient of wrongs' to right would make some sense of the catastrophic destruction of life that had taken place and the enormous blood sacrifice Britain had made in destroying Germany. Because surely the overcoming of a commercial competitor merely to furnish the greasy till could not have been worth the destruction of the most prized manhood of a generation?

It had to have been worth more than that. And in the advance up the Tigris and Euphrates to the Garden of Eden, in the recapture of Jerusalem for Christianity, in the return of God's Chosen People to the Promised Land, it could, at last, be all made sense of.

Storrs was explicit, in the concluding passage of his Chapter, about what England was engaged in — which was in making the Arabs scapegoats for the sins of Europe:

> "Zionism is admittedly a departure from ordinary colonizing processes; an act of faith. To this extent impartiality is condemned by Zionists as anti-Zionistic; he that is not for me is against me — a Mr. Facing-both-ways, like a neutral in the War. Their attitude may be judged as anyhow constructive: you cannot make omelettes without breaking eggs: 'to do a great right do a little wrong.' Will anyone assert that Palestinian Arabs can hope to have the predominance they expected, and but for Zionism, would have enjoyed, in

Palestine?... The fact remains that we have supported Zionism; and we must continue to support it with undeterred but unhustled moderation and justice.

Nothing great has ever been easy, nor accomplished without deep searchings of spirit... I could never understand the dullness of soul in Europe which failed to perceive that Zionism, for all its inherent difficulties and gratuitous errors, is one of the most remarkable and original conceptions in history." (*Orientations*, p.401.)

The Great War was the greatest 'act of faith' indulged in by the British State. And it was a catastrophe. In that great 'act of faith' neutrality was not permissible. So if Britain was ever minded to be impartial in the administering of Palestine it was quickly disabled by Zionist reminders that there could be no fence-sitting in great acts of faith. And the greatest 'act of faith' that was the Great War for civilization was an omelette that had just involved the breaking of an enormous amount of eggs. So what was the breaking of a little more between friends?

What was the difference between the Zionist programme for Zion and Britain's Zionist programme? It is this: The British, desiring to keep hold of the final dish, wanted to break the eggs over time, and to keep them simmering in perpetuity; whereas the Zionists wanted to break the eggs very quickly to make sure there was no ambiguity and the victims would accept their fate.

### The Wrong Jews And The Right Jews

We have already noted that no distinction was made by Britain between one Jew and another until a distinction was made between Zionist and other Jews. This only became a problem to the British Empire when it began to try to manage its Imperial Colony of Jews in Palestine.

The British Statesmen who provided for the Jewish Colony in Palestine, and their officials who administered it, had an idealistic perception of it because of their religious upbringing. And deep religious impulses had been stirred within them as the land of the Old Testament came into their possession.

But were the inheritors of Zion the people who the British imagined them to be? Storrs was shocked by the abuse he received from Zionists, in Zion and in America, when he did not prove Zionist enough for their liking. And since they were a Special People, of whom he was in awe, he wondered if he was, after all, in the wrong?

And then it occurred to him that he was not wrong, because the type of Jew he was familiar with and admired was, perhaps, different to the bulk of the Colonists who were abusing the British in the Colony Britain had established for them:

"What made some of us think that we might not be wholly and always in the wrong was the relative lack of success then enjoyed by the Jewish Commission with considerable sections of local Jewry. Modern working Zionism had its origin, certainly its mainstream, in Russian Jewry, for which Britain was to provide and America to furnish a National Home... The spirit

294

of the living creed, predominantly Russian, was reflected in the personnel, particularly the permanent personnel of the Commission, and in the outlook of the Commission not only upon the Administration but upon all the Sephardim of the Near East, indeed upon all Jews other than the Ashkenazim from the Northern and Central East of Europe. In England we had known of the Sephardic or Spanish as the 'Noble' Jew. In the new land of Israel he was if not despised at any rate ignored as a spineless Oriental. Yet it was this same Eastern background that would have rendered the Sephardim, had the Commission deigned to employ their services, ideal agents for dealing or negotiating with the Arabs, with whom they had maintained a close and friendly contact ever since the Expulsion from Spain in 1492." (*Orientations*, p.380.)

There seems to be a strange lack of logic in Storrs's admiration for the Sephardim, who had no desire to be Colonizers, and who were therefore useless to the Imperialist project, and his distaste for the Ashkenazim, who were the motor force of Zionism, and the building blocks of the British Jewish Colony.

But perhaps he reasoned that it was a contradiction best not thought about, lest it reveal more problems and questions, including the issue of the advisability of the project itself. Storrs simply made this comment:

"The religious Jews of Jerusalem and Hebron and the Sephardim were strongly opposed to political Zionism, holding that God would bring Israel back to Zion in His own good time, and it was impious to anticipate His decree." (*Orientations*, p.353.)

To counteract the influence of the religious Jews, Avraham Kook was appointed the first Chief Rabbi of British Mandate Palestine. Rabbi Kook had welcomed the deaths of millions in the Great War as a sign of the salvation of the Jews and the Coming of the Messiah (Israel Shahak and Norton Mezvinsky, *Jewish Fundamentalism in Israel*, p. x). He followed the beliefs of the *Mizrachi* movement, arguing that the settlement of the land of Israel by Jews must precede, instead of follow, the arrival of the Messiah and would hasten his coming. And the logical extension of this was the belief that the Jews should occupy the Old Testament lands of Judea and Samaria as instructed by the Book of Deuteronomy.

And so the Colony started with an expansionist, irredentist mission.

The God of the English proved to be the God of the Zionists. And so the Jews of the Ottoman Empire, like their Moslem neighbours, were forced out of their lives of contentment to be eternally disrupted by the working out of the Balfour Declaration and the expansion of the Colony it put in place under Imperial auspices.

### A Little Loyal Jewish Ulster

Storrs, as Governor of Jerusalem, set out what he imagined the Jewish Colony might become in this emotional passage:

"In spite then of non-Zionist and anti-Zionist Jews, world Jewry was at last within sight of home. No more would an infinitesimal minority out of all her sixteen millions creep to Jerusalem for the privilege of being allowed to die on sufferance as if in a foreign country. No longer would the Jews remain a people without a land, in exile everywhere... Civilization had at last acknowledged the great wrong, had proclaimed the word of Salvation. It was for the Jews to approve themselves by action worthy of that confidence: to exercise practically and materially their historic 'right.' The soil tilled by their fathers had lain for long ages neglected: now, with the modern processes available to Jewish brains, Jewish capital and Jewish enterprise, the wilderness would rejoice and blossom like the rose. Even though the land could not yet absorb sixteen millions, nor even eight, enough could return, if not to form the Jewish State (which a few extremists publicly demanded), at least to prove that the enterprise was one that blessed him that gave as well as him that took by forming for England 'a little loyal Jewish Ulster' in a sea of potentially hostile Arabism." (*Orientations*, pp.357-8.)

Before the War, the Arabs had been unaware of the principle of self-determination. The Ottoman State had done nothing to foster nationalism in order to subordinate people to its dominion, as England had, so there was no need of such a concept. The Arabs were made aware of the concept of self-determination by their exposure to the War.

The War propaganda led peoples across the globe to understand the idea of self-determination as a general political principle, for which the War was being fought, and which would be universally applied after it was done. However, it soon became clear that self-determination was not for universal application — it was a prize that was in the gift of the Allies who won the Great War. And it was only to be applied in cases that suited the interests of the victors in that War.

The British Mandate for Palestine had one fundamental difference from the other Mandates that were awarded. All the other Mandates were instituted on the premise that the Mandated Power would bring the inhabitants of these countries considered unfit to govern themselves up to a level whereby, in the future, they were capable of self-government. But, in the case of Palestine, the inhabitants were to be kept under control by the Mandated Power while another group of people were brought in from outside — until they achieved such numbers that *they* would be capable of government. And then, and only then, would self-government be awarded.

Essentially, the scattered Jews of the world, though not at present resident in Palestine, were given as much right to the country as the actual inhabitants — until the time came that the build up of Jews in Palestine was sufficient enough that they could become the predominant receivers of government. As the Zionist writer J. Stoyanovsky pointed out in 1928:

"The present population of Palestine is only a part of the much larger population whose connection with Palestine has been internationally recognized. The Jewish people as a whole may be considered, for this purpose, as forming virtually part of the population of Palestine. The Mandate System has been applied to Palestine not merely on account of the inability of its present population to stand alone, as is the case with the other Mandated territories, but also, and perhaps chiefly, on account of the fact that the people whose connection with Palestine has been recognized is still outside its boundaries. The Mandatory power thus appears not only as a Mandatory generally given to this term but as a kind of provisional administration in the interest of an absent people. In this capacity the Mandatory has assumed an obligation not toward the actual but the virtual population." (*The Mandate For Palestine*, p.41-2.)

The self-determination that was applied to Palestine involved a very novel application of the concept indeed. Self-determination is usually based on the people who had been inhabiting a region over a sustained period of time. But in this instance the right to self-determination of the actual inhabitants of the region was being over-ridden by a right of self-determination based on a two thousand year old Book and the view that the land should be possessed by those most likely to develop it to its fullest, and contribute to 'progress'.

That, of course, is usually called colonialism, rather than self-determination (England's idea of planting 'energetic' Jewish Colonists into the land of Palestine and clearing it of the 'lazy' Arab fellah, in order to develop it into a Garden of Eden, was a precedent taken up by the Nazi settlers who went to colonize Poland.)

The British scheme for Palestine did not envisage the establishment of an independent Jewish state. It was realised that in the past Jewish states had been conducted in a way that did not lead to stability and tended more toward catastrophe. A Jewish state would have been anticipated to go the way of all the others in 1918 but one was possible under British auspices—if a balancing act could be accomplished between the Jews and Arabs.

But if Britain imagined that the Jews could be turned into a loyal garrison of England's interests in the region they were to be disappointed. The Jewish colonists were not content to meekly accept a role within a communal grind with the Arabs, in the Imperial interest and in perpetuity. They were of far more substantial stuff than the other group which Britain was embarking on a similar project with, the Ulster Protestants, and had ideas of nationhood of their own.

The Jews might have started out like the Protestant planters in Ireland, in that they were given land, but they almost instantly turned out to be more like the Irish Catholics, in that they felt they were being denied nationhood by the British.

The British objective of establishing a Home Rule State of Jews, or a Jewish Dominion, in Palestine, for strategic purposes, had that one potential flaw—that the Zionists, like the Irish, might really want more. The Jews might even become whole-hearted nationalists and desire political independence. And what would become of Imperial plans then?

This possibility momentarily concerned some in the Imperial periodicals during the War. But, like many other potential problems of the Post-War world that were being created in the waging of the War, it was a problem that was quickly wished away and left for another day. But it is very difficult to read the following passage, with the knowledge of what transpired, without getting the impression that the author was hoping, rather than knowing, that his description would match reality. Again, this is from *The New Europe*, with the author this time being the Anglicized Jew Albert M. Hyamson:

"A common fallacy is the belief that the aim of Zionism is the creation of an independent Jewish State, into which a vast body, perhaps the majority, of the Jews of the Diaspora, will migrate. To those who hold that view Zionism is an Imperialist movement, one aimed at the conquest, perhaps peaceably, if not, forcibly, of the Holy Land, carrying with it, presumably, the ousting of its non-Jewish populations. But this is very far from the truth. To responsible Zionists the attainment of the status of an independent State in Palestine is not a matter of practical politics at the present day. The Jewish people is not ripe, nor can it be in the near future ripe, for independence. In the political sphere all that Zionism asks immediately is autonomy for the Jewish population, present and future, of Palestine, self-government in domestic, in internal matters, an extension of the autonomy which the Jewish colonies already enjoy under the Turkish regime, independence in matters of education, of local government, of religion—gas and water Home Rule one might say, but rather more than that: cultural Home Rule. As the Jewish population increases the area covered by this system of Jewish autonomy will increase. It will not increase at the expense of the non-Jewish population, nor will its liberty, its right to self-government, diminish the liberty or the rights of its neighbours. There is room in Palestine for at least another million Jews without displacing the inhabitants. Palestine is an empty land, a deserted land, not a desert, one that has been deprived of its people. For its regeneration a population must be provided and it is only from the Jewries of the Dispersion that the population will come. That it is quite practicable for self-government of this character to be enjoyed by the Jewish population, is shown by the experiments of the past thirty years. During that period between forty and fifty self-governing Jewish settlements, ranging in size from three or four thousand inhabitants to less than a hundred, have sprung up. The Turkish Government has granted an autonomy that is practically complete. The only grounds of interference by the Central Government are in respect of taxation... and serious crime...

The relationship between these Jewish colonies and their Arab neighbours is in every respect friendly. The benefit to the latter is direct and is admitted...

Zionists do not desire to obtain absolute control of Palestine... They want ... the protection of a Power that will secure the land against all possibility of outside aggression. Politically, the fondest dream of the Zionists is the incorporation of Palestine in an Empire whose basis is liberty and justice..." (*The New Europe,* 27 September 1917.)

So why did this Ottoman Garden of Eden for Arab and Jew so quickly become a Hell on earth under British auspices?

It would have been a realistic calculation to assume that there would be no real conflict of interest between Arab and Jew, provided that Britain honoured its agreement with the Shereef of Mecca and Britain recognised an Arab State at the end of the War. Faisal, who was to be the King of that State, agreed to accept the Balfour Declaration, on condition that Britain honoured its commitment to accept the Arab State. However, Britain divided the Arab State with France, and then divided its own share of the spoils into a series of puppet-states. And that put the position of the Jews and Arabs in the new State of Palestine on an entirely different footing than Hyamson may have imagined.

According to the *Encyclopaedia Judaica,* Albert Hyamson was an English Zionist Jew who became anti-Zionist after serving as Britain's Chief Immigration Officer in Palestine in 1921-1934. He published several books including *A History Of The Jews Of England* and also a general reference work, *Dictionary of Universal Biography.*

Hyamson was the Director of the Department of Information which the British Foreign Office set up in 1917 to spread propaganda amongst Jewish communities about the Balfour Declaration. Part of his work was to organise aeroplanes to drop leaflets over Germany and Austria.

In 1898, during his visit to Palestine, the Kaiser had spoken favourably of the Zionists and increased autonomy for the Jewish settlements. But the Ottoman Administration rejected any formal autonomy, restricted land transfers, and preserved the arrangements which proved conducive to good relations between Arab and Jew. Hyamson obviously believed that England could preserve good relations in the region, as the Turks had done, and build a substantial Jewish colony at the same time. But subsequent events proved how mistaken he was.

Britain, in attempting to turn the Jews, made a fatal miscalculation in its ecstatic state of Biblical fervour. If Jews were mere mercenaries of Germany, as Britain believed, why could they not become mercenaries of Britain? It was never considered that turning the Jews into nationalists of Zion might cause them to cease being mercenaries. Would they then not see themselves, after their return to Zion, as real nationalists with national independence as their aim—the only objective worthy of self-respecting nationalism? And would that not make them repel the Imperial motherland (which was not really a mother to them at all but really just a surrogate)?

Finally, what would be the attitude of thoroughgoing nationalists, imbued with notions of religious and racial superiority, towards a large and hostile group within their midst? That question arose strongly in 1947-48, and has not gone away.

Ronald Storrs was defamed by Zionists as an anti-Zionist and anti-Semite for his conduct as Governor of Jerusalem. What they seemed to have found fault with was his declarations of neutrality between Jew and Arab and his failure to promote the Zionist interest sufficiently. Apart from Ernest Bevin and Sir Edward Spears, he became the most disliked Englishman in the Zionist world. And yet *Orientations* reveals him as being truly under the Zionist spell and in awe of the Zionists.

It is true that by the 1940s he had come to despair of Zionism and, like Hyamson, to see the experiment as a terrible mistake. When contemplating a note for a 1948 edition of *Orientations* he wrote the following:

> "Re-reading these chapters I compared what Britain had done for Zionism with what Zionism had done to the British, to the peaceful inhabitants of the Holy Land and to the Middle East, to Judaism and to world Jewry, to the fair name of the United Nations, to the Anglo-American relationship, upon which the future of humanity depends—then, in the speech of our book of common prayer—'I held my tongue and spake nothing.' I kept silence, even from God's words, but it was pain and grief to me." (Rory Miller, *Sir Ronald Storrs And Zion: The Dream That Turned Into A Nightmare, Middle Eastern Studies,* July 2000, p.138.)

Britain made the nightmare of Zion possible and then suffered before washing its hands of it. Storrs should have appreciated that, knowing his Bible well and realising he was the successor of Pontius Pilate. But there was no escaping the nightmare for 'the peaceful inhabitants of the Holy Land and the Middle East'.

### The British Zionist Fraud?

*The Irish News* had commented on the Balfour Declaration briefly in the context of a potted history of Jerusalem on the day of its publication in *The Times*:

> "In Palestine General Allenby is beating the Turks. He has captured Gaza— the scene of Samson's final display of untoward might—at last; and he may press on to Jerusalem, fifty miles away. The ancient capital of the Jewish Kingdom has stood many sieges. It was an old centre of population 3,000 years ago—before David the Psalmist extended and beautified it. Jerusalem was attacked by the Egyptians, the Philistines, the Israelite 'seceders,' the Assyrians, and the Babylonians between 1000 B.C. and 300 B.C. The Greeks plundered it after the death of Alexander of Macedon, and again at various periods down to the advent of the all-conquering Romans, into whose possession it came under Herod. In 70 A.D. the Jews revolted against Rome, and Titus captured their capital and levelled it to the ground... The Persians assailed it in the year 614; and 28 years thereafter the Caliph Omar and his Islamites seized upon it. Since that date it has been controlled by Mahommedans—with a brief interval. The Arabs were succeeded, as masters of Jerusalem, by the

Seljuk Turks; and the atrocities committed by these ancestors of the present Turkish nation inspired Peter the Hermit with the idea of preaching a 'crusade.' Godfrey of Bouillon and the Christians of the West rescued the city in 1099; but it was retaken by Saladin in 1187. The Egyptians appeared on the scene as conquerors in 1247; but the Sultan Selim I. annexed it to the Turkish Empire in 1517. Now a new chapter will be added to the long and troubled history of the 'Holy City.' A great scheme of Jewish 're-colonisation' has been adumbrated; but we cannot observe any evidence of sincere enthusiasm for the project amongst the masses of the world-scattered Hebrew race. Perhaps they are, with characteristic prudence, awaiting events before definitely committing themselves: or a vast majority of them may prefer the 'flesh-pots' available amongst the Gentiles to the prospect of figs and olives in the land of Solomon and Judas Maccabeus." (*Irish News* 9th November 1917.)

*The Irish News* piece is an extremely partisan reading of history. All the violence and destruction directed by Christians at Jerusalem is ignored, the only atrocities mentioned are the work of the Turks.

It seems that Peter the Hermit and Redmondite Ireland had a lot in common. Atrocity propaganda directed against Moslems inspired the Crusaders in 1099 to 'rescue the city' of Jerusalem (by massacring up to 10,000 around the al-Aqsa Mosque, and wading in the blood of surrendered civilians). It reappeared again through Redmondite Ireland during August 1914 to inspire Liberal England and its Irish annex to partake in the secular crusade against Prussianism. And it continued in *The Irish News's* history lesson on Jerusalem, as the Last Crusade closed in on Jerusalem.

*The Irish News* noted that there was not a great deal of enthusiasm for a return to the Homeland on the part of the Jews. They seemingly preferred the comfort of the Gentile 'flesh-pots' to a life of pioneering hardship in colonial work. But the Imperial Power, which *The Irish News* supported, had the objective of changing all that, in alliance with the small Zionist movement.

By 1921 though *The Irish News* began to show scepticism about what was happening in Palestine, believing that the Zionist scheme was a fraud, and just a cover for British conquest. It saw Palestine, like its Governor did, as 'a little loyal Jewish Ulster'. On 7th September it had an editorial on *The Holy Land*:

"England is committed to an immense and revolutionary experiment in Palestine. Mr. Arthur Balfour—curiously enough, when his political record as a condemner and enemy of small nations is recalled—was the chosen exponent of the policy which he declared was adopted to make Palestine 'the national home for the Jewish race.' But are the members of the Jewish race—95% of them—anxious to make the Holy Land of the Christian world their 'national home?' Apparently not... Mr. Henry Morgenthau is a Jew; he is also one of the most eminent men in the public life of the United States... He acted as U.S. Ambassador in Constantinople until America came into the war; he knows the Jewish world; he knows the Near East; and he has written recently: 'Zionism is the most stupendous fallacy in Jewish history; a surrender, not a solution, a retrogression into the blackest error, and not progress toward the light.' These are stern words of condemnation for the policy England is seeking to carry into effect at the point of the sword. Mr. Morgenthau proves that the Balfour scheme is a physical and economical impossibility. Zionists had been working for 30 years in the same direction before the British took possession of Palestine; they had spent millions; 'and in 1914 all they had accomplished was the return of 10,000 Jews to Palestine.' During the same period 1,500,000 of the scattered race emigrated from Europe to the U.S.A. The Jewish population of the world is 13,000,000. There are now 5,000,000 people in Palestine. That small and rather barren country cannot support more than an additional 1,000,000 even under the most favourable conditions. Fully 85% of the present inhabitants are Mohammedans — and there are as many Christians as Jews. Where is there room for the Children of Israel in their 'National Home?' Mr. Henry Morgenthau hammers the delusion mercilessly. He reveals the hypocrisy behind the British scheme: 'Politically, Zionism is ridiculous. British influence must be omnipotent on both sides of the Suez Canal. Moreover, Britain cannot afford to trifle with the susceptibilities of its Moslem subjects.' ... Yet the British Government are maintaining a Governor, a host of administrative officials and a large army in Palestine at an immense annual cost on the pretence that they intend to accomplish an impossibility and establish a new state, predominantly Jewish."

Morgenthau had been behind a petition, signed by thirty other prominent American Jews, including Adolph Ochs, the publisher of *The New York Times*, to President Wilson, protesting at the establishment of a Jewish State in Palestine. The petition stated that the setting up of such a State would be 'utterly opposed to the principles of democracy... for which the world war was waged'.

It was never imagined in 1921 — or if it was, no one suggested it as a possibility — that the problem of living space in Palestine brought about by the moving in of Jews under Imperial auspices might be ultimately resolved by the moving out of the present inhabitants.

What appeared to Morgenthau and to *The Irish News* as British hypocrisy was, in fact, the product of reconciling, in the post-War situation, the different promises made to the different parties Britain had involved in its War. Looked at from the vantage point of the pre-War world, it looked as though England was about to grab Palestine for itself on the pretence of installing a small nation in its historic homeland.

But Britain was no longer master of the situation it had brought about. Before it had even occupied the area, it had promised Palestine to the Arabs as part of a much larger Arab State in return for their insurrection against the Ottomans. At the same time it had promised the same land to the Zionists, in order to encourage the American Jews to change sides in the War, thus removing a major obstacle to U.S. participation. And it used the pretence of fully supporting the democratic anti-imperialist demands of President Wilson to guarantee America's entry into the war.

So England had restrictions on what it could do when it began to administer Palestine after the War, and it had a balancing act to perform between the League of Nations, the Arabs and the Jews — all within the Mandate constriction. (The Jews, of course, gradually got the best of this balancing act and the Arabs, the worst.)

Britain probably calculated that the situation it created in Palestine, with two antagonistic peoples competing against each other in a small territory, would ensure its continued control of the territory — since Palestine could never be trusted to govern itself. In this context, Britain facilitated the steady immigration of Jews into Palestine so that it could ultimately hand over a limited form of self-government to them, when they had attained a majority, while itself remaining as overseer to manage the process. At the same time Britain reassured the Arabs; Britain probably anticipated trouble ahead but nevertheless believed the trouble could be kept within bounds and handled by its power.

The Imperial Power, however, was not the Ottoman Empire and neither was it what it used to be. Circumstances, that it had been directly responsible for, conspired against it. And after these circumstances also brought about another World War, and the mass killing of European Jews, British Palestine came under pressure, with the result that the Imperial Power finally walked away from the mess it had created, leaving behind the Arab nationalists it had cultivated, and the Jewish nationalists it had made functional, to settle accounts.

Ireland may have expressed joy in the recapture of Jerusalem for Christendom but it did not fight the Great War to establish a Jewish Colony in Palestine and see the native inhabitants driven out. If any Redmondite leader had proposed such a thing, it is pretty certain they would not have recruited many soldiers on the basis of it. Colonisation and the destruction of native peoples were not popular causes in Ireland given its history in this respect. But that is the problem with joining a war as an outsider in a state of blind belief in those who launched it and in wilfully remaining blind to the secret purposes of the war even when they began to be evident in the way it was conducted. War is a catastrophic activity and catastrophe on a large and wide scale was definitely the outcome of the Great War that Redmond signed Ireland up for.

### *The Arabs And The Balfour Declaration*

The effect of the Balfour Declaration on the Arabs is best described in a passage of George Antonius's 1938 book, *The Arab Awakening*:

> "In those parts of the Arab world which were in direct touch with the Allies, the Balfour Declaration created bewilderment and dismay, even among those who were not aware of the exact nature of the British pledges to the Arabs. It

was taken to imply a denial of Arab political freedom in Palestine... In the occupied part of Palestine, the British command did their best to conceal the news, as though they had a bad conscience about it.

When the news reached King Husain, he was greatly disturbed by it and asked for a definition of the meaning and scope of the Declaration. His request was met by the despatch of Commander Hogarth, one of the heads of the Arab Bureau in Cairo...

The message which Hogarth had been instructed to deliver had the effect of setting Husain's mind at rest, and this was important from the standpoint of the Revolt. But what is equally important from the point of view of the historian is that the message he gave the King, on behalf of the British Government, was an explicit assurance that 'Jewish settlement in Palestine would only be allowed in so far as would be consistent with the *political and economic freedom of the Arab population*'. The message was delivered orally, but Husain took it down, and the quotation I have just given is my own rendering of the note made by him in Arabic at the time. The phrase I have italicised represents a fundamental departure from the text of the Balfour Declaration which purports to guarantee only the *civil and religious rights* of the Arab population. In that difference lay the difference between a peaceful and willing Arab-Jew co-operation in Palestine and the abominable duel of the last twenty years. For it is beyond all reasonable doubt certain that, had the Balfour Declaration in fact safeguarded the political and economic freedom of the Arabs, as Hogarth solemnly assured King Husain it would, there would have been no Arab opposition, but indeed Arab welcome, to a humanitarian and judicious settlement of Jews in Palestine.

In his reply, Husain was quite explicit. He said to Hogarth that in so far as the aim of the Balfour Declaration was to provide a refuge to Jews from persecution, he would use all his influence to further that aim...

In the months that followed, Husain gave ample proof of the sincerity of his attitude. He sent out messages to his principal followers in Egypt and in the forces of the Revolt to inform them that he had had assurances from the British Government that the settlement of Jews in Palestine would not conflict with Arab independence in that territory; and to urge them to continue to have faith in Great Britain's pledge and their own efforts to achieve their freedom... He caused an article to be published in his official mouthpiece, calling on the Arab population in Palestine to bear in mind... the duties of hospitality and tolerance, and exhorting them to welcome the Jews as brethren and co-operate with them for the common welfare... reflecting the general Arab attitude toward Jewry prior to the appearance of political Zionism on the scene." (*The Arab Awakening*, pp.268-9.)

King Hussein was to find out, as did John Redmond, that it was dangerous to place trust in British promises, particularly verbal ones. But, like Redmond, he had the greatest trust in the goodwill of his patrons, despite all the evidence they offered to the contrary in their actions. That was because, when one joined with Britain in a compact, again like Redmond, there was great difficulty in going back.

Other Arabs were not so willing to trust to verbal assurances. Seven prominent Arabs, living in Cairo, who had been made privy to the Hussein-McMahon correspondence, and who had worked for the Arab Revolt, drew up a statement demanding that the British Government clarify their attitude to the future of the Arab region as a whole. This was presented to the Arab Bureau and then to London in early 1918.

On June 16th 1918 the Foreign Office presented its reply — a reply that was extremely important not only for its content but also for the effect it had on the Arab world.

The *Declaration to the Seven* is probably the most important statement of policy made by Britain to the Arabs, although it is now forgotten outside the Arab world. It was significant in that it was made public and because of its confirmation of previous pledges to the Arabs, made in plainer and more straightforward terms.

In the Declaration, the British divided the region into four categories. The first two categories comprised the Arab territories that were 'free and independent before the war', and the territories that were 'liberated from Turkish rule by the action of the Arabs themselves'. In these two categories, roughly comprising the area from Aden to Aqaba, at the start of the Red Sea, the British recognised 'the complete and sovereign independence of the Arabs inhabiting those territories'.

The third category comprised the Arab territories 'liberated from Turkish rule by the action of the Allied armies'. This area roughly comprised Mesopotamia and Palestine. To this category England promised 'that the future government of these territories should be based upon the principle of the consent of the governed'.

The fourth category was made up of the 'Arab territories that were still under Turkish rule', including the greater part of Syria and the vilayet of Mosul, to the North of Mesopotamia. The statement regarding these areas expressed the British desire 'that the oppressed people in those territories should obtain their freedom and independence' and to work for that objective.

The *Declaration to the Seven* had the desired effect of reinvigorating the Arab Revolt and removing doubts about the future raised by the revelation of the Sykes-Picot Agreement and the publication of the Balfour Declaration. And, a few days before the Armistice with Germany, an Anglo-French Declaration appeared, announcing the intention to set up national governments chosen by the populations themselves in popular elections.

This latter Declaration had to be hurriedly issued when unrest swept Syria during October 1918. The unrest occurred when the leaders of the Arab Revolt met those they had 'liberated' in Damascus and Beirut. The 'liberators' found that the 'liberated', having received a great deal of information about the Allied double-dealings from the Turks, were sceptical about the sincerity of the Allied promises.

### How The Arabs Lost Out

After the War, the Arabs got the part of the Arab world they already ruled in everything but formality—the Arabian Peninsula. The Peninsula could never be a place for European colonization, no European wanting to live there, so Britain did not worry about having to administer it. The fact that nobody was aware of the rich oil deposits in the area at the time was also fortunate for the Arabs. The Peninsula could be controlled, in any case, by the Royal Navy, around its coasts. And just to make sure, the Arab chieftains were each paid a subsidy to keep them in general order and prevent them from dealing with other Powers. King Hussein became titular sovereign of the Hejaz and other States were created in Najd, Yemen, Asir and Shammar.

At the Peace Conference, the issue was always going to be what to do with the northern Arab lands of Syria, Palestine and Iraq. In 1919 the status of these areas was that of Occupied Enemy Territory, with their populations subject to military law and Occupied Enemy Territory Administrations. These administrations were represented as provisional to the settlement at Paris and the various Allied declarations indicated that they were to hand over to Arab administrations freely elected by Arabs.

When Faisal arrived in Paris to represent the Hejaz at Versailles, he was informed that his invitation was not in order and he was politely sent off to London. (The French claimed that the Hejaz was not officially recognized as one of the Allied States). So, like the elected Government of Ireland, he found himself locked out of the Peace Conference.

In London Faisal was surprised to find that there was a dispute going on between Lloyd George and Clemenceau over the Sykes-Picot Agreement. This was the Agreement that he had been informed, by the Allies, was an obsolete set of preliminary discussions that lost all relevance when the Arabs entered the War.

Clemenceau insisted on the continued validity of the Agreement whilst Lloyd George argued that the Agreement had been annulled due to the absence of one of its signatories, Russia, from the table of victory.

Lloyd George was not trying to renege on Sykes-Picot because of the promises made to the Arabs, but because he wanted to grab oil-rich Mosul from the French, and to make sure that Palestine was awarded to Britain rather than to an International administration; and so he denied the validity of the entire agreement.

Faisal had gone to Paris to claim his dues as representative of one of the victorious Allies of the War. But, instead, he found himself under pressure to assent to the giving away of Palestine to England and the Zionists. The British Foreign Office wanted to present the French with a *fait accompli* at the Peace

Conference by revealing an Arab-Zionist agreement that England should control Palestine. And to do this they needed Faisal's signature. Lloyd George employed a negotiating manoeuvre that he was to use against the Irish in the Treaty negotiations a couple of years later. Faisal was persuaded by the British (including his old comrade, Colonel Lawrence) that they were his main hope, and if he did not give his consent to an agreement with the Zionists, the French would tear up all agreements and disregard all promises made.

The Arab view was that Palestine, as an Arab territory, was an integral part of Syria. Syria was a self-contained geographical unit with well-defined natural frontiers and an interdependent economy stretching from the coast to the interior. It had cultural and historical traditions of unity from before the times of the Crusades, stretching back to the seventh century. But the League of Nations Supreme Council decided that the only way of satisfying the designs of both England and France was to divide Syria between them. So Faisal was placed in a dilemma.

He was, however, persuaded by the Zionists that they had no intention of working for a Jewish State, if Palestine was cut off from the rest of Syria, and were only interested in furthering their mutual interests.

Faisal decided to consent to the Agreement on the general condition that Britain fulfilled her pledges on Arab independence. With that Britain insisted that the Arabs take their place at the Conference with two seats. Faisal believed he had secured Arab rights, with American backing, when President Wilson agreed to the King-Crane Commission to investigate the democratic wishes of the population in Syria. Faisal believed Britain's backing of it demonstrated that it intended to fulfil its pledges on Arab independence, as agreed. But the real reason for England's support was the belief that the Commission's report might prise the French out of Syria. A confident Faisal then returned to Damascus to take control of things, awaiting the Commissioners.

Before the arrival of the Commissioners, elections were held in Syria (including Lebanon and Palestine) and a representative General Syrian Congress met in Damascus in July 1919. It passed resolutions calling for the recognition of an independent Syria (including Lebanon and Palestine) with Faisal as King, repudiation of Sykes-Picot and the Balfour Declaration together with the proposed partition of Syria to create a Jewish State in Palestine; rejection of the tutelage of the Mandate system; and an independent Iraq.

In the meantime England withdrew its support from the King-Crane Commission when it was decided to extend its investigations to the British areas of influence, in Palestine and Mesopotamia. And Wilson had to insist on its mission going ahead with American delegates alone.

The King-Crane Commission is the most objective and independent source of information on the situation in the area. In August 1919 it made its Report. It recommended a great Arab State consisting of Syria, Mesopotamia, Iraq and Transjordan and advised the ending of any attempt to set up a Jewish

State in the area. It suggested that the Mandate system be put in place, but for a strictly temporary period, so that the Mandated Powers did not use it as a cover for extending their Imperial ambitions. It found that, if the Arabs had to come under any supervision, they would prefer to come under an American Mandatory administration. It also recommended that only two mandated areas be established—for Iraq and for Syria (including Lebanon and Palestine). And it strongly advised that there should be no Palestine.

The establishment of a state based on the Balfour Declaration, the Commission found, could not

"be accomplished without the gravest trespass upon the civil and religious rights of existing non-Jewish communities in Palestine" and

"the non-Jewish population of Palestine—nearly nine-tenths of the whole— are emphatically against the entire Zionist program."

The Commissioners had started out predisposed to the Zionist idea, but in conversations with the Zionists found that they looked forward to a complete dispossession of the non-Jewish inhabitants by various schemes of purchase. As a result, the Commissioners saw the Zionist ambition as a violation of the Allied War aims and recommended that their project be strictly limited.

However, the British and French suppressed the Report, seeing it as the wrong conclusion, by making sure it was kept secret until after the United States had signed up to Versailles. In fact the Commission's Report was suppressed and did not see the light of day for three years. By that time the Middle East had been reconstructed without the Americans in the way the Imperialists wanted it.

On 8th March 1920, the General Syrian Congress, acting on the basis of the War propaganda, declared the independence of Syria (including Lebanon and Palestine) as a sovereign State under Faisal as King. But the French and British refused to recognize it.

On 25th April at the San Remo Conference it was decided that the whole region was to be placed under Mandates with Syria broken up into three: A truncated 'Syria', under France; Lebanon under France; and Palestine under Britain. Iraq as a whole was given to Britain. The provisions were made public on the 5th of May.

The Mandates had been assigned, not by the League, but by the Supreme Council, composed of Britain, France and Italy. The San Remo Conference disregarded all the findings of the King-Crane Commission. And so the Mandates merely represented a division of the spoils amongst the Imperialists, modified only in so far as was necessary to reconcile their conflicting claims— with America out of the way.

The French Army then moved on Damascus to repress the General Syrian Congress. Despite the pledges England made to Hussein in the McMahon correspondence to uphold and maintain an Arab government in the Syrian interior, British forces conveniently evacuated, leaving the Arabs to their fate. Arab Resistance was crushed with hundreds of deaths and the French invited Faisal to leave, which he did on 28th July 1920.

Some historians have blamed French intransigence and cultivated the impression that in all this the French acted more disreputably than the English. But the French made the point that they had made an Agreement with Britain over the possession of the Middle East in 1916 and were not party, or indeed privy, to the separate Agreement Britain made with the Arabs around the same time. It was England who was double-dealing, bringing the Arabs into the War on false promises, to obtain possessions for Britain. The French acted in the straightforward and honest way of Imperialist practice. It was England who cheated the Arabs of what they had been led to believe they were fighting for.

## *Why The Arabs Lost Out*

George Antonius, writing in 1939, questioned Britain's motives toward the Arabs and Jews in Palestine, in view of the shambles it had created, and asked why the Arabs were turning out to be the losers in the mess:

"Where Great Britain's policy appears altogether indefensible is in the period after the War when the incompatibility of her promises to the Arabs and to the Jews had become manifest; when it became clear that the Zionists were out for a Jewish majority and were using the Balfour Declaration as a means and the label of National Home as a screen to establish the Jewish state, and that the Arabs were determined upon defending their own existence as a majority for the sake of their existence on the land... History shows that a conflict of that kind, if allowed to develop, can only be resolved in blood... There were enough indications in the earliest years of the mandate in Palestine to show them what to expect. Not only in such warnings as they had had from the penetrating report of the King-Crane Commission... but also in the opening acts of the tragedy itself. They saw that Zionist colonization involved the actual wiping out of villages and the eviction of the peasantry; that the money which the Zionists brought and the resulting prosperity... did not make up in Arab eyes for the loss that all that a peasant holds dear and sacred in his village surroundings; that the peasants were defenceless against the process of dispossession and the legalised but relentless pressure that went with it...

Yet seeing that, the British Government remained to all outward appearances unmoved. It is not easy to arrive at the underlying motive of their attitude: whether it is that they are more deeply committed to the Zionists than they allow to appear, and more amenable to their pressure; so that they believe that a Jewish state would be a stronger and more dependable ally of Great Britain's than an Arab state in that important corner of the world; or that they are above all concerned with retaining for as long as they can their absolute strategic and economic hold on Palestine... Even now their policy has turned Palestine into a shambles and they show no indication of a return to sanity." (*The Arab Awakening*, pp. 397-8.)

One reason why the Arabs failed to get their State and the Jews got theirs is revealed in the report of one senior official in the India Office made during October 1914, as England planned to make war on the Ottoman Empire:

> "The strength of our position vis a vis the Arabs has lain in their own divisions and in their hostility to Turkey. The substitution of an Arab confederacy might well result in the withdrawal from us of a loyalty that has been paid to us, less because we are loved, than because the Turks are hated. Moreover, Pan-Islam is a danger that must be steadily borne in mind, and it seems highly probable that eventually a consolidated Arabia would be a far greater danger, alike in Africa and Asia, than the Jewish free-masons who now control the Caliphate." (Stuart A. Cohen, *British Policy In Mesopotamia 1903-14*, p.306.)

The Arabs were of use to England as a political lever against the Turks and in the destruction of the Ottoman Empire. Once the Arabs had helped destroy the Ottoman Empire, a different situation arose. The important thing then was to prevent the Islamic peoples of the region from acquiring a new State that might give them power and influence over their destinies. And at the same time the objective of making the Jews into a nationalistic people to prevent their future participation in conspiracy and internationalism was to be carried through (In 1921 the British rejected Abdullah's proposal of incorporating Transjordan into Palestine because it would interfere with the Zionist project).

Before Britain had instigated the Arab Revolt there had been no nationalism of any consequence amongst Arabs. But having been encouraged to fight a war for their own State and been inspired by notions of nationality from their Imperial sponsors, it was hardly likely that they could be returned to their pre-War contentedness. The genie could not be so easily put back in the bottle!

### Islam And Progress

It was Gladstone who said of the Koran; 'as long as that accursed book remains on earth the world can know no peace'. (*New York Times*, December 20th 1914.) That might have been more accurate if it had been said of the Book that was closer to the Grand Old Man's Heart—particularly its Old Testament. But it was very wide of the mark with regard to the Koran and Islam. And the problem the Imperialists found with Islam was precisely the reverse—Islam led to too much of a peaceful existence for its adherents.

Thomas Lyell, a British Officer in the Administration of Mesopotamia, wondered why Islam, which he took to be a most reactionary force in the world, proved so popular and vigorous a religion among people. Here are some of his thoughts on the subject:

> "Islam imposes upon its followers an intellectual tyranny that is unbelievable

to those who have not lived in its midst. It is an example of an extreme theocracy without God. It is utterly impossible for Moslem powers to keep abreast with the general advance of civilisation, for intellectually they are incapable of expansion. Originality of thought is sin...

Yet in spite of this hopeless system—a system which is as rigid as is possible to conceive, which admits of no originality, no progress, which is narrower than the narrowest Calvinism, which is intellectually and morally dead, and which holds its followers bound hand and foot to a legalism that kills all aspiration and strangles at birth every effort—in spite of all this, Islam is the great rival of Christianity, and in those parts of the world e.g. Africa, where the two proselytise side by side, it is making headway against our own faith... When the official religion of all the progressive nations is being supplanted by that of those peoples who are universally renowned for obscurantism, decadence, and political corruption, the matter becomes one of the pressing political questions.

The soul-killing system of Islam is, from one point of view, its strength. It has acted on the individual and, through the individual, on the mass. Such terms as 'the unchanging East' are a criticism of Islamic influence. The number of Moslems in China is negligible, in Japan they are almost non-existent, and we find those countries daily advancing towards a realisation of national soul-consciousness. On the other hand, moving westwards to India, we see a vast upheaval in process, a strenuous bringing to birth of something—it may be a monster—but something, which is inflicting hideous pangs on the country. Now I do not believe for a moment that there is a desire for progress, as we understand it and as it is understood in Japan or China. It is rather the very opposite, a desire to be left alone...

*'Inshallah bukra'* ('God willing, tomorrow') is the cry throughout Arabia. The individual will refuse to stir himself. He has no sense of cohesion for the common good. He lives for himself alone, and is supremely content in the knowledge of his own superiority. Islam demands from the faithful no individual effort, and it is this fact which secures it the mission field.

The Moslem is excessively proud, and between Moslem and Moslem there is, in one sense, a real brotherhood... It must indeed be admitted that Islam is far preferable to Animism, and it is over this primitive and degraded faith that the Moslem missionary attains his chief power. He demands nothing from the convert save the recitation of a formula, and submission to the rite of circumcision, to which, however, most savage tribes have already submitted. He offers a membership of a huge society; he plays on the innate antagonism of colour against the white races; and he works for converts among those who, like himself, have no desire for progress and all the effort that progress implies. The Moslem missionary as a rule does not settle among his converts, but passes on, leaving his flock in precisely the same moral condition as of old...

Our unique gifts for colonisation have placed upon us a responsibility far wider than we often trouble to realise. The mind of the heathen cannot possibly comprehend the difference between a Christian in name and in deed. To him all white men are Christian... The effect of climate on the moral character is great, and, coupled with the slackening of the laws of convention so rigorous at home, frequently works havoc with the white man abroad. The inconsistency has been remarked over and over again by Moslems to our great detriment...

Islam offers him an assurance of heaven, and an obviously attractive heaven at that: also the friendship of all Moslems wherever he may be... Finally (and this has great influence), he has been given a definite sense of superiority over, and union against, the most-disliked white man. It is not unknown that the English in general, but more especially the commercial class, are most heartily disliked by the majority of the indigenous peoples abroad." (*The Ins And Outs Of Mesopotamia*, pp. 132-9.)

Although Moslems, and other 'simple' peoples who converted to Islam, seemed to want to live in this unprogressing world that England thought intolerable, it appears they just could not be allowed to do so.

Within Islam and the political expression of it, the Ottoman Empire, devotees found peace and contentment. It was the Christian West that was always unsettled within itself, bent on progress, and determined to deny peace and stability to everywhere else, including the Islamic world and its hinterland.

England, for one, could not find contentment within its own religion, the religion it had constructed for the purposes of State. It had shaken off Catholicism in the name of the progress of its State and then found its State Protestantism to be inadequate to its deeper desires. When a more fundamentalist variety of its State religion emerged, England tore itself apart in a conflict over it and then restored the original variety, with the representatives of the fundamentalist variety being punished by exclusion from the political process for a century and a half. Then came the greatest disruptive force of the missionary work of Liberal fundamentalism, which did not quite know whether it was Imperialism or some sort of civilizing Christianity.

Islam offered a stable existence and contentment to its two to three hundred million followers and, despite being adverse to proselytizing, was a very infectious religion attracting many more devotees, on this basis. It was the first real religious democracy.

Maude Royden, an English writer of the 1930s, noted that Islam had a much more universal appeal for humanity than Christianity. In 1939, commenting on the Moslem, she wrote:

"His God was of such transcendental greatness that before him all worldly differences were nought and even the deep and cruel cleavage of colour ceased to count. There are social ranks among Moslems as elsewhere, but fundamentally (that is to say, spiritually) all believers are equal: and this fundamental spiritual equality is not a fiction as so commonly among Christians; it is accepted and is real. This accounts very largely for its extraordinarily rapid spread among different peoples. It accounts for its strength to-day in Africa, where the Christian missionary preaches an equality which is everywhere mocked by the arrogance of the white races and the existence of the colour bar. The Moslem, black, brown or white, alone finds himself accepted as a brother not according to his colour but his creed." (*The Problem of Palestine*, p.37.)

But the Moslem was not allowed to live unhindered in this egalitarian and unprogressing world of contentment. He (and she) had to be brought into the global market of free-trade and progressed in the manner of the West.

### Islam And The West

After the victories of Kemalist Turkey in 1922, *The New York Times* looked with foreboding on Ataturk's potential effect on the Islamic world. In an article entitled *Kemal As He Looks to the Mohammedan World* a writer suggested that:

"Were the Mohammedan peoples to win in the near future their independence and to liberate themselves from the European domination, the greatness of the most powerful European nations would be seriously shaken and the future of Europe would be gloomy and disquieting...

England succeeded in arousing, against the Turks, the Shereef of Mecca, Hussein, the direct descendant of the Prophet, a man of indomitable energy and large ambitions. A treaty, negotiated and concluded between him and the British Government, promised the independence of the Arabs in Mesopotamia, Syria and Hedjaz. The dream of Hussein... seemed to become a reality and he declared war on the Turks. His son, Feisal now King of Mesopotamia, was given the command of the Arabic Army that fought with the English troops under General Allenby for the liberation of Palestine and Syria. In the first days of October, 1918, Feisal entered Damascus, victorious and a Liberator... But presently problems arose and new troubles raged. The Treaty between England and the Shereef was contradicted by the famous promise of Balfour to establish a Zionist State in Palestine and by the secret Sykes-Picot Treaty, between France and England, affirming the rights of France in Syria and England in Mesopotamia... The Shereef of Mecca dreamed of an immense Arabic empire and found himself reduced to a meagre and insignificant Kingdom of Hedjaz. The people of Palestine found themselves governed by a very small Jewish minority and threatened with a rising wave of undesirable Zionists. Damascus, the Eden of the East, the proud city of the Omayyada, the door of the Kaaba, one of the most holy cities of Islam, fell under French mandate and control. Mesopotamia was subjected to an English mandate, with Bagdad, the once famous capital of the Abbasids, the enchanted city of the Arabian Nights, bewildered by the Khaki of the British officers. And Egypt, now the richest and most brilliant centre of Arabic and Mohammedan culture, strove in vain to liberate herself from the strong grasp of English domination. Thus all the hopes of the Arabic world were frustrated. The King of Hedjaz and his sons, having revolted against the Turks... are no more the heroes of Arab independence." (17th December

1922.)

The Arab world was worked up by the West with Western nationalist passions and the promise of a state. And then it was duped by the West, when the War was over, and left to go hang. It was not surprising then that the Arabs began to reject the Western Liberalism that had disgraced itself in relation to them, and to reject those who had made an alliance with it for the purposes of destroying the Islamic State.

After the Western Powers had divided up the Arab lands at the Peace Conferences, Hussein found himself discredited, with no political leverage and dependent on Britain. In the summer of 1921, England attempted to place its alliance with Hussein upon a formal basis, using Colonel Lawrence as emissary.

The Treaty Britain offered to Hussein involved him signing up to clauses restricting his sovereignty as King of the Hejaz and recognising the 'special position' of Britain in Palestine and Iraq in return for a subsidy and protection. In effect, Hussein was being required to legitimise the breaches of faith the Arabs had been subjected to by England in return for 'protection'. Hussein refused to sign but two years later Britain returned with the Treaty. This time the negotiations centred on Britain's requirement that Hussein declare support for their rule in Palestine. Hussein refused until a guarantee of Arab rights was forthcoming from the British.

It was not surprising that, after the behaviour of the West in the region, there should be a revival of Wahhabi fundamentalism, spreading into Hussein's territories. Ibn Saud, Chief of the Wahhabi Sect, had his base at Riyadh, uncomfortably close to Mecca. (The sect was founded around 1720 by Mohammed Ibn Abd al Wahab in reaction to what were seen as departures in faith and practice from the Koran. Wahhabism was a Unitarian Puritanism of a very rigid type which held that everything not done by the Prophet, or that was not the custom in his days, was sin. All unnecessary adjuncts to worship, like rosaries and charms, were taken to be the offensive attributes of the Sunni and Shiah idolators. The Wahhabis regarded pilgrimages to the Holy Shrines of the Saints as an abomination and twice sacked Medina and Mecca, plundering the Shrine of the Prophet and distributing its treasures among its fighters.)

The Wahhabi revival enabled Ibn Saud to absorb the neighbouring territory of Shammar and then to march into the Hejaz in October 1924, taking control of Mecca in the following year. When Hussein requested help from his former ally, Britain told him they had no business interfering in a religious war, despite all they had done in this area to undermine the Ottoman State.

Hussein was by then an object of ridicule in England. He had made himself expendable by not providing Britain with the last of its requirements of him — legitimising its rule and influence over the Arab lands it had cheated him of. Britain therefore meekly accepted the incorporation of the Hejaz into the

Wahhabi State of Saudi Arabia. (Two years previously, in 1922, when 3,000 of Ibn Saud's Wahhabi followers, who did not accept the Imperial borders, rode across the line in the sand, as they had always done, between 'Arabia' and 'Jordan, they were slaughtered by British aeroplanes and armoured cars).

It is unsurprising, given the Arab experience of Western democracy, that Ibn Saud was successful in bringing about the Saudi development on the Peninsula. Saudi Arabia, the Islamic theocracy, whose rulers are chosen by Allah rather than the people, has become a pillar of the Western world, despite overthrowing the liberator of the Arabs and being a negation of everything the Great War was supposedly fought for, and the Ottoman Empire destroyed. In May 1927, Britain concluded the Treaty of Jedda with the House of Saud, recognising Ibn Saud as sovereign and independent ruler of Saudi Arabia, including the Hedjaz. There was no requirement for him to recognize Britain's 'special position' in the region.

## *From The Ottoman Empire To 9/11*

The destruction of the Ottoman Empire was a case of extreme political vandalism in which the traditional lives of Arabs, which they had contentedly led for centuries, suffered lasting disruption. The Islamic State, in which they existed was torn down, and then the Arabs, promised an alternative Islamic State, were forced into alien political structures and arrangements that made no sense to them and which were established merely to suit the Imperial purposes of Britain and France. When they later objected to these arrangements they were mown down by machine-guns and bombers.

British Imperialists argued that the Arabs were not ready for self-government and had to be taken care of by Protecting Powers. But, if that was truly the motivation of British policy, why was it that the amount of self-government and independence given to the different Arab 'nations' was almost inversely proportional to their political development? Why were Syria and Iraq set up under direct foreign administration and the inland areas of Arabia and other backward Sheikdoms were granted the independent privilege of States?

The destruction of the last great Islamic political expression in the world, an event that deprived Moslems of their own overarching State for at least a century, is one of the most important forgotten aspects of the Great War on Turkey. And any sign that a State including Moslems might emerge as a regional Power now immediately provokes recourse in the West to the Hitler analogy (to describe its leader), fears of the destruction of civilization, and increasing mention of the nuclear option.

Islam has undergone something of a renaissance lately—but it is not the type of rebirth that the West was expecting. The Moslems have been deprived of their own State for the best part of a century, a State in which they could have achieved an orderly and responsible development in their own way. States

315

tend to exert a moderating influence on people's aspirations, whereas the lack of structure tends to set people toward radicalism and fanaticism.

Instead there is a collection of balkanised fragments and client-states in the Moslem world that are no good for the self-respect of one of the major cultures of the world (and Moslems have suffered an even greater interference since the end of the restrictions of the Cold War has emboldened the West.)

The response of some Moslems to the predicament they have found themselves in is a consequence of the Imperial re-ordering of the Middle East that began in 1914 with the Great War and the West's insistence on remodelling them on Liberal principles for globalising purposes. And there is little doubt that the vapour-trails of the aeroplane attacks of September 11th 2001 lead right back to the British conduct of the War against the Ottoman Empire and the cheating of the Arabs afterwards.

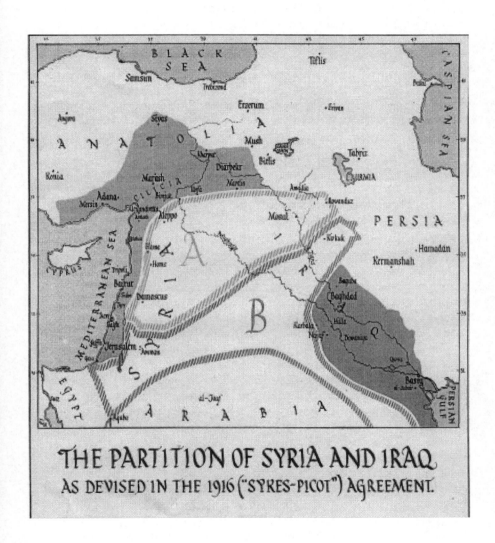

# THE PARTITION OF SYRIA AND IRAQ
## AS DEVISED IN THE 1916 ("SYKES-PICOT") AGREEMENT.

317

# VI. The Conquest of Mesopotamia and the Making Of Iraq

The most famous Irish soldier in Mesopotamia is Tom Barry. Tom Barry was one of the 'liberators' of Mesopotamia from the Turks, although he didn't know it at the time. He had not joined the British Army to liberate Mesopotamia, or indeed to fight the Turks. Or even for John Redmond and Home Rule. He frankly admitted:

"I was not influenced by the lurid appeal to fight to save Belgium or small nations. I knew nothing about nations, large or small. I went to war for no other reason than that I wanted to see what war was like, to get a gun, to see new countries and to feel a grown man." (*Guerilla Days in Ireland*, p.2.)

Barry was one of those Irishmen, therefore, described by the Taoiseach's website:

"The British Army in Ireland provided a convenient outlet for young men interested in soldiering... which offered regular income, attractive uniforms and the opportunity to travel abroad."

The career of Tom Barry in the Irish Republican Army has lately come under some scrutiny, and criticism. But his service in the British Army, which he seems to have joined for no other reason than to have an adventure, mindless killing included, is not commented on. Bombardier Tom Barry of the British Army in Iraq has been a largely forgotten aspect of the Great War.

Another individual, however, personified Ireland's Great War on Turkey better than Bombardier Tom Barry. That is Frank 'The Pope' Flanagan, cousin of the first Taoiseach, William Cosgrave. And he is mostly forgotten too.

Flanagan got his name 'The Pope' from his time at Clongowes, a Jesuit school, where he displayed an ardent Catholicism—which must have been very ardent indeed considering the Catholic enthusiasm of the time. He attended a Jesuit seminary for a time. Like his father, he became a member of the Irish Parliamentary Party, and he was a great friend of Tom Kettle and T.P. O'Connor. He joined the Irish Volunteers in 1913 and helped to create a famous diversion on horseback that enabled the arms to be landed at Howth in July 1914.

After the split in the Volunteers, Flanagan remained with the Redmondite wing and in December 1914 he enlisted in the Royal Artillery and was made a Captain. In May 1915 he was released from service to take part in an important Irish Party delegation to Paris, which played a part in influencing Italy to join the Allies.

In December of that year Flanagan was posted to Salonika with the Royal Artillery to support the 10th Division under Bryan Mahon, who became Flanagan's Commander in Chief. This was followed by a posting to Egypt and onto Afghanistan during 1916.

In 1917 Flanagan was sent to join the Mesopotamian expedition and he took part in the recapture of Kut and then the capture of Baghdad under General Maude. He was given a post in the British administration of Iraq, becoming assistant administrator of the Hilla Province, the district around Babylon. After an argument with Arnold Wilson, the Colonial Administrator of Iraq, Flanagan was returned to his battery. But the dismissal saved his life, as his replacement was killed by insurgents a few days later in the house that Flanagan had occupied.

Flanagan left behind an autobiography detailing his experiences but it has not been thought worthy of publishing as yet. So, unfortunately, Flanagan's words cannot, at present, enlighten us as to the views of an Irishman in the British Imperial service against the Ottoman Empire. Tom Barry has not written much about his military career in Mesopotamia. So it is to British sources that we must go to examine this forgotten aspect of the Great War on Turkey.

### To Bagdad With The British

Arthur Tillotson Clark wrote *To Bagdad With The British* in 1918 when England had achieved its objectives in Mesopotamia and Palestine. Its first Chapter, *Preparing The Play, 'On To Bagdad!' — England In The Persian Gulf And The German-Bagdad Railway*, serves as a good introduction to Britain's aims in invading Mesopotamia, putting these in historical context:

"Back in 1914, as the war was approaching, over 72,000 laborers were working on the Berlin-Bagdad Railway, trying to shove it through the Taurus mountains... Mesopotamia, lying right between Palestine and Persia, was the key position... Now, in 1918, when both Bagdad and Jerusalem are under British protection, we have a glimpse of the real importance of the war in Mesopotamia, for the campaigns in Mesopotamia and Palestine have worked together to block the deep-laid plans of the Huns. They are far from Egypt and far from India...

When India became a colony of England, one of the first steps of the new government was to encourage and protect trade between her new charge and the renowned city of Bagdad. Away back in the days when the first New England colonies were just starting, a British force was fighting the Portuguese in the Persian Gulf. That was the beginning. Not many months ago a British force entered Bagdad. About half a century after England's arrival in the gulf, Turkey moved her border down through Mesopotamia to the top of the Persian Gulf. There was no opposition to this. One look at the country was enough to bring the British sailors in the gulf to the conclusion that Mesopotamia was a place for Turks, or for wandering Arabs, not for them. England's task was to get rid of the hostile powers in the gulf and to keep peace there, that there might be trade between India and Persia and Bagdad. Little did it matter who owned Mesopotamia. No one saw ahead two hundred years to the ambitions of a Pan-German monarch.

In 1622, by a treaty with the Shah of Persia, England took up the burden of keeping men-of-war in the Persian Gulf. Persia, with its soil rich in mineral deposits, its great endless plateaus and its high natural sea wall on the east side of the Persian Gulf, gained through British ousting of Portuguese and Dutch, her only harbor and outlet to the world. To the west of the gulf lay Arabia, the home of countless wandering tribes, neither governing nor governed. Above the gulf, between these two countries — no one knows just where the borders are — lay Mesopotamia, the land 'between the rivers.'

As time went on there still arose no occasion for England to be interested in the future of that blighted country. The right of trade through it was important, but that country which controlled the Persian Gulf controlled the important part, the trade route between the Tigris and the rest of the world. All the rest of Turkey faced the Bosphorus, but Mesopotamia faced south. The British men-of-war and the British flag became more and more objects of respect both to Persians and to Arabs.

Aggressive measures... gradually put an end to... piracy, and gave England the official status of protector of the Persian Gulf, with rights in the disposal of the lands on its coasts. Thus, finally, a quarter of a century before the Great War began, England's constant guardianship of the Persian Gulf for more than two hundred years, to the great benefit of both Arabia and Persia, was officially as well as unofficially rewarded. Her 'wedge' in the gulf was a respected fact...

Perhaps the British wedge would have reached up to Bagdad. But the chance was gone. The moves of Turkey and Germany, with ideas of greater depth than anyone imagined, were about to commence. A few years after the first great treaty between the British and the Arab chiefs, the new Yali of Bagdad, the Turkish governor of the District, marched a good-sized army through Mesopotamia and started after the Arabian towns on the shore of the Persian Gulf. But England was overlord of the gulf and hers was the power of disposal of lands on the Arabian and Persian shores...

With the accession of William II to the German throne a new light appeared on the situation. Out of a most casual difference between Turkey and England developed a colossal struggle... With the visit of the Emperor to Constantinople in 1889 began the war against the British in Mesopotamia. For years it had been concealed; now it was in the open, but fruitless. The plans of the Kaiser were deep. England was in a little difficulty with Turkey over the war in Egypt, relations between the two countries were not too good in the Persian Gulf, and the Sultan was quite ready to ally himself, or sell himself, to Germany for the rich rewards which would come from the Kaiser's schemes. As Defender of Islam and protector of the Turkish throne, Emperor William was master of Turkey.

Turkey needed cultivation, especially the part of Turkey known as Mesopotamia. A railway through there would do wonders. It would also be a boon to India. The slogan, 'Hamburg to the Persian Gulf,' grew in popularity as the realization came of the true purpose — 'Berlin to Bombay and Cairo.' ... It would indeed be a fine thing to have another railway through Asia, and especially in this part. Asia has few enough railways as it is. But there was certainly something queer about the plans of the aforesaid concession. It was curious that, if the railway were for commercial reasons, the proposed route across should carefully leave out all the regions which gave promise of better agricultural districts and go by the shortest possible route across the barest desert... It was hoped by Germany that the duty charges on goods sent over the line would in time bring into the Turkish treasury from England, which was the chief trader with the East, enough to pay for the line. But in the meantime Germany would become possessor of the land through which the railway would run. By the clever ruse of a railway she would annex practically all Asia Minor, Palestine and Mesopotamia, perhaps Persia...

It speaks well for England's actions in the gulf that every one of the Arab Sheikhs at the head of the districts which Germany was trying by all manner of means to acquire, stood firm by Great Britain and refused to let any land go without her consent...

England, some years before, had secured the right of trade up the Tigris, and the Lynch Brothers were carrying on a prosperous trade between Basra and Bagdad. Against this Germany started a line of trade with the Persian Gulf. The Hamburg-American line ran some boats to the gulf, treating all the nation's head-men to music and wine — to win them heartily to Germany. Even these means failing to give her control in the gulf, Germany played the last card, the card that has worked so successfully with other nations since the outbreak of the war. She put the matter in the hands of the big diplomats of the countries; disguising the important matters as unimportant, sliding through agreements before their real significance could be grasped, proposing, under pretext of playing a square game with Turkey, a plan that meant nothing but the helping of Germany, Turkey's master. Perhaps if the British guardians in the gulf were too alert for any under-hand work to succeed, the diplomats in London, so far away, might be more easily influenced.

Fortunately nothing was signed before war broke out. Even a few days delay in the declaration of war might have told. From the job-trader in pearls to the deep-dyed plottings of villain diplomats, every sort of German intrigue had been tried. In the meantime the railway was being built. The section from Bagdad to Samarra was just completed. Enough materials were piled up at Basra to run a line across the Persian frontier and enable the troops of Germany's vassals to move against India. Germany in India! Germany in Egypt! The very thoughts make one shudder...

But with the war came a little British camp on the island of Bahrain, not so very far from Basra. Was that little camp a part of the World War? Indeed it was — and a much more important part than it thought. It was starting something more than a war between Tommies and Turks. The British Empire was at war with the German Empire to maintain England's right to her position in the East and to vouchsafe to India and Egypt the liberty and peace gained through the strong protecting arm of Great Britain.

In the land where Assyria and Babylon fought for the mastery of the East, where a Caliph of Bagdad claimed allegiance from the great wall of China to the Atlantic, now Turks and Arabs, as tools of Germany, were to contend against the power of England — her navy, her British troops, and her dusky warriors of India." (Arthur Tillotson Clark, *To Bagdad With The British*, pp.7-25.)

As Tillotson describes, England had, for many a year, had her eye on Mesopotamia, with a view to absorbing it into its Indian Empire.

In the first six months of 1914 Lt. Colonel Ryder of the Survey of India was engaged in an extensive mapping of the area north of Fao, under the guise of doing a Survey of the boundary between the Ottoman Empire and Persia. The Survey assumed great military importance when the British Indian Expeditionary Force embarked at Fao and penetrated northward with accurate maps and information of military value on the opening day of the War on the Turks.

### Another Soldier In Mesopotamia

Major R. Evans, a serving soldier, has given an interesting view of the expedition in his 1926 book entitled, *A Brief Outline Of The Campaign In Mesopotamia*:

"A military campaign is waged in order to enforce a policy. In 1914, the policy of Great Britain was to support France and to bring about the defeat of Germany and her allies. Further, Great Britain sought to uphold this policy by securing the stabilisation of her position in India... She aimed at keeping India quiet, and Persia, Afghanistan and Arabia neutral—or at least not actively hostile. Finally, she desired the military defeat of her declared enemy, Turkey, in order to remove a menace to her communications with the East and leave her Ally, Russia, a free hand to concentrate upon the struggle with Germany... To give effect to this policy in the middle east, Great Britain initiated three campaigns:—one—an offensive—aimed at the vital centre of Turkey, Constantinople; one—a defensive—to protect the Suez canal; and a third—an offensive defensive (offensive politically, defensive strategically)—to uphold her prestige at the head of the Persian Gulf and prevent a coalition between Turk and Arab. Of these three, the campaign in Mesopotamia was almost purely political in its object and the effect which it was designed to have upon the general war-plan. Its purpose was to produce a definite political result in a limited territorial area and to protect one point of minor strategic importance— the Anglo Persian Oilfields... Unfortunately this phase of policy came to an end all too quickly. Suddenly political aspirations became almost limitless; the objective of the campaign became Baghdad—for the reason that it was essential for ensuring the security of India... Granted that the security of India was an entirely justified aim of British policy in the Middle East; granted that the protection of the oil fields and of the territorial area at the head of the Persian Gulf were political and strategical necessities in Mesopotamia, would not it have been better had policy and strategy remain content with military penetration into Mesopotamia as far as the line Ahwaz-Amara-Nasiriyeh, and no further? ...

So much for the first aim of British policy in the Middle East. As for the second, the overthrow of Turkey, our attitude in Mesopotamia could affect that but little, unless Turkey were foolish enough to divert her resources from the decisive point to a secondary theatre of war. Turkey was not to be beaten in Mesopotamia—a handful of her troops might be...

Turkey was attacked by Russia in the Caucasus, while Great Britain carried out her protective measures in Mesopotamia and in Egypt. Then, at the Dardanelles, we aimed a blow at the vital centre, a blow which just failed to get home because the enemy was a little better prepared to parry it than we were to deliver it. Subsequently, the weight of attack shifted to the Tigris and to Palestine." (pp.128-32.)

'Suddenly political aspirations became almost limitless'—that is how it must have looked to the soldier on the ground. Imperial policy made little sense to the commanders in the field who were told that they were advancing into Mesopotamia to protect India. They realised they were over stretching their lines in pursuit of an objective which did not seem to merit the extent of the operations they were engaged in. And even in 1926, when Britain had conquered Mesopotamia and Palestine, Major Evans was disinclined to believe that he had been involved in the execution of a long-term plan to destroy the Ottoman Empire and grab one of its best parts.

The Indian Expeditionary Force came to grief eighteen miles from Baghdad, at Ctesiphon, where a powerful Turkish counter-attack, led by a German commander, drove it back. General Townsend, who commanded the British forces, was forced to surrender the remnants of his army at Kut-el-Amara shortly afterwards. Even Bombardier Tom Barry could not save them.

The British Cabinet authorized the payment of two million gold pounds and the surrender of the force's forty field guns to the Turks if they allowed Townsend's army to escape. Presumably it believed that the Turks were open to financial inducements. But the Turkish commander refused and secured a major blow to British prestige in the region.

## Trade And The Flag

*The Irish News* tried to account for the Baghdad expedition through an economic motive. Manchester Capitalism had an interesting relationship with Baghdad, despite the German 'penetration' of the area, which *The Irish News* pointed to in its editorial of 7th December 1915, *Baghdad And After*:

"Up to the declaration of war last year nearly 90 per cent of Baghdad's annual trade, valued at £2,500,000, was with Britain and India. Lancashire's trade with the city was immense; the principal importers there were represented by agents in Manchester 'who understood the requirements of the market, and by reason of local standing and long connection obtained credit and financial facilities which they could not obtain elsewhere without long probation.' Perhaps Baghdad's importance as a trading centre helps to account for the progress of the expedition beyond Kut-el-Amara. As usual no fault was found with the enterprise until those engaged in it were compelled to retreat. Men who become mightily wise after the event... have become a veritable plague in every country."

The Irish News was frustrated with the armchair generals in England who used every military setback to effect more Unionist control over the levers of power in London. The Dardanelles And Mesopotamia Commission, which inquired into the debacle at Kut in mid-1916, found that cost-cutting by the Liberal Government led to an army being sent into Mesopotamia that was more suited to Indian border expeditions, than to fighting a World War. The expedition had been sufficient to capture Basra from the unprepared Turks. But it had not been up to the Liberal Imperialist ambitions that took it up to Baghdad and disaster at Kut. And the Report of the Commission was another nail in the coffin of the Asquith Government.

It is not clear if *The Irish News*, however, approved or disapproved of the attempt to grab the Baghdad textiles market by a military expedition. But the commercial angle taken in the Editorial suggests that the Devlinites had a very naïve understanding of British designs in the area.

British commercial interests in the region were undoubtedly considerable. Stuart Cohen, author of *British Policy in Mesopotamia, 1903-1914,* puts the total tonnage of ships calling at Basra in 1900-02 at 478,000 with those flying the British Ensign at 453,000 tons. Since 1859 the British-owned Euphrates and Tigris Steam Navigation Company had dominated the river trade. And the British Consul, or 'Resident,' at Baghdad, lived in the largest building in the town, with a Sepoy Honorary Guard, surrounded by a growing Indian community.

It was certainly the case that commercial rivalry with Germany played a part in Britain's conquest of Mesopotamia. In a 1925 book, *The Heart of the Middle East*, an English writer, Richard Coke, described the differences between German and English commercial methods, differences that resulted in Britain losing the commercial battle with Germany. This is what Coke wrote of the English business community in Mesopotamia and the contrast with the Germans there:

"In the towns the latter were popular, they were clever, they were energetic, they pulled well together and they had money to spend; they mastered the language and the habits of the country quickly, and they mixed freely with the people. The British, whether engaged in official duties or in business, appeared somewhat aloof and careless, and the impression grew among local businessmen that the representatives of English firms did not care very much whether they sold their goods or not, so long as they were left in peace to enjoy quiet and gentlemanly lives adorned by all that a good name, a regular salary and a host of native servants could provide. The quick-witted German soon began to make serious inroads into the trade monopoly which the English had held for two hundred years, and he used all his wiles to play upon the imagination of the ignorant but by no means dull inhabitants of the Mesopotamian towns...

The military power of Germany, her aggressiveness, her hardness, her cruelty were left out of the picture; and it was as a sort of Europeanised American that the German came to Mesopotamia, full of schemes for setting the country on its feet, full of modern democratic notions, ready to mix with the people as an equal, the apostle of 'push and go' as against the maddening, if gentlemanly, indolence of the Turk and the Englishman." (*The Heart of the Middle East,* p.130.)

Coke's was not an isolated voice. The files of the Foreign Office show Edward Grey, in August 1907, expressing concern that 'the whole of Mesopotamia is overrun by German commercial travellers.' (see Stuart A. Cohen, *British Policy in Mesopotamia, 1903-1914*, p.53.)

Coke confirms that it was not German military conquest that concerned England in Mesopotamia but the fact that because Britain was getting the worse of its commercial competitor the gradual process of penetration, which was meant to lead to British conquest, was being interrupted and ultimately threatened. And, according to Coke, Britain was not going to concede the work of centuries without a fight:

"Contrary to the general opinion in Great Britain, the British connection with Mesopotamia did not begin with the war; the war was but the culmination of a series of incidents extending over a very long period of time, in which Britain more and more assumed the right to interfere with, or to control the internal life of the country. The British economic connection was an accomplished fact one hundred and fifty years ago, and may still easily remain an accomplished fact a hundred and fifty years hence; facts are stubborn things, and such a connection will hardly be easily broken either by the enunciation of pleasing political theories, or by the rodomontades of an ignorant and prejudiced press. Great Britain has been slowly conquering Mesopotamia for many years, and, having accomplished the conquest, she is honour bound to accept the consequences of her actions. She cannot withdraw her support from the territory whose previous government she has persistently undermined and finally destroyed, without a serious reflection on her honour and as a colonizing nation." (p.11.)

The last couple of lines of this passage refer to an argument within the British ruling class about what to do with Mesopotamia once it had been conquered from the Turks; we shall deal with this question later. Coke's idea was that since England had spent so much time and effort working its way into the territory, and had gone to the extent of a military conquest to prevent a commercial rejuvenation of the area by another Power, it should at least make good its intentions and take the region in hand in the traditional Imperial manner. His argument was conducted against those who, in the interest of saving money, wanted to establish the façade of an Iraqi national government under British supervision.

### George Louis Beer

If *The Irish News* really wanted to know what England was doing in Mesopotamia, it could have done worse than consult a book by George Louis Beer called *African Questions At The Paris Peace Conference With Papers on Egypt, Mesopotamia And The Colonial Settlement.*

Beer was described in the inside page of this book as 'Chief of the Colonial Division of the American Delegation to negotiate peace and alternate Member of the Commission of Mandates'. He was a strong Germanophobe, and the first non-Briton to be a member of the *Round Table* group. He was the historian of the British colonial system in pre-Republican America and wrote a series of Anglophile studies on the British Empire in the eighteenth century, which he published in the period after 1890. When the British *Round Table* Group began to study the causes of the American Revolution, so that such a thing would never occur again, they wrote to Beer and began a close and sympathetic relationship with him.

George Beer was one of the chief supporters of American intervention in the War against Germany in the period 1914-1917. With his high level connections within the British ruling class, Beer was very much in the know about Imperial intentions in the War and post War—with regard to Mesopotamia, in particular.

Beer realised that if the general public were told that Britain had come about the possession of Mesopotamia in some accidental kind of way they would be keen to get shot of it in a time of hardship—in an 'easy come easy go' manner. So he wanted to dispel the notion that the conquest of Mesopotamia had somehow come about as some accidental by-product of the Great War on Germany. He stressed that there were good strategic reasons why England had had her eye on Mesopotamia for some time and that the conquest of the region had been entirely deliberate and planned. Under the heading '*Strategic Importance of Mesopotamia and the Persian Gulf*', Beer wrote in 1923:

> "It was not due to mere military expediency, to a desire to strike a fresh enemy in a weak spot, that, shortly after Turkey's entrance into the war in the autumn of 1914, a force was thrown from British India into the region at the head of the Persian Gulf and a campaign was inaugurated against the Turks in Mesopotamia. For not only is Mesopotamia potentially one of the richest of the world's undeveloped regions, but the head of the Persian Gulf commands a very valuable trade route and is one of the world's chief strategic points. As the outlet for a rich hinterland, it is destined to have some of the importance of a Trieste or an Odessa and, because of its situation upon a potentially great world route, it may in the distant future rank with a Panama and a Suez. But

even under conditions existing before the war, its value was great. In 1902, Admiral Mahan wrote that 'the control of the Persian Gulf by a foreign state of considerable naval potentiality, a fleet in being there based upon a strong military port. . . would flank all the routes to the Farther East, to India, and to Australia.'" (*African Questions* p.413.)

On 5th May 1903 Lord Lansdowne, who had been Viceroy of India, laid out in the House of Lords what was the British Empire's Munroe Doctrine for the Gulf and surrounding area. The Persian Gulf was British and England would regard any other Power's presence in the region as being hostile to its interests.

Thoughts of territorial acquisition naturally led on to dreams of colonies. Beer pointed out that Mesopotamia was not only an Imperial annexation but could also provide the basis for a new British colony in the area:

"The great problem of the future will be to meet the demands of Asiatic peoples for more land. Their numbers are gaining rapidly. This is markedly true of British India, whose population increased in the ten years between 1901 and 1911 from 294 to 315 million. Indian opinion demands some satisfaction for its vital economic needs in return for its sacrifices during the war, and hopes to find an outlet for its surplus people in East Africa and Mesopotamia where the native populations are sparse. The Moslems in India could furnish many valuable settlers who should be able to live in harmony with the native Arabs of Mesopotamia. Moreover for centuries close commercial relations have been established between India and the countries bordering on the Persian Gulf." (p.420.)

One MP in Westminster, on 22nd March 1916, described Mesopotamia as 'the prize for which the Indian Army is fighting' and said he looked forward

'to see the banks along its rivers populated and cultivated by flourishing Indian colonies transported from the banks of the Indus'.

And no word was ever uttered by the Government to discourage such aspirations (Arnold Wilson, *Loyalties Mesopotamia, 1914-1917,* p.154.)

The Indian Army of the British Empire did most of the fighting in the conquest of Mesopotamia and what better way to reward them and see to the security of the conquered territories than to establish a colony of Indians there, as Cromwell had done in Ireland with his soldiers.

Beer further speculated on the future of Mesopotamia, despite the fact that by then it was widely known that the Arabs had been promised it by Britain as part of a new Arab State for their Revolt against the Ottoman Empire:

"It has been suggested by some that it should form part of an independent New Arabia which should include the bulk of the four to seven million Arabs within the Turkish Empire or on its borders. Although a distinctly virile and able stock, the Arabs are apparently still too uneducated politically for so extensive a project." (pp. 420-1.)

He dismissed proposals for an International Protectorate and opted for a preferred solution of the attachment of Mesopotamia to the British Empire (or Commonwealth of Nations, as it is was being rechristened). And it was within this ambit that the Arabs were to receive their political education.

Under another heading, *'British Policy and German Methods'*, George Louis Beer, commenting on Admiral Mahan's view that control of the Persian Gulf was vital for England, wrote:

> "British statesmen fully realized this and while establishing no naval base of their own in the Persian Gulf, they steadfastly refused to let any other Power to do so... [they] resolutely opposed the establishment of naval stations connected with transcontinental railroads under foreign, and perhaps hostile, control. As a result, there was at one period considerable friction with Russia, whose expansionists aimed to reach these warm waters; and later, there was even more trouble with Germany over the projected Bagdad Railway and the German attempts to gain a foothold in the Persian Gulf." (p.414.)

### The Thieves of Baghdad

In November 1916 another, more powerful, British Army, under Sir Stanley Maude, advanced from Basra, capturing Kut and then Baghdad.

The Irish *Independent* of 12th March 1917 greeted the fall of Baghdad in the following way:

> "The capture of Bagdad is an event of great military and political importance. The city lies on the main route to Persia—and to India. It was by means of the Bagdad Railway that Germany hoped to open her way to the Persian Gulf and to shatter the prestige of England in the Far East. The defeat of the Turks must react upon all German schemes of expansion. The very foundations of the Ottoman Empire will be shaken by General Maude's victory... The Arab tribes, which were none too friendly to the Turks, will most probably bestir themselves to be rid of the hated oppressor. From Mesopotamia to the shores of the Red Sea and the Levant the news will travel that the rule of the Turk is near its end. In Persia and in Afghanistan where Turko-German intrigue has been busy since the war, the reaction will be decisive. The bungling in early stages of the Mesopotamia campaign undoubtedly tended to lower England's prestige in the Mohammedan world, but the mischief then wrought is now, thanks to General Maude, and his gallant troops, in a fair way being undone."

The Arab world did not feel oppressed by the Ottoman Empire as *The Independent* made out. The Arabs were Moslems and they felt at ease within the vast, loose Moslem State. There were a few nationalist intellectuals, mainly centred around Basra, but the masses knew little of such European sentiment outside the American Missionary Schools. Arnold Wilson, the future Colonial Civil Commissioner of Mesopotamia, who had studied and lived in the region for many years, noted that there were no Arab aspirations for living under a different government:

"The Arabs of Mesopotamia themselves had scarcely given the matter a thought: they had always regarded themselves as part of the Turkish Empire, and had never desired anything more than some form of autonomy under the Sultan." (*Loyalties Mesopotamia, 1914-1917,* p. 17.)

It was only with the working up of racial divisions between Arab and Turk by the British, that nationalistic feeling began to develop. And it did so only because of the extraordinary situation that was developing from the War.

The mischief had only just begun for the inhabitants of Mesopotamia with the arrival of the British there. On March 19th the *Freeman's Journal* reported the *Proclamation issued by Lieutenant-General Sir Stanley Maude to the people of Baghdad.* And the *Freeman* made no comment on the obvious parallels between the British conquest of Ireland and the criticism directed at the record of and the promises made by the Ottoman administration in Mesopotamia.

The reader can compare the subsequent history of the British creation of the State of Iraq with the promises made by their 'liberators' of 1917:

"To the people of Bagdad vilayet! In the name of my King and in the name of the people over whom he rules, I address you. Our military operations have as their object the defeat of the enemy and the driving of him from these territories.

In order to complete this task I am charged with absolute and complete control of all the regions in which British troops operate, but our armies do not come into your cities and lands as conquerors or as enemies but as liberators.

Since the days of Halaska, your cities and your lands have been subjected to the tyranny of strangers, your palaces have fallen into ruins, your gardens have sunk in desolation, and your forefathers and yourselves have groaned in bondage. Your sons have been carried off to wars not of your seeking; your wealth has been stripped from you by unjust men and squandered in distant places. Since the days of Midhat, the Turks have talked of reforms, yet do not the ruins and wastes of today testify to the vanity of those promises?

It is the wish not only of my King and his people but it is also the wish of the great nations with whom he is in alliance that you should prosper, even as in the past, when your lands were fertile, when your ancestors gave to the world literature, science and art, and when Bagdad city was one of the wonders of the world. Between your people and the dominions of my King there has been a close bond of interest. For two hundred years have the merchants of Bagdad and Great Britain traded together in mutual profit and friendship.

On the other hand, the Germans and the Turks who have despoiled you and yours, have for twenty years made Bagdad a centre from which to assail the power of the British and of the Allies of the British in Persia and Arabia. Therefore, the British Government cannot remain indifferent as to what takes place in your country now or in the future, for, in duty to the interests of the British people and their Allies, the British Government cannot risk that being done in Bagdad again which has been done by the Turks and the Germans during this War.

But you, people of Bagdad, whose commercial prosperity and whose safety from oppression and invasion must ever be a matter of the closest concern to the British Government, are not to understand that it is the wish of the British Government to impose upon you alien institutions. It is the hope of the British Government that the aspirations of your philosophers and writers shall be realised, and that once again the people of Bagdad shall flourish, enjoying their wealth and substance under institutions which are in consonance with their sacred laws and their racial ideas.

In Hedjaz, the Arabs have expelled the Turks and Germans who oppressed them, and proclaimed the Shereef Hussein as their King and his Lordship rules in independence and freedom, and is the Ally of the nations who are fighting against the powers of Turkey and Germany. So also are the noble Arabs, the Lords of Koweyt, Nejd and Asir. Many noble Arabs indeed have perished in the cause of Arab freedom, at the hands of those alien rulers the Turks who oppressed them. It is the determination of the Government of Great Britain that these noble Arabs should not have suffered in vain. It is the hope and desire of the British people and the nations in alliance with them that the Arab race may rise once again to greatness and renown among the peoples of the earth and that it shall bind itself together to this end and in unity and concord.

People of Bagdad, remember that for twenty-six generations you have suffered under strange tyrants who have ever endeavoured to set one Arab against another in order that they might profit by your dissensions, That policy is abhorrent to Great Britain and her Allies, for there can be neither peace nor prosperity where there is enmity and misgovernment. Therefore, I am commanded to invite you, through your nobles and elders and representatives, to participate in the management of your civil affairs in collaboration with the political representatives of Great Britain, who accompany the British Army, so that you may be united with your kinsmen, north, south, east and west, in realising the aspirations of your race."

So much for Colonel Tim Collins! It was all said and done in the same way ninety years ago. What was it that Marx said about history repeating itself a second time as farce?

General Maude's speech was written by Mark Sykes, who had previously helped carve up the Arab lands in a secret agreement with the French in the Sykes-Picot Agreement — unbeknown to the residents of Baghdad. These were surely the modern thieves of Baghdad.

Arnold Wilson commented on the content of Maude's Declaration in his book, *Loyalties Mesopotamia 1914-1917,* and pointed out that Sykes, the speech writer, had written a declaration which conflicted with his own Agreement with the French:

"If this [speech] meant anything, it meant that the Allies viewed with benevolence the idea of a united or federated Arabia, a conception wholly incompatible with the Sykes-Picot agreement, a Federation in which the

Wahhabis of Najd, the 'Lords of Koweit and Asir,' the Sunni Arabs of Syria and the Shi'ahs of Iraq, not to mention the usual minorities, would by some means unite to realize their presumed aspirations to govern each other." (*Loyalties Mesopotamia, 1914-1917*, p.239.)

According to Wilson it was also far from clear that the local Arabs desired a change of masters at all:

"To induce Arabs to come forward and participate in the civil administration was exceedingly difficult, in the absence of an honest and straightforward announcement as to the form of government to be set up after the war... By no means all the leading Arab families of Baghdad or of the Wilayet were anti-Turk; on the contrary, the landed gentry and the subordinate civil clerical staff who had remained in Baghdad were on the whole inimical to an Arab regime such as was outlined in General Maude's proclamation. In their hearts they preferred the Turk, with all his failings, to the unprobed complications of an Anglo-Arab condominium. Turkish rather than Arabic was the language of polite society, and leading families boasted of their Turkish affinities rather than of their Arab forebears. Many had been educated in Constantinople; all had been taught to regard Constantinople as their cultural centre... the Sublime Porte still enjoyed prestige." (*Loyalties Mesopotamia, 1914-1917*, pp. 241-2.)

Wilson knew that England had not come to the Arab lands as 'liberators'. And he saw the contradiction of posing as such whilst maintaining, in all the proclamations made to the Arab rulers and people of the region, that Britain had gone to War with Turkey only with the utmost reluctance. Britain was occupying their lands, it was suggested, merely as a by-product of her conflict with Turkey and Germany.

Here are some examples of these proclamations, translated and reproduced in Wilson's *Loyalties* book. Interestingly, a number were issued before England had even declared war on the Turks (5th November 1914.):

"To the Arab Rulers and Shaiks in the Persian Gulf and their Subjects.

Since the Crimean War, when France and Britain voluntarily went to war to preserve the integrity of Turkey, it has been one of the supreme objects of the British Government to preserve inviolate the Ottoman Empire.

Now, by their own act in foolishly intervening in the struggle between Germany and all the other Powers, the present rulers of that Empire would be wilfully preparing their own destruction, and it seems impossible to hope that their Empire can any longer be preserved..." *(S.G. Knox, Lieut. Col., 31st October 1914.)*

"Let it not be hidden from you that the Great British Government has to its great regret been forced into a state of war by the persistent and unprovoked hostility of the Turkish Government instigated by Germany for her own ends..." *(P.Z. Cox, Resident, Persian Gulf. 5th November 1914.)*

"Issued on behalf of the General Officer Commanding the British Forces in Occupation of Basra, To the Notables and Public of the Town.

As is well known, Great Britain has, in the past, always displayed friendship and regard for Turkey..." *(P.Z. Cox, Lieut. Col., Political Officer to the Force. 22nd November 1914.)*

General Maude himself, the conqueror of the city, objected to the text of Sykes's speech. It was full of the propagandist rhetoric of the 'war for small nations' and it did not say why the British Army was in Mesopotamia or who was going to rule the region. So Maude felt that the Arabs would get ideas above their station—ideas that would be dangerous if they were left in the air. Maude was told by London to get on with it, but in his administration of the city there was no room for Arab participation.

When Maude's Proclamation was discussed in the British Parliament there were mixed feelings amongst the Members, whose thoughts seemed to be drawn to nearer home:

"The Speaker of the House of Commons referred to it as containing a great deal of oriental and flowery language not suitable to our western climate. Mr. Devlin suggested that a similar proclamation would be apposite in Ireland, and Mr. S. McNeill suggested in writing it Sir Stanley Maude, who was an Irishman, was probably thinking of the Irish situation...

Mr. McVeigh returned to the charge the following day, asking whether the War Cabinet was aware that Sir Stanley Maude proposed, 'on behalf of Great Britain and the Allies, to force Home Rule on the Arabs without regard to the views of those who might desire to remain under Turkish rule; whether the Arabs have agreed amongst themselves as to the form of government they desire... and whether, in urging the Arabs to remain a united nation north, south, east and west, he had the sanction of the War Cabinet.' He too was perhaps thinking of Ireland." *(Loyalties Mesopotamia, 1914-1917, p.240.)*

The references to Ireland were pertinent. The Arabs had never desired any other government than the Ottoman structures they lived under, yet a form of Home Rule was being forced upon them, whereas in Ireland, where the demand of the overwhelming majority had been for at least the same, all sorts of violence had been threatened by the major Party of State against the Government proposing it.

A couple of weeks after Maude's Declaration, the War Cabinet issued the following instructions to its new administration in Baghdad, when it enquired over Britain's intentions in Mesopotamia:

"Basra is to remain permanently under British Administration... Baghdad to be an Arab State with local ruler or government under British Protectorate in everything but name. It will accordingly have no relations with foreign Powers... Baghdad to be administered behind the Arab façade as far as possible as an Arab province." (P.W. Ireland, *Iraq: A Study in Political Development*, pp. 96-7.)

Arnold Wilson recalled that 'At no time during the year [1918] did any doubts arise in our minds as to our future intentions in Iraq.' (p.99.) But he became concerned at the Twelfth of President Wilson's Fourteen Points, issued in January of that year, which stated that

> "the nationalities now under Turkish rule should be assured an undoubted security of life and an absolutely unmolested opportunity of autonomous development."

Wilson saw that this, and statements emanating from Allied leaders designed to convince the U.S. of their good intentions in the East, denying that there were any plans for Imperial annexations, obviously conflicted with what he knew about Sykes-Picot and from internal memoranda he had received from London.

When Wilson asked his political masters in London about the future arrangements for governing the area, in the light of these conflicting messages, he was fobbed off and told to use his own initiative. So he just got on with the job in the only way he knew.

### Imperialism And Small Nations

Before the Great War it was assumed in England that history was progressing from the National to the Imperial. Numerous articles were written in Imperial publications recognising this historical line of development. Just one example was W. F. Monypenny's '*The Imperial Ideal,*' contained in a section called *Principles of Empire,* within the 1905 collection, *The Empire And The Century.* Monypenny, an Ulsterman, was Assistant Editor of *The Times* before he went to South Africa to become Editor of the *Johannesburg Star.* Later, during the Home Rule crisis, he wrote a book called *The Two Irish Nations.*

Monypenny's article is worth quoting, to give the reader an appreciation of how the future was seen in England prior to the Great War—a vision that Arnold Wilson and his fellow administrators in the Indian Empire would have shared as they took the reins in Mesopotamia:

> "Among the many remarkable changes of the last generation none is more remarkable than the change in the political ideas uppermost in the minds of men, and in the political aspirations to which these ideas give direction and impetus—a change which is perhaps most perceptible in our own country and among our own kindred, but which can also be traced among every other people with any claim to civilisation. Thirty or forty years ago the word 'Nation' and its derivatives were on the lips of all. Political enthusiasm was concentrated on the redemption of subject nationalities, or in the bringing together of severed national fragments; or, where national unity had already been attained, in the development of political freedom and the extension of political privilege from the few to the many. The national ideal, in fact, was the great formative influence in political thought, the guiding principle of diplomacy, the inspiration of

political parties. Today the words 'Empire' and 'Imperialism' fill the place in everyday speech that was once filled by 'Nation' and 'Nationality.' In the never ending struggle of political principles, authority rather than liberty seems at the moment to have the upper hand; power and dominion rather than freedom and independence are ideas that appeal to the imagination of the masses; men's thoughts are turned outwards rather than inwards; the national ideal has given way to the Imperial...

From the time of the Crusades... Europe has, from small beginnings and, at first, by tentative steps, been overrunning the world: she has been stretching out her hands over the remainder of the globe, and been drawing it under her control or within the orbit of her civilization. In some cases, of which the United States is at once the typical and the most splendid instance, she has planted new nationalities of European origin in what were waste or thinly-populated regions of the earth. In others, as in the case of the Russian Empire, she has extended an existing European nationality far beyond the bounds of Europe... Yet again — and here India is the typical and crowning illustration — where no question of nationality was involved or could for ages arise, she has reduced to a condition of independence an immense population incapable of providing a civilized government for itself; has established a reign of justice and order, which is the first condition of order in civilization; supplied the initiative and momentum that could not be found among the governed; and entered on the tremendous task of raising them to their own plane of civilization by an effort, which, to be successful must last for ages...

Asia has succeeded to Africa as the chief field of ambition; all the greater nation states of Europe have joined in the race... and eagerly seized a share in the 'white man's burden.' During the last quarter of a century the absorption of the unoccupied or weakly-held portions of the earth, and the reduction of the uncivilized or semi-civilized States to a dependent position, have proceeded at such a pace that the end is almost in sight. The partition of Africa is almost complete. Eastern Asia is emerging from the melting-pot, and it is beginning to be possible to foresee the lines on which it will be reconstructed; and it is only in the case of Turkey and the other Mohammedan countries of Western Asia that the future is still wholly dark, and that great conflicts must too probably precede the final solution." (pp. 5-16.)

Prior to August 1914, it was believed in ruling circles in England that nations had been seen off and the future was Imperial. The general thrust of British Imperial thinking prior to the Great War was that small nations were giving way to the Imperial Super-State and the whole world was coming within its sway, in an inevitable progression of history. Most parts of the earth would become part of the British, French and Russian Empires or of the great expansionist State of America.

Part of the reasoning behind the Unionist resistance to Irish Home Rule was the idea that Home Rule for Ireland would be an unnecessary backward step in the movement of history.

As Monypenny noted, only the Ottoman Empire, which was not a real empire at all in the British sense, remained as an anomaly in this historical process. But 'great conflicts must too probably precede the final solution' of that aberration.

But then came the Great War, and, in order to take Liberal England with it, the Government raised the rallying cry for small nations. And Nations and Nationalism were to have another innings, after all.

## Arnold Wilson and Mesopotamia

Arnold Wilson arrived in the Middle East in 1904 as assistant to Sir Percy Cox, Resident in the Persian Gulf. At the commencement of War with Turkey he became a Political Officer with the Indian Political Service. As British military forces captured areas from the Turks they were handed over to ready-made administrations, products of the Indian Civil Service. Political Officers, almost entirely products of the Public Schools, brought with them the knowledge and experience of governing the Indian Empire and acted as intermediaries between the British armies of occupation and the civil population they ruled. Many had cut their teeth in recent years in the Gulf Sheikdoms, specialising in establishing British control behind the façade of local elites. But they carried with them the world of the Indian Empire and naturally saw the conquest of Mesopotamia as an absorption of territory into it.

In March 1918, Cox was posted to Teheran to conclude a Treaty with the Persians and Wilson was appointed acting Civil Commissioner of Mesopotamia. Wilson brought with him an Indian Civil Service, Indian laws, and an Indian Police Force, and he immediately proposed a plantation of Punjabis to help cultivate the unpopulated plains of the country. He envisaged Britain annexing (or establishing protectorate over) the area and remaining in it for generations. Thomas Lyell, one of Wilson's Officers, understood it like this:

"That self-government for these people may be possible, say, one hundred years hence, is perhaps true; but to suggest such a thing at the present time is the veriest eyewash and camouflage." (*The Ins And Outs of Mesopotamia*, p.148.)

Strong and purposeful government was not only an Imperial prerequisite for Mesopotamia, it was also essential because the character of the local people made it the only way of bringing about progress:

"Mesopotamia... has been reduced from a state of world-famous productivity and fruitfulness to a sterility which was accurately described by a British Tommy as 'miles and miles and miles of damn all.' There are, it is true, still tracts of land of marvellous beauty and fertility; but as a whole it can only be regarded as a desert, and the blight of the land has fallen on the inhabitants thereof. Its past history is one of perpetual feuds and bloodshed. ..

Ever since the country passed from the hands of the Persian Empire into those of Islam, it has always needed the strongest and most severe Governors, since none of weaker calibre could cope with its peoples." (*The Ins And Outs of Mesopotamia*, pp.155-6.)

Lyell, aware of the War propaganda, and the promises of self-government made to the Arabs, asserted that it would be the utmost folly to return this area immediately to its people, who would simply compound the hash that had been made of the country in the past. And this would have been the view of his boss, Arnold Wilson.

When Wilson arrived in Mesopotamia he began to act on the 'Principles of Empire' described by Monypenny—the understandings that had been inculcated into the Imperial governing class. He saw his mission as being similar to that undertaken by the Empire in India: to install 'a civilized government' with 'a reign of justice and order... the first condition of order in civilization' and to enter 'on the tremendous task of raising them to their own plane of civilization by an effort, which, to be successful must last for ages.' And he believed that 'no question of nationality was involved or could for ages arise' in the area.

Wilson's reminiscences about his time in Mesopotamia are contained in two volumes: Volume I, *Loyalties Mesopotamia, 1914-17, A Personal and Historical Record,* and Volume II, *Loyalties Mesopotamia, 1917-20.* At the start of the *Preface* to the Second Volume he has a quotation from one of Cromwell's speeches, from 12th September 1654:

"You have been called hither to save a Nation,—Nations. You had the best People, indeed, of the Christian world put into your trust, when you came hither... Through the blessing of God, our enemies were hopeless and scattered... If by such actings these poor Nations shall be thrown into heaps and confusion, through blood, and ruin and trouble—all because we would not settle when we could, when God put it into our hands—to have all recoil upon us; and ourselves... loosened from all known and public interests;... who shall answer for these things to God?" (*Mesopotamia 1917-1920 A Clash Of Loyalties,* pp. x-xi)

It is clear from this that Arnold Wilson believed that having obtained the power of life and death over peoples, having defeated the enemy and conquered his territory, that the responsibility lay with England to govern purposefully and in the interest of progress.

### Shiah, Sunni and Kurd

The intention, at the start of the British conquest of Mesopotamia, was that it would be governed as a colony by an Indian administration. The region was earmarked to be annexed to British India, making the Arabian Sea and Persian Gulf into a British lake.

Wilson did not imagine that a state would be constructed out of the three *vilayets* loosely comprising Mesopotamia. The name Mesopotamia, 'the land between the rivers', is not quite accurate a term to describe the three *vilayets* since 'Mesopotamia' is really a topographical expression which does not encompass the mountains of the North, where the Kurds lived, or, indeed, the Shatt al-Arab. The phrase 'Al-Iraq', 'the lowland', was a topographical expression as well, not a political one, and it did not apply to the mountains in the North either. In fact, no single name applied to the disparate regions that were combined to form Iraq, because history never imagined them to form a distinct area.

Just before the War with Turkey, Wilson had made an extensive survey of the region, with a view to advising the Liberal Government of the territory they ought to add to the Indian Empire once the Turks were driven out. Wilson concluded at this stage that only the Basra vilayet should be incorporated into British India. Wilson had had experience of India with its conglomeration of princes, faiths, and races. He did not wish to disturb the rich and intricate miscellany he found in Mesopotamia, that had preserved itself down the centuries within a stable framework of existence, by cobbling it all together and combining it in a State. He therefore initially only advised London to incorporate Basra into British India, as Burma had been attached to it in previous years.

But then, of course, 'suddenly political aspirations became almost limitless'.

The intention of Britain when it first came into possession of Baghdad apparently was to attach Basra to the Indian Empire and to make the Baghdad *vilayet* part of the new Arab State—or 'Arab *façade*' as the British Government saw it. This policy at least had the advantage of fulfilling the promise to Shereef Hussein—in name anyway—of an Arab State, whilst not cobbling together Shiah Basra and Sunni Baghdad into some kind of political entity, under a local puppet ruler.

The Basra *vilayet* consisted overwhelmingly of a Shiah Muslim population. But the Shiah were also heavily represented in the area around Baghdad and constituted about 1,500,000 of the 2,700,000 people of the three *vilayets* that ultimately went to make up Iraq. An alliance between clan chiefs and the religious leaders based in the four Holy Cities of Karbala, Kadhiman, Samara and Najaf, was the main source of leadership amongst the Shiah. The *Hawzas*, religious seminaries in Karbala and Najaf, are, to the present, the source of much of the Law, which can be freely interpreted by the Priests, or Mujtahidun, (unlike Sunni doctrine which is rigidly derived from the *Sunnat* of the Four Great Legalists). Acknowledging the power of the Clergy among the Shiah, which Wilson called the 'Persian Clergy' because of where they tended to train, the Turks governed the Basra *vilayet* through either the Imams or the Chieftains of the local tribes.

The cornerstone of Shiah doctrine was the Imamate, which is entirely different from the Sunni devotion to the Caliphate. It originated with Imam

Ali and the fatal attack he suffered at Kufa whilst praying. The devotion to Ali and the Imamate arose from the desire for a spiritual head with a divine quality, rather than a purely religious head (the Sunni Caliph) with merely human attributes. Because of the Sunni denial of the divine quality of the Imamate, the Shiah saw them as heretical renegades. And the Shiah had no interest in the political question of the Caliphate, which they took to be a merely earthly matter, of little consequence.

A reading of Arnold Wilson's memoirs and Thomas Lyell's book reveals that the British administrators saw great difficulties in governing the Shiah, due to the predominance of religion in their lives, the strength of religious authority over them, and the fact that this insulated them from the wider (Sunni) Moslem world, and the world beyond that. Lyell suggested that:

> "Cursed, as the country is, with the presence of the Holy Cities, it is foredoomed to stagnation unless there comes a speedy reform, either from without or within. The former would imply a civil administration of such power that the strength of the Mujtahidun could be shattered. A reform from within would imply a change of faith..." (*The Ins And Outs of Mesopotamia*, p.86.)

Lyell speculated on the conversion of the Shiah to Christianity to make them more amenable to progress but gave up the idea because the Shiah honoured Christ second to the Prophet Mohammed and it would be like asking them to exchange a subordinate for a superior.

So Wilson and his Officers believed that the only solution to the reactionary character of Shiah Islam was in a strong direct Imperial governing that would remake them for progress by interfering in their world of stagnant routine.

The Baghdad *vilayet*, in the centre of the country, had the greatest concentration of Sunnis. But they were only a majority in the city itself and in Samarra. There were also communities of Shiah (who were in the majority in the *vilayet*), about 20,000 Christians and 60,000 Jews (mostly in Baghdad). The Sunnis tended to look outwards to the greater Muslim world; they were more likely to be loyal subjects of the Ottoman State, and to constitute its local bureaucracy and law agencies. Sunni landlords helped govern the region, and the educated served as administrators and army officers in the Ottoman Army. Here, unlike in the south, there was a more developed Ottoman administration and the Turks had actually made some effort to collect taxes.

Wilson used the ex-Ottoman Officials to establish a workable administration in the Baghdad area. However, one of the Shiah Ulema of Karbala apparently commented:

> "When a man pulls down a public latrine because it smells too bad, it is a mistake to build the new one with the same bricks!" (*The Ins And Outs of Mesopotamia*, p.84.)

The remaining region of Mesopotamia, Mosul, in the north, was considered the most backward by Wilson and it was the most hostile to being placed within any kind of Arab construction. The chief group here, the Kurds, were Muslims. But they were not Semites like the Arabs. Wilson took them to have been descendants of the ancient Medes people, horse-riding kin of the Persians. That explained their yearning for independence, their pastoralist existence, and their relative poverty, Wilson thought. He saw them as being like the Afghans, divided into tribes and deeply resistant to any centralised authority, even to one operated within the Kurdish community itself. But on the whole, their reputation was not high. As Lyell observed:

"For general brutality and villainy we have to go to the Kurds... A more untrained savage it would be hard to find. The brutalities inflicted on our soldiers after the surrender of the Kut garrison were committed by Kurds. Most of the Armenian massacres were carried out by the Kurds, at the instigation of the Turk. The latter know that murder, loot, and rape are the natural activities of these gentry... I would wish to make clear that where, in this book, I refer to the Moslem, I do not include the Kurd, although that is his official religion. He is beyond the Pale. There let us leave him." (*The Ins And Outs of Mesopotamia*, pp.107-8.)

On 25th March 1919, a debate took place in Parliament initiated by Asquith in which the former Prime Minister argued that, in the interests of economy, the British Empire in Mesopotamia should confine its commitments to Basra. The serving Prime Minister, Lloyd George, replied:

"I cannot understand withdrawing from the more important and more promising part of Mesopotamia. Mosul is a country with great possibilities. It has rich oil deposits... It contains some of the richest natural resources of any country in the world... What would happen if we withdrew? ... If we did not undertake the task probably some other country would, and unless some country were to undertake the task, Mesopotamia would be exactly where she is today, or probably much worse. After the enormous expenditure which we have incurred in freeing this country from the withering despotism of the Turk, to hand it back to anarchy and confusion, and to take no responsibility for its development would be an act of folly and quite indefensible." (*Freeman's Journal*, 26 March 1919.)

The Kurd in Mosul could not be left 'beyond the Pale', because he lived above some large deposits of oil. And yet the Kurdish majority, who did not, were left under 'the withering despotism of the Turk' without a worry.

*The Times* of March 27th, 1920 made this comment on Lloyd George's plans for Mesopotamia:

"The Prime Minister made statements about the future of Mesopotamia which require further elucidation. He said that when the Treaty of Peace with Turkey has been finally decided, the British Government would 'claim the right' to be the 'mandatory Power' for Mesopotamia, including the vilayet of Mosul... Judging from some passages in his speech, even Mr. Lloyd George himself has never grasped the full and dangerous significance of the adventure he now advocates...

The Prime Minister's reply conveyed the impression that he has only the very haziest idea about what he proposes to do in this region, which has been the grave of empires ever since written history began... Mr. Asquith says — and he is entirely right — that if we hold a line in the mountains of Northern Kurdistan we shall sooner or later be driven to advance to the shores of the Black Sea, or even to the Caspian. His view is in complete accord with every lesson to be derived from our history as an Empire. We have never drawn one of these vague, unsatisfactory frontiers without being eventually compelled to move beyond it. We cannot incur such a risk in the Middle East, and the cost in money and the strain upon our troops are alike prohibitive factors."

The British Empire had desires that were beyond its means in 1920. And apparently everyone realised that, however deep-seated and ingrained these dangerous impulses were, it was better not to be led into temptation. But temptation is highly irresistible.

### The Problem of Promises And Allies

The Sykes-Picot Agreement had assigned the Mosul *vilayet* of the Ottoman Empire to France but in December 1918 the French, in return for a free hand in Syria and a cut of oil reserves in the area, yielded Mosul to Britain to go along with Basra and Baghdad in making up 'Irak' or Iraq.

General Maude's speech in Baghdad had implied the establishment of a great Arab State stretching from Syria to Arabia (with Hussein of Mecca in charge). And in truth this Arab State (perhaps excluding the Saudi region) would have been the second best option, after the retention of the loose Ottoman structures, for social and political development in the area. It would have preserved the great diversity of the area with the minimal amount of friction between the elements living side-by-side within it.

Arnold Wilson's colonial administration, which originally aimed at a simple absorption of Mesopotamia, at least had the benefit of letting things be to a considerable extent in the task of gradual improvement.

But Britain now decided to go for the worst of all solutions, balkanising the Middle East and cobbling together two and three-quarter *vilayets* of the Ottoman Empire (Baghdad, Mosul and most of Basra) to make up a new nation-state of Iraq.

Although the peoples of these *vilayets* had lived side by side in relative peace within the large Ottoman entity, there was no sense of unity amongst the Sunni, Shiah and Kurdish inhabitants and they were now simply to be combined in the strategic interest of Britain.

Wilson later explained in *Mesopotamia: A Lecture,* given in 1920, how the Sunni, Shia, Christians, Arabs and Kurds were effectively incorporated into the loose Ottoman structures but were very unsuitable material for combining in a national State:

"All these discordant and irreconcilable elements were loosely governed and prevented from falling into more serious and extensive forms of anarchy by the Turks—an alien government but Islamic in structure and tradition, with the prestige and authority of 200 years behind it in Mesopotamia, and a continuous military record in Asia of much greater antiquity... It was a bad government from many points of view... but my belief is that were a plebiscite to be taken to-day in Iraq on the issue of Turkish v. Arab Government there would be a large majority in favour of the return of the Turk... Arab national feeling exists, but not yet as a unifying factor."

Wilson was appalled at the idea of constructing a nation-state out of these elements. He believed that this was a most unstable unit for development and such a State was just not viable. He explained in his Lecture:

"The population is so deeply divided by racial and religious cleavages and the Shiah majority after two hundred years of Sunni domination are so little accustomed to holding high office that any attempt to introduce institutions on the lines desired by the advanced politicians would involve the concentration of power in the hands of a few."

When the British occupation spread across Mesopotamia to the *vilayets* of Baghdad and then on to Mosul Wilson accepted that these should be incorporated into the British Empire—particularly with the oil resources found to be available in Mosul. But Wilson, whilst he maintained an opposition to an Arab State, also believed that Mesopotamia could not be made into a nation-state. He explained why in the *Preface* to his second book on Iraq, *Mesopotamia 1917-1920 A Clash Of Loyalties*:

"The conception of Arabia as an independent entity was not unfamiliar to the educated minority, but the idea of Iraq as an independent nation had scarcely taken shape, for the country lacked homogeneity, whether geographical, economic, or racial. Separatist tendencies were strong in Basra; it was scarcely to be hoped that the wilayets of Basra and Baghdad would maintain their existence as an autonomous state without the revenue it was hoped might eventually be derived from the economic resources of the Mosul wilayet. Yet three-quarters of the inhabitants of the Mosul wilayet were non-Arab, five-eighths being Kurdish, and one-eighth Christians or Yazidis. The Kurdish problem proved insoluble. The tribesmen were disunited and intractable; their leaders had no common policy, and agreed only in their opposition to any form of government which would bring them under Arab domination... The simpler Arabs of the Basra and Baghdad wilayets were under the influence of the priesthood of Najaf and Karbala—spiritual tyrants whose principal ambition was to stem the rising tide of emancipation." (pp. x-xi.)

The problem was that the British Government, in getting involved in so many messy entanglements with Allies, merely to just about hold its own in the War, had made so many conflicting promises, that sorting out all the payoffs was taking time, and this was building up great pressure in the conquered Ottoman territories:

"It was impossible seriously to consider the terms of peace with Turkey until our account with Germany was settled... Turkey was for the moment defenceless, beaten to her knees. The whole burden of the campaign against Turkey in the Dardanelles, in Syria, in Iraq, and in Persia, had been borne by the British and Indian forces. Yet our Italian and Greek allies, with shrill and discordant voices that brooked no refusal, demanded territorial compensations that would have reduced Turkey to a State little larger than pre-war Serbia. The French demanded the fulfilment of the Sykes-Picot Agreement. The Arabs, represented by their self-constituted champion, King Husain, having obtained, with British assistance, the temporary governance of Syria, talked of a federated Arabia. Ibn Sa'ud, whose star was just beginning to arise, abode in his breaches like Asher, awaiting the moment when he, too, should make good in his own way his claim to be heard. The Kurdish tribes across the frontier, in Turkey, had been given to understand, by the Allies, through their representatives in Constantinople, that they, too, were to determine their future government and would be given their independence." (pp. 140-1.)

As pressure began to build up on Wilson from the Arabs, who felt they were about to be cheated of the various things they had been led to believe they would get, he moved to a position of gradual devolution of power, through legislative councils, but still under British executive control. But he was not allowed to publish his proposals.

### The Anglo-French Declaration

On 8th November 1918, a Declaration issued by the Allied Supreme Council arrived in Baghdad seemingly signalling the intention of establishing nation-states in the region. The Declaration began with the assertion:

"The end which France and Great Britain have in view in their prosecution in the East of the war... is the complete and definite liberation of the peoples so long oppressed by the Turks and the establishment of national governments and administrations drawing their authority from the initiative and free choice of indigenous populations..." (*Mesopotamia 1917-1920 A Clash Of Loyalties*, p. 102.)

Thomas Lyell was a member of Arnold Wilson's staff in the administration when the Declaration arrived and he remembered his reaction:

"I was the first person to read the document with its startling order for immediate publication. I cannot believe that it was originally intended as anything more than sentimental eyewash, an appeal to a Europe revelling in the emotional reaction produced by the war...

It has been recorded that, at the Versailles Peace Conference, the possibility of self-government for Mesopotamia was discussed. Three very high politicians from Whitehall are said to have made the following remarks:

1st Politician. 'I fear that the country may be badly governed.'
2nd Politician. 'The country will be badly governed.'
3rd Politician. 'The country ought to be badly governed.'

This bears out my contention that our *beaux sabreurs* were perfectly well aware of what self-government in Mesopotamia must produce.

It is, in my opinion, a truism that the British Empire has never taken any 'interest' in a country from motives of 'pure philanthropy.' Why, indeed, should it? The Empire is a business concern first and foremost, and, by this standard it has fully justified itself in whatever parts of the world it has absorbed. But the benefit has always been mutual... For the first time in our history we appear to be acting the part, not only of philanthropists, but of philanthropists full of folly." (*The Ins And Outs of Mesopotamia*, pp. 158-9.)

The Declaration was a bombshell to the British administrators in Baghdad. Arnold Wilson telegraphed the India Office in response to a request for information as to how the Declaration might affect Mesopotamia:

"I should not be doing my duty if I did not first of all record my conviction that the Anglo-French Declaration of November 8, in so far as it refers to Mesopotamia, bids fair to involve us in difficulties as great as Sir Henry MacMahon's early assurances to the Sharif of Mecca... The Declaration involves us here on the spot in diplomatic insincerities which we have hitherto successfully avoided and places a potent weapon in the hands of those least fitted to control a nation's destinies.

I would emphasize the almost entire absence of political, racial or other connexion between Mesopotamia and the rest of Arabia... The Arabs of Mesopotamia will not tolerate that foreign Arabs should have any say in their affairs, whether those Arabs come from Syria or from the Hijaz. In practice they dislike and distrust both. National unity means for them unity of Mesopotamia, and not unity with either Syria or Hijaz...

The average Arab, as opposed to the handful of amateur politicians of Baghdad, sees the future as one of fair dealing and material and moral progress under the aegis of Great Britain, and is clear-sighted enough to realise that he would lose rather than gain in national unity if we were to relinquish effective control...

I can confidently declare that the country as a whole neither expects nor desires any such sweeping scheme of independence as is adumbrated, if not clearly denoted, in the Anglo-French Declaration...

The world at large recognizes that it is our duty and our high privilege to establish an effective protectorate and to introduce a form of government which shall make possible the development of this country..." (*Mesopotamia 1917-1920 A Clash Of Loyalties,* pp. 104-5.)

Truth had become very problematic for the British Empire by this time. Wilson was aware of the false promises made to the Arabs to secure their services against the Ottoman Empire. He saw them as false promises because he had the traditional Imperialist understanding of Britain's mission in the world and that mission did not include expending blood and treasure on the conquering of territory just to give it away to races unfit for government. So he knew that some kind of insincerity was going to be involved in his dealings with the Mesopotamian Arabs and did not like the idea.

Wilson also saw a number of dangerous implications of the Declaration for the region—if it was taken literally by the subject peoples:

> "The promise that indigenous populations should exercise the right of self-determination regarding the form of national government under which they should live was considered, not unnaturally, to imply that they should also be free to choose whether they desired France or Great Britain to be the mandatory power, or whether they wished their freedom to be limited by any sort of mandate... The pronouncement was, moreover, incompatible with the Balfour Declaration of November 1917 regarding a National Home in Palestine for Jews.
>
> Its promulgation was a disastrous error, the perpetration of which was forced upon the Allied Powers by President Wilson: it encouraged aspirations amongst Armenians and Assyrians, Chaldean and Syrian Christians, which neither the Allies nor the United States did anything to further, nor did these Powers do anything in later years to mitigate the penalty which the Armenians suffered as a result of their confidence in Christendom and in the U.S.A. Well might they say of the latter, with Byron—'I trust not for freedom to the Franks, they have a King who buys and sells." (*Mesopotamia 1917-1920 A Clash Of Loyalties,* p. 103.)

Wilson was correct in saying that the Balfour Declaration was, in the first place, wholly inconsistent with the Anglo-French Declaration of November 1918. If the Declaration of November 1918 meant anything, it meant handing over Palestine to the Arabs, and it was highly unlikely that they would consent to the establishment of a Jewish State in their midst. In fact, British power would have to be used against the actual inhabitants while a Jewish population was brought in and built up in order to form a government. And that was a complete negation of all the Declarations for self-determination.

Wilson was also concerned that the Declaration would encourage minorities within the remains of the Ottoman Empire to rise up and demand self-determination. These uprisings, encouraged by the Allied Declaration, would be unlikely to secure aid from the Allies and would result in disaster for the peoples concerned.

Wilson was assured by London that the Declaration was meant for Syria rather than Mesopotamia, to alleviate Arab suspicions of the French. But he was also informed that the annexation of Mesopotamia was, at that point, off the agenda of the British Government. London stated that no formal Declaration would be made of establishing a Protectorate but it was envisaged that the country would be governed as Egypt was between 1882 and 1914—which might be described as informal Protectorate (before it became a Protectorate at the Declaration of War). Iraq would be ruled under a British High Commissioner, with Arab Ministers 'informed' by British advisors, but with no Arab Head of State.

Discussions went on during 1919 and early 1920 at State level about the different merits of annexation, Protectorate and informal Protectorate. The trend was away from the Imperial governing of the past, but it was not until after the insurgency of summer 1920 that the Empire ultimately changed course.

### An Iraqi View of England in Mesopotamia

In an *Annex* to *A Clash Of Loyalties* Arnold Wilson has an account of Gertrude Bell's visit on 6th February 1919 to the Naqib of Baghdad. This was in the period when there was great uncertainty as to Britain's intentions in Mesopotamia and talk of Mandates, or some form of indirect rule, was in the air.

For years before the British occupation Gertrude Bell had journeyed across the region, as she recounted in her 1907 travel book, *The Desert and the Sown*. She used her position as a rich foreign woman to secure the hospitality of the Arabs, and she knew the tribes and their elders, the religious hierarchies, and geography of Mesopotamia, Syria and Arabia well. Having secured employment in the occupation bureaucracy in Mesopotamia, she had gradually become an 'Arabist' and an opponent of Wilson. But she found the Naqib to be a supporter of Wilson's traditional Imperialist view—to the victor, the spoils. This is what he told her (The Turkish word *Khatun* roughly means 'noble woman'):

> "The English have conquered this country, they have expended their wealth and they have watered the soil with their blood... Shall they not enjoy what they have won? Other conquerors have overwhelmed the country. As it fell to them so it has fell to the English. They will establish their dominion. Khatun, your nation is great, wealthy and powerful: where is our power? If I say I wish for the rule of the English and the English do not consent to govern us, how can I force them? And if I wish for the rule of another, and the English resolve to remain, how can I eject them? I recognize your victory. You are the governors and I am the governed. And when I am asked what is my opinion as to the continuance of British rule, I reply that I am the subject of the victor. You, Khatun... have an understanding of statecraft. I do not hesitate to say to you that I loved the Turkish government when it was as I once knew it. If I could return to the rule of the Sultans of Turkey as they were in former times, I should make no other choice... The Turk is dead; he has vanished, and I am content to become your subject." (p. 338.)

The Naqib, in his conversation with Bell, then turned to the subject of the new notion of self-determination:

> "What is all this talk... and what is its value? I trace it to America and I hear

the voice of (President) Wilson. Does Shaikh Wilson know the East and its peoples? Does he know our ways of life and our habits of mind? You English have governed for 300 years in Asia and your rule is an example for all men to follow. Pursue your own way. Do not submit to guidance from Shaikh Wilson. Knowledge and experience are your guides." (p. 339.)

The Naqib may, or may not, have been representative of opinion in Baghdad or Mesopotamia. As Arnold Wilson said, in a country with so many disparate elements, opinion was very hard to gauge. But what the Naqib was surely correct about was England's 'dog in a manger' attitude to governing the country. The Arabs expected the British, particularly with their long history of conquest and governing in Asia, to exercise purposeful government, like the Ottomans. They probably expected the British to stay indefinitely, until someone emerged who had the power to eject them. But what turned up was most unexpected. Whilst Britain did not seem to have the will to govern purposefully the peoples the Ottomans had successfully administered, and who the British Army had now conquered, they continued to occupy their country, preventing any other form of functional authority from emerging, from within or without.

### Govern Or Evacuate

Arnold Wilson and Gertrude Bell were called to Versailles to address the Peace Conference at the Hotel Majestic. Arnold Toynbee remembered meeting them and, in a review of Wilson's Mesopotamia books for the Royal Institute of International Affairs, he recorded his memories:

"They brought a breath of fresh air into the place; for these were people who, by a rare exception, had come through the War without having lost the pre-War state of mind. Iraq had been perhaps the only country involved in the War where the work of destruction had been overshadowed by the arts of peace. Here, behind a military front, successive provinces of a derelict empire had been taken in hand and set on their feet. The English people who had been doing this work in Iraq during the War came to the Peace Conference under the impetus of it. They were full of confidence and drive. They presumed that the constructive work that they had in hand would be preserved and carried forward. They were soon undeceived." (*International Affairs*, September 1931, p.708.)

On the 28th June 1919 the Treaty of Versailles was signed. Article 22, which set up the League of Nations, included a clause dealing with territories that had been taken from the defeated countries

"which are inhabited by peoples not yet able to stand by themselves under the strenuous conditions of the modern world."

To these people,

"there should be applied the principle that the well-being and development of such peoples form a sacred trust of civilization and that securities for the performance of this trust should be embodied in this covenant."

This civilizing process, Article 22 declared,

> "should be entrusted to advanced nations who by reason of their resources, their experience or their geographical position can best undertake this responsibility and who are willing to accept it, and that this tutelage should be exercised by them as Mandatories on behalf of the League."

So the peoples of the world who had borne no responsibility for the Great War, who had been innocent victims of the conflict, and who had only wished to be spared its devastations, were to be placed under the civilizing hand of those who had been responsible for the killing of tens of millions and the destruction of Europe and the East over the previous five years.

On 1st May 1920 England 'accepted,' at the San Remo Conference, the Mandate for Mesopotamia. A concerned Arnold Wilson made the following assessment of the suitability of the Mandate system for Mesopotamia:

> "The application in Arab countries of the mandatory principle seemed to me to be inconsistent with the interests of the inhabitants of the territories to which it was applied. If the system was merely a subterfuge to enable the supervising Power to exercise dominion… in substance without the form, and so to pander to the misconceptions of President Wilson, it was unworthy and did not deserve to endure. If, on the other hand, it was intended to be a reality, it was unworkable, for it contained within itself the seeds of decay and dissolution. There was no 'competent authority' to exercise ultimate power: it was the worst kind of diarchy… The very foundations of such organized life as existed in Iraq had been shaken by four years of war. The first principle to be re-established in men's minds was that of authority. It was difficult to envisage this under the mandatory system.
>
> It was clear that the acceptance of the Mandate, as framed, would be followed almost immediately by a demand for complete and unfettered freedom from any form of tutelage, for which I believed Iraq to be unfitted, owing not only to lack of competent administrators or to the absence of national feeling, but also on the broadest economic grounds. Its geographical situation, its long history of decay, the low repute of its principal products in the world's markets, all pointed to the benefits to be derived from close association with a larger and more advanced unit of government." (*Mesopotamia 1917-1920 A Clash Of Loyalties,* p. xi-xii.)

Wilson saw the Mandate system as either a despicable con-trick on the Arabs or a pandering to hopeless idealism at the expense of a people's welfare by those with the duty of care. The cardinal principle of Imperialism was that government should rest with those with the power and ability to govern and not be based on religion, race or nationality. There lay chaos.

Appalled at what he saw as the dereliction of duty that the Empire was now engaging in Wilson told the Secretary of State for India on June 9th 1920 that they should either govern or evacuate Mesopotamia:

> "Having set our hand to the task of regenerating Mesopotamia, we must be prepared to furnish alike men and money to maintain continuity of control for years to come. We must be prepared, regardless of the League of Nations, to go very slowly with constitutional or democratic institutions, the application of which to Eastern countries has been attempted of late years with such little degree of success.... If His Majesty's Government regard such a policy as impracticable or beyond our strength (as well they may) I submit that they would do better to face the alternative, formidable and from the local point of view, terrible as it is, and evacuate Mesopotamia." (*Mesopotamia 1917-1920 A Clash Of Loyalties,* p. 270.)

Wilson put his reasoning behind this view at the end of the *Preface* to his second book on Mesopotamia:

> "As Sir Henry Maine remarked with reference to India: 'the British Nation cannot evade the duty of rebuilding upon its own principles that which it unwittingly destroys.'" (*Mesopotamia 1917-1920 A Clash Of Loyalties,* p. xiv.)

Wilson also urged a reconciliation with Turkey and a recognition of its territorial integrity from Constantinople to the Caucasus, arguing that if England did not have the power, or will, to take the region in hand and give it stable government, then the Turks should be allowed to do so. (*Mesopotamia 1917-1920 A Clash Of Loyalties,* p. 239.)

### Insurgency in Iraq, 1920

*The Irish News* reported the outbreak of the Mesopotamian insurgency in its editorial *Wars, Actual and Potential,* of August 6th :

> "'Dissatisfaction' was spreading North of Baghdad, and a 'small British column' was sent out to arrest the spread of that most condemnable feeling, or sentiment, which follows upon the advent of British troops armed with cannons, tanks, and machine guns amongst rude and ungrateful populations who believe they are entitled to live their own free lives as God ordained, not as the owners of the armaments desire... The British War Minister in the House of Commons announced that 366 individual members of the column... were killed, wounded or 'missing.'... It is to be feared the 'missing' officers and soldiers—281 in number—have perished for the most part. Mr. Winston Churchill, the war maker, could only hope that the worst had not happened. These casualties were severe and resulted from a serious battle. The Arabs of Mesopotamia and Syria are natural-born fighters. England and France must slaughter them in tens of thousands before a War Minister in London or Paris can boast that 'disaffection' has been dissipated by shells and bullets... in fulfilment of the historic Westminster pledge that the 'rights and liberties of small nations' shall be restored and respected."

From July to October 1920 Britain was involved in a war in Mesopotamia.

Ex-officers of the Great War began volunteering for policing duty, as they did in Ireland in the shape of the Black and Tans.

Major General Sir Frederick Maurice explained to the London *Daily News*:

"We are in for a long and costly bout of guerrilla warfare in a country with a damnable climate against an enemy who has no capital to be occupied and no main body to be routed.

It is pitiful that we should have to call the Allies, to protect whom we accepted a mandate from the League of Nations, enemies, but it is no use blinking at the facts. The Arabs of Mesopotamia have become our enemies, and, willy-nilly, we have now to treat them as such. We cannot withdraw now without endangering interests which extend far beyond Mesopotamia.

In the East it pays to make concessions when they are obviously not induced by fear. To retire before trouble is to induce an avalanche. It is for this very reason that all wise men have deprecated the extent of our commitments in Mesopotamia. Now we have to see a most unpleasant business through and to convince the Arab with bombs and shells that we are his friends." (August 23rd 1920.)

The maintenance of prestige was always an important consideration in Imperial governing, particularly in the East, where the Oriental had to be continually shown the superiority of the white man. And there could be no backing down to a challenge—for there lay ruin. Even if the long term intention made the issue an irrelevancy, it was always a good idea to give the natives a damn good hiding so that they would know their place in the future. And that is what Britain proceeded to do in Mesopotamia in the summer of 1920.

Politicians, and even military men, do not speak so candidly about their work today. But the bombing and shelling of people to convince them of Britain's friendship was no contradiction in Imperial affairs in those days. It was tried and tested in South Africa between 1899-1902 when England invaded the Transvaal, killed tens of thousands of Afrikaan civilians in concentration camps and then turned the Boers into 'fast friends'. So much so that they tried to repeat with Redmond, and then Collins, in Ireland, the exercise which they had completed in South Africa with Botha and Smuts. But, whilst things seemed to work out for the best for the Empire before 1914, they all started to go wrong after the Great War. It was as if Midas had lost his golden touch.

When the 'liberated' people in the new State of Iraq realised that their 'liberators' were the new oppressors, who were intent on cheating them of their declared dues, they became increasingly discontent and went into revolt.

From the summer of 1919, the Sunni and Shiah started to come together in response to the situation they found themselves in. Arnold Wilson had tried to prevent this. The British assaults on Persia, and their efforts to make it into a British Protectorate, had antagonised particularly the Shiah population around Karbala and Najaf. With the relinquishing by the Bolsheviks of the Russian claims in Persia, the British had seen a vacuum and sent forces from

Mesopotamia to establish control in the former Russian zone. The Shiah of the Basra *vilayet,* bound to Persia by close ties of religion and kin, were suspicious of British aims, and alarmed at their incursions.

The Sunni Moslems' discontent was due to events both in Baghdad and in the wider Arab world. And, in the month of Ramadhan, Sunni and Shiah began to visit each other's Mosques to honour the birth of the Prophet and other Moslem saints. Wilson then knew there was trouble ahead.

Here is how Lyell explained it:

> "Sir Arnold Wilson was in a most intolerable position. The Anglo-French Declaration had inspired the leaders of the people with hopes far beyond their wildest dreams. They had been further encouraged by the inquiry [The American King-Crane Commission. P.W.] into their own ideas of what government they desired. And then nothing happened, for the Civil Commissioner was not yet permitted to make that definite announcement of future policy which would have worked wonders and saved many lives.
>
> The idea grew that to inquire, or consult them, did not pledge us to any consideration of their opinions. They were to be baulked of their glorious future. Then came the expulsion of Feisal from Syria by our allies and, presumably with our consent, if not approval. It was now clear that, having obtained all we could from Mecca, we were ready deliberately to break faith with Hussein. There was no further hope for the future of Mesopotamia.
>
> Out with the British tyrants. The revolution burst upon us..." (*The Ins And Outs of Mesopotamia*, pp. 167.)

### *A Lesson in Air Control*

According to General Sir Aylmer Haldane, 70,000 soldiers were sent out to destroy the insurgents and 'pacify' the civilian population. Haldane had been brought out of semi-retirement to command the British Indian Army in 1919 and wrote a book about it later. In it he described what he thought of the character of the insurrectionists and the Iraqis in general:

> "The tribes of Iraq, although generally speaking, they may be described as eager, fierce and impetuous, are not given to showing fanatical instincts when they are likely to come into contact with a power or strength superior to their own... The settled Arab of Mesopotamia has no fanciful notions as to dying the death of a hero, such as are associated with the Ghazi of Afghanistan or the Arab of the Sudan. The mainstream of his actions comes from... the hope of getting plunder, more especially if it can be easily obtained with a minimum of risk to life or limb." (*The Insurrection in Mesopotamia, 1920,* p.27.)

With such character, the people of Mesopotamia should have been easily governable by Britain and the insurrection should not have amounted to very much. But it lasted over three months and left at least 10,000 dead or wounded.

The British counter-insurgency operation proved costly in terms of men and money. According to a 1994 account this led to an innovation in Imperial policing:

"Winston Churchill, as Colonial Secretary, was sensitive to the cost of policing the Empire; and was in consequence keen to exploit the potential of modern technology. This strategy had particular relevance to operations in Iraq. On 19 February, 1920, before the start of the Arab uprising, Churchill (then Secretary for War and Air) wrote to Sir Hugh Trenchard, the pioneer of air warfare. Would it be possible for Trenchard to take control of Iraq? This would entail the provision of some kind of asphyxiating bombs calculated to cause disablement of some kind but not death... for use in preliminary operations against turbulent tribes.

Churchill was in no doubt that gas could be profitably employed against the Kurds and Iraqis (as well as against other peoples in the Empire): 'I do not understand this squeamishness about the use of gas. I am strongly in favour of using poison gas against uncivilised tribes.' Henry Wilson shared Churchill's enthusiasm for gas as an instrument of colonial control but the British cabinet was reluctant to sanction the use of a weapon that had caused such misery and revulsion in the First World War. Churchill himself was keen to argue that gas, fired from ground-based guns or dropped from aircraft, would cause 'only discomfort or illness, but not death' to dissident tribes people; but his optimistic view of the effects of gas were mistaken. It was likely that the suggested gas would permanently damage eyesight and 'kill children and sickly persons, more especially as the people against whom we intend to use it have no medical knowledge with which to supply antidotes.'

Churchill remained unimpressed by such considerations, arguing that the use of gas, a 'scientific expedient,' should not be prevented 'by the prejudices of those who do not think clearly.' In the event, gas was used against the Iraqi rebels with 'excellent moral effect' though gas shells were not dropped from aircraft because of practical difficulties." (Geoff Simons, *Iraq: From Sumer to Saddam*, pp. 179-181.)

Britain had introduced chemical warfare into the Middle East, in the shape of mustard gas, during the Battle of Gaza in 1917. And the effectiveness of air power in the region, where there was little cover and villages were densely populated, became apparent to the Royal Flying Corps in the battles North of Jerusalem during early 1918.

Sir Arthur 'bomber' Harris—of Dresden and Hamburg fame—in his book *Bomber Offensive*, written in 1947, recounted what happened in Iraq in 1922 when the Air Ministry took over the defence of the new client-kingdom.'Bomber' Harris learnt his craft in Mesopotamia and later described the process of policing by bombers, or, as it was known,'*air control*':

"When I got to Irak, or Mespot as we called it, in those days, Sir John Salmond had just taken over the air control of the country and most of the very large army forces which the British taxpayer refused any longer to support there had departed. A rebellion had broken out in 1920, because the Arabs there had been led to expect complete independence and had got instead British army occupation... The military control of Irak was transferred to the RAF entirely in order to save money... the decision to hand control of the country to the RAF—which was of course Winston Churchill's—was made in 1921 and took effect on 1 October, 1922...

The truculent and warlike tribes which occupied, and still largely controlled after the rebellion, large parts of Irak... had to be quelled, and in this our heavy bombers played a large part. We were hundreds of miles up river near Baghdad and in the centre of thoroughly turbulent and wholly unpacified tribes on whom we were endeavouring to impose government of local Baghdad Effendis whom the tribesmen have naturally held in utter contempt for time immemorial. When a tribe started open revolt we gave warning to all its most important villages by loudspeaker from low flying aircraft, and by dropping messages that air action would be taken after 48 hours. Then, if the rebellion continued, we destroyed the villages and by air patrols kept the insurgents away from their homes for as long as necessary until they decided to give up, which they invariably did." (p.21-2.)

After one bombing raid on Iraq in 1924, Harris wrote:

"they now know what real bombing means, in casualties and damage; they now know that within 45 minutes a full-sized village can be practically wiped out and a third of its inhabitants killed or injured by four or five machines which offer them no real target, no opportunity for glory as warriors, no effective means of escape."

(This quote is from a 1990 book by David Omissi, *Air Power and Colonial Control: The Royal Air Force 1919-1939,* which is an important source of information on the origins of terror bombing.)

In Iraq, in the 1920s, the RAF flew most of its missions against the Kurds—who have always resented rule from Baghdad. For ten years the RAF waged an almost continuous bombing campaign in the oil-rich, mountainous northeast region of Iraq against these people, to whom Britain had earlier promised autonomy. The Iraqi Air Force—which the British established, built up, trained and equipped—carried on this work from Baghdad after the Iraqi client state became nominally independent in 1932.

Arnold Wilson later condemned the air control used in Mesopotamia to attack 'undefended places' in an address to the Grotius Society in 1932, explaining why it was a poor substitute for government of the traditional variety:

"To attack such a place by dropping bombs by aeroplanes is clearly a breach of International Law... There is no subject better calculated to test the wisdom of the Army Commander and strain the conscience of civil administrators than the question of bombarding places inhabited wholly or mainly by non-combatants, even though they may have been warned (perhaps in mid-winter) to leave the place and fly to the neighbouring hills or fields. Yet in this matter

His Majesty's Government has, of recent years, set the pace, and created a new set of usages of war by using the Royal Air Force, in support of the Civil Power, to suppress disturbances which are often primarily, if not solely, 'political' in origin. There is no doubt whatever that the bombing of towns and villages is accompanied by little danger to the airmen; that it is cheap, spectacular and temporarily effective. My own view is that it is not, in the long run, effective, and that it is contrary both to The Hague Convention, to the usages of war as laid down in The Manual of Military Law, and to the larger interests of this country and of humanity at large. The ineradicable defect of action by air is that even though warning be given, the onslaught is sudden, the damage indiscriminate; there is no locus penitential and no chance of a friendly parley under a flag of truce and timely surrender after a few shots. To allow a belligerent to employ any measure at his own will because it is likely to abbreviate fighting is to set back the clock of International Law." (*The Laws of War In Occupied Territories*, pp. 27-8.)

But the use of 'Air Control' became too attractive and cheap an alternative for the government of the Empire's subjects, with detrimental effects for both the governing and governed. Previously, the hands-on style of the Indian Political Service had created a useful relationship with local elites and some of the general populace but the expedient of policing or governing from the air placed a distance between rulers and ruled:

"Perhaps the most serious long-term consequence of the ready availability of air control was that it developed into a substitute for administration. Several incidents during the Mandate period indicate that the speed and simplicity of air attack was preferred to the more time-consuming and painstaking investigation of grievances and disputes. With such powers at its disposal the Iraq Government was not encouraged to develop less violent methods of extending its control over the country." (Peter Sluglett, *Iraq Under British Occupation*, pp. 268-9.)

Whatever might be said about the former Imperialism, it certainly confronted the Imperial subject with a more beneficial face than the latter version, which confronted the ruled impersonally with only bombs and machine-guns from the skies. The blueprint for the American and British bombing strategy of the late 20th-early 21st century against Iraq, Serbia, Somalia, Afghanistan and Iraq (again) was developed by Britain as soon as she saw the possibilities of the aeroplane as a weapon of war. And as Wilson noted 'His Majesty's Government... set the pace, and created a new set of usages of war'.

Britain displays great continuity in its military affairs, across land, sea and air. As the fields of conflict extended to different spheres, Britain maintained the same principles of warfare. It applied the logic of the methods of the Boer War concentration camps and of the Great War naval blockade of Germany to Iraq, by destroying the women and children of the fighting men in order to defeat the combatants.

The British State was unique in 1920 in having an independent air force and air ministry. In other countries, air forces were arms of the navy or army and designed to support and complement military operations against enemy military forces on the sea and land. But in setting up an independent air force and air ministry, Britain set out to make war against civilians its primary method of warfare, replacing the blockade. (Sir Samuel Hoare described this method as 'terrorism' in 1939, before it began to be employed by the R.A.F. to goad Hitler into attacking London). David Edgerton puts it like this in his *England And The Aeroplane—An Essay On A Militant And Technological Nation*:

> "The primary context for the study of the development of aviation is English grand strategy which ... cannot be understood in the usual schemes of political history... I see the basic strategy of the English state as one of relying on technology as a substitute for manpower, and using the technology to attack enemy civil populations and industry, rather than armies. I label this 'liberal militarism', a term I use as an aid to analysis, as an 'ideal type' of warfare." (p. xv.) ['ideal type' means pure type, or category, with no positive connotation.]

Liberalism is often mistakenly thought of as anti-militarist and anti-imperialist. But it has been shown, in the catastrophic wars it has been responsible for, to have the impulse of expansionist aggressiveness much more than conservativism has. Liberal militarism, according to Edgerton, was produced by combining Liberal Imperialism's desire for cheapness in the waging of war, funded by private business, with the Liberal understanding that war was fundamentally an extension of commerce. Or, in other words, war was only worth it for the purposes of extending British trade and seeing off commercial competitors.

It is no surprise then that the neo-conservatives in the U.S. administration who in recent years occupied Iraq on the cheap, using air-strikes 'to accomplish democracy', were liberals in orientation.

The bombing of civilian populations was originated and perfected by Britain in 'policing' operations on the frontiers of India-Afghanistan and Iraq in the inter-war years, in a kind of apprenticeship for things to come. In civilian bombing Britain led the world. It taught Mussolini a thing or two when he copied the British methods in Abyssinia in the mid-1930s, his air-force supplied with oil from the British possessions in the Middle-East by British companies — despite the League of Nations sanctions which the British were publicly supporting. And when, in the thirties, Hitler wanted to conclude limitation agreements on bombers, England turned down the deal because it wondered how it could police its Empire with a limited number of airplanes to drop bombs on natives who wouldn't pay their taxes.

Britain's lesson taught other, more recent, 'dictators' it had groomed — and then fallen out with. Saddam Hussein was not the first to use chemical weapons against the Iraqi population 'with excellent moral effect'.

During the inter-war period the British employed 'police bombing' elsewhere in the Empire: in the client state of Transjordan; against the Pathan tribesmen on the northwest frontier of India; in the Aden Protectorate (now southern Yemen); and against the Nuer pastoral farmers of the southern Sudan. Schemes of aerial 'policing' similar to that practised in Iraq/Mesopotamia were set up in the Palestine Mandate in 1922 and in the Aden Protectorate in 1928. Bombers were active at various times in policing British rule in Egypt and nomads in the Somali hinterland.

The Chief of the Air Staff, Sir Hugh Trenchard, had great ambitions for his bombers, according to Omissi. In a paper written early in 1920, when some politicians feared a social revolution in Britain, he suggested that the RAF could even be used to suppress 'industrial disturbances or risings' in Britain by bombing working class districts. Churchill, who had experience of suppressing industrial disputes himself with armed force, decided such a thing was impolitic to say and told Trenchard never to refer to his proposal again – at least not in writing.

The officers, like Arthur Harris, who thrived in their work and served their bombing apprenticeships against the Kurdish villages in Iraq furthered their careers and went on to greater things in Palestine and then Dresden and Hamburg.

### The Irish News And The Insurgency

The escalating conflict in Mesopotamia prompted *The Irish News* to pen the following editorial on what Britain was calling the 'little war' in *Mesopotamia*:

"It is not a 'little war' but a desperate struggle between an army of invaders and a people 'rightly struggling to be free' that is now raging in Mesopotamia... The people are nearly all Arabs—men in whose hearts the passion for freedom burns with traditional intensity... When British forces invaded Mesopotamia, in pursuance of the Allies campaign against Germany's Eastern ally, the late Sir Stanley Maude issued a famous 'Proclamation' to the people of Baghdad, announcing in high-blown and gorgeous Oriental phraseology that he and his troops had come as deliverers, and that Mesopotamia was to be freed forever from the Turkish yoke and constituted an independent State. The Mesopotamians believed Sir Stanley Maude; they helped him to complete the task of destroying Turkish power; they guided and fed his armies, and fought side by side with the 'deliverers.' The Turks were driven out; the British took possession of the country; and they proceeded to fasten on the people's necks a yoke of slavery more galling than that of the defeated Sultan... the English are slaughtering the Mesopotamian Arabs and these sons of the desert are hitting back so shrewdly that a war of serious dimensions is proceeding—and the fact cannot be hidden any longer. Point '9' of President Wilson's vanished

'14' Points provided that 'non-Turkish nationalities in the Ottoman Empire should be assured of autonomous development.' England and France publicly accepted this 'Point' amongst the others. No sooner was peace declared than the process of enslavement and spoliation were begun in Western Asia...

The history of the Western Alliance since the signing of the Armistice is a continuous chapter of shameless, blood-guilty 'breaches of faith.' All the lands between Mesopotamia and Ireland have been foully betrayed...

The stern resistance offered by Mesopotamia's 3,000,000 people to the invaders will probably concentrate attention on their struggle; until they have been crushed by the weight of numbers and by superior armaments. Hordes of Indians are being hurried from their own country to bring their Asiatic brethren to a condition of servitude alike unto their own... Human blood is shed in torrents that Mesopotamian oil may flow into British speculators' tanks..." (*The Irish News,* August 20 1920.)

This is a fundamental departure from the Redmondite Imperialism of the Great War. It is quite reminiscent of the anti-Imperialist position of Ireland during the Boer War. (And it is a far more radical position that one would ever see in *The Irish News* today.)

*The Irish News* retreated from Redmondite Imperialism when the 'war for small nations' began to be proved to be a con-trick, right across the world. It will never be known if the support for Imperialism might have continued if Britain had done right by Ireland and Redmond had become Prime Minister of a Home Rule Government. But there was just too much evidence about, by 1920, that millions had died for nothing (although that seems to be forgotten now).

Here is *The Irish News* editorial of 5th August, *Treachery's Harvest*, that should give food for thought to the present day celebrators of Ireland's common sacrifice in the Great War. Simply put, it blames Britain for the twentieth century:

"The cup of the English Coalition Government's iniquities is full to overflowing. Mr. Lloyd George and his colleagues were returned to power on false pretences by the excited and deluded British people in December 1918. During the brief intervening period the victors in that frenzied General Election have betrayed the vital principles on which the hopes of all nations were based after the war, flouted their own professions, made useless — and worse — the sacrifice of millions of human lives, and hustled the peoples of the world to the verge of ruin. Another month may see ruin irretrievably brought on Europe and Asia if the hands of those enemies of mankind are not stayed... From Ireland in the West to China in the East countless millions groan and tremble under the evils wrought by Great Britain's rulers under the inspiration of Sir Edward Carson. The 'Old World' is a unit in misery now. The same causes that produced 'pogroms' and riots... are directly responsible for chaos and confusion in Germany, for the greater part of the horrors that devastate Central Europe, for Poland's impending fate, for chaos in Egypt and India, for bloody strife in Syria and Mesopotamia, and for the train of events that are turning China and Japan into discontented and ambitious multitudes who may become a direful menace to Christianity and civilisation any day."

I don't suppose that *The Irish News* would have described it as *Our War* in 1920. To claim ownership or any degree of responsibility for such a catastrophe by those who were experiencing its effects would have been madness. But it shows how far Ireland has come since then.

Of course, it was not the malevolent influence of Lord Carson on the Coalition Government that started the rot. The rot had set in much earlier — in the period when the Home Rule Party had supported the Liberal Government that set the train of events in progress which resulted in the Great War. But this does not nullify the validity of the observations *The Irish News* made about the Coalition and its doings. It was just that the Devlinites were deluded about the nature of Britain, a delusion brought about by Home Rule promises, and not dispelled until those promises proved empty, at home.

To claim the Great War as *Our War* would have been extremely foolish. So in 1920 blame had to be pinned on others for it. Even Redmondites felt that way in those days.

### The Empire Changes Course

Having crushed the rising in Mesopotamia what was England to do with Iraq?

On 27th August 1920 *The Irish News* produced another editorial on Mesopotamia, called *Punic Faith:*

"The English Government have now discovered that they 'have never wavered from the policy of setting up an independent Arab State in Mesopotamia, with the advice and assistance of the Mandatory Power.' By way of preparing Mesopotamia — a region which is described as 'three cities and a waste of swamps and deserts, with oil wells in a corner' — for perfect independence, the Government 'occupied' the country with nearly 100,000 armed men, proceeded to establish a 'Civil Service' of Englishmen on a scale that might make Dublin Castle, Whitehall or Washington envious of Baghdad, took possession of the oil wells, brought English women and children into the habitable places with the obvious intention of 'settling them,' as the wives, sisters and children of English military officers and members of the C.S. administration are ensconced in Hindustan, and behaved exactly as conquerors act in a territory which they mean to hold until the end of time... Now Sir Percy Zachariah Cox, who had been roaming about as a soldier and 'political agent' in Eastern lands for many years, has been sent to Baghdad; his mission is 'to set up an independent State to be governed in accordance with the wishes of the people.'... Rightly or wrongly, the ancient Romans regarded the Carthagenians as never failing traitors to their pledges and promises: hence the phrase 'Punic faith.' The Mesopotamians will either be entrapped and subdued or exterminated. If Sir Percy Cox were the most immaculate and honest of all 'political agents' since the days of Abraham's Mesopotamian treaties, he would not deserve a moment's trust while he was associated with the present Prime Minister of England."

What *The Irish News* observed was the beginning of a sea-change in British policy in Mesopotamia. And it was prophetic in its warnings about trusting Sir Percy Cox.

Between the Armistice and the middle of 1920, there had been a long running struggle between the British Foreign Office and the India Office over what to do with Mesopotamia. The Foreign Office, which had been involved in the deal with Hussein, were strong supporters of rewarding the Hashemites with positions at the head of the new Arabs states Britain was constructing. This placed it against the India Office, which had a more traditionally Imperialist conception of what to do in the region; the India Office had been funding Ibn Saud, Hussein's rival in Arabia, and supported Arnold Wilson in Mesopotamia. The India Office always had its eye on India and did not like the disruptive effects it understood the Foreign Office's sponsoring of Hussein would have on the Moslems of the Indian Empire, with the treachery shown to the Caliph at Constantinople, the assaults on the Holy Cities and the pretence that Hussein could take over the Caliphate.

Ultimately this struggle was won by the Foreign Office, when the Cabinet decided to remove Wilson in June 1920 (although he was left in place, unaware of the decision, until September, when Cox was due back from Persia). But Lloyd George only finally resolved it in December by placing the Colonial Office, headed by Churchill, over both Mesopotamia and Palestine, and leaving the Foreign Office in control elsewhere in the Middle East.

The supporters of the Foreign Office and the Hashemites waged their campaign openly in the British Press. *The Times* and other leading opinion formers in England led the attacks against Arnold Wilson in the Summer of 1920, putting the responsibility for the insurgency and its cost on the 'extravagant administration of the Indianisers'.

That 'extravagant administration of the Indianisers' was made to appear as some kind of aberration in Imperial affairs by *The Times* when, in fact, it was very much the norm of a former world, cut off in its prime.

Here is an example from *The Times* Leader writer of 21st August:

"We are confronted by insurgence which extends from Mosul to within 150 miles of Basra… We are saddled with the task of reconquering Mesopotamia once more, and the ironical feature of the situation is that we are not now fighting Turks, but the very inhabitants whose welfare was declared to be 'a sacred trust of civilization.'

Order will eventually be restored, but only at a considerable sacrifice of life, at a cost which will upset Mr. Chamberlain's battered Budget, and still more, and with the prospect of consequences which may leave the people of Mesopotamia permanently hostile to any form of British control. The policy of the Government is demonstrated to be inherently wrong and extremely foolish. Immersed in the contemplation of problems elsewhere, the Cabinet allowed the British Administration in Mesopotamia to pursue unchecked a course that was bound to end in disaster. The controlling authorities in Baghdad, who do not appear to have been seriously amenable to anybody, were permitted to plan schemes of control absurdly in excess of local requirements, to create hundreds of lucrative posts for officers, mostly inexperienced in the task of 'civilizing' backward races, and to impose taxation which was too heavy for the people to bear."

*The Times* wanted Imperial control on the cheap. It did not want the Mesopotamians to be free of Britain and it was not an enthusiast for autonomy on the basis of 'national rights', despite all the War propaganda. Before the War, it had been one of the greatest opponents of Irish Home Rule. But now it realised that Britain could not afford its expanded Empire in the old way and a new policy, which would balance the books, was needed, with some moral gloss applied to it. *The Times* believed that whilst London had taken its eye off the ball the old policy—the default position—totally inappropriate to the new circumstances, had re-emerged.

*The Times* was joined by Colonel Lawrence, who had now assumed cult status in England, as 'Lawrence of Arabia', after Lowell Thomas's film show in Covent Garden during the winter of 1919-20. On August 8th Lawrence penned a sarcastic comment in *The Observer* over British military policy in Mesopotamia: 'It is odd that we do not use poison gas... Bombing the houses is a patchy way of getting the women and children.'

In a letter to *The Times* of August 22nd 1920, Colonel Lawrence, the by-now War celebrity figure, exclaimed:

"Our government is worse than the old Turkish system. They kept fourteen thousand local conscripts embodied, and killed a yearly average of two hundred Arabs in maintaining peace. We keep ninety thousand men, with aeroplanes, armoured cars, gunboats and armoured trains. We killed about ten thousand Arabs in this rising this summer. We cannot hope to maintain such an average: it is a poor country, sparsely peopled; but Abd el Hamid would applaud his masters, if he saw us working... How long will we permit millions of pounds, thousands of imperial troops, and tens of thousands of Arabs to be sacrificed on behalf of a form of colonial administration which can benefit nobody but its administrators?"

That question had never been asked in the past, when the Empire in its great civilizing mission had provided employment opportunities across the globe for the sons of the English Upper and Upper Middle-classes. In those pre-Great War days the Manchester Capitalists of earlier times, who thought

359

the Empire a mere financial balance sheet, were mocked by the New Imperialists, who saw it lasting a thousand years.

But now the Empire, its great civilizing mission, and the white man's burden, were all a liability to an exhausted, cash-strapped people in hock, up to their eyes, to the Americans.

## The Indian Empire Replies

On 8thJuly 1920 *The Times* published an editorial about *The Amritsar Debate* in the House of Commons. This debate was over the Hunter Commission's report into the killing of nearly 400 Indians by Brigadier-General Dyer's forces the previous year. Rebuking Dyer it noted that 'Events like those at Amritsar will obscure our national purpose and betray the ideals that inspire it.' And it stated clearly the change in Imperial ideals that had come over the governing of the Empire since the Great War:

> "The growth of the ideal of nationality, freed by the breaking of many ancient fetters, has not been confined to Europe; it has expanded swiftly over Asia... The newer conceptions of the rights of European peoples embrace also the subject races of our far possessions. For an Empire based on organized force or organized commerce the people of this country have substituted, in their own minds, the conception of a British Commonwealth founded on the willing cooperation of free peoples. That they have done so is, in our opinion, no small vindication of our national repute for genius in government. Nevertheless such an ideal, though it be the lodestone of true statesmanship, is not everywhere to be immediately achieved; and its consistent pursuit must necessarily spell many difficulties and involve many problems... Moreover the difficulties are all the greater because the rate of progress has been accelerated by the war... If we are to continue to hold India, we can only do so by the good will of the Indian peoples, secured by our own past record and sealed by our proved capacity to adjust our rule to the progress of the world."

How could 'subject peoples' of the Empire be free? By being freely subjected to the Empire, of course. And how could talk of holding the Empire be reconciled with the goodwill of subject peoples? Squaring that circle would presumably be the 'vindication of our national repute for genius in government'.

In 1924 'Al Carthill' wrote a very prophetic book about the Indian Empire called *The Lost Dominion*. 'Al Carthill' was Bennet Christian Kennedy (1871-1935), the senior Justice in the Bombay High Court. Carthill's book is a warning to the post-War administration in London not to depart from the traditional form of ruling the Indian Empire and Moslems by encouraging bogus notions of national rights and democracy amongst the natives, in the spirit of the propaganda that was used to win the Great War.

Carthill is very interesting because he reveals the traditional Imperial understanding that went into governing Moslems in the Empire. And, I think, this should be firmly borne in mind both in relation to propaganda about

Ottoman misrule and in understanding why England's actions after the Great War proved so destabilizing and disastrous for its own Empire and subjects.

What Carthill was particularly concerned with, after the Great War had run its course, was the export of ideas of democracy from Britain, where they had served a historically constructive purpose, to the East, where, he believed, they were both inappropriate and could only do enormous damage. He believed that there was a great danger of exporting English political culture, which had become infused with Liberal notions, to the East:

> "The culture was English — that is, it was permeated with Whig and Liberal ideas all very unfavourable to racial predominance, despotism and bureaucracy. Such a culture was easily convertible into a means of propaganda of vague humanitarian, atheistic, and subversive ideas, masquerading under the form of democracy and self-determination." (pp.159-60.)

The old Whig Party that ruled the Empire had understood this situation, according to Carthill, but the Liberal Imperialists did not. They had preserved continuity with the foreign policy of the Unionist administrations, but at heart they were Liberals, who had to justify to the tail of the Liberal Party their wars and their governing of conquered territories. But the Glorious Revolution, unlike the French, was not for export:

> "the real Whig knew that the gospel of 1688 was revealed, and the blood of the martyrs, Hampden and Russell, and Sidney and Titus Oates, was shed certainly for the Englishman; probably for the Scot, possibly for the Colonial and Irishman, but in no way for the foreigner, and least of all for the man of colour." (pp.64-5.)

Carthill was not suggesting that the ideas of democracy were being seriously applied to the governing of the Indian Empire but simply that it was dangerous to give the Indian any notion that England believed in them, outside of Britain — despite all the War propaganda.

Carthill advised the Government of India to say boldly to the Indian that Britain was continuing its high mission of civilizing, which it would not falter in carrying through, maintaining the executive in its own hands, and meeting agitation, sedition and revolt with the necessary force. If not, the Government would appear weak, and would have to resort to massacre, as it did at Amritsar:

> "Massacre, as part of the activities of Government, is by no means in itself abhorrent to the mind of the Oriental, and the Indian was familiar enough with it. There are several forms of political massacre, and there was nothing about any of them which was repugnant to the Indian. There is the massacre that is the resource of the weak Government. If offences are not punished from time to time, and particularly if dangerous agitation is tolerated, then it invariably happens that the Government must ultimately abdicate or fight. In England, where the divergences between parties are not vital, the Government

abdicates... There are, however, precedents in British history which tend to show that, when the occasion arises, the British will display a surprising energy and thoroughness in this branch of administration. The 'administrative massacre,' as this kind may be called, is, of course, familiar enough to the Oriental." (pp.93-4.)

The reason why what happened in England between 1912-14 was so serious was that the forces worked up in the conflict over Home Rule seemed to rule out the possibility of abdicating and increasingly veered toward the possibility of fighting—and that was a precedent the British State had avoided for two centuries.

Carthill became disenchanted with the policy being enacted by London with regard to India, Mesopotamia and the Middle East. Even before the Great War, the British Indian Administration was aware of the Liberal Imperialist manoeuvring with Arabia. Calcutta was totally against the policy of creating a new Caliph at Mecca to displace the Sultan. It was thought that this manoeuvre would involve Mecca and Medina in politics and would be a disruptive influence on England's Moslem subjects in India. So the British Indian Administration was against the meddling from Egypt and London, believing it far better to 'let sleeping dogs lie' in the Holy Places so as to keep the Indian Empire quiet.

The British Indian Empire was actually quite alarmed at the thought of the wholesale destruction of the Ottoman Empire. The administrators of India were still orientated against Russia, and many of them viewed the obsession with Germany as a temporary interlude in the Great Game against the Czar. They understood that the arrangement with Russia over Persia would simply divert Russian expansionism to the Balkans. When Germany was beaten, they reasoned, the Russians would be down at Constantinople and threatening the Indian Empire as before. And it had been a tenet of British Foreign Policy from Disraeli to Lord Salisbury that a Russian conquest of Constantinople would have a very detrimental effect on Britain's hold over its Moslem subjects in the Indian Empire—which was always understood to be firmly based on the matter of England's prestige.

The objective of the Indian Empire was gradually to absorb chunks of the Ottoman Empire, along the Persian Gulf and Eastern Arabia, without promoting a cataclysm in the region that would stir up its Moslem subjects in unpredictable ways. The Indian Administration worried during the pre-War period, believing that Britain had surrendered its leverage on the Ottomans through a series of policy decisions beginning with Gladstone's tirade against 'the unspeakable Turk' in 1894, after the 'Armenian massacres'. This, it was thought, let the Germans in. And, with the replacement of the Sultan by the Young Turks, England seemed to have relaxed its efforts, believing that the control of its Moslem subjects did not depend on the Caliphate in Istanbul as much as it did with the Sultanate in power. Finally, and most importantly, was the alliance of Britain with Russia, Turkey's traditional foe. From there on, it seemed, there was no going back to good relations between Britain and Turkey and everything was a holding operation until the opportunity arose for the Empire to move in for the kill.

The very things that Carthill warned London about exporting to the Indian part of its Moslem Empire were what London foisted on the Arab part in order to destabilize the Ottoman State and what it gave to Mesopotamia afterwards. And the consequences of this are with us still.

Arnold Wilson had called on Britain to govern or evacuate. But England did not want to do either in Iraq. It wanted to find a way of staying in Mesopotamia, without bearing the cost of governing it. England desired power over the region, without the responsibility or expense of tending to its good government.

Sir Percy Cox was sent for by London and the dilemma was put to him. Cox pronounced it capable of a solution, whereby Britain neither governed nor evacuated the country, but maintained control at low expense.

### Arnold Wilson Departs

The result of this policy was seen in the disastrous attempt to nurture the new State of Iraq into a nation-state within the British sphere of influence. It was suddenly decided that Iraq should become a nation-state, in the spirit of the war propaganda which had encouraged such notions, and because it was considered important to lure America into world responsibility by humouring the ideals of President Wilson. The objective became to create an Arab puppet state in which Britain could pull the strings to secure its political and economic interests — and all at a low cost.

As a first step, the Colonial Commissioner, Arnold Wilson, was replaced by his superior, Sir Percy Cox, in October 1920.

At a complimentary dinner held for Arnold Wilson on his imminent departure from Baghdad, the former Civil Commissioner for Iraq outlined his view that all the problems that now beset the Empire had their root in the decision to adopt Nationalism as a War objective in 1914, in preference to the old belief in an Imperial future for the world. Sound judgement had been led astray by War propaganda, argued Wilson, and the subsequent attempt to shoe-horn the world into the newly favoured structures in the spirit of the new morality, and in defiance of material forces, was destined to be disastrous:

> "The last few months have saddened us all; doubt has replaced hope. Why, we ask, should these things have occurred?... Time was when ideas which had their birth in the East had a profound influence on Western thought. We are now seeing the opposite process at work.

> The end of the nineteenth century witnessed the revival of Nationalism in

Europe and Asia—a reaction of the man in the field and in the street from the conception and existence of great Empires... Nationalism is the basis of the latest Peace Treaties. We entered the war to protect the rights of small Nations and no idea appealed more widely to the many races composing the British Empire. Critics of Nationalism as a constructive policy were silenced; doubters were perforce dumb; Nationalism held the field, and every official utterance of the Allies, and of the spokesmen of the Associated Powers, emphasized this as the basis for future policy.

The seed of Nationalism was sown broadcast at home, but the Army that landed at Basra in 1914 was animated by no such ideas. Our mission was to beat the Turk and we did so...

The seed of Nationalism had grown in Europe meanwhile, and the plant had borne fruit in the East. The Sharif's revolt was proclaimed as a national movement of Arabs against the Turks, and in return for the co-operation of Arab forces the Allies pledged themselves to respect and further Arab aspirations...

Each fresh victory in Mesopotamia involved a further advance inland until as a result of the Armistice we found ourselves responsible for the wilayets of Mosul, Baghdad and Basra, pledged to the policy enunciated by General Maude, but still unable without reference to our Allies to give effect thereto... We had been told that we could not act until the Peace Conference had come to a decision... Mesopotamia itself was quiet, but the seed we ourselves had sown was growing; the new wine was fermenting in the old bottles... Our orders were clear: we were not to build. We could not know what the Peace Conference would decide, but we could, and did foresee that delay meant trouble. Demobilization, however, went on until May 1st last we only had 5,000 British and 30,000 Indian combatants in Mesopotamia.

During this month the Supreme Council of the Peace Conference conferred the Mandate on Great Britain, but took no decision as to the form of government to be set up; that was held to involve consultation with local opinion—no easy task. It was at this critical moment in the history of Mesopotamia that certain men, more ambitious, more short-sighted, more impatient and less wise than others, saw fit to foment under a constitutional guise a movement which within two months became frankly revolutionary, fanatical and anarchic."
(*Mesopotamia 1917-1920 A Clash Of Loyalties,* pp. 318-9.)

In his Preface to *A Clash Of Loyalties* Wilson outlined the other problem of governing Mesopotamia connected to the attitude of the Imperial Government in London:

"In England the government of the day was distracted by financial and political problems of the utmost gravity at home and abroad; the press gave no useful guidance in any direction; publicists offered little but the broken lights of sentimentalism and pacifism. The British Empire had won the war, and in so doing seemed to have lost faith in its mission and belief in the obligation, imposed on it alike by self-interest and duty, to uphold the principles of authority and of good government for which it stood, until these principles had taken root and could safely be entrusted to an indigenous authority. I felt then, as now, deeply—even passionately—that the welfare of the people of the Middle East and India, no less than the existence of the British Empire, depended upon our facing our responsibilities... My innermost beliefs were in all humility those expressed by Cromwell: 'We are a people with the stamp of God upon us... whose appearance and whose providences are not to be outmatched by any story.'" (*Mesopotamia 1917-1920 A Clash Of Loyalties,* p. x.)

Wilson, looking back in 1931, wrote that he believed he was witnessing an unnecessary collapse in the Imperial will to govern in 1920, which amounted to no good in the world, for the Empire or its subjects:

"Neither in Iraq nor, later, in Bombay... did I find any trace of despondency or lack of belief in our duty, our ability, and therefore our right to exercise at our discretion in foreign countries whither our armies had penetrated, so much authority as would enable the populations concerned to keep in step with the rest of the world, and under our aegis, to develop in a political and economical sense. 'Defeatism,' which may be defined as the anticipation of moral or physical defeat, and the acceptance in advance of its implications, was nowhere evident... I then believed, as did Lord Curzon twenty years earlier, that the eastward trend of our responsibilities was destined to increase and not diminish... bringing also a mutually beneficial increase of international commerce...

There seemed in 1920 no sufficient reason why we should prematurely surrender the reins of government in the East, or seek to hand on a torch which as yet burned so feebly...

Much has happened since those days. We have for the moment lost faith of ourselves. For a beacon-light we have substituted a round table, and we tend to rely on the pious resolutions of Geneva to accomplish much that could be more hopefully and more nobly secured by unilateral action." (*Mesopotamia 1917-1920 A Clash Of Loyalties,* pp. 318-9.)

Such was the price of the decision in August 1914 to enter into a War on Germany and to continue waging it to the death, even when the Germans proved unlikely to break. And as the *Entente* was foundering, it became essential to enlist the services of the United States to complete the job. As a result, when the British Empire had finally achieved the pinnacle of its worldwide power it found itself exhausted and lacking the will to govern in the old way. And yet it could not bear to do the decent thing—it could not evacuate.

What must the 56 year old Arnold Wilson, as a volunteer pilot officer, have thought in his last moments on earth, on 31 May 1940, in the skies over Dunkirk, when he could see the Empire's Army below, run off the continent by those whom the Great War had been waged to destroy? Would he have been tempted to wonder, where had it all gone wrong?

## A Lesson in Electoral Democracy

Sir Percy Cox, Gertrude Bell and the 'Arabists' who replaced Wilson in the British administration in Baghdad, had the intention of forcing the Sunni and Shiah Arabs, and the Kurds into an artificially constructed State of Iraq under British dominion. But they failed to see the problems involved in imposing the son of Britain's ally, Sharif Hussein of Mecca, on the Arabs and Kurds of Basra, Baghdad and Mosul. The 'Arabists' imagined that Shereef Hussein's son Faisal, who had been previously expelled by the French from Syria, would be an acceptable figurehead for most Iraqis. It was probably known that the Kurds were unlikely to welcome an Arab head of State under British tutelage, but they no longer mattered in the scheme of things.

Gertrude Bell was a highly experienced traveller in the Middle East who had written extensively about it and its people in publications, letters and diaries. She always maintained that there was nothing that could be described as nationalism in the region, that authority was local and traditionally based, and that it would be very wise not to disturb this state of affairs, but to leave well alone, as the Turks had done. In 1917, in *The Arab of Mesopotamia*, for instance, she had written:

> "The tribes of Iraq have advanced but little beyond the Moot Court, and should the shaping of their destinies become our care in the future, we shall be wise to eschew any experiments tending to rush them into highly specialised institutions — a policy which could commend itself only to those who are never wearied by words that signify nothing." (p.21.)

But sometime in 1919 Bell had a change of heart that is hard to explain, and which negated all the understanding she had accumulated over her years of travel.

Bell became an enthusiastic supporter of imposing a Hussein on Iraq, believing that the Mesopotamian Shiah would take to Faisal as a direct descendant of the Prophet Muhammad and the Sunnis would accept him as one of their own.

Arnold Wilson had been aware of the feeling amongst Mesopotamian Arabs against the imposition of an outsider on them as their head and counselled against such a move. The Naqib of Baghdad, who was a relative of Faisal's, had warned Bell:

> "The Hejaz is one and the Iraq is one, there is no connection between them but that of the Faith. Our politics, our trade, our agriculture are all different from those of the Hejaz... As regards the government of Mesopotamia my detestation of the present Turkish administration is known to you, but I would rather a thousand times have the Turks back in Iraq than see the Sharif or his sons installed here." (*Mesopotamia 1917-1920 A Clash Of Loyalties,* pp. 340.)

The 'Arabists' believed they could make Iraq governable by creating what they would call 'two majorities' out of the three communities. The theory was that any two of the three groups could combine, allowing the two to constitute a majority, against the other. Thus, Arab and Kurdish Sunni Muslims could dominate the Arab Shiah; or, if the two Arab communities, Shiah and Sunni, combined, they would have a majority over the Kurds.

An election was organised to legitimise the new concoction of Iraq. But when the popular and consequential candidate, Said Talib, returned to contest it he was kidnapped by the British and deported to Ceylon. The election, therefore, had one candidate, Faisal, the son of the Shereef of Mecca, who had issued the *Jihad* against the Turks on Britain's behalf. He duly won and became King of Iraq. Thomas Lyell, a Staff Officer under Arnold Wilson commented in his book:

> "When... the Colonial Office was induced to put Feisal, son of the Sharif of Sunni Mecca, on the throne of Shia Iraq, it can be understood that it was utterly against the people's wish." (*The Ins And Outs of Mesopotamia,* p. 84.)

This fraudulent exercise was Iraq's first experience of how Western democracy worked and it seems to have made a lasting impression.

An account of these events, which took place between March and August 1921, is given in *Arabian Days* by St. John Philby (father of the spy, Kim). Philby was, in 1921, Adviser to the Ministry of The Interior in the Provisional Government of Iraq, conducted under the authority of the British Civil Commissioner for Mesopotamia, Sir Percy Cox. The Interior Minister was Said Talib. The following extracts are from the chapter, *Iraq in the Making*:

> "One day about the end of March, Saiyid Talib told me he was giving a dinner party at his house to all the consular and diplomatic representatives at Baghdad, the leading businessmen of the European community and a number of local notables... The host was as merry as anyone else, perhaps more so, and at the end of the dinner he rose to unburden his heart of some of its political overload. The gist of his speech was that, rumours of the appointment of Faisal as prospective King of Iraq having become widely current, he wished to make it clear to those present and to the British Government that the people of Iraq did not want Faisal and would not tolerate his imposition on them: 'If you doubt my word, here is Shaikh Muhammad of the Rab'ia, the land of forty thousand braves and Shaikh so-and-so of such-and-such, a tribe with thirty thousand men, at this very table; ask them and they will tell you what the people think.' One of Saiyid Talib's guests, a businessman named Tod, hastened after the meal to tell Gertrude Bell all that had passed at the banquet, and Gertrude Bell told Cox the following day."

Talib was invited by Lady Cox to take tea with her and Sir Percy the following Saturday. Philby had also been invited to dine with a Captain Cox at the *Alwiya Club* that night:

> "When we reached the Club another officer came forward to explain that he was acting as our host, as Cox had been suddenly called away on urgent

business. 'Terrible business, isn't it?' He managed to whisper in my ear as we trooped into dinner. He assumed of course that I knew everything.

Saiyid Talib, had, at Sir Percy Cox's orders, been kidnapped while a guest at his house, and had been carried off in an armoured car to a launch waiting downstream to take him to Basra and internment in Ceylon. The details of the story must be told:

Lady Cox was, I am convinced, an entirely innocent party to the plot, which was cleverly planned even to the cutting of all vital telephone lines, including my own. Cox himself had gone off to the races, leaving an apology with Lady Cox, with whom was Gertrude Bell when Saiyid Talib was announced. While tea was in progress Major E.W. Bovill and Captain Cox dropped in casually, as it were, and partook of tea, after which they took their leave. Ten minutes later Saiyid Talib rose to go and Gertrude Bell escorted him to the front door of the Residency, saw him to his car and withdrew. As the chauffeur started the car he found the drive blocked by a number of lorries. Saiyid Talib was about to expostulate at such discourtesy when Bovill and Captain Cox appeared from behind a lorry apologizing for the obstruction and asking him to regard himself as their prisoner. They had instructions to arrest him and convey him forthwith to an undisclosed destination. The wiliest man in Arabia had walked into the simplest of traps, from which there was no possible escape. So he went quietly.

My wife was horrified, and I was furious. I called upon Cox and asked if I could see him to discuss what had happened. 'Certainly,' he replied, 'any time you like, I'm free now.' So I drove round contemplating immediate resignation, and drove back after a three hour interview as a member of the Iraqi Cabinet, in fact as Minister of the Interior vice Saiyid Talib! Cox had been quite frank about the deportation of Saiyid Talib, and I realised that he could not have taken me into his confidence before the event. I most certainly would have warned my friend against that tea-party; and there is no saying what Talib Saiyid might have done to counter the intrigue against him. All that was Cox's business and his responsibility. I expressed my disapproval of his action, which I interpreted as meaning that Talib Saiyid had to be got out of the way to make the path clear for Faisal. But he assured me that there had been no intention of imposing Faisal as King on the people."

Philby replaced Talib at the Ministry of the Interior and one day received notice that Faisal was heading for Basra. Churchill then announced this to Parliament:

"Churchill told Parliament that Faisal was on his way to Mesopotamia to present himself to his people as a candidate for the throne; the Government's best wishes for his success went with him, and it was hoped that Iraq would appreciate this new opportunity of realizing its aspirations. We all knew what that meant. But, strangely enough, the declared policy of free elections still stood, and that did not look good for Faisal and his small minority of supporters in the country. But the British Government has always had a knack of reconciling the irreconcilable."

Philby was at the head of a large civic reception that met Faisal as his boat docked in Basra and he stood for the first time on the soil of the country he was to become King of. But the Minister of the Interior told Faisal that he stood little chance of winning an election. Faisal's displeasure at this remark was communicated to Cox who asked Philby at a meeting:

"'Surely you understand now what the British Government want.?' 'Of course I do,' I replied. 'What I can't understand is why the Government, if it wants and intends Faisal to be King doesn't appoint him in a straightforward manner instead of insisting on the farce of an election. Anyway, I am too committed by the assurances I have given all round to take part in rigging the elections.' 'I understand,' said Cox, 'but I don't see how your attitude can be reconciled with you remaining in your post.' 'If I am expected to rig the elections,' I replied, 'I have no desire to remain in my post, and if you nominate my successor I will go straight round from here and hand over to him.' 'Thank you Philby,' he said, 'I'm sorry you can't see yourself round to helping us' ...

So ended my official connection with Iraq and Cox. The electoral law, at which we had laboured, was thrown on the rubbish heap, and instead of the proposed elections Cox organised a plebiscite on the single question: 'Do you want Feisal to reign over you?' Ninety six and a half per cent of the *ad hoc* electorate answered the question in the affirmative and Faisal was crowned on 21 August 1921."

There is only one other account of these events and it is found in a notorious 1956 biography of T.E. Lawrence by Richard Aldington, veteran of the Great War, poet and author of the famous 1929 novel *Death of A Hero*. Aldington takes up the story where Philby's account left off:

"Sir Percy Cox had promised that starting with a representative provisional government, the Irakis would go on to free elections to a constituent assembly, which would determine a future constitution of the country, and, if desired choose the future head of State. Now, all of this had been determined and promised before the Cairo Conference, and if it had been carried out honestly, nobody could say truthfully that Irak had not been allowed to choose its own form of government. But such a representative body would not have chosen Feisal, and the determination had been reached to impose him on the country. According to Lawrence, Sir Percy Cox protested to Cairo against presenting Feisal as a *fait accompli*, and said he had promised the Baghdad Arabs that the election of a king should be free as an election in England. And Lawrence says that Mr. Churchill replied that they should be, as in England electors have a choice between candidates which are selected by the parties and that an English election is not therefore free at all. If this is true, Sir Percy was very easily satisfied; for this was how the election was carried out...

Saiyid Talib had, by Sir Percy Cox's orders, been kidnapped while a guest in his house... The other candidates for the throne were simply ignored, and

Cox organised a plebiscite on a single question: Do you want Feisal to reign over you? As the alternative was the continuation of undiluted foreign rule which the Irakis wanted to be rid of, it is hardly surprising that 96 per cent of those voting said 'Yes.' The analogy with elections to a British Parliament is striking. Thus, a typical example would be for the Government to kidnap and exile the local candidate who was hostile to themselves, and send down a supporter of themselves brought in from Northern Ireland with the single question: 'Will you have Mr. So-and-So to represent you in Parliament?' As the only alternative would be no representation at all 96 per cent of the constituents would vote 'Yes.' And Liddell Hart would obviously highly approve since he wrote that 'Feisal's election by the people was as free as elections in England.'" (*Lawrence of Arabia, A Biographical Enquiry*, p.305-6.)

Thus the nation-state of Iraq began life and was introduced to democracy. Meanwhile back in England, Lord Winterton declared in Parliament in July 1920:

"Prince Faisal is the John Redmond of 1915. He is a moderate Nationalist, anxious to come to terms, and in his country are hundreds of Arab Sinn Feiners who say 'Away with this man, and let us have people who will have nothing to do with the French or the British.'" (Elie Kedourie, *England And The Middle East*, p.206.)

Winterton had fought with Lawrence during the Arab Revolt and he was a vocal advocate of installing the Hashemites on the thrones of the Arab nation-states Britain had erected in the Middle East.

Before the War Winterton had been one of the foremost opponents of nationalism and nation-states — within the British Empire, at least. Other MPs failed to remind Winterton that, as a Die-Hard, he had formed a paramilitary group in the Home Counties to be called to duty when Redmond's Home Rule Bill became Law. But by 1920 Redmond had begun to be seen by Unionists as a moderate and they forgot their own role in bringing the gun into Irish politics against him. And Winterton was urging Britain to give to Iraq what he had been prepared to oppose through armed rebellion, in much more limited form, to Ireland only a decade previously.

Elie Kedourie comments in his book, *England And The Middle East*, on the long-term effects of Britain's conduct of policy in Iraq:

"The 1921 settlement... justified and sanctioned violent and arbitrary proceedings and built them into the structure of Iraqi politics. The men who came with Faisal believed that their success was due to the use of violence and that they had triumphed over the British, and compelled them to change their policy, by the use of violence. It was a lesson that would sustain them both in their relations with the British and in their conduct of public affairs. Now they were masters of a country the population of which was heterogeneous in the extreme... All these disparate groups were now to be ruled by successful men of violence, between whom and any of these groups disagreement would be solved by arbitrary and violent action. The 1921 settlement... organised a central government, able to use all the modern techniques of administration, and handed it over to these men to use as they liked; authority was drained from all localities and communities and concentrated in them; a group at odds with them would either be crushed wholly and finally or, if it could, would uphold its cause by the sword." (p213.)

By 1922 Faisal had fallen out of favour for showing some independence of mind and Sir Percy Cox complained to Churchill:

"Faisal unmistakably displayed the cloven hoof. I have endeavoured to be absolutely straightforward and frank to him, and to treat him like a brother, but there you are, when he is scratched deep enough the racial weakness displays itself." (cited in Helmut Mejcher, *The Imperial Quest For Oil*, p. 81.)

The Iraqis continued to be ruled by a British *protégé* until 1958, despite being granted formal independence in 1931 under Faisal. The emptiness of this status was demonstrated during the Second World War when Churchill invaded Iraq after its government attempted to assert its independence and neutrality and refused to facilitate British troop movements. That is not an episode that is widely known about in Britain or Ireland—since the impression must be maintained that it is only Germans who do such things.

The lesson in democracy that Britain gave to the Iraqis at the moment of the foundation of their State is another forgotten episode of the Great War on Turkey. Experience shows that it was of great importance in determining the political character of the Iraqi State from then on. In the 1920s, it was fresh in the minds of many in Britain and for years there was a campaign of character assassination directed against Said Talib. But, as memories faded, the episode has been left to drop from the record.

However, I read in certain articles at the time of the latest invasion of Iraq that some Iraqis opposed to Saddam Hussein mentioned the name of Gertrude Bell in a derogatory fashion to American officials, accusing them of seeking to become 'the new Gertrude Bell'. So I presume that the Said Talib episode has never been forgotten in Iraq.

Britain, and now America, have seen to that, of course.

# TURKEY UNDER THE TREATY OF PEACE.

The Sèvres Treaty

Constantinople and a narrow strip of country around it are all that is left to Turkey in Europe. The control of the Straits is placed in the hands of an international commission. The new terrritory acquired by Greece is shown by the dotted lines. The ultimate possession of Rhodes is to be determined by a plebiscite.

# VII. Another Greek Tragedy

Having seen off President Wilson at the Peace Conference Lloyd George got down to the traditional business of Imperialism. But, since America was not available to provide for, and support, British Imperial interests, and since the exchequer and army were depleted, Britain required others to assist in the continued work of the Empire. And that is where M. Venizelos and Greece came back on the scene.

In some publications I have seen the war fought between Greece and Turkey, that came out of this situation, referred to as the Greco-Turkish War. But that is about as misleading as describing the conflict over the Treaty in Ireland as the Irish Civil War.

A conflict between Greece and Turkey did figure within that war, but it was fundamentally a proxy-war of Britain on the Turks, using the military forces of the regime they had established in Athens, to impose a punitive peace settlement on the Turks.

In this conflict Ataturk's Turkey succeeded in wearing down and whittling away the alliance against them, until all that was left was the issue between Britain and Turkey, which was finally decided at Chanak and settled at Lausanne. But the tragedy was what happened to the Greeks.

### Constantinople And Asia Minor—What Should Be Done?

There is a very interesting book called *The Great Problems Of British Statesmanship* by J. Ellis Barker, a thoughtful Imperialist writer, and long-term associate of Joseph Chamberlain. It was published in 1917 and was a discussion of what the Empire should do about some of the major strategic issues that it was clear would emerge after the War. Barker discusses the problem of Constantinople exhaustively and decides that it should go to Russia, despite the regime change in Moscow. His argument was that the possession of Constantinople would, contrary to previous thinking, actually weaken Russia and make her vulnerable, as Bismarck thought, by stretching her resources over a length of territory that was undefendable. But Barker finished his book before Russia became clearly Bolshevik, and that option was closed off for Britain.

Then Barker discusses the problem of Asia Minor and concludes that:

"The question of Asiatic Turkey is undoubtedly a far more difficult question than that of Constantinople. Constantinople and the Straits are, as I have shown, not the key to the Dominion of the World, as Napoleon the First asserted, but merely the key to the Black Sea. Former generations, uncritically repeating Napoleon's celebrated dictum, have greatly overrated the strategical importance of that wonderful site. The importance and value of Asiatic Turkey on the other hand can scarcely be exaggerated, for it occupies undoubtedly the most important strategical position in the world. It forms the nucleus and centre of the Old World. It separates, and at the same time connects, Europe, Asia, and Africa, three continents which are inhabited by approximately nine-tenths of the human race." (p.56.)

This is very similar to Halford Mackinder's 'heartland' argument—'he who controls the heartland controls the world.'

Barker argues that such an important strategic region should be placed under the guardianship of a European Power—and guess which one:

"If the European Powers should decide to place Turkey under a guardianship, a single, a strong, a non-military and therefore non-aggressive Power experienced in managing Mohammedans should be selected. The only Power possessing these qualifications is Great Britain. Great Britain might convert Asiatic Turkey into another, and a greater, Egypt. Outwardly it would remain an independent State with Sultan, &c. However, an inconspicuous representative of the guardian Power, called Adviser or Consul-General, would control the Turkish administrative and executive absolutely by controlling the entire finances of the country.

Asiatic Turkey, like Egypt, would not need, and should not possess a real army. A police force and a gendarmerie, possibly supported by a few thousand soldiers in case of internal troubles, should suffice. The entire energy of the Asiatic Turks should be concentrated upon the development of the country. Only then would Turkey cease to be a danger to other nations and to itself. Great Britain would derive no benefit from its guardianship, except the benefit of peace. Her activity on behalf of Europe would be distinctly unprofitable to herself. It is true that the Turks would have to pay salaries to a number of British officials—a paltry matter—and that Great Britain might possibly provide some of the capital needed for developing the country.

However, Great Britain will, after the War, have no capital to spare for exotic enterprises. All her surplus capital will be required for developing the Motherland and Empire. Besides, she has no superabundance of able administrators available for the service of Turkey and of other semi-civilised States. Great Britain would see in a guardianship over Turkey rather a duty than an advantage...

The aim of the British Government and of all Europe should be to enable Turkey to govern herself. But in order to be able to govern herself Turkey must be taught the art of government, and Great Britain might be her teacher.

If, on the other hand, the Powers should not be able to agree to a British guardianship, it would become necessary to divide Asiatic Turkey into zones of influence. In that case, the Turks would probably be restricted to a comparatively narrow territory in the centre of Asia Minor. Being cut off from the sea and lacking great natural resources, the few million Turks would scarcely be able to retain their independence for long. Asiatic Turkey in its totality would be partitioned by the Powers. Great Britain would probably claim the control, in some form or other, of both Mesopotamia and Arabia as her share. However, it seems very doubtful whether the partition of Asiatic Turkey would prove a final one. It is much to be feared that it would lead to a disaster perhaps as great as the present War." (pp.103-4.)

England's decision to take on the destruction of the Ottoman Empire created more problems than solutions, as Ellis Barker was well aware. Barker believed that it was necessary to create a large buffer-state — 'a gigantic Switzerland' — out of Turkey, to restore stability to the region. Of course, Barker came from another world — the purposeful Imperialist world from before the Great War, that had Britain as a great civilising Power, capable of what Barker imagined. But the War had changed everything.

But Barker's suggestions were very close to those which the British Government adopted and attempted to follow through between 1919 and 1922.

### Venizelos Claims His Spoils

The Greeks went to the Paris Peace Conference in Paris to claim the spoils of victory, having abandoned their neutrality for promises of territory in Europe and Asia Minor. Here is what Arnold Toynbee said of the claims the Greeks made at that Conference:

> "At the Paris Conference Mr. Venizelos, on behalf of Greece, put forward startling demands. He asked for the whole of Western and Eastern Thrace up to the Black Sea and the Chatalja lines, and for the entire vilayet or province of Aidin, in Western Anatolia, with the exception of the one sanjak or department of Denizli, but with the addition of a corridor to the south coast of the Marmara. The first claim meant interposing a continuous belt of Greek territory between Turkey and other European states and between Bulgaria and the Aegean. The second meant taking from Turkey the richest province and principal port of Anatolia, bringing a large population under Greek rule, and leaving the two nations, with these new seeds of discord sown between them, to face one another along an immense land frontier." (*The Western Question in Greece And Turkey*, pp.68-9.)

When England was confronted by the claims of its Allies after the War — the things that they had been promised, or led to believe were to be their rewards for joining the Great War for civilization — their demands were seen as 'startling'. Did these countries not realise that they had been promised things in the heat of battle, in the hour of crisis, when it was felt that without the addition of another new ally, without a further extension of the War, Germany would never be beaten? Did they not realise that England had made promises it could not or would not keep, promises that conflicted with other promises made to others? Could they not just go home now that the job had been done and the world was safe for civilisation, and leave Britain to the burden of reordering it in everyone's interests, as was its duty?

No, these selfish people wanted pay-back!

Neither Edward Grey nor Lloyd George ever told Venizelos in 1915 that his demands were 'startling'. And if they did, which I presume for the sake of diplomacy they would not have done, the Greek Premier never let on to the Greek people. So, many people in Italy, Serbia, Rumania, Arabia, Greece etc. expected much more for their sacrifices in saving civilization than they were going to get when the victors unrolled the new maps of Europe and Asia.

What is even more startling about this is that Arnold Toynbee knew better. Toynbee had been appointed to the Political Intelligence Department established by the Foreign Office in March 1918. The Political Intelligence Department was set up to give a greater focus to British War aims, by employing specialists in certain areas that could be consulted about what to do with captured territories. Toynbee joined Harold Nicolson and Allen Leeper in the Greek Department. All three were Balliol graduates and were enthused with the ideas of *The New Europe Group* which envisaged a Europe redrawn along lines of national self-determination with arbitration from the League of Nations on minority problems. (This was the Group which originated the idea of re-ordering Europe by constructing artificial Buffer States between Germany and Russia).

Toynbee and his colleagues in the Political Intelligence Department recommended that, in the Peace Conference, Greece be enlarged by an enclave around Smyrna and the possession of all the Aegean Islands. And they also suggested that it would be wise to evict the Turks from Constantinople and to establish an Arabian Caliphate.

Now England had a different agenda, and this demanded that the Allies (and in particular, Italy) be characterised in the War for civilisation as selfish grabbers — or 'irredentists' (a word which now began to take on a derogatory connotation) — so that they could be cheated of the fruits of victory.

Basil Thomson noted that, after participating in the winning of the War, Venizelos was in for a shock at the Peace:

> "The Armistice brought a rude awakening to that versatile statesman. King Constantine had stipulated for conditions if his country were to join the Allies: Venizelos had joined them without conditions. In the Peace Conference he was to learn a fact that he ought to have known from past history — that the victors in a great war are realists before all else and have no room for sentimental attachments to their small allies. The Greek army was almost intact; Venizelos believed he could use it for bargaining purposes. He offered an army corps to join the ill-considered Allied expedition against the Bolsheviks in the Ukraine. The Allied expedition failed; the Greek contingent was decimated and the Bolsheviks wreaked vengeance upon the Greek colony in Southern Russia which numbered about 100,000 people." (*The Allied Secret Service In Greece*, pp. 234-5.)

Perhaps the Greek adventure in Southern Russia should have taught Venizelos the dangers inherent in a campaign in Anatolia. But no! And I presume that the Bolsheviks remembered what the Greeks had done when the possibility of an alliance with the Turks later emerged.

In May 1919 Venizelos, concerned that Greece was not about to share in the harvest of victory, appeared in Paris and demanded a hearing from the Triumvirate who were dividing up the world—Lloyd George, Clemenceau and Wilson. There he produced a forged Turkish Proclamation indicating that Christians living around the Smyrna district were about to be massacred by Mohammedans. He sympathised with the Triumvirate in their desire to demobilize their armies and save money and offered them his services to prevent the spilling of Christian blood, which they would not like on their consciences. The Triumvirate ceded to the Greek the right to occupy Smyrna on the conditions that the occupation would be temporary, pacific and restricted.

A major concern in 1920 for Britain, along with punishment of the Turks, was how to cheat the Italians out of the spoils of war—the spoils which they had been lured into the war for—*Italia Irredenta*, and beyond. The Italians had been promised the Smyrna area and a substantial piece of Asia Minor under the Treaty of St. Jean de Maurienne as well as the unredeemed regions to the North and East of the Italian State. But they had been trumped by Venizelos. So Lloyd George urged the Greeks to land at Smyrna quickly to head off the Italian claim.

The cheating of Italy by Britain played a large part in the coming to power of Mussolini and Fascism in the country. But the loss of Smyrna can only be looked upon as a blessing for the Italians—and a curse for the Greeks.

Under the new British plan the Smyrna region, which had substantial Greek and Armenian minorities, was to have its own autonomous parliament, and after five years it would decide whether to become part of the Greek State. Given that this mixed-population area was to be occupied, the Turkish population would in all likelihood begin to leave, in one way or another, making a Greek annexation of it a distinct possibility in the future. In 1918 the Greeks had successfully cleared out the Jewish quarters of Salonika and planted Greeks in their place, so Smyrna looked forward to a similar prospect.

And that is how the Greek adventure in Asia Minor began.

### Lloyd George And The Greeks

Lloyd George was an admirer of the Greeks and he believed that, with his assistance, they would become a great people again. He had, from his schooling, an affection for them, as for the Jews, and felt compelled to restore them to their former glories. He had the Gladstonian dislike of the 'unspeakable Turk', whom he took to be of a much inferior race to the Greek, and he had a great regard for Venizelos, 'the greatest Greek since Pericles', whom he believed to be a man after his own image. In fact, Venizelos seems to have captivated most of the Allied leaders with his charm and powers of persuasion.

However, when, in December 1919, the French Premier, Clemenceau, met Lloyd George, he urged Britain to respect Turkish integrity and to pull the Greeks out of Smyrna. But Lloyd George refused, believing the Greeks to be useful in advancing British interests in the area.

Arnold Toynbee saw Lloyd George's admiration for Venizelos as a secondary factor in his courting of the Greeks. The primary consideration was the strategic interests of Britain. Here was the reasoning:

> "The British Government cannot keep troops mobilised in the East to enforce eventual terms of peace upon Turkey; Greece can provide the troops and enforce the terms with British diplomatic and naval backing, and she will gladly do so if these terms include her own claims. If Greece makes these claims good through British backing, she will have to follow Britain's lead. She is a maritime Power, a labyrinth of peninsulas and islands, and territories that she covets in Anatolia are overseas. In short, if Turkey can be dominated by the land-power of Greece, Greece can be dominated by the sea-power of Great Britain, and so the British Government can still carry out their war-aims in the Near and Middle East without spending British money and lives." (*The Western Question in Greece And Turkey* (1922) p.74.)

So the Greek demands were no longer 'startling' and England and Greece could do business again, to their mutual benefit.

At the close of the War, the British Empire had a million men at arms in the Middle and Near East. But Britain was in financial hock to the United States as a result of its miscalculation of the strength and length of German resistance. The Prime Minister had also made some rash promises in order to win the 1918 General Election. Apart from the hanging of the Kaiser, he had promised to demobilise the conscripted men as quickly as possible. The War propaganda that had been used to inspire the recruits had been on the lines of seeing off the Prussian evil, and since that had been done and the Hun defeated, it was only reasonable that the men be released from service, rather than being retained for further Imperial adventures.

As a result of the great territorial gains made by the British Empire's War on the Ottomans, the Imperial forces found themselves overreached and without the possibility of reinforcement. So surrogates were necessary in completing British ambitions in the region. One of the most important considerations was Mesopotamia. England needed to keep the Turks away from the area as Imperial rule bedded down, and this could only be accomplished by the distraction of a Greek army in Anatolia. Lloyd George could use the Royal Navy to enforce some of the Imperial will, but he had to rely on the Greek Army to do the rest.

The great thing about the plan was that the Greeks could be cut down to size by the Royal Navy if they ever overstepped the mark—with regard to Constantinople, for instance. Athens could be flattened at any time by the guns of the battleships of the Mediterranean fleet (and the diaries of C.P. Scott show that Lloyd George did in fact contemplate this).

The Allies landed Greek forces at Smyrna during May 1919, six months after the Armistice with Turkey. Smyrna was one of the best harbours in the world and Lloyd George hoped he could occupy it cheaply, using the Greek

Army. The Greek troops were sent to Smyrna with a Mandate from the Allied Supreme Council—although this was in violation of the terms of the Armistice with Turkey. There was provision for dealing with disorder under its terms, but the only evidence of disorder was the forged document that Venizelos, who himself wished for a Greek colonisation there, had presented to the Allies.

The Greeks landed off Allied warships under the cover of general troop movements to maintain order. The Turks had been expecting a small British occupation force but they were aghast to find the ancient foe, with their expansionist designs on Anatolia, landing from the British warships. Under the protection of the *Entente* forces, the occupying Greeks, in front of the world's press, proceeded to conduct a massacre of around four hundred townspeople from the Turkish districts of Smyrna (after local Turks had supposedly fired a few shots).

Lloyd George acquiesced in the Greek advance into Anatolia, within a few days of their arrival in Smyrna, despite the fact that the Greeks were only authorized to occupy the town and its hinterland. And this seemed to mark the start of the development of a new Pontic state in Asia Minor with Smyrna as its nucleus.

### The Peace Conference And Constantinople

Hanns Froembgen has the following interesting account of the way the Turkish Government was humiliated at the Peace Conference in Paris:

"The Allied Peace Conference had assembled in the Champs Elysées... The Treaty of Versailles had been signed; peace had been dictated to Germany, and now they could slowly turn their attention to the South-East and consider the Oriental question.

Actually, the secret pacts for the partition of Turkey, signed before the War and supplemented and amended at various times during the War, had the largest say in the dictation of peace; but there were at the same time certain squabbles and jealousies among the victors which made the matter more difficult. As a grand gesture, they had invited to Paris the Grand Vizier, whom they proposed to hear.

A squat figure... the Tiger, Clemenceau, sat in an arm-chair at the head of the big conference table... Next to him could be seen the massive Welsh skull of Lloyd George. The third delegate, the Italian, was the reserved, gentlemanly Count Sforza. Surrounding the three big men were a crowd of satellites, secretaries of state and departmental experts.

There was an oppressive atmosphere in the room, which reminded one of a court of justice. The door opened, and into the centre of the 'U' shaped table stepped the brother-in-law of the Ottoman Sultan, Grand Vizier Damad Fend Pasha, in appearance—save for the Turkish fez—a typical English gentleman. With a dignified bearing and stern, steady features, he advanced into the room, followed by his suite, under a crossfire of glances from the big, feared men who were assembled to share out the world and decide the fate of nations.

Greetings were cool and formal; the Tiger gave a slight snort; and Lloyd George's head transformed itself into an untakeable fort.

The Grand Vizier was too much a man of the world and too skilful a diplomat to show surprise at the extreme coolness of his reception. But for the first time an uneasy feeling of depression overpowered him on realizing that he was there not to be treated on equal terms, but as a helpless defendant in the dock.

Damad Ferid began to state his case, but his words, he could not help noticing, fell on empty ears. The judges of the world were not listening to him. In the Tiger's eyes there was a look of scorn, a gleam of hatred. The Grand Vizier cited Wilson's fourteen points in support of the sacred principle of self-determination for the nations. The Ottoman Government acknowledged that principle. They were willing to accord self-administration to the Arab provinces and desired to remodel themselves in harmony with the rest of the civilized world and contribute their share towards the tasks of civilization. The entry of Turkey into the War—the Imperial Ottoman Government freely admitted it—was a crime. But the guilt lay with the men who held power at the time, Enver, Talaat and the Members of the Committee of Union and Progress, who, without reasonable justification, plunged the country into war....

A chair was suddenly pushed back, and the Tiger jumped up to attack this last sentence. Here was a chance for him to use his claws. They had heard, from the mouth of the Grand Vizier of the Ottoman Empire, that Turkish statesmen bore the guilt for the crime of war. That confession substantially simplified the trial and clarified the position. Outside that the Grand Vizier seemed to have already forgotten that his country was completely in the hands of the Allies and that it was the place of the conquered to remain silent.

The Tiger warmed to his subject. Did they remember the Levantine proverb—Where the Turk treads no grass will grow? Had they forgotten that the Ottoman race had always been barbarians by nature and that the world had never known anything from them save brutalities and atrocities? Was it not, therefore, perfectly natural that the military clique should get together with a similar clique in Berlin to destroy human civilization and freedom? Who would attempt to estimate the number of war crimes with which the Turks had aroused the disgust of the whole world?

'Be silent, your Highness! Relieve Paris of your presence! You will honour us by returning to your country as quickly as possible, where you may yet have the opportunity of dedicating yourself to the tasks of civilization!'" (*Kemal Ataturk,* pp.106-7.)

At the first meetings of the Allies about Constantinople in 1919, the English strongly argued that the Turks should be evicted from the city, whilst the French held the contrary opinion. Britain toyed with the idea of removing the Sultan, as it had the Kaiser, and putting the Turks out of Constantinople completely. One suggestion by the former Prime Minister, Asquith, was to 'Vaticanize' the Sultan—leaving him in his palace as Caliph but taking away his temporal authority and control of Constantinople from the Turks.

There were strong elements in the British State who were in favour of placing the city under 'international control'—which would probably have meant British control. France, though, which had extensive commercial interests in Constantinople, was opposed to expelling the Turks and handing over control of the city entirely to Britain.

Gaston Gaillard noted the importance of another factor, which he believed to have altered the British position:

> "The fear of Bolshevism... brought about in 1920 a complete change in British ideas concerning Turkey and Constantinople. The London Cabinet realised that the Turks were the first nation that the Bolshevist propaganda could reach, and to which the Moscow Government could most easily and effectually give its support against British policy in Asia Minor, which would make the situation in the East still more complicated. So, in order not to drive the Ottoman Government into open resistance, England first showed an inclination to share the view, held by France from the outset, that the Turks should be allowed to remain in Constantinople." (*Turkey And Europe*, p.97.)

Britain had sent invasion armies into Russia to bring down the Bolshevik Government but the effect of this action had been a strengthening of support for them. The survival of the revolutionary government put a complicating factor in the politics of Europe and Asia—the fear of the revolution spreading. So it was decided that the Sultan had to be worked with.

The news that the Turks were to stay in Constantinople provoked a sudden wave of hostility in Britain, emanating from a range of interests, including the Protestant churches and most of the Press. A memorandum was handed to Mr. Lloyd George and printed in *The Times* of February 23rd. It was signed by, among others, the Archbishops of Canterbury and York, the Bishop of London, Lord Cecil, A. G. Gardiner (former editor of *The Daily News*), Lord Bryce (former ambassador to the United States), the well-known writer Hugh Seton-Watson, and Professor Burrows, Principal of King's College, along with other academics and clergy. It protested that the chance to expel the Turk from Byzantium was about to be lost and Christianity would pay the price.

This led to a debate in the House of Commons on February 26th, on the retention of the Turks in Constantinople, in which Lloyd George said:

> "When the peace terms are published there is no friend of the Turk, should there be any left, who will not realise that he has been terribly punished for his follies, his blunders, his crimes, and his iniquities. Stripped of more than half his Empire, his country under the Allied guns, deprived of his army, his navy, his prestige— the punishment will be terrible enough to satisfy the bitterest foe of the Turkish Empire, drastic enough for the sternest judge. My right hon. friend suggested that there was a religious issue involved. That would be the most dangerous of all, and the most fatal. I am afraid that underneath the

agitation there is not only the movement for the expulsion of the Turk, but there is something of the old feeling of Christendom against the Crescent. If it is believed in the Mohammedan world that our terms are dictated by the purpose of lowering the flag of the Prophet before that of Christendom, it will be fatal to our government in India...

Mr. Lloyd George went on to state that the Allies had contemplated maintaining only the spiritual power of the Sultan, but unfortunately this scheme did not seem likely to solve the difficulties of the situation. For Constantinople had to be administered at the same time, and it is easier to control the Sultan and his Ministers in Constantinople than if they were relegated to Asia Minor." (*Turkey And Europe*, pp.108-9.)

So the Sultan was to be kept as a puppet in Constantinople where he was easier to control, with a gun to his head, to do the Imperial bidding—with the British fleet and army occupying the Straits and Constantinople, to ensure his continued cooperation.

A combination of factors led to this decision—including the fear of Bolshevism, the opposition of the Indian Office who feared the effect on Moslems in the Empire, the lack of money to engage in a further round of conflict and America's unwillingness to share the Imperial burden.

This ridiculous scheme, to hold a nation in perpetuity at the point of a gun, was the start of the blundering that characterised the behaviour of the Empire after the Great War.

### The Treaty of Sèvres

A year after the British declaration of War on Turkey, Asquith outlined his '*Only Terms For Peace*' to Parliament. *The Freeman's Journal* of 15th November 1915, reported Britain's intentions with regard to the Ottoman Empire in these terms:

"The Turkish Empire would be torn to fragments, and Armenia, Syria, Palestine, Mesopotamia and Thrace divided amongst those who would develop those once fair places now desolated under alien rule. The Turks would be generally penned up in central Anatolia, where they would be compelled to learn to work instead of massacre."

That was not the advice of the de Bunsen Committee. But the Asquith Government could not resist taking the best bits of the Ottoman Empire for England and for those who had contributed to the War, and then confining the Turks to a large Anatolian desert concentration camp where they would be made to labour for their past sins.

By 1920, only Lloyd George and Churchill remained of the Liberals present in the Coalition of May 1915. But the intentions of the Coalition towards the Ottoman Empire were carried over into the Treaty of Sèvres.

The Treaty of Sèvres was a drastic punitive settlement aimed at reducing the former Ottoman State to a small inland Anatolian rump under Allied economic and military control. The victorious Allies had already disposed of the Ottoman's Arab possessions at San Remo in April 1920. France had received a Mandate over Syria and Britain Mandates over Palestine and Mesopotamia. The Treaty of Sèvres confirmed these provisions as well as the establishment of Hejaz-Arabia in the South.

In the negotiations leading up to Sèvres, the French had desired a demilitarized Turkey under the financial control of the Allies but without any partition of its territory amongst the Allies. However, Lloyd George and Lord Curzon insisted on a distribution of territory and the Greek colonial project; they got the French to accept that by conceding France's financial demands over Constantinople. Britain retained the occupation of the Straits and Cyprus for itself. The Turkish Army was reduced to a small token force. Economically, the detested Capitulations were to be extended and the national finances of Turkey placed under Allied supervision. Greece was to receive the valuable territory of Turkish Thrace, to the West of Constantinople and the Straits, plus some islands guarding the approaches of the Dardanelles and the great port of Smyrna and its hinterland in Anatolia – an addition of 1,700,000 to its population.

Furthermore, the Treaty provided for the establishment of an independent State of Armenia and an autonomous Kurdistan carved out of eastern and southern Anatolia. It was estimated that an Armenian State would need about 15,000 soldiers to establish it and get it up and running. So it was offered to America — who failed to take up the opportunity of carrying out the Imperialist's dirty work for them, and Armenia was forgotten about.

The Turkish delegation objected to the terms imposed on them by the draft Treaty at Sèvres but the Allies issued a 'note' to them informing them of the reason why they were being punished, if they needed an explanation. It was published in *The Times* of 19th July 1920:

"The Turkish Government would appear to think that its responsibility in the great war is less than its allies and it is therefore entitled to lenient treatment. The Allies cannot accept that plea.

In the opinion of the Allies, Turkey voluntarily joined a conspiracy against the liberty of all nations at a time when its tyrannical purpose had become revealed to all. They consider that Turkey was thereby guilty peculiar treachery to Powers which for more than half a century had been her steadfast friends... The Turkish delegation does not appear to appreciate the loss and suffering which Turkey's intervention has caused to humanity. The extent of Turkey's liability is not to be gauged merely by the cost of overcoming the Turkish armies. By gratuitously closing a great international waterway in the face of the Allies and so cutting off the communications between Russia, Rumania and the Western Allies, Turkey certainly prolonged the war by not less than two years, and caused a loss to the Allies of several millions of lives and thousands of millions of pounds. The reparation that Turkey owes to those who, at terrible cost, have re-established liberty for the world is far greater than she can ever pay. The Allies are clear that the time has come when it is necessary to put an end once and for all to the empire of the Turks over other nations...

The Allies can make no modifications in the clauses of the Treaty which detach Thrace and Smyrna from Turkish rule, for in both areas the Turks are in a minority... the freedom of the port is guaranteed by the Treaty, its inhabitants will have the strongest interest in making their town the port of the hinterland, and under an honest government will serve the interior more effectively than ever. The arrangement is analogous to that introduced at Danzig.

As regards the regime of the Straits, there can be no question of the necessity of taking effective measures to prevent another betrayal of the cause of civilization by a Turkish Government...

A BAG AND BAGGAGE HINT

In conclusion the Allies would point out that the Treaty has not the character attributed to it by the Turkish delegation... the Treaty even leaves Constantinople as the capital of Turkey. In view of the misuse made by the Turks of their power in the past, the Allies have had grave doubts as to the wisdom of this step. If the Turkish Government refuses to sign the peace, still more if it finds itself unable to reestablish its authority in Anatolia, or to give effect to the Treaty, the Allies, in accordance with the terms of the Treaty, may be driven to reconsider this arrangement by ejecting the Turks from Europe altogether."

In many ways this Treaty was similar to that imposed on Ireland a year or so later. The terms were dictated to the minor party and the offer was a 'take it or leave it' affair with the threat of blockade, war and reoccupation of the country hanging over the delegations that met the British. And there was the insistence that the Turkish Government repress the Kemalists and the Turkish democracy just as the Free State Government were expected to deal with the Republicans who remained loyal to the Irish democracy — or face the consequences of the Imperial Power doing it itself.

The difference lies in the tremendous short-term success of this British project in Ireland but its catastrophic failure in Turkey.

It is also noteworthy that the British wanted to make Constantinople into a kind of 'free city,' like Danzig. The Middle East should be thankful that Ataturk prevented this development, in the light of the use made of the European 'free city' in restarting the European conflict a couple of decades later. Ataturk's success is the main reason why Turkey was able to negotiate the Second World War largely in peace.

### Sèvres And The 'War of Extermination'

Another English view of Sèvres was presented in an article called *The Turkish Treaty* by Leland Buxton, in the *Problems of Empire Series,* published by the Imperial publication *Foreign Affairs. Foreign Affairs* magazine was described as Britain's 'Journal of International Understanding' by its publishers. And it appraises the Treaty's chances as a going concern in a much more realistic manner than did those who imposed it. So much so that it is worth reproducing almost in its entirety.

It was written in mid-1920 and it is very perceptive in its assessment of the mistakes Britain was making in seeking to impose this settlement on the region:

"While the creation of a Greek Empire is perhaps the worst feature of the Turkish settlement, there is little cause for satisfaction in any part of the Treaty. If its object is to make our own position in the Middle East secure against Turkish aggression in the future, it is totally ineffective. Turkey will, quite possibly, become a more formidable military power than she was before the war. She is not surrounded, like Bulgaria, by hostile States, and it is quite impossible for the Allies, under present circumstances, to conquer and occupy the whole of Anatolia, where the Nationalists are supremely indifferent to the orders of the Government at Constantinople. We have no means, therefore, of enforcing either the military clauses of the Treaty or those dealing with the protection of minorities...

One of the most important sections of the Treaty is that which creates a 'Commission of the Straits,' with its own flag, budget, and police, to control the navigation of the Bosphorus, the Sea of Marmora, and the Dardanelles. 'In the case of threats to the freedom of passage of the Straits,' says the official summary of the Treaty, 'special provision is made for appeal by the commission to the representatives at Constantinople of Great Britain, France, and Italy, which powers under the military provisions of the Treaty, provide forces for the occupation of the zone of the Straits;' the naval and military commanders of the Allies will then (it is hoped) take the necessary steps. The Commission is to consist, for the present, of representatives of the British Empire, France, Italy, Japan, Greece, Rumania, and of the United States, if that Power is willing to participate. An element of comedy is supplied by the provision that Russia and Bulgaria (who are vitally interested in the freedom of the Straits) shall have representatives on the Commission if and when they become members of the League of Nations. In other words, they are indefinitely excluded from participation, and it will doubtless be one of the objects of Greek policy to prevent Bulgaria's admission to the League.

The League of Nations is also to serve as a convenient excuse for preventing, as far as possible, the resumption of German trade with Asia Minor. It is declared that the members of the League are to enjoy complete freedom in the use of the ports of Constantinople, Smyrna, Alexandretta, etc. Thus all the members who trade with Turkey are furnished with an additional motive for keeping the ex-enemy States outside the League of Nations for a long period. The League does not figure largely in the Turkish Treaty, but it has provided the Supreme council with some welcome opportunities of gratifying its innate love of cant.

Whatever advantages we may hope to gain by inflicting further injuries on our Christian enemies, there is little doubt that we shall suffer terribly for the crusading enthusiasm of Mr. Lloyd George... According to the Peace Treaty, Turkey practically loses her independence and is placed under the tutelage of three Christian Powers; while the conditions under which the Sultan remains at a semi-internationalised Constantinople, almost under the guns of the despised Greeks, will certainly not diminish Moslem resentment. To avoid the suspicion that the British Empire was hostile to Islam, it was essential that Turkish suzerainty, at least, should be retained over the greater part of Eastern Thrace, with its sacred city of Adrianople, and over the 'Jazirat-ul-Arab' (i.e., Syria, Mesopotamia, and Arabia), which has a peculiar holiness in the eyes of all Moslems. An important party has long existed among the Turks which was in favour of provincial autonomy throughout the Empire, and there is no doubt that the Ottoman Government would now give the inhabitants of the Arab provinces what they desire, i.e., the right to mismanage their own affairs with the least possible interference from any central government. As the great majority of the population would prefer the suzerainty of the Sultan to that of any Christian Power, a wise statesmanship would have left the Turks and Arabs to come to a mutual agreement.

The Allied statesmen, however, had the mentality of concession-hunters, and a particularly keen scent for coal and oil. Although the precise arrangements made among themselves have not yet been published, it is clear that Italy, as usual, gets the smallest share of the spoils, and neither the coal of Eregli, nor a sphere of influence in Southern Anatolia, will compensate her for the aggrandisement of Greece. Syria, Mesopotamia and Hejaz are declared to be independent states, but this is a fiction which deceives nobody; humbug has become such an ingrained habit with the Big Two that it has ceased even to amuse. 'The selection of mandatories is to be fixed by the principal Allied Powers,' and not by the peoples chiefly concerned. In practice, of course, France is to have a Protectorate over Syria, and Great Britain over Mesopotamia, Palestine and Arabia. These things outrage the feelings of Moslems throughout the world, but they do not rankle in the minds of the Turks like the Greek annexation of Thrace and Smyrna, especially as the British and French do not habitually persecute those who differ from them in race or religion.

In the case of the Treaty with Turkey, there was no clamour for vengeance from France, and it was open to Great Britain, therefore, either to initiate a policy of conciliation or to insist on that of the Big Stick. Mr. Lloyd George, largely under the influence of M. Venizelos, has chosen the latter course, and the consequences will be disastrous for the British taxpayer. We have driven the Turks into the arms of the Bolsheviks, and have made the Pan-Islamic danger a reality. From Khiva to Cairo, from Adrianople to Delhi, we have fanned the flames of fanaticism and organised the growing animosity against Christians in general and against the British in particular. The menace to our Eastern Empire becomes more formidable month by month. When a great nation allows its foreign policy to be dictated by a Balkan statesman, it must expect to suffer." (*Foreign Affairs, Problems of Empire Series No. 2, Special Supplement, July 1920*, pp. xii-xiv.)

In the same publication there is another interesting article entitled *Self-Determination And The Turkish Treaty* by '*Q.*' It is worth reproducing because it deals very well with the ingenious uses made by Britain of the principle of self-determination—a principle that could have a myriad of interpretations and applications to suit policy:

"Although peace has not yet resumed its sway over mankind and is not likely to do so for many a decade yet if the 'governing classes' continue acting as they are acting to-day—how distant seem the days of war when the noblest of principles were being advertised with an eloquence that had all the appearance of sincerity! The most notable of these and the special product of the mentality of the war is the principle of self-determination which, chameleon-like, takes on the hue of political surroundings in various parts of the world.

Montenegro, perhaps the smallest of the small nations of the world, in the interests of which we were told the war was waged, must submit to Serbia because, reversing the Japanese proverb, it is better to be the tail of a bull than the head of a cock, and she is doomed to lose her individuality because the autocrats at the Peace Conference table have decreed that Serbia must have a respectable size and population. There, according to Lord Curzon, the advantage of being part of a larger unit outweighed the inestimable possession of liberty which the people of the Black Mountain had evidently cherished for long centuries. But, when the Mussulmans of India merely ask the Premier not to interfere in the purely Muslim question of an adjustment of the undeniable right of the Arabs to autonomy within the scheme of Ottoman Sovereignty, so that the most essential religious institution of the Khilafat might not languish for want of adequate temporal power for the defence of the faith, he asks them whether he is to deny to the Arabs, because they are Muslim, the independence that has been given to the Czecho-Slovaks and the Yugoslavs, as if the Muslims of Egypt, supported by their Christian compatriots, had already had their undoubted independence recognised at 10 Downing Street, and as if the Arabs, ruled over by the Ottoman Khalifa did not need, in these days of large dominating empires, the support of their Muslim brethren of Turkey to withstand the pressure of so-called protectors and mandatories?

Again, when Ireland has so clearly determined what her future shall be, she is told by the Premier that: 'it is of no use talking about self-determination. If the Rt. Honourable gentleman (Mr. Adamson) supports self-determination, he must go the full length of planting an Irish Republic in Ireland ... Self-determination does not mean that every part of a country which has been acting together for hundreds of years shall have a right to say, we mean to set up a separate republic.....There must be that limitation to the application of any principle, otherwise you might carry it to every fragment and every locality in every country throughout the world. When you lay down a principle of that kind, you must lay it down within the limitations which common sense, which tradition will permit.'

And yet apparently if the starving population of blockaded Arabia—

387

promised immunity from attack and molestation—is made to demand separation from the Empire, to which the most sacred ties and traditions had bound her for many centuries, these great almoners at the Peace Conference table are so lavish in distributing the largesse of liberty that no consideration of the kind that overruled self-determination in Ireland, could check their generosity at other folk's expense. As for Smyrna, one wonders whether even the limitation of common sense was present in the Premier's mind at San Remo, let alone the limitation of tradition.

But the last connotation of self-determination is evidently the best. There is oil in Mosul, and the only self-determination that is therefore possible, is that the British shall demand a mandate in Mesopotamia. Verily as a member of the Indian Khilafat Delegation has said, the Prime Minister is pouring Mosul oil over the troubled waters of Mesopotamia!

All these interpretations are ingenious enough in their own way, but even they will not assist the Government in justifying its decision with regard to Thrace and Smyrna, or even with regard to so-called 'Armenia.'

Take the case of Thrace. it can hardly be forgotten how pressure was brought to bear on just such another Government in Turkey as Great Britain has set up there to-day under Damad Ferid Pasha, when Kamil and his colleagues were being urged early in 1913 to surrender Thrace to the Balkan Allies even before Adrianople had fallen. That was neither in accordance with the earlier formula of the Asquith government: 'No changes in the territorial *status quo ante bellum* as the result of the war' when the result of the war was feared to be in favour of Turkey, nor was it consistent with that Government's subsequent formula: 'The fruits of victory for the victor,' when unexpectedly it was the 'rank outsiders' that turned out to be the victors. Those who had any vestige of conscience left had protested against this 'Concert of Cowardice,' as a writer in the Daily Mail characterised this strange combination of the Powers against Turkey, and apart from the fact that Adrianople had not until then fallen and Thrace was still unoccupied by the Balkan Allies, the general argument used on the occasion against this spoliation of a brave but unfortunate nation was that 60 per cent of the population of Thrace was Turkish and Muslim...

And what is the story that these figures tell? The Treaty assigns to Greece the whole of the Turkish Vilayet of Adrianople or Eastern Thrace, leaving to Turkey in Europe only a strip of territory near Constantinople up to the Tchataldja lines. That, too, is entirely included in the 'Zone of the Straits' to be controlled by a Commission of the Powers which include Greece, Rumania and Bulgaria, but excludes Turkey herself.

According to the official census taken in 1914, the Muslim population of the Vilayet of Adrianople or Eastern Thrace to be ceded to Greece, was 360,000 or 57 per cent of the total, as against 224,000 Greeks or 35 1/2 per cent. Western Thrace had already passed out of Turkish sovereignty in spite of the fact that its Muslim population was 362,000 or 69 per cent as against 86,000 Greeks or 16 1/2. per cent. Taking the two together the total Muslim population of Thrace is 722,000 or 62 1/2 per cent as against 310,000 Greeks or 26 per cent.

The territory now to be ceded to Greece includes the second Muslim city of the Ottoman Empire, Adrianople, dear to Turks on account of its many sacred and historical associations. And yet there is not even a semblance of the exercise of self-determination, for fully knowing what the verdict of the people would be, the principal Allied Powers have taken no plebiscite. And it must not be forgotten that there is a considerable Bulgar element even in Eastern Thrace which is even more anti-Greek than the Turks, while in Western Thrace it nearly equals the Greek population.

This was the region covered by Mr. Lloyd George's pledge given on the 5th January, 1918, when he said: 'Nor are we fighting . . to deprive Turkey of its capital or of the rich and renowned lands of Asia Minor and Thrace which are predominantly Turkish in race.'

This pledge was emphatically repeated on the 26th February this year, when in the House of Commons the Prime Minister said:

'It was given... after full consultation with all parties. The Member for Paisley and Lord Grey acquiesced. There was a real desire to give a national statement of war aims, a statement that would carry all parties with it, and all agreed... It was a carefully prepared statement, it was not a speech in the ordinary sense of the term. It was a declaration... That declaration was specific. It was unqualified, and it was very deliberate. It was made with the consent of all parties in the community... that was a perfectly deliberate pledge.'

The case of Thrace is bad enough in all conscience, but that of Smyrna is worse. Here there is no pretence of the people being predominantly Christians. The official census of 1914 shows that as against 1,250,000 Mussulmans there are only 300,000 Greeks, 20,000 Armenians, and 40,000 other elements, but since in the town of Smyrna itself there is quite a large minority of the Greeks averaging 24 per cent. against 42 per cent. Muslims, whom Turkish tolerance allowed not only to live but to prosper, Smyrna and a good deal of adjoining territory — the richest of the 'rich and renowned homelands of the Turk in Asia Minor' — are to be lopped off from the Turkish Empire and placed under the administration of the Greeks with the 'option' to decide five years later in favour of annexation with Greece, but not in favour of reversion to Turkish administration!... Muslims could discover no justification for this action except the desire of Greek capitalists to exploit the rich and renowned lands of Asia Minor, which are admittedly the homelands of the Turks. If this state of affairs was allowed to continue he declared that not only would the Turk be driven out 'bag and baggage' from Europe, but that he would have no 'bag and baggage' left to him even in Asia. He would be paralysed, commercially and industrially, in a land-locked small Emirate in Asia Minor, the speedy bankruptcy of which was certain. The application of the principle of self-determination, he contended, would entirely rule out the Greek claim in this fertile region, which obviously tempts the greed of the capitalist and the exploiter...

But it is forgotten, both in the case of Thrace and of Smyrna, that in 1898 there were 7 million Turks in Turkey in Europe, in Thessaly and in the Islands, but that at the present time there are only 2 million Albanians and Turks in the

Balkans. As many as 3 million have disappeared from the world, in the recent wars and the massacres that followed; but even then as many as 1million emigrated to Thrace and Turkey in Asia. And yet, if M. Venizelos is to be believed, they swelled the figures of Turkish population neither in Thrace nor in Smyrna. Five years hence, that is, if Mustafa Kemal and the Nationalists permit the Treaty to be enforced, M. Venizelos would have the satisfaction of announcing to the world a unanimous decision in favour of the annexation of Smyrna and the surrounding territory to Greece. We know what happened to the Muslim population of Crete; and we also know what happened to the peaceful and prosperous Turkish community in Thessaly. In the latter there are to-day villages bearing Turkish names such as Sakaalar, Maimounlar, Inebeilar, etc. But as a Turk has put it, they are all empty of Turks.

This is what Venizelist Hellenism and Lloyd Georgian self-determination mean, and if Turkey submits to this treaty, Smyrna will have self-determination with a vengeance. Only other people spell it differently. They call it extermination." (*Foreign Affairs, Problems of Empire Series No. 2, Special Supplement, July 1920,* pp. xvi—xix.)

That is the background to the Greek tragedy that was to unfold in Asia Minor, upon the prompting of Lloyd George. Self-determination was recognized as a 'war of extermination' by 'Q' and that is what it proved to be.

### Suppression Of Democracy, Turkey 1920

In early 1919 Britain began to suppress the Irish democracy which came into being after the 1918 election. About a year later it did the same in Turkey.

Wanting to get Mustapha Kemal out of the way, Britain persuaded the Sultan in Constantinople to send him to Eastern Anatolia, to control Turkish forces that were preparing to resist the establishment of an Armenian State. But, having got there, Kemal resigned from the Army, united with these forces, and signed the *Amasia Protocol* on June 9th 1919, declaring his intention to resist the occupation and also the Sultan, as its instrument. This was a rival source of power to the puppet regime in Constantinople and became the nucleus of a new Turkish national development.

Kemal presided over a National Congress held in July at Erzurum, in Eastern Anatolia, and then in Sivas in September 1919. From these conferences was issued the *Milli Misak* or National Pact. This pact proposed a peace with the occupying forces on the basis of self-determination for the Arabs south of the Armistice line; the opening of the Straits to free commerce; full rights for non-Turkish minorities; the retention of all non-Arab Moslem-majority areas of the Empire (Anatolia, Eastern Thrace and Mosul included); and abolition of the Capitulations.

If this declaration had been issued by one of the new national constructions of the *Entente* in central Europe ('Czechoslovakia' or 'Yugoslavia') it would have been trumpeted as a great product and realisation of the war for small nations. But instead it was taken by Britain as a declaration of war—in the same way it took the establishment of *Dáil Éireann* after the democratic decision of the 1918 election. Not in my Empire!

The new political expression of the Turkish national will influenced the Sultan to dismiss his Premier Damad Ferid Pasha. A new, more representative, parliament came into existence in January 1920—the first really representative assembly Turkey had ever had. It declared support for the National Pact. The *Entente* viewed this development with concern and told the Sultan to repress it. As Churchill candidly put it:

> "The Allies were loyal to the principle of representative government: accordingly the Turks had voted. Unhappily, they had almost all of them voted the wrong way." (David Walder, *The Chanak Incident,* p.76.)

To force the Ottoman government to submit to the Allied peace terms, and to control events in Turkey, the British Government authorised a military occupation of Constantinople on March 16th 1920. British forces marched into Constantinople, arrested the Nationalist leaders in the city and occupied the various Ottoman Ministries. The leading Deputies and leaders in the Constantinople Parliament were arrested by British Intelligence Officers and it was shut down. The representatives of the Turkish democracy were sent to internment in Malta.

A week later Mustapha Kemal opened the Turkish Grand National Assembly in Ankara, which was attended by, among others, those Deputies who had managed to escape the Allied repression of Parliament in Constantinople.

Gaston Gaillard has the following account of these events in his 1921 book *Turkey And Europe.* I have included a long extract to reveal the details of how it was that Britain, in repressing the Turkish Parliament, set off the chain of events that led to a national war of liberation:

> "At the beginning of the armistice England had deported the members and chief supporters of the Committee of Union and Progress, and later on the high functionaries who had been arrested by Damad Ferid Pasha, and were about to be court-martialled. One night fifty-four of the latter out of about 130 were suddenly deported to Malta for fear they should be set free by the population of Constantinople... The British even evinced a desperate, undignified animosity and an utter lack of generosity in regard to the Turkish generals who had defeated them. They had, as it were, carried away the spirit of Turkey...
>
> On Tuesday, March 16, the Allied troops, consisting mostly of British soldiers, under the command of General Milne, occupied the Ottoman Government offices. It might seem strange that the Allied troops in Constantinople were commanded by a British general, when the town was the residence of General Franchet d'Esperey, commander-in-chief of the inter-

Allied troops on the Macedonian front, who, in the decisive battle in which he broke through the Bulgarian front, had had General Milne under him... But, after the defeat of Bulgaria in October, 1918, the British Government required that the troops sent to the Constantinople area should be led by a British general.

In this way General Milne assumed command of the British troops stationed round and in Constantinople when Admiral Calthorpe had concluded the armistice with Turkey, and as a consequence General Franchet d'Esperey, though still commander-in-chief of the Allied forces in European Turkey, was now under the orders of General Milne, commander of the Constantinople garrison and the forces in Asia Minor. ...

Thus all the plans of the French headquarters were altered by England, and to her advantage; at the same time part of our endeavours was broken up and annihilated under the pressure of the Pan-Russian circles that urged France to intervene in Russia, and the French policy in the East was wholly at the mercy of England...

A note added that for a short time the political administration would be left to the Turks, but under the control of Allied officers. Martial law was proclaimed, and, in case of resistance, force would be resorted to.

The Ottoman Government gave no answer, and an hour later all the measures mentioned by General Milne were carried out. As these operations took a whole day, all the means of transport and communication were temporarily stopped. At the War Office the soldiers on duty attempted to resist the British forces. A skirmish ensued, in which two British soldiers were killed, and an officer and three soldiers wounded; nine Turks, including an officer, were killed, and a few more wounded.

At the same hour a Greek destroyer steamed into the Golden Horn, and cast anchor opposite the Patriarch's palace. Before this, General Milne had had a few deputies and senators arrested, together with a few men considered as having a share in the Nationalist movement... Reouf Bey and Kara Vassif Bey were considered as representing in the Turkish Parliament Mustafa Kemal Pasha and the people who ensured the transmission of his orders. All these men were arrested illegally and brutally... Among the men arrested that night, Jemal, Jevad, and Mahmoud Pasha, all three former Ministers, were insulted and sent to prison in their nightclothes, with their arms bound. Their doors and windows were broken open, and their Moslem wives were threatened... Some children of thirteen or fourteen were also arrested and thrashed. Eight Turkish soldiers on duty at Shahzade-Bashi were killed in the morning while they lay asleep on their camp-beds, and the censorship probably suppressed other deeds of the same kind.

The Ottoman Government could not understand how members of Parliament could be imprisoned, especially by the English, the founders of the parliamentary system... England, to enhance her influence over public opinion, got control over the chief newspapers which were not friendly to her. Jelal Noury Bey, the director of the *lleri*, a radical newspaper, and Ahmed Emin Bey, the director of the Vakit, were deported. The Alemdar, the Peyam Sabah, the Stamboul, edited by Refi Jevad, Ali Kemal, and Said Mollah, which, since the first days of the armistice, had praised the English policy, fell into English hands...

On March 21, 1920, the British at Skutari requisitioned the police courts, the law courts, the police station, the town hall, and the prison, thus almost completely disorganising the administration of the town. In the note signed by the High Commissioners, this occupation was described as a measure of guarantee, with a view to the execution of the treaty that was going to be forced on Turkey.

Yet it seemed rather strange that such measures should be taken before the treaty was concluded—or was it because the English, being aware the treaty was unacceptable, thought it necessary to gag the Turks beforehand, or even sought to exasperate them ?—for if the Turks offered resistance, then the English would have a right to intervene very sternly, and thus could justify the most unjustifiable measures of repression. What would England and the United States have answered if France had proposed such coercive measures against Germany in addition to those of the armistice?

It was stated in this note that the occupation would not last long, and was no infringement upon the Sultan's sovereignty, that it aimed at rallying the Turks in a common endeavour to restore prosperity to Turkey in accordance with the Sultan's orders; but it also threatened that, should disorder last longer in Asia Minor, the occupation might be extended and the provisions of the treaty might be made harder, in which case Constantinople would be severed from Turkey...

Finally, the very day after the occupation of Constantinople, General Milne, who commanded the British troops of occupation, enjoined the Salih Pasha Cabinet to resign under pretence that it no longer enjoyed the Sovereign's confidence. The Grand Vizier refused to comply with the English general's request, as the Government had the confidence of the Chamber and the Sovereign need not apply to the commander of the forces of occupation for permission to communicate with his Ministers.

After incarcerating a good many deputies, senators, and political men, as has just been seen, the general gave the Grand Vizier to understand that orders had been given for the arrest of the Ministers in case they should attempt to go to their departments.

In order to spare his country another humiliation, Salih Pasha handed in his resignation to the Sultan, who, following the advice of England, charged Damad Ferid to form another Cabinet. It requires all the reasons that have been previously given to enable us to understand why England threatened and humbled Turkey to such an extent—the only Power left in the East that could be a factor for moderation and peace.

Mustafa Kemal never recognised the Damad Ferid Cabinet, and only after the latter had resigned and Ali Riza Pasha had been appointed Grand Vizier did he consent, in order to avoid another conflict with the Sultan, to enter into negotiations with the Constantinople Government. Salih Pasha was charged by the Minister to carry on the negotiations with the Nationalists, and repaired to Amasia.

There it was agreed—first, that the National Organisation should be officially recognised as a lawful power which was necessary to the defence of the rights of the country, and should have full liberty of action side by side with the Government; secondly, that the Cabinet should avoid taking any decision sealing the fate of the country before Parliament met; thirdly, that some appointments should be made in agreement with the National Organisation, after which the latter should not interfere in the administration of the country.

Besides, as Mustafa Kemal said later on in a speech made before the Angora [Ankara] Assembly, though the Sultan had been represented by some as lacking energy, not maintaining the dignity of the Imperial throne, and not being a patriot, yet the reason why he had fallen under English tutelage was that he had seen no other means to save both the existence of Turkey and his throne. The question whether Parliament should meet at Constantinople or in a province brought on a first disagreement between the Government and Mustafa Kemal, who finally yielded.

But, owing to the occupation of Constantinople, Parliament soon found itself in a precarious condition, and the National Organisation decided to hold its sittings at Angora. After all these events a deputy, Riza Nour, at the sitting of March 18, 1920, raised a protest against the occupation of Constantinople and the incarceration of some members of Parliament by the Allies, which measures were an insult to the dignity of the Turkish Parliament, and a contravention of the constitutional laws and the law of nations.

This motion, carried unanimously by the Ottoman Chamber and signed by the Vice-President, M. Hussein Kiazim—the President, for fear of being prosecuted by the British authorities, having left his official residence—was forwarded to the Allied and neutral Parliaments, and the Ottoman Chamber adjourned *sine die* till it was possible for the deputies to carry out their mandate safely.

Ahmed Riza, former President of the Chamber and Senate of the Ottoman Empire—who, after the failure of Damad Ferid's mission to Paris, had addressed an open letter to M. Clemenceau on July 17, 1919, almost the anniversary day of the Constitution—joined in that protest and commented upon the treatment some members of Parliament had undergone, as follows: 'It is contrary to all parliamentary rights and principles throughout the world and to the legal dispositions that guarantee the inviolability and immunity of all members of the Turkish Parliament to arrest representatives of the nation while they are carrying out their mandate. So the armed interference of the foreigner with our Chamber cannot be in any way excused or accounted for. Such an arbitrary intrusion, especially on the part of England, that is looked upon as the founder of the parliamentary system, will bring everlasting shame to British civilisation.

After the illegal arrest of several of its members, the Turkish Parliament adjourned *sine die*, as a token of protest, till the deputies are able to carry out their mandate freely and safely... Who is to examine the Peace Treaty to-day, and who is to give its assent to it now the nation has been deprived of its representatives? Of what value will be a treaty thus worked out secretly, behind closed doors, and concluded in such conditions? How can the signature of the members of the Government be considered as binding the nation? For the new Ministry does not yet represent the Ottoman nation, since no motion of confidence has hitherto been carried by a chamber which does not sit; and so it cannot be looked upon as being legally constituted. Whatever may happen, the nation alone can decide its own fate. If, at such a serious juncture, when its very existence is at stake, it were not able to defend its own cause and its own rights freely through the peaceful vote of its own mandatories, it would be looked upon by the whole of mankind as the victim of most unfair treatment, the responsibility of which will one day be determined by history.'" *(pp.153-168.)*

Britain, by suppressing all democratic expression in Turkey—in order to do what it willed to the Turks—created a situation where the nation removed itself from its capital and reformed in its heartland. Its representative elements (those which had not been interned) drifted off to the new national expression and the modern Turkish State was born in Anatolia.

### *The Treaty And 'Civil War'*

The Sultan was presented with the Treaty in July 1920 with the message, sign or else. Gaston Gaillard describes the signing of it, under the threat of war:

"Turkey was granted a period of ten days, expiring on July 27 at 12 midnight, to let the Allies definitely know whether she accepted the clauses of the treaty and intended to sign it... As soon as the Grand Vizier came back to Constantinople a conflict arose between the latter, who maintained Turkey was compelled to sign the treaty, and some members of the Cabinet...

On July 20 the Sultan summoned a Council of the Imperial Family, including the Sultanas, and on July 22 the Crown Council, consisting of fifty-five of the most prominent men in Turkey, among whom were five generals, a few senators, the members of the Cabinet, and some members of the former Government. The Grand Vizier spoke first, and declared Turkey could not do otherwise than sign the treaty. All the members of the Council supported the Government's decision, with the exception of Marshal Fuad, who had already used his influence with the Sultan in favour of the Nationalists and who said the Turks should die rather than sign such a peace, and of Riza Pasha, who had commanded the artillery before the war, who said Turkey did not deserve such a grievous punishment and refused to vote. Turkey had been at war for ten years, which partly accounts for the decision taken. Therefore the order to sign the treaty of peace was officially given...

Then the question arose how the treaty—which now admitted of no discussion—after being enforced and carried out by arms, before the delay for acceptance granted to the Ottoman Government had come to an end, against all rules of international law and diplomatic precedents, could solve the Eastern question.

Of course it was alleged that the Greek offensive in Anatolia had nothing to do with the treaty of peace presented to Turkey, that it only constituted a preventive measure in support of the treaty and it was not directed against the Stambul Government, but against Mustafa Kemal's troops, which had broken the armistice by attacking the British troops on the Ismid line.

Yet this was but a poor reason, and how was it possible to justify the Greek attack in Thrace, which took place immediately after? The fact was that England and Greece, being afraid of losing their prey, were in a hurry to take hold of it, and neither Mr. Lloyd George nor M. Venizelos shrank from shedding more blood to enforce a treaty which could not bring about peace.

Now that the Allies had driven a Government which no longer represented Turkey to accept the treaty, and the latter had been signed, under English compulsion, by some aged politicians, while the Greeks and the British partitioned the Ottoman Empire between themselves, was it possible to say that all the difficulties were settled? The signature of the treaty could but weaken the tottering power of the Sultan. Moreover, England, eager to derive the utmost benefit from the weakness of Turkey, raised the question of the Caliphate; it was learned from an English source that the title of Caliph had been offered to the Emir of Afghanistan, but the latter had declined the offer. On the other hand, how could Mustafa Kemal be expected to adhere to the decisions taken in Constantinople?

It was to be feared, therefore, the agitation would be protracted, for an Anatolian campaign would offer far greater difficulties than those the Greek army had had to overcome on the low plains along the sea; and at Balikesri, standing at an altitude of 400 feet, begin the first slopes of the Anatolian uplands. As a matter of fact, Turkey was not dead, as Mr. Lloyd George believed, but the policy of the British Premier was doomed to failure—the same policy... which was paving the way to the secession of Ireland, and may one day cost Great Britain the loss of India and Egypt." (*Turkey And Europe*, pp. 254-9.)

## Civil War Or National War?

The following extract describing the sequence of events after the signing of the Treaty is taken from Hanns Froembgen's *Kemal Ataturk*. Froembgen refers to the conflict between the Treatyites and Kemal's Anti-Treatyites as a civil war. But I doubt if it is seen in Turkey as such. Turkey still has a strong and vigorous national culture, which was preserved and strengthened by what Ataturk did in 1919-22. It does not call a conflict between those who signed a Treaty at the point of a gun, and who subsequently attempted to impose it on the rest of the nation, and those who resisted it, a civil war. It understands it to have been a liberation war by the Turkish democracy:

"NOTICES posted in the principal streets and squares of Constantinople proclaimed a State of Siege. Damad Fend had for the second time assumed the responsibilities of the office of Grand Vizier. Shouts echoed through the streets. The Sheikh-ul-Islam called for the death of the rebels. Who would gain paradise must kill the Nationalists, who had been declared outlaws and on whose heads a high price had been set by the Padishah...

Anatolia was aflame. Risings occurred in all parts of the country. The Sultan's emissaries spent liberally of the English money with which they had been furnished, and they had no difficulty in finding deluded people who could be persuaded to fight for the Sultan against Mustafa Kemal. In addition, the summons of the Sheikh-ul-Islam was not without effect. Nationalist troops were despatched to all parts of the country, but owing to their weak numbers and the vastness of the country they were unable to quell all the outbreaks.

Anatolia was in a state of civil war.

Angora itself was a huge camp. People from all parts streamed into the little city, which was unable to accommodate even a small fraction of their number. Generals lived in stables and deputies slept in the open. When their day's work was done, they wrapped themselves in their over-coats, stretched out on the ground, and slept as well as the cutting steppe wind would allow. All differences in rank had vanished; the common emergency made all persons equal.

The National Assembly, which represented the revolutionary party, sat in the building formerly occupied by the Young Turk Committee of 'Union and Progress.' The assembly room was a long, narrow apartment with the Turkish flag hanging from one of its walls. The deputies, officers and civilians sat on plain wooden chairs. The President's chair, in front, was occupied by Mustafa Kemal.

This was the centre of the revolution, where work never ceased. During the evenings and nights two mean paraffin lamps provided necessary, though inadequate, illumination. The Executive Committee of the Great National Assembly was the revolutionary Government of Turkey. Mustafa Kemal was its President and Dictator.

Among the many persons who reported to the Dictator in Angora there was a short, unprepossessing man in the uniform of a colonel, but when Mustafa Kemal recognized him his delight was evident. Quickly the news spread through Angora that Colonel Ismet, after an adventurous journey from Constantinople, had arrived at the headquarters of the Nationalist Government. Who was Ismet? A newcomer, an unwritten page. At the Ministry of War he was supposed to have been working in secret for the revolution. Mustafa Kemal had long talks with the little colonel and aroused a great deal of astonishment by entering Ismet's name in the list of Ministers of the Revolutionary Government. Then it was announced that he was to receive command of the entire army... The appointment gave rise to a number of fierce arguments and angry scenes...

Sultan Vahideddine had not been idle. Further batches of Imperial troops had been sent out to Anatolia, and while the Kemalists were well occupied in quelling the risings which had broken out in all parts of the country, the Caliphate Army was steadily approaching Angora.

Vahideddine was within sight of the day when he would again be master of the land and in a position to establish his tribunal of vengeance.

At Sèvres, near Paris, the Allied Supreme Council had arrived at its decision regarding the peace conditions. Eighteen months had elapsed since the conclusion of the Armistice, and for eighteen months the Turkish people had existed in cruel uncertainty of their fate. Now they were to know. The victors had come to an agreement, and the dictated peace waited for signature.

As May of the year 1920 drew to its close, the Big Three published the conditions of the Peace. Even Sultan Vahideddine turned pale on being informed of them.

Constantinople and the Straits were to be placed under international control, and the Sultan, as Head of the Mohammedan religion, was to remain at the Golden Horn and reside under the eyes of the English. South Anatolia, Kilikia and its capital Adana were to fall to France, Italy was to receive the territory of Adalia, and Smyrna was to become Greek, in which instance the Greeks would be acting as stewards for England. Cut off from all access to the sea, Turkey was to have central Anatolia and Turks were to live in what may be described as a sort of Indian reservation. The Arab provinces were to be placed under British and French mandates. A new Armenian Republic was to be created in the Eastern Provinces and along the Black Sea.

It was Mustafa Kemal's special care that every peasant was made aware of the conditions of this dictated peace, which in vindictiveness and madness exceeded all others. All at once Anatolia grew calm, and the noise of fighting ceased throughout the land. Soldiers of the Caliphate Army held their rifle-butts aloft as a sign that they wished to fraternize with the Kemalists, and marched to Angora to place themselves under the banner of the Grey Wolf. The risings suddenly died down. All eyes turned to Mustafa Kemal, the man who had predicted what would happen and the man who summoned them to resist the victors and the traitors in their own land. The remaining loyal Imperial troops fled back to the Straits, hotly pursued by the Kemalists. Near Constantinople, on the Asiatic side of the Sea of Marmora, the British had dug themselves in. The loyal troops made for this position. The Kemalists, without a moment's life of ease in the capital and hastily dispatched to reinforce the position at Ismid on the Sea of Marmora, where fierce fighting was already in progress.

The Kemalists were the first at their destination and reached the coast before the British were able to arrive. Soon shells were flying across the Bosporus, several of them falling on the headquarters of the British High Commissioner. In the rear of Constantinople, in European Turkey stood a Turkish army corps that had gone over to Mustafa Kemal. It was set on the march. The British thus found themselves caught between two fires, held in the two arms of pincers. Stambul cheered itself hoarse, while in Pera the houses were hastily shut and barricaded. After a few days the fright was over.

Mustafa Kemal had been merely staging a demonstration. The main force of the Nationalist Army was still in the centre of Anatolia, where a big task still confronted it. But the Allies now knew what they might expect — and they had hardly expected such an answer to their dictated peace! The Grey Wolf was now very much on the alert. Everything depended now on what Sultan Vahideddine would do.

Vahideddine actually had little choice. Either he bowed to the revolution, subjected himself to the will of the hated rebels, or he complied with the wishes of the victors. A decision was not difficult. England at least guaranteed him his throne. What would the Grey Wolf be prepared to guarantee him? The Sultan laughed bitterly. He knew precisely the goal at which Mustafa Kemal was aiming. Victory by the Grey Wolf meant the last of the throne of Osman. Did the Anatolians realize what goal they were fighting for? Punish everybody, leaders as well as followers! declared the Sultan. Put an end to this state of affairs, this Empire without territory, whose power did not extend beyond the limits of its own capital! Only England could now bring salvation from the Nationalists. England!

Vahideddine signed the Peace Treaty. He had now played his last card. It was the Grey Wolf's turn to show his hand. All Anatolia shouted and cheered when Mustafa Kemal pronounced the Grand Vizier, Damad Fend, a traitor and deprived him of Turkish citizenship.

The Grey Wolf was wise enough not to aim his blow directly at the person of the Sultan-Caliph.

The Allied Supreme Council in Paris were placed in a position of considerable embarrassment. In particular the French were seriously alarmed. It was no longer a secret that General Gouraud had been obliged to approach the Grey Wolf for an armistice in Kilikia, and that he had been forced to enter into negotiations with the Angora people just as though they were regular Government. France cursed the whole East. There was war in Africa, war in the mandatory territory in Syria and war in Kilikia, while the bulk of the troops were in station on the Rhine. It was an unenviable position.

The Peace Treaty was ready and had actually been signed. Treaty? At the moment it was worth little more than a scrap of paper. In the circumstances there seemed little likelihood of being able to enforce its conditions.

There was only one way of enforcing them, and that was through the use of military persuasion.

Lloyd George was the first to draw this unwelcomed conclusion. The French shrugged their shoulders. England had had the pick of the booty, then let her pull the chestnuts out of the fire! To France the treaty was not worthy a new war in the East. They had already had a foretaste of the joys of mastery in Kilikia. Italy was in no position to furnish an expedition. What was the position of England?

Lloyd George found himself in a somewhat awkward position. The army at home had just been demobilized, and it was hardly to be expected that the men would relish being summoned to the Colours again.

Then there came to his rescue a country to whom the Treaty was well worth an expedition: Greece burned for a chance to extend its conquests in Anatolia — and Greece was ready. Venizelos had not allowed grass to grow under his feet. In Smyrna and in the Province of Aidan Greek armies were already there, prepared to march. Lloyd George, thrilled and delighted, seized the offer with both hands and showed that he was both grateful and generous. England would assume the responsibility for equipping the Greek troops: money was no object. The Greek army was to have the very latest equipment for the campaign and English officers were to be attached to the staff. All Venizelos had to do was to find the men, 200,000 of them, eager, fresh soldiers, who had not had a world war behind them.

The British fleet was to open the way. Great grey hulls again ploughed the waves of the Bosporus. Sultan Vahideddine prayed to Allah. Neither God nor the devil could save Mustafa Kemal now." (pp.130-4.)

What happened in 1920 was that Lloyd George, having imposed a Treaty on the captive Turkish Government in Constantinople, found he was not able to impose it on the Turkish nation. So he agreed to the Greeks providing the military muscle to impose the Treaty of Sèvres on the Turks in parallel to the efforts of the Sultan.

Finance and support were provided to Venizelos and the Greek Army through Sir Basil Zaharoff, who owned most of the shares in the shipbuilding yards of Vickers and Co. and who, with a huge fortune he made in business, subsidised several organs of the British Press. Zaharoff had also been a confidential adviser of M. Venizelos, and had an influence over Lloyd George, owing to services rendered to the Prime Minister at election time.

According to the scheme planned by Venizelos, the Turkish Nationalist army, which was concentrated in the Smyrna area, could be routed by a quick advance of the Greek forces, numbering 90,000 men, who would capture an important railway junction on the railroad from Smyrna and Adana-Ismid. This was the only line of communication Mustapha Kemal possessed, and cutting this off would force the Nationalists to withdraw towards the interior of Anatolia, breaking the Turkish resistance.

At first, all went well for the Greeks as they quickly began to advance deep into Anatolia toward their objective. The other Greek Army occupied Thrace and captured Adrianople in July 1920.

On August 10th 1920 the Sultan capitulated to the Treaty of Sèvres and signed up to all the Allied demands. Greece was granted a five year administrative mandate in the Smyrna zone with the possibility of annexation, after a plebiscite. It was also granted the whole of Eastern Thrace up to the Constantinople Peninsula. All of this, of course, was currently under the possession of the Greek Army, along with the whole north-west of Anatolia up to the Maeander and Eski Shehir Rivers. Venizelos returned to Athens in triumph with thoughts on obtaining Constantinople in time.

The British calculation was that Mustapha Kemal would bow to the reality of force and accept the Treaty—or risk greater partition of Turkey, harsher treaty terms and the loss of Constantinople for good. They viewed the Greek Army as a useful weapon to be employed against him, if he did not concede to the Imperial requirements.

## The New Byzantium

On 16th November 1920, *The Irish News* described what it saw as the elevated position of *The New Greece*:

> "Greece has become an important factor in the European hegemony since the War; almost an 'Empire,' in fact. It sprawls all over the Levant in the new maps of Europe; territories are now ruled from Athens that had never been conquered—politically, at least—by heroes of the days of old. Agamemnon and his army fought for ten years to capture a solitary city on the coast of Asia Minor. Alexander of Macedon carried his flag to Egypt and India; but his conquests were evanescent and his 'Empire' had begun to vanish before the mighty General died. But Alexander was not a Greek... The Greeks of today, like the Coalitionist majority in the British Parliament 'did well out of the War'—to outward appearance. Turks, Bulgarians and other races will never let them rest, however: what they won by 'diplomacy' must be held by the sword."

The *Megali* or 'great idea' of a Hellenic Empire encircling the Aegean had been born with the Greek independence movement in 1821. The centre of this dream of a Greater Greece was, of course, the acquisition of Constantinople. The former Byzantine capital was in the possession of the Allies in 1918 but it would not have been ridiculous for Greece to calculate that if the Greek Army conquered in Asia Minor, on behalf of themselves and the British interest, a new Greek State on both sides of the Aegean might prove an acceptable guardian of the Straits and the City.

*The Irish News* piece was a very perceptive piece of writing. The Greeks, like the 'hard-nosed' businessmen of the Tory backbenches, had done very well out of the War. But appearances were deceptive. The Greeks had achieved a vast expansion of territory, but not through their own efforts on the battlefield. The new Byzantium, conquered through the diplomacy of Venizelos, did favours for the Allies and benefited from their military power. But now it was the overextended Allies who were relying on the military power of the Greeks to sustain their hegemony in Asia Minor, and General Metaxas and the Greek General Staff had already calculated that such a project was foolhardy and unsustainable.

The idea that Greece could provide good government to the Smyrna region, where a mixed population lived, and a large proportion were deeply hostile to Hellenic rule, was extremely rash and foolish. Turkey was the leading State in the region, with hundreds of years of experience in administering areas of mixed population within the Ottoman Empire. The Greek State had been in existence for less than a century and its experience of ruling peoples of other races, for a mere ten years, had not been noticeably successful; it had been Constantine's opinion that the Greek State required a generation to consolidate itself, rather than take on any further responsibilities elsewhere.

## The Greek Democracy and Venizelos

It was not Allah or the devil who intervened, but the Greek democracy, reasserting itself. Venizelos, despite his triumphal return to Athens, was thrown out of power in the Greek General Election of 1920.

When Venizelos returned to Athens in July 1917, behind the French Army, a General Election was urged upon him to legitimise his authority. Venizelos declined a contest, however. By November 1920 his Government had exceeded its term of office, under the Constitution of Greece, by eighteen months. The Venizelist dictatorship might have gone on for years to come had his sponsors not grown uneasy at his conduct of affairs and pushed him into an election to renew his mandate.

Venizelos decided to fight the election against King Constantine, even though the former King was not a candidate and remained in exile after his forced abdication. His replacement, King Alexander, had died from a monkey bite and Constantine was invited to return to Athens with the defeat of Venizelos by Gounaris and the pro-neutrality former Ministry. Venizelos, still believing in his star, and having deluded himself into believing he was the representative of the Greek people, thought a contest with the ex-King would be ideal.

Venizelos could have put the matter to the test by declaring a Republic and becoming President. But Venizelos must have made the calculation that that would have meant civil war—and what would have become of the new Byzantium then?

A welter of books were published in London, around 1918-19, celebrating the 'victory of Venizelos' and the downfall of Constantine. These were carried along by the British propaganda in favour of Venizelos and against the Greek King. But in 1920 it was all shown to be spin.

What the election showed was how much Venizelos's power rested on foreign arms and how little on the support of the democracy. The Greek people understood that they had been forced into the War through foreign intervention and Venizelos had returned with a foreign army. They resented these infringements on their independence and wanted to reassert their independence and sovereignty. The result was a massive defeat for the Greek Premier as a huge majority voted for the opposition and 'Constantine'.

On November 30th *The Irish News* explained this curious turn of events to its readers in *What Happened in Greece*. And it did so in a brutally honest and accurate way:

> "M. Venizelos is in Nice; a pleasant place beloved of idlers. He would prefer lively little Athens; but, like Aristides of old, he is not wanted by the Athenians now. Ex-King Constantine may be quietly wending his way to the Greek capital... and the Hellenic people are to decide the big issue: will Constantine reign again?
>
> If they say 'Yes' what will the Allies do?...

402

Greece is still 'at war' with Turkey—though what Turkey consists of at the present moment few outside the circle of 'secret diplomacy' understand. A Sultan still exists somewhere; there are also the redoubtable 'Kemalists,' who appear to be at war with everyone they meet—except the Bolshevists of Russia. It has been suggested in England that when Constantine's friends and relatives re-join the Greek Army, that noble institution will rapidly become demoralised; and, anyhow, that England and the Western Allies will not finance the military adventures in the Near East to which Greece has been committed by M. Venizelos. If funds for warfare are stopped, Greece must become peaceable— a good thing for Greece, though her withdrawal from the strife in the Levantine regions will make the situation awkward for the conquerors of Syria and Mesopotamia...

Most people forget that England is still 'at war' with Turkey; therefore the Home Rule Act of 1914 awaits the passing of the Partition Bill and its own passage into that British haven from which no treaties return...

'German influence' in the Near East is the bugbear before which the Western Allies shudder. Constantine is the Kaiser's brother-in-law; the fact that he is the King of England's first cousin does not count. Constantine's wife is a resolute lady: she has more than her share of that 'Teutonic doggedness' which was boasted as a distinctly English characteristic—a grand 'Anglo-Saxon' foil to 'the mad fool-fury of the Celt'—up to the 1st August, 1914...

The Allies chased this 'royal pair' from Athens; be it noted that they were not hunted out by the Greek people, but by the dominating Western Powers. And in this fact lies the explanation of M. Venizelos' downfall at the recent elections, and of the 'movement' in favour of the exiled sovereign's return to his throne, palace and responsibilities...

Because Constantine was dethroned and hoofed out by foreigners, with the assistance of Venizelos, the Greek people ejected Venizelos, thus resenting and revenging the outrage on their national dignity committed by the strangers from the West. That is what happened in Greece... We say nothing for or against the German cousins of the 'Anglo-Saxons'—beyond suggesting that in their most beclouded moments they did not manifest a tithe of the brutal stupidity shown by the English Government in that Government's relations with America, Russia, Egypt, Greece and Ireland."

Here we have another facet of *Our War* that Redmondite and Devlinite Ireland was none too keen to take responsibility for.

In fact, there are strong overtones of disillusionment with the English democracy and scepticism about her promises in this editorial. The Irish context—or Northern Catholic context, to be precise—is illuminating. *The Irish News* had enthusiastically recruited for the British War effort among Belfast Catholics on the understanding that the Home Rule Bill, which had been placed on the Statute Book in August 1914 and suspended for the course of the War, would be brought into operation at the end of the conflict. But two years on there was no Home Rule Act. And when *was* the War going to end?

When Turkey was finally done?

Peace had been celebrated two years previously in November 1918—the official finish of the War. But since then Britain had maintained a naval blockade on Germany, causing the death by starvation of up to a million civilians to May 1919. Then a war had been launched on its former ally, Russia, when she had gone too far after replacing the Czar. And the War with Turkey continued all the time, leading to other wars in Mesopotamia, Palestine, Afghanistan, Arabia, Persia, Egypt etc.

The demobilised Northern Catholics, who had fought and died for Home Rule and the 'rights of small nations' in Britain's war on Germany and the Turk, had returned to find a pogrom waged against them in Belfast and proposals put forward to cut them off from the rest of the country, and place them under the rule of those who had organised the resistance against Home Rule. They found that the U.V.F., the illegal pre-War army that had defied the British Government with German guns, and had waged a terror campaign against Catholic Belfast through 1920, was about to become the security forces of the British State in the locality.

That is why *The Irish News*, the enthusiastic supporter of Imperialism and fierce propagandist for the 'great English democracy' against the Hun in August 1914, and against those Irish who doubted the change in Britain's ways, was feeling cheated and was developing a degree of healthy scepticism by October 1920.

### Britain Pulls The Plug On Greece

After nearly six years of interference in the affairs of Greece, England now began its formal withdrawal. And its withdrawal was to prove as disastrous to Greece as England's first fatal overtures had been to her in 1914-15.

The new Greek Government was warned by Britain that, if they accepted Constantine back to Athens, there would be consequences. Two Notes were presented to the Greeks after the fall of Venizelos. One declared that the recall of King Constantine would be considered as a confirmation by the Greek people of the hostile attitude taken by the Greek Government to the Allies during the War (they had remained neutral, which translated as hostility). The second was a warning that financial help would therefore be withdrawn. But the Greek Government persisted in behaving as an independent country.

So, having done the Allied bidding in their Asian Minor military adventure, the Greeks were now to be left high and dry, with their army in the middle of Anatolia, because they exercised their democratic right in choosing their own rulers.

Why was Britain acting like this and abandoning its instrument in the Near East?

The Tory backbenchers were certainly growing uneasy at reports of increased Turkish resistance to occupation after the Greek advance into the

Anatolian interior—and the awful expense of it all. Apparently, and quite worryingly for the Coalition Cabinet, they began to utter the old phrase from a previous era, from the time of a long lost foreign policy: 'the Turk is a gentleman.'

The instincts of a former world fed into anger against the Greeks, who had the temerity to recall their King, a man who had put his country before the Allied cause. So the Coalition began to be put under pressure by its backbenchers—who had been very quiescent and tolerant of the Coalition up until then—to restrict its expansionist designs on Turkish territory. And there was some talk in Parliament and the Press that the Jews were behind it all again.

The reinstitution of Constantine gave Britain the cover necessary to begin to abandon its Greek catspaw. As David Walder puts it:

> "Greek action in Anatolia had originally been tolerable and possible within the framework of a grand design, however ill conceived. Now the grand design was fading away. The Allies began to recall the cost of assisting Greece. The British taxpayer alone had lent nearly £16 million since 1914... had not the return of Constantine wiped the slate clean?" (*The Chanak Incident*, pp.92-3.)

When the tide began to turn against the Greeks on the battlefield their usefulness to England was found to be negligible, and they were now left to their own devices. Arnold Toynbee later explained the great change in British policy in the following context:

> "During the War, the Eastern 'side-shows,' though frequently criticised, were rightly regarded as a technical military problem. They were a part of the general conduct of the War, and a comparatively small proportion of our man-power and material resources was involved in them. The public let them be, and the diplomatists made their secret agreements on the supposition that the men and money available in the East for military purposes during the War would remain at their service for political purposes after it. But from the moment of the armistice, public opinion began to assert itself. The main operations on the Western front had been terminated by complete victory; why should subsidiary fronts be kept in being? The soldiers who had been defending the heart of France, Italy, and England were being demobilized; why should their comrades be kept under arms to hold down unwilling populations in outlandish Eastern countries, where neither they nor their families had any interests at stake? And why should the taxpayers, on whom the national struggle for existence had imposed crushing burdens, accept further burdens for the sake of their diplomatists' professional struggle for power...

There had been a growing opposition in the Press and the Parliaments. Confessions about the strength of the respective military forces in the East, their casualties, their cost of maintenance, and about the budgets of the civil administration in the occupied territories, had been wrung out of unwilling Governments and subjected to unanswerable criticisms... Official resistance had been very stubborn, and at first the unspent momentum of the War and the distraction of the public mind enabled the officials to carry on. They were not prevented from embarking on costly aggressive operations in Russia, though they were forced to break them off; and as recently as the summer of 1920 the French Government found ways and means of conquering Syria and the British of reconquering Mesopotamia. But it was always a losing battle, and the last offensive ended in rout…

Substantially, the Western nations… have re-established an effective, though belated, limited, and rather negative 'democratic control' over their public servants, and they have realised more quickly than the 'experts' that the days of Oriental dependencies are numbered. Under post-War conditions — especially political conditions — these pieces of property are going to bring in diminishing returns, and their owners, the Western nations, have therefore begun to liquidate them." (*The Western Question in Greece And Turkey*, pp. 58-60.)

The War for democracy had the quite unintended consequence of creating the semblance of a democracy in Britain. The 1918 election was the first election in Britain where the majority of people voted. It was conducted in the aftermath of four years of intense democratic propaganda which depicted the mass killing of millions of people as a sacrifice for democracy and civilization. The mass participation of the population in the War through conscription also had democratic consequences. The election itself was called with almost indecent haste by Lloyd George in order to maximise his mandate for government and the Prime Minister worked up the new democracy in irresponsible ways to secure it.

The Statesmen who before the War had been used to governing in the former manner, in disregard of the general populace, and who during the War had got attuned to governing as a small cabal, in spite of Parliament, were presented by the new democracy with restrictions of a new type. Coupled with this, the great expenditure of blood and treasure which they had resorted to in order to see off Germany left much less room for manoeuvre than in the past.

And so a half-baked Imperial policy emerged, unwilling and unable to do one thing or another. And the first victims of this were the Greeks, who were left to their fate under the burning skies of Anatolia.

### British Revision And Mixed Messages

In December 1920, the Greeks had advanced deep into Anatolia, to Eskisehir, the important Railway junction. Finding stiff resistance from the Turks, they retired to their original positions. In early 1921, the Greeks resumed their advance, but again met stiff resistance from Kemal's forces, who were fighting in an increasingly effective manner.

The Greek advance was halted for the first time at the Battle of Inonu on January 11th 1921. By March the Allies began to realise that Turkey was not done, after all, and was in fact a force to be reckoned with. This setback led to Allied proposals to amend the Treaty of Sèvres at a conference in London, where both the Turkish Revolutionary and Ottoman Governments were invited.

The Allied Powers assembled in London to revise the Treaty of Sèvres. Calogeropoulos, the new Greek Premier, and Gounaris, now the Greek War Minister, apparently accepted Allied terms that Greece end its military occupation of the Smyrna district. Gounaris was increasingly concerned with the safety of the Greek population in the area that the expansionist policy of Venizelos had put in danger. However, the Turkish delegation refused to be pressurised into a modification of Sèvres by the Allied Ministers at London and stated that they would have to return to Angora to submit any revisions to the National Assembly.

Mixed messages were coming at the Greeks from London and they were compounded by Lloyd George's continued moral support for the Greek adventure in contacts with them through private channels and in Parliament. Walder notes:

> "The British were no longer the allies of Greece; they supplied no arms, no money or assistance. They had no control over the decisions of the Greek King, his politicians or his generals. Yet the Turks could not believe this and were convinced that all Greek actions were somehow inspired by the machinations of Lloyd George...In Churchill's words, the Greeks still believed 'the great man is with us, and in his own time and by his own wizardry he will bring us the vital aid we need.'" (*The Chanak Incident*, p. 123.)

This Pilate-like washing of the hands by Britain presented King Constantine with a dilemma: The Allied Supreme Council had ordered the halting of the Greek advance and the British had withdrawn support; but Lloyd George and his Ministry were winking the Greeks on, where Venizelos had left off.

Even as England was giving all the appearances of being a moderating influence on the Greeks and a reconciling force between Greek and Turk at the London Conference, British Statesmen were urging the Greeks on in private, at the same venue. Basil Thomson described the muddled confusion Britain was now practising in relation to the Greek expansion into Anatolia:

> "The catastrophe that befell Greece was largely due to the fact that members of the British Cabinet were at cross purposes as regards the British policy to be followed at this crucial juncture as is shown by the following incident.
>
> On the day when M. Gounaris was to arrive in London, March 9th, Sir Maurice Hankey, in a casual conversation with a member of the Greek Delegation, counselled moderation, saying that the Greek army in Asia Minor should refrain from any rash action against the Kemalists. This message had hardly had time to reach M. Calogeropoulos, when an urgent message from Mr. Lloyd George was brought to him personally. In substance it was to the effect that the advice which Sir Maurice had given might be disregarded and

that the Prime Minister (Mr. Lloyd George) saw no objection to the Greeks undertaking an offensive against the Kemalist forces if the safety of the Greek army called for it—in other words to imposing peace by force of arms. This secret suggestion, made behind the back of the Conference, must have been made without consulting the British General Staff who had been convinced ever since Venizelos obtained the consent of President Wilson, M. Clemenceau and Mr. Lloyd George to his occupation of Smyrna, that the Greek army was quite unequal to the task." (*The Allied Secret Service in Greece*, pp. 243-4.)

Thomson commented that Gounaris was 'scarcely to be blamed for trusting to the support of the British Prime Minister' particularly since

"Mr. Lloyd George was egging him on, behind the back of the Conference, to obtain a settlement by force of arms." (p.248.)

British enthusiasm for the Greek adventure rose and fell with the fortunes of the Greek Army, and its ability to perform the role that the Imperial Power had invested in it:

"This duality of policy within the British Coalition Cabinet was maintained throughout the Greek campaign in Asia Minor. It was the main cause of the Greek disaster. Whenever a Greek success was announced Mr. Lloyd George sang a paean in praise of Greek valour, patriotism and efficiency; whenever there was a check he effaced himself and left Lord Curzon to do what he could do by diplomacy to find a way out of the muddle. And while Greece was left to feed on words from the British Prime Minister France and Italy were busy signing treaties of friendship with Kemal and furnishing him with money and war material." (p.248.)

When the Greek Army was winning, force of arms was the answer and when it suffered setbacks diplomacy was used to minimise the damage for Britain. And this appeared to be a clever strategy to obtain the maximum political gain for Imperialism, on the cheap, through its Greek catspaw. The possibility that the strategy might end in disaster not just for the Greeks, but for the Empire too, does not seem to have been considered.

King Constantine and his Ministers were placed in a dilemma. They had not originated the Greek adventure in Asia Minor, on the contrary they had actively opposed it for years. But they also realised that there was no going back in the war of conquest and extermination that Venizelos had launched with British support. A retreat would leave the Greek inhabitants of Anatolia, who had been implicated in the ethnic cleansing of Turks from the Greek occupation zone, at the mercy of the advancing Turkish army.

But most of all they trusted in Britain. Arnold Toynbee was there and knew why the Greeks still persisted in their reckless adventure, that was to end in catastrophe:

"Nothing struck me more forcibly during the eight months that I was with the Greek Army and public, than the universal belief that Great Britain, or rather the Prime Minister, wielding the resources of Great Britain, would see them through. It was one point on which all Greeks—Ottoman subjects and Hellenic, literates and illiterates, Royalists and Venizelists, civilians and soldiers, privates and generals—were in enthusiastic agreement. 'With Great Britain supporting us we are not afraid of anything.' ... 'Lloyd George is supporting us, and he will throw the resources of Great Britain into the scale if we can't do the job ourselves.'—But Mr. Lloyd George isn't an autocrat. He can only help you if public opinion lets Parliament vote him the men and money.'—'Oh, you will vote them. You know your own interests. You know how useful a Greater Greece can be to a naval Power like yours.' ... 'Oh! We know all about British policy. We have watched you for years. We have seen you throw dust in people's eyes before. You will be with us alright when the moment comes." (*The Western Question in Greece And Turkey*, pp. 98-9.)

Constantine may have believed that with Lloyd George on his side all would be well, or he may have just reasoned that the only way of retaining British help was by doing its work on the battlefield. Whatever the case, he decided to stake all on the test of battle and ridding Anatolia of Kemal once and for all.

The Greek Army, whom the British had effectively washed their hands of, embarked on a spring offensive aimed at the new Turkish capital of Angora. All went well at first, as the Greek Army with its morale buoyed up by the arrival of the King, captured Eskishehir, the important railway junction considered to be the key to controlling the rest of Anatolia. And Lloyd George was singing the Hellenic praises in Parliament again and taunting the backbenchers with, 'I told you so!'

### The Greek Disaster

At the high point of the Greek advance, a small section of the Greek Army made a retreat from Khoja-Ili. *The Irish News* published a report from the *Manchester Guardian's* Special Correspondent in Constantinople made on July 15th.

The Liberal *Manchester Guardian* had been traditionally anti-Turk, in the Gladstonian manner, so its coverage could not be said to have a pro-Turk agenda against the Greeks. It was prophetic as to the mayhem that Britain's policy of using the Greeks as a catspaw to further their strategic ambitions would ultimately cause in the region:

"NEAR EAST CRISIS.
TRAGEDY THREATENED IN ASIA MINOR.
THE GREEKS AS PAWNS...
The Greek retreat in the district of Khoja-Ili... has been voluntary, premeditated, and leisurely, and yet the Greek army (as I have witnessed myself) has attempted in cold blood to ruin and uproot, if not to exterminate the Turkish population in the area it had decided to abandon, with the necessary consequence

that the Christian population of the same area could not venture to await the entry of the Turkish Nationalist troops, and therefore—though more fortunate than the Turks insomuch as none of them has been massacred—have still been ruined and uprooted in their turn (abandoning, in their flight, much of the property which they had stolen from their Turkish neighbours a few days before). After this sample of the Greek army's conduct in such circumstances, what have we to expect if, in the course of the far more serious military operations which the Greek Government have insisted on carrying out... their army were compelled to make a general retreat? In such a retreat the discipline of the Greek army would further be relaxed than it is at present... The Greek and Armenian minority in this great region... will be forced to leave the country again, and though most of them will this time escape with their lives, they will lose most of their property, and probably will never be able to return to their homes. The Turkish majority will suffer worse still, for they will not only be ruined but partly massacred, and the remnant will be left without the means to reconstruct a desolated country... The Greeks, if they impose their terms on Angora, will, in any case, be ruined by the effort of holding what they seize, while if they lose, their lavish expenditure of lives and money will have been still more obviously in vain...

When the (Allied) Supreme Council, against the unanimous opinion of their expert advisers, allowed Greek troops to disembark at Smyrna in the Spring of 1919, they deliberately inoculated the mixed population of Western Anatolia with the germ of racial warfare which had hitherto been confined, on the whole, to the north-eastern provinces and to Turkey in Europe... (All nationalities now sigh for the golden age of Abdul Hamid!) But on the whole, the local Greeks and Turks managed to get on with one another in Western Asia Minor until the fatal Greek landing in 1919...

And this is where the Allies are so gravely to blame. All along they have pushed the Greeks forward as pawns to save themselves the trouble of working out the Turkish problem and by so doing have increased the number and confusion of the pieces on the board. The Greek forces were put into Khoja-Ili by the British Government a little more than a year ago, because at that moment the Nationalist forces were on the point of surrounding a British battalion at Ismid, and the British Government could not decide either to come to terms with the Nationalists or to fight them with British soldiers. The Greek troops that have devastated Khoja-Ili, in the course of their departure, first came there with the assistance of the British Navy." (*Irish News*, 25th July 1921.)

It was really saying something when *The Manchester Guardian* could proclaim that: 'All nationalities now sigh for the golden age of Abdul Hamid!' For years the organ of Gladstonian Liberalism, with its distaste for the Turk, had called Sultan Hamid, 'Abdul the Damned'. But now these were the good old days of the Ottoman Empire!

At this point in the War, Lloyd George announced that the Treaty of Sèvres was scrapped and it was up to the Greeks and Turks to fight it out over Anatolia, with the winner taking all. Britain declared itself neutral in the conflict—although it had inspired it.

But, at the same time, the Prime Minister reiterated that England was still at war with the Turks—and therefore incited the Greek Army to continue on!

This was the crucial moment of the War. The Turkish commander, Ismet, wanted to fight on to regain the junction at Eskisehir but Kemal arrived, saw that the Turkish Army was going to be destroyed in a great encirclement, and ordered the retreat. As H.C. Armstrong put it:

> "This retreat... gave up Turkish soil (over 100 miles) and Turkish men, women and children to the national enemy who would burn, rape and destroy. But that did not complicate his decision. He saw the problem as a military one; if they had stood and fought at Eskisehir the Turkish main army would have been wiped out." (*Grey Wolf*, p.145.)

In the National Assembly at Angora there was a degree of panic and Kemal's opponents rounded on him. So Kemal proposed that he be elected dictator for three years and if he failed he would take full responsibility and would pay the price. Through this effective manoeuvre he united supporter and opponent behind him.

Kemal had located the new capital at Angora because any invader would find it much harder to attack a Turkish administration there than in occupied Constantinople—it was safe from the Royal Navy, in particular. Angora was a small provincial town on an arid plain in the middle of nowhere. But it was located in a fatal environment for an attacking army. The surrounding desert was either blisteringly hot, or freezing cold, and neighbouring areas were prone to malaria. Moreover, an attacking army risked their lines becoming dangerously extended and exposed in the vast Anatolian heartland behind it.

That is what happened to the Greeks. Kemal surrendered territory to the attackers, until they were drawn into the most hostile of conditions at the line of the Sakarya River, fifty miles from Ankara, with their supply lines stretched. Kemal positioned himself with two river tributaries guarding his flanks and a railway at his rear to maintain his supplies and aid reinforcements. Since the Turks faced a larger Greek force, Kemal ensured all the advantages lay with the Turkish defenders and all the disadvantages with the Greek attackers.

The Turkish defensive positions were located on a series of heights, and the Greeks had to storm them to occupy the higher ground. The Turks had to conserve men, for the Greeks held the numerical advantage, so they surrendered some positions. The crucial moment came when the Greek Army attempted to take Haymana, 40 kilometers south of Ankara, but the Turks held on.

The advance into Anatolia had lengthened the Greek lines of supply and communication and they began to run out of ammunition. The battle of Sakarya, fought during August-September 1921, lasted twenty-one days before the Greeks, unable to break through, went into a full retreat.

Gounaris made a last appeal to the British Foreign Secretary for money to maintain the Greek Army in Anatolia—otherwise he said he would be forced to pull Greek forces out of Asia Minor altogether. When there was no reply, he went to London in a bid to save the Greek population around Smyrna. Basil Thomson takes up the story:

"Gounaris now demanded a meeting with Lord Curzon on the plea of urgency, but on the ground that he had pressing business in the House of Lords, Lord Curzon referred him to an Under-Secretary. Mr. Lloyd George was equally inaccessible. Gounaris waited vainly for a fortnight and then resolved upon the evacuation of Asia Minor. He sent the preliminary orders before leaving London and advised the British Government of what he was doing. But before he had time to reach Athens a letter was received from the British Foreign Office in reply to his letter of February 15th enlarging upon the patriotism and discipline of the Greek soldiers, and expressing the hope that these qualities would not fail them at this difficult moment; that the wisest way out of the situation was to hasten a diplomatic settlement; that it was hoped that M. Gounaris would take heed of the counsels that might be given him in a spirit of confidence and in good faith. It was an appeal to him to revoke the evacuation order.

Gounaris, who had been stamped… as a rabid pro-German, was in reality of all the Greek statesmen the most susceptible to British influences, and this proved to be his undoing. Once more relying on the words of British Ministers he complied. Great as may be the responsibility of Mr. Lloyd George a year earlier, one cannot acquit Lord Curzon of his share since he induced the Greek Government to continue a hopeless struggle from which Gounaris might have extricated her. Both Statesmen forgot that war is not waged with fine phrases but with guns, shells and munitions, and of these the Greeks had no more left."
(*The Allied Secret Service in Greece*, pp. 250-1.)

Many accounts give the impression that Lloyd George was a lone advocate of Greek military conquest in Anatolia within the Cabinet. But it is more accurate to see the Prime Minister as the ideological core of support for the Greeks with this support radiating outward to the other Ministers who were altering their position in line with how they saw the Greek adventure contributing to Imperial interests.

The British Prime Minister was still not short of good advice for the Greeks, however, even at this critical moment. Thomson reveals:

"It was said that when the Greek debacle began, Mr. Lloyd George advised Gounaris not to ask for an armistice, reminding him of the mistake made by Ludendorff in 1918." (p.253.)

And in the House of Commons on August 4th the British Premier made a notorious speech declaring that 'Greek victory was imminent,' copies of which were circulated to the Greek Army at the front.

On August 26th 1922, in a surprise attack the Kemalists broke the Southern front of the Greeks, surrounding and destroying half their army. The survivors fled at the double for Smyrna and the coast.

The Greek retreat turned into a rout; the Greeks left a trail of burning towns, desecrated Mosques and massacred civilians, which the advancing Turkish army encountered on its way to the coast. Greek civilians fearful of the vengeance of the Turks fled with Constantine's army back to the port of Smyrna, which became crowded with the remnants of the Greek army and thousands of refugees. Turkish forces entered Smyrna in early September 1922 as the Greeks, and other Christian inhabitants, fled panic-stricken in numerous ships, as the town burned around them.

## The Irish News and the 'Unspeakable Turk'

Below are *The Irish News* editorials commenting on the Turkish victories and the Greek retreat in Asia Minor. They were all written during September 1922:

"WHAT OF THE CHRISTIANS?

The territory known as Asia Minor has been described as 'a sort of bridge between Europe and Asia' ... Before the latest series of massacres there were more than 1,000,000 Christians in Asia Minor, 600,000 of these being Armenians. Probably 300,000 Armenians have been slaughtered since the beginning of the World War; but even yet the Christian population of the historic Peninsula cannot be much less than 2,000,000.

What is to become of them now that the noble 'Christian' Powers of Europe mean to accept the military defeat of the Greeks as an accomplished fact and to leave Asia Minor at the disposal of Kemal and his bloodthirsty hordes.

Smyrna itself is a proud city: its population is equal to that of Belfast; it is the seat of Catholic, Greek and Armenian Archbishoprics; it is a great manufacturing and trading centre—because Christian peoples have been allowed to live and work there in comparative security. When Kemal and his Turks take hold of Smyrna, what fate is in store for the 2000 years-old city?

The Turks... are unchanged and unchangeable. They were addicted to ruthless massacre when their baleful shadow first emerged above the Eastern horizon: in the long and hideous record of their national career as authors of atrocities nothing more utterly fiendish was laid to their charge than the deeds of the past five or six years...

The beaten Greeks are seeking an Armistice, hoping that Europe's 'Christian' Powers may do something to save the Christians from utter extinction during the interval. But the French papers—some of them at least—urge the Turks to keep the French '75s' at work and to thrust the Christian Army out before any European nation plucks up courage enough to intervene. France is taunting England with the failure of the offensive undertaken by the Greeks under English patronage and England is afraid to say 'boo' to the Turks lest the Mohammedans of India might cause trouble there though Downing Street must feel encouraged by the news that in some parts of the Indian Peninsula

Mohammedans and Hindus are merrily cutting each others throats again...

With France to back them... Turkey has been... made more powerful than at any period since the Treaty of Berlin was forced upon the Russian deliverers of the Christians 44 years ago by Bismarck and Beaconsfield and the restoration of the Turk is the work of the same trio... Greece might have saved the situation but the Greeks find themselves betrayed and deserted..." (September 6th 1922.)

The next editorial dealt with the origins of the Turks—they came from a race of nomad horsemen from the central Asian steppes and *The Irish News's* racial conception of history compared them unfavourably with Genghis Khan and the Mongols:

"MOSLEMISM *REDIVIVUS*

About 1,000 years ago the honest Mongols who inhabited Central Asia could not tolerate any longer the aggressive savagery of a horde of murderers and robbers called the Turks, and the Mongols drove their unruly neighbours westwards into Armenia and Asia Minor. In these places the barbarians found native races more amenable to 'irregular' tactics than were the Mongols of the Far East. The fugitives became conquerors, they crossed into Europe and captured Gallipoli in 1358; a little later they were at Adrianople... as the years passed their power was carried farther and farther into Europe at the point of the scimitar...

From the middle of the fifteenth century onwards the reign of the Turks in Europe was marked, year after year, by aggressive militarism against the Christian Powers and by cruelty of the most odious and barbaric kind practised on the conquered Christian peoples...

The brutal 'Empire's' progress Westward was stayed but its rulers and their fanatical swarms of barbarians maintained almost continuous warfare, they robbed, tortured and slaughtered without cessation; regions that had been fertile and rich since days before Abraham owned flocks herds in Mesopotamia withered into Aridity under their blighting rule...

But the Turkish power declined... and the emancipated Christian nations of the Balkans—Greece, Serbia, Bulgaria and Macedonia—drove the persecutors into Constantinople just before the Christians began their own Great War.

Turkey declared for Germany in that War: it was prophesied, and promised, that the Sultan and all his entourage would finally be expelled from Europe when the Allies had won their victory. But the Allies made a hideous mess of the peace; thereafter they quarrelled bitterly; England urged Greece to rescue the wretched remnants of the Christian population left in Asia Minor; France promptly armed and equipped the Turks, and lent them a full measure of 'moral support.' England abandoned her Greek protégés, in fear of the French, the Turks, and Mohammedans of Hindustan...

Austria, Hungary and Poland were powerful nations when they barred the path to the Atlantic against the Moslem armies; they are broken, bankrupt and powerless now...

By their decisive victory over the Greeks in Asia Minor the Turks have re-established themselves and consolidated their power and supremacy over the Moslem world...

The Turks are Asiatics; they fought and won in Asia; it is not the Moslem millions in India alone who will rejoice and learn to look on the Giaour with contempt: the Japanese and Chinese will be confirmed in their conviction that Asia is the exclusive heritage of the Asiatics. Turks are already nibbling at the British occupation of Mesopotamia—called 'Irak' as if to disguise it: and the Arabs of that ancient but rather unhealthy territory who had been revolting against English domination already will gather fresh determination and energy from the happenings over their border...

The Turk has not merely 'got a new lease of life' as a force for evil: he has been placed on a pedestal higher than he had occupied since the Crimean War. As 'statesmanship' the Allies conduct of Near and Middle Eastern 'problems' is wholly worthy of the Treaty of Versailles." (September 9th 1922.)

It was hard for *The Irish News* to imagine a situation in which 'the Japanese and Chinese will be confirmed in their conviction that Asia is the exclusive heritage of the Asiatics'. What would the world come to then? What would happen if those races, 'those lesser breeds without the law', as Kipling called them, were left to their own devices to rule themselves? Britain was to find out when, under American pressure, it decided not to renew its alliance with Japan, a country which had protected British assets in the Far East during the Great War.

That was a view characteristic of the racial theories of Imperialism. But in its estimation of the effects of the Statesmanship of the Empire it was very near the mark. The inability of the Imperial Statesmen to deal with the situation they had themselves engineered, and the inspiration that Mustapha Kemal provided to 'those lesser breeds', began the unravelling of Britain's Empire in the region.

"NEAR EASTERN CHAOS

More than 500,000 terrified Christians fugitives preceded the Turkish Army into Smyrna. Where are they now?... And at least 1,500,000 Christians are either dead or alive in the regions through which the Turkish forces marched to Smyrna. Their fate, at the hands of Kemal's barbarous 'camp-followers' cannot be imagined without a shudder... 'An early announcement of British policy' is imperatively demanded. The 'policy' that has placed 2,000,000 Christian people helplessly and wholly at the mercy of a Turkish army flushed with victory and fanatical hatred of the Greeks has been pursued by the English Government since the Armistice was signed. It is too late to alter it now—too late for the Christians who were promised protection and safety in Asia Minor as a slight reward for their services to the Allies against the Turks in the Great War." (September 12th 1922.)

I do not know to what extent the Greek, Armenian and other Christian peoples served those who wished to destroy the Turkish State. But if they acted as a fifth column for the Imperialist Powers, in return for protection, it is not surprising that this foolish misjudgement marked the end of the Christian communities in Asia Minor. And the behaviour of the Greek Army, described in the editorial below, can only have hastened the process:

"PERILOUS NEAR EAST
Every country in the world has a direct interest in the development of the situation brought into existence by the Turkish victories in Asia Minor.

True, the well-armed and ably-generalled Kemalists defeated only a Greek Army which seems to have been little more than a mob when the testing time came. Modern Greeks fight well—when they are winning. They 'fall to pieces' when the tide turns against them. But to the Moslems of Asia and Africa that Greek Army stood for the armed might of Christendom. A decisive triumph for the Crescent over the Cross has already been proclaimed amongst millions of ignorant fanatics from North-West Africa to Eastern Asia. By this time the news has reached the farthest Soudan and the remotest passes between India and Afghanistan. Moslemism is resurgent and it is led by generals who know how armies can be used and by politicians who hold the 'statesmen' of the Occidental nations in well-deserved contempt.

Millions of Christians are within the zone of fire in Asia Minor. The Turks are, undoubtedly, massacring them already. According to an American Correspondent who travelled in the wake of the contending forces, the Greeks behaved in a fashion eminently calculated to inflame the furious passions of the Turkish population. Those Greeks were incendiaries and plunderers even as they fled ignominiously before Kemal's troops.

'Without giving battle at any point since the fall of Ushak,' writes the American Observer, 'it (the Greek Army) laid waste the countryside, burning villages, destroying bridges, leaving hopeless confusion behind... The Greek Army has evacuated but it has left Anatolia in ruins.' This phraseology is painfully familiar; the sentences seem like an excerpt from Mr. Cosgrave's recital of irregular ravages in his speech of Monday last...

The evacuation of Constantinople by the Allies, the unconditional surrender of Adrianople, the cession of Trace: these are the Kemalist terms... But the British have declared that the Turks shall not have Constantinople, and soldiers and warships have been placed in position and fitted for battle against the victorious Kemalist legions in the famous city and in the neighbourhood of the Dardanelles. Thus the train is laid for a gigantic explosion." (September 13th 1922.)

The last editorial in this series, below, reveals the extent of the Devlinite disillusionment with Imperial policy in the East. Essentially, *The Irish News* was preparing its readers for another change in British foreign policy in which the Turk was to be rehabilitated to save the face of the Empire—becoming speakable of again as a gentleman. And such a change in policy would make a mockery of the Irish sacrifice at Gallipoli to win 'the freedom of the Straits':

"THE TURK ON TOP

The London *'Times'* asked yesterday: 'Have England and France yet awakened to the fact that they stand face to face with the most serious crisis which has confronted them since 1914?'

It was an amazing question: and the leading English journal's answer to its own query was still more astonishing, 'Not quite,' said the *'Times'* : 'but they are gradually awakening to it.'...

Mustapha Kemal and his victorious hordes will awaken the sleepers of London and Paris.

The Turks have sacrificed Smyrna on the altar of their triumph... they might have tolerated the existence of Smyrna were it not for the fact that its traders and manufacturers and the majority of the workers were hated and despised Christians — Greeks and Franks of various nationalities, Armenians and Britons, and Americans; Catholic, Greek, and Armenian Archbishoprics were established in Smyrna; probably 85 per cent of the trade and industries were in Christian hands: the noble Turk does not 'earn his bread by the sweat of his brow' while he can plunder his neighbours — and when he cannot live by plunder, his women work on his behalf.

So Smyrna was given to the flames. By this time it is doubtful if much more than blackened ruins remain

of a city that was great and famous long centuries before the Turkish barbarians emerged from Central Asia.

Massacre and incendiarism went hand in hand at Smyrna. The qualities that have characterised the Turk throughout the ages have survived — and waxed stronger. He is still the remorseless and bloodthirsty savage of Oriental history. The great Christian Powers are awakening to a sense of the gravity of the crisis: they have actually decided to keep the Turk out of Europe for a few weeks — until they have fashioned some kind of excuse for letting him in and presenting him with Constantinople and Thrace...

The Turk has won: anyone who thinks otherwise is deceiving himself. The Turk has traded, as usual, on the jealousies and wretched rivalries of the European rulers who call themselves Christians; and he has played the centuries old game more successfully than at any period of his fiendish history.

Of course, he will give a 'guarantee' that the precious Straits shall be 'free.' Why should he refuse to sign the most stringent document that the 'statesmen' of London, Rome and Paris can indite? Freedom of the Straits had been secured by various solemn treaties before the Great War; on the day after the honest Turk threw in his lot with Germany, the solemn Treaties were not worth the ash in the bowl of a smoked out chibouque. Officers and men of the British Navy and the survivors of the forces that were sacrificed at Gallipoli can bear testimony to this historic fact.

417

Behind the Turks are the Russian Bolshevists. Efforts to drag Germany into the muddle are being made in England; when the surrender to Moslemism in arms is announced, the British public will be told that perfidious Germany was responsible for all the trouble in the East, and that the necessity for curbing her on the Rhine compelled England, France and Italy to rest content with Mustapha Kemal's assurances about 'the freedom of the Straits.'

We cannot forget our own plight at home for a moment; but we must not ignore happenings elsewhere that may, and most probably will, react on the affairs of every country in the world." (September 16th 1922.)

The Irish News reporting of 'Smyrna's Inferno of Blood and Flames' recalled all the Redmondite atrocity stories about the Germans in Belgium. Under the sub-heading *'Smyrna Horrors—Great Fire Still Raging: Massacre of Christians',* the paper's correspondents reported:

"1,300 Christian refugees had taken refuge in the College near where the fire started. The fate of the girl pupils is unknown. ALL OF THEM HAVE BEEN CARRIED OFF BY THE TURKS. Prior to the fire there were massacres that carried on into the night in the midst of the flames. It is impossible to estimate the number of people killed." (September 16th 1922.)

We do not know what happened to the girls—but perhaps they ended up in a harem, passing some babies tossed on Turkish bayonets on the way! And there may even be a book in it for the contributors to *Our War.*

### The Irish News, Atrocities and Arnold Toynbee

The coverage of the *Irish News* in the days between the rout of the Greek Army in Asia Minor and the Chanak incident at the Dardanelles makes interesting reading. It presents a noticeable contrast with that of the *Catholic Bulletin* during the same period.

The Devlinite *Irish News* was a supporter of the Great War on Germany and Turkey. During the Home Rule struggle the objectives of Irish Nationalism and English Liberalism merged and Redmondite Imperialism was the outcome. *The Irish News* fully supported all the extensions and escalations that British Imperialism engaged in from the war for democracy and small nations. But around 1920 *The Irish News* began to realise that what it was hoping for, in the world of Imperial triumph, was not what was occurring.

In the Middle East the British Empire was also disappointing *The Irish News.*

The Devlinites did not have a foreign policy as such, in the true sense of the word, since they were a mere annex of British Imperial policy. However, they did have a view of the world, and that view tended to be Hibernian. The view taken by *The Irish News* of foreign affairs was an extension of its Hibernianism at home—a narrow Catholic Nationalism that was very different from the Republicanism of the 'sectarian' *Catholic Bulletin.*

Arnold Toynbee railed against what we now know as 'the politics of the last atrocity', forgetting perhaps that atrocities have a very useful function for governments when they wish to engage populations in war (as shown in his own work at Wellington House).

But Toynbee had a different function in 1922—getting the public to see sense after they had been engaged, through atrocity propaganda, in a mass slaughter to save civilization. So those, like *The Irish News*, who wanted another war because of new atrocities had got to get a grip on themselves and realise that there was more to politics than wars over atrocities waged by sentimental do-gooders.

If only such an attitude had prevailed in August 1914, one is tempted to think!

This is what Toynbee wrote of the malevolent effect of 'atrocities' on the public mind in 1922:

"As people read of them, they have the double luxury of being confirmed in their views (for they seldom read the other side) and of giving way to moral indignation. They write to the Press or petition the Government to take active measures against the offending nation. They rarely reflect that previous measures of the kind for which they appeal may have provoked the very atrocities that have just aroused their feelings. Because they are indulging their feelings, and not using their reason as they would use it in circumstances where they were more directly responsible for what was to be done, they thirst for vengeance and forget to look for remedies. Thus they overlook the obvious and fundamental fact that atrocities are committed in similar exceptional circumstances by people of every nation and civilisation, and that whatever may be the duties of Governments, the mission of philanthropists is not to punish crime but to remove the cause.

This was the sentimental link between British public opinion and Mr. Lloyd George's policy towards Turkey and Greece, but it was no more the motive for the British Government's constancy than hostility to King Constantine was for the French Government's volte-face. In either case sentiment screened supposed interest, and British policy was slow to change because co-operation with Greece against Turkey, did, on a short view, seem better calculated to serve the interests of Great Britain than those of France. The Greek campaign in Anatolia did temporarily lighten for the Allies the task of controlling the Black Sea Straits... Thus there was a positive British interest to be served by employing Greece as a pawn... Mr. Venizelos did play his part according to the understanding. Without any expenditure of British money or lives, the littoral of the Straits was cleared by the Greek Army's advance and the Nationalists driven away into the interior. This was a substantial service, and the British Government, who had accepted it in order to extricate themselves from an awkward position, were committed by it more deeply than before to the Anglo-Greek *entente* in virtue of which it had been rendered.

The Greek Army was so immediately convenient that British statesmen ignored the fact that its presence in Anatolia had really created the hostile movement which it showed so much obliging readiness to combat, and the still more serious fact that this movement was potentially stronger than the force which had called it into being. They only slowly realised that the Greek military position in Anatolia must ultimately prove untenable, and that when the inevitable evacuation occurred, the Straits would not only be left uncovered but might be exposed to attacks from a military Power driven into hostility towards Great Britain on account of her support of Greece—a Power which did not exist at the time of the original Greek landing at Smyrna." (*The Western Question in Greece And Turkey*, pp. 91-2.)

*The Irish News* expected Britain to continue with the Crusading against the Moslem Turks without understanding that Imperialism brings with it many more considerations than Crusading. Crusading was only an awakened impulse of a transitory nature, produced by a long suppressed religiosity, in the conquest of the Holy Land, that disappeared when circumstances changed.

In August 1914 the Irish were fed principles in vast quantities so that they could engage in an Imperial War, and they were given atrocities so that they could hate the Hun. But now they were being told that such things were unimportant and delusional and they should readjust.

And people wonder why Ireland spent half a century trying to forget the Great War!

### Ireland and the East

Apparently, at the high point of their advance into Anatolia, just before the crucial battle with the Turks, the Greek Chief of Staff withdrew 20,000 soldiers and sent them to gather outside Constantinople. This was probably a last desperate throw of the dice by the Royalist commanders to shake themselves free of the British and look after Greek interests. But the Greeks were warned off and, however that happened, their army melted away.

Then came the battle in Anatolia which turned into full retreat for the Greeks and destroyed the dream of a new Byzantium and a Christian return to Constantinople.

At the crucial moment of the Greek campaign in Anatolia *The Irish News* published an editorial, entitled *The Seething Orient,* which is worth considering:

"'East is East and West is West, and never the twain shall meet, till earth and sky stand presently at God's Great Judgement Seat'. So Rudyard Kipling wrote many years ago, and the truth enshrined in the couplet becomes more plainly manifest as the years pass by.

Kipling meant that the Eastern and Western races of men were so different, radically and essentially—in moral standards and mental outlook—despite their common human nature, that they could not unite on a basis of mutual understanding and appreciation. But the East and West have been meeting since before the dawn of history—occasionally in friendly intercourse, more frequently in the clash of battle. The East is ancient; it is not really 'unchanging,' but it has altered very little since the days of Alexander of Macedon. Christianity came out of the East—the Near East—into the European territories of Pagan Rome; but it was not spread Eastwards; and when Mohammed appeared, six centuries after Christ, with a creed to be forced with fire and sword, he and his successors conquered territories into which the light of the Gospel of Peace and love had not penetrated. Mohammedanism is the dominant factor in the lives of the more virile Asiatic races—always excepting the Japanese, who stand apart. Mohammedanism is struggling against Occidental influences now from the north-westerly coast of Africa on the Atlantic to the shores of the Pacific: the struggle is not against Christianity, for the aggressive European nations have definitely abandoned the religious plea that served invaders West and East of old—that Henry II advanced in Ireland and English rulers of later dates in Hindustan...

The Turks held the leadership of Mohammedanism for centuries. They were remorseless conquerors and merciless persecutors; more than once they seemed destined to secure supremacy over Europe and to change the future of the world. But they were beaten back, and back, slowly but surely. They managed to survive in Europe because the Christian Powers hated and feared one another more than they did 'the unspeakable Turk.' And now a Greek Army is apparently pressing to defeat the last embodiment of Turkish military prowess: and the scene of the conflict is ancient Angora, 220 miles E.S.E. of Constantinople. When the Greeks have won that battle, will they annex an immense territory in Asia Minor? And how can they hold their Asiatic conquests if they refrain from seizing Constantinople?" (*Irish News*, 6th September 1921.)

The impulse of *The Irish News* was Christian, of an age before secularist Imperialism came on the scene and began to make Christianity incoherent—in comparison to Islam, at least. The Irish, it seems, remained Christian enough that they could not easily alternate between seeing the Turk as 'unspeakable' and then as a 'gentleman', as Imperial policy dictated.

The Belfast newspaper rooted for the Greeks and other Christians using the most ignorant Christian prejudices against Islam and the Turks. It stated that 'Mohammed appeared, six centuries after Christ, with a creed to be forced with fire and sword.' And yet Islamic expansion was stopped on the borders of France over one thousand years ago. It existed peacefully in Spain for a number of centuries in a highly civilised form, and when it was driven out by a Crusade Spain reverted to a more barbarous state for hundreds of years.

Islam was never a proselytizing religion like Christianity. It was Christianity that sent missionaries and Crusading armies into Moslem lands to spread the 'Gospel of Peace and love' during the last millennium and accompanied the globalising Imperialism of the great Powers across the world, destroying other cultures and their beliefs in the name of progress.

Added on to the religious impulse in *The Irish News* was the Imperialism of the Kipling era—the vigorous new Imperialism of late Victorian England.

When *The Irish News* agreed with Kipling that
> "the Eastern and Western races of men were so different, radically and essentially in moral standards and mental outlook"

it was not upholding the view that there was an equality of diversity between them. It believed that the East was inferior to the West in 'moral standards and mental outlook'.

The attitude taken by *The Irish News* to the East is very different to the Young Ireland interest in the Orient in Charles Clarence Mangan's poetry translations between 1837 and 1846. Mangan did not find a 'Seething Orient' of lower 'moral standards and mental outlook'. His *First Article* on *Persian and Turkish Poetry* contains the following appreciation of the East — along with an explanation for the ignorance of the West, and in particular the Western Orientalist, in understanding it. It is worth setting down as a handy antidote to Kipling and *The Irish News*:

> "Asia was the cradle of the human race, was man's primeval world. We look to it from childhood as the land of the sun... The coldest of cosmolities must feel that it is the great Caravanserai at which he is oftenest disposed to put up in the resting pauses of his pilgrimages... If he would know how empires were founded, how society was formed, how civilisation originated, Asia must be his book of reference...
>
> It is a matter of regret that the old Orientalists... were men who had been taught to think, rather than men who had learned to think. They had acquired, perhaps, a knowledge of history but they had not acquired any knowledge of the principles upon which the great events and great characters of history should be judged...
>
> They regarded the Asiatics as a subordinate and degraded caste of mortals, without troubling themselves to anatomise with too much curiousness the reasonings they had arrived at their conclusions by. Europe stood with her face to the light; Asia lay buried in shadow; the contrast was undeniable and was made the most of...
>
> The old Roman, as he looked with contempt on the barbarian Teuton and Briton, could scarcely have imagined a period when Germany and England would contest the victory of intellectual pre-eminence with the majestic mistress of the world...
>
> The old Orientalists were unfortunately so organised as to be incapable of viewing the existing condition of Asia as it stood in relation to the system of the world from its beginning...
>
> They tested the genius, habits and prejudices of one continent by the genius, habits and prejudices of another; and because the two continents differed — because the moral character of Europe was reckoned austerer than that of Asia, because Asia was not Europe, the literature of Asia was pronounced unworthy of comparison with the literature of Europe." (*The Dubliner, The Lives, Times*

*and Writings of James Clarence Mangan*, pp.95-6.)

*The Irish News* had not forgotten Mangan and it curiously included one of his translations in an editorial published as General Townsend moved in on Baghdad in late 1916.

But *The Irish News* coalescence with Kipling is a world away from Mangan and Young Ireland. The liberal and outreaching national culture of Young Ireland had been ground down by 1914 into a very narrow nationalism with all the prejudices of the British Imperialist outlook and the puritanical Catholicism of Cardinal Cullen. It was an odd combination. But it is easily explainable in terms of historical causation.

Just after Mangan had written his appreciations of the East and made his translations of its poetry, there had been the Great Famine of 1847-8. One of the major effects of the Famine was that it facilitated the remoulding of Irish Catholicism from the complexities of the old Irish Church to the reconstructed fundamentalist Romanism of Maynooth. And Irish nationalism, from the time of Daniel O'Connell onwards, developed around that reconstructed Church, and its society, to form the intolerant and narrow Catholic-nationalism that emerged in the middle of the nineteenth century.

That Catholic-nationalism then made an accommodation with British Imperialism in the course of its desire for Home Rule. And that accommodation involved moving away from the old sceptical and disrespectful attitudes toward the British State and taking on instead the racial and social attitudes inherent in English society, as Britain was seen in a more favourable light. Irish nationalists began to aspire to be a junior partner to Britain in the lordship of the world, instead of being one of the lorded over races. In doing this, it was fitting to take on the outlook and horizons of Imperial Britain and leave behind the character of the dispossessed who sympathised with the lots of similar peoples.

By 1914 Irish Nationalism and English Liberalism had become intertwined, particularly after the conflict with Unionism over Home Rule—which facilitated the Redmondite development by providing an antagonism within the British State that the new Nationalism could find a continuity against, with which to undergo its Imperialist transformation. And this was extended in 1914 to hostility towards Liberal England's enemies in its Great War for civilisation—Western and Eastern.

Mangan came to his appreciation of the Ottomans and the East through his Germanism. But no one could indulge in such sentiments within the atmosphere created by mainstream Nationalism in the service of Liberal England during August and September 1914. If Mangan had lived in Dublin then he probably would have been run out of town and treated in the manner of a Kuno Meyer.

That is the historical background to the attitude of *The Irish News* towards the Turks, as expressed through its editorial comment on the Turkish national liberation war and the Chanak crisis.

423

Eleutherios Venizelos, Prime Minister of Greece, 1910-15, 1924

# VIII. Chanak And Imperial Decline

The Suez crisis of 1956 is often seen as the event that marked the demise of the British Empire. But if Suez was the end, Chanak in 1922, was the beginning of the end. The end, therefore, took a long time and it took in another World War.

At Suez, Britain thought it could still do independent military things of great world wide consequence. It found that it couldn't when America said no. Chanak had resulted from Lloyd George's confidence that Britain did not need America to do its work in the world. It could carry on, regardless of the position it had found itself in at the Armistice with Germany.

At Chanak, when Britain believed it was at the pinnacle of its power, it attempted to impose its will on an enemy which it had defeated a few years earlier. The enemy had refused to accept the peace terms imposed upon it and had resurrected itself and dared the victors to do their worst. But the victors were then scattered, one by one, by the resurrection, until only England was left—last man standing. Then Britain, the chief amongst the victors, after declaring it would do its worst, found that it could not, or would not. It backed down. And that set a trend in backing down that was to last a couple of decades, with very serious results for the Empire and the world it stood astride of.

Of course, that trend was reversed, in the worst possible way, in 1939, when the Imperial spirit seemed to be willing again. But the flesh found itself, by then, to have become incredibly weak. Britain declared a World War over a ridiculous issue and found itself unwilling and incapable of fighting for it. And others had to finish the job it had started, with fifty million perishing in the process.

But Chanak is where it all started to go wrong—and not in Ireland, despite what the Tory Diehards said. The Diehards opposed the appeasement involved in the Irish Treaty, Indian representation in the Raj, and the ending of the Egyptian Protectorate. But they collaborated in the greatest act of appeasement of all, at Chanak—to out-appease the great appeaser, Lloyd George.

## The 'Chanak Incident'

The 'Chanak incident' is virtually written out of British history—or written down as a mere 'incident'. It is mentioned in the downfall of Lloyd George's Coalition Government, but only in passing, without explanation of its wider significance. There are clues to what happened in the writings of the some of the participants, such as Churchill, but the impression given is that the whole affair, including the instigation of the Greek adventure that preceded it, is one that is best forgotten.

After the liberation of Smyrna, the Turkish objective was the recovery of Constantinople from the British, and Eastern Thrace from the Greeks. But Mustapha Kemal found his way barred by British forces stationed at Chanak on the Asian side of the Dardanelles. A stand-off ensued with something of the character of *High Noon*.

There is a book about *The Chanak Affair* by David Walder (a Tory MP), which tries to explain it away. But it was written in 1969 when the British Empire was no more—or had not been re-imagined yet.

*The Chanak Affair* was not written with the purpose of explaining the significance of Chanak for the Empire but rather of putting a gloss over it. It explains Chanak as a kind of triumph of British reasonableness over momentary British recklessness. British reasonableness had become the dominant idea by 1969, particularly amongst the Heathite Tories who were attempting to make the necessary post-Imperial readjustment and point Britain in a different direction to the past. But, of course, the Empire was not built, and could not have been built, on reasonableness. And it was often expanded through recklessness of catastrophic proportions, as Lord Roberts had pointed out back in 1914.

Chief among the reckless was, of course, Churchill. The arrival of Kemal's forces at Chanak transformed Churchill's attitude to the Turks. Whilst Churchill had previously advised Lloyd George against his Greek adventure as military madness—and argued for placating the Turks to ensure British interests in the region, he now reversed his position. He saw Kemal's challenge to Britain as one that could not be backed down from without losing the tremendous aura of invincibility that Britain had won at great cost in the war. 'Chanak had now become a point of great moral significance to the prestige of the Empire,' Churchill warned the Government. And he stated at a Cabinet meeting that if the Turks took Gallipoli and Constantinople the whole war would have been in vain.

Lloyd George, at the same meeting, described the Straits as 'the most important strategic position in the world,' the lack of which 'had added two years to the war'.

The British Cabinet decided to resist Kemal by force and determined this should not be a bluff. In the meantime Britain began to scratch around for suitable allies that would do the bulk of the fighting for them, to keep costs down and prevent a new call-up. Suggestions included France, Serbia, Rumania and Bulgaria and the nations of the Commonwealth and Empire.

Churchill was asked to draft a telegram to the Dominions on 16th September 1922 asking for support; and then to prepare a press statement announcing this support. (Since this was an Empire and Commonwealth requirement it was taken for granted that it would be given).

However, in his excitement at the prospect of a new war, Churchill forgot about the time difference (over the weekend) between Britain and her Colonies and released his press statement too early. As a result, the Colonial Prime Ministers embarrassingly read of the Imperial call to arms in their Sunday papers before they were even given the courtesy of being asked for their agreement.

Here is part of Churchill's extravagant communiqué – the declaration of a statesman who saw himself directing the forces of an Empire at the pinnacle of its power which would have no truck with any defiance of its will:

"The approach of the Kemalist forces to Constantinople and the Dardanelles and the demands put forward by the Ankara government... if assented to, involves nothing less than the loss of the whole results of the victory over Turkey in the last war... That the Allies should be driven out of Constantinople by the forces of Mustapha Kemal would be an event of the most disastrous character, producing, no doubt far-reaching reactions through all Moslem countries, and... through all states defeated in the late war, who would be profoundly encouraged by the spectacle of the undreamed of successes that have attended the efforts of the comparatively weak Turkish forces... The reappearance of the Turk on the European shore would provoke a situation of the gravest character throughout the Balkans, and very likely lead to bloodshed on a large scale in regions already cruelly devastated." (*The Chanak Affair*, pp.224-5.)

Churchill could not have made it any clearer – the defeat of Kemal was life or death for the Empire.

### August 1914 Revisited?

An interesting contrast is revealed between the editorials of Southern and Northern newspapers in Ireland during the period around Chanak. The coverage of events in the Middle East is much more extensive in the Devlinite *Irish News* than in the Free State *Independent*. In its editorial, *The Balkans Again*, *The Independent* comments on September 19th 1922:

"There may be a new war. Well don't worry. Ireland is busy setting up house. We haven't time for outside concerns."

*The Independent* should have thought again—because it evidently did not know its Treaty.

In August 1922, the Treaty conflict in the South began to change in character. The Free State forces had largely gained control of most towns and won the war of territory; the Republican forces had began guerrilla type activity in response. What *The Independent* meant when it said that 'Ireland is busy setting up house' is that the Irish Republic was being disestablished through military force in favour of the Irish Free State—a house acceptable to the Empire and in line with the Treaty.

*The Independent* was becoming the newspaper of the Free State during this period and it was leaving behind the activist Imperialism of the Redmondite period. That is not to say that it was leaving behind the British influence in its understanding of foreign affairs. That was still there in its world outlook. And that can be seen in contrasting its view to that of *The Catholic Bulletin*.

An independent Irish viewpoint on the world did not emerge within the popular press until the publication of the *Irish Press* in 1931. This paper was the newspaper of independent Ireland. All the other papers had been adaptations from the Home Rule era, in one way or another.

The North-East, unlike the South, was still Redmondite, or more correctly, Devlinite. *The Irish News* was hesitantly veering toward a Free State position for the purposes of adapting to what the bulk of the nation was doing in the South, but it was doing so within the ambit of the Devlinite Imperialism of the previous decade or so. That is understandable. To the Northern Catholics, the Irish 'Civil War' was a travesty and a disaster. The main concern in the North was for the conflict between Nationalists in the South to be over so that the main part of the nation could exert itself on behalf of the Northern part of the nation again. That is mainly why *The Irish News* took the Free State side. But the Catholics of Belfast remained Hibernian/Devlinite in orientation—despite the British/Unionist provocation that was encouraging them in a Republican direction.

It also goes to prove that Catholic West Belfast, unlike the rest of the country, had been reasonably content with Home Rule and the participation in Imperial affairs that went with it. Belfast was a British city, unlike anything in the South, and it took a continued interest in the affairs of the State it remained part of, and what it was doing in the world. In fact, in this case it would not be inaccurate to say that the *Irish News* believed the Empire should be doing *more* in the world. Its opponents were the Unionists/Conservatives, who wanted to do less in order to save money.

That is why there are references sprinkled about *The Irish News* about the continued importance of events in the East, when the Free State *Independent* does not want to know about anything but Treaty housekeeping.

Irish Nationalism had not been just a benign influence on British Imperialism in the Redmondite period. A number of Redmondites had believed that Ireland could actually enhance Imperialism by providing it with a spiritual dimension to go with its materialism. At the start of the war, Redmondites helped work up the anti-War Nonconformist Liberal backbenchers into a War frenzy by penning War atrocity stories for the Liberal Press. And now they rallied to the cause again in Belfast against the Turk—expecting their work to bear the same fruit.

But they were to be disappointed.

In 1914, the Redmondites had a degree of influence in the British Government, (which was then Liberal and had fought side by side with the Irish Nationalists in the Home Rule struggle and against the Tory House of Lords). But, by 1922, the Liberal Government had given way to a Coalition made up largely of Conservative Unionists, with a Liberal Prime Minister. And the influence of the Redmondites within Imperialist circles had also been reduced to insignificance by their decimation in the 1918 election. In the same election the great British Liberal Party had itself been decimated. By 1922 both Liberal Imperialism and Irish Imperialism were numerically inconsequential (the latter being reduced to Joe Devlin and T.P. O'Connor) and had been superseded by other forms of politics in both countries.

There is a fashion today for counter-factual history. Here is a counterfactual that Irish revisionist historians ought to consider: What would have happened if the British Unionists had won one of the two 1910 General Elections and had ditched Irish Home Rule as they pledged in their manifesto? Would Redmond have supported England in August 1914? Would there have been a Great War in August 1914 at all? Might it have been conducted without the Liberals and been a purely Balance of Power war in the old tradition?

If the answer to the first question is 'no' where does that leave Ireland's Great War and Commemoration? As a mere by-product of its desire for Home Rule, I would say: a blood price that had to be aid for Home Rule on the Statute Book.

There was a concern in England during August-September 1922, due to the situation in the East, that things had reached a pass similar to the situation which presented itself to Edward Grey in August 1914. And a resumption of world conflict was a distinct possibility. The Tory press created a great palaver about it, to prevent any repeat, and Lloyd George and his cabal had to proceed in a very sensitive manner to avoid bringing their administration down.

If the Conservatives had been inspired by the Devlinite agitation in 1922 with regard to the Turks, as the Liberals had responded to the Redmondite War propaganda against the Hun in August 1914, British Imperialism would have done even more damage in the Middle East than it actually did.

It was undoubtedly a good thing for Britain and the world that Irish Republicanism detached the Irish Imperialists from the patrons they aspired to work for and made them irrelevant when it came to the bit over Chanak.

## The Catholic Bulletin's View

*The Catholic Bulletin* had been a Home Rule publication, having been founded in 1911 during the Home Rule era. It had initially attempted to preserve unity between Home Rulers and Republicans in late 1914. It had tried to adopt the initial Redmondite position of Ireland raising a defence force to protect the island from invasion. It did not realise that this was just a staging post for Redmond and his colleagues for an advance to a full Imperialist position of war on Germany. And it proved incapable of holding such a position for any length of time, in view of the Redmondite insistence that neutrality was an impossibility in a War for civilisation.

So *The Catholic Bulletin* felt its way to a Republican position, which it held onto during the split over the Treaty in 1921-22.

The period in which the Turks succeeded in rolling back the Treaty of Sèvres and the Greek invasion coincided with the period of Truce, Treaty and Treaty War in Ireland. Like *The Irish News*, *The Catholic Bulletin* followed international events closely; particularly those relating to British imposed treaties. At the time J.J.O'Kelly, 'Sceilg', Republican Minister and Deputy Speaker of Dáil Éireann edited the *Bulletin*. O'Kelly was opposed to acceptance of the Irish Treaty and took interest in what was happening with regard to British attempts to impose the Treaty of Sèvres on Turkey.

The *Bulletin* began to take a special interest in Mustapha Kemal, seeing that he was achieving something that many people in Ireland believed impossible—facing down a Treaty imposed by Britain and backed by Imperial military power. At this time, of course, Britain was achieving her objectives in Ireland through engineering a fatal division in the national movement by the means of imposing a Treaty through the threat of 'immediate and terrible war'. But, in Turkey, the Anti-Treaty forces had achieved a victory beyond the wildest dreams of most and those who had signed the Treaty (of Sèvres) were moving out, 'bag and baggage'.

The retreat from the Treaty of Sèvres, that the *Bulletin* witnessed, was the first sign of a British Imperial blundering that was to characterise the period between the two wars on Germany. Ireland had been an inspiration for others in the world struggling for their freedom—up until the 1921 Treaty. But it was now Mustapha Kemal and the new Turkey that was proving to be the inspiration for people fighting for independence against Imperialism.

The first evidence of this Imperial blundering was shown in the way the British architects of Sèvres had, in just over a year, undone something that Imperial Statesmen had spent an entire century constructing. They had ended the enmity between Russia and Turkey that British foreign policy had encouraged throughout the nineteenth century and driven the two countries to cooperate for the first time since the days of Peter the Great (The Bolsheviks had renounced Russia's Imperialist demands in the region and moved to aid the Turks against the Imperial Powers).

Then, once Kemal had showed the substance of the Turkish will to resist the Treaty imposition, Britain had not risen to the challenge and had instead, in early 1921, tried to revise Sèvres by inviting the Kemalists to a conference in London. Kemal refused any revisions to Sèvres until the Greeks withdrew from Anatolia, and again Britain hesitated, and did nothing but abandon its catspaw. And then Kemal got a new Treaty of an entirely different kind.

One of the most interesting aspects revealed in reading the *Catholic Bulletin* was the differing stance between it and the *Irish Independent* and *Irish News* on the conflict between Greece and Turkey. How did the *Catholic Bulletin* find itself on the side of the Islamic world against the champions of Christianity at *The Irish News* and *The Independent*? That does not seem logical if one thinks of the *Bulletin* as a narrowly Catholic sectarian publication, as Roy Foster, Margaret O'Callaghan of Queen's University, and other revisionist historians have presented it.

*The Irish News* was a Devlinite newspaper that was published under the auspices of the British State. But *The Independent* aspired to be the newspaper of the new Irish State. However, *The Independent* was stuck in the narrow confines of British thought parameters, accepting Imperial propaganda about evil, backward races incapable of government, etc. whilst *The Catholic Bulletin* had the broad humanism supportive of democracy and the emancipation of the dispossessed.

The *Bulletin* has had a bad press in academia for its relentless war of ideas against the Imperial rearguard in the Free State. It understood that in the 1920s and 1930s Irish independence had not been accomplished (despite what the revisionists believe today) and everything was still in the balance. It believed that Ireland would not be truly independent until it had established an independence of mind and it set out to combat the ideas that attempted to reconcile Ireland to the Imperial mindset.

One can only say that the *Bulletin* was justifiably concerned, given what has happened in Ireland over the last few decades.

### High Noon at Chanak

Here is how *The Irish News* reported the unfolding of events with regard to the *High Noon* situation that was now developing at Chanak. It started off in quite hopeful mood, believing that it was on the side of the big battalions:

"PREPARING FOR THE STRIFE

No ingenuity can reconcile the divergent views of the British and French Governments on the situation brought about by the defeat of the Greeks in Asia Minor... Mr. Lloyd George and his colleagues are sufficiently emphatic they will fight rather than give the Turks even a semblance of control over the invaluable Straits, and they will stand by Rumania, Jugo-Slavia, and Greece, small nations whose very existence cannot be secured for a year if the Turk obtains a foothold on the European continent again...

Mustapha Kemal may not wait... Then there is the colossal Shadow of Bolshevism lowering on the Russian frontier. The Bolsheviks have supplied the Turks with gold, with provisions taken from the starving Russian population... Lenin and Trotsky have a well-defined policy and object; they will promote trouble everywhere — in the Near East and the Far East, in Ireland, America and Australia, if they find an opportunity, so that the anarchic conditions which they seek to establish the world over may spring from bloodshed, confusion and general chaos. They will help to get the Turk back to Constantinople and Thrace: his eviction can be accomplished at the Russian giant's will when Mustapha Kemal has played his part as a helper in the destruction of Europe.

Mr. Lloyd George is to be made a scapegoat by the English politicians who have opposed him virulently within the past twelve months. In a sense he deserves the fate to which his English enemies would consign him. He... encouraged the Greeks to fight the Turks: but he did not support the Greeks, and he left them to defeat at the hands of the Moslems supplied with Russian gold and French '75s.' ...

France has secured herself against... damage to her prestige. That rather intangible French asset will be improved if the Turks get Constantinople; if the Turks win, England will be classified with Greece by the Moslems; and here the divergence of interests between the two Powers is vital...

The reveille is ringing throughout the British Empire again; Australia will respond without delay; Australians and Irish fell in thousands so that the Turks might be driven out of Gallipoli. If the Turk re-enters under Bolshevik auspices, 'hell will be let loose' in the Balkans once more." (September 18th 1922.)

*The Irish News* believed that behind the Kemalists were the Bolsheviks.

Mustapha Kemal had indeed established a working arrangement with the Russian Communists—but it was on *his* terms. The Bolsheviks tried to gain influence in Turkey but they were rebuffed by the Kemalists and the Turkish Communists were suppressed. An effective relationship between the two countries was set up, to the mutual benefit of both, by the Soviet Commissar for the Nationalities, Josef Stalin. Stalin was a Georgian and knew the region well. He realised that Turkey should not be divided and weakened by Communist intrigues but supported in order to do maximum damage to British Imperialism in the region. So Stalin organised the first significant Soviet aid to be supplied to a foreign people struggling against Imperialism, despite their anti-communist nature, to great effect.

*The Irish News* view of Kemal as an instrument of Bolshevism undoubtedly owed its inspiration to the British Press. All the disturbances that were occurring across the Empire during 1920-22 were put down in some respect to Jewish-Bolshevik conspirators. Many Imperial Administrators and sections of the British Press formed the argument that Bolshevism was an extension of the German-Jewish conspiracy against the British Empire, that had assumed new forms after the defeat of the Kaiser. Behind it all was 'the hidden hand' of Jewish financiers. And it was no accident that an English translation of the *Protocols of The Elders of Zion*, in a book entitled *The Jewish Peril*, which drew attention to the Jewish backgrounds of many of the leading Bolsheviks, appeared during 1920 in London (One sees references in the English Press about this time also to the 'Spanish Jew', DeValera. Perhaps he was a Sephardim!)

It was not even beyond the bounds of speculation for this section of the British ruling class that Islam was involved in the German, Jewish, Bolshevik intrigues that led to the revolts across the Empire! And Kemal, the Bolshevik catspaw, was a running theme of Devlinite reports.

What was really at issue with regard to control of the Straits and Constantinople? *The Irish News* explained to its readers in its next editorial:

"TROUBLED STRAITS
The narrow strait connecting the Aegean Sea with the Sea of Marmora is called the Dardanelles on the Aegean side and the Hellespont on the Marmora side.

That was the Strait which the British navy failed to ford in February, 1916. Had the naval operations against the Straits and the military effort in the Gallipoli Peninsula—or either—been successful at the beginning of 1916, the World War might have been brought to an end before the close of that year. Russia was then a potent factor... it was a bold attempt; but it was ill-judged; and it fell through ignominiously—after many thousands of lives had been vainly sacrificed.

Warships in the Sea of Marmora would have Constantinople at their mercy. The Bosphorus connects the Sea of Marmora with the Black Sea; it is right under the walls of the former Turkish capital. Free communication with the Black Sea, into which the mighty Danube flows, is absolutely essential to the trade and commerce of Central and South-Eastern Europe, and to the commercial interests of all the world's countries that trade with Russia, Austria, Hungary and Rumania.

No one in Europe really believes that the Straits would be free if the Turkish power was re-established at Constantinople and restored at Gallipoli. The tragedy of 1916 would be re-enacted if the Turks, under Bolshevist inspiration and guidance, chose to quarrel with any Christian Power in the course of a few years. Mr. Lloyd George declared yesterday, in reply to Australia's prompt response, that 'the Empire cannot consent to sacrifice the results of the gallant struggle and the final victory of its sons in the Eastern theatre.' But the fruits of the final victory will be sacrificed at the end of this diplomatic contest. Mustapha Kemal is the arbiter of destiny... he will not force the issue; he can afford to wait, and play the diplomatic game. In return for some kind of an 'understanding' or 'guarantee' that the precious Straits will be free, the Turkish leader and his troops will be allowed to enter Constantinople without the firing of a shot; they will also get Adrianople and the better part of Thrace...

The Die-hards are using the crisis as a weapon against Lloyd George; there is no enthusiasm for the policy of combat—not even the faintest shadow of approval—amongst any political party in England, nor, if appearances are not deceptive, amongst any section of the English people...

The organs of English opinion in India seem to have been terrified out of their wits by the bare idea of a war between England and Turkey. Why? Well, Reuters Correspondent cabled the following significant message from Bombay yesterday:-

'The Kemalist victories are being celebrated by Mahommedans in India and yesterday was celebrated as a day of prayer and thanksgiving at the behest of the Khalifat Committee. Moslem quarters were gaily decorated and processions marched through the streets, cheering Mustapha Kemal and waving Turkish flags. Mosques are crowded with worshipers.'

Now it can be understood why the '*Times of India*' and the '*Bombay Chronicle*' became hysterical when Lloyd George's 'call' sounded in their ears. India's Moslems number 70,000,000; and a majority of that multitude can fight as well as pray...the 70,000,000 prayerful Moslems of India will believe, not unjustifiably, that the British Empire has been defeated and humiliated." (September 19th 1922.)

433

The next series of editorials act as a running commentary on the failure of the Imperial will at Chanak in the face of the Kemalist resurgence:

"BAD—WHATEVER HAPPENS

England has definitely committed herself in armed opposition if the Turks invade the 'Neutral zone'—an achievement credited to Kemal's troops in some quarters already...

The protagonists are Turkey Redivivus and England. If war breaks out, these will be the combatants.

We believe war will be avoided. The Turks are flushed with victory... If Mustapha Kemal and his men are assured of success via negotiations, why should they run the risk of conflict with England? And were a conflict forced on England, present-hour domestic differences would be sunk in a gigantic and desperate effort to achieve victory. Whoever believes the contrary has failed to read aright the lessons of English history during the past 260 years.

Whatever happens—war or peace—England stands to lose immeasurably through the triumph of Mustapha Kemal and his Turks.

If peace is made—which is probable—all Islam will be convinced that the Turks who were beaten in Palestine and Mesopotamia and practically hunted out of Europe into the wilds of Anatolia a few years ago defeated England as truly and thoroughly as they smashed the Greeks...

This grave consideration is before the English Government hour after hour. War against the victorious Turks would have its serious perils; furious Moslems might be roused to 'direct action' in India: but Lloyd George and his colleagues are asking themselves —would it not be wiser and safer to face this risk than to hand over Constantinople and Thrace to Mustapha Kemal, and thus convince the Moslem world that England feared to put the issue to the test of force?..." (September 21st 1922.)

"STILL RATHER DOUBTFUL

Perhaps Mustapha Kemal may be induced to wait for a few weeks—by which the date of a Conference can be fixed...

If the English forces had cleared out of Chanak before the threatened advance of the Turks who had just made the Islamic millions thrill to the news of decisive victories over the Greeks and with the utter rout of the Christians at Smyrna, England's domination over the East would not be worth a year's purchase.

Those who argue conscientiously that the destruction of English power in the East would be a just and meritorious achievement—good for the Eastern peoples and good for the English themselves—are entitled to hold their honest opinions. But while the English think otherwise they cannot afford to lose another fragment of the prestige on which their dominance over the East depends altogether: and that prestige would have been lost without hope of redemption had General Harrington's troops scuttled out of the little fort on the Asiatic side of the Dardanelles...

Englishmen who assert that war must not be risked on any account have valid arguments on their side. Imperialism as a policy is decrepit to the point of death—perhaps it will never be revived. 'O, for an hour of Palmerston!' was a common exclamation for more than half a century whenever an English Government displayed signs of hesitation or 'weakness' in dealing with Turks, Russians or Spaniards, Irish or Portuguese or any other people who ventured to cross the path of the Imperialist juggernaut.

Palmerston's name has not been printed in London since the end of the Great War." (23rd September 1922.)

"THE GREAT CLIMB-DOWN

A remarkable document has been addressed to the 'National Assembly' of the Kemalist Turks by 'the three Allied Governments.' Its text is published elsewhere; it might be abbreviated, without altering its meaning, into a few simple lines—thus :-

'Please, good and kind Mr. Turk, come into a conference with us: take Thrace, Constantinople, Adrianople—anything you want; only be merciful enough, out of the fullness of your charity and in accordance with our humble request, to refrain from sending your armies against the English troops at Chanak until these troops can be withdrawn without utter discredit to England in the eyes of her Mohammedan 'subjects'. O, Turk, pray hear and heed our appeal, and you shall be brother in the League of Nations!'

The wisdom of yielding to the Turk after he had beaten an undisciplined and disheartened horde of Greeks is a matter for the Powers directly concerned. Nothing can be gained by discussing the point now. But, for the sake of whatever little regard for Truth and Common Honesty that has been left to the world by its rulers, let there be no attempt to disguise or hide the simple fact that a handful of the Turks who were signally defeated in the Great War have come out of the recesses of Asia Minor into the borders of Europe and terrified the 'triumphant' Western Allies into the most abject surrender in modern history." (September 25th 1922.)

"A GALLIC VICTORY

France has won a diplomatic victory of surpassing magnitude over England...

England, through her Government, has surrendered to the Kemalist Turks— nominally: her real surrender was made to France, for she would have been compelled to face and cope with French hostility in the open had she not humbled herself before Mustapha Kemal. France meant to stand by the terms of the Angora Treaty made and signed without England's consent or knowledge. When the English Government realised this fact, they abandoned their own position rather than challenge an open breach of an 'Alliance' that has long been a mockery and a delusion...

England has a knack of 'getting back a share of her own'. She has not done with France yet. As the French know their neighbours thoroughly, the contest between the two nations henceforward must prove absorbingly interesting to detached observers. It may end in disaster to both." (September 26th 1922.)

France remained unimpressed with the British call to arms at Chanak, despite four visits by Curzon to Paris. The other European 'allies' also declined and the response from the Empire was embarrassingly lukewarm (only New Zealand offered to help), despite the moral blackmail Churchill resorted to about 'the sanctity of our graves at Gallipoli' (which E.M. Forster wrote a reply to). And the British public and press expressed widespread astonishment that they might be going back to War, given Lloyd George's election pledges of rapid demobilization, and so soon after the 'war to end all wars'.

The Alliance between England and France which had been formed in 1904 to deal with Germany started to become 'a mockery and a delusion' as soon as Germany had been beaten. Both countries had differing reasons for the *Entente Cordiale*. France was encouraged to join with England because of irredentist considerations concerned with Alsace-Lorraine. Britain had looked upon the alliance as a exercise in the readjustment of the Balance of Power Policy to deal with Germany.

In 1914 Britain aimed to destroy Germany's commerce and capture large areas of territory from the Ottoman Empire. This process began to involve the destruction of the Ottoman Empire, which would mean that the Russian and French Allies would also pick up a cut of the territory in the area. So the object, from Britain's point of view, was to make sure that she maximised her gains and minimised those of her Allies — her future rivals in the new Balance of Power.

But one of her Allies was counted out during the War, before the knock-out blow could be landed on Germany. Russia collapsed and then reneged on her part in the effort against Germany, and, worse still, it went Bolshevik. So she was absent when the vultures gathered around the carcass of the Ottoman Empire.

However, France remained, and therefore Britain could not conclude the Peace entirely in the way she wanted.

During the course of the war, France had made the greater sacrifice in terms of men and materials and she was determined to protect herself from Germany in the future by establishing a Rhine frontier — with the Palatinate forming a Buffer State between France and Germany. Marshall Foch, the Commander of the Allies, argued that France was as entitled to this security, as Britain had been when she set up the Belgian Buffer State in the 1830s to keep Antwerp from any major power. Clemenceau, the French Premier, who had experienced the debacle of 1871, concurred with this view. But despite setting up Buffer States in other parts of Europe, this was one Buffer State that Britain did not want.

A month after the Armistice with Germany, Clemenceau met with Lloyd George in London. The French understood that they had received a British commitment to supporting French requirements in Europe, in relation to Germany, in return for deferring to England's desires in the Middle East.

However, when it came to the bit, Britain refused to allow France to gain the security of a Rhine frontier against Germany, despite a degree of acquiescence existing in the Rhineland for it. Britain was still operating the Balance of Power policy and France was replacing Germany as the object of it. And the presence of a strong French State amongst all the small Buffer States that were created, and which the French wanted to add to with the Rhineland and Bavaria, was unacceptable to London.

England blocked the French requirement for a Rhineland frontier with the argument that the Empire had fought the War for self-determination, and the Rhenish people were undoubtedly German. And the French could not counter this argument with reference to the Middle East, where Britain showed no respect for such principles, because the Mandate system only applied to the backward races who, supposedly, could not as yet govern themselves.

The French became very disillusioned with the peace that Britain arranged in 1919-20. Whilst the British imposed a much harsher peace on Germany than the Germans had on the French in 1870, with the scuppering of the Kaiser's fleet and the appropriation of the cream of the merchant navy, England refused to countenance French demands for the security of their land frontiers.

The French had their own interests in the East and their businessmen had greatly profited by the Capitulations which the Sultan granted to foreign capitalists. This led the majority view within the French Government to be against the destruction of the Ottoman Empire at the start of the War. But, once the British had shown their intention of breaking up and colonising as much of it as possible, the French were left with no choice but to grab their share. France had historic links with the Syrian *vilayet*, which also contained substantial Christian Maronite communities, so she demanded this slice of the Ottoman Empire.

As early as 1917, Lloyd George tried to make a deal with the Turks through the arms dealer, Basil Zaharoff, which would have given Britain all of Mesopotamia, Palestine and Arabia and cut the French out of Syria. The Sykes-Picot Agreement had been dropped by Britain when their armies occupied Damascus. Then, according to the French Press, a secret agreement was made between the British and the Sultan with the Sultan promising to support a British mandate over Turkey and control of the Straits in return for material aid against his nationalist opponents. This involved excluding the French from the territory around Syria which Britain had agreed in the Sykes-Picot arrangement should go to France. The French were concerned at the secret British manoeuvres and decided to cut a deal with Kemal himself.

The Balance of Power reflex in British policy can be seen in the following extract from Arnold Toynbee's 1922 book, *The Western Question in Greece And Turkey*, where France seems to be taking the place of Germany, three years after the defeat of the Hun. Toynbee says of France:

"During the twenty years before the armistice, her cultural property in the Ottoman Empire had been trespassed upon by Germany; indeed, she had been violently evicted from it by Germany after the outbreak of war. She had a cultural Alsace-Lorraine to recover in the East as well as a political Alsace-Lorraine in Europe, and in both cases she wanted an 'integral' restitution. She regarded both assets as her property, and the acquisition of them by others as robbery, and on the whole it is less odious to be robbed by one's enemies than one's allies. This is perhaps the fairest statement of the French point of view. One might put the same thing in another way by saying that France was eager to step into Germany's shoes and appropriate her monopoly of influence over Turkey by carrying on the German policy of diplomatic cajolery, intellectual bedazzlement, financial control, and studied disinterestedness in the Ottoman Government's treatment of subject populations. But this less charitable formulation is also really less correct, for the German policy was nothing but the policy invented for France nearly four centuries ago by Francis I and habitually practised by her till Wilhelm II filched it from her." (pp.88-9.)

That is a pretty good summary by Toynbee of how Britain saw the Balance of Power. For England in 1900, Germany was becoming the new France, in other words, the main enemy to organise an alliance against — to redress the Balance of Power. But now that Germany was defeated, France 'was eager to step into Germany's shoes', which were, of course, really French shoes all along! And that was undoubtedly the truth of the matter — France had been the object of the British Balance of Power for centuries. Germany had only stepped in France's shoes for a decade or so!

Under the Sykes-Picot Agreement that divided the Ottoman Empire up between the *Entente,* France had been awarded a vast zone including Cilicia, East Central Anatolia, and Western Kurdistan. This award had been confirmed by the Treaty of Sèvres. But the French found themselves incapable of holding this territory against Kemal's forces. So France cashed in its chips with Kemal, ceding all its spoils to the loser in the War, in an agreement of 20th October 1921. And she gave up a large amount of surplus weaponry to the Turks, including some artillery, which proved very useful to Kemal in dealing with the pawns of England in Anatolia.

So Britain, who was operating a Balance of Power policy against France in Europe, suffered a pay back in the East as the Balance of Power manoeuvre was turned against her by the Turks and the French.

The last line of *The Irish News* editorial proved remarkably prophetic. Britain was to bring back Germany as a counter-weight to France in its Weimar construction and then, more dangerously in its Nazi manifestation. The Balance of Power game was played until the balance got out of control in relation to Herr Hitler. And, when Britain tried to redress the balance with another drastic change of policy, it did indeed 'end in disaster to both' England and France, in May 1940.

438

## A Tribute To Ataturk

The final series of *Irish News* editorials recognises the measure of the man who beat the British Empire:

### "MUSTAPHA KEMAL

As the Turkish leader did not get the Allies' humble petition for mercy until Monday morning, the 'movements' of his cavalry within the 'neutral zone' behind Chanak which drew a stern warning from General Harrington were probably unauthorised, and will now be suspended... There is no valid reason for Turkish aggressiveness in that area, now that General Harrington's masters have surrendered to the Oriental gentleman who is, like Julius Caesar, Brian Boroihme, Napoleon, and other great men of history, both a soldier and a statesman. The French have now discovered that the Turks did not set fire to Smyrna! Lord St. Davids, an English Liberal Peer, has painted the Greeks in colours black as the smoke out of Etna's crater. The 'treacheries' of King Constantine are daily recalled by English politicians and newspapers...

But, while awaiting developments, let a tribute be paid to the personality of Mustapha Kemal. He is a real leader. He knew all along what he wanted. He went the right way about getting it. Circumstances were largely on his side, but few men could have utilised even favourable circumstances more dexterously or effectively. As an individual he deserves the success which he has achieved. He has resurrected the Turks, exalted the Bolsheviks, and finally smashed the Western European *Entente*." (September 27th 1922.)

### "A TERRIBLE 'GAME'

For the moment the situation depends on the upshot of a really terrible 'game.' Kemal's men are not merely within the 'Neutral Zone' which the Allies are pledged to hold sacrosanct; they are cheek by jowl with the British garrison at Chanak, and each side is hoping that the other will fire the first shot, and so be represented as blameable for the conflict...

But the polite Kemalists have no right to come within 30 miles of the British entrenchments. Their appearance within the defined boundaries of the 'Neutral Zone' is an act of defiance and aggression that would have been forcibly resented an hour after they had crossed the line of demarcation by any Power not thoroughly afraid of them...

War can be avoided if the Turks inflict a humiliation more disastrous than actual military defeat on England. If England is not prepared to accept such humiliation and see her 'Eastern Empire' walking away from her in the course of a few years, she must curb the Turks. One party or other will win; and a victory for the Turks at this juncture will mean a deathblow to Britain.

These are the simple facts: and they are keenly realised at Downing Street. Whatever happens, these days are 'big with fate' for 'the Empire on which the sun never sets.'" (September 30th 1922.)

### "TRYING TO AVOID WAR?

The Turks have graciously consented to withdraw a little way from

Erenkeuy, a small fort nearer to the Dardanelles entrance than Chanak and about 10 miles from the position occupied by the British. That is paraded as a great concession. But they are still moving quietly toward Ismid... only 50 miles from Constantinople. Ismid would be a natural base for a Turkish advance against the great city wrested from the Greeks...

But the pathway to a sort of compromise is in the process of construction...

Mustapha Kemal will win... His victory will mark the beginning of the end of the British Empire in the East..." (October 2nd 1922.)

The British Cabinet sent an order to General Harrington, the commander of British forces at Chanak, to give the Kemalist forces an hour to withdraw and to engage them if they failed to comply. Large reinforcements to back up the threat were promised to him.

But, despite being warned that he was purely a military man who should do his duty as instructed, Harrington decided, on his own initiative, not to deliver the ultimatum. He then entered into talks with Kemal to defuse the situation. And the British Press, right across the political spectrum, treated Harrington as a hero for doing so. As *The Irish News* put it:

"WAR AND POLITICS

General Sir Charles Harrington's military record is creditable; he appears to be gifted with the instinct of statesmanship also. It is probably quite unjust to accuse the British Government of an eager desire to wage war on the Kemalist Turks; but it is certain that Sir Charles Harrington could have begun a war at any moment during several days without exceeding his instructions in the slightest degree... General Harrington's success depended on his ability to persuade the Turks that they could get all they wanted without firing another shot..." (October 13th 1922.)

The British signed an Armistice with Kemal at Mudanya. But this was not an Armistice turned into a defeat like the one four years previously at Mudros, or with Germany—or if it was, the Turks turned it into a defeat for the British Empire.

Occupying *Entente* forces began to withdraw from Constantinople and on October 19th Turkish troops entered the Straits and the City. The Turks then moved into Thrace and nobody stopped them.

### Fall of Lloyd George and The Coalition

*The Irish News* believed that an era was drawing to a close with the British appeasement of Mustapha Kemal:

"In other days when English Party politicians vied with one another in their professions of devotion to the principles of Liberty 'as far as Poland is' and to the interests of Humanity, a Government who had behaved like the Welsh Wizard and his colleagues would have been assailed by hosts of angry rhetoricians for the disgraceful hesitancy and ineptitude of their dealings with

440

the Turks. It was thus William Ewart Gladstone attacked the Near-Eastern policy of Disraeli while the story of the 'Bulgarian atrocities' was blazoned before England and the world: and the hideous deeds exposed by M'Gahan and utilised by Gladstone with such effect that the powerful Tory Government were hurled ignominiously from power in 1880 were mere trifles when compared with Turkish ebullitions of fiendishness since 1914. Now the outcry against an English Government is that the Turkish march on European Christian peoples was temporarily stayed until these Christians could clear, 'lock stock and barrel,' out of the cities, towns and *vilayets* in which their homes, their properties, and their land have been fixed for centuries.

Quite justifiably, as a political controversialist, Mr. Lloyd George dwelt on this marvellous change. England is no longer the rescuer of oppressed peoples, 'the friend of freedom in every clime.' The Czars and the Bombas, and the Sultans, and the Thebaws, and the Prempehs of the earth can oppress, and torture, and massacre, and get drunk, and offer up human sacrifices at their will and pleasure henceforward and the watch-dog of Liberty in London will never dream of growling. That is the new dispensation. Mr. Lloyd George himself has adopted it—in unison with Mr. Bonar Law: but he holds that he and his Government were right when they thrust British troops and warships in the way of the conquering Moslems who, having massacred a million and a half Christians in Asia Minor within the past six years, were marching triumphantly over the blood-soaked ruins of Smyrna to Constantinople, with its defenceless Christian population of more than 500,000, and to Thrace, whose population is 60 per cent Christian...

Our interest in this spectacle of the Welsh Wizard at bay is twofold. First of all our concern with the effect of the struggle between Mr. Lloyd George and his enemies on the fate of the Irish Settlement. There seems to be no reason for apprehension. If Ireland stands by her side of the International Treaty, England will not venture to repudiate hers, no matter what Government may rule her. And we cannot divorce ourselves from the world outside Ireland. The future lot of many nations may depend on the great struggle now fairly opened across the Irish Sea." (October 16th 1922.)

The Devlinites were naïve to the end about England's intentions in the world. During the past half century England had indeed posed as 'the rescuer of oppressed people'—when these people were minorities in other Empires or States which Britain wanted to destabilise. But England was never the same in its own Empire—that really should have been clear in Belfast.

The Christians of Asia Minor had lived under Ottoman rule for centuries. For most of that time, they had got on with their living—their trade and their religion unmolested. Their communities grew and prospered over hundreds of years. But then came Britain in 1914 and sought to be 'the rescuer of oppressed people' in the Ottoman territories, using the Christian Greeks as a catspaw to rescue them.

It was Gladstone who expressed the desire to remove the Turk 'bag and baggage' from Europe. It was the last Liberal Prime Minister who set off the chain of events that led to the centuries-old Christian communities of Asia Minor leaving 'bag and baggage' for Europe and beyond.

On 20th October *The Irish News* reported the fall of the Lloyd George Coalition:

"NO MORE COALITION
Mr. Lloyd George and his colleagues have duly resigned; Mr. Bonar Law will be Prime Minister of England for a brief space.

The immediate fate of the British Coalition Ministry depended on the vote of the Tory MPs and members of the Government who met at the Carlton Club yesterday. Mr. Austen Chamberlain demanded from his Party a vote of confidence in himself and his Cabinet colleagues. He was confident until a late hour on Wednesday evening that the Vote would be passed by a large majority. Then began a series of incidents which altered the situation altogether...

When the *puissant* Sir George Younger jumped into the arena and convened a meeting of the Unionist Association for next Tuesday, Tory MPs realised that their own authorities were against the Coalition... This process was accelerated yesterday morning by the news that a Die-hard Tory had been returned for the once overwhelming Liberal division of Newport, in Lloyd George's own Wales...

But the deciding factor against the Coalition at the Tory meeting was the reappearance and action of Mr. Bonar Law... He 'came down' on his own side; he is to succeed Mr. Lloyd George.

And so ends the British Coalition Government formed after the General Election of December, 1918, with a majority of 249 over 'all other Parties combined'—and with an actual majority of 322, because 73 Irish representatives never went to Westminster...

Mr. Lloyd George won that General Election in Great Britain. Sir George Younger cleverly deprived him of that victory...

The managers of the Tory Party... had a clear majority of 130 over Coalition Liberals, Labourites, and all other groups. They could have kicked the Prime Minister out at any time and carried on as a Government on their own account... The Tories bided their time; the Coalition Government's popularity and power faded month by month...

At the close the crisis was artificially produced. There was not a protest from the Tory ranks while Lloyd George was mercilessly dragooning Ireland, betraying the cause of liberty in many lands... the bulk of the Tory Party became Die-hard when at last he decided to stand up to the Turkish protégés of Disraeli and Salisbury and to save from bloody extermination those remnants of the Christian peoples in the Near East ..." (October 20th 1922.)

The Chanak *debacle* was the event that drew together Conservatives who wished to withdraw support for the Coalition and reestablish the party division in British politics. To head off the revolt, the Coalition leaders conceived a plan to call an election before the opposition could collect itself at the Tory Party Conference in November. The idea was to use up all the Tory election funds in a Coalition campaign, thus installing the same government in power for another five years.

But the Coalition leaders miscalculated. Bonar Law, who was seriously ill with throat cancer at the time, came back from retirement to lead the opposition at a Carlton Club meeting and put himself forward as an alternative Prime Minister. At the same time a by-election result in which an independent Conservative candidate trounced a Coalition Conservative, as well as Labour and the Liberals, galvanised resistance to Lloyd George, who resigned. Bonar Law became Prime Minister and called a General Election that the Conservatives won with a healthy majority.

Britain suffered a change of government as a result of Chanak that was much more than a replacement of an administration. It was a moral collapse, or at least the start of one, of great significance. From this point onwards, great uncertainty crept into the conducting of its foreign affairs and those of Empire. The Empire that thought itself as being at the pinnacle of its power, having vanquished its Carthage, found that it had overextended itself and was caught between a rock and a hard place. It could not govern its Empire purposefully but also could not let its subjected peoples go. It began to be seen as a paper tiger by upstart adventurists, like Mussolini and Hitler, who built up their reputations by engaging in brinksmanship with it over its balance of power game—a game it no longer had the skill or will to play with authority. And, instead of being a source of stability and constancy in a new world rid of evil, it turned out to be an erratic agent of further catastrophe.

Churchill called the new administration that followed the Coalition's fall 'a Government of the Second Eleven'. Birkenhead described the new Ministry as 'second class intellects whose mediocrity frightened him'. And Bonar Law's short premiership was followed by more mediocrity over the next decade and a half of Baldwin/MacDonald governments of the 'Second Elevens'.

During this period all the successful Treaties dictated by Britain to the vanquished began to be undone by those who sensed the decline of the Imperial will. And Britain itself blundered about in the world in an increasingly purposeless and erratic manner that ultimately led to the catastrophe of 1939-45.

*The Irish News* was right—it was witnessing the start of the setting of the sun on 'the Empire on which the sun never sets.'

The second part of *The Irish News* editorial of October 20th concerned the effect the fall of the Coalition would have on Ireland:

"The history of the Lloyd George Cabinet's relations with Ireland, and of Ireland's position and performances, cannot be written fully as yet. We know the situation in our own country as it stands; we have got to make the best of it:

443

and the best can be made of it if we, or some amongst us, are not mad enough to forfeit what has been gained and to make our losses irretrievable...

The future of Ireland is in the hands of Irish people now—more truly than at any previous period of our national history. It matters little to us what kind of English Government follows upon the forthcoming General Election. If the people of the Twenty-six Counties dispose of irregularism, establish a stable Administration, and turn their attention soberly and practically, to the great work of Reconstruction and Reunion, Ireland will live, and flourish, and become great amongst the free nations, whether Great Britain is ruled by Die-hards or Communists. But if irregularism finally defeats the people's efforts to redeem their country and themselves, Ireland will, more hopelessly than in 1800, be 'chained to the wheel of the foe by links that the world cannot sever'—and which no sane community in the world will raise a finger to break for the lifetime of the youngest amongst us who may see this century out." (October 20th 1922.)

Although Mustapha Kemal had been recognised for his great abilities as a Soldier and Statesman he had not proved an inspiration to *The Irish News*. What the Turks had done was unthinkable in Catholic Belfast. West Belfast was not in favour of the vigourous independence movement that Mustapha Kemal represented in Turkey, and which it saw in the 'irregularism' of Southern Republicanism. It was for close cooperation with Britain within a unified Ireland—one day. Whilst the rest of the country had moved in a seamless fashion from the Home Rule Party to Sinn Fein, Catholic Belfast had remained largely faithful to Joe Devlin's objectives.

It would take another half century of life in the Northern statelet before something of the spirit of Mustapha Kemal emerged amongst the Catholics of the North.

## *A Black and Tan's Complaint*

H.J. Simson, I believe, was a former Black and Tan who, after the Irish Treaty of 1921, went to do the Imperial work in the former Ottoman territory of Palestine.

In 1937 Blackwoods published his *British Rule, and Rebellion*, a kind of recommendation to the political and military leaders of the Empire about how they could rule their subject races more effectively. It contains sections on Ireland and Palestine in which the author complains about the incompetent appeasement of the Imperial Power toward its subjects and recommends ways in which they could be dealt with in future.

Here are a few extracts from the first chapter, *Rule and Rebellion,* in which it is suggested that things have changed somewhat, in the couple of decades since the Great War, in the Empire's will to govern:

"During that period of twenty years, there has been encouragement of self-expression and a crop of rebellions, within the sphere of British rule. At the

444

same time, there has been hesitation on the part of the ruler to apply force, in striking contrast to the lack of hesitation on the part of the ruled to appeal to force. The most recent example of this state of affairs was provided in 1936 in Palestine." *(British Rule, and Rebellion, p.3.)*

Simson elaborates on this point later on in the Chapter:

"There is no reason whatever to suppose that we have made any progress in the last sixteen years in ability to deal with well-organised rebellion on modern lines. The lack of progress is in no way due to lack of force... In her own Imperial sphere... Britain has adopted a bewilderingly easy-going attitude toward factions or races which take up arms and appeal to force in their own interests. So much is this the case that it seems that she positively encourages resort to force where she governs. One can hear it said to-day, all the way from the Far East right home to the front door, that if you want to get something out of the British, the best and quickest way to get it is to start shooting...In the Imperial sphere where she has enough force, she emphasizes conciliation and suppresses any mention of sanctions till it is long overdue. Then when she has to use force to frustrate appeals to violence, she seems to be quite incapable of using it effectively... we are perhaps the greatest world power which has ever existed... We seem unable to keep peace among those who live inside our rule, but keep on lecturing about peace to those who live outside it. In fact, neither we nor our arrangements are easy to understand." *(British Rule, and Rebellion,* pp.12-19.)

After Chanak there was no consistency evident in the governing of the Empire's subjects. When previously force was applied, it was measured and appropriate to the exerting of sufficient authority to accomplish the Imperial will (for example, South Africa). But, in the period after Chanak, conciliation alternated with brutal suppression in incomprehensible turnabouts of policy. Faceless airmen were used as tax-collectors. The subjects could not understand or comprehend the will of the masters and therefore did not behave as subjects should.

The view that was exasperating Simson could be described as the modern (or post-Chanak) Imperial view. In the pre-Chanak days authority was exerted. Force was employed first, no questions asked, and the moral aspects of it were dealt with later. As Lionel Curtis put it: 'The purpose of force is to give time for morality to bed down'. And since morality was defined by the situation created by the use of force then the moral case most often supported the previous use of force. So it was with the conduct of Imperial affairs during the previous century, and so it was with the Boer War and the Great War.

But, with regard to Turkey, force was employed (or as much as could be mustered), and it failed. So the morality of the situation had to be redefined in favour of the situation that the successful defiance of force had created. And that was very difficult for Britain. So an expunging of history took place until Simson dealt with Chanak in the context of the new morality that had come about as a result of the successful resistance of Mustapha Kemal.

The new morality that was applied presented the whole affair as a kind of settling of things, to the benefit of all, by a wise and benevolent Britain. The Empire, the most powerful force in the world, chose conciliation over force, when it could easily have dispatched the uppity subject with a bloody nose if it had so pleased.

That, of course, is a travesty of the truth, although it is a necessary fiction in the affairs of modern Britain.

Simson realises (having been a Black and Tan) that the decline in the Imperial will began in Ireland with the calling of a truce with the IRA in 1921. But that will, which was seemingly lost on the battlefield, was substantially recovered by the statesmen in the conference room with the signing of the Treaty and its successful implementation, as the Irish Republic was put into reverse towards Home Rule.

There was talk in the British press of making Michael Collins 'the new Botha' after the success of the Treaty, and before he was shot. But nothing could be made of Mustapha Kemal after Chanak. And the world was never the same again.

### The British Bluff at Chanak and In Ireland

The *Catholic Bulletin* understood the meaning of what it was beginning to see in 1922. The *Bulletin* was opposed to the Irish Treaty and saw, in the events that led up to Chanak, signs that it had been right about the Treaty and the threat of 'immediate and terrible war' that had ensured its signing. The *Bulletin* had urged defiance of the Treaty and the calling of the British bluff on it as an alternative to 'civil war'. But Collins and the Treatyites preferred 'civil war' to calling the British bluff.

It is not the case that the *Bulletin* felt the British threat of war was not real. It knew its history and it had a great interest in world affairs—so it knew all about England and how it worked.

Collins decided not to call the British bluff, in conjunction with the other plenipotentiaries who signed the Treaty. Others believed that, if it was put up to Lloyd George, and his bluff was called, he might have blinked and not have had it in him to go for it.

Just before the Treaty negotiations started, the battle of Sakarya in September 1921 took place. This was where the Greek advance into Anatolia was stopped. At this point Lloyd George would have been a very worried man, with all his plans for the region facing catastrophe. And his mind, faced with the choice of waging 'immediate and terrible war' in Ireland, or not, would surely have been in turmoil.

It is impossible to gauge how the Irish and Turkish situations would have interacted in practice, and in Lloyd George's mind, and what would have come out of it.

446

If the Irish had stonewalled and not implemented the Treaty during 1922, if the national movement had stayed united in defiance of it, and if the Coalition 'of all the talents' had fallen, as it did after Chanak in November, what would the new British Government have done to Ireland? Of course, we will never know. But is it likely that the Governments of Stanley Baldwin and Ramsey MacDonald would have done what Lloyd George, Churchill, Balfour, Birkenhead, etc. were incapable of? It is extremely doubtful—if their record in dealing with Ireland and other affairs over the next decade and a half is examined.

Strangely enough the Free State Government was led to fear the fall of the Coalition and the assumption of power by a Bonar Law/Diehard administration. That helped the British enormously in hurrying along the implementation of the Treaty in Ireland. But when one looks at Chanak and the Treaty of Lausanne it must be concluded that Lloyd George was truly the master of bluff – with regard to the Irish.

### How England Rewrites History

On the subject of King Constantine of Greece *The Irish News* penned this well-chosen appreciation of his career on the occasion of his second downfall, after the Greek disaster in Anatolia, during September 1922:

> "Ex-King Constantine's experiences as a monarch have been unique in history—certainly in the modern history of Royalties. He may be described hence-forward as a Double-Ex-King.
>
> A large majority of deposed sovereigns accept their fate, resignedly or reluctantly, and cease to worry the world after their departure from their thrones. In many cases efforts to 'come back' are made—more often unsuccessfully than effectively. But Constantine was (1.) forced to abdicate (2.) re-established in his powers, prerogatives and privileges by the army, with the all-but-unanimous approval of the people; and (3.) kicked out again—this time, also, with the cordial assent of the people...
>
> The Greeks made a scapegoat of their King. Constantine was not altogether an admirable person, perhaps; but he pursued the policy in the Middle East that had been initiated by M. Venizelos: and the approval given to that policy by England in the days of Venizelos was continued when the restored King took it up and prosecuted it—to his ruin, as events transpired." (September 29th 1922.)

In recent years England has undertaken the rewriting of the history of Ireland and has devoted considerable resources to doing this. It has established centres in academia designed to produce a new Irish history that will replace the history of Ireland written by independent Ireland. It has attracted and patronised young Irish historians for its project, and academia—being one of the last vestiges of patronage in society—has trained even younger Irish historians in similar manner. And the whole thing has paid enormous dividends in confusing the

Irish mind so that it is malleable to the British State interest. That has been demonstrated in the rehabilitation of the Great War and the British militarism associated with it but it will also have served its purpose when a situation comes about when a an alteration of world-view might prove vital.

If Irish history and its view of things is to be altered, it is certainly worth enquiring where this new source of history is coming from and how it was constructed—or how such things were done in the past to those who believed in Britain.

After the Great War and the subsequent Greek disaster in Anatolia, Britain was aware of the catastrophe she had brought to Greece. But Britain does not dwell on these things—if it did the mind of the nation might not be in the state required when the necessity of doing them again might arise (as it did with Greece only a decade and a half later, during the Second War on Germany).

But history must be written. Perhaps it can be left to be forgotten in the future and the less said the better about some things. But some record must be produced so that if anyone looks for answers later on they will come across a version of events that will at least deter them from looking any further.

With regard to Greek affairs, England assigned one of its foremost historians, Arnold J. Toynbee, to the project of creating an account that, if not absolving England of all responsibility for what happened to Greece, at least deflected the blame onto other parties—Venizelos, the Greeks, France etc. And ultimately the whole affair assumed the atmosphere of a terrible tragedy that really could never be imagined before the event and which originated in the base characteristics of a foreign people who did not possess the qualities of those who interfered with them—it being a typical failing of these inferior breeds that they just do not know when to stop, when the game is up, and when discretion is the better part of valour, as England does.

British historians seem to develop, as a reflex, the ability to write history in the service of their State. That ability includes the skill of adjusting accounts to justify policy changes in retrospect, so that the reader's understanding of the behaviour of British Statesmen is reprogrammed to the retrospective context, and the actual context of decision-making is lost to the rubbish bin of history.

Arnold Toynbee adjusted from being a vigorous anti-Turk propagandist at Wellington House during the Great War to being a considerate apologist for the Turks after it. When the Turks were earmarked for destruction he vilified them as evil personified, and when they re-emerged as a force to be reckoned with, after it was thought they were down and out, he understood them and what they were about.

What is noticeable about British propaganda writing in the service of the State, from Wellington House to Chatham House, is how they borrow and utilise information from each other and sources are shared across them. A picture or impression is built up in the reader's mind about the Germans or

Turks that is constantly reinforced by similar pictures from slightly different angles in various publications.

Brendan Clifford mentioned a similar thing to me. About twenty years ago he went through a large number of reference books in search of information about Said Talib and found that they were entirely circular, all controlled from one source. He found that Stephen H. Longrigg of Chatham House was the central controller of what was said in a wide range of publications about Talib.

The *Round Table* Group that established Chatham House were the innovators of this technique. And interestingly they had the same word for their meetings, where ideas were thrashed out, as Wellington House — calling them 'moots'.

Toynbee was appointed Director of Studies at Chatham House in 1925 and maintained this post for thirty years. He was without doubt the dominant intellectual influence at Chatham House and its publications are a product largely of his directing.

The Chatham House writing of history could be said to be the official British history of the Middle East. It was the version accepted by the British State and the British people, largely because it was the only systematic and coordinated centre of thought that went into understanding the affairs of the Middle East. It was therefore the authoritative version of thinking on the region from which all other thought developed.

Chatham House became such an influence because it did not confine itself to academic ideas. Journalists, newspaper people, men of State, politicians and public servants all mingled and exchanged their views with academics. So that Chatham House had an influence in the State far beyond the usual academic circles.

Chatham House, like its predecessor, Wellington House, did not produce knowledge for the sake of knowledge. It saw the most important activity in the world as the power to influence the mass of people through the production of ideas. And it viewed the disasters of humanity as the result of misinformation and ignorance.

But there is something very peculiar in the Chatham House view that the disaster of the Great War was a result of misinformation and ignorance amongst the masses — when many of its leading lights spent their time working up the masses with the same misinformation from Wellington House in order that they should sacrifice their lives and take those of others.

### Atrocity Propaganda Again

In a previous chapter I noted how Toynbee changed his opinion about atrocity propaganda — from producing it in the Great War to condemning it as a malevolent factor in human affairs afterwards. With regard to Toynbee's post-war declaration about the dangers of atrocity propaganda, the following account about the Wellington House publications of Turkish atrocities against the Armenians is interesting:

"Half a century after these events, Toynbee claimed that the British government had issued the Blue Book for a special purpose, of which he was unaware at the time, and, he believed, Bryce was also unaware. According to Toynbee, the Russian armies, when retreating across the Polish-Lithuanian frontier in the spring of 1915, had committed barbarities against the Jewish diaspora there, and the advancing German armies had tried to exploit them. Jewish-American journalists, invited to the German occupied Russian territories, had sent 'lurid' dispatches to American papers, and the British government in London had been seriously perturbed.

Thus in February 1916, the New York American had advised the whole American people to demand that Christian England and Christian France restrain the 'savagery' of the barbarous allies. Toynbee believed the government was worried lest American Jewry might retaliate against the Allies by throwing its weight into anti-British scales in the debate in the United States. The 'considerably worse' barbarities committed against the Armenians had provided the British government, according to Toynbee, with 'counter-propaganda' material against Central Powers. Noel Buxton, as well as Asquith and Stanley Baldwin, asserted that the British government did make use of the Armenian tragedy to win over American support during the war. Noel Buxton, who had 'a close and lasting' relationship with Colonel E. M. House, President Wilson's confidential adviser on foreign affairs, 'believed' that the account of the sufferings of the Armenians had a 'great influence' upon American opinion.

The description of their expulsions and massacres, as documented in Bryce's Blue Book, had been one of the 'moving factors' in President Wilson's 'decision to enter war'. Asquith who was Prime Minister when the Blue Book was issued in 1916, and Stanley Baldwin, Prime Minister in the 1920s, also had similar views... they stated that Bryce's Blue Book was 'widely used for allied propaganda in 1916-17 and had an important influence upon American opinion and upon the ultimate decision of President Wilson to enter war'." (Akaby Nassibian, *Britain and the Armenian Question, 1915-1923*, p.81.)

After the Great War, the resurgence of Turkey under Ataturk necessitated a different approach, even to 'atrocities'. According to Toynbee in 1923:

"In judging Greek and Turkish atrocities, Westerners have no right to be self-righteous. They can only commit one greater error of judgement, and that is to suppose that the Turks are more unrighteous than the Greeks. Much mischief has been done in the Near and Middle East by this common Western opinion. The argument generally advanced is that Turks have committed a very much greater number of atrocities upon Greeks than Greeks upon Turks since the two peoples first came across each other. The fact is true but the deduction is fallacious, because a second factor has to be taken into consideration, and that is the opportunities enjoyed by the two parties for respective ill-treatment." (*The Western Question in Greece And Turkey*, p.269.)

Toynbee goes on to point out that the Greeks did not have the upper hand in history over the Turks for nearly as long as the Turks did over the Greeks, and points out that, whenever they had the chance, the Greeks perpetrated as much or more violence than the Turks did in similar circumstances.

What Toynbee was doing was rehabilitating Turkey in the service of the changing requirements of British Foreign Policy which had to settle accounts with the re-emerged presence of the Turkish State in the East, and dump the Greeks as inconsequential. That was a tricky thing to do with any honest consistency, considering the Wellington House propaganda that Toynbee had lent his name to only a few years before—vilifying the Turk from every conceivable angle. But Toynbee was a first class mind and he set about his task with considerable skill. And here is a sample of his work:

> "In attempting to express and explain the Turkish point of view, I am not seeking to suggest that it is right, or to deny the charges brought against the Turkish nation and Government for their treatment of subject peoples during the past century. Their crimes are undoubtedly exaggerated in the popular Western denunciations, and the similar crimes committed by Near Eastern Christians in parallel situations are almost always passed over in silence. At the same time, the facts substantiated against the Turks (as well as against their neighbours) by authoritative investigation are so appalling that it is almost a matter of indifference, from the point of view of establishing a case, whether the embroideries of the propagandists are counterfeit or genuine. The point which I wish to make is that, if our aim is not simply to condemn but to cure, we can only modify the conduct of the Turks by altering their frame of mind, and that our only means of doing that is to change our own attitude towards them. So long as we mete out one measure to them, another to the Greeks, and yet a third to ourselves, we shall have no moral influence over them." (*The Western Question in Greece And Turkey*, p.29.)

*The Western Question in Greece And Turkey* is concerned with building up the former enemy, the Turk, at the expense of the former ally, the Greek. Toynbee goes through the centuries to demonstrate that the Greek is not all he was cracked up to be in England and the Turk was not, after all, undiluted evil.

> "The best commentary on all this false history and false sentiment which prejudice the thoughts of the Western public about the Greeks and the Turks (on the rare occasions when it thinks about them at all) is the judgment of those Westerners who speak from personal experience. They are few in number, but they are mostly educated men, and the different vocations which have drawn them to the Near and Middle East enable them to see the situation from independent points of view. Some have gone as business men, others as soldiers, others as doctors, others as consuls, others as missionaries. Any point on which the majority of these diverse first-hand observers agree, cannot easily be dismissed as a delusion; yet they are almost unanimous in the verdict that, as an individual human being in the local environment, the Turk is not the Greek's inferior. They find him no less honest in his dealings, no less admirable in his character, and no less pleasant as a companion. This consensus among

Westerners who have had direct relations with both nationalities cannot possibly be the product of Turkish propaganda. In the first place, the people who hold this view have formed it as the result of experience; and, secondly, the Turks, as a nation, are almost ludicrously innocent of the propagandist's art. The difference between Western and Middle Eastern social conventions has restricted those forms of personal contact on which propaganda (as well as the more reputable forms of self-revelation) largely depends. The revolution in the position of Turkish women, which has been in progress for the last ten years, is beginning to break this barrier down, but it is still there.

In addition to this material obstacle, there are subjective inhibitions. The Turks are aware of the prejudice against them that exists in Western minds, and are inclined to despair of the possibility of overcoming it. This pessimism arises partly from discouraging experiences and partly from pride, for the Turks have not lost possession of their distinctive Middle Eastern civilisation. It may have been a failure; it may even be inherently inferior to that of the West, yet it is, after all, a system of life which is a law unto itself and has its own standards and ideals. The more the West displays contempt and aversion, the more it discourages the Middle East from the pursuit of a *modus vivendi* and impels it to retire into itself. If there is any question of propaganda, it is on the other side. This questionable art, which is unfortunately characteristic of Western culture (the very name having originated in the bosom of our greatest Western institution, the Roman Catholic Church) has been acquired by the Greeks with uncommon virtuosity. The Greek colonies in the principal urban centres of the Western world, with their intimate affiliations — through business, naturalisation, and intermarriage — with 'influential circles' of Western society, are admirably equipped for practising it. They will themselves be the first to admit that they have not neglected their opportunity. This is not to their discredit, but it does suggest that the influence of propaganda is to be traced in the second-hand opinions of the majority of the Western public that has stayed at home, rather than in the first-hand experience of the minority that has been in contact with the Greeks an the Turks in their native surroundings...

The Greek assumes a character which he does not possess. He poses as a scion of Ancient Hellenic society, who has rejoined his long-lost Western brother after an interval of adversity, due to the accident of a brutal barbarian conquest. The Westerner, on his side, starts from the generous assumption that the only essential difference between them consists in his own accidental better fortune, and that if the Greek bears the marks of what he has been through, it is only delicate to draw a veil over a temporary infirmity. From the moment of contact, however, these mutual assumptions begin to break down, and the process of disillusionment is so awkward, and sometimes even painful, for the Western party to the relationship that he tends to bring it to an end and to avoid its renewal. In fact, he often cherishes a quite unjust resentment against the Modern Greek, because the latter does not come up to expectations which he would never have entertained if he had exercised his judgment. It is not to the interest of either Greeks or Westerners that this source of misunderstanding should be perpetuated." (*The Western Question in Greece And Turkey*, pp.36-40.)

Here is the start of Toynbee's account, in service of covering up what England did to the Greeks between 1915 and 1922 (which enabled them to do the same when the occasion demanded again in 1941-2) and inserting a false memory. The reader should bear in mind G.F. Abbott's penetrating account of these events in comparison to Toynbee's work of State:

"A game played with living pieces may be a cruel spectacle, and, half through her own fault, Greece has been the principal victim. The fault is only half hers, for at first she struggled hard not to be drawn into the rivalries between the Powers, and the struggle cost her her internal unity. But instead of commonsense and moderation prevailing, as since the armistice they have begun to prevail in the West, they were overborne by the pressure of the *Entente* Powers and the imperious personality of Mr. Venizelos; and Greece, more than ever divided at home, was pushed into that foreign policy of reckless aggrandisement towards which the blind herd-instinct under the surface of her politics was all the time impelling her. At last, fatally at war within herself and at the same time fatally united for war against a neighbouring nation, she was brought to a point from which she could neither reach internal or external peace, nor retreat without loss or even disaster. The world has sympathised with the personal tragedy of Mr. Venizelos. There is a greater pathos in the national tragedy of his country…

Mr. Venizelos… grasped at such excessive territorial prizes that he failed to secure the greater prize of peace. Being a statesman of great force and great charm of character, he has been able to give ample effect to his policy, and when it has been mistaken, his country has therefore suffered its consequences to the full…

Neutrality, during the whole period during which we respected the King's legitimate claim to insist upon it, was more prudent for Greece, and more dignified, than the purchase of territory by intervention; and it makes for the general betterment of international relations if small states always and everywhere keep as clear as possible of the rivalries between Great Powers. Indeed, King Constantine was not alone in his views. Possibly a majority among the politically educated people in Greece agreed with him…

Every event… raises controversial issues. Did the elections and by-elections of 1915 prove or not that Mr. Venizelos was supported by a majority of the Greek nation? If he was, had the King a right to dismiss and exclude him from office? Did her treaty with Serbia legally and morally bind Greece to fight when Bulgaria intervened? Had the Allies received a genuine invitation from Mr. Venizelos's Government to land at Salonika? Which side was morally the aggressor in the fight at Athens on the first of December 1916? Was the will of the Greek nation or the military power of the Entente the real cause of Mr. Venizelos's triumph over King Constantine between his flight from and return to Athens? These controversies lie behind the horizon of this book; many of them had only an ephemeral interest; others are incapable of settlement." (*The*

*Western Question in Greece And Turkey*, pp.63-8.)

The fact that Toynbee, unlike George Abbott, does not deal with the important issues that are central to the undermining of Greek neutrality—issues which he characterises as 'ephemeral'—speaks volumes. These acts of interference in Greek neutrality by England and France encouraged the fatal Greek adventurism that would ultimately lead to catastrophe in Asia Minor and the Greek mainland itself.

But the blind spots that British writers have when discussing the behaviour of others in the world are truly amazing: Greece is accused by Toynbee of having a 'foreign policy of reckless aggrandisement,' of lacking 'commonsense and moderation,' of desiring 'the purchase of territory by intervention.' And she is admonished for entering the war when it 'makes for the general betterment of international relations if small states always and everywhere keep as clear as possible of the rivalries between Great Powers'. Wasn't all this the very means by which England fought and won her Great War and wrecked the world for the next century in the process?

Finally, *The Irish News* got its view of the Turks largely from the British War propaganda of Wellington House. So where did that leave the Irish view, once England changed course again?

Suspended in 1914 one presumes.

# IX. The Catholic Bulletin
## On 'Our War' (1922)

The Catholic Bulletin referred to 1922 as 'the tragic year of 1922'. It was in 1922 that the harvest of victory became clear. The Armistice of November 1918 had ended the military confrontation between the Allies and Germany on the Western front. But the War continued almost everywhere else—by land, sea and air.

The commentaries of The Catholic Bulletin from 1922, reproduced below, provide the reader with an illuminating picture of the result of the Great War— as the 'chickens came home to roost'. And we see a very different Catholic Bulletin to that presented by Roy Foster etc—speaking up for the Islamic world and Bolshevik Russia.

These commentaries provide an insight that no history book will give as to conditions of life for the peoples of Europe and Asia after civilization had been saved and small nations had won the right to self-determination. This was the world which the British and Redmondite War effort against Germany and Turkey produced. It was a shattered world of ruins in which great Empires had been destroyed, societies been returned to the elementals and forces let loose that would take generations to work themselves out. These were the achievements of Our War.

MATTERS OF THE MOMENT

"IT is a tragic commentary on the statesmanship of Europe that, while it could agree without any difficulty in projecting a destructive war in 1914, involving the loss of five million lives on the field of battle, it has not yet, though four years have passed since the cessation of hostilities, agreed on the terms of a constructive Peace. To even attempt unravelling all the alleged items of disagreement is out of the question here. Generally they are spoken of in terms framed to preclude investigation except by profound experts. Reference to the actual conditions of existence of the peoples of Europe, occasioned by the penalties of the Treaty of Versailles is singularly absent, and it is supposed that until some ghastly disaster like that which reduced the Russian nation to little more than an animated skeleton, overtakes them the human aspect of the European crisis will be studiously avoided.

Conference after conference, each in turn exciting world-wide interest, has met and ended with no apparent definite result. Their object, the Reconstruction of Europe, has been boomed in the press, in the same way that Civilisation, and the Freedom of Small Nations, was boomed in 1914. But just as in that year Civilisation, in reality Empire, connoted, so at these conferences the Reconstruction of Europe connoted the same evil and immoral thing...

In the East, as in the West, the deceit, duplicity and craftiness of British policy is... being trenchantly exposed. The following extract from the official organ of the Kemalists- Hakimlet Millie, is a reply to the recent British pro-

455

posal to send a Commission to inquire into the treatment of Christians:

'There still exist in Turkey a few People who suppose that we can come to an arrangement with Britain, and who imagine that Britain may one day be brought to have benevolent sentiments towards Turkey. To these persons we point out that the whole Oriental policy of Britain for the last hundred and fifty years has been a deceptive policy, aiming methodically at the destruction of Turkey and the suppression of our sovereignty. It is always Britain who places obstacles in the way of our efforts to restore peace. It is Britain and Britain alone who desires our extinction. She aims at seeing the Near East and the Middle East peopled by Moslems submitted to her authority. It is this policy which brought about the union of Kemalist Turkey and Russia against a common enemy, an event which has greatly perturbed the British statesmen. Turkey and Russia now constitute twin factors of liberty in the Orient, standing at the head of all the oppressed nations of the East. The latest criminal manoeuvre of Britain has been to leave our peace counter-proposals unanswered, and to demand an inquiry into our treatment of Christians: an inquiry which we shall naturally refuse. Britain is acting in the Orient as the confirmed enemy of all Moslem aspiration.'

Lieut.-Col. Herbert, M.P., at a recent meeting in London, of the Near and Middle East Association stated that 'the awful things that had happened in Asia Minor were the result of the policy of our Government. The policy of Mr. Lloyd George and the Government had been the policy of using minorities as a weapon in Asia Minor.'

The overwhelming evidence, manifest in the Foreign Press, of the awakening of all nations to England's responsibility for the unrest, anarchy and misery that exist, and have existed throughout the world, is possibly the explanation of Lord Robert Cecil's vicious censure of the British Government's flagrant betrayals of the Assyrians, Armenians, and people of Mesopotamia within the past three years. Lord Robert characterised England's violations of the pledges given to these peoples as ' one of the blackest pages of British diplomatic history.'

Regarding Mesopotamia the noble Lord said that where, instead of the independence that was guaranteed by a Proclamation published in Bagdad and re-affirmed in 1918, an autocratic, bureaucratic system of an Indian type of Government was established, in which Mesopotamians had practically no share whatever, until through pressure from various quarters a different policy was adopted." (September 1922)

\* \* \*

"The victorious Christian allies, steeped in materialism, and flushed with lust for loot, knew that they could treat with indifference and with contempt the Gospels of Christ in any settlement which they in their strength, might be pleased to impose on Europe but they were either miserably ignorant, or foolishly defiant if they acted on the same assumption with reference to the Koran in their efforts to dismember and purloin the Turkish homelands.

To the Muhammedan, the world over, the Koran is still the Koran—the religious standard of faith and, at the same time, the civil code of law, and finally the bond of nationality. On texts of the Koran are founded the decisions of the cadis in Muhammedan States; it is the source of the maxims of the doctors of the law and of the supreme religious council. To a victorious Christian power the Holy Bible is only the Holy Bible, if it can he quoted in the interests of an expanding Empire. The Koran is the law of Turkey and of the Muhammedan world; the Treaty of Versailles is the law of Europe. In seeking to install that law, and the law of Sèvres in the place of the Koran, the victorious Allies, particularly Great Britain, have outraged the sentiments of the entire Muhammedan people. This immeasurable resentment may be slightly visualised in the person of Mustapha Kemal Pasha. By his victories he has taught these so-called Christian powers that if throughout the great Barbaric War, and throughout the Specious European Peace, they could manifest a braggart independence of Christ, they must, at least, respect Muhammed.

The immediate cause of the war between Turkey and Greece may be regarded as the Treaty of Sèvres, signed on August 10, 1920. This Treaty, signed on behalf of Great Britain by Sir George Grahame, is the crystallised expression of the agreement reached between the Allies, during the war, to not only confiscate and partition the Turkish Empire, but to partition the Turkish homeland in Asia Minor. 'It was based,' said the Daily Herald, 'like all treaties concluded by the Coalition Government, on the principle of loot. The strong powers bargained among themselves for how much they could get.'

The Treaty of Sèvres is also the crystallised violation of solemn proclamations made, and pledges given, by the British Government, during the war, to Indian Mohammedans. The first pledge was given in a proclamation published at the outbreak of war between Turkey and Great Britain by the Indian Government, presumably with the sanction of Downing Street, and was to the effect that the Holy Places of Islam would not be violated or brought under non-Moslem dominion in consequence of hostilities. The second pledge was given in a speech by Mr. Lloyd George on January 6, 1918. In this speech, the British Prime Minister stated that they were not fighting to deprive Turkey of its capital, or of the rich and renowned lands of Asia Minor, and Thrace. On these con-ditions, we may add, the Indians were induced to fight in the Great War for Civilisation.

To fully appreciate the fulfilment of these pledges, it is necessary to refer to the secret agreement of May, 1916, made between Great Britain and France. This is now known as the Sykes-Picot Agreement. Under it Syria, from Tyre to Aleppo, Cilicia, and Southern Armenia were to be within what is called the French 'Sphere of influence'. The Syrian districts of Damascus, Aleppo, Urfah, Deir, Mosul were to be Independent Arab districts, subject to French influence. Under the same agreement Palestine was to be constituted an International Territory from the Jordan to the Mediterranean, and Haifa and Mesopotamia were to be within the British 'Sphere of Influence.' When, therefore, the British Prime Minister's pledge was given, Islam had already been betrayed.

457

The Treaty of Sèvres, with some modifications gave the force of law—if we might use the term in connection with international looters, to this Agreement. By it Syria, the Great Lebanon, Mesopotamia, Palestine and Haifa and Arabia are declared to be independent of Ottoman rule. The administration of Mesopotamia was then entrusted to Great Britain, by the Supreme Council of the Allies, while a Mandate for the administration of Palestine was recently given to the same power by the League of Nations.

In connection with the present war, however, it will be noted that Great Britain's loot of Mesopotamia and Palestine is kept well in the background while the loot of Greece-Thrace is made to figure most prominently in the thieves' den of Turkey's appropriated possessions. On the subject of Thrace, Professor Toynbee, a recognised authority on Near Eastern questions, says in a letter to the Manchester Guardian:

'The Turks have never in their worst moments of adversity, renounced their claim to Thrace. It is inscribed in their 'National Pact', and in their hour of victory it is inconceivable that they should forego any fraction of it. Now, the present possessor of Thrace is Greece. She is not only in military occupation of the province, but holds the sovereignty in virtue of the Treaty of Sèvres, and that document, though never ratified, has at least been signed and constitutes a title which it is essential, from the Turkish point of view, to extinguish.'

In parenthesis, it is illuminating to review the policy of the *Irish Independent* on the international situation. The rumour, though we believe it is that of a wag, that this newspaper has been invited to join the League of Nations, owing to its large circulation of British propaganda, lends interest to its profound views. In an editorial of September 19, the *Independent* says: 'The Kemalists want to come back to Thrace. In other words they aspire to tear up the Treaty (of Sèvres) and gain their footing in Europe.'

The Kemalists never recognised the Treaty of Sèvres. Mr. Morgenthau, for several years Ambassador of the United States in Constantinople, recently informed a representative of *The Times*, when discussing the Nationalist movement which has crystallised under the guidance of Mustapha Kemal Pasha into a powerful manifestation of military power, that this movement arose primarily as a patriotic protest against the attribution of Smyrna to the Greeks and the presence of armed forces of foreigners in Constantinople: 'It was a furious refusal to tolerate the Treaty of Sèvres and the almost unlimited foreign interference prescribed in that document.'

The *Independent* article continues: 'His place (the Turk's) is not in Europe and it is to the interest of the Christian nations to keep his pretensions within bounds...'

On September 21, the same journal seriously delivered itself thus: 'for ourselves we have expressed the opinion that the Turks first of all should be kept as far from Europe as possible, because they are haters—sincere haters, no doubt, of the Christian faith.' Naturally, since Christian nations have outraged the Fifth and Seventh Commandments in their thefts of goldfields, diamond mines, and oilfields, and in the means adopted to obtain their possession.

458

As a matter of general education we would recommend to the *Irish Independent* a volume recently published on *'The Western Question in Greece and Turkey'*, by Professor Toynbee. The author in the preface says: 'I had certain opportunities for first-hand study of Greek and Turkish affairs, and during the European War I edited, under the direction of Lord Bryce, the *Blue Book* published by the British Government on the treatment of Armenians.'

Professor Toynbee on the subject of atrocities says: 'In judging Greek and Turkish atrocities, Westerners have no right to be self-righteous. They can only commit one great error of judgment, and that is, to suppose that the Turks are more unrighteous than the Greeks.' The author then justifies his argument by authentic instances and graphically describes the conduct of the Greeks on their landing at Smyrna in May, 1919.

In the *Manchester Guardian* the evidence of an eye-witness of Christian atrocities was recently published. The witness stated:

'Ever since the Balkan wars of 1912-13 a most barbarous persecution of Moslems by Christians has gone on. I witnessed the exodus of unfortunate Moslems in 1913... both Serbs and Montenegrins boasted to me freely that if I returned in two years I should find none (Moslems) remaining... If Christians expel large masses of Moslems from Europe, confiscate their property, hunt them like beasts, massacre a large number en route, the wretched survivors who reach safety in Asia will very naturally try to make that last refuge safe by getting rid of members of the religion which has so tortured them. Had Great Britain intervened in 1913 on behalf of the Balkan Moslems it is highly probable we should have had the Turks on our side in the late war, in which case many pressing problems of to-day would not have arisen. Instead of which we allowed Germany to assume the task of protecting Moslems!'

The righteous, justice-loving *Independent* concludes its article with the pious hope that 'the Turks may be pacified with Constantinople, but that the Allies, as interested in the Black Sea, and therefore in the Straits, will be firm on the two main questions, the freedom of the Straits and the freedom from Turkish control of Thrace.'

'The freedom of the Straits' has an old familiar ring about it. It summons up memories of the 'freedom of small nations'—and the ocean of blood that was shed in its hypocritical cause. Great minds, we are told, think alike, and we are not surprised to find, therefore, that the British Prime Minister entirely agrees with the *Independent* on this subject. In a statement made to foreign press representatives Mr. George said 'The freedom of the Straits is of vital interest to us as a maritime and commercial power, and to civilisation throughout the world...'

There is no end apparently to this cant about civilisation. It has proved, however, an excellent dope in Ireland, and we do not know of any finer medium for its administration than the Irish Press.

The civilisation which the 'freedom of the Straits' portends is the subject of a fine analytical article in the *Daily Herald*, by Mr.Brailsford, from which we take the following extract:

'We shall get no further in piercing this mystery until we note that the Freedom of the Straits becomes a controversial issue only in the event of war. In peace the Straits will always be free, and always have been free in modern times. No one suggests that even the extremist of Turkish Nationalist Governments would interfere with shipping unless war supplied a compelling motive. War, however, is, unfortunately, not a rare event in these latitudes. From the Italian expedition to Tripoli until to-day, there have, in eleven years, been only rare and negligible intervals of peace. The whole controversy turns, then, upon the Freedom of the Straits in time of war. To whom in time of war shall they be open? To whom shall they be closed? And who, above all, shall have the right to open and to close them? The right in this case means practically the power. There are several alternatives. The guardian of the Straits may be a single Power, or some international grouping of Powers. Throughout the nineteenth century it was held to be one of the chiefest British interests to maintain Turkey in this position. During the Great War we were fighting to make Russia her successor. How does the case stand, if you substitute a group of Powers for the single guardian? So long as a group remains united in its belligerent interests, it will act in time of war like a single Power. It will open the Straits to its friends and close them to its enemies. That is the scheme of the Treaty of Sèvres, the scheme which enlists the apparently unanimous enthusiasm of the British Press. Apart from the minor Commission which performs the humble but useful duty of a harbour and police authority, the effective custody of the Straits falls to the three chief Allies— Britain, France, and Italy. Russia has no place among them, nor Germany, nor any of the neutrals. No Black Sea State (though theirs is the primary economic interest) has a share in this military and naval power. It is a part of the Allied dictatorship over our hemisphere. It might, and doubtless would, be used like that of a single Power, in time of conflict, to blockade Turkey, Bulgaria, or Russia, or to close the waterway to German shipping. And if the group should break up, what then? Why then, of course, the supremacy of the British Navy would make us masters of the Straits, as we are masters of Suez and Gibraltar."

This is precisely what the *Irish Independent* requires.

The measure of resentment felt by the Indian Mohammedans, on account of their disgraceful betrayal by the British Government, in the Treaty of Sèvres, may best be estimated by recalling the sensational telegrams of the Viceroy of India, on behalf of the Government of India, to Mr. Montagu last March. This telegram states:

'We feel it our duty again to lay before his Majesty's Government the intensity of feeling in India regarding the necessity for a revision of the Sèvres Treaty. The Government of India are fully alive to the complexity of the problem but India's services in the war, in which Indian Moslem soldiers so largely participated, and the support which the Indian Moslem cause is receiving throughout India, entitle her to claim the utmost fulfilment of her just and equitable aspirations. The Government of India particularly urge... the following three points, namely: The evacuation of Constantinople; The suzerainty of the Sultan over the Holy places and; The restoration of Ottoman Thrace (including Adrianople) and Smyrna. The fulfilment of these three points is of the greatest importance to India.'

Lord Northcliffe, who visited India, in January of this year, described the situation, which had there arisen, in an interview with a representative of his own paper—*The Times.*

'Returning,' he said, 'to India after twenty-five years' absence, I am shocked at the change in demeanour and acts towards Whites by both Hindus and Mahomedans, and especially Mahomedans, who were formerly most friendly. For the first time in Indian history Hindus and Mahomedans are now acting in close combination. I have interrogated over a hundred Moslems of every class and sect and they are unanimous. In the Dutch Indies, Malay States, Ceylon, Madras, Southern India, Hyderabad, Central India, the United Provinces, the Punjab, Rajputana, and Bombay the attitude of Moslems is now one of sullen silence or outspoken hostility. A distinguished loyal Mahommedan, a Judge, who was educated at Oxford, whither his son is now proceeding, said to me: 'The most dangerous sign is that our women are now becoming infected with the anti-British poison, and all students of Islam know what that means."

Proceeding to explain the reason for this remarkable change Lord Northcliffe quoted from well-informed sources. 'In effect they state that Indian Mahomedans who are communicating with all Moslem countries intensely resent our policy regarding Turkey and feel most deeply the slight they consider has been put upon the Caliphate.' The following programme if carried out would, argued Lord Northcliffe, heal the wounded sentiments:

(1). They contend that the British should again recognise the Sultan as head of Islam and Warden of the Holy Places, Mecca, Medina, and Baghdad, and grant free access to them to all Moslems.

(2). Adrianople should be returned to Turkey. Adrianople is a Holy City, and its loss would never cease to rankle.

(3). The whole of Asia Minor should be handed over to Turkey, not excepting Smyrna, for the Turks regard Asia Minor as their homeland, and they resent the splitting up of the land of their birth."

The Mohammedans number between 250,000,000, which is the British estimate and 400,000,000, which is the Muhammedan estimate. With this gigantic power behind his throne we await, with the keenest interest, the action of Mustapha Kemal Pasha. To what extent he is actually influenced by Muhammedan sympathy we do not know. We do know, however, from the address of the Khalifate delegation, presented to the British Viceroy in India in January, 1920, that: 'The requirements of Islamic law are so definite and of such a binding nature that they cannot be reduced by a hair's breadth to suit the desires of the Allied and Associated Powers.' The Khalifate delegation, it is understood, have never yielded in their demand for ' exclusive Moslem control over what Moslem religious authorities call the 'island of Arabia,' a region that includes Palestine, Syria and Mesopotamia also, and the continuance of the Khalifa's wardenship of the Holy Places of Islam.'

'These are the limits set by Allah, and none shall transgress them.'"

* * *

"Practical protests, against this transgression, have frequently been made of late, not only in Egypt and India, but in Mesopotamia. On August 23, it appears that Sir Percy Cox, the British Governor of Mesopotamia, was insulted when attending King Feisal's palace for the purpose of offering his congratulations to this British-appointed monarch on the anniversary of his accession. A crowd, it appears, blocked the way as High Commissioner Cox entered the Serai through which his cars had to push their way. The steps to the king's reception room were also unbecomingly crowded.

'As the High Commissioner ascended the steps,' writes the *Times* correspondent, 'a clapping arose in response to a remark which the High Commissioner was unable to hear . . . The remark which evoked applause was ' Down with the Mandate.'" The result of this demonstration is told in a further communication from the *Times* correspondent which says:

'The two important events in Iraq politics during the last fortnight were the arrest and deportation of a number of extreme Nationalists by order of Sir Percy Cox, the High Commissioner, and the vehement protest made by the High Commissioner against the discourteous treatment meted out to him on the first anniversary of King Feisal's accession. While the resignation of the Nakib's Cabinet last week is represented as due to Ministerial resentment of King Feisal's interference in departmental work, there is much more than that in the affair. For some time past the King has displayed an inclination to discard his British friends (to whom he owes his throne), and identify himself more closely with the programme and the aims of the extremists. The British Army in Iraq is now in the throes of transferring its responsibilities to the Royal Air Force, and it is reported that there will be very few British military officers left in the country after October 1.'

The following are brief notes by the *Times* correspondent, on the chief men arrested for political offences in Mesopotamia:

'Ja'afar Chalabi abu Timman is a well-known Baghdad merchant, and was Minister of Commerce until he resigned last week. He obtained his appointment in the Cabinet through the influence of Kadhimain religious leaders. A capable man of business, he deals chiefly in Persian trade. Shortly after the Armistice he visited Persia to engage in anti-British propaganda. Hamdi Pachahich, a Sunni, and a well-educated citizen of Baghdad, was a Turkish official in pre-war days, but declined to take any part in the administration of Iraq under the British mandate. Some months ago he was offered, and declined, the position of Director of Public Security. Sheikh Mahdi Basin al Hilli is a Hillahs man, who normally lives at Nejaf, but who for some time past has made his headquarters in Baghdad, where he has been engaged in political agitation. He is a Shiah, and is blind. He is also a poet, whose verses are well known and appreciated throughout Iraq. The texts of his poems are usually based on hatred of the British, and he would like to see the British evacuate the country altogether. Sheikh Ahmed al Sheikh Daud is a well-known and well-educated Sunni, who was a Judge in the Turkish Administration. Abdul Ghafur al Badri was an officer of the Turkish Army and fought against us in Mesopotamia during the war. A good soldier but a poor politician. A Sunni from Samarra, he was director and owner of the *Istiklal*, a Baghdad newspaper, suppressed some time ago because it attacked the Provisional Government.'"

\* \* \*

"Mustapha Kemal Pasha may be described as one of Islam's distinguished Trinity of Patriots. Gandhi, now a prisoner in a British dungeon in India, is perhaps the most famous, while Zaghoul Pasha who occupies a similar position in a British residence at Gibraltar is considered the most uncompromising. They are united by deep religious bonds, by a respect for the home of Islam and by a determination to prevent its partition. Last year at Mecca sorrowful pilgrims from Egypt, India, and Asia Minor spoke of these incorruptible patriots and of the English betrayals of Islam. All Islam is now laughing and rejoicing at the embarrassment of this so-called pious Christian Power whose shameful acquisition of Turkish Holy Places and territories has been suddenly exposed to the gaze of nations by the victorious march of Mustapha Kemal.

Cleverly enough the British Government through sections of its Press has sought to hide its own guilt, or to justify its designs, by focussing attention on Turkish atrocities. The *Irish Independent*, for example, in an editorial of September 18, informs its readers that thousands of Greeks and Armenians have been massacred and hundreds of thousands are destitute and at the mercy of the Turkish soldiery—a position where 'death is often preferable'. In its news columns, the same journal seeks to influence the Irish mind with huge pieces of print intimating that '100,000 Christians perish in the East! Awful scenes in Smyrna! Heaps of Dead'— and so on.

It is of interest, in this connection, to recall one of the last public statements of Lord Northcliffe—indeed, it might be regarded as a deathbed confession, on the subject of Belgium. The great Director of Propaganda said:

'There is an inclination in the mind of the public to exaggerate the amount of damage done to Belgium by the Germans. Any student of the war knows that the Germans did comparatively little damage in Belgium. The German Army lived in Belgium for years, spent money there, and I say without hesitation that Belgium is the most prosperous country I have seen since 1 left New Zealand...'

This was written last June. But though three years had passed since the conclusion of the war the *Irish Independent* continued its campaign against the Germans. In May 1921, an editorial informed us that those who are at pains to question the responsibility of Germany for the Great War cannot deny that 'her method of waging it in Belgium was an . . . outrage on the chivalrous practice of nations.'

Seeing the conditions of Europe, for the past few years, it may be that Irish newspapers feel that they have on their pages, as it were, the blood of thousands of young Irishmen whom they induced to volunteer for service, in the British army, in a cause which was regarded by all sincere people as a quackery from beginning to end; a view which time has justified—and that, therefore, to save their faces they must continue to protest their justification by the reiteration of old falsehoods. Lord Northcliffe, however, had the courage to confess the lie. We do not know of any man who was more capable to speak, on this subject, than the late Lord Northcliffe, considering that he left £30,000,000 in America during the Great War for propaganda, employing at the same time 10,000 agents for the purpose of pushing British ascendancy and maligning the Irish and the German peoples.

The objects of the German-atrocity propaganda from 1914 onwards were to arouse hatred of Germany, enlist sympathy with England and to obtain recruits for the British army. The Turkish-atrocity propaganda has the same objects in view. Lord Northcliffe's programme for capturing American sympathy comprehended:

'Efficient propaganda, carried out by those trained in the arts of creating public goodwill and of swaying public opinion as a definite purpose is now needed, urgently needed. To make a beginning, efficiently organised propaganda should mobilise the press, the Church, the stage, and the cinema, press into active service the whole educational systems of both countries and root the spirit of goodwill in the homes.'

It will be observed that Lord Northcliffe placed the Church in the uncomplimentary position of second fiddle, clearly intimating that the Press was now the influential authority in all countries, it having usurped the former power wielded by the Church. The unbecoming reference to mobilising the Church will be resented, we are sure, by all good Catholics. It is most undignified.

With regard to Turkey, the mobilisation of the Irish Press, in the interests of England, would appear to have been adequately effected. The *Independent* in its account of the burning of Smyrna says:

'Mustapha Kemal is giving the finishing touch to organised massacres, acts of incendiarism and atrocities on a large scale. About 100,000 Christians, mostly Armenians and Greeks, perished. The entire quarters were set on fire by the soldiery and infuriated populace. The main thoroughfares are covered with corpses. . . Many Englishmen and officials have been ruthlessly killed, and the Greek and Armenian bishops have been crucified... About 300,000 are doomed to extermination.'

In a leading article of September 19, the *Independent* definitely states that 'the Kemalists have seized and burned Smyrna.' Yet, the English *Sunday Express* in its editorial of September 29, intelligently enquires:

'Who burned Smyrna? Mr. Lloyd George believes that the Turks burned it, but his information may not be conclusive. There are advices accusing the Greeks of having set it on fire. As a rule a victorious army does not burn its own city when it recaptures it. Therefore, it is difficult to believe that the Turks burned Smyrna as soon as they wrested it from the Greeks. The Greeks, on the other hand, burned all the towns on the line of their retreat. Therefore, it would not be surprising if they set fire to Smyrna before they evacuated it. The victor does not usually throw away the spoils.'

The *Irish Independent* says he does! The conduct of the Greeks, on the line of their retreat, is confirmed by a resident of Smyrna who says in a letter published in the *Sunday Times* that: 'The news to-day is very bad! One of our British officers stationed out here, who has just returned from an expedition up the line, has told us that he takes back everything complimentary he ever said about the Greeks. Certainly the way they are behaving in retreat seems to be too horrible for words—the soldiers, I mean and they are getting quite out of hand in the town.' This statement was made under the date of September 5. The correspondent of the *Times* at Constantinople wiring on September 12 stated that: 'The Turks are behaving well at Smyrna town.' Elsewhere, in the same paper appears this account: ' Official advices from Smyrna state that the city is quiet and that the Turkish commander has his troops well under control. As a consequence the British naval detachment has been withdrawn, except for a small force which has remained to protect the Consulate, which remains open. All British subjects who wished to leave have been safely embarked.'

The *Daily Herald* of September 18 reported that the Greeks had admitted responsibility for the burning of Smyrna, and that the Greek battleship Kilkos increased the havoc by shelling the Turkish quarter. This report concludes thus: 'The Turks are now alleging that Greeks and Armenians are guilty. An Adana message (transmitted by Reuter's Paris correspondent) says that the authorities at Smyrna have arrested some Greeks and Armenians, who have confessed to having set the town on fire.'

The *Echo de Paris* asks why the Turks should burn a town they have just conquered and recalls the Greeks' impudent words that if they were obliged to evacuate Smyrna they would 'leave their enemies only ruins.'

In this, as in all matters, the only brief we hold is on behalf of truth, our main concern being to present our readers with the true facts of national and international situations as they arise. But we find of late that the space at our disposal considerably handicaps our good intentions, it being entirely inadequate to deal with the vastly increased propaganda of late of the Irish Press. Truth is the basis of our Catholic Doctrine. We are a Catholic country, a Catholic people. Protests have frequently been made against the importation of foreign, impure, newspapers. Yet, with our usual inconsistence we support Irish newspapers on whose word no reliance can evidently be placed. It is a very painful matter, involving as it does, a contempt of our religion and our Church, whose foundation is Truth itself. We have waited in vain for a protest... We are not alone in our views regarding Irish press facilities for English propaganda. The following extracts from an admirable letter of Mr. O. Grattan Esmonde to the *Irish Independent* illustrates this:

'I cannot refrain from expressing my astonishment at your leading-article of to-day, and the prominence you are giving to virulent English propaganda directed against the Turkish army, who are on the point of freeing their native land from the invader. May I point out that every single dispatch that you have hitherto pub-lished, describing supposed atrocities and massacres, has been of English or Greek origin. Most of them have come direct from Athens. We, who have suffered more than any other nation in the world from English propaganda, have no right to accept it when directed against another nation which for four years has been fighting for its life, and whose leaders have in public and in private expressed their sympathy and admiration for Ireland. I notice to-day that the Armenian Archbishop, who was massacred last week, has turned up safely in Greece. The same fate awaits at least ninety-per cent of the 120,000 Christians, slaughtered by Reuter's news-agency this morning! It is more than probable that at least three zeros have been added inadvertently to the correct number of the victims. France and Italy, the traditional defenders of the Christians in the Near East, are sufficiently well-informed not to he taken in but, at the other side of the globe, Australia and New Zealand are being stampeded into war by the British Government, who control the cables, and are at liberty to pour out atrocity-propaganda without fear of contradiction. The new Turkish army and the Turkish National leaders are clean fighters, and the same type of men as those who have carried through the evolution in this country. Are we also to be stampeded into war with them solely in order that England may retain control of the Straits, and—by that means—of the eventual Russian Oil Supply

O. Grattan Esmonde.

The statement, in the *Independent*, that Englishmen had been murdered in Smyrna was subsequently contradicted in an English newspaper, but the contradiction, so far as we know, was not published in the *Independent*."

\* \* \*

"The collapse of the Treaty of Versailles, like that of Sèvres, is now an accepted fact. Even the impotency of the League of Nations is acknowledged, notwithstanding the sermon preached by the Archbishop of Canterbury, at Geneva, on the eve of the opening of the League early last month. His Grace took the following for his text: 'Seek ye first the kingdom of God and His righteousness and all these things shall be added unto you.'—St. Matt. VI. 33. All things shall be added unto you. How appropriate! Loot of German territory in Africa; loot of Turkish territory here, there, and everywhere; the debasement and degeneration of European peoples; the starvation and extermination of the Russian people who are not capitalists, and so on *ad infinitum*. These things constitute England's kingdom of God. Even our own good Catholic citizens of the British Empire must surely blush for this blasphemy of the Sacred Word which is their life and their consolation in suffering. The speech of this Archbishop was inspired by Lloyd George who recently called on the Churches to fight in the battle of Peace and who, at the same time, was filling the coffers of the Greeks with money to drive the Turks out of their territories. Lord Robert Cecil speaking in August on the defeats of the League of Nations, controlled by the Supreme Council in London, said that he reckoned as one of

466

the League's most deplorable failures, its futile attempt to do anything adequate for the alleviation of the Russian famine. With regard to the Safeguarding of Industries Act he declared it to be absolutely opposed to the whole purpose of the League which had claimed the necessity of economic unity in Europe.

This general breakdown of Treaties and Covenants—intimating a grave mishandling of delicate situations—negotiated by the Coalition Government is, no doubt, partly responsible for the following views of the *Spectator*, August 16, regarding the Irish Treaty:

'What we ought to have done—granted that we had determined on a fundamental change of policy—was to scout any idea of half measures, and boldly to adopt the policy of complete severance. We should have given South Ireland that complete Republican independence which the majority of its people desired; if the Government were afraid to go so far as this, it would have been better to do nothing. If we are right as to what will be the course of events the Government must be prepared to take the initiative, and, by anticipating, to prevent an attack on Ulster. They had better give South Ireland that Independence which she will certainly take sooner or later, but while giving it they must also make those terms for the protection of the Southern Loyalists which we have so often described in these columns. The protection of the North from invasion needs no stipulation. There is a duty from which the British people will not shrink, no matter what the cost."

The foregoing views have been not infrequently expressed by the *Spectator*, and, in this connection, it is interesting to recall that the anniversary of the famous admission by Mr. Lloyd George, in the House of Commons, that the Irish people had declared in favour of an Independent Ireland, with a republican form of Government, will occur on the 3rd of this month."

(October 1922)

"MATTERS OF THE MOMENT

The British House of Commons has now to face a rejuvenated Eastern world keenly alive to the aims and to the tricks of England. In this connection, it is of importance to record the views of Mustapha Kemal Pasha expressed in an interview with the special correspondent of the *Chicago Tribune*:

'I would call to mind that in former days it was not the Turkish Government which closed the Straits, but England, interested to do so against Russia. The freedom of the Straits is our desire. We believe it is in con-formity with the desires of the whole world except of a single Power—England, which is interested in closing them if they are closed by England herself. England has not expressed openly this view to its allies, but it main-tained the Greeks on the Dardanelles, using them as an instrument in closing this waterway. Great Britain always said it was interested in the freedom of the Straits, but this cannot be true. If it were true there would be no differences of opinion between the British and Turkish Governments, because we have repeatedly declared for a free passage of the Dardanelles. If Great Britain desires the freedom of the

Dardanelles there is no question. If she is for closing the Straits either through agents or directly by herself the world must define the position. In view of the present position of the armies of the Grand National Assembly the Straits are already in our hands or under our influence. But we have no desire to take advantage of the position or interfere with their freedom. It remains for the rest of the world to unmask England and get to the bottom of her attitude. I am sure that France, Italy, and the United States are aware of the real idea of the British. It remains for them to declare and publish it. The British declared a neutral zone. It is not neutral, but a scheme to protect the remnant of the Greek army. It is true that the aim of the British Government in denying us the free passage of the Dardanelles is to protect Greece. Therefore, we do not find it just and reasonable that other Powers should share this view with the British Government. The British Government has two aims in its present attitude... (1) To save the remnant of the Greek army (2) to keep possession of both the Dardanelles and Constantinople. Even if it does not keep possession of Constantinople the British Government hopes to maintain its possession of Gallipoli, which means indirect control of our capital. The present British Government is resorting to every sort of intrigue in order to fool other Powers. At the present moment they wish to deceive other Powers in order to drive them into an adventure, but I do not think these other Powers will lose their reason in so far as to fall in with Great Britain. If the British nations leaves its affairs in the hands of statesmen like Lloyd George for any length of time it will be creating irreparable breaches in the foundations of the British Empire. In view of the recent pronouncement of the British Government that she is ready to evacuate Constantinople to Turkish claims, that city is no longer a national question', I suggested: 'It is not a question of readiness to evacuate Constantinople but of being forced to retire,' returned his Excellency quickly. 'By force I mean moral pressure of public opinion throughout the world.' 'But,' added Kemal Pasha, ' one can never fully believe or place confidence in the words of Lloyd George.'

Kemal Pasha might well have added—or of any British Minister."

\* \* \*

"Turkey's outlook on the question of the Straits is shared by Russia. A recent Note despatched by the Soviet Government to the British Government points out:

'The freedom of the Straits is, above all, necessary for the Powers adjoining the Black Sea—Russia and her allies and Turkey—who hold the greater part of the Black Sea coast. As early as 1920, in the national pact for which she is fighting, Turkey recognised the freedom of the Straits for the commerce and shipping of all nations, proving the regulations were established by the interested States. The Russo-Turkish Treaty signed in Moscow on March 16, 1921, contains in its fifth clause Russia's confirmation of the freedom of the Straits for commercial vessels at the same time indicating that their international status would be determined by the Black Sea Powers.

The Soviet Government does not consider that the interests of Russia require the enslavement of a section of the Turkish people. For this reason it denounced the former treaties of the Tsarist Government.

The Soviet Government repeats its previous declaration that Russia will not recognise any decision taken without her participation and against her interests. Russia and Turkey have come to an agreement as to the forms in which the freedom of the Straits must be realised in practice, and Russia warns the Western Governments against the repetition of mistakes founded on ignorance of the vital interests of the States affected.

The freedom which Great Britain has in view is merely equivalent to the desire of a great maritime Power to control a route of vital importance to other States and constantly to subject the latter to its menace. This menace is directed, above all, against Russia and Turkey. Great Britain is sending armed forces into the Near East and is seeking to draw France and Italy, Jugo-Slavia, and Rumania into the war against Turkey.'"

\* \* \*

"The People's Commissary for Foreign Affairs—Georgiy Vasilevich Chicherin, on his return to Moscow, stated, in the course of a long pronouncement on the international situation, that Russia had decided to seek separate agreements, not with the Governments but with the 'capitalist powers' of foreign States. Her choice, he added, lay between French, German and British capital. French capital had already been sunk in various German industrial concerns; French capital had captured Polish Silesia and was now putting forward a plan for a 'Continental agreement' which would include Czechoslovakia and Austria. If French capital succeeded, Chicherin continued, in amalgamating with the Rhenish Westphalia mining industry of Germany then Great Britain would be faced with a formidable economic rival on the Continent. In the meantime, 'British industry is losing its overseas markets. South Africa, South America, Egypt, India, Japan and to a certain extent China, are beginning to develop industries of their own.' Chicherin then stated that the 'various sections of the British Empire which had gained political freedom are simultaneously attaching themselves to England by economic ties,' and as an example the Russian Minister quoted Ireland."

\* \* \*

"It is highly amusing to turn from all these pronouncements— characterised by national dignity and high-minded patriotism to the 'sour grapes' articles of the London *Spectator*.

'We cannot act,' this journal declares, quoting Mr. Bonar Law, 'as the policeman of the world—Mr. Bonar Law was perfectly right.' And, with pleaded magnanimity, it continues; 'If for the sake of humanity we decide to hold up and restrain the Turks by force in the event of the worst occurring we can accept only our fair share of the task.'"

\* \* \*

"While the Near Eastern crisis may be said to have precipitated the General Election in England, the real determining factor, in bringing about a change in Government, was England's terror of the immediate danger of complete isolation. Speaking at Bradford on October 24, Viscount Grey said:

'We have come perilously near to complete isolation. We have seen Germany and Russia come together. The Genoa Conference will be remembered mainly because during that conference the agreement between Germany and Russia was signed. Well, you may say, and say truly, that the coming together of those two countries under conditions which at present exist was not due solely to British foreign policy, that it was due at least as much, or more, to French foreign policy. Very well, let us admit there is a good deal of truth in that. Then Turkey and Russia have come together, and there, I think, the responsibility is more upon British policy than upon French policy. (A voice: Why?). Because British policy has been pro-Greek in the war between Turkey and Greece. And then we see now in the Near East in this last crisis, France and Italy drawing together and Great Britain becoming isolated. I think in this Near Eastern crisis the Coalition Government would have achieved complete isolation if it had not been for the two visits of Lord Curzon to Paris. Believe me, isolation is a position which is not safe even for something so strong as the British Empire. We are dependent greatly on foreign trade. The United States is separated from other continents by an ocean and thousands of miles of water. We are separated from Europe only by the channel, which is a less barrier under modern conditions of big guns and aircraft than a river was fifty years ago. We cannot contemplate isolation with equanimity from our Allies and from other countries that were neutral in the war. From people who go abroad there comes the same story that British influence abroad is not what it was. It counts, no doubt, because we are still, compared to other European countries, a strong country comparatively, but that moral influence which we used to have, which came from the fact that our policy could be depended upon, has gone.'"

* * *

"The evolution of the isolation of England has been going on since the signing of the Treaty of Versailles. One cannot, however, point to a particular incident and say definitely that it is the cause. Disagreement with France over the eternal Reparations problem is certainly one important factor in the creation of England's precarious position. England's attitude on this question possibly prompted France to negotiate on her own account what is called the Angora Agreement (1921) and which definitely widened the breach between the two countries. The Paris correspondent of the *Daily Herald* describes this Agreement thus:

'The Angora agreement tore up the Treaty of Sèvres, overthrew the balance of power in the Near East as it existed on Armistice Day, and broke down the supremacy of the Shell-Royal Dutch oil trust in Asia. It also ranged France definitely on the side of the Turks—and behind France, the unknown, incomputable power of Standard Oil. The Angora agreement also (and history may

470

prove this abundantly) threw the first stone at the precarious war alliance of the Allies.'

Under the Treaty of Sèvres (1920) the Dardanelles, the navigation of the Straits, the Sea of Marmora and the Bosporus together with the port of Constantinople were placed under international control, that is to say, under the control of the British Navy. The correspondent of the *Daily Herald* adds:

'But the Angora Agreement had an Annexe, which dealt with the economic relations between the two countries, in this all-important Annexe, Turkey accords to France most-favoured nation treatment in all commercial transactions, tariffs, and customs dues; allots to French capitalists the execution of public works in Turkish territory, and promises to France the exploitation of that portion of the Bagdad Railway which runs through Turkish territory.'

In addition, it is believed that a secret clause in this Annexe conceded to French oil companies the exploitation of the oil deposits in Turkish territory (present or future) and cancelled all previous concessions made by Turkey to British or Germano-British groups. The correspondent of the *Daily Herald* concludes:

'This agreement has been the most powerful factor in the relations between the Western Powers and the Near-Eastern crisis. It is at once the cause of the British intransigence against the Turks, and the reason why France refuses to join in any war that England may declare against Kemal.'

The isolation of England matured with the successful revolutions of the Russian and Turkish peoples who, in their Treaty signed at Moscow, on March 16, 1921, decided that 'each of the contracting parties agree to recognise no peace treaties or other international conventions imposed by force upon the other contracting party.'

A further contribution to the isolation of England was the Rapallo Agreement concluded between Germany and Russia. The British Government is at the moment, therefore, faced with an alliance, or alliances, between Germany, Russia and Turkey and, at the same time, with an unwillingness on the part of France to go to war with any people save the Germans."

\* \* \*

"In the course of one of its leading articles on the British General Election the *Irish Independent* said: 'We in Ireland are no longer concerned for the fate of parties and policies on the other side of the Channel...' A few days later, this journal belied its editorial statement by devoting actual pages to the results of the Election! In any event it is unmitigated nonsense to suggest that any of His Britannic Majesty's Dominions can afford to view with indifference a British General Election. Quite recently Lord Curzon pointed out, when discussing the foreign policy of the British Empire, that 'initiative and executive action must for geographical reasons remain in the Foreign Office,' while the ex-Colonial Secretary, Mr. Winston Churchill, declared so far back as August last that: 'when the king declares war all subjects of the British Empire and all the Dominions of the Crown are from that moment at war...'

Many of the election speeches were almost exclusively devoted to Ireland. Some illustrated that our country had not yet ceased to be of interest to dear old England, while others reflected the great achievement of the Treaty, or demonstrated the merits of British diplomacy. Mark in the following extract from Mr. Bonar Law's speech the tone of the superior Englishman—we should really say Canadian:

'A country so demoralised as Ireland in no circumstances can be put right quickly or easily. It will require great patience, but if we are satisfied now that the Provisional Government are honestly trying to carry out the treaty, we will have patience and give them every chance to make it a success.'

In the course of the Election Address of Mr. Winston Churchill there appears the following significant passage: 'My earnest hope is that north and south may come together as the years pass by in some form or other which they will themselves devise, and I believe that Ulster has it in her power to render in her own way and at her own time an enormous service to the British Empire.'

In his speech at Caird Hall, Dundee, on November 13, Mr. Churchill said that:

'He had read with satisfaction that that mischievous and murderous renegade, Erskine Childers the Englishman who was inspired by an equal measure of hatred both for this island and the one in which he had now taken up his abode, had been captured by the Free State troops. No man had done more harm or shown more malice to bring the greatest curse upon the common people of Ireland or had shown more malignant hatred to the land of his birth. 'I have every faith in the Irish people,' said Mr. Churchill. (A voice— What about the past?) 'That is another matter,' retorted Mr. Churchill. 'This is the time to draw the sponge of oblivion across the horrid past.' Mr. Churchill's unsuccessful candidature was, we understand, largely due to Labour opposition. At one of his meetings a huge crowd displayed a banner on which was a cartoon depicting Mr. Churchill as an octopus, dripping with blood, encircling Ireland, Mesopotamia, Antwerp, and other places. Another banner, we understand, bore the following inscription: 'Vote for Churchill and you vote for the graveyard.'

At the conclusion of the election all the candidates gathered in the counting room, 'Mr. Churchill standing apart from the others, his face tense, and his lower lip tightly bitten between his teeth, the picture of a man who knew already that he was beaten.'

Sir Hamar Greenwood, another unsuccessful candidate, did not forget the island of his lies in his election speech at Sunderland. Note the subtlety of the description of the Settlement: 'the great result stands out that the Government of Mr. Lloyd George made a Peace Treaty with the Irish people and has handed the Government of that country to the two Irelands... it will remain in history the greatest achievement of any Government of any time in the history of this country. Viscount Birkenhead triumphed in the diplomacy of the settle-ment.'

We take the following from the *Irish Times* of November 3:

'It perplexed the sagacity of Queen Elizabeth, it defeated the genius of Cromwell. Pitt failed and nearly every great statesman in English history has applied his mind to it and has not yet succeeded in finding a remedy. . . Why should we lavish treasure on that campaign when there are men in Ireland who have undertaken the task in alliance with us, and who, when they are given time, will successfully carry out that task, and who have behind them the overwhelming body of opinion among the Irish people themselves?'..."

(December 1922)

"FAR AND NEAR

For nations and peoples, at home and abroad, the year 1922 has been one of prolonged agony. Horrible as was the World War in its toll of life and in its unnatural methods of destroying humanity, it is incomparable in tragedy and pathos to the fratricidal strifes, the tyrannies, the assassinations, executions and enforced famines that have characterised the existence of Western and Eastern nations during the year that is now drawing to a close as we pen these lines.

In the nature of things, we cannot see how these appalling conditions could have been avoided, since prevailing international relations are governed by 'Treaties' all of which have been inspired by unbridled cupidity—subtly disguised as justifiable vengeance and warrantable apprehensiveness. The authors of those 'Treaties' indefatigably seek to hide their guilt by referring to the World War as the cause of the economic downfall of Europe, whereas the actual cause has been the character of the so-called Treaties of Peace.

All these 'Treaties,' particularly the 'Treaty of Versailles'—ratified by Parliaments and acclaimed by Christian peoples with every manifestation of sacred and profane approval, proclaimed, in effect, that the Natural Law of Self-Preservation no longer applied to certain countries of the continent of Europe. In other words, that, in addition to capitulation, national suicide was demanded. These 'Treaties' prescribed, furthermore, a new code of moral laws for the vanquished nations. The Moral Law ordained for Germany under the 'Treaty of Versailles' obliged that country to surrender its territories, its revenues, its railway rolling stock, its agricultural machinery, its merchant ships with a gross tonnage of nearly five million tons, its cattle, its sheep and poultry, its horses, its coal and coke, its dyestuffs and chemical drugs. Obedience to this Moral Law involved, necessarily, the abrogation of the Natural Law of Self-Preservation, with the result that Germany is to-day exhausted economically, financially, physically, socially and spiritually.

The existence of this condition of general bankruptcy is borne out by a contribution to the current number of the *Fortnightly Review*, from which it appears that the entire situation of Germany is one in which every economic law, and every principle of business is disregarded or violated. The whole position, it is maintained, is impossible and cannot long continue. In the first place, the temper of the German people is no longer what it was. They are exhausted with their long struggle to make a depreciating currency pay for a rapidly increasing cost of living. For a long time their daily fare has been short of certain elements generally considered necessary for physical well-being. The intellectual classes are practically starving; they have lost all standing, and materialism has swept them into the rubbish heap. The question of daily bread is the all-absorbing thought and topic of conversation.

The Moral Law ordained for Hungary, under the 'Treaty of Trianon,' obliged that country to surrender the best part of its territory, its revenues for cost of reparations, eighty-eight per cent. of its forest land, all its salt mines, all its sea-going ships, whether the property of the State or private individuals, its river steamers and barges, more than one half of its output of coal, its iron works, its mines, its agricultural estates serving the purposes of cattle breeding, and its live stock. The Moral Law prescribed for Hungary comprehended, moreover, the surrender of the rights and interests of her nationals in any public utility undertaking, or in any concession operating in Russia, Turkey, Germany, Austria or Bulgaria; the delivery by her to each Allied and Associated Power of all securities held by her nationals, and relating to property situated in the territory of that Allied or Associated Power, including any shares or debentures of any incorporated company.

Again, obedience to this Moral Law involved the annulment of the Natural Law of Self-Preservation. The result is described by Lord Newton thus:

'Hungary, which in 1914, was a prosperous self-contained country of about 18,000,000 inhabitants, is now reduced to a State of about 7,000,000, with only a third of its former territory left, its former economic prosperity has been destroyed, and it now consists almost entirely of an agricultural population surrounded by hostile neighbours, cut off from the sea, and fenced in by prohibitory tariffs. Worse than all, millions of Hungarians have been transferred, without any opportunity of expressing their wish, to alien States of an inferior civilisation. Our (i.e., the British) policy towards Hungary since the war has been marked by a narrow-minded pedantry and intolerance which may be justified on technical grounds, but which is certainly not practical, as a bankrupt and powerless Hungary is no advantage to us... We acquiesced in the merciless mutilation of Hungary, we made no effort to prevent solid blocks of Hungarians being incorporated into alien and hostile States, we have ignored the oppression and misgovernment of Hungarians in Transylvania in flat defiance of the Minorities Treaty, we have refused to allow to the Frontier Commissions the latitude which would to some extent have remedied the territorial injustice of the Trianon Treaty, we have joined in the preposterous prohibition of any Hapsburg as a possible King, we have even acquiesced in the contemptible attempt to wring financial reparations out of this bankrupt people and to all the appeals made to it, the British Government have replied that the treaty must lie carried out in its entirety.'

The Moral Law prescribed likewise for Austria reduced that country to such extremes that its Chancellor was actually obliged to visit neighbouring States and beg for alms. The fate of Austria in September was then believed to have been sealed—the country was bankrupt and the people starving. People so far extreme in their occupations as manual labourers, printers, employees of coffee-houses, metal workers and landlords could not live on their earnings, the cost of all necessities having increased in one week by ninety per cent. Meanwhile, being without hope, 'they seek oblivion in drink to the ruin of the finances and the health of the race.'

Over and above every other consideration it is clear, we think, that the 'Treaties' referred to amply demonstrate that the actual arbiters of the Natural Law, the Moral Law, and every other law, for that matter, are those Powers possessing the greatest navies and armies, and not the Author of nature Himself. It would, therefore, seem useless, and a waste of valuable time, for distinguished thinkers and writers to lay down in their works on ethics that treaties 'that offend against the Natural Law are quite invalid, or that a treaty having for its object the unjust subjugation of a particular nation is likewise invalid.' Of course, it may be argued that this is ethical idealism and that idealism in ethics is most praiseworthy and often expedient, whereas, on the contrary, idealism in patriotism is always fanaticism. But patriotism alone can make a treaty invalid, at least render it nugatory, as in the case of the 'Treaty of Sèvres' by which Turkey was partitioned and robbed of her territories.

What determines, in this world, the validity of a 'treaty' is simply and solely the bayonet—not ethics. We live in a world where machine-guns and black troops regulate economic conditions, as they do the natural and the moral laws. These are solid facts of which every student of contemporary affairs is cognisant. What, however, rings out from the forests of European misery and anguish is the question, to the effect, that if, according to ethical teaching, 'treaties' which contravene the natural and moral laws, are invalid, why does not, for example, the Archbishop of Canterbury, who addressed the delegates to the Genoa Conference, openly and publicly say so. It is, indeed, an unchristian and unconsoling reply which says, that this silence has been expedient in the interests of the British Empire.

Fratricidal strife in Greece arising out of the 'Treaty of Sèvres'—already reviewed in the Bulletin, culminated in the execution of five Greek ex-Ministers and a former Commander-in-Chief.

Apart from the general interest which attaches to all foreign affairs the execution of the ex-Ministers and the War itself, between Greece and Turkey, make a special claim on our attention. What surpasses all comprehension, in the history of Greece, during the past five years is the extraordinary extent to which the Government of that country allowed itself to be made the 'catspaw of England' or as a Kemalist paper recently graphically said, 'the Hangman of England.' What the Greeks did, and were prepared to do, for England was summed up by the *Temps*, so far back as March last, thus:

'In appearance it is only a question of stopping a war between the Greeks and the Turks. But in reality the war is between the Turks and the English. The Greek army disembarked at Smyrna at the wish of the British Government, desirous of preventing the occupation of that city by the Italians. It (the Greek army) advanced into the interior with the approbation of the British Government. It will evacuate Asia Minor if such a course pleases the British Government—it is therefore England which is at war with the Turks.'

Of course, the Greeks were not acting gratuitously. Their reward was to be, according to Venizelos, 'a degree of satisfaction' theretofore undreamt of, in the form of a considerable portion of Asia Minor which England, through the 'Treaty of Sèvres,' had been kind enough to assign Greece. But the whole scheme of the 'Treaty of Sèvres' was to vest the control of the Straits in the British Navy. This control could not be achieved until Turkey was destroyed— that is to say, until Turkey was forced to acquiesce in the conditions of the 'Treaty of Sèvres.' Hence the interest of the British Government in the war between Greece and Turkey.

The outstanding and determining features of the Near Eastern situation were and are the successful revolution in Soviet Russia, whom England sought first to destroy, expending one hundred millions in the adventure, and the subsequent alliance between Russia and Turkey which resulted in the isolation of England in the Near East, her only friend or rather 'hangman' left being the far too credulous Greek.

The main charges made against the executed ex-ministers—M. Gounaris, Protopapadakis, Stratos, Theotokis, Baltazzis and General Hadjianestis, were that they—'Withheld the Allied Note of December 8, 1920, which dealt with the imposition of an economic blockade in the event of the return of King Constantine. Although the Prime Ministers of Great Britain and France declared on several occasions openly that Greece could not rely on any support while King Constantine was on the Throne, they did not insist upon the necessity of the King abdicating, they did not resign themselves, and they concealed the truth from the people.

Ordered from London in March, 1921, the opening of the campaign in Asia Minor before mobilisation had given the required results, thus causing the first defeat of the Greek army.

Decided upon the Angora campaign against the advice of the competent Commander-in-Chief.

Entrusted the Powers with mediation, giving them *carte blanche*, notwithstanding the resolution of the National Assembly that the Treaty of Sèvres represented the minimum national claims.

By agreement with Great Britain renounced part of the credits promised by the Powers.'

During the course of the trial it was frequently stated that General Stratigos (imprisoned for life) had received while in London encouragement from Mr. Lloyd George and Lord Curzon, while the Chancellor of the Exchequer was stated to have sent M. Gounaris a letter promising financial support. The frequent visits of Greek ministers to London, the speeches and correspondence of British Prime Ministers, and finally the amazing revelations of the private secretary, M. Chrussachi, to M. Gounaris leave no doubt of England's complete responsibility for the whole sanguinary business. M. Chrussachi says that Lloyd George's speech of August 4, 1922, in which a glowing account of the prospects of Greece was given was actually reported in Greek Army Orders, while Athens, according to another source, was, as a result, thrown into a delirium of flag-waving.

In an editorial on these revelations the *Morning Post* wrote:

'We have no doubt that Mr. Bonar Law is right about the Cabinet Secretariat, and that it took no share in the negotiations with the Greek representatives. That it may be all quite true; but it does not interest us, nor does it concern M. Chrussachi, who never made any such allegation. What he said was something entirely different, and very much more personal to Mr. Lloyd George. He alleged that after the Conference had elaborated a revision of the Sèvres Treaty, and after M. Gounaris had expressed his willingness to accept that revision, Mr. Lloyd George, through Mr. Philip Kerr, intimated that the Conference proposals need not be taken too seriously, and that an immediate Greek offensive would suit the British book admirably. Here is a statement, not that the Cabinet Secretariat, but Mr. Lloyd George, through his own Secretary, intervened. It is a very grave statement, for what it amounts to is this — that while the late British Government were working for peace, and had arranged a settlement which the Greeks would probably have accepted, Mr. Lloyd George was working secretly and behind the backs of his own colleagues in the opposite direction, and was egging the Greeks on to war. The late Prime Minister is actually alleged to have sent a message to the Greek representative to make an ' immediate Greek offensive,' in other words, to prosecute the war.'

Of course, if the Greeks had succeeded then the British Cabinet would have known its Prime Minister's policy. Most certainly it would. As a matter of fact the British Cabinet knew nothing about the Great War until the Armistice, nor about the policy of reprisals in Ireland during the Black and Tan regime. It is only when the policy of conquest and rapine fails that Viscount Grey or Asquith or Lloyd George is responsible. Who would dare to associate so sacrosanct an institution as the British Cabinet with the attempted plunder of Turkey by Greece?

Through the execution of the Greek ministers, the world has been given an exhibition of England's meanness, duplicity and hypocrisy which in itself should be an unforgettable lesson for the nations of the world for all time. When Greek arms were successful, Greek ministers were received with welcome and warmth in London; when they failed, the doors of Downing Street were closed to M. Gounaris and his colleagues. When the news of the executions reached London, the British Government was shocked and despatched a sanctimonious Note of horror to Greece breaking off diplomatic relations. In this connection it is interesting to note a telegram received by Reuter's Agency from a Greek semi-official source which says:

'The Greek public is still at pains to understand the British Government's intervention in favour of these ex-Ministers, which has gone to the length of a diplomatic rupture. Great Britain did not intervene in the reign of terror and political assassination which were upheld during the past two years in Greece by these very men, so why should it intervene now to save them from their just and lawful punishment?'

The virtuous *Spectator* was quite overcome with horror, and wrote:

'The Court Martial delivered judgment in the early hours of Tuesday morning, and within a few hours the condemned men were all shot. M. Gounaris, who was extremely ill with para-typhoid, was carried from his bed in a hospital and was propped up against the wall to be shot. The horror with which this brutal and 'dark ages' method of removing those who have failed is held in this country is true to the instincts of our people. The British Government were only interpreting those instincts when they instructed Mr. Lindley, the British Minister at Athens, to protest in advance against the death penalty. When the Greek Government, which is probably dominated by the revolutionary Committee, refused to give way, Mr. Lindley left Athens.'

We thoroughly appreciate this generous expression of utter detestation of a callous crime, and our sympathy goes out to the offended English people whose noble instincts have on many occasions rescued civilisation from disaster. One instance will suffice. Some years ago, in a country whose geographical position is between 51 26' and 55 21' N. latitude and from 5 25' to 10 30' W. longitude—what its real name is now, we frankly do not know— a man named James Connolly was wounded in battle. Subsequently this man was condemned to death, but his wounds would not permit of his walking to the place of execution. So he was carried there in a chair. And in the chair he was shot dead, he being unable to stand.

We have not a copy of the *Spectator* for the year 1916 before us, but we are sure it was moved as deeply then, at this illustration of the 'dark ages' methods, as in the case of M. Gounaris. In this connection we may say, however, that the keenest appreciation of the instincts of the British which we have read for some time appeared in the Kemalist newspaper, *Peyam-Sabah*, and was written by the Nationalist leader Aka Givundouz, who said:

'When it came to my knowledge that celebrations were being organised in honour of those who won by the bayonet at In-Onou the strangest of feelings came over me. I do not know what reason to ascribe these feelings to, but the very same sort of feeling had come over me on another occasion— on my return from Malta, when everybody asked me 'What have you seen? What do you think?' This only I can tell you, that from what I have seen at Malta, from what I have heard at In-Onou, from what I have felt at Sakaria, one thing stood out definite, unshakable, eruptive like a volcano, stable and firm like the faith in God, infinite like time and darkness—Hatred against the British. Hatred against the British—in whose vocabulary impudence stands for sang-froid, meanness and vileness for truthfulness, insolence, hatred, and despotism for virtue and civilisation—must be the fundamental principle and basis of every true religion, whether founded on the Bible or not. No, I should not have said it must be, because, in fact, it is and shall be. It is the British who sow discord and trouble amongst you, O servants of Christ. You should, therefore, know that, if the commandments of the Holy Spirit are ten in number, the eleventh should be Hatred against the British. In the yellow flames of the altars of the idolators, in the overthrow of the dark and dumb idols of those who worship the fire there is one pinnacle—Hatred against the British. There is a typhoon which soaks with blood the cradles of the innocent, devastates the hearths, and causes the foam of blood to cover lips that wish to smile—it is England. On the breasts of the Greek corpses which you have laid low in the Sakaria, on the breasts of the corpses which you will surely lay down to-morrow at Smyrna—there is the British Evzone, on their backs there is the sign of the British, in their hearts there is the British. O sages, who pursue your brainwork, let hatred against the British illuminate your minds. Look round and see. Besides England, is there any other Power helping Greece or besides Greece, has England any other friend? O army of righteousness and of the people, on the day of your victory all the world will spit on the shameless face of the British, and on the day when you plant your standard on your national frontier mankind will breathe in peace and without fear. My greetings to the unknown martyrs who have fallen. My greetings to the wounded heroes, who have no bandage. My greetings to those in the trenches!'

Downright falsehood and despicable treachery were exemplified in the attitude of the ex-British Cabinet on the subject of the letter of M. Gounaris of February 15 last, to the Marquess Curzon. This letter pointed out that unless Greece received immediate assistance in credits and war-material a withdrawal would be necessary—a withdrawal amounting to a complete evacuation of Asia Minor. Lord Curzon replied with a letter which suggested that they should carry on, even if it did not give this advice in so many words. The result was disaster to the Greek army.

The following gentlemen, all members of the late British Cabinet, declared that they had not seen the letter which M. Gounaris had written: Mr. Lloyd George, Lord Birkenhead, Sir Robert Home, Sir L. Worthington Evans, Lord Lee, Mr. A. Chamberlain, Mr. H. A. L. Fisher, and Mr. T. J. MacNamara.

It is unnecessary to deal with more than a few of these gentlemen, who are all 'honourable men.' Mr. Chamberlain, in the first instance, stated in the British House of Commons that he had 'not seen this letter.' A search was subsequently made of the State papers left by him at his office, and among them was found a copy of the letter written by M. Gounaris. 'It bore in the corner a tick, which is the customary method by which Ministers indicate that important papers have been read by them.'

Sir Robert Home, Chancellor of the Exchequer, did not see the letter! A search among the papers left by him revealed, however, a copy of the letter itself.

Neither Mr. Lloyd George nor Lord Birkenhead saw the letter! The records of the Foreign Office show that copies were sent to them on February 26. With regard to Lord Birkenhead, we can only give his first and second utterances in the British House of Commons: 'I am confident no such document was ever sent to me. I am confident that these papers were never circulated.'

And the following letter addressed to the *Morning Post* by Mr. Cecil Hayes: 'Before the Gounaris letters affair passes away, may I, in the public interest, call your attention to an astonishing conflict shown by comparing two separate statements on different dates made by Lord Birkenhead. Both statements were made in the House of Lords; the first on March 30th last, and the second on December 11th, last Monday. Both statements referred to the same matter—his failing eyesight.

The statement of March 30th (when he applied for a month's leave in the House of Lords) contained these words ' I am sorry to say that for the last month or two I have had some anxiety in regard to my eyesight which has made it almost impossible for me with any comfort to read written documents. . . and there were almost two months in which I was never able to attend to the duties of the Cabinet, because I gave exclusive attention during that period to my Judicial work.'

On December 11th (last Monday) he said ' These circumstances, of course, did not prevent me from reading, or becoming acquainted with, my foreign Office papers...I was in the habit of going through the Foreign Office papers with scrupulous accuracy, so far as I knew them, two or three times a week, with a colleague.'

Not even a 'first-class' brain can reconcile these two conflicting statements. In one statement he was never able to attend to the duties of the Cabinet; in the other, he attended to the duties of the Foreign Office with scrupulous accuracy.

No hint of failure to read the letters being due to failing eyesight was given by Lord Birkenhead on December 7th, the day he made his charge against Lord Curzon. Such hint was reserved for the day of atonement, December 11th, when the charge had petered out."

It will be remembered that, when the Dominions were asked to join in the Near East war, the British Foreign Minister stated the appeal had been made without his knowledge—that its authors were solely Lloyd George and Churchill. We now suggest that Lord Curzon's papers should be examined, for obviously no reliance whatever can be placed on the word of a British Minister.

On the whole, we think, the new Greek Government is to be heartily congratulated on the fact that its diplomatic relations with England have ceased...

A hint of the Eastern outlook on the Irish settlement was given by Mr. Saklatvala, recently, in the British House of Commons. Mr. Saklatvala is the first Indian Labour Member to take his seat in the British House of Commons. In the course of his speech, he said:

'In reference to Ireland, I am afraid that I shall strike a jarring note in the hitherto harmonious music of this House. I am well disciplined and trained in the general principle of the Labour movement, namely, that the happiness of the world depends on international peace, and that international peace is possible only when the self-determined will of the people of each country prevails in each country. I deplore greatly these elements still existing in the Irish Treaty that are not compatible with that great and wholesome principle. It is no use denying the fact, for we shall not in that way create peace in Ireland. As a House we say that we are giving this Irish Treaty with a view of bringing peace to Ireland, but we know that it is not bringing peace. Either we are actuated by the motive of restoring thorough peace in Ireland or we are doing it as partial conquerors in Ireland. Everyone knows that the Treaty has unfortunately gone forth as the only alternative to a new invasion of Ireland by British troops. As long as that element exists the people of Ireland have a right to say that the very narrow majority which in Ireland accepted the Treaty at the time, accepted it also on this understanding—that if they did not accept it the alternative was an invasion by the Black-and-Tans of this country. The Irish Treaty all along continues to suffer in Ireland from the fact that it is not a Treaty acceptable to the people as a whole. If it were possible in some way in the preamble of the Treaty or by an Act of this House to allow the people of Ireland to understand that their country's constitution is to be framed by them as a majority may decide and that the alternative would not be an invasion from this country, but that this country would shake hands with Ireland as a neighbour, whatever shape or form that Government took, it would be quite a different story. Otherwise, whatever we may do, however many treaties we may pass, however unanimous the British may be in their behaviour towards Ireland, Ireland will not be made a peaceful country. As in 1801 England gave them a forced Union, so in 1922 England is giving them a forced freedom. We must remove that factor. Unless we do so we shall not be giving to the Irish the Treaty of freedom which we have all decided mentally that we are doing. When I say so, I put forward not my personal views but the views of ninety per cent. of those Irishmen who are my electors. They have pointed out to me that, whereas under the threat of renewed invasion the Dail only passed the Treaty by a majority of barely half a dozen votes, Irishmen who are not under that threat—Irishmen who are living in Great Britain—have, by a tremendous majority, voted against it. As long as those factors continue to exist, the Irish Treaty is not going to be what we—in a sort of silent conspiracy—have decided to name it. The reality will not be there. The reality is not there. Before I conclude I wish to refer to one point which is conspicuous by its absence from the King's Speech. If in the Empire, this House and this Government are going to take the glory of the good, they will also have to take the ignominy of anything disgraceful which happens outside this country. This Government may not be responsible. This House may not be responsible. The people of this country may not be responsible. Yet there is something like a public voice and public prejudice, and if this Government and this house are proud of their association with the Colonies and the Empire, this Government and this House will also have to satisfy this country as well as outside countries, why the policy of the South African Government in hanging and shooting workers, was permitted and was kept quiet. We are still calling Ireland a part of this Empire, and it is only last week that four young working-class lads, without an open trial and without even fair notice to their families, were shot dead. Even on the night before, their families were told that everything was all right, but on the following morning, when the mother of one of them went to convey a bundle of laundry to her son, she was informed that the poor boys had been executed. These acts might be described as the acts of independent governments. Either these governments are independent or they are part of this Empire. If they are part of this Empire, then the Government in the centre of the Empire must see to it that a policy of this kind does not go without challenge and without, at least, protest from this House, if nothing else can be done.'"

* * *

"The story of the world for the year 1922 is thus, in every sense, a tragic one. Nor unhappily is there the slightest indication that the New Year will see a change for the better..."

(January 1923)

## *Note on the Executions of the Royalist Ministers and Commanders*

In Greece a military coup under General Plastiras overthrew the Royalist Government and sent King Constantine and Prince Andrew (father of the present Prince Philip of Britain) into exile. The new rulers of Greece had two generals and four ministers tried and shot for their failure in Anatolia. Interesting information came out at their trials regarding continued British government support for the offensive, even after Westminster had seemingly washed its hands of the Greeks.

*The Daily News* of November 30th 1922 published the following report of an interview with Venizelos concerning British protests at the executions of the Royalist Ministers:

"M. Venizelos approved of the executions of the five Ministers and the Commander-in-Chief whom he believed to have been guilty of a criminal betrayal of Greek interests... He declared that the men were condemned by a legally constituted court and that therefore Great Britain had no right to protest against their executions. The British Government and the British public made no protest when Mr. Erskine Childers was executed. Why therefore all this indignation when Greece condemns men who were sworn enemies of the State?"

# X. The Treaty of Lausanne

Having lost the military confrontation with Ataturk in Anatolia and at Chanak England determined to recover with a Treaty what it had lost on the battlefield—as it had done in Ireland.

On the Monday before Lord Curzon, the British Secretary of State, was due to go to Lausanne to negotiate a settlement with the Turks, he made the following speech to businessmen in the City of London 'where his declaration that the Government would stand firm against Kemalist aggression was received with loud cheers.':

> "The developments in Turkey he characterised as 'the most definite menace to the peace of the world... The Nationalists, flushed with victory over the Greeks, have run riot during the past few days. They have deposed the Sultan and abolished the temporal power of the Caliph. I wonder what the Moslems of the world will think of this... The Nationalist Party has assumed the Government of Constantinople and has called upon the Allied Powers to withdraw—the fleet of Great Britain, if you please—to withdraw at their bidding from the Bosporus, the Sea of Marmora and the Dardanelles. They have abolished the capitulations and mixed courts, abolished the national debt, and repudiated the national obligations. These pretensions cannot be tolerated. They have no conceivable justification. They are an affront to the Allies and a challenge to Europe... Turkey must learn that there is a limit even to the concessions which we can make to her, and that we cannot purchase peace at the cost of humiliation or disgrace. Turkey must realise that the strength of Britain and the might of Europe are a rock against which she will hurl herself in vain."
> (*Irish Independent*, 9th November 1922.)

First, a word about Lord Curzon, who figures so prominently in this story. Curzon was the 'truly Imperialist' Viceroy of India that the Imperial Civil Servant, Charles J. O'Donnell of Donegal, had such a low opinion of. O'Donnell had seen Curzon's flamboyant new Imperialism partitioning Bengal on religious lines and presiding over a repeat performance of the Irish Famine on his watch in India, during 1896-1902. Like Trevelyan, Curzon denied famine relief on the basis that it would have weakened the moral fibre and self-reliance of the natives. The famine was let rip, food was exported and public spending cut, and 19 million died, according to *The Lancet*. (See Mike Davis's *Late Victorian Holocausts* for this forgotten aspect of Imperial rule.) Then, in 1903, Curzon presided over the famous Delhi Durbar where the money he saved on famine relief was blown on the most spectacular display of Imperial pomp in history, to celebrate the accession of Edward VII.

According to his City of London speech, Curzon went to Lausanne in 1922 with the objective of keeping the British Fleet at the Straits, controlling Constantinople, maintaining the Capitulations, forcing the Turks to pay reparations... or else!

## Froembgen's Account of Lausanne

The Lausanne Conference started on November 20th 1922. General Ismet (who later took the surname, Inonu) led the Turkish delegation. Mustapha Kemal remained at home, like DeValera—on the end of the telephone. The Turkish delegates were to contact him if his judgement was required.

The other parties to the proceedings were Britain, France, Italy, Japan, Greece, Rumania and Serbia. Russia participated later at Turkey's request and the U.S. acted as observers. The conference broke down on February 4th 1923 and reconvened on April 23rd. The Treaty was signed on July 24th 1923 after Turkey, Britain, France and Italy ratified it.

One of the more humorous aspects of Lausanne was the appearance of Lord Curzon in extravagant and exotic attire, when he met the Turkish delegation. Curzon sought to present the image of a colonial Proconsul in order to overawe his opponents. But instead he looked like a 'Court eunuch' to the Turks. In the unfolding drama this guise of the British negotiator was perhaps indicative of more than just Curzon's sense of apparel.

We reproduce Hanns Froembgen's entertaining account of the negotiations at Lausanne—as a contrast to what happened in the Irish Treaty:

> "THE representatives of some dozen States stared coldly at the small, slightly built man in the frock-coat, who appeared in the doorway of the conference hall. So that was Ismet Pasha, Count Palatine to the Ghazi, the great soldier.
>
> Mussolini's expression was openly hostile, Poincaré's was no more encouraging, and England's representative, Lord Curzon, was obviously at some pains to emphasize an attitude of reserve and so make clear to the Turk that they did not recognize him.
>
> In order to accentuate the inferiority of status, the Turkish Delegation had been provided with ordinary chairs, while the other delegates had armchairs. Ismet glanced round the room, and his eyes came to rest on the chairs. He understood their significance.
>
> Why were there no armchairs, he desired to know? There was a certain amount of embarrassed coughing, after which it was explained that owing to the shortness of time it had been found impossible to procure more armchairs. Good, said Ismet, then we'll return when the omission has been remedied. Lord Curzon bit his lip. In the twinkling of an eye the armchairs were in their place. Ismet's determination not to be hoodwinked and brow-beaten had passed its first test.
>
> The Peace Conference was then officially declared open, and Poincaré and the other delegates addressed the assembly. They expressed satisfaction that at last they were able to come together and confer on certain modifications of the Treaty of Sèvres.
>
> Ismet politely and quietly objected. They could not proceed on that assumption. The Kemalist Government would have nothing to do with a Treaty of Sèvres. Negotiations could only be pursued on the basis of the Armistice of

Mudania, which, they were aware, he had concluded as victor. The first, unalterable condition was discussion on terms of perfect equality—or...

This bombshell took the Conference members completely by surprise. But whether they liked it or not they were obliged to submit. Since the days of Mudros the situation had entirely altered. They were not dealing now with an Ottoman Empire defeated in the World War, but with a Kemalist Turkey that had been victorious in the Anatolian mountains.

Could they adjourn the Conference before it had begun? That would have been a leap in the dark. England wanted to reach a settlement, and Mustafa Kemal wanted to reach a settlement. It was decided to preserve a sense of realities and to attempt to come to an agreement. Ismet saw that he had not deceived himself. His bold front and resolute attitude had made an impression. His faith in the political wisdom of his most powerful and most important partner in the negotiations had proved justified.

Lord Curzon gave proof that he possessed that leading virtue of a statesman—the ability to acknowledge reality, no matter whether it happened to be agreeable or disagreeable. The Allies continued to stress the unity which existed among themselves. Ismet, who was slightly deaf, on this occasion displayed a pair of uncommonly sharp ears. He heard immediately the slightest discord, which from time to time disturbed the harmony of the discussion, and took these rather over-emphasized allusions to unity for what they were—an admission of the contrary.

On the face of it his position may not have appeared a very favourable one, but as a Kemalist he knew that an individual was more than a match for a multitude. In numerous instances this had been proved in history.

Once more they attempted to overawe him with the methods which were used all too often and with extreme thoroughness at the Peace Conferences in 1918/9. They desired morally to drive Turkey into a position of defence and began to cast up the question of War Guilt.

The small, rather deaf general immediately opened a counter-attack. It was a question, he complained, which the victors were constantly putting to the defeated, and he refused categorically to enter into any discussion about it. In order to arrive at any definite decision about the matter it would be necessary to review in all details the history of the last thirty years, and the Turkish Delegation had neither the time nor the inclination to enter upon such academic and practically worthless discussions.

Their demands were equally as clear as they were simple and just. They desired for the new Nationalist State complete independence in political, economic and military matters. The Turkish Delegation pointed out that the Allies themselves had gone to war simply and solely to secure self-determination for the nations.

Two years ago it would have been impossible for such words to be used, but at this Conference Right was once more a powerful weapon, or in this case the justice-seeking had fought for, and secured for themselves, a position of might.

In the first phase Ismet was victor. Now began the main part of the Conference. Clearly it was a tight issue between the two protagonists, Ismet and Curzon. The rest receded into the background, had only secondary roles to perform.

Turkey and England were anxious to establish a new relationship that was to be free of all ambiguity and sources of conflict. First the numerous misunderstandings, which had been accumulating for centuries, had to be cleared out of the way. On both sides there was suspicion, mistrust, contempt, hatred.

Ismet introduced a new tone to the proceedings, displaying a candour to which diplomacy had hitherto been a stranger. Every nation had right to exist. When governments were prepared honourably and unreservedly to recognize this principle, there should be no great difficulty in harmonizing the various interests.

Kemalist Turkey had no ulterior motives to serve. It had not the least intention of making war on any other nation. All it demanded was justice and recognition and assurance of the liberty which it had just secured, at the cost of great sacrifice, with the sword. Ismet knew that it would not be easy to convince Conservative England of the genuine non-aggressive intentions of the new Turkey. Not two years ago Mustafa Kemal had been described in London as a bandit. This had not been forgotten in the Kemalist camp.

Days, weeks, months passed. The Conference was still in session in Lausanne. It was not so much a conference as a fight, a hard-fought duel between Ismet and Curzon. The others were merely spectators, go-betweens. Ismet was no diplomat of the old school. He had no desire or intention of tricking his partner in the negotiations. England was to be satisfied. The legitimate interests of the Empire were to be respected. A Peace was to be concluded that was acceptable to both parties.

At the same time, the small, deaf general — he made a habit of having everything repeated in order to gain time to compose a ready answer — drew a well-defined boundary where all concessions ceased. The defeat in the Great War was fully acknowledged. As the price of that, Mustafa Kemal was prepared to pay over all non-Turkish provinces. It was a high price, and the fact that Mustafa Kemal paid with a light heart, without reserve or ill-feeling, made it no less valuable to England. On the contrary, England had no need in future to worry about interference from the Kemalist side.

Soon the vexed question of the Straits was occupying a prominent position in the negotiations. Hardly had the name 'Dardanelles' been mentioned when spectres of the past made their unwelcome entry to the scene. For a good two hundred years the Straits had been one of the chief danger points in European politics. The problem was rendered even more complex by the confusion of treaties which had been formed round it. Old, unforgotten grievances and threats were reawakened.

It was almost as though the men who died on Gallipoli might be heard uniting in the chorus: Enough of this interminable wrangling! Solve the question once and for all; free Europe of this source of peril!

In the treatment of this question of the Narrows Soviet Russia had been admitted to the Conference to have an opportunity of stating its case. The scene underwent a change. The real opponents now were Tchitcherin and Curzon. Tchitcherin demanded that Turkey should acquire full and absolute sovereignty over the Straits. The Straits are free. Turkey is the sole prophet of Freedom. That was the claim made by Soviet Russia.

Curzon now had an opportunity of confirming that Ismet was a statesman of no mean ability. The Turkish general subjected his zealous Russian ally to a sharp scrutiny. As a Nationalist this solution of the Straits Question was very acceptable to him, but he knew that it was not to be achieved at this Conference, that it would not be achieved at Lausanne.

England returned an unconditional 'No!' to the Russian demand. England intended to continue to occupy the Straits and could afford to be unyielding. If Ismet adopted the Russian standpoint as his own, the Conference would break down and the situation would remain obscure and pregnant with dangers. Peace would recede farther than ever. Sooner or later guns would fire again.

That might suit very well certain, far-aiming Soviet Russian plans. But Turkey's urgent need was peace. England discovered herself in a similar position. Much to everyone's surprise, Ismet ignored the Russian demand. Turkey certainly was not willing to act as door-keeper of the Narrows for the Russians. She did not wish to become a Russian pawn in the game against England.

Turkey was pursuing an essentially independent, national policy and was not going to allow herself to be taken in tow by any foreign Power. And so Ismet accepted the compromise which England offered. Freedom of the Straits and demilitarisation of its shores. That meant abandonment of sovereignty over one of the most important areas of the Nationalist State. The Turkish nation had bled for complete independence. Had not Ismet given away too much at Lausanne?

Already grumbles were heard in Angora. There were many men in association with the Ghazi who had taken a distinct dislike to the small, semi-deaf general, and they knew, too, of the extent to which he enjoyed Mustafa Kemal's confidence. It was a risky thing to attack the Grey Wolf. On the other hand, there was nothing to prevent people from attacking Ismet.

It was spread about that Ismet, in respect of the Straits Question, let his country down at Lausanne. In far-off Angora Mustafa Kemal placed himself before his paladin and defended and approved his attitude.

Turkey desired and must have peace. She had to pay the price of it to England. Politics was the art of doing what was possible. Granted, it was intolerable that they should have a demilitarized zone and that they should not be in a position to defend Constantinople against possible violent measures undertaken by a foreign Power. But had Constantinople the same crowning importance to the new Turkey that it had possessed for the old Ottoman Empire?

Constantinople, said Mustafa Kemal, was no longer a Turkish city in the strict Nationalist sense. Constantinople was an international city. It had revealed itself to be the chief centre of reaction. The curiously mixed population, consisting for the most part of elements who were bitterly opposed to the new order of things, at the present could not be relied on and had no claim to any sort of confidence. Through the removal of the Russian danger in the East the Straits had lost a great deal of their significance to the new Turkey. But for England the question remained as urgent as ever. England could and would not, make any concession. Her obstinacy was aimed not so much at Turkey as at Soviet Russia. They must learn to distinguish the upper from the lower notes in the political concert. In this case it was shrewd statecraft to show a certain willingness to yield.

The Conference in Lausanne continued. In general there were no great difficulties in coming to an agreement concerning the frontiers of the Nationalist State. That was not to be wondered at, since Mustafa Kemal had already as good as drawn them with his sword. However, a definite decision with regard to the Turkish-Irak frontier led to some sharp disagreement. Both Ismet and Curzon claimed the Province of Mosul.

England demanded the union of Mosul with Irak, not simply on account of Mosul oil but, principally, for strategical reasons. The *Vilayet* of Mosul was the doorway to Irak. Suddenly the world became filled with suspicion of the men in Angora.

Would Mustafa Kemal, after a short breathing space, summon the Arab peoples to fight against England? Was his ultimate goal the revolutionizing of all Mohammedans? The echo of his victory had reached the Islamic world, where it had had a tremendous effect. He was being called the Messenger of Allah and a second Mohammed. All the hopes and all aspirations towards independence on the part of the Eastern peoples were inspired by the man who had seized unto himself the sword of Osman and who had employed it so successfully against the Christian world.

People suddenly began to ask themselves, did he meditate uniting the Eastern races in a new invasion of Europe? Western imagination, excited and overstrained in the Great War, feared that the spirit of Genghis Khan had risen from the plains of Central Asia and descended upon the leader of New Turkey. The atmosphere in the Conference room was charged.

Ismet was not willing to give up claim to Mosul. The majority of the inhabitants of the *Vilayet* were Turks. The position from the point of view of Right was perfectly clear. Quite so—said Curzon—perfectly clear. England was *de facto* possessor of the territory by reason of her victory on the Palestine front.

There was not one right for victors and one right for defeated. There was a single Right, and that was on the Turkish side. The inhabitants of the *Vilayet* were Turks and by reason of the National Pact should have their place within the new Nationalist State. Moreover, the territory was not occupied until after the conclusion of the Armistice of Mudros. So Ismet argued. Curzon contradicted. The *Vilayet* was populated by a Kurdish majority. The Kurds were not Turks.

Ismet grew indignant. For centuries the Kurds had lived side by side with the Turks, they were a brother race. It was impossible that they should be given to Arab Irak. Furthermore, two years ago they took up arms against the British.

What did that prove, Curzon parried? Had the Turkish Government never been called upon to deal with revolts in their occupied territories? On both sides tempers began to rise and it became evident that there was no prospect of an agreement on this point being reached. Was the Conference to collapse on a part-question?

Ismet again gave proof of his qualities as a statesman and of his sue of responsibility. He accordingly proposed leaving the Mosul question entirely out of the programme of the Conference for the present. The interested parties might then have an opportunity later of coming to an amicable arrangement. Until such time the *status quo* would be binding on both parties.

No less serious difficulties were caused through the Turkish demand for an exchange of populations with Greece. About two million Greeks lived in Anatolia, although a large percentage, admittedly, had fled with the defeated army. Mustafa Kemal was determined to make Anatolia a purely Turkish land. The foreign minorities must be uprooted and expelled, unfortunately by a violent process. This would entail great misery and suffering to those concerned, but history knows no mercy when her hand is forced. But consider how much misery this motley collection of races brought to the East! In them lay one of the chief causes of the disaster of the old Ottoman Empire. Turkey for the Turks! On this question Ismet was unyielding.

The Conference agreed in principle. The materialization of this sole instance in history of a mass deportation was to be the subject of discussion at a later date.

The negotiations grew more dramatic as the Conference proceeded. Presently came the trickiest and most difficult question of all — that of the capitulations. Ismet demanded the complete removal of all privileges which had formerly been granted by the sultans to foreigners in consideration of loans. The *Dette publique*, the International Debts Administration, real ruler of the old Ottoman Empire, must disappear, and with it all the many forms of control, concessions and restraints. Away with the inextricable tangle of treaties and contracts, through which no man could possibly find his way!

The desire was to clean the slate of the past centuries, Ismet explained.

This matter affected the Allies' most vital interests. The system of capitulations was a convenient and certain method of maintaining a control over the Ottoman Empire. Now this was to come to an end, the Turk desired to be master in his own house. The Ottoman Bank, which held the exclusive right to issue notes, was controlled principally by French capital. Such conditions were intolerable to the Kemalists.

The Allies endeavoured to make it clear to Ismet that Turkey without the help of the European Powers simply could not exist. The country had been bled dry, was backward and devastated; what could it do without external aid? The financial experts drew horrible pictures of what might be expected if Turkey carried her independence to this stage. Turkey could only survive with the assistance of loans. But—the delegates smiled coolly and sarcastically to themselves—who would be willing to grant loans to an economically ruined land?

No one need worry himself unduly about that, retorted Ismet, New Turkey would defend herself as tenaciously against foreign money as she had done against foreign soldiers. She would work for her own recovery entirely with the means at her disposal.

The people in Angora were wished luck, but at the same time it was pointed out to Ismet that Turkey lacked everything that, in a civilized State, was essential as the *prima facie* basis of economic independence. The country not even possessed a proper legal code; all it had was the Sheria, the ancient Islamic ecclesiastical code. Ismet wore a superior smile. They would very soon alter that.

A bitter struggle continued. No concession was to be got out of Ismet, not the slightest foreign privilege, not the merest suggestion of the old capitulations—they were a disgrace, worse even than ruin! In the face of this heroic attitude on the part of the war-seasoned soldier all legal and commercial arguments lost their force. They automatically collapsed.

But Curzon and his allies were not willing at once to admit themselves beaten. In particular, the French were unwilling to give up all hope. Poincaré, the representative of close-fisted petty bourgeoisie, saw a danger to French savings. An endeavour was made to reach a compromise.

Ismet again stated that his decision was irrevocable. Curzon now became ruffled and threatened to take his departure. Ismet shrugged his shoulders. If his Lordship was prepared to take responsibility on his own shoulders . . .!

It was eight in the evening. Lord Curzon drew attention to the fact his train left at nine. So Ismet still had an hour in which to reconsider the matter. He hoped to be able to take pleasant memories back to London with him. The two men bowed to each other. Ismet left and returned to his hotel, which was immediately invaded and overrun by the French delegates. The French implored the Turkish general to accept the compromise. There was still time. The train had not yet left the station.

Ismet expressed regret. He could not consent to any sort of compromise nor tolerate any veiled capitulations that were irreconcilable with the honour of an independent State. The Frenchmen attempted fresh entreaties, then flattery. Monsieur Bompard reminded him that Marshal Foch had elected to conclude an armistice with the Germans rather than march to Berlin. Ismet Pasha, too, was a great soldier.

*Eh bien*, said Ismet, and at Mudania I acted in very much the same way that Marshal Foch acted at Compiègne. What was there to stop the Nationalist army from marching to Athens, or for that matter to Constantinople?

Lord Curzon waited on the platform, watch in hand. Already the train had been held up half an hour. His Lordship then lost patience, but decided to wait a few more minutes. No signs of Ismet.

Curzon stepped into the train, the door slammed, and the train slowly set itself in motion and vanished into the darkness. The Conference had broken down. Uncertainty and peril again cast their shadows over the East. Would war break out again? Was mankind to suffer still more misery?

In Angora a bitter debate in the Great National Assembly continued for nine days. Everybody who had been angered by the dethronement of the Sultan, and all those who were jealous of the personal power of Mustafa Kemal, pounced on Ismet. He was treated as a man who had been defeated. Clumsiness was the mildest of the terms which were applied to him.

Mustafa Kemal allowed the storm to subside, again showing that, despite being a man of action, he could wait when necessary. With the present Parliament no work could be done. The Opposition had nothing better to do than drag out the debates, argue about matters which were of no concern, and produce greater confusion.

Mustafa Kemal, the Victor, had only just begun. His next great task was reconstruction of the State. This implied ruthless destruction of many ancient Turkish traditions and, in their place, the creation of new traditions: it was a leap from the Middle Ages to the twentieth century.

It was a fight that could not be won while there were individuals working at cross-purposes with the Government. As at Sakaria and Dumlu Punar, all national forces had to be mobilized and a united national will formed. The path to this unity was to be paved by the creation of a Party sworn to give unconditional support to the aims and policy of the Ghazi. Moreover, it was to be a Party representing the will of the entire nation, not a particular group of parliamentary deputies.

While the Opposition was still hurling abuse at Ismet, Mustafa Kemal launched his blow. He dissolved the National Assembly. It had functioned for three years. Meanwhile, the situation had radically changed. It was now right that the people should be consulted.

Mustafa Kemal went into the country as a preacher and was given an enthusiastic reception by the people. He mingled with Anatolian peasants, listened to their needs and wishes, induced awestruck people to talk and express their opinions—most of them had never in their lives seen a real pasha at close quarters, let alone a Chosen One of Allah—explained the situation to them, canvassed, and organized them. In little, out-of-the-way villages local groups of the People's Party were formed, on strictly military lines, which owed allegiance to their President.

The election for the new National Assembly ended in a sweeping victory for the Ghazi. Not a single member of the Opposition gained a seat in the Assembly. Unity of will had been achieved. The creative work of State reconstruction could begin.

At the commencement of April Ismet went again to Lausanne. The Peace Conference resumed its deliberations. In the place of Curzon Sir Horace Rumbold appeared as head of the British Delegation. Ismet stuck to his old tactics—as far as possible satisfaction of British desires for the purpose of establishing a frictionless relationship between the two countries. Sir Horace, a calmer and more diplomatic man than Lord Curzon, approved of his efforts. Between Turkey and England there were no longer any disagreements which made the prospect of an amicable settlement impossible. The question of the Straits had been solved in a manner satisfactory to Great Britain. It had meant a great sacrifice to Turkey, but that sacrifice had been made.

Regarding Mosul, they were to arrive at a settlement after the conclusion of the Peace Conference. In the matter of the exchange of population England acceded to Turkish demands; and to relieve the Straits Pact of some of its mess, a concession was made. Turkey was accorded the right to maintain twelve thousand soldiers in the Straits Zone.

France was chiefly interested in the economic questions. The same France, who, at the critical hour, had placed the trump cards in the enemy's hands, and who, dissatisfied with the early stages the Conference, had encouraged Ismet to be unyielding. Poincaré, the time fully occupied with the Ruhr adventure, now found himself facing an England that had settled its account with Turkey and who had no further interest in French requirements.

Ismet's clever tactics now became apparent. With the aid of France he had acquired from England practically everything that Turkey demanded, in order to have a satisfied England with which to check-mate France. England pressed for a conclusion of the Conference and had not the remotest intention of sending a single soldier to champion the interests of the French *rentier*, whose part Poincaré now began to take—admittedly, with a considerable display of anger and with extremely little skill.

And so Ismet, by agreeing to a few, negligent limitations, was able to prevail with the Turkish claims on the question of capitulations.

In Lausanne, on the afternoon of 24 July, the bells began to peal. Peace at last, peace after nine years' terrible war!

Ismet, as the representative of an independent State enjoying equality of status, signed the Treaty. England showed an attitude of cool contentment. France felt that she had been cheated and was exceedingly downcast. Italy too was disappointed. Garroni and Montagna had given themselves great pains to please Ismet and had seldom failed him with support. He had made use of it in the same way that he had played the French help.

Ismet, it must be admitted, was extremely suspicious of his friends. He knew that Italy expected to earn a rich reward for her services. But in that she would be disappointed. Turkey was certainly not going to permit any extension of foreign economic interests. Would Italy remain on amicable terms when she saw that her hopes had been deceived?

The Conference concluded without excitement or ceremony. Only one speech was made and that by the Swiss Federal President Scheuer, in his capacity as host, who addressed a few words to the delegates. He made reference to the fact that in Lausanne a peace had been concluded by peaceful negotiations, not by dictatorial methods. Now was the time, he said, for these peaceful principles to be extended over the whole world, in order that humanity might be relieved of a grievous burden. No nation should be denied the right and duty of contributing to that end.

The incredible had been achieved, Mustafa Kemal had carried his programme through. Turkey was free. Military limitations were no longer the subject of discussion at Lausanne, and political and economic shackles had been shaken off. The victory was complete.

The nation worshipped its deliverer, called him Saviour and Messenger of Allah. The whole Islamite world was stirred. From near and far deputations pilgrimized to Angora, bringing costly presents and paying homage to the man who was considered as the new champion of Islam, as an instrument of the one true God, who sent Mohammed into the world as his prophet.

Osman's throne was vacant. Silence reigned in the rooms and apartments of the Yildiz Kiosk. The servants had departed and vanished. Officials appointed by the Kemalist Government were now in occupation of the administrative offices. Refat Pasha was Governor-General and energetically engaged in restoring order in the capital.

The Army of Occupation was preparing for its departure. By the terms of the Peace Treaty the capital had to be evacuated by the autumn. There was still time for the troops to feel a breath of the fresh breeze which blew across the Bosporus.

The new masters indeed had nothing in common with the masters of yesterday. There was no trace in them of the peaceful lassitude and laziness of the Oriental. They lived at twentieth century pace. They applied themselves to the practical work of administration with the same fanatical zeal that their earliest ancestors had shown when they descended upon the people of the East and the Christian world with their scimitars." (pp.175-188.)

The Lausanne Treaty, unlike the Anglo-Irish Treaty, was negotiated with long and hard deliberation spread over an eight-month period (the Turkish delegation withdrew for a three-month interruption in the middle of the proceedings when it was not happy with what was happening). Turkey refused to have terms imposed upon her that would dilute her sovereignty, even though Britain fought tooth and nail to maximize her Imperial influence over the region. The Turkish delegation also refused to be bullied into a take it or leave it deal imposed by an arbitrary deadline. When Curzon said his train was standing at the station and it was 'now or never' the treaty remained unsigned by the Turks. Curzon, after delaying his train in the expectation they would submit, left empty-handed on his train. The British returned a few months later and the Treaty was signed on July 24th 1923.

On reading Froembgen's account of the negotiations at Lausanne, with the Irish Treaty negotiations in mind, I was reminded of something James Clarence Mangan said of the Turks in his admiring introduction to *Arabian, Persian and Turkish Poetry*:

"The truth is that the Moslem has more faith, humanly speaking, than the Englishman… He reverences with deeper emotion, cherishes sympathies more comprehensive, has a roomier capacity for the reception of mysteries of all sorts. He does not start objections, and moot evidences, and balance probabilities... Not he: of such huckstering and shabbiness his soul has an intuitive contempt. He takes the higher ground... It would never occur to him to immure himself within a given circle of petty practicalities... and hence it is that he is always tranquil, always untouchable..." (*The Dubliner, The Lives, Times and Writings of James Clarence Mangan*, p.109.)

Maybe that is why the Turkish delegation was so effective in the negotiations at Lausanne. As Froembgen's account shows, Ismet took the 'higher ground' from the start and refused to be descended to the 'petty practicalities' by Curzon. In the negotiation of the Irish Treaty the Irish plenipotentiaries found themselves 'huckstering' over the details and losing the higher ground to the British—with the result that, when all was said and done, despite the concessions made to them, they found themselves back in the Empire, whilst the Turks became an independent nation.

### An American Jurist on Lausanne

Philip Marshall Brown served as Secretary to the U.S. Embassy in Constantinople before the Great War before becoming a Professor of International Law at Princeton in 1915. He was Associate Editor of the *American Journal of International Law* and was the author of *Foreigners in Turkey* (1914), *International Realities* (1917) and a number of other books.

*Foreigners in Turkey* was published at the moment (September 1914) when the Ottoman State moved to abolish the exterritorial privileges granted to foreigners known as the Capitulations. Brown traced the origin of these exterritorial privileges to the Ottoman conquest of the Byzantine capital, which maintained a system of privileges itself. When the Moslem Ottoman Empire, which identified the State and Religion, came to rule over non-Moslems it granted these communities the right to exercise their own laws over their members. Around 1740 the Sultan gave French citizens extraordinary privileges in the Empire and these were gradually applied to other Westerners. By the Nineteenth Century these had become the Capitulations, protected by the Western Powers through their financial control over the Ottoman Exchequer.

The extraordinary privileges enjoyed by Westerners included absolute jurisdiction of consular tribunals over their nationals, immunity from visits to their domiciles from the Ottoman authorities except in cases of murder or armed revolt, freedom from arrest or imprisonment by the Ottoman State, complete freedom of trade and immunity from search by port authorities and the right to run their own postal services.

When the Young Turks sought to remove the Capitulations it was taken almost to be an act of war by some in Britain and it is mentioned in many works as a cause of the hostility toward the Turkish Government in England and France.

In 1923 Professor Brown turned his attention to the negotiations at Lausanne in the periodical he edited, the *American Journal of International Law*. At the point of writing, the conference had stalled and broken up with Curzon's train having left the station. Brown knew Turkey well and was able to make an informative estimation of the changing situation in the region that was to be reflected in the Treaty. What he noted was that the Allies, in exporting notions of nationalism and 'self-determination' in the East, had proved enormously successful where it was least intended, with momentous consequences:

"The Eastern Question... is essentially a Western Question. It concerns quite as much the nationalistic ambitions and rivalries of the European Powers as it does the peculiar interests and problems of the peoples of the Near East. Unlike previous conferences such as the Congress of Berlin, the Congress of Lausanne found itself confronted, not by an abject conquered 'Sick Man,' but by an invigorated, re-awakened nation determined at all costs to maintain what it believes to be the sovereign rights of the Turkish people. The result has been it was found necessary at Lausanne to seek a conciliatory adjustment of the Western and Eastern questions...

The ferment of nationalism, as expressed in the alleged principle of the 'right of self-determination,' has produced amazing results in Turkey as well as in other countries... A lethargic people who believed in a theocratic state and who for centuries had maintained an indifferent, if not indulgent, attitude to their non-Moslem neighbors have shaken off their apathy  and are now asserting the literal claim of 'Turkey for the Turks.' They have stripped their Caliph of his political functions as Sultan. They have divorced the Moslem church from the State, and have established a genuinely democratic govern-ment in Angora. Democratic by instinct, though respectful of leadership and authority, the Turks have dedicated themselves to the colossal task of the re-generation of their nation.

A melancholy aspect of this manifestation of nationalism is the fervid con-viction of the Turks that in view of the nationalistic aims of the Greeks and Armenians and the danger of European intervention in their behalf, it is no longer possible to permit such alien elements to remain within the Turkish nation. The Armenians have been dispersed and exterminated as a national community enjoying special privileges under the Sultans. The Greeks have been likewise dispersed, largely as a result of the disastrous adventure in Asia Minor. Turkey and Greece have agreed, with the approval of the United Na-tions, to exchange populations, though the Greeks in Constantinople have been allowed to remain in a rather precarious state bereft of former privileges as a national community under their Patriarch, while that high official has been allowed to remain on his historic throne of Byzantium shorn of his political and judicial functions. In such tragic ways has the principle of self-determina-tion affected the ancient civilizations of the Near and Middle East.

The policy of the Angora Government toward the European Powers and toward foreigners in general is indicated in their absolute determination to abolish the hateful regime of the capitulations under which Turkish sovereign rights in fiscal, economic, educational, judicial and other respects were practically ignored. Privileges and concessions originally granted by the voluntary action of the Turks to foreigners and non-Moslem subjects alike became transformed through successive wars, interventions and diplomatic intrigues into irksome exactions that formed the basis of a kind of international suzerainty over Turkey. The Turkish customs tariff could not be altered without the consent of the European Powers, and then only at the cost of other concessions by the Turks. Their finances… came largely under foreign control. Valuable concessions and monopolies were obtained by methods fair and foul… The various foreign missionary establishments acquired exceptional privileges that left them practically independent of Turkish supervision and control. The foreign post offices crept in insidiously and deprived the Ottoman postal service of a large revenue, as well as enabling foreigners to evade provisions of Turkish law relating to customs duties and to censorship.

The extraordinary juridical privileges acquired by foreigners made them almost entirely immune from Ottoman jurisdiction and resulted in an intolerable disregard of Turkish laws and sensibilities, as instanced in the maintenance of foreign brothels which the police could not close or control. Foreigners in Turkey before 1914 enjoyed so privileged a status that they were not only free from the restraints of Turkish law but free from the restraints of their own laws.

The unyielding attitude of the Turks at Lausanne is not difficult to understand: in fact it commands considerable sympathy and respect…" (*The Lausanne Conference, American Journal of International Law*, April 1923, pp.290-2.)

At the conclusion of the negotiations and the publication of the Treaty, Professor Brown penned another article comparing the Treaty of Lausanne to its predecessor, the Treaty of Sèvres. He did this to show how much Ataturk had overturned the Treaty that had been imposed on the Turks by Britain and France. Here is his evaluation of Ataturk's achievement on the battlefield and then at the conference:

"The Treaty of Sèvres of August 20, 1920… was an old-fashioned treaty, like that of Versailles, imposing the harsh terms of a relentless victor. Neither treaty revealed much magnanimity or statesmanship. The Turks were able successfully to resist the imposition of The Treaty of Sèvres. The measure of their success may be seen by a comparison of the more important terms of the treaty compared with those of Lausanne signed on July 24 1923.

In 1920, the Sultan's Government, under pressure from the Allied Powers in Constantinople, was constrained to accept the Enos-Midia boundary which left to Turkey only so much of European territory as was represented by Constantinople and a small hinterland for the protection of the capital. In 1923, the Turks received back approximately their old boundary line with Bulgaria and Western Thrace, which remained with Greece, including the Holy City of

Adrianople which holds the tombs of the early Sultans. In 1920 they agreed to surrender Smyrna with a large outlying district to the Greeks, though retaining a fictitious sovereignty subject to extinction by a plebiscite to be held under the auspices of the League of Nations. In 1923 they regained this territory without any restrictions whatever. In 1920 they agreed to an independent Armenia and ultimately to an independent Kurdistan. The Treaty of Lausanne makes no mention of either.

The Treaty of Sèvres provided an absolute guarantee of the freedom of the Straits by leaving Greece in control of the European shore of the Dardanelles, while the Treaty of Lausanne leaves Turkey in complete control from the Aegean Sea to the Black Sea.

The Treaty of Sèvres, though recognizing the inability of Turkey to make 'complete reparation' for its responsibility for the World War, imposed the obligation to pay for 'all loss or damage suffered by civilian nationals of the Allied Powers in respect of their persons or property through the action or negligence of the Turkish authorities during the war and up to the coming into force of the present treaty.' (It will be recalled how this phrase 'damage suffered by civilian nationals,' was distorted in the case of the Treaty of Versailles to include pensions and separation allowances.) A financial commission was imposed on Turkey with the most sweeping powers of national receivership. The Treaty of Lausanne merely provides for the payment by Turkey of its foreign debts due before October 29, 1914, in a manner convenient for Turkish finances, and also for a *pro rata* distribution of the obligations represented by the revenues represented by the former portions of the Ottoman Empire.

The Treaty of Sèvres re-imposed the regime of the Capitulations abolished by the Turks on October 1, 1914, whereby foreigners had acquired so privileged a status as to be contemptuously independent of Turkish jurisdiction and to reduce the sovereignty of the nation to a fiction... The Treaty of Lausanne explicitly provides for the 'complete abolition of the Capitulations in Turkey from every point of view.' ...

The Turks at Lausanne stood firmly and consistently on the platform of their National Pact of 1919, which asserted the right of Turkey to a full sovereign status on an equality with all other nations. That they were so successful was due to two facts: First, that the Allied Powers were disunited and mutually distrustful; and second, that the Turks, after the landing of Greek troops at Smyrna, in May, 1919, had been aroused to a supreme national effort. They were willing to fight for their principles and for the last stronghold of the nation in the mountains of Anatolia, while the Allied Powers, on the other hand, were utterly unprepared after the terrific strain of the World War to sacrifice any more lives or treasure...

When the Allied Powers, therefore, met the Nationalists at Lausanne, they were at a humiliating disadvantage. The Turks, who had been humiliated many times before and compelled to yield to threats and bluster, now had the delicious satisfaction not merely of resisting the European Powers but ultimately of imposing their own terms. Nor was the old diplomacy of bazarlik (bargaining) any longer of avail: there was little left with which to bargain.' (*The Lausanne Conference, American Journal of International Law*, January 1924, pp.113-5.)

Lloyd-George recognized, in a debate in the House of Commons on 6th June 1924, what a turnabout Lausanne had been for the Empire compared with Sèvres and previous policy:

> 'I believe it is a complete reversal of the decisions taken at Paris... In three important parts it is a complete departure from the decisions taken... First of all, with regard to Smyrna and South Eastern Anatolia, that was a reversal. The Straits is another. You... had a demilitarised zone, to be occupied and garrisoned by the Allies. Now, you have a demilitarised zone depending entirely upon Turkish Declarations. What were their declarations worth in the late war? Then there is a guarantee of Turkish neutrality by the British Empire. Surely that is a vital distinction. If there is any attack upon their zone, upon Constantinople, upon the Straits, the British Empire by this Treaty is bound to come in—horse, foot and artillery, with all its resources —to defend them from whatever quarter the attack comes. Is not that a vital difference? What is the third departure? The surrender of the capitulations. You surrendered there British rights which had been enjoyed by the traders of this country for centuries. That was not in the Paris arrangement. That was not in the Treaty of Sèvres... It is a, perfect farce... These are three serious departures." (*Irish Independent*, 7 June 1924.)

The Treaty of Sèvres was a treaty dictated by the victors to the vanquished —or so the victors thought. The Treaty of Lausanne was a treaty negotiated between comparative equals. As Curzon later remarked, when his bluster to the businessmen of the City had been shown to be without substance, Sèvres was

> "dictation of terms at the point of the Bayonet ... Only when the terms had been drawn up was the beaten enemy admitted, to be told his sentence. ... Far otherwise was it at Lausanne. There the Turks sat at the table on a footing of equality with all the other powers.' And he also admitted: 'Hitherto we have dictated our peace treaties. Now we are negotiating one with the enemy who has an army in being while we have none, an unheard of position."

Curzon had demanded and threatened and the Turks had said: 'You and whose army?' And that was that.

There was still a great *potential* disparity of power between the two parties to the Treaty (which Britain used to good effect) and there was still the British military occupation, which restricted what it was possible for Turkey to retain of its Ottoman possessions. (The major victory Britain secured in the Treaty was the holding on to the oil-rich Mosul region to the north of Mesopotamia that their forces occupied. This meant that they pushed the local inhabitants, the Kurds and local Turkomen, into the new state of Iraq.)

On the question of the Straits the British Admiralty had desired the ability to 'hammer at the gates of Constantinople and force the Turks to open the door into the Black Sea.' (A.L. Macfie, *The Straits Question*, *Middle Eastern Studies*, May 1979, p.235.) Presumably this was to get at Russia, if the need arose.

Turkey was prepared to agree to the free passage of commercial vessels and a more limited passage of warships. The Turks won back the right to close the Straits to its enemies in the event of war and to stop and search neutral vessels suspected of supplying them. However, Turkey was forced to agree to demilitarise a 15 mile wide zone with an international commission to oversee traffic through the Straits—although the Turkish Army could cross the demilitarized zone as it desired and station forces in Eastern Thrace.

These provisions were superseded by another Treaty signed at Montreux on July 20th 1936, which conceded full sovereignty to Turkey over the area, as the Turks took advantage of the decline in British power (just before DeValera did).

The Treaty permitted Turkey to remilitarise the Straits and imposed new restrictions on the passage of warships. Turkey was authorised to close the Straits to all foreign warships during wartime or when it was threatened by aggression. Additionally, it was authorised to refuse transit from merchant ships belonging to countries who were at war with Turkey.

A number of specific restrictions were imposed on what type of warships were allowed passage through the Straits. Non-Turkish warships in the Straits must be under 15,000 tons. No more than nine non-Turkish warships, with a total aggregate tonnage of no more than 30,000 tons, may pass through at any one time, and they are permitted to stay in the Black Sea for no longer than three weeks. The number of foreign warships permitted in the Straits at any one time is also restricted to one. The Black Sea states, including the Soviet Union, were given more leeway, being authorised to send capital ships of any tonnage through the Straits, but only one at a time and specifically excluding aircraft carriers. They were also permitted to send submarines through the Straits, if they gave prior notice.

As far as I know it is still in force today, with some amendments. It was recently in the news over the Georgian aggression in South Ossetia when the Russian Ambassador to Turkey pointed out that there were ten NATO vessels in the Black Sea. Russia's Ambassador to Ankara made his protest after the U.S. demanded to use the Straits to send two ships carrying aid to the Georgians in a move that would have violated the Convention. Turkey did not allow the passage of another two United States naval vessels, which exceeded the weight limit defined in the convention, instead allowing three lighter warships to pass through the Straits.

That was another demonstration of how seriously the Turks take their sovereignty, even when the Great Powers rattle their sabres (in comparison to other nations which turn a blind eye under pressure).

What made all the difference between the two Treaties of Sèvres and Lausanne was the Turkish will to defend its sovereignty—demonstrated on the battlefield over the previous couple of years.

*The Irish News* gave this, rather begrudging, recognition to the achievement of the Turks on 20th July 1923:

> "It is now history that the Turks have emerged from the peace negotiations victorious. Not alone have they salved a great portion of their losses, and minimised the humiliation of their defeat in the field, but they have outwitted the best diplomacy of Europe and made it look foolish. In addition they have created feelings of distrust amongst the Allies which will keep the Western Chancelleries so busy watching and checkmating one another that Angora will be little troubled with supervision in its schemes for the restoration of Turkey's former power in Europe as well as Asia... That is the net result of the great campaign which was going to free Europe from the last traces of the Moslem, and bring sweetness, civilisation, and progress into the dark places of Asia."

The Treaty of Lausanne was an immensely successful Treaty compared to the other post-War, dictated, Treaties. It brought stability that has lasted near on a century whilst the other, imposed, treaties produced another World War within a generation. The Treaty marked the birth of a new State, created by the struggle of its own citizens rather than the gift of the Imperialists. It set the new Turkish State apart from all others in the region by being independent of the Imperial powers. And it stood the test of time as a result.

### Ireland Makes Peace with Turkey

The Lausanne Treaty came into force on August 6th 1924 after Turkey, the British Empire (including the Irish Free State), France and Italy ratified it.

Another forgotten aspect of the Irish Great War on Turkey which the *Catholic Bulletin* examines is the implications for the Dominions of the Treaty of Lausanne—Ireland being one by this time, having returned to the Empire via the Treaty.

The May and June 1924 editions of the *Catholic Bulletin* throw light on an event the reader may not ever have been aware of. The Irish Free State was confronted with something it had not fully bargained for in signing up to the Treaty of 1921—its obligations in war to the Empire, of which it had pledged itself to be a loyal part.

The Treaty of Lausanne, which Britain alone signed, pledged the Empire to defend the 'neutrality' of the Straits (against Turkish or perhaps Bolshevik infringement). The Empire, of course, meant Ireland as well!

The following was written by an American commentator on the doctrines of war and neutrality within the British Empire:

> "In the case of the British Commonwealth the subjects of war and neutrality are peculiarly intertwined, partly because of the uncertainty as to the sepa-

rate statehood of the members, and partly as a result of the continuance of certain doctrines of a common British nationality and of a common Crown. In a word, there can be no right to separate neutrality in the British Commonwealth if the entire Empire is placed at war by the action of one government of the Empire." (H. McD. Clokie, *International Affairs: The British Dominions And Neutrality, American Political Science Review*, August 1940, p.737.)

If the Empire declared war, Ireland would be regarded as being at war with whoever the Empire had chosen to go to war with. The only thing at issue for Ireland, as a Dominion, was the 'extent of belligerency' it chose to adopt. What that meant was how many soldiers it was to provide to the Empire, how it was going to raise these soldiers, and what other materials and facilities it would contribute to a war. But there was no doubt it would be at war.

The above consideration was written in 1940 so it applies even more strongly to 1924 before there were any developments in the administration of the Empire. In 1931 the Statute of Westminster gave the Dominions of the Empire the right to give advice to the Crown in the event of the prospect of war. But how many wars start like that and how much consideration would the Crown, or the British Prime Minister exercising the Crown Prerogative, give to Irish advice?

It was not until the 1937 Constitution that Ireland took the power to make war on its behalf away from the Crown and gave it over to Dail Éireann. And it was not until the Second World War that this was proved to have taken place in substance.

The British did something very curious with the Treaty of Lausanne in 1924. They stipulated that it had to be ratified by the Parliaments of the Dominions as well as the Imperial Parliament, even though no plenipotentiaries of the Dominions had been involved in its negotiation or signing. This was a different procedure than that used with regard to the other post-war peace treaties (and the Washington Agreement) where the Dominions had their own representatives involved and signed up separately to the Treaties.

It could be argued that the Dominions had been at War with Turkey and therefore they had an interest in formally ending it. But in the Treaty of Lausanne Britain also made commitments on behalf of its Dominions that might have resulted in them being involved in future wars on behalf of the Empire, with Turkey, or indeed, Soviet Russia.

Canada, for one, was very unhappy at this. And, since the status of the Irish Free State, according to the Treaty of 1921, was supposedly the same as that of the Canadian Dominion within the Empire one would have expected the Free State to have the same concerns. But no!

It was suspected at the time that Britain was not best pleased with the Treaty of Lausanne, in fact had begun to realise the extent and consequences of its surrender, and was trying to slide out of it. It was doing so by making a commitment that Britain realised, after its call to arms over Chanak and the negative response that received, its Dominions would also be unhappy with.

It was hoping then that the refusal of one or more Dominions to ratify could leave the Imperial Parliament free of the procedure of surrender and leave its hands free on the Straits for the future. It could take a similar attitude to Lausanne as it took to the League of Nations, after America's decision not to sign up.

I think it is impossible to gauge the truth of this in the light of Britain's incomprehensible behaviour in the post-war period.

We reproduce part of the debate which took place in Dáil Éireann when the Minister for External Affairs, Desmond FitzGerald, introduced a motion to ratify the Treaty of Lausanne. FitzGerald seemed to be at a loss in his realisation that he was concluding peace with the state that Ireland went to War with on the 5th November 1914. FitzGerald was part of the movement which developed in opposition to that War and which became the national movement that founded an independent Republic. In fact the 1916 rising could be said to have been conducted against Britain in partial alliance with the Turks, since the Ottomans were allied to the Irish Republic's 'gallant allies in Europe'.

It seems to have come as a bit of a shock to him, and to the Free State Government, that Ireland was still at War with the Turks – just as in Redmond's days. It appears that the Free Staters were under the impression that the business with Turkey had nothing to do with them. Perhaps it was wishful thinking or maybe they did not fully understood what the Treaty of 1921 really meant.

John Redmond had not been consulted over the British decision to make War on the Ottomans in 1914 and now the Irish Free State was being told to ratify a treaty of peace with Turkey that England had concluded herself, and to sign up to a future war – if Britain deemed it necessary!

It is one of the forgotten aspects of Ireland's Great War on Turkey. Welcome back to the Empire: 'And Pharaoh said: I will let you go, but you will not go very far.'

"Dáil Éireann—1 July, 1924

"TREATY OF LAUSANNE.—MOTION TO ACQUIESCE IN ITS RATIFICATION.

MINISTER for EXTERNAL AFFAIRS, Mr. Desmond Fitzgerald (Cumann na nGaedheal): I beg to move: —That the Dáil, in order that the state of peace may be established beyond all reasonable doubt as between Saorstát Eireann and the Turkish Republic, authorises the Executive Council to acquiesce in the ratification of the Treaty of Lausanne, provided that it be clearly understood that (unless the Oireachtas shall hereafter undertake such commitments by legislation) the Saorstát thereby incurs no commitments other than the definite establishment of peace.

I think I had better give a little explanation and a little historical statement about this. The Treaty as it stands effects, or purports to effect, roughly three things. One is a clear definition of a state of peace with Turkey, between the ratifying parties on the one side and Turkey on the other. It makes certain conventions with regard to the protection of the Straits, and it has also an arrangement which permits of the submitting of contract cases, and other similar cases, to a body known as a mixed arbitral tribunal.

When the Saorstát came into formal legal existence, the position was that the condition of war which had been declared on November 5th, 1914, had not been formally declared at an end, owing to the non-ratification of the Treaty of Sèvres. Further negotiations for a Treaty had already been begun at Lausanne. These negotiations had been suspended but were recommenced in February, 1923. During the later stages of the negotiations we were kept informed of their progress, but it will be observed we were not consulted as to the initiation of these negotiations, nor were we invited to be represented by an Irish pleni-potentiary at Lausanne. When the Treaty became due for signature, we were not invited to be signatories. It will also be seen that when we came into exist-ence, a state of technical war might be held to exist and that a Treaty of Peace was already being negotiated to establish a state of peace beyond question, and to settle various legal questions connected therewith.

The Irish Free State, therefore, cannot in any way be held responsible for the existing circumstances, and for that reason the Executive Council do not propose to ask the Dáil to recommend ratification, as by doing so the Dáil might appear to be accepting *post factum* responsibility. At the same time, it might be held that a state of war exists between the Irish Free State and the Turkish Republic. A Treaty of peace has been negotiated and signed, purport-ing to be made on behalf of all the nations of the community. The negotiation of that Treaty has been very protracted, extending over a period considerably more than a year. That Treaty cannot be constitutionally ratified without the acquiescence of the Irish Free State. To start negotiations now for a new Treaty might easily lead to considerable complications in the Near East. The main feature of the Treaty is the declaration of peace, and as that appears to be the only aspect of the Treaty really affecting the Irish Free State, we think that we may safely acquiesce in its ratification. The two other main features of the Treaty are the Convention with regard to the Straits. Great Britain, under this Convention, would be bound, under certain circumstances, to take such war-like steps as might be decided upon by the Council of the League of Nations.

Ireland and the other nations of the Commonwealth are not in that posi-tion... The Executive Council will, therefore, acquiesce in the ratification of the Treaty on the clear understanding that unless the Oireachtas shall hereafter undertake such commitments by legislation the Saorstát incurs no commit-ments other than the definite establishment of peace; on the clear understand-ing also that in the initiation, negotiation and signature of any future Treaties the terms of the Imperial Conference Resolutions shall be rigidly adhered to; and on the assurance given that the existing form of Royal Title be used in the preamble, that steps are now taken to put Royal Titles used in the preamble in accord with fact as brought about by the Treaty of December 6th, 1921.

The Treaty is an extremely long document, going into many details, practically all of which are of no interest to this country, and do not affect this country in any way. Clause 1 declares a state of peace to exist. As I have said, it might be argued that at the present moment we are in a technical state of war with Turkey. On the other hand it might be argued that we are not. We propose to make it perfectly clear beyond all reasonable doubt, as we say in the resolution, that we are not at war with Turkey. There may be some question about the Straits Convention. Under the Straits Convention in this Treaty if the Council of the League of Nations decide that warlike action should be taken Great Britain is certainly committed to warlike action. Other members of the British community of nations would not be committed by any decision of the Council, but the matter might go before the Assembly of the League of Nations...

I do not need to remind Deputies that Clause 49 of the Constitution states that this country cannot actively participate in war without the express sanction of the Oireachtas, and, therefore, as we pointed that clearly out, and as our joining the League of Nations was subject to the acceptance of that letter, we cannot be committed to any warlike action under this Treaty... If we refuse to ratify it, the only course I see would be that the whole negotiation would have to be begun over again, which would involve the British Commonwealth, and France and Italy and Japan, and Turkey as well as other countries in a secondary way. The negotiation of it took over a year, and I feel that, on the whole, it is better to recommend that we acquiesce in its ratification than that we should run the risk that would be inevitable in postponing some such Treaty being made for another year or more, that the negotiation of another Treaty would take.

Major Brian COOPER (Cumann na nGaedheal): I agree that the ratification of this Treaty is necessary, and I shall vote for it if it is pressed to a division. There was one thing the Minister said that I cannot allow to pass without comment and contradiction. He said that the only feature that affected the Irish Free State is the conclusion of peace. I did not follow the proceedings at Lausanne very closely. But I do know that great and deep consideration was given to one question, and that question is embodied in the Treaty, and that is the question of the custody of the graves in Gallipoli. That is a feature that affects this country, and very many people in this country, most deeply indeed. From the slopes of the beaches at Sedd-ul-Bahr, where the Dublins and the Munsters were dashed to death, to Kiretch-Tepe-Sirt, where the Tenth Irish Division was bombed out of existence without being able to make reply, the slopes of the Gallipoli beaches are enriched with Irish blood, and Ireland's glory never shone more brightly or more gloriously than there. There were men of every creed and class there, men who a year before had joined in the Volunteers with General Collins and other men of very different opinions. They fought, lived and died side by side like brothers, and now the Minister tells us that the details of this Treaty are of no interest to this country. Is it of no interest to an Irish mother to know whether her son's grave is exposed to the jackal and coyote? I am more concerned with peace with Turkey than any

Deputy in this Dáil, because I am the only Deputy who fought against Turkey, and while I thank God that peace has come, because I know what war is, I say we have a vital interest in this Treaty; and, that we should have been represented at Lausanne. Though I would not stand in the way of peace, I will not allow the Minister to say that it is no concern of ours.

Mr. DARRELL FIGGIS (Independent): I am not rising to make any opposition to this Resolution, because I think that the form of words adopted by the Minister, the definite form of words, does preserve the dignity and freedom of this State... The Minister referred to Article 49 in the Constitution, which states that the Irish Free State shall not be committed to active participation in any war without the consent of the Oireachtas. In the form of words used it has been implied that although Ireland may not be committed to active participation that she actually is, nevertheless, in a state of war, although she actively may not participate in that state of war—that, for example, if between any European Power and Great Britain a state of war broke out, that we in the Free State might decide to have no active participation in it, but that nevertheless a state of war would exist...

Mr. Patrick BAXTER (Farmers' Party): I must express my surprise at the apparently safe passage which this Resolution is going to get through the Dáil... I take it that this resolution means the ratification of the Treaty or acquiescence in it. I cannot find out when the negotiations started, what mandate these people had, and whom they represented. I have yet to learn what authority there was from anyone in this country to declare war with Turkey, or to negotiate a Treaty of peace. I do not think any such authority was ever given by the people of this country. Under these circumstances I cannot see why we should be called upon to acquiesce in the ratification of a Treaty that will make for peace with Turkey. We were not consulted about any declaration of war, and neither were we consulted in the negotiations for a Treaty of peace. If we acquiesce in the ratification of this Treaty I take it that we would be bound by the words in the Treaty, and that our action would not be governed by the words of the resolution. The Treaty will be a binding document. From my point of view I do not think the people of this country gave to the representatives of the British Empire a mandate to negotiate a Treaty on their behalf with Turkey. If we acquiesce in the ratification of the Treaty, and agree to its terms, even though our signatures may not be on it, at a later stage, if that Treaty is broken, will not this country be at war again? I agree that we may not be committed to any act of war, and may not be called upon to take up arms and fight these people, as no matter what any Treaty may demand, the will of the people will decide what action is to be taken. If the Treaty were broken would we not be at war again, technically? Although we may not be disposed to take any action that would really mean an active war for us, the other people would be in a position to make war on us. We would then be called upon to defend ourselves, and be drawn into the conflict because we left to the people of another country the right to negotiate a Treaty, and later acquiesced in the ratification of that Treaty. That is something I do not feel in a position to agree with. I recognise the difficulties that will be created by refusing to ratify this Treaty—that we would still be, technically, at war with Turkey. If peace is to be made with Turkey it seems to me that it ought to be possible for this State directly to negotiate peace either through Notes or, if necessary, by having a representative there. That is the only way the sovereignty of this State, and its right to make a Treaty, can be maintained. If the Dáil accepts the resolution and agrees that a Treaty made between the representatives of Britain and other peoples at Lausanne, is to be accepted, it seems to me, the Dáil is agreeing that the people of another country can make a Treaty, in which our interests are concerned, and that it can be brought to the Dáil at any time for acquiescence. That is not a position I am prepared to take up.

Mr. Thomas JOHNSON (Labour Party): I am not able to follow the arguments of Deputy Baxter, though I think his desires are in accord with my own. I notice that the Minister mentioned the date, November 5th, 1914, as the date on which war was declared against Turkey by the British Crown. At that time, as a matter of fact, without the desire of Deputy Baxter or other members of the Dáil, the majority of the people of Ireland had not decided up to that date to renounce their association with Britain, and were largely represented in the British Parliament. Even Deputy Baxter will agree that, technically, Ireland was at war with Turkey. A change in relationship has taken place since that date. It seems to me that the case the Minister has made is very satisfactory. War was declared on behalf of, and with the legal acquiescence of, Ireland, in November, 1914.

International procedure seems to require that there should be some form of declaration of peace. If there had been an absolute separation of Ireland from the British Commonwealth, no doubt the international arrangements would be such, that Ireland could make formal peace with Turkey independent of anything that had been done by any of the other powers that were at war with Turkey. Whether we like it or not, that situation has not been arrived at, and consequently it seems that some other method is necessary. When the war was begun in November, 1914, it was a war entered into on behalf of Ireland, and, as has been pointed out, very many Irish soldiers entered into it. Consequently, the method of notifying Turkey in the formal way adopted by the Resolution seems to me to meet with acceptance.

I do not accept as a corollary at all the statement of Deputy Baxter, that if at some future date the present Treaty were broken, it would automatically make Saorstát Eireann a formal enemy of Turkey. The alternative position should be looked at. We do not know the effect of non-acceptance of this Resolution, or of any such resolution, or perhaps more important, the non-approval of the state of peace, and what it is going to result in for the eastern portion of Europe. I do not know very much about the terms of this Treaty. I do know that it has been looked upon by publicists throughout the world as a diplomatic victory for Turkey, and that there are many people in England who would not be averse to failure to ratify the Treaty. Large numbers of people are rejoicing at the delay that has taken place in doing so, and they seem to suggest—not in so many words but there is a certain current which seems to underlie their views — that it would be a very good thing for the Powers, outside Turkey, if this Treaty were not ratified...

We recognise that, as a matter of fact, the Free State of its volition, having arrived at a stage of conscious and actual nationhood, formally set down in writing, and accepted by the Powers of the world through the League of Nations, has never considered itself at war with Turkey. There is, technically, as a matter of international relation, a state of war still existing. We want to remove that former state of war and notify everybody that we are not only actually at peace but formally at peace...

Mr. FITZGERALD (Cumann na nGaedheal): First of all, I want to explain that I think Deputy Cooper did not understand the point of view I was taking. I was considering the difference between our agreeing to this Treaty and our not agreeing to it. I recognise that there are many Irish people who are deeply interested in the graves in Gallipoli. I recognise that so much that I have made certain arrangements about our relations with the Imperial War Graves Committee. I was considering solely the difference, whether Ireland were an international person who acquiesced in this ratification or if Ireland were not. As a matter of fact, those graves in Gallipoli are, I think, administered by the War Graves Commission, and although this Treaty does consider this matter, actually, if Ireland were entirely outside this Treaty these graves would be still looked after, and not left to the coyote and the jackal. Although that is the fact, I quite agree with the Deputy that I should have made it clear that there were other matters of interest to us in the Treaty, inasmuch as it puts an end technically to a state of war in Europe. That is of interest to us independent of our share in it.

I think Deputy Baxter has not quite noticed the clear connotation of the words of the resolution. If he looks at it clearly he will see that the resolution does not, in any way, say that we are in a technical state of war at present. I think it could be argued two ways. There are various opinions. It may be held on one side that once war is declared war exists until it is formally declared that it ceases to exist. On the other hand it may be held that war only exists so long as an active state of war is there and that at the end of any period of time, when peace has existed, peace exists technically as well as actually. That has been held but there has never been any definition as to how long it requires a state of peace to exist before it — a technical state of peace — can be said to exist. Therefore, if the Deputy reads the resolution he will see that it is so worded in order that peace may be established beyond all reasonable doubt. At present the Turkish people may say: 'We are technically at war.' On the other hand they may equally say: 'We are not technically at war.' In order to remove all doubt on that point, if the Deputy will read the words of the resolution he will see that he has put too definite a connotation upon the words.

Deputy Baxter asked what authority the British had to negotiate peace on our behalf. I thought I stated clearly in my opening statement that we could not recognise that this Treaty in being negotiated for, without every State being represented, had been negotiated properly, and I quite agree with him that we could have every reason for protesting and saying that as we were not there we refuse all responsibility in the matter. I explained, however, in my opening statement that the Treaty was negotiated over a period of a year. We have every reason to be angry. We were not invited to send our representatives there, nor were we invited to be a signatory, but the question arises, shall we nurse our anger and shall we put our own anger—our own pride if you like — before the well-being of the peoples of Eastern Europe? In this matter, weighing up one thing with another, I think it is better for us to be generous, if you like, and say that, although we may say we have been wronged we are prepared to be wronged rather than that ill should come to others. We must remember also, and I think I made it clear, that this thing which happened in regard to the Lausanne Treaty must not be regarded as a precedent, and if the same thing happens again we must refuse to have anything to do with the ratification of any similar Treaties. That is a thing upon which the whole Dáil can be entirely agreed. The Deputy says that he thinks that in acquiescing to the terms of this resolution we will be bound by the whole Treaty. The terms of the resolution make our attitude perfectly clear. I, myself, believe, and the Government that negotiated this Treaty also believe that we are committed to no active thing other than the clear definition of peace, where a lack of clearness may exist with regard to peace. We are stating exactly where we stand. If it is considered that our acquiescence in ratification of this Treaty only binds us so far as we are agreed, then there is no need for any stipulation about it. We have no nationals involved.

Mr. BAXTER (Farmers Party): Would the Minister say what would happen, in the event of the Treaty being broken—where would we stand?

Mr. Denis GOREY (Farmers Party): We would be at war.

Mr. FITZGERALD (Cumann na nGaedheal): We hereby make it clear that we are at peace with Turkey. As I said, there are two opinions: one that a technical state of war exists, merely because war has been carried on and, another, that a technical state of war exists because a formal declaration of war has been made. If the Treaty is broken in such a way as to lead to war, this legislature can, by its own volition and by its own act, decide that Ireland is going to take part in that war. If this legislature decides that Ireland would not take part in that war I would refer the Deputy to Article 49 of the Constitution..."

# XI. The Catholic Bulletin
## On The Defeat of England At Lausanne
## (1923-4)

*The Catholic Bulletin* devoted an enormous amount of coverage to the negotiations at Lausanne and the Treaty that followed (it should be remembered that the *Bulletin* was primarily a religious periodical). Its reporting amounted to about twenty pages in twelve editions, over a period of a year, in which the Treaty and its significance were commented upon.

In April 1923, to keep its readers well informed, the *Catholic Bulletin* took the unusual step of publishing the official (British) record of the proceedings at Lausanne. It did so without comment, believing, presumably, that no comment was necessary. And the *Bulletin*, being of the Anti-Treaty mind that went into the making of Fianna Fail, contrasted the performance of the Turkish and Irish plenipotentiaries in their respective settlements with the British.

I have seen *The Catholic Bulletin* criticized for its relentless war of ideas waged against British influence in Ireland during the 1920s and 1930s. This criticism, of course, has come from those wanting to reestablish those ideas in Ireland today—so that the Irish would see the world in the same way the British State sees it.

I think what *The Catholic Bulletin* did was very important in establishing independent Ireland when many thought the mere signing of a Treaty would accomplish it. Independent Ireland was not a fact in 1921—it had to be fought for in various ways for another quarter of a century before it was begun to be achieved.

I think we owe some gratitude to Ataturk because Turkey's example provided some of the inspiration and will to carry on the struggle that was necessary for such an achievement.

The Catholic Bulletin clearly saw what happened at Chanak and then Lausanne as a turning point that had important implications in world affairs— and for Ireland in its future relations with the Empire. It saw these events as 'a great defeat for England' at the hands of a small nation fighting for its freedom. That understanding was acted upon over the coming two decades by DeValera to achieve for Ireland what Ataturk had done for Turkey.

Here are extracts from *The Catholic Bulletin* concerning the British Empire and Turkey during the years 1923-24:

"FAR AND NEAR

THE BETRAYAL OF GREECE

The Bucharest *Adeverul* quotes the case of Greece as a warning to those small countries that place too much trust in the promises of the greater Powers, and goes on to say:

'Greece entered into war, because she was urged to do so by England. The Greek people were tired of war and that is why they voted out the Venizelists and summoned Constantine back to the throne. But Constantine did not have the courage to pursue the policies which the Greek people called upon him to follow. He moved along the same pro-British procedure of Venizelos and in consequence the Greek people have had to pay the terrible price of this policy. They lost not only Smyrna but they were obliged to evacuate Thrace. When in the spirit of honour and patriotism they resisted the demand that they should evacuate Thrace, this is the answer approximately that was made to them: ' If you refuse to obey, you will have to deal not only with the Kemalists, whom we should allow to pass freely into Europe but also with us, your great Allies of yesterday, your powerful protectors, who will block your seaports without the slightest delay.'

What a beautiful lesson the case of Greece is for the lesser nations. Alliances with great Powers and their friendship are bestowed on the lesser peoples as long as the great have need of the little fellows. Beyond this a narrow selfishness is the supreme rule in their political relations.

What in private life would be considered as treacherous and immoral conduct becomes transformed in international politics to an unchanging principle.

\*　　\*　　\*

PATRIOTISM IN THE NEAR EAST

It is a significant fact that the British Government has failed, with one very notable exception, to carry out its programme at all the conferences which have been held since the conclusion of the World War. Its defeat at Lausanne was, undoubtedly, the most humiliating, since it was inflicted by the representatives of 'an impoverished Ottoman State of not more than seven million inhabitants.' Despite the fact that on the occasion of practically every manifestation of Turkish sovereignty and independence at the Conference, a British warship was dispatched to Constantinople, the great delegates of Angora remained adamant. These delegates, we may add, were supported magnificently by their Army, their people and their Press, all of whom were patriotic to the heart's core. Discussing the Peace Treaty before an audience of five thousand people, Mustapha Kemal Pasha enquired whether they would accept it. The answer was a unanimous cry—'No!' Describing the terms as unbecoming to the dignity of an independent nation he added, 'Turkey can boast of her pacifism. If we make war it is because we are forced to do so to safeguard our existence. The Western Powers aimed at causing the Ottoman Empire to disappear. We Turks are not afraid of Britain. If Britain thinks she can intimidate us she will soon find this a mistake.' The patriotism of the Turkish Press was, likewise, a source of strength and inspiration to the Angora plenipotentiaries. 'If you cannot do anything, O Pasha, come back,' wrote, for example, Ileri, 'and place yourself at the head of your troops. Then, if the whole world is against us, and we are beaten, the historian of the future will say: they died rather than submit to barbarian rule.'

Two factors which determined the defeat of England, at Lausanne, were the loyalty and adherence of the Angora plenipotentiaries to the Declaration of Independence or National Pact, made in January, 1920, and the mutual fidelity of Turkey and Russia to Article 1 of the Treaty signed between these countries on March 16, 1921. First, as to the National Pact, *Birlik*, a Turkish bimonthly, in explaining the genesis and aims of the Turkish Nationalist movement, says that at the end of the World War the British forgot their pledges and there followed the invasion of the Gallipoli peninsula and Constantinople. A certain number of 'self-respecting and more virile Turks,' it adds, 'escaped to Anatolia and there organised the Grand National Assembly of Angora.' It will be recalled that on May 16, 1920, the British took possession of the Turkish Parliament at Constantinople, and all the Ministries, and imprisoned, at Malta, 150 of the most patriotic Turks. The prisoners seized every opportunity for considering and discussing their future plans and, on their release, they repaired to Angora where, with those who had escaped, they formed two-thirds of the now famous Assembly.

The National Pact comprehended the recognition of the political, economic and judicial independence of Turkey, and unconditional restoration of Constantinople and the Straits, giving due respect to the rights of the interested Powers in the freedom of the Straits for commerce and communication. In pursuance of its further objects the Grand National Assembly 'decreed resistance to the occupation of Asia Minor by the Greeks. The advance of the Greeks toward Anatolia started the Greco-Turkish war in which the Greeks,' adds *Birlik*, 'received every kind of support from England whose imperialistic aims required the prostration of Turkey which would facilitate the annexation of the latter's possessions—Palestine, Mesopotamia and Constantinople.'

The Turkish bi-monthly then proceeds to discuss the Treaty of Sèvres thus: 'In 1920 the Allied Powers concluded among themselves an agreement which was the culmination of the work of the spoliation of Turkey. This treaty was not accepted by the Angora Turks. In the years 1920 and 1921 several conferences took place between the Turks, the Greeks and the Allies but no substantial change in the Treaty could be secured. The Angora Government, however, succeeded in concluding several separate treaties with different Powers in Europe and Asia—Soviet Russia, France, Italy, Persia, Afghanistan, Ukraine and Caucasian Republics, most of these recognising definitely the right of the Turk to the provision of the National Pact. These treaties were concluded between the various Powers and the Grand National Assembly at Angora, and not with the Government of the Sultan at Constantinople. The Sultan had been forced to declare the Kemalists as traitors to Turkey. The Angora Assembly, finding the Sultan and his Government prisoners in the hands of the British and virtually their puppets, declared themselves to be free from all obligations to the Sultan, claiming, at the same time, that the Angora Government was the only one entitled to speak in the name of the Turks.'

As the British Government, at the Lausanne Conference, aimed at making the Turkish delegates tear up the Declaration of independence of their Parliament, they should, from their experience, have sent ministers whose personalities were more impressive and alluring than those of Lord Curzon and his companions.

Second, as to the factor of the Treaty between Turkey and Russia.

This Treaty was signed on March 16, 1921, and ratified on March 21, 1921. The text recites the solidarity existing between the two countries in the struggle against Imperialism; the fact that any difficulties created for either of the peoples aggravated the position of the other and finally the desire to establish between themselves permanent, sincere friendship, based on their mutual interests. Article I provided that each of the contracting parties agreed not to recognise any peace treaties or any other international acts the acceptance of which would be imposed by force on either countries.

Lord Curzon, in the first instance, devoted his entire energies towards smashing this agreement, that is to say, towards driving a wedge between the two countries. Alternately he protested England's friendship for Turkey and for Russia, but in vain. Each country remained true to itself, to its principles, and to its bond. England was confronted with stone walls of patriotism, faithfulness and loyalty, which reduced her battleships to the potency of tin cans. 'It was clearly the wish,' declared M. Chicherin, 'to separate Turkey from Russia. The Allies scheme allowed free passage in time of war, which would expose the south coast of Russia to attack. The proposal would oblige Russia to arm herself and the guarantees were quite illusory for Turkey. The Allies proposal,' he continued, 'violated the independence of Russia, would lead to naval armaments and was an obstacle to international peace.' And the spider, Curzon, in reply said: 'Let me invite M. Chicherin to recognise our goodwill towards Russia.' This, after England's 'one hundred million' efforts to destroy Soviet Russia. While such Satanic hypocrisy, impudent condescension and superior patronage might influence less resourceful representatives of a country, they failed utterly to deceive or impress the representatives of the Russian people.

It was recently announced on the continent that a further agreement or treaty of a military nature had been reached between Russia and Turkey.

On the last day of the Conference, Ismet Pasha stated emphatically that the Conference—a polite way of referring to England—had been aiming at the exploitation of Turkey. Lord Curzon answered that the Turkish intractability was incredible, while someone else said it was a crime. Our readers will be particularly interested in the description of the final scenes by one of the foreign correspondents of the British press. We read:

'Ismet Pasha, the head of the Turkish Delegation, has refused to sign the Near East Peace Treaty. Ismet left the hotel smiling at 7.45 in the evening, replying to journalists that he had not signed... Following Ismet's departure the French and Italians sent representatives at 8.25 after Ismet to make him another offer, and Lord Carton delayed the departure of his train half an hour in order to give M. Bompard and the Italian representative, who were engaged in this last effort with Ismet, an opportunity to inform him of the result of their attempt. Lord Curzon and Sir Eyre Crewe left for the station here at 9.30 tonight. M. Bompard had not returned, but a member of the delegation said: 'We gather that the last attempt has failed, but we are still not quite certain.' Lord Curzon's time limit, however, had been reached. But in any case it was then definitely reported that the Franco-Italian effort had failed. M. Bompard and Marchesi Garroni said farewell at the station. Within five minutes of the time fixed for the Marquess Curzon's departure the fate of the Treaty was still in the balance. Ismet had had his way on many matters. The Allies had agreed to whittle down what remained of the judicial Capitulations until they were almost unrecognisable. Foreign judges, who were to preside over trials affecting foreigners and who in courts of last instance were to form a majority of the bench, were to step down from that eminence and their place be taken by a somewhat shadowy foreign jurist who, in cases where foreigners were concerned, would hold a sort of watching brief for them. The war indemnity was reduced from fifteen gold millions Turkish pounds to twelve. Article Sixty, which was notoriously an endeavour to perpetuate the dead and buried Tripartite Agreement in the interest of Italy, has been jettisoned. Limitation of the number of the Turkish garrison in Eastern Thrace was dropped, and the Turkish demand that the new States amputated from the body of the Ottoman Empire should bear their share of the Ottoman Public Debt whether or no bondholders consent, was accepted in, principle. This latter concession, of course, involved a great sacrifice on the part of France, as a great majority of bondholders are French. On the whole, Ismet could fairly claim that he had made good use of his extension of that time limit, and if he had agreed to sign a Treaty he would have been signing a document offering considerably more advantage to Turkey than did the Treaty presented to him last Wednesday. But although much had been given in these last hour discussions it was not enough for Ismet who, after sitting up nearly the whole of the night with his councillors in unbroken conclave produced a fresh set of arguments and demands, which were handed to Lord Curzon at one o'clock this afternoon. In course of the afternoon Lord Curzon, M. Bompard, and Marchesi Garroni were considering these arguments, and experts were flitting between the Beau Rivage and the Lausanne Palace hotels in search of elucidation of what was not clear in Ismet's latest version of Turkey's last words. Meanwhile all luggage was packed and seats and sleeping-car berths booked on the train which leaves for Paris tonight. Visitors to the Turkish headquarters during the afternoon found that Ismet's proposals contained an offer to Lord Curzon that the Mosul *vilayet* should be dropped from the Treaty and left for settlement between England and Turkey within a space of one year. He had further asked in respect of Capitulations that the foreign legal advisers, who were to watch over foreigners' interests in Turkish courts, should be nominated by the Turks, and also demanded further modification of the financial clauses. After two hours consultation M. Bompard and Sir Horace Rumbold departed up the hill to the Lausanne Palace hotel for another argumentative tussle with Ismet. On their return discussion in Lord Curzon's room was resumed, and evidently by arrangement a telephone message was sent to Ismet requesting him to come down to the Beau Rivage. He arrived shortly before six with Riza Nur and a company of uncommonly dour-visaged experts, who filed into the tea room while their chiefs mounted to the chamber in which the heads of the Allied delegations were in council. The Turks wanted the whole series of economic questions reserved for further discussion. The Powers were willing to reconsider questions of contracts and concessions, but the Turks insisted on the whole economic chapter being suspended. With regard to Capitulations they declined to accept our reduced formula – although gravely modified to-day, and we were unable to agree to an alternative scheme proposed by them this morning. Every appeal was made to the Turks from all sides, but they remained unshakeable. Lord Curzon wrestled with Ismet Pasha for two hours before he abandoned hope (He had already been wrestling with him for practically three months!) One might almost say that it was with the train whistle sounding in his ears that he gave up the battle for lost—at least for the time being.'

A day or two later the *Daily Mail* followed with an editorial on the Conference in which the following amusing sentence occurred:

'It is a curious subject for thought that if Lord Curzon had missed his train that Sunday evening, peace with Turkey might very well have been signed.' It would have been a much more curious subject for thought if Lord Curzon had sent Sir Horace Rumbold, in a taxi, to an influential adviser of Ismet, and who was also a friend of Curzon, and succeeded, in this way, in procuring the signatures of the Angora delegates to the Treaty.

*   *   *

BRITISH DOMINIONS AND WAR

In a recent session of the Canadian Parliament the question of the liability of the British King's Dominions to send troops, to the assistance of the British armies, in the event of a declaration of war by England, was raised by Mr. Mackenzie King: 'We are content,' he declared, 'to rest our action on the principle that the making of war, which is a matter affecting the lives and happiness of all the people, should not be determined by a few individuals, but is a question to be determined by Parliament alone.'

The ex-Colonial Secretary, Churchill, declared over and over again that when the King declared war all his dominions and subjects were at war. The obvious corollary to this is that the King's Dominions must participate, with or without the consent of their parliaments, in whatever hostilities are undertaken. The *Times*, commenting editorially on Mr. King's speech, said:

'The actual outbreak of a war comes always with terrible swiftness. So long as the centre of international friction lies in Europe, London will always be overtaken by the final rush of events before Ottawa. An instant decision might have to be made. It might even be difficult for the British Government to consult its own Parliament before it advised the King to declare war. It might well be impossible, with all the will in the world, to wait for the judgment of the Dominion Parliaments. And, once Great Britain was at war, Canada would be regarded by international law and by foreign Governments as being *ipso facto* at war, too. The King cannot be at war in one part of his realm and at peace in another part of it and the declaration of war is almost the only Royal prerogative which is not delegated to a Governor-General. We believe that this position, arising as it does from the inexorable facts of geography, is understood and accepted by the mass of well-informed opinion in all the Dominions. It is understood, too, that it is not, as it might seem at first sight, a negation of the principles of self-government and equality. The actual outbreak of a war is the outcome of a more or less protracted conflict of policy; the actual decision is usually more or less predetermined by a course of action which has been shaped long beforehand. And every one knows that in shaping that course in determining, that is, the really decisive factors on which peace and war depend—the Dominions can nowadays share equally with Great Britain.'

Well-informed opinion in the Dominions has not, apparently, grasped the essential fact that foreign Governments do not recognise their separate existence. Wherever their home may be the world regards them merely as loyal members of the British Empire, or simply Britishers...

(March 1923)

\* \* \*

FAR AND NEAR

Foreign Supplement

Official Minutes of the Final Meetings of the Lausanne Conference according to a British Blue Book issued March 8, 1923 (Command 1814) The *Times*, March 9:

'The final meeting was held in Lord Curzon's room at 5.40 p.m. Lord Curzon, in opening the discussion, reminded Ismet Pasha that the Allied Powers had the day before put forward the final concessions which they were prepared to make. The Turkish Delegation had had full time to examine these concessions, and their reply had, in fact, been received that afternoon... 'The Treaty,' said Lord Curzon, must be signed here and now. 'There are only a few hours left. The world is looking for a solution, and we must find one before we leave this room.

Lord Curzon then turned to the text of the letter received that afternoon from the Turkish Delegation. He expressed the hope that Ismet Pasha would realise that it was now out of the question to reopen, or even to reserve, any large number of the questions raised in that document. The Conference could not at this moment enter upon a further stage. The Allies had considered very carefully, in their intense desire for peace, whether it would be possible for any or all of them to make further concessions at this eleventh hour. Lord Curzon, for his part, was willing to make such a concession on a point of the greatest importance namely, that of Mosul. Ismet Pasha had asked that the settlement of this question might be postponed for the period of one year for direct discussion between his Majesty's Government and the Turkish Government. Lord Curzon regretted that he was unable to consent to any alteration in

515

the actual words of the Treaty, since the matter was already, as stated in the Treaty Article, been referred to the League of Nations and was now in the hands of that body.

Lord Curzon was prepared, however, in a spirit of friendship and conciliation, to suspend the result of his appeal to the League of Nations for a period of one year... This concession, the importance of which he need scarcely underline, was absolutely the last which Lord Curzon was prepared to make. He was glad, however, at this final moment to make this offer to Ismet Pasha, but he could only do so under two conditions—namely, that if the two Governments failed to reach a direct understanding the intervention of the League would be resorted to in the manner originally proposed, and that the *status quo* existing in that region should be preserved during the year in which these discussions might continue.

Lord Curzon continued 'I wish you to realise, Ismet Pasha, that I have given up more than I thought possible. I have done this for the sake of peace. If within the next two hours we do not conclude peace, there will be no peace; we cannot wait and I do implore you to accept, in the spirit of the concluding words of your own letter, the concessions which we have made and to realise that we have now come to an end.'

Ismet Pasha stated that ... there was one point which he wished to raise at once... namely, that of the Greek indemnity...What the Turkish Delegation wanted was the fixation of the sum to be paid by Greece in the way of reparation...

Lord Curzon pointed out that Ismet Pasha's proposal was not in the least a helpful one at that stage. It was impossible within the two hours that still remained to fix a definite figure for Greek reparation, and it would be far better if Ismet Pasha could accept the formula which had been shown to him under which all his rights and claims were reserved.

At this moment Ismet Pasha stated that he was not contented with the discussion as it was proceeding. Might he and his two colleagues adjourn into another room for a few moments to discuss the situation? Ismet Pasha, Riza Nur Bey, and Hassan Bey accordingly left the room at 6.30 and returned without Hassan Bey at 6.45.

Ismet Pasha said that he accepted Lord Curzon's proposals regarding Mosul. He also accepted the proposed formula as regards the payment of an indemnity by Greece, subject, however, to the omission from it of the reference to Greek claims against Turkey.

Ismet Pasha, continuing his reply to the Allied proposals, explained that the declaration which the Turkish Delegation had proposed was the maximum which he could accept in the matter of judicial guarantees for foreigners in Turkey. As regarded the economic clauses of the Treaty, the Turkish Delegation were unable to accept the Allied proposal for the adjournment of the discussion on certain of these clauses. If Turkey were to accept the economic clauses of the Treaty as now proposed by the Allies, she would be placed in a position of economic servitude.

Lord Curzon exclaimed against the use of such a term as applied to the economic clauses of the Treaty in their present form. He could not accept these declarations as the last word of the Turkish Delegation on judicial guarantees and economic clauses. It was incredible that Ismet Pasha should refuse peace on these two points.

Turning to the economic proposals, Lord Curzon pointed out that Ismet Pasha had made a splendid fight for his country, and was winning for Turkey a very good peace. Did he really intend to leave the field owing to his refusal to accept the Allied proposals on the two questions now under discussion?

Ismet Pasha replied that for years Turkey had suffered for her independence. And now for months the question of the judicial guarantees had been discussed. What the Allies now proposed was the Capitulations in another form. It was impossible for Turkey to accept them. Only on that very day in a spirit of extreme conciliation he had offered a declaration giving the Allies the promise of foreign assistance in the Turkish judicial system. He could do no more. With regard to the economic clauses, the Allied proposals would deprive Turkey of all economic relief. Turkey could not live under the economic regime proposed. All the great diplomatists in the world were gathered together in that room, and they were refusing Turkey peace in spite of all his (Ismet Pasha's) concessions.

The Marquis Garroni pointed out that the economic and financial regime which was being offered to Turkey was far more liberal than any regime offered to any country which had been beaten in war by the Allies. M. Bompard begged Ismet Pasha once again to reflect. His responsibility was great and terrible.

Lord Curzon pointed out that there was one hour left in which peace could be made.

Ismet Pasha declared that it was impossible to make peace on the terms proposed. The Allies had the will and the power to decide in Turkey's favour.

Curzon's appeal to Ismet Pasha—Lord Curzon begged Ismet Pasha to reflect again. Your Excellency could make peace if he wished. He could easily justify what he was doing before his own Parliament if he desired. Lord Curzon knew what public opinion in England would think, and he knew that he would be blamed if, after all the concessions made by the Allies, Turkey still refused peace. Did his Excellency realise what his present decision, if persisted in, might mean? Did it mean that Allied and Turkish soldiers were to begin fighting again? Did it mean that, when he (Lord Curzon) had just agreed to make one more concession and to meet his Excellency as regarded Mosul, there was to be fighting in the streets of that town? Did it mean that British, French, Italian, and Turkish soldiers would be shooting at each other again in the region of the Straits? Was there to be fighting at Chanak, at Ismid, and in the streets of Constantinople? Did it mean that the horrors of Gallipoli were to be renewed? On the verge of peace were blows again to be struck? It was unthinkable. His Excellency (Ismet Pasha) had known the triumphs of war. He had also known its horrors. It was incredible that anyone like him should take this terrific responsibility on his shoulders. Lord Curzon could not imagine any humane man in such circumstances, and at such an hour, taking this burden upon himself.

Ismet Pasha said that he well remembered the tragedy of the war. But he knew that he was not now responsible. He had done all that was possible.

M. Bompard declared that it was tragic to hear such an answer when Ismet Pasha had before him a draft Treaty which placed Turkey on her feet again. . . He begged Ismet Pasha to reflect again and not to be obstinate.

Lord Curzon asked Ismet Pasha once again to remember the personal concessions which he himself had made to his Excellency. There was the question of the ships requisitioned by Great Britain before the outbreak of war with Turkey. There was the question of Mosul. On both of these questions he (Lord Curzon) would have great difficulty in defending before public opinion the concessions which he had made to Ismet Pasha. He had made them, however, because his Excellency had personally told him that they were the two points on which he considered concessions to be necessary in order to enable him to sign the Treaty of Peace. When, however, the concessions were made to Ismet Pasha the latter had raised objections on judicial and economic questions.

Ismet Pasha must understand, however, that if these generous concessions were not now accepted by Turkey, Lord Curzon would be forced to withdraw them all. If the peace, for the purpose of concluding which they were offered, was not secured, these concessions must be taken away and Lord Curzon would never offer them again.

Ismet Pasha declared that . . . he had conscientiously considered his position and he could go no further.

Riza Nur said that... some of the Allied claims had not yet been discussed at all in any sub-commission. How could the Turkish Delegation be expected to accept them straight away? It was only recently that the Allies had sent the Turkish Delegation a draft declaration regarding judicial capitulations and now the Turkish Delegation had put in a counter-declaration in reply.

Lord Curzon said that...when he came here to conclude peace there was a strong feeling in England in favour of Turkey, in spite of the fact that Turkey had attacked Great Britain in 1914 and was England's enemy. There were many in England who remembered the old traditions of friendship between England and Turkey... When, the day after to-morrow, he was back in London and told England how he had fought, and how at the last moment he had failed and why he had failed, people in England would say that it was impossible to negotiate with Turkey and that it was impossible to enter into friendly relations with her. . Was Turkey really going to throw away the friendship of England for the sake of the questions now at issue?

Ismet Pasha replied that he had spoken in conscientious conviction. If his modest proposals were not accepted, England would to-morrow ask why Lord Curzon could not make peace. It would be known that Turkey had merely refused the judicial and economic proposals of the Allies because they were irreconcilable with Turkey's independence. For Turkey this issue was vital. For the Allies it meant little. Why should the work of months be allowed to fail over this? The responsibility rested on the Allies and not on the Turkish Delegation.

Lord Curzon feared that there was nothing more now to be done. They had worked for peace for the last two hours. Riza Nur interposed to point out that the Turkish Delegation had done all they could. If they gave way further on the points under discussion, the Treaty would not be ratified by anyone.

Lord Curzon refused to accept this statement. Only a few days ago Lord Curzon had asked Ismet Pasha whether, if the latter signed a Treaty it would be ratified, His Excellency had said 'Yes', and had added that if he returned to Angora with a draft which was not signed it would be torn up, but if he returned with a signed Treaty it would be ratified without delay.

Riza Nur replied that Ismet Pasha could only sign something which the Turkish people wanted.

Lord Curzon observed that it was now twenty minutes to eight. Soon after nine o'clock he must be in the train. He would ask Ismet Pasha in the short interval before he left to talk the matter over again with his friends. If he could come back in, say, half an hour, there might still be time in which to conclude peace. Let him discuss the points again with his friends and experts. Let him once again reflect. Lord Curzon and his colleagues would then be happy to see him again. Lord Curzon concluded by pointing out that this might be the last time he would ever see Ismet Pasha. He wished to carry back to London a memory of friendship and he would like to sign a common pact of peace and friendship with Ismet Pasha before he left.

At this point Ismet Pasha and Riza Nur rose and took their leave, and the meeting closed at 7.45 p.m.'

NOTE—The *New York Nation*, warning the American people against the League of Nations, describes that institution as a very convenient noose in the hands of the imperialist garrotters, and it quotes the case of Turkey, thus:

'Ismet Pasha promised Lord Curzon that Turkey would enter the League of Nations. Lord Curzon remarked sardonically: 'This makes many things easier,' the point being that England holds a mandate for Mesopotamia under the League of Nations, and that it is by virtue of this mandate that she is claiming for Mesopotamia, the Mosul oil regions. Turkey once a member of the League will have put her head in the noose. She will have subscribed to the control of the League and must abide by its judgments. The League Council—controlled by Great Britain—will determine the boundaries of Mesopotamia. It will declare the Mosul oilfields to be part of Mesopotamia rather than of Turkey. England will get the oil. Turkey, a member of the League, will have practically no voice in the decision.'

Since the foregoing was written the Grand National Assembly has rejected the Lausanne draft treaty, and Turkey, presumably, will not now enter the League of Nations.

(April 1923)

\* \* \*

FAR AND NEAR

TURKEY AND IRELAND

Writing on the subject of the peace Treaty signed at Lausanne on July 24, the *Irish Times* in an editorial of July 25, says: 'There is some analogy between the birth of the new Turkey and the birth of the Irish Free State. In both cases a treaty has ended—or ought to end—a secular conflict that was a nuisance to the whole world. In both cases the weaker Parties have made surprisingly good bargains with the stronger Powers...' With even this qualified analogy we cannot agree, much to our regret. New Turkey has been born free, enjoying the full use and control of all its limbs and faculties. The Irish Free State, alas! has been born deficient in faculties, sadly deformed in many features, and short of a limb. The *Irish Times* would have been nearer to the truth if it had stated that there was some analogy between the conceptions of the movements which resulted in the births of the new Turkey and the Irish Free State. It would also be correct to say that there was some analogy in the environments which excited the forward movements in Turkey and in Ireland. Both countries were confronted with the same external enemy; both countries possessed political parties whose actions were considered inimical to the achievement of liberty and independence. The exponents of Young Ireland and of Young Turkey charged those of Old Ireland and of Old Turkey with treason, corruption and of siding on all occasions with the alien enemy. Furthermore, the political commitments of the moderate parties in both countries led directly and indirectly to the respective Declarations of National Rights made by the new generations of Patriots, and to the establishment of native parliaments based on those Declarations. In Ireland British Home Rule Acts were repudiated, and National Independence declared, by a public proclamation in 1916. This Proclamation of Independence made known:

'... the right of the people of Ireland to the ownership of Ireland, and to the unfettered control of Irish destinies to be sovereign and indefeasible... Standing on that fundamental right and again asserting it in arms in the face of the world, we hereby proclaim the Irish Republic as a Sovereign Independent State..."

The foregoing was confirmed on January 21, 1919, by the elected representatives of the Irish people in Parliament assembled. In January, 1921, in an address to foreign nations, signed by the President of Dáil Éireann, and by all the members of Dáil Éireann present, the following declaration was made:

'The Irish people claim ... their right as a nation to determine freely for themselves how they shall be governed... On no other basis is peace possible. .. We shall not surrender our national right—nor will force compel us. Our cause is the common cause of humankind. To that cause we have pledged ourselves and our people to remain faithful unto death.'

The Constitution adopted by Dáil Éireann in January, 1919, invested Dáil Éireann with full legislative powers.

Similarly, the policy of the Palace, of the Porte, and of the moderate, compromising, politicians in Turkey led to the establishment of the native parliament at Angora, to the promulgation of the National Pact, to the repudiation in arms of the Treaty of Sèvres, concluded with the 'moderate' Turkish party and by which Turkey was partitioned and her sovereignty destroyed, and finally to the repudiation and the deposition of the Sultan who had declared, at the instigation of England, that the Turkish patriots were traitors.

The analogy between the causes of Young Ireland and of Young Turkey is illustrated in the National Pact and by the following declaration of Independence made by the Grand National Assembly at Angora in November, 1922:

'In virtue of the Fundamental Law the Sovereign rights of the Turkish people are vested in an inalienable, undivided, and irrevocable manner in the moral person of the Grand National Assembly as the sole and only emanation of the people. The Assembly has decided not to recognise any other body or power not issuing from itself. Therefore it does not recognise, within the frontiers defined in the National Pact, any other form of government. Consequently the Assembly esteems that the form of government existing at Constantinople based upon personal sovereignty has been relegated to the past from March 16, 1920.'

It would be correct to say, also, that there was some analogy between the methods employed by the British Government at the Irish Peace Conference, held in London, and those employed at the Turkish Peace Conference, held at Lausanne. The representatives of the Governments of Dáil Éireann, and of the Grand National Assembly, were threatened with the renewal of immediate war, if the Treaties proposed were not acceded to and signed. In the case of Turkey, battleships were actually dispatched in confirmation of Lord Curzon's threats. With regard to Ireland, the rumour was prevalent during the fatal week, when the Articles of agreement were under discussion, that troopships were ready to land in the event of the Dáil rejecting the Treaty. Here ends, however, whatever analogy exists. The representatives of the Government of Dáil Éireann having signed the Articles of Agreement, under threat of war, the native Irish Parliament accepted, by a small majority, the situation created. On the other hand, the representatives of the Grand National Assembly, at Lausanne, refused to sign the Treaty proposed, notwithstanding a similar threat, while the National Assembly itself subsequently endorsed its delegates' action. Mustapha Kemal Pasha, last March, addressing this Assembly when the draft Treaty proposed was under consideration said: 'Turkey was not a land of slaves. The nation had announced its decision. The time of hesitation was passed. . . It is the inherent right of Turkey to enjoy financial, economic, and administrative independence... What would life be without independence? Nothing.'

It is ludicrous to suggest that there is any analogy between 'the surprisingly good bargains' obtained by Ireland and Turkey.

We do not think the *Irish Times*, when suggesting this analogy, can have had present to its mind the minimum programme to which the Parliament of Ireland (1919-1921) was committed. This programme was embodied in various declarations and resolutions. One of these forbade the recognition, within Ireland, of any other body or power not emanating from itself. The recognition of the Government of Northern Ireland was a flagrant violation of Dáil Éireann's National Pact, and it is in relation to that Pact only, and not in relation to what the Parliamentary party had achieved or hoped to achieve, that 'the surprisingly good bargain' is to be judged. The extraordinary success of the Turkish nation is due to the persistent and rigid adherence of its delegates at the Peace Conference, and of the National Assembly, at home, to the minimum terms of the Angora Pact. Hence we have the condition in the Treaty, signed on July 24th, 'Providing for the withdrawal of the Allied military, naval, and air forces from Constantinople and the Straits within six weeks from the ratification of the treaty of peace.' If the *Irish Times* had said that there was an analogy between the Treaty of Sèvres (1920) and the Anglo-Irish Articles of Agreement (1921) there would be some case for argument. By the Treaty of Sèvres the 'moderate' Turkish party acquiesced in a permanent occupation of the Straits; it renounced all claim to Eastern Thrace; it handed over large tracts of Asia Minor to Greek rule; it agreed to pay reparations and it agreed to continue the special regime for foreigners known as the Capitulations. The Irish Treaty acquiesces in the occupation of Irish harbours by British warships; in affording Aviation facilities for the British Air Forces; in the Partition of Ireland; in the overlordship of the King of England; in the payment of part of England's war expenses for the suppression of a commercial rival; in the occupation by British troops of the area under the control of the Northern Government; and, finally, in the renunciation of Ireland's right to Independence as a sovereign nation by accepting its merge in the British Empire. Under the Lausanne Treaty, Asia Minor remains integrally Turkish. Instead of paying reparations Turkey receives a strip of territory (the smaller Karagatch enclave) in lieu of reparations from Greece, while Eastern Thrace is recognised as Turkey's domain.

The events following the signing of the Treaties demonstrate the absence of the faintest analogy between the birth of the New Turkey and the birth of the Irish Free State. On the day the Lausanne Treaty was signed, Constantinople had a public holiday. A salute of 101 guns was fired, while the town was beflagged and processions headed by bands perambulated the streets. At night there were illuminations and torchlight processions. At Lausanne joy-bells announced the tidings of peace.

Since the birth of the Irish Free State Ireland has been in a state of mourning. The 'successful bargain' which she made, and the degree of peace which she reached, with England, has been demonstrated in the incessant tolling of dead-bells, in the disfigured streets of the capital beflagged with ruins, in the processions of mourners following their executed dead, and in the filling of the jails with men and women unprecedented in numbers since Cromwell's peace.

What an analogy. (September 1923)

\* \* \*

## FAR AND NEAR
### NATIONALISM versus IMPERIALISM.

While ultra-imperialism in London is endeavouring to save England from perdition, revolutionary nationalism challenges the ascendency of the British Empire throughout the East. In the *Contemporary Review*, Dr. Arnold J. Toynbee points out that in 1918 it seemed as though practically the entire Middle-Eastern world would be absorbed in the British system. Britain's quiet rival, Russia, had disappeared from the scene. There were British troops in the 'Russian Zone' of Persia. Also in Trans-Caspia. Also in Trans-Caucasia. British power had supplanted Turkish power in Iraq, Palestine and Arabia, and even in Constantinople and Anatolia it seemed that the Turks 'would reconcile themselves to a British ascendency.' What has changed all this? Dr. Toynbee suggests Angora:

'Angora is much more than the capital of the new Turkish national State; it is a focus from which revolutionary nationalism has been spreading... Had we succeeded in establishing a moral hold over the last independent Moslem State, our ascendency would hardly have been disputed elsewhere: and the whole Islamic world, from Bengal to Constantinople, and from the African lakes to the Caucasus might have been drawn into the wake of the British Empire, except for a few French and Italian dependencies scattered here and there as enclaves. Looking back on this position to-day, the Turks, Egyptians, Afghans, and Indians whom an English visitor meets at Angora have a way of smiling and professing ironical gratitude to Mr. Lloyd George. It was your late Prime Minister, they explain, who saved Turkey from herself. Had he given her one touch of kindness, one friendly stroke or gentle word, she would have licked his hand and we might all have lost our independence forever. Fortunately, he preferred to kick her till she showed her teeth and summoned up her last energies to fight for her existence and, as it turned out, we have gained far more by defiance than we could ever have gained by conciliation.'

Conciliation is now impossible it seems, for Dr. Toynbee considers that 'the psychological moment has passed' and 'it is no longer conceivable that the Oriental peoples will consent to work out their destinies within the framework of the British Empire.' For—

'They have been alienated by unhappy experiences—the Turks by the deportations to Malta and by the inter-allied régime in Constantinople, the Egyptians and Indians by events which are too painfully familiar to require mention—and they are convinced that our system stands, as far as the East is concerned, for a Western ascendency, both in political and in personal relationships. Therefore they will have none of it, for equality of status with the West lies at the back of all their demands, and is the ultimate stimulus of their action in every sphere. They are willing to trade with us, as they have always done, and they intend to master our economic methods, but not at the sacrifice of personal equality and political independence and we shall not change their sentiments by substituting the word 'Commonwealth' for 'Empire' or by giving them progressive instalments of representative institutions.'

'The chief danger of our position is,' concludes Dr. Toynbee, 'that we do not yet know our own minds, while men's minds in the East are travelling so fast that we have little time left for making decisions.'

(November 1923)

\* · \* \*

## FAR AND NEAR

Looking round the world for an instance of brilliant achievement during the year, we see 'Turkey head of the class.' After centuries of rule by Mahomedan Caliphs, Mahomedan Kings, Sultans and Princes it was proclaimed in 1923 that Sovereignty belonged absolutely to the Turkish people, while Mustapha Kemal Pasha was then elevated to a dignity never before enjoyed by a ruler in Islam—President of the Republic of Turkey.

(January 1924)

## FAR AND NEAR
### TURKISH TREATY RATIFICATION

'India and New Zealand agreed very early on ratification, Canada replied that she would agree. She raised one or two constitutional points... The Irish Free State had no difficulty . . . Australia and South Africa have agreed to ratify the Treaty.' —The Prime Minister of England.

THE foregoing is taken from Mr. Ramsay MacDonald's speech in the British House of Commons on April 1 at the second reading of the Treaty of Peace (Turkey) Bill and to which the following amendment had been moved:

'That this House declines to proceed with the second reading of this Bill until it has received a definite statement as to whether the Dominions and India have been fully informed of the liabilities in which the Empire must be involved by the guarantee of the demilitarized zones on both sides of the Straits contained in Article 18 of the Straits Convention annexed to the Treaty, and as to whether the Dominions and India are prepared to ratify the Treaty with the Straits Convention.'

Opposition to the Bill, directly, was offered on the ground that it ratified the undertaking given by Great Britain, at Lausanne, to defend Turkey against any attack on Constantinople, or any other part surrounding the Straits. The view was openly expressed that this guarantee might involve the British in war within the lifetime of the present generation. With regard to the consent of the Dominions, the Prime Minister, in opposing the amendment which was subsequently withdrawn, stated, in addition to what we have already quoted, that the British plenipotentiaries—Lord Curzon and Sir H. Rumbold—were appointed with the knowledge and approval of the Dominions; that the Dominions had been kept in touch with all stages of the negotiations, and that, therefore, their Governments were fully aware of the obligations to which the signatures of the plenipotentiaries pledged them. Further, that the Treaty, when signed, was printed and circulated to the Dominions three months before the Imperial Conference, and that though it was explained and discussed at the Conference, no objections had been raised to its contents.

It now appears, according to the Press, that the Prime Minister of Canada has, on behalf of that Dominion, repudiated the obligation resulting from the negotiations, and that the Labour Party in Australia has also repudiated it. Mr. MacDonald has stated that the Irish Free State had no difficulty, thereby implying that it had given its unreserved acceptance of the guarantee which may one day involve the Irish people in war. Since those representatives of the people who attend the Free State Legislature have not been consulted, on the subject of this serious commitment, we beg to enquire what the position would be in the event of a declaration of war involving the application of the guarantee. According to Article 49 of the Constitution the Irish Free State, save in the case of actual invasion, 'shall not be committed to active participation in any war without the assent of the Oireachtas.' In our humble opinion, the assent, which, according to the Prime Minister of England, has been given by the Free State Government, to the ratification of the Treaty with Turkey, is an assent to an active participation, in certain contingencies, in a future war, and that, in these circumstances, therefore, Article 49 of the Constitution has been violated or, rather, treated as non-existent. It will be argued, of course, that the assent of the Free State government is not ratification by the Oireachtas, but against this it would appear that ratification by the Dominions was not provided for in the Treaty.

*   *   *

TREATY SIGNING

The procedure, relative to the signing of the Peace of Lausanne Treaties has been discussed at great length in the English Press. The Peace Treaties, and also the Washington Agreement, were signed separately on behalf of the Dominions and India, by their own plenipotentiaries. Those which pledged the British Empire to obligations were not merely signed by Dominion plenipotentiaries, but negotiated in constant consultation with a whole panel of plenipotentiaries, each of whom had full powers on behalf of his Dominion. Britain alone signed the Treaty of guarantee to France, and to that instrument was attached the clause now expressly used in the absence of Dominion signatures, exempting from the Treaty any Dominion which did not in fact ratify it. In the case of the Treaty of Lausanne a different method of procedure, it would seem, was adopted. The Straits Convention, which gives a territorial guarantee to Turkey, and, in certain eventualities, agrees to defend it against attack was negotiated by British plenipotentiaries alone, and it did not contain the usual clause exempting the Dominions unless they ratified it separately. If this version be correct it might be argued that the Dominions were exempted from liability, though it would now appear, for the reasons mentioned by Mr. MacDonald, that the British Government regards the Dominions as parties to the guarantee.

So many contradictory statements have been made, that it is almost impossible to get a glimpse of the truth. Our opinion is, that the British Government, itself, hoped to evade the ratification of the Treaty with the Turks, and that the omission of the clause referred to, was intended to facilitate the dishonouring of England's bond. We have the advice of one of our nationalist Dublin newspapers, that, should the Turkish Treaty come before the Free State Legislature, it should not be ratified. That is surely enough. Solicitous for Irish interests, as this paper generally pretends to be, there are moments, when as though talking in its sleep, it protests its love for England.

*    *    *

ENGLAND'S SURRENDER

Readers of the *BULLETIN* will remember the Supplement published last year describing Lord Curzon's final interview with Ismet Pasha and others. The very superior person proved on that occasion the most inferior. Threats and blandishments failed to induce the Turkish plenipotentiaries to agree to Curzon's terms. It was Curzon's second failure. His first, if we remember rightly, was the partition of Turkey by the Treaty of Sèvres. If this was not Curzon's personal failure it was, at any rate, England's failure. The Treaty, which was eventually signed and agreed to by Turkish patriots, has been described as 'deplorable' from the British point of view. This fact, we must grasp, if we are to get to the bottom of all the misunderstandings with regard to the alleged responsibilities and liabilities of his Britannic Majesty's Dominions. It should be remembered that the Lausanne Treaty was written and signed in the French language — the English was merely a translation. Therefore, the official document of a treaty, as the honourable Lloyd George pointed out, had been in both languages. The change, said the Welsh liberator of twenty-six counties of Ireland, was more than a mistake; it was significant of the fact that 'we had gone back in authority and prestige in our dealings with foreign powers.'

It had been, indeed, been a grave surrender on the part of British representatives.

The whole Treaty was a stupendous British surrender. British politicians and the British Press thundered that it was a treaty which might have been signed by a vanquished Power so far as British interests were concerned. Privileges, like Capitulations, which the mighty British had treasured for generations vanished like smoke. These, the only constant protection for the precious life, the honest liberty; the valuable property of every British trader in Turkey was ignominiously surrendered. Then the poor Christian minorities, for whose welfare England's great heart ever beats, particularly those in Belfast, were thrown to the Turkish dogs. Finally, above all things, England who had incited the Greeks to war against Turkey, finding it opportune, suddenly somersaults and guarantees the defence of the nation she relentlessly sought to destroy. This policy has been excellently described by the author of '*The Lost Dominion*'—a sensational book recently published on India. He says:

'It is an old policy of England to sacrifice her friends to her enemies. The idea is that your friend is your friend, and will support you anyhow. Your enemy will be so pleased at being allowed to punish your friend that he will forget his old grudge against you, and perhaps himself become friendly. And the policy is often successful enough, especially when the friend is helpless and the enemy placable.'

If there be a god of nations how he must despise this treachery, not less treacherous when euphemistically styled opportunism!

This policy has failed with the Turks who refused to budge until an essential clause of the Lausanne Treaty had been complied with. Ramsay MacDonald has told part of the story, and when reading Ramsay MacDonald bear in mind his motto. He expressed it quite recently at an insignificant meeting in London: 'Never,' advised the Prime Minister of England, 'say you will do anything, but within reason, always keep people expecting that you are going to do it.' Irish ex-members of the British Parliament will recognise that the new pupil has learned a thing or two from his masters.

*  *  *

### WEMBLEY, PRAYER AT

And Ramsay MacDonald asks, speaking on the Turkish Treaty: 'Need we ratify?' Then in a hushed voice: 'We must ratify.' We can hear the heart-breaking words hissing faintly across the floor of the Mother of Parliaments. 'Otherwise,' continues the Bolshevist Prime Minister, 'there is going to be no end of the state of war.' But British honour presently asserts itself, rising on high above the horrors of the cold-blooded, Christian-massacring Turk, above the murders of Ireland, the murders of Egypt and India; 'we must ratify the Treaty' — not because England gave her bond, be it noted, but 'because it could be ratified over our heads by three other powers.' A few days later the Bishop of London, at the opening of the Wembley exhibition, stood at the right hand of England's king, and Ireland's king and Canada's king, and India's Emperor, and, to the left hand of the High Commissioner of the Irish Free State, in a beautiful uniform of gold and blue, and thus spoke:

'Grant that our ideals and aspirations may be in accordance with Thy will, and help us to see ourselves as others see us. As we have mastered Nature that we might gain wealth, help us to master the social relations of mankind that we may gain justice and a world of brothers. Make us determined to live by truth and to found our common life on the eternal foundations of righteousness and love.'

Then the Lord's Prayer was recited reverently by the multitude while Sir Edward Elgar, a lonely figure in black, raised his baton for the massed choirs above him to sing Palestine, or rather 'Jerusalem.'

The Bolshevist Minister continues in a dramatic whisper: 'It must be ratified because during the months of delay Turkey has been becoming more suspicious (of the eternal foundations of righteousness and love), more and more pressing and has declined absolutely, and in the most point-blank way, to make any appointments to any of the Committees or Commissions provided for in this Treaty until such time as the Treaty has been ratified.' He lifts the curtain a little. 'One of the outstanding points is the boundary of Iraq. I have been pressing... I have been cajoling.' He was endeavouring, you understand, to master the social relations of mankind that 'we' might gain justice and a world of brothers, but he failed. 'I have been doing everything I could to get Turkey to appoint its representative upon that Commission. The reply is definite. No, not until you have ratified the Treaty.' What a contrast—the Irish Free State ratified the Anglo-Irish Treaty without waiting for the appointment of the Ulster Boundary commissioners! Truly, Ireland must be colonised by some such nation as the Turks before she will gain her liberty.

*   *   *

Mr. Ramsay MacDonald, in his official position as Bolshevist Prime Minister of England, has been doing his best in another direction. We quote from his speech in the British House of Commons:

'Mr. MacDonald: Canada replied that she would agree to what his Majesty's Government did.

Sir E. Grigg: Are we to understand that Canada has ever intimated her readiness to accept this obligation as binding upon Canada?

Mr. MacDonald: The Canadian Government has said, with a full knowledge of the Treaty, that she would be perfectly willing to accept the decision of the Government, and would take no exception to what his Majesty's Government did.

Sir E. Grigg: Does Canada accept the obligation herself?

Mr. MacDonald: Canada accepts the obligation, having been represented by Lord Curzon at Lausanne with her full knowledge and consent.'

Now here is what the Prime Minister of Canada actually said in the Canadian House of Commons early in April:

'We were asked shortly before the present session of Parliament whether the Government would signify its concurrence with the ratification of the Treaty and Conventions in question. We take the position that not having been invited to the Lausanne Conference, and not having been represented there, and not having for the reasons I have mentioned signed the Treaty, the Treaty does not impose any obligations on Canada; and the parts of the Empire on which it does impose obligations are the only parts that should sign and ratify it.

As we do not regard the Treaty as imposing obligations on Canada, we do not feel it necessary to submit the Treaty to Parliament for its approval . . . we make it quite clear again that with respect to the course pursued at the Lausanne Conference we had no exception to take with respect to its procedure. However, we pointed out that it must be apparent, quite apart from any action or representation on the part of Canada, that a different procedure had been followed at Lausanne from that followed at Versailles and Washington, namely, the direct representation and participation by fully authorised plenipotentiaries, formally signed by Canadian representatives, approved by parliament and the assent of His Majesty on behalf of Canada.'

Help us, said the Bishop of London, to see ourselves as others see us. We are doing, my lord bishop, all we can on this side to help you to realise your ideal. As we have suggested, a misunderstanding with the Dominions might eventually enable England to escape her obligations.

*   *   *

## DOMINION STATUS

It is of more than academic interest to consider whether Lord Curzon, or any other British Foreign Minister, could sign a treaty on behalf of Canada. Two years ago, says the *Solicitor's Journal* and *Weekly Reporter*, we published a series of four articles in which we endeavoured to explain the novel theory of the British Constitution which has been evolved by General Smuts. Perhaps we ought to say, 'revived' because prior to Cromwell's Protectorate the same theory was generally held by the Cavalier, as opposed to the Roundhead, party. The essence of this view is that, in each self-governing Dominion, and possibly in every Colony, the Sovereignty rests not in the King in Parliament, but in the King as Monarch of the colony in question. The British Empire, according to this view, is a Confederation of States under one Monarch and the claims of the British or Imperial Parliament to legislate for the Colonies are legally defensible only on the fiction that the King has delegated to Parliament his powers to grant Constitutions to or otherwise legislate for his Colonies. Needless to say, this view is not in accordance with the accepted Constitutional creed as laid down by Dicey and other authorities. But, at the Treaty of Versailles, it received by the admission of the Dominions as separate signatories of the Treaty, a tacit recognition. This recognition has now been carried one stage further by the assent of the Crown to the action of the Canadian Ministry in negotiating a separate Treaty with the United States relating to disputed fishing rights and similar matters. This Treaty (1) was negotiated by the Dominion Ministry without the formality of submission through the British Foreign Office (2) did not receive the signature of the British Ambassador to the United States on behalf of the King, although Sir Auckland Geddes informed the Prime Minister of Canada that he had been instructed to sign, and was refused permission to do so on the ground that his signature was not necessary and (3) was signed by the Canadian Minister of Marine and Fisheries on behalf of the King. Clearly the King's assent was given, not on the advice of his responsible Ministers in England, but on behalf of his responsible Ministers in Canada. This is a far-reaching precedent and clearly implies the theory that Canada is not a State subordinate to the Imperial Parliament, but a sister-State confederated with it under the same Monarch.

The statement made by the Prime Minister of Canada corroborates the views expressed in this article, namely, that the King's Canadian Ministers, not having been invited to Lausanne and not having been represented there, the Treaty did not impose any obligations on Canada. If the Irish Free State enjoys the same position as Canada in the Imperial scheme of things, if it is not a State subordinate to the Imperial Parliament, but a sister-State, why has it no difficulties at all in the matter of the Lausanne Treaty?...

\* \* \*

## JACOBIN TURNED JINGO

Lloyd George spoke at length against the ratification of the Lausanne Treaty. He was afraid the guarantee might one day involve the Empire in a war with Russia. 'Russia now might be pacific,' he said, 'but revolutionaries were apt to develop into Imperialists.' He remembered Lord Morley once shaking a finger at him and saying: 'There is nothing worse than a Jacobin turned Jingo.' The Treaty, he added, was a humiliating Treaty; it was a cowardly Treaty and it might well be a calamitous Treaty. From his knowledge of the Versailles Treaty, the Sèvres Treaty, and the Anglo-Irish Treaty, there is no one, we daresay, more qualified to discriminate between a cowardly and an honourable treaty than David Lloyd George. We forget the exact figure which, according to a French paper, was offered to Mustapha Kemal Pasha to sign the original and rejected Lausanne Treaty. But it was sufficiently substantial to purchase renunciation, if renunciation was for sale. It was not. Little wonder indeed in the prayer of the Bishop of London: 'Grant that our ideals and aspirations may be in accordance with Thy will, and help us to see ourselves as others see us.'

(May 1924)

\* \* \*

FAR AND NEAR

LAUSANNE TREATY

The *Irish Independent*, which is one of Turkey's most dangerous enemies, advised the Free State, some months ago, not to ratify the Lausanne Treaty. 'This Treaty,' it said, 'will come before the Oireachtas. In the circumstances it should not be ratified.' We have already dealt with the circumstances and expressed the opinion that England did not want the Treaty ratified at all. On the other hand the *Irish Times* in its editorial of June 7, makes the subject the excuse for extravagant sarcasm. It says:

'Mr. Ramsey Macdonald announced in the House of Commons, in the course of the debate, that the Canadian Government had agreed now to accept the Treaty and to acquiesce in its ratification. The Free State remains. Mr. Macdonald said that he had been engaged in an effort to 'clear away difficulties' and that he hoped that the explanations which he had given would enable the Free State Government to advise the ratification of the Treaty. We share the Premier's hope. The Free Stale is holding up the business of the whole world. The fact that it is a full member of the League of Nations has defined its international status once and for all, and to refuse point-blank to ratify this Treaty would be merely childish. If the Treaty contained new clauses which by any chance might prejudice Free State interests now or in the future, the opponents of ratification might have a case; but, as everybody who has read the Treaty knows, no such clauses exist. Ratification in this case is a purely formal matter, and the Free State Government will not forfeit one iota of its prestige by following the example of Canada.'

Anyone who has read the Articles of Agreement is aware of the provisions and safeguards with regard to the British Army and Navy in time of war. The Free State is therefore committed in advance to stand by England, and the Free State's ratification or non-ratification of England's treaties does not make the slightest difference; whatever the consequences of such treaties may be, the responsibilities remain unaltered, so far as the Free State is concerned. There is no analogy with regard to Canada in a matter of this kind."

(June 1924)

*   *   *

# Bibliography / Bibliographical Index
(with pages on which the works cited appear)

Abbott, G.F. (1922) *Greece And The Allies 1914-1922* p150, 151, 158, 159, 164, 179-181

Ahmed, Feroz *Great Britain's Relationship With The Young Turks 1908-14*, Middle Eastern Studies, July 1966 p78

Albin, Pierre (1915) *From Agadir to Sarajevo* p40

Aldington, R. (1955) *Lawrence of Arabia, A Biographical Enquiry*, p 369

Allen, William E.D. (1934) (under the pen name of James Drennan) *BUF, Oswald Mosley And British Fascism* p25

- (1919)*The Turks In Europe—A Sketch Study* p 25

*The Lausanne Conference, American Journal of International Law*, April 1923 p 496

*The Lausanne Conference, American Journal of International Law*, January 1924 p 496-7

Anon. (1915) *The Dardanelles: Their Story And Their Significance In The Great War, By The Author of 'The Real Kaiser'* p 123

Antonius, G. (1938) *The Arab Awakening* p57, 251, 252, 303-4, 309

Armstrong, H.C. (1932) *Grey Wolf, Mustafa Kemal: an intimate study of a dictator* p 411

Barry, T. (1949) *Guerilla Days in Ireland* p 318

Batzaria, Nicolae (1916 ?) *Din Lumea Islamului* p 74

Beer, G.L. (1923) *African Questions at The Paris Peace Conference* p 326-7-8

Bell,G. (1907) *The Desert and the Sown* p345

- (1917) *The Arab of Mesopotamia* p 366

Benson, E.F. (1918) *Crescent and Iron Cross* p194-6, 274-5

Brandes, Georg (1913)*The World At War* p 49, 60

Buchan, J. (1915) *The Thirty-Nine Steps*

p 201-2

- (1916) *Greenmantle* p 203-6

(1915) Interdepartmental Committee under Sir Maurice de Bunsen on 'British Desiderata In Turkey-in-Asia'. Report p 249

Burrows, R. M. in *The New Europe*, 9th November 1916 p 151, 162

- in *New Europe* 19 October 1916 p174

Buxton, Leland (1920) *The Turkish Treaty*, in the *Problems of Empire Series,* in *Foreign Affairs magazine* p 384-6

'Al Carthill' (B. C. Kennedy) (1923)*The Lost Dominion,* p 276-8, 361

Casement, R. (1913) *The Problem Of The Near West* in *The Crime Against Europe* p 83-86

*The Catholic Bulletin* for 1922 p 22

*The Catholic Bulletin* September, October, December 1922, January 1923 p 455-482

- March, April, September, November 1923, January, May, June 1924 p 509-531

Chevrillon, A. (1917), *England And The War (1914-1915)* p 115

Chomsky, N. (1983), *Fateful Triangle* p293

Churchill, W. (1923) *World Crisis* p 119, 121, 167, 169

Clifford, B. (1988) *The Dubliner, The Lives, Times and Writings of James Clarence Mangan* p 422, 493

Cohen, S. (1976) *British Policy In Mesopotamia 1903-14* p 234, 310

Coke, R. (1925) *The Heart of the Middle East* p 324-5

Collinson Owen, H. (1919) *Salonica And After: The Sideshow That Ended The War* p 185

- in Irish News, 1 January 1919 p 208-9

Cooper, Major B. (1918) *The Tenth (Irish) Division in Gallipoli* p17

Cooper Willis, Irene (1928) *England's Holy War* p 146, 147, 178-9

Court Repington, Charles (1924) *Policy And Arms* p 120

Crawfurd Price, W.H. (1915) *Light On The Balkan Darkness* p 154

Curtis, Lionel in *The Round Table* December 1918 p 212

Dáil Éireann Debate on the Treaty of Lausanne, 1 July 1924 p 502-8

*Daily News* 23 August 1920 p 349

Darwin, F. ed. (1887) *The Life and Letters of Charles Darwin*, p36

Davis, M. (2001) *Late Victorian Holocausts* p483

Disraeli, B. (1852) *Lord George Bentinck: A Political Biography* p269-70

Dixon-Johnson, C.F. (1916) *The Armenians* p31

Edgerton, D. (1991) *England And The Aeroplane—An Essay On A Militant And Technological Nation* p 354

Egerton, G. *Britain And The Great Betrayal* in *Historical Journal*, December 1978 p229

Ellis Barker, J. (1917) *The Great Problems Of British Statesmanship* p373-4

Evans Lewin, P. (1916) *The German Road To The East* p64

Evans, R. (1926) *A Brief Outline Of The Campaign In Mesopotamia* p322

Eversley, Lord and Chirol, V. (1923) *The Turkish Empire From 1288 To 1922* p 51

Fabre-Luce, A. (1926) *The Limitations Of Victory* p87

*Foreign Affairs, Problems of Empire Series No. 2, Special Supplement, July 1920* p 384-390

*Freeman's Journal* 10 November 1914 p 112, 137

5 April 1915 p 155

19 April 1915 p 108

23 February 1915 p 125-6

24 April 1915 p 153

editorial 30th October 1915 p16

15th November 1915 p 167, 382

19 March 1917 p 329-30

26 March 1919 p 339

Frobenius, H. (1914) *The German Empire's Hour Of Destiny* p 113

Froembgen, Hanns (1935) *Kemal Ataturk* p126-131, 139-143, 379-80, 396-400, 484-493

Fromkin, David (1989) *A Peace To End All Peace* p 47, 192, 270

Gaillard, Gaston (1921) *Turkey And Europe* p 40, 78, 381, 382, 391-5, 395-6

Gilbert, V. (1923) *The Romance of the Last Crusade—With Allenby to Jerusalem* p 261-2

Gregory, A. and Paseta, S. ed. (2002) *Ireland And The Great War: A War To Unite Us All?* p14

Goodwin, J. (1998) *Lords of the Horizon* p30

Grigg, John (1973) Biography of Lloyd George p 263

H.M.S.O., *Military Operations, Egypt And Palestine* p 237

Haldane, A. (1922) *The Insurrection in Mesopotamia, 1920* p 350

Hamilton J. (2004) *God,Guns and Israel* p 257

Harris, A. (1947) *Bomber Offensive* p351

5th 'Herbert Samuel' lecture 20.10.1961 p 283

Hibben, Paxton (1920) *Constantine I And The Greek People* p 155, 171-2, 173, 188

*The Historical Journal* (1975) *Wellington House And British Propaganda During The First World War*, p193

*Historical Journal*, December 1978, p 229

Horne, C.F. ,Austin, W.F. and Ayres, L.P. (1923) *The Great Events Of The Great War* p 59

Horne, J. and Kramer, A. (2001) *German Atrocities 1914: A History of Denial*

Howe, Frederic (1919) *The Only Possible Peace* pp 65-68, 71, 218-20, 221-227

- (1925) *The Confessions Of A Reformer* p218

- (1915) *Socialised Germany* p218

Hurgronje, C.S. (1917) *The Revolt In Arabia* p57, 243-8

Hyamson, A. M. in *The New Statesman* 21 November 1914, *The Future Of*

*Palestine* p 253-4
- (1908) *A History of the Jews of England*
- in *The New Europe* 27 September 1917 p 298-9
Hyamson, A. M. (1950) *Palestine Under The Mandate* p 256
- (1951) *Dictionary of Universal Biography*

Ireland, P.W. (1937) *Iraq: A Study in Political Development* p 332
*Irish Independent,* 6 November 1914 p 109
  7 November 1914 p 109
  12 March 1917 p 328
  9 November 1922 p 483
  7 June 1924 p 498
*Irish News* 2 November 1914 p110
  4 November 1914 p 111
  5 November 1914 p 111
  12 February 1915 p 112
  4 April 1915 p 157
  23 September 1915 p 161
  30 October 1915 p 166
  20 November 1915 p 116
  7 December 1915 p 323
  Editorial December 1915 *The Gallipoli Tragedy* p15
  9th December 1915 p 168
  14 September 1917 p 186
  9 November 1917 p 300-1
  16 November 1920 p 401
  30 November 1920 p 401
  11 December 1917 p 260
  1 January 1919 p 208-9
  19 May 1919 p 211
  5 August 1920 p 356
  6 August 1920 p 348
  20 August 1920 p 355-6
  27 August 1920 p 357
  25 July 1921 p409-410
  6 September 1921 p 420
  7 September 1921 p 301
  September 1922 p 413-8
  18 September 1922 p 431
  19,23,26 September 1922 p 433-35
  27 September 1922 p 439
  29 September 1922 p 447
  2,13,16 October 1922 p 440-1
  20 October 1922 p 443-4
  20 July 1923 p 500
Jastrow, M. (1917) *The War And The*

*Bagdad Railway: The Story Of Asia Minor And Its Relation To The Present Conflict* p 60
Jellicoe, E.G. (1924) *Playing The Game* p 48

*The Jewish Chronicle, 13 November 1914*
  Editorial *What About Palestine? p 252*
John, R. (1988) *Behind The Balfour Declaration: The Hidden Origins Of Today's Mideast Crisis* (The Institute for Historical Review, 18221/2) p 264, 269

Kedourie, Elie (1970) *The Chatham House Version* p237
- *Young Turks, Freemasons and Jews, Middle Eastern Studies,* January 1971 p 271-3
- (1956) *England And The Middle East,* p 370
Klieman, A. S. *Britain's War Aims In The Middle East In 1915, Journal Of Contemporary History,* July 1968 p 249
Kinross, Lord (1977) *The Ottoman Centuries—The Rise And Fall of The Turkish Empire* p 91

Lawrence, T.E. (1922) *Seven Pillars Of Wisdom,* p 20, 239-40
- Letter to *The Times* 22 August 1920 p 359
Lewis, Bernard (1996) *Cultures in Conflict; Christians, Muslims And Jews In The Age Of Discovery,* p 41
Liddell Hart, Basil (1934) *History Of The First World War* p 101
Lowes Dickinson, G. (1917) *The European Anarchy* p71
Lyell, T. (1923) *The Ins And Outs Of Mesopotamia* p 235, 238-9, 310-2, 335-6, 339, 343, 350, 367

McCarthy, J. (1880) *History of Our Own Times* p41
McCarthy, J. (2001) *The Bryce Report: British Propaganda and the Turks* p206-7
McD. Clokie, H. *International Affairs: The British Dominions And Neutrality, American Political Science Review,* August 1940 p 501

Macfie, A.L. *The Straits Question In The First World War*, *Middle Eastern Studies*, July 1983 p103, 132

Mackenzie, Compton (1932) *Greek Memories* p 163, 170, 176

Mackinder, H. (1919) *Democratic Ideals and Reality* p 270

Magnus, L. (1915) *The Third Great War* p114

Malcolm, J. Memorandum to Members of the Royal Commission on Palestine (1936) p 269

*The Manchester Guardian* 20 March 1917 p 286
- 9November 1917 p259-60
- in *Irish News* 25th July 1921 p 409-10

Mangan, C. C. *The Dubliner, The Lives, Times and Writings of James Clarence Mangan* p 422, 493 see B. Clifford

Marder, Arthur (1952) *Fear God And Dread Nought: The Correspondence of Admiral of the Fleet Lord Fisher of Kilverstone* p95
- (1961-70) *From TheDreadnought To Scapa Flow: The Royal Navy In The Fisher Era, 1904-1919*

Marlin, Randal (2002) *Propaganda And The Ethics of Persuasion* p193-4

Massey, W.T. (1919) *How Jerusalem Was Won—Being The Record Of Allenby's Campaign In Palestine* p 262

Maxse, Leo in *NationalReview* 1901-02 p 42

Mejcher, H. (1976)*The Imperial Quest For Oil* p 371

*Middle Eastern Studies*, January 1970 p 257

*Middle Eastern Studies*, October 1988 p 285

Miller, R. *Sir Ronald Storrs And Zion: The Dream That Turned Into A Nightmare, Middle Eastern Studies,* July 2000 p 300

Molho, R. *The Jewish Community Of Salonika And Its Incorporation Into The Greek State 1912-19* in *Middle Eastern Studies*, October 1988 p 285

Moltke, Count Von (1893) *Germany and Palestine,* from *Essays, Speeches and Memoirs* p51

Monypenny, W. F. *'The Imperial Ideal,'* in the 1905 collection, *The Empire And The Century* p 333

Nassibian, A. (1984) *Britain and the Armenian Question, 1915-1923* p450

*The New Europe,* 9th November 1916 p 287
17 January 1917 p 210-11
on 19th April 1917 p 255, 258
27 September 1917 p 298-9
27th September 1917 p 279,280

*The New Statesman* 21 November 1914, *The Future Of Palestine*p 253-4

*New York Times* 5th November 1910 *Islam's Call To Kaiser, Emperor Hesitates to Answer Appeal to Save Persia from Aggression* p 58
5th March 19 p54
30th April 1916 p64
25 November 1917 p70
9 January 1918 p 69
17 December 1922 p 313

O'Donnell, Charles J. (1924) *The Irish Future With The Lordship Of The World* p 178

O'Neill, H.C. (1920) *A History Of The War* p 118, 135

Omissi, D. (1990) *Air Power and Colonial Control: The Royal Air Force 1919-1939* p 352

Palmer, Alan (1987) *The Banner Of Battle; The Story Of The Crimean War*, p26

Pasha, Djemal (1922) *Memories Of A Turkish Statesman* p 93, 95-99, 104

Pears, E. (1916) *Forty Years in Constantinople* p 105-6

Peterson, H.C. (1939) *Propaganda For War* p199
- *British Influence On The American Press 1914-17, American Political Science Review*, February 1937 p 199

Philby, St. John (1948) *Arabian Days* p 367-8

Powell, E. Alexander (1924) *The Struggle For Power in Moslem Asia* p 28

Price, G.W. (1918) *The Story of the Salonika Army* p182, 184, 187

Quigley, Carroll (1981) *The Anglo-American Establishment : From*

*Rhodes to Cliveden*, p 213
- 1966 *Tragedy and Hope* p 230-1

RTE, *Our War* (2008) published in conjunction with the Royal Irish Academy, p 5

Rankin, Lt.-Col. Reginald (1914)*The Inner History Of The Balkan War* p79-83

Raymond, Ernest (1922) *Tell England* p7

*The Round Table* March 1918 p 281-2
December 1918 p 212
December 1918 p 229
March 1919 p 214
March 1920 p230

Royden, M. (1939) *The Problem of Palestine* p312

Sacher, H. ed. (1916) *Zionism And The Jewish Future* p

Salah, Zaki (1957) *Mesopotamia 1600-1914, A Study in British Foreign Affairs*, Baghdad 1957 p 62, 69, 73

Sciaky, Leon (1946) *Farewell To Salonica, City At The Crossroads* p29, 284-5

Sidebotham, H. (1918) *England And Palestine: Essays Towards The Restoration Of The Jewish State* p 259

Simons, G. (1994) *Iraq: From Sumer to Saddam* p350-1

Simson, H.J. (1937) *British Rule, and Rebellion* p 444-5

Sluglett, P. (1976) *Iraq Under British Occupation* p 353

*The Spectator* 12 August 1916

Stannard Baker, Ray (1927-39) *Life and Letters of Woodrow Wilson* p215

Starke, Joseph Anthony (1921)*Light And Truth After The World Tragedy* p 39, 71, 75

Storrs, R. (1937) *Orientations* p 238, 288-9, 290-2, 293

Stoyanovsky, J. (1928) *The Mandate For Palestine* p 296-7

Sykes, Mark *The Clean-Fighting Turk, A Spurious Claim* letter in *The Times* 20 February 1917 p 27, 190, 191

Talaat *Posthumous Memoirs of Talaat,* in *The New York Times Current History*, No. XV., October 1921 p 99

Tansill, C. C. *America Goes to War* p 215

Tennant, M. *Recollections* p 105

Tillotson Clark, A. (1918) *To Bagdad With The British* p 319-22

Thomson, Basil (1931) *The Allied Secret Service in Greece* p 106, 148, 149, 152, 170, 181, 376, 407-8, 412

Thomson, M. in *The Times,* 2 November 1949 p 265

*Time Magazine* 28th March 1932 p 10

*The Times*, Editorial 31 October 1914 p 101
27th September 1917 p280
27 March 1920 p 339
8 July 1920 p 360
19th July 1920 p 383
21 August 1920 p 358
2 November 1949 p 265

Toynbee, A. (1922) *The Western Question in Greece And Turkey* p 375, 378, 405-6, 408-9, 419, 438, 450-4

Tumulty, Joseph (1921) *Woodrow Wilson As I Know Him* p 229

Unattributed *The Turkish Empire From 1288 To 1922* p 51
- *The King Of The Hejaz And Arab Independence* p 241
- *Life of Laurence Oliphant* p 256
- 1905 collection, *The Empire And The Century* p 333
- *The World War I Collection—Gallipoli and the Early Battles*
*1914-16*, p 50

Verete, Mayir in *The Balfour Declaration And Its Makers* in *Middle Eastern Studies*, January
1970 p 257

Walder, D. (1969) *The Chanak Incident* p 391, 405, 407, 427

Walsh, Pat (2003) *The Rise And Fall Of Imperial Ireland* (Athol Books) p22

Weizmann, C. (1949) *Trial And Error:The Autobiography of Weizmann* p 266-8

White, Henry and Nevins, Allan (1930) *Thirty Years Of American Diplomacy* p68

Wilson, A. (1930) *Loyalties,*

# Index

The Great War on Turkey is largely forgotten in Ireland, no less than elsewhere, despite the fact that it was probably the biggest military action Ireland ever took in the world. That war lasted from 1914 until 1924 - when the Irish Free State ratified the Treaty of Lausanne and finally made peace with the Turks, along with the rest of the British Empire. It made the Middle East (including Palestine and Iraq) what it is today, and had the catastrophic effects on the Moslem world that persist to the present.

Ireland's part in the Great War on Turkey was an embarrassment to Republican Ireland and its historians and the details of the War became forgotten. The more recent historians of a revisionist disposition and the Remembrance commemorators have also refrained from remembering it, for other reasons.

This book, the first history of Ireland's War on Turkey, explains why the British Empire really made war on the Ottoman Empire and why Irishmen found themselves part of the invasion force it sent to Gallipoli. It describes the forgotten political and military assault launched on neutral Greece and the devastating effect this ultimately had on the Greek people across the Balkans and Asia Minor. It explains the reasons for the establishment of Palestine and Iraq and why the United States was repelled from the League of Nations by the behaviour of the British Empire in the conquered Ottoman territories after the War.

It concludes on a positive note, describing the great achievement of Ataturk in leading the Turkish nation to independence from the Imperialist Powers. This was an event that Republican Ireland could only marvel at, from the confines of the Treaty and the British Empire - an Empire whose demise Ataturk set in motion through the successful Turkish war of independence.

Athol Books
2009
ISBN 978 085034 121 8